The Victorian Ghost Story

Edinburgh Companions to the Gothic

Current Series Editors
Andrew Smith, University of Sheffield
Ruth Heholt, Falmouth University

Co-founding Series Editors
Andrew Smith, University of Sheffield
William Hughes, University of East Anglia

This series provides a comprehensive overview of the Gothic from the eighteenth century to the present day. Each volume takes either a period, place, or theme and explores their diverse attributes, contexts and texts via completely original essays. The volumes provide an authoritative critical tool for both scholars and students of the Gothic.

Volumes in the series are edited by leading scholars in their field and make a cutting-edge contribution to the field of Gothic studies.

Each volume:
- Presents an innovative and critically challenging exploration of the historical, thematic and theoretical understandings of the Gothic from the eighteenth century to the present day
- Provides a critical forum in which ideas about Gothic history and established Gothic themes are challenged
- Supports the teaching of the Gothic at an advanced undergraduate level and at masters level
- Helps readers to rethink ideas concerning periodisation and to question the critical approaches which have been taken to the Gothic

Published Titles
The Victorian Gothic: An Edinburgh Companion
  Andrew Smith and William Hughes
Romantic Gothic: An Edinburgh Companion
  Angela Wright and Dale Townshend
American Gothic Culture: An Edinburgh Companion
  Joel Faflak and Jason Haslam
Women and the Gothic: An Edinburgh Companion
  Avril Horner and Sue Zlosnik
Scottish Gothic: An Edinburgh Companion
  Carol Margaret Davison and Monica Germanà
The Gothic and Theory: An Edinburgh Companion
  Jerrold E. Hogle and Robert Miles
Twenty-First-Century Gothic: An Edinburgh Companion
  Maisha Wester and Xavier Aldana Reyes
Gothic Film: An Edinburgh Companion
  Richard J. Hand and Jay McRoy
Twentieth-Century Gothic: An Edinburgh Companion
  Sorcha Ní Fhlainn and Bernice M. Murphy
Italian Gothic: An Edinburgh Companion
  Marco Malvestio and Stefano Serafini
Irish Gothic: An Edinburgh Companion
  Jarlath Killeen and Christina Morin
Queer Gothic: An Edinburgh Companion
  Ardel Haefele-Thomas
Comic Gothic: An Edinburgh Companion
  Avril Horner and Sue Zlosnik
The Vampire: An Edinburgh Companion
  Nick Groom and William Hughes
The Victorian Ghost Story: An Edinburgh Companion
  Andrew Smith

Visit the Edinburgh Companions to the Gothic website at:
www.edinburghuniversitypress.com/series/EDCG

The Victorian Ghost Story

An Edinburgh Companion

Edited by Andrew Smith

EDINBURGH
University Press

Edinburgh University Press is one of the leading university presses in the UK. Publishing new research in the arts and humanities, EUP connects people and ideas to inspire creative thinking, open new perspectives and shape the world we live in. For more information, visit www.edinburghuniversitypress.com.

© editorial matter and organisation Andrew Smith, 2025
© the chapters their several authors, 2025

Edinburgh University Press Ltd
13 Infirmary Street, Edinburgh EH1 1LT

Typeset in 10.5/13pt Sabon LT Pro
by Cheshire Typesetting Ltd, Cuddington, Cheshire

A CIP record for this book is available from the British Library

ISBN 978 1 3995 2149 9 (hardback)
ISBN 978 1 3995 2151 2 (webready PDF)
ISBN 978 1 3995 2152 9 (epub)

The right of Andrew Smith to be identified as the editor of this work has been asserted in accordance with the Copyright, Designs and Patents Act 1988, and the Copyright and Related Rights Regulations 2003 (SI No. 2498).

EU Authorised Representative:
Easy Access System Europe
Mustamäe tee 50, 10621 Tallinn, Estonia
gpsr.requests@easproject.com

Contents

List of Figures   viii
Acknowledgements   ix

    Introduction: Victorian Ghosts   1
    Andrew Smith

PART I: HISTORICAL CONTEXTS

1. Gothic Fiction, Romanticism and the Origins of the Nineteenth-Century Ghost Story: 1764–1832   17
   Dale Townshend

2. The Ghost Story: 1830–70   34
   Anthony Mandal

3. The Ghost Story: 1870–1900   51
   Nick Freeman

4. Neo-Victorian Unquiet Spirits: Encounters with Nineteenth-Century Ghosts   66
   Marie-Luise Kohlke

PART II: CRITICAL CONTEXTS

5. Economics   85
   Andrew Smith

6. Ghostly Machines and Mechanical Ghosts: Industrialisation and Victorian Haunting   99
   Bridget M. Marshall

7. The Ghost Story as Written by Victorian Women Writers   114
   Lucie Armitt

8.	The Victorian Ghost Story and Colonialism *Melissa Edmundson*	129
9.	Religion *Alison Milbank*	146
10.	The Victorian American Ghost Story *Jeffrey Andrew Weinstock*	160
11.	Victorian Christmas Ghosts *Tara Moore*	176

PART III: AUTHORS

12.	Charles Dickens *Scott Brewster*	195
13.	Rudyard Kipling *Minna Vuohelainen*	210
14.	J. Sheridan Le Fanu *William Hughes*	225
15.	Margaret Oliphant *Valerie Sanders*	241
16.	Charlotte Riddell *Helena Ifill*	255
17.	Vernon Lee *Ardel Haefele-Thomas*	270
18.	Henry James *Luke Thurston*	285
19.	M. R. James *Roger Luckhurst*	300

PART IV: PLACES

20.	Haunted Landscapes *Emma McEvoy*	317
21.	Maritime Ghost Stories *Joan Passey*	332
22.	The Victorian Haunted House *Emma Liggins*	347

23.	Haunted Libraries and Museums *Darryl Jones*	364
24.	Pyramids *Andrew Smith*	379

Notes on Contributors   393
Index   399

Figures

1 Clarkson Stanfield's final plate in Charles Dickens's
   The Haunted Man and the Ghost's Bargain   181
2 John Tenniel's image for Chapter 1 of Charles Dickens's
   The Haunted Man and the Ghost's Bargain   182

Acknowledgements

Editing this volume has generated a network of scholars with whom it has been a pleasure to work. Many thanks for your excellent contributions and for responding so positively to my editorial queries and promptings. Thanks also to Jackie Jones at Edinburgh University Press for her enthusiastic adoption of the project and to William Hughes, the co-series editor, for his positive response to the initial book proposal and for his chapter contribution to this volume.

Friends and colleagues who have supported my earlier work on the ghost story include Angela Wright, Dale Townshend and Jerrold E. Hogle. Thanks to them for their encouragement on those ghostly projects. Other support has been more oblique but also important and I would like to thank the good folk of Sheffield Ukulele Club for their unique brand of musical respite care.

Finally, and as always, I would like to thank my wife, Joanne Benson, for her love, tolerance and support during the period in which this book was edited.

For Avril Horner and Sue Zlosnik

Introduction: Victorian Ghosts
Andrew Smith

This volume bears testimony to the complexity and diversity of the Victorian ghost story. The Victorian ghost story's engagement with issues about class, gender and national identity demonstrates the extraordinary adaptability of the form during the period. This complexity, however, was not always acknowledged by ghost story writers themselves. Famously, Dickens took the view that:

> There is no end to the old houses, with resounding galleries, and dismal state bedchambers, and haunted wings shut up for many years, through which we may ramble, with an agreeable creeping up our back, and encounter any number of ghosts, but (it is worthy of remark perhaps) reducible to a very few general types and classes; for, ghosts have little originality, and 'walk' in a beaten track. (Dickens 1990: 112)

Dickens's objection is that the ghost story is too reliant on familiar textual props. Dickens was, of course, a great innovator of the ghost story form (see Scott Brewster's chapter on Dickens in this volume) and if there is a sense of fatigue here there is also an implicit rallying cry to make the ghost story do something different. Dickens politically moulded the ghost story to reflect his social reformist ambitions, as witnessed in *A Christmas Carol* (1843) by Scrooge's transformation after encounters with the ghost of Jacob Marley and time-travelling spirits. As we shall see, engaging with the social, political and economic issues of the period is a key driver in the innovation of the Victorian ghost story. The ghost becomes the figure who draws attention to what is lost and what might be regained in tales that address an often fragile confidence in the social and economic authority of the Victorians. Scrooge, for example, cannot keep the world at bay despite his initial self-isolation. Marley will find him in his home (a home which had once belonged to Marley) in order to drive him out into a world which Scrooge can only change by going back into social circulation and using his money as a force for good.

It is important to note that in these tales private places are potentially haunted ones. In the ghost story you lock yourself in with the 'monster', meaning that your private space does not shield you from danger. The moment when Scrooge encounters Marley's spectre points to two crucial characteristics of the Victorian ghost story. First, ghosts gain a proximity to the subject because in the haunted home there is nowhere to hide. This troubling proximity indicates that the ghost frequently functions like a double (Marley was Scrooge's business partner) which makes visible an uncomfortable truth that the haunted do not want to acknowledge. In Freud's account of the double in 'The Uncanny' (1919), he notes of the uncanny that 'many people experience the feeling in the highest degree in relation to death and dead bodies, to the return of the dead, and to spirits and ghosts' (Freud 1990: 364). It is this return (as in Marley's spectral liminal return) which becomes the starting point for Scrooge's reflections on his own social liminality. The second characteristic is that ghosts are not always obviously Gothic because the ostensible Gothic double is not there simply to haunt, but also to enlighten. Marley is, for Scrooge, a deeply unsettling presence, but he is there to help him – indeed, to save his soul. As he tells Scrooge, '"you have yet a chance and hope of escaping my fate. A chance and hope of my procuring"' (Dickens 1985: 63). Ghosts are thus not always inherently evil (although sometimes they are, as this collection testifies). They are not the same as other 'Gothic' figures. In the Victorian period it is difficult to find selfless vampires, for example, who function in the same way as Marley.

Why the ghost functions like this can be accounted for in psychological and political terms. The issue of proximity speaks to a form of internalisation that, as noted above, the ghost makes visible as a type of double. Scrooge changes, but this has political as well as psychological consequences because he now sees how money can be used in a better, more charitable, way which enables social reform.

The example here of Scrooge and his psychological and political transformation should not, however, be read as identifying a model of spectrality which fits all ghosts, but it helpfully identifies aspects of the ghost story that are played out in a number of contexts explored in this volume. The political narrative of transformation, for example, can be seen in tales that address the role of women's work in the period, as a type of spectral work made culturally and economically invisible. Tales that examine the colonial contexts of Ireland, India and Egypt often represent spectres as figures which challenge colonial authority. There are other tales in which the ghost is a more malevolent entity, as in the stories of M. R. James where the spectre's motivation is often unclear and fear is generated out of the seemingly random nature of ghostly attack. The places that are haunted, whether they are *dâk*-bungalows in Kipling, M. R. James's libraries or Haggard's museums, manifest ghosts which respectively appear to challenge colonial authority, orders of epistemology and collections of purloined artefacts. The ghost therefore symbolises the possibility of resisting often quite specific manifestations of authority, and in this instance of the colonial context (discussed in depth in this volume by Melissa Edmundson and in chapters on Kipling, Le Fanu, and haunted pyramids), there are issues of territorial rights which are explicitly addressed. It would, in this instance, be tempting to claim the status of radical freedom fighter for such ghosts but in reality the ghost is an ambivalent figure who represents a possible colonial revenge, but also a type of horrifying otherness which needs to be defeated. The Egyptian mummy, for example (analysed in the chapter on haunted pyramids) is a type of ghost, a dead-undead figure who frequently seems to have legitimate revenge on their side, but mummies are also often monstrous unappeasable figures who represent a terrifying supernatural presence. This ambivalence reflects a political hesitancy in which the colonial subject may find themselves subject to the very depersonalisation which they had foisted, in often explicitly racial terms, on the colonial other. Decoding this type of projection and the implicit doubling which underpins it reveals the political and moral uncertainties of the period. The vestigial human presence in the ghost also represents in projected form the anxiety that the human may also be freighted by the spectral. At one level this reflects anxieties about death but also fears about life, which underlines the metaphysical fragility which also challenges the seemingly politically and economically secure world of our Victorians.

The colonial context is mentioned here because it also emphasises the fact that ghosts are, usually, highly territorial. Jacob Marley, for example, does not stray much from his old haunts, which represents his tragic adherence to finance. Ghosts can appear to be static, inhabiting houses and territories which once belonged to them, but they transcend the type of repetition that Dickens had lamented in his account of the formulaic ghost story. That ghosts haunt different places in different ways is explored here in Joan Passey's chapter on haunted seascapes, and Emma McEvoy's chapter on haunted landscapes. Such hauntings address the dangers of maritime travel and the role of folklore in shaping emerging environmental concerns. Laying the ghost to rest requires addressing the ghost's (and society's) needs, such as the need for environmental reform during a period of rapid industrialisation. As noted above, ghosts are ambivalent figures but they draw attention to where power, of various kinds, has been abused.

It is clear that Victorian ghosts are the product of their age and address often quite specific social concerns. The ghost may not always be a malevolent figure but their ontological and metaphysical uncertainty poses a problem for a society which has placed some confidence in science and the progress with which it was associated. The ghost suggests that the past cannot so easily be left behind, or rationalised. These issues are also a matter of individual exploration, as the chapters on specific authors illustrates. The different contexts of gender, class and nation are variously addressed in the ghost writers analysed here in chapters on Charles Dickens, Rudyard Kipling, J. S. Le Fanu, Margaret Oliphant, Charlotte Riddell, Vernon Lee, Henry James and M. R. James.

There have been many important critical contributions made to our understanding of the ghost story. Julia Briggs's *Night Visitors: The Rise and Fall of the English Ghost Story* (1977) examined many of the writers explored in this volume. Her landmark study acknowledges that the figure of the double provides an important reflection on the political and psychological dramas of the period. She argues that the double emerged '[o]ut of an alienation, to which the decay of supernatural beliefs contributed' (Briggs 1977: 19). Briggs's observation helps to illuminate some of the new psychological shifts in a century characterised by the emergence of developing ideas about the self, culminating in Freud's idea of the psychologically haunted subject. Whether ghosts represent the possibility of radical transgression has also been critically discussed. Luke Thurston (whose chapter contribution on Henry James forms part of this volume) in *Literary Ghosts from the Victorians to Modernism: The Haunting Interval* (2012) argues that the radical ghost resists the structure of the ghost story. For Thurston the ghost should be seen as a rebellious entity when it defies attempts to explain its presence. In this instance the narrative of the ghost story functions like a 'host' who has invited in a rebellious ghost (or 'guest') which challenges the type of calm induced by the presence of familiar narrative props. For Thurston ghost stories are tales about metaphysically transgressive guests whose existence asserts an unresolvable tension between 'narrative reality and an absolute otherness' (Thurston 2012: 3). This view of the ghost story stands as a counter to Dickens's jaded assessment of the form outlined at the beginning of this chapter. Ghosts can thus function as radical entities which challenge the grounds on which meaning is asserted. That the ghost can also function in an explicitly politically radical way has been explored by Vanessa D. Dickerson in *Victorian Ghosts in the Noontide: Women Writers and the Supernatural* (1996). Dickerson notes that:

The ghost stories written after the 1850s, but especially in the last decades of the century, would be written in a climate of change and reform marked by such developments as the agitation for women's rights to education, employment, and suffrage; the passage of the married women's property bills; and the rise of the New Woman. (133)

For Dickerson the period witnessed the radical repositioning of the female-authored ghost story from the 1860s, after what she identifies as the moralistic and politically conservative turn taken in sensation fiction during the era. The issue is examined by Lucie Armitt in her chapter, 'The Ghost Story as Written by Victorian Women Writers', in this volume.

Other studies of the ghost story have explored the implications of the literary and cultural contexts of the form. Simon Hay in *A History of the Modern British Ghost Story* (2011) argues that such tales dwell on the persistence of historical trauma. He also explores the relationship between the ghost story and other literary forms, such as realism. In *The Ghost Story 1840–1920: A Cultural History* (2010) I examined a number of ways in which the ghost story could be related to economic, colonial and gendered contexts, as well as exploring the influence of spiritualism. Nick Freeman, the author of a chapter in this volume which surveys developments in the ghost story between 1870 and 1900, wrote a chapter, 'The Victorian Ghost Story', for the edited collection *The Victorian Gothic* (Smith and Hughes 2012), also published in this series of Edinburgh Gothic Companions. In it he elegantly outlined the solution to the problem of the formulaic tale that had troubled Dickens, which is that 'the ghost story represented a challenge few writers could resist – how to make new wine from some very familiar, even stale, grapes', a challenge which 'ensured experiment and innovation' (106) during the period. This collection bears witness to this spirit of innovation which is manifested in the broad range of topics and issues that our ghost story writers engaged with.

This book is divided into four parts: 'Historical Contexts', 'Critical Contexts', 'Authors' and 'Places'. The first part provides a critical overview of specific periods which witnessed innovations and developments in the ghost story. The section begins with an assessment of how ghost narratives from the eighteenth century, and the Romantic era, established themes and issues that were inherited by our later Victorian writers. It concludes with an analysis of how neo-Victorian ghost stories reflect on, and provide a critical reassessment of, the Victorian ghost story.

In 'Gothic Fiction, Romanticism and the Origins of the Nineteenth-Century Ghost Story: 1764–1832' Dale Townshend surveys the ghost narratives which influenced the later Victorian ghost story. He discusses the important role that Shakespeare's ghosts played in the writings of Horace Walpole and Ann Radcliffe, before analysing the emergence of new forms of romantic spectrality in the work of Walter Scott and Mary Shelley. Townshend also explores how a number of supernatural narratives published in *Blackwood's* magazine generated themes that were explored in the Victorian ghost story.

Anthony Mandal in 'The Ghost Story: 1830–1870' examines developments in the periodical press, exploring how short fictions appeared in increasing numbers in both book collections and within the pages of magazines, resulting in a rich and variegated golden age for the Victorian ghost story. This chapter discusses a range of writers who made significant contributions to the development of the genre in this 'golden age'. They include the last works of Romantic fabulists like Scott and Hogg, whose contributions laid the foundations for the generation of authors who followed. Writers explored include Charles Dickens, Elizabeth Gaskell, Edward Bulwer-Lytton and Rhoda Broughton.

Nick Freeman's 'The Ghost Story: 1870–1900' provides a comprehensive overview of the developments in the ghost story from Dickens to the early writing of M. R. James. He explores how tales address concerns about industrialisation, educational reform, colonialism and gender. The chapter also examines the issues which characterise the *fin de siècle* ghost story, including its engagement with the type of 'real' ghost stories explored by the Society for Psychical Research (founded in 1882). Writers discussed include Mary Elizabeth Braddon, J. S. Le Fanu, Rudyard Kipling, Margaret Oliphant and Bram Stoker, among others.

In 'Neo-Victorian Unquiet Spirits: Encounters with Nineteenth-Century Ghosts' Marie-Luise Kohlke examines neo-Victorian novels, including Marghanita Laski's *The Victorian Chaise-Longue* (1953), Joanne Harris's *Sleep, Pale Sister* (1994) and Barbara Chase-Riboud's *Hottentot Venus: A Novel* (2003). Kohlke considers the relationship between haunting and familial or national genealogies, and the role of neo-Victorian locations in facilitating spectrality. Neo-Victorian spectres, she argues, expose sociocultural traumas and unacknowledged historical offences ranging from child labour and sex abuse to racist persecution. She concludes that neo-Victorian ghosts prove most effective when they produce 'haunted readers', who are left to question the persistence of inimical 'Victorian' social conditions and forms of discrimination into the present day.

Part II explores the different critical contexts that can be applied to the ghost story. Some of these relate to the political and economic contexts which shaped the ghost story. Others reflect on national (American) and seasonal (Christmas) contexts. The important role played by gender, colonialism and religion is also addressed in this section.

In 'Economics', I discuss how the various economic crises of the 1840s and 1870s influenced the representation of money in the ghost story. Dickens's Scrooge is a miser during the 'hungry forties' and his attempt to hoard money in a period of economic recession makes him aware of ghosts (such as Marley's and others), whose spectrality renders them incapable of helping those in need. The chapter also explores how texts such as Charlotte Riddell's *The Uninhabited House* (1875), Wilkie Collins's *The Haunted Hotel* (1878) and the anonymously published 'The Ghost in the Bank of England' (1879) associate spectral money with ghosts at a time when money seemed to be in danger of becoming lost (or invisible).

Bridget M. Marshall in 'Ghostly Machines and Mechanical Ghosts: Industrialisation and Victorian Haunting' focuses on representations of ghostly workers and haunted machines as a response to the world-altering changes of the Industrial Revolution. Ghostly workers were all too often the result of industrial machinery that seemed to come to life at the same time that it took the lives of workers. Machines thus made ghosts but also were themselves ghostly, often haunting and haunted. Marshall analyses how the evolving technology of the industrial age created new ways to haunt an already haunted world in writings by Charles Dickens, Samuel Butler, Frances Trollope and others.

In 'The Ghost Story as Written by Victorian Women Writers' Lucie Armitt considers how haunted domestic spaces became gendered in the work of female writers of the Victorian ghost story, who explore the spectral labour undertaken by women in the home. In addition, Armitt explores how the politics of property ownership and the sexual politics of the writing of the romance were addressed. Writers discussed include Emily Brontë, Charlotte Riddell, Vernon Lee and Edith Nesbit.

Melissa Edmundson in 'The Victorian Ghost Story and Colonialism' examines the colonial contexts of the Victorian ghost story. She argues that as the British travelled, they brought their ghosts with them, and within colonial regions these ghosts changed into new and terrifying forms, ones which show the British as haunted by their attempts to conquer and oppress Indigenous peoples. The chapter explores ghost stories set within colonial regions and also examines how the colonial ghost returns to Great Britain as a form of haunted memory. Authors surveyed include Bithia Mary Croker, Arthur Conan Doyle, Ernest Favenc, Rudyard Kipling, Florence Marryat, Rosa Mulholland, Alice Perrin, G. M. Robins and H. G. Wells.

In the chapter titled 'Religion' Alison Milbank argues that it is paradoxical that the ghost story should rise to such prominence in the nineteenth century, at a period of growing challenge to Christian belief. Moreover, Enlightenment thinkers, and Kant in particular, relegated religion to the level of practical reason and separated phenomena, experienced by the senses, from noumena, to which we have no perceptual access, and in which category the supernatural was to be placed. The chapter focuses primarily on J. S. Le Fanu, Elizabeth Gaskell and Margaret Oliphant. In all three cases the afterlife is more real in some ways than the diurnal world because in their ghost stories the noumenal is restored to full presence.

Jeffrey Andrew Weinstock in 'The Victorian American Ghost Story' argues that ghost stories inherently reflect anxieties concerning loss and death, and desires for an afterlife and justice. He analyses how these general anxieties and desires were conditioned by the culturally specific contexts and the personal experiences and tastes of individual American authors during the period. He argues that the Victorian American ghost story was influenced by, and used as a means to address, issues such as the subordination of women, slavery and its aftermath, westward expansion, spiritualism and the epistemological uncertainty introduced by postbellum scientific advances. Writers explored include Ambrose Bierce, Mary E. Wilkins Freeman, Nathaniel Hawthorne, Henry James and Edgar Allan Poe.

The final chapter in this section explores the importance of the seasonal Christmas ghost story. Tara Moore in 'Victorian Christmas Ghosts' explores this culturally important context in which ghost stories became a staple of Christmas celebrations. While frequently devoid of Christmas as a setting, these ghost stories nonetheless made their appearance each December from the middle of the century onwards. Writers discussed include Charles Dickens, Elizabeth Gaskell, Jerome K. Jerome and M. R. James.

Part III explores the work of specific authors who have made an important contribution to the development of the Victorian ghost story. Scott Brewster in 'Charles Dickens' charts and evaluates the contribution of Dickens to the development of the Victorian ghost story. His chapter examines how Dickens's stylistic inventiveness extended the generic possibilities of the ghost story. Brewster argues that these ghost stories revolve around haunting, memory and nostalgia, community and isolation, money and social conscience, but that the allegorical function of the ghost is never settled for Dickens. This chapter shows that, in a period fascinated and daunted by the invisible and unseen, the ghost represents for Dickens a figure of doubtful *and* privileged perception, allowing us fleeting, enigmatic glimpses of the excluded or forgotten within Victorian culture.

Minna Vuohelainen's chapter on Rudyard Kipling analyses Kipling's contribution to the development of the ghost story between the mid-1880s and the early years of the twentieth century. Kipling's earliest ghost stories, published in the Anglo-Indian press in the 1880s, demonstrate a solid understanding of the established conventions and commercial potential of the genre while transporting its familiar tropes to the Anglo-Indian world. By the early twentieth century these generic experiments had evolved into increasingly sophisticated, proto-modernist explorations of hauntings characteristic of the modern world. The chapter examines the recurring preoccupations in Kipling's body of supernatural fiction, which includes issues associated with spectral encounters in the Anglo-Indian home, the dramas of the colonial frontier, and the transformative experience of technology.

Williams Hughes's chapter on Joseph Sheridan Le Fanu acknowledges Le Fanu's important influence on the ghost story tradition, but also argues that the critical focus on a narrow range of texts has distorted Le Fanu's legacy. In order to correct this, the chapter addresses the often overlooked Irish narratives, *The Purcell Papers* (1880), which form a significant component of Le Fanu's short fiction. These narratives tend to consider historical subjects and to balance, on the one hand, an indulgent nostalgia for the morals and manners which ostensibly pertained before the Union with, on the other, an uneasy contemplation of the anarchic behaviour and pervasive superstition supposedly suppressed by the imposition of an anglicised culture. This chapter therefore provides new insights into Le Fanu's contribution to the ghost story.

Valerie Sanders's chapter on Margaret Oliphant argues that Oliphant's supernatural tales tackle emotional longing and inertia in dysfunctional families. The chapter begins by contextualising Oliphant's interest in the dead and her sometimes dystopian concept of the afterlife. The chapter also provides an overview of the themes of her ghost stories before focusing on five of the most important: her novella, *A Beleaguered City* (1879), 'The Open Door' (1882), 'The Lady's Walk' (1882), 'Old Lady Mary' (1884) and 'The Library Window' (1896). Sanders argues that Oliphant's contribution to the genre emphasises the ghost-seers' frustrations with their home lives, and the ghosts' longing for emotionally fulfilling relationships beyond the grave.

In the chapter on Charlotte Riddell, Helena Ifill notes that Riddell was known as *the* novelist of the City, specialising in depicting the lives of businessmen, their families and associates, and these figures often appear in her ghost stories. Riddell's representation of gender is also unusual as she experiments with masculine personas in a more sustained manner than her female contemporaries. This chapter demonstrates how Riddell's ghost stories allowed her to explore her ongoing fascination with business, capitalism and speculation, whilst proving liberating (as they did for so many Victorian authors, especially women) in terms of both content and form.

Ardel Haefele-Thomas's chapter on Vernon Lee explores how Lee utilised the ghost story to explore the danger of bigotry and fanaticism within the specific context of the anti-sodomy laws of the time. Within this historic context queer persecution could not be ignored and this is addressed at different levels of explicitness in Lee's writings. Stories examined include 'A Wicked Voice' (1889–90), 'Oke of Okehurst; Or, The Phantom Lover' (1886) and 'Amour Dure' (1887), as well as Lee's essay 'Deterioration of Soul' (1896) in which Lee confronts the persecution of decadent writers (many of whom were also queer) and the vilification of publications like *The Yellow Book*.

In the chapter on Henry James, Luke Thurston traces the shifting scenarios of the Jamesian ghost story, from the period of the American civil war to the turn of the century, arguing that they provide a vital index of artistic turbulence and self-discovery in James's writings. A range of topics and anxieties are mapped across the stories, from questions of identity and belonging to the uncertain relation between imagination and reality. The chapter argues that James's ghosts challenge conventional reading practices, as a way of disturbing the constrictive and repressive protocols of Victorian bourgeois culture. Exploring some of the key critical responses to *The Turn of the Screw* (1898), Thurston shows how James addresses the undying question of what links the imagination and the real.

Roger Luckhurst's chapter on M. R. James examines James's tales within the context of the club tale, popular at the time, which provided an epistemologically safe place for discussion. Luckhurst argues that James's tales are overdetermined by a set of mutually reinforcing homosocial 'clubbable' worlds. To the closed circuit of Eton and King's College can be added the worlds of college politics, medieval scholars, rule-bound donnish clubs, Cambridge faculty who published occasional ghost tales, and James's own highly ritualised Christmas gatherings. This chapter reconstructs these frames but also addresses how the tales represent issues about persecution, paranoia and sexuality.

Part IV on 'Places' consists of five essays which explore various environments that have shaped the Victorian ghost story. These include landscapes and seascapes, but also other places and spaces such as the haunted house, haunted libraries and museums, and haunted pyramids. Which spaces are haunted, and how and why, provides another way of thinking about what it is that the Victorian ghost makes visible.

In 'Haunted Landscapes' Emma McEvoy examines the haunted landscapes of Britain, India and the Arctic. Gaskell's 'The Old Nurse's Story' (1852) provides the starting point for a consideration of the landscape as spectacle and an examination of how ghost stories reframe and render uncanny other landscape traditions. The chapter considers the geographies of haunting, focusing on what can happen in the haunted landscape that cannot happen elsewhere. McEvoy draws on the insights of eco-Gothic criticism to consider the landscape in relation to environmental concerns, and examines the interpenetration of folklore and literary tradition.

Joan Passey analyses seascapes in her chapter 'Maritime Ghost Stories'. The chapter investigates the recurrence of the ghostly sea in nineteenth-century literature and culture. It situates the sea as a specific locus of contemporaneous anxiety about a transatlantic slave trade, colonisation, scientific survey and a growing global economy. The Victorian spectral sea is a site of inevitable return, the resurgence of the repressed, an alien territory, resisting habitation, where language and rationality become meaningless and dissolved. From the *Flying Dutchman* to the *Mary Celeste* to voices screaming up from the waves, Passey demonstrates the ways in which nineteenth-century seascapes gave up their ghosts.

The idea that the home could be, or could become, haunted is a popular anxiety addressed during this period and Emma Liggins's chapter, 'The Victorian Haunted House', examines the importance of the haunted house in the development of the Victorian ghost story. She draws upon debates about the domestic uncanny, the gendering of space and the roles of (invisible) servants within Gothic fiction. The chapter provides an overview of the ghost story's investment in strange, dark and eerie places, particularly remote ancestral mansions and the borders of their surrounding estates, as well as rented urban accommodation on the wrong side of town. Writers discussed include Joseph Sheridan Le Fanu, Lettice Galbraith, E. Nesbit, and Henry James.

A notable theme in the Victorian ghost story is a fascination with scholarship and knowledge and Darryl Jones's chapter, 'Haunted Libraries and Museums', examines this in depth. The chapter notes that the period witnessed the beginnings of the antiquarian ghost story, in which learning and scholarship is figured in uncanny terms. Tales about colonial acquisitions also address the morality of colonialism in tales which hint at the possibility of revenge against the colonisers who have turned culturally prized possessions into publically displayed museum artefacts.

The final chapter, 'Pyramids', explores the colonial context of haunted spaces by focusing on haunted pyramids. In this chapter I explore how the ghost story responded to the 'Egyptian Question' of the period. In the nineteenth century Britain's protection of its economic interests in the Suez Canal looked to many like an illegitimate form of colonialism, while the tomb excavations in the Valley of the Kings resembled a form of grave-robbing. Egypt provided a different colonial context for British imperialism than that of India or Africa and the ambivalence with which it was regarded is reflected in tales of vengeful mummies, who often appear to have right on their side. The chapter examines writing by Henry Rider Haggard, Arthur Conan Doyle, Kate and Hesketh Prichard and Bram Stoker, amongst others.

All of the chapters in this companion have been specially commissioned. They provide an authoritative account of the Victorian ghost story and all of its varied engagements. The book outlines the important historical phases of the ghost story and engages with the important critical contexts which shaped the form. The volume also evaluates the contributions made to the ghost story by specific authors and explores the places and spaces haunted by ghosts. Victorian ghosts provide us with an insight into the preoccupations of the period. These varied spectres speak to us about how the Victorians conceived of the world and their often precarious place in it.

Works Cited

Briggs, Julia. *Night Visitors: The Rise and Fall of the English Ghost Story*. London: Faber, 1977.
Dickens, Charles. *A Christmas Carol*, in *The Christmas Books*, vol. 1, edited by Michael Slater. Harmondsworth: Penguin, 1985, pp. 45–134.
———. 'Christmas Ghosts' from 'A Christmas Tree', in *The Signalman & Other Ghost Stories*. Stroud: Alan Sutton, 1990, pp. 110–16.
Dickerson, Vanessa D. *Victorian Ghosts in the Noontide: Women Writers and the Supernatural*. Columbia and London: University of Missouri Press, 1996.
Freeman, Nick. 'The Victorian Ghost Story', in Andrew Smith and William Hughes (eds), *The Victorian Gothic: An Edinburgh Companion*. Edinburgh: Edinburgh University Press, 2012, pp. 93–107.
Freud, Sigmund. 'The Uncanny', in *Art and Literature: Jensen's 'Gradiva', Leonardo Da Vinci and Other Works*, edited by Albert Dickson. Harmondsworth: Penguin, 1990, pp. 339–76.

Hay, Simon. *A History of the Modern British Ghost Story*. Basingstoke and New York: Palgrave Macmillan, 2011.
Smith, Andrew. *The Ghost Story 1840–1920: A Cultural History*. Manchester: Manchester University Press, 2010.
Thurston, Luke. *Literary Ghosts from the Victorians to Modernism: The Haunting Interval*. London: Routledge, 2012.

Part I

Historical Contexts

Chapter 1

Gothic Fiction, Romanticism and the Origins of the Nineteenth-Century Ghost Story: 1764–1832

Dale Townshend

As literary critics and cultural historians have often observed, Gothic writing of the late eighteenth and early nineteenth centuries comprises only one, relatively brief episode in the longer history of the Victorian ghost story, a form of supernatural storytelling the origins of which ultimately recede into the mists of ancient oral culture (Killick 2016; Belsey 2019). In her foundational *Night Visitors* (1977), for example, Julia Briggs noted that 'Ghost stories are as old and older than literature', a claim that she proceeded to illustrate through reference to the encounters between humans and supernatural entities figured in the Babylonian epic *Gilgamesh* (c. 2100–1200 BCE); in Homeric poetry of the eighth century BCE; in the Old Testament; the Icelandic eddas of the thirteenth century; the Old English epic poem *Beowulf* (c. 700–1000 CE); and in selected works by Lucian and Pliny the Younger (Briggs 1977: 25–6). With its focus fixed more narrowly on the English tradition, Sasha Handley's *Visions of an Unseen World* (2007) has charted the extent to which various forms of preternatural narrative permeated English culture between c. 1660 and 1800, revealing their presence across a broad cultural field that includes dissenting and Anglican theology; print culture; Graveyard poetry; the notorious Cock Lane ghost of 1762; in national and local constructions of the English landscape; and finally, by way of conclusion to her study, in the Gothic fictions and dramas of Horace Walpole, Ann Radcliffe, Matthew Gregory Lewis and other writers from the 1760s onwards. As Handley figures it here, the Gothic is only one manifestation of a trans-media preoccupation with the preternatural in eighteenth-century English culture, its ghosts, contra E. J. Clery's influential argument in *The Rise of Supernatural Fiction, 1762–1800* (1995), continuing to perform important philosophical, theological and scientific work and engaging contemporary readers for whom the existence of spirits remained a distinct possibility (Clery 1999: 13–32). Indeed, if Gothic ghosts for Handley bear any singularity at all, it might be said to lie in the self-consciously fictional register with which this particular mode engaged with the preternatural, an approach rather different from the religious, political, antiquarian and scientific concerns of other media. The consigning of the ghost to the realm of Gothic fiction from Walpole's *The Castle of Otranto* (1764) onwards, Handley shows, was the culmination of a process of distinguishing between fact and fancy that commenced with the publication of Daniel Defoe's apparition narrative, *A True Relation of the Apparition of One Mrs Veal, the Next Day After Her Death, to one Mrs Bargrave, at Canterbury* (1706), and the passing of the Stamp Acts of 1712 and 1724, which sought to differentiate factual – and thus taxable – news from fictional and sensational forms of reportage (Handley 2016: 95–100, 216). If, before the advent of Gothic fiction, apparitions roved freely across such media as religious sermons, scientific tracts, antiquarian writing, poetry, drama, cheap print and political discourses, it was because, as Handley puts it, 'a settled genre of ghost stories had yet to emerge' (Handley 2016: 210). It is precisely the emergence of the 'settled genre of ghost stories' that I wish to chart in this chapter, that is, the ghost story as we have come to regard it in its most recognisable form as a shorter, self-contained work of prose fiction that generates a certain readerly *frisson* through graphic depictions or subtle suggestions of spectres, hauntings and other forms of supernatural encounter.

Though by no means the first example of supernatural storytelling in British culture, Walpole's *The Castle of Otranto* was nonetheless foundational to what, in time, would become the nineteenth-century ghost story. The narrative practically teems with ghosts and other supernatural phenomena: a painted portrait comes mysteriously to life and issues forth as an 'infernal spectre' (Walpole 2014: 25); doors in the castle slam shut as if by the work of an 'invisible hand' (25), so that the servant Bianca legitimately comes to believe that 'This castle is certainly haunted' (39); the guilt-stricken Manfred momentarily mistakes Frederic for a 'dreadful spectre' (76) or 'ghastly phantom'(76); Theodore regards the good Alfonso as an 'unsatisfied shade' (87); the apparition of a skeleton 'wrapt in a hermit's cowl' (98) appears before Frederic; and in the narrative's closing moments, the ghost of Alfonso, 'dilated to an immense magnitude' (103), appears in order to proclaim Theodore his true and legitimate heir as the castle falls to the ground in ruins around it. In several of these instances, the manifestation and apprehension of ghosts is licensed by the examples of Shakespeare's *Hamlet* and *Macbeth*, a gesture borne in Walpole's assertion of the virtues of a 'Gothic' or natively English supernatural tradition against the critiques levelled at the Bard by Voltaire and other French neoclassicists

(Townshend 2008). But they are also firmly of the order of 'the darkest ages of [C]hristianity' that the Protestant Walpole, in the guise of the translator William Marshal, decried in *Otranto*'s first Preface, an aspect of the 'empire of superstition' that was peddled by the 'artful priests' of the Counter-Reformation who sought to 'confirm the populace in their ancient errors and superstitions' (Walpole 2014: 5).

Some of the major Gothic fictions published in *Otranto*'s wake contained episodes that, with hindsight, might be regarded as important moments in the historical development of the Victorian ghost story. In the fourth volume of Ann Radcliffe's *The Mysteries of Udolpho* (1794), for instance, the heroine Emily St Aubert, having fled the eponymous castle, takes up residence at the Château-le-Blanc, the Gothic pile in France to which she and a number of other characters have made their way. The white double to the dark Udolpho, the Château-le-Blanc, Emily soon learns, is too thought to be haunted: mysterious music haunts the battlements; the castle contains an uncanny portrait of a woman who, though consciously unknown, is all too familiar; and the housekeeper Dorothée tells Emily the unhappy story of the castle's previous owner, the late Marchioness de Villeroi, who is believed to haunt the tapestried bedchamber on the north side of the castle in which she died some twenty years earlier. When Dorothée accompanies the terrified but no less curious Emily by night to the haunted apartment in question, she claims to see her mistress's ghost stretched out on the pall that is laid on the draped bed on which the marchioness died. Shocked by the housekeeper's reactions, Emily involuntarily peers behind the bed's curtains, but only to observe the blackness of the funereal pall itself. Looking again, however, she watches in terror as the velvet pall moves, lifts up into the air and then moves again. In a notable reversal of precedents established in the interactions between Emily and the servant Annette concerning the apparent haunting of Udolpho earlier in the narrative, it is the superstitious servant who allays the middle-class heroine's fears on this occasion – '"It is only the wind, that waves it, ma'amselle"', she explains (Radcliffe 1998: 535) – and, thus chastened, Emily is momentarily embarrassed by the intensity of her reactions. But when both women look at the marchioness's bed for the third time, 'the pall moved again, and, in the next moment, the apparition of a human countenance rose above it' (Radcliffe 1998: 536). Screaming in terror, heroine and maidservant flee the deserted bedchamber, both thoroughly convinced that it is haunted by the ghost of the Marchioness de Villeroi.

Ludovico, one of Montoni's servants who has accompanied Emily to France, is determined to put such superstitions permanently to rest, and elects to spend a night in the castle's north apartment. '"I will engage,"' he confidently boasts, '"that no spectre shall disturb the peace of the chateau after this night"' (Radcliffe 1998: 545). Armed with nothing more than an old book of romances that the superstitious Dorothée has lent him, he settles into the supposedly haunted room, reading there, by the light of a flickering fire, 'The Provençal Tale', one of the stories in the old anthology that is included in full in Radcliffe's narrative. Being 'strongly tinctured with the superstition of the times' (Radcliffe 1998: 552), this interpolated tale tells the story of Baron de Brunne, a nobleman of Bretagne (Brittany) who is visited by a mysterious stranger as he retires one night to bed. Of a 'noble air, but of a sorrowful and dejected countenance' and dressed in the habiliments of a knight, the stranger is 'of a tall and majestic stature, and of dignified and courteous manners' (Radcliffe 1998: 552, 553), yet when the baron questions him as to his identity, he replies only with silence and the promise that he will reveal to the baron a 'terrible secret' if he accompanies him to the nearby forest (Radcliffe 1998: 553). Pressed by the baron once again, the knight reluctantly introduces himself as Sir Bevys of Lancaster, a famed English knight who, as he cryptically communicates, was 'benighted' in the neighbouring forest upon his return from the Holy Land (Radcliffe 1998: 554). Despite his misgivings, the baron reluctantly follows Sir Bevys into the forest's darkest recesses, and it is here that he is shown the bloody corpse of a man with a ghastly wound on its forehead. When the baron inspects the body further, he is chilled to discover in its features 'the exact resemblance of the stranger his conductor' (Radcliffe 1998: 556). Sir Bevys, it becomes clear, is the ghost of the English knight who was murdered in the forest upon his return from the Crusades, and who now, in the form of a spectre, makes of the baron two requests: 'inter the body in [C]hristian ground, and cause his murderers to be punished' (Radcliffe 1998: 556). The baron oversees the burial of the ghostly knight's body in the chapel of his own castle, and although no account is given of whether Sir Bevys's murderers are ever apprehended or whether the spectre, having been at least partially appeased, is content to disappear, the narrative at this point breaks off as Ludovico closes the book, falls asleep and begins to dream vividly of yet another ghostly encounter involving the face of a man that stares intently at him over the high back of his armchair. When, the next morning, it is discovered that he has disappeared from the marchioness's chamber, Radcliffe momentarily lends credence to the servants' superstitions: the apartments in the north of the Château-le-Blanc do, indeed, appear to be haunted and Ludovico, while passing the night there, has seemingly been carried off by a spectre. In fact, it is only several chapters later that *The Mysteries of Udolpho* provides a material explanation for this event, for as Ludovico comes to reveal, he had been abducted by a band of ruffians or pirates who, for many years, had secreted the spoils of their plunder in the castle's vaults and who deliberately fabricated tales of the castle's haunting so as to keep its inhabitants at bay and thus to prevent their crimes' detection. The supernaturalism of 'The Provençal Tale', for its part, remains intact, and even as it features as merely a short inset narrative within a longer Gothic romance, it was certainly received by members of the Romantic literati as a short, self-contained work of supernatural fiction in its own right: William Hazlitt described it as the 'greatest treat' that Radcliffe's pen has provided 'for the lovers of the marvellous and terrible' (Hazlitt 1819: 252); Walter Scott, applauding Radcliffe for her abandoning of the explained supernatural in the piece, praised the 'admirable ghost-story' that Ludovico reads in the narrative of the haunted chamber (Scott 1824: xxvii); and Leigh Hunt, equally impressed by both the story of Ludovico's disappearance and 'The Provençal Tale', extracted and presented both as a composite and exemplary manifestation of super-natural storytelling in *A Book for a Corner* (1849).

A three-volume Gothic romance comprising several shorter narratives, inset ballads and poems, Matthew Gregory Lewis's *The Monk* (1796) included at least two tales of the supernatural that, together, lead us closer to the terrain of the nineteenth-century ghost story. In the first of these, the story of the Bleeding Nun, as it is told by Don Raymond in the second volume, is the ghost of Beatrice de las Cisternas, a figure who, in many ways, is the double of the titular monk Ambrosio, and who is said to haunt a chamber in the Castle of Lindenberg, Germany. Derived from Johann Karl August Musäus's 'Die Entführung' (translated as 'The Elopement' or 'The Abduction') from his five-volume *Volksmärchen der Deutschen* (1782–7), Lewis's story tells of how the heroine Agnes contrived to disguise herself as the Bleeding Nun in order to escape from her confinement in the Lindenberg Castle and run away with her beloved Raymond. Plans go horribly awry, however, and Raymond elopes not with his disguised lover but with the ghost of the Bleeding Nun herself, a 'real' supernatural entity who appears thereafter at his bedside over a succession of nights so as to taunt him repeatedly with her ghastly refrain: '"Raymond! Raymond! Thou art mine! / Raymond! Raymond! I am thine!"' (Lewis 2004: 156). The mouldering skeleton of her body concealed in a nearby cave, this spectre, like the ghostly Sir Bevys in 'The Provençal Tale', demands of the living a proper burial in consecrated ground, a duty with which Raymond himself is charged. This, together with the exorcism that is performed by the Wandering Jew, is sufficient to appease Beatrice's restless spirit. Although this act provides a conclusion of sorts to the story, the existence of the supernatural itself remains unchallenged, Lewis's narrative technique remaining in the end considerably different from that of Radcliffe.

A second, equally significant supernatural story in *The Monk* is 'Alonzo the Brave and Fair Imogine', a ballad that the novel's other heroine, Antonia, peruses in the third volume and a reworking of Gottfried August Bürger's 'Lenardo und Blandine' (1776) as well as his extremely influential ballad of supernatural seduction 'Lenore' (written 1773; published 1774; first translated into English in 1796). Lewis's version in 'Alonzo the Brave' tells the story of the titular lovers who are separated from one another when Alonzo, a knight or warrior, is called away to Palestine to join the Crusades. Swearing perpetual fealty to her lord, the beautiful Imogine makes to him a weighty promise: '"If e'er I, by lust or by wealth led aside, / Forget my Alonzo the Brave, / God grant, that to punish my falsehood and pride / Your ghost at the marriage may sit by my side, / May tax me with perjury, claim me as bride, / And bear me away to the grave!"' (Lewis 2004: 271). Convinced of his beloved's fidelity, Alonzo departs, but no sooner has he left than Imogine's affections stray as she is captivated by a wealthy and attractive baron. On the day of her marriage to her new object of desire, a silent and inscrutable knight arrives at the wedding feast, the visor of his helmet drawn; when he uncloses it, he reveals to the horror of all, and in lines that would be tirelessly replayed, burlesqued and parodied throughout the period, the decrepit head of a skeleton: 'The worms they crept in, and the worms they crept out, / And sported his eyes and his temples about' (Lewis 2004: 273). This mysterious stranger, it is clear, is the ghost of the once beloved Alonzo, returned from the afterlife so as to exact the terms of the faithless Imogine's initial promise to him: '"Behold me, thou false one!"' he ominously cries, '"remember Alonzo the Brave!"' (Lewis 2004: 273). Seizing Imogine, the spectre disappears with his lover through the floor, dragging her into a hellish afterlife in some strange subterranean realm. Four times a year, at midnight, forever thereafter, so the penultimate stanza of the ballad relates, the spectre of Imogine appears to dance with her Skeleton-Knight in the hall of the baron's castle, the throng of ghosts that accompany the couple cavorting around them while drinking blood from skulls that have been newly torn from the grave.

If, through the elaborate process of allusion, doubling and repetition that structures *The Monk*, neither of Lewis's two supernatural tales is, strictly speaking, entirely discrete from, or independent of, the longer Gothic romance in which they occur, their afterlife in late eighteenth- and early nineteenth-century British culture certainly made of them something approaching the short and self-contained ghostly fictions of the Victorian period. As Franz J. Potter has shown, Lewis's romance all but galvanised contemporary publishers' interests in bringing Gothic chapbooks to press (Potter 2021: 29–50), with the supernaturalism of the Raymond, Agnes and Bleeding Nun story, in particular, proving particularly popular in such titles as Sarah Wilkinson's *Castle of Lindenberg* (1796) as well as such anonymous chapbooks as *The History of Raymond and Agnes* (1803) and *Almagro & Claude* (1803). In these and other examples, a fictional account of the supernatural that is left wholly unexplained takes the form of a short story in prose; as Diane Long Hoeveler thus argues, it is to the Gothic chapbook that we should look for examples of ghost stories in the period prior to their heyday in the mid- to late nineteenth century (Hoeveler 2018: 25).

Yet, when M. R. James, the undisputed master of the British ghost story in the first three decades of the twentieth century, looked back on the Gothic fictions of Radcliffe, Lewis and their contemporaries, he was struck by just how unamenable their work was to the mode of storytelling that, as he famously put it, was 'written with the sole object of inspiring a pleasing terror in the reader' (James 2013: 411). Indeed, what emerges from the many articles that James wrote on the subject, as well as from the numerous paratexts that he penned for various collections of short supernatural fiction, are the clear differences that he saw between the nineteenth-century ghost story, on the one hand, and early Gothic writing, on the other, the latter a mode upon which he reflected at some length in the essay 'Some Remarks on Ghost Stories' that was published in *The Bookman* in December 1929. While conceding that *The Castle of Otranto* is 'perhaps the progenitor of the ghost story as a literary genre', James here went on to opine that 'I fear that it is merely amusing in the modern sense', thus situating Walpole's text at considerable remove from the pleasurable discomforts of the ghost story as he had formulated them in the Preface to his seminal *Ghost Stories of an Antiquary* (1904) and elsewhere (James 2013: 411, 406). Radcliffe's romances, in which 'ghosts are far better of their kind', he continued, were marred by the 'exasperating timidity' that demanded that they be explained away, while Lewis's *The Monk* was 'odious and horrible without being impressive' (James 2013: 411). Although James was willing to countenance the significance of supernatural ballads in the larger genealogy of the British ghost story that he sketched out in this essay, claiming that 'we must not forget that the ballad is in the direct line of ancestry of the ghost story', he was more drawn to the traditional ghostly ballads collected in Thomas Percy's *Reliques of Ancient English Poetry* (1765), the 'fine ghost stories' that Walter Scott had contributed to Lewis's *Tales of Wonder* or to those anthologised in Scott's *Minstrelsy of the Scottish*

Border (1802–30) than to 'Alonzo the Brave' or any other ghostly ballad that 'Monk Lewis' himself had written (James 2013: 411).

As it soon becomes clear, James's reservations with the work of his Gothic forebears are founded on two points of contention, the first the conventional historical settings of these narratives and the second the Radcliffean tendency to dispose of the supernatural via the narrative contrivances of the explained supernatural. 'I think that, as a rule, the setting should be fairly familiar and the majority of the characters and their talk such as you may meet or hear any day,' he wrote in the Preface to *More Ghost Stories of an Antiquary* (1911); 'A ghost story of which the scene is laid in the twelfth or thirteenth century may succeed in being romantic or poetical,' he continued, though 'it will never put the reader into the position of saying to himself, "If I'm not very careful, something of this kind may happen to me!"' (James 2013: 406). While, unlike the detective story, which 'cannot be too much up-to-date', a 'slight haze of distance' is desirable in the ghost story, the medieval or renaissance settings of so many Gothic novels and romances, James explained in 1924, was too 'antique' to engage the reader effectively, for 'some degree of actuality' is the 'charm' of the best ghost stories, an actuality or sense of plausibility that is strong enough 'to allow the reader to identify with himself with the patient' and to ward against the tendency for the reader of an 'antique story' to 'fall into the position of a mere spectator' (James 2013: 408). 'Roughly speaking,' he later elaborated, 'the ghost should be a contemporary of the seer', as it is in such effective examples of supernatural storytelling as Shakespeare's *Hamlet* and Charles Dickens's *A Christmas Carol* (1843), for it 'cannot be said too often that the more remote in time the ghost is the harder it is to make him effective, always supposing him to be the ghost of a dead person' (James 2013: 417). Actuality of setting, however, was not to be confused with a cultivated sense of facticity, and James was clear that any ghost story that, in the tradition of the apparition narratives of the late seventeenth and early eighteenth centuries, made claims to being based on verifiable truth was not a form of spectral writing with which he shared any affinity (James 2013: 410). As he put it in an article, 'Ghosts—Treat Them Gently!', that was published in the *Evening News* in April 1931, such 'veridical' ghost stories were utterly distinct from the ghost story in its self-consciously literary forms. Yet, as his comments on Radcliffe suggest, it was the tradition of the explained supernatural that James thought to be particularly inimical to the generation of the ghost story's pleasurable terrors. As he reasoned in the Introduction to V. H. Collins's collected *Ghosts and Marvels* (1924), while it was not amiss in the ghost story 'sometimes to leave a loophole for a natural explanation', such an aperture should be so narrow 'as not to be quite practicable' (James 2013: 407). 'The reading of many ghost stories has shown me that the greatest successes have been scored by the authors who can make us envisage a definite time and place,' he wrote in 'Some Remarks on Ghost Stories', but who, 'when the climax is reached, allow us to be just a little in the dark as to the working of their machinery. We do not want to see the bones of their theory about the supernatural' (James 2013: 415). By this line of reasoning, the fictions of Ann Radcliffe and her school, all populated by ghosts that eventually give way to the powers of reason and rationality, were a far cry from what James took to be the more successful ghost stories of such nineteenth-century British writers as Dickens, Joseph Sheridan Le Fanu, Edward Bulwer-Lytton, Wilkie Collins, Rhoda Broughton, Mrs Henry Wood and Margaret Oliphant.

Faintly damning of the work of Walpole, Radcliffe and Lewis though they are, James's comments are nonetheless useful in distinguishing these and other early manifestations of the Gothic mode from the Victorian ghost story proper, as it were, providing, as they do so, a salutary corrective to the tendency to regard eighteenth-century Gothic fiction as simply an immature adumbration of the form, or the shorter spectral narratives that comprise it as little more than nineteenth-century ghost stories 'in the making'. They also provide a way of situating in relation to the history of the Victorian ghost story the brief Gothic fictions and fragments that were published in periodicals in the late eighteenth and early nineteenth centuries, a mass of rich and fascinating material to which Robert D. Mayo first drew critical attention and which has been mined in the numerous collections and anthologies of shorter Gothic tales that have been published since the 1990s (Mayo 1950; Baldick 2009; Morrison and Baldick 1995, 1997; Macdonald 2020). Though often demonstrating a fleeting interest in the supernatural, the Gothic short stories published between c. 1780 and 1830 in such periodicals as *The European Magazine, The Universal Magazine of Knowledge and Pleasure, The General Magazine and Impartial Review, Walker's Hibernian Magazine, The Edinburgh Magazine* and the *Lady's Monthly Museum* are distinct from the Victorian ghost story insofar as they are almost invariably set in 'ancient' Gothic times and in strange and unfamiliar locales. The medieval, feudal settings of such narratives are quite different from the more quotidian if not mundane settings of the Victorian ghost story, an aspect of the form upon which James reflected in his article in the *Evening News* in April 1931 (James 2013: 416–17). James's reservations with 'veridical' ghost narratives and his comments on the importance of fictionality more broadly, moreover, are useful in distinguishing another prominent strand of early nineteenth-century spectral writing from the ghost stories written and published later in the century. In a continuation of the tradition of the apparition narratives of Defoe, Joseph Glanvill and others, such beguiling titles as the chapbook anthology of 'real' supernatural narratives *Tales of Superstition; or, Relations of Apparitions* (1803), T. M. Jarvis's *Accredited Ghost Stories* (1823) or John Timbs's pseudonymous *Signs Before Death, and Authenticated Apparitions: In One Hundred Narratives* (1825) all offered 'truthful' accounts of ghosts, often at the expense of the generation of a 'pleasing terror'. While acknowledging the significant place that the spectral narratives of the late eighteenth and early nineteenth century occupied in the history of the British ghost story, M. R. James remained poignantly aware of the numerous points of difference between the two traditions.

It was, indeed, the innovations that were introduced to the writing and publication of shorter supernatural fiction during the Romantic period that would prove to be the crucial point of transition between early Gothic writing and the Victorian ghost story, and it is to a brief account of these that I turn in the remainder of this chapter. The first factor at stake pertained to relations of confluence, according to which Romantic essayists, poets, novelists and short-story writers self-consciously drew upon earlier Gothic traditions yet modified them with a number of small but significant inflections, anticipating the nineteenth-century ghost story as they did so. That the gathering of Lord Byron, Percy Bysshe Shelley, Mary Wollstonecraft Godwin, Jane (Claire) Clairmont and John William Polidori at the Villa Diodati, Geneva, in the summer of 1816 constituted a formative moment in the development of nineteenth-century literature, Gothic, Romantic and otherwise, has long been established (see Callaghan and Wright 2020). Looking back on the genesis of *Frankenstein; or, The Modern Prometheus* (1818) in the 'Author's Introduction' to Henry Colburn and Richard Bentley's Standard Novels edition of the text in 1831, Mary Shelley famously made mention of the 'volumes of ghost stories, translated from the German into French' that the group read as they whiled away the bad weather, a reference to *Fantasmagoriana* (1812) (Shelley 1992: 7), Jean-Baptiste Benoît Eyriès's anonymous French translation of the first two volumes of *Gespensterbuch* (1810–11), a collection of German ghost stories by Johann Apel and Friedrich Schulze that, itself, claimed to have been based on orally transmitted tales of the supernatural (Van Woudenberg 2020: 42–3). Although none of the completed fictions to have emerged from Byron's legendary storytelling competition – Shelley's *Frankenstein*, Polidori's *The Vampyre: A Tale* (1819) and his *Ernestus Berchtold; or, The Modern Oedipus* (1819) – is a ghost story in any strict sense, they ultimately took their inspiration from a collection of short German tales of the supernatural, at once replaying the German influences upon a writer such as Matthew Gregory Lewis in the 1790s and anticipating the formative effects that other German ghost stories such as Heinrich von Kleist's 'Das Bettelweib von Locarno' (1810) [The Beggar Woman of Locarno] and E. T. A. Hoffmann's 'Der Elementargeist' (1821) [The Elementary Spirit] and 'Die Bergwerkezu Falun' (1819) [The Mines of Falun] would have on British ghost story writers later in the nineteenth century. Certainly, the influence of German tales of the supernatural on the development of the Victorian ghost story cannot be over-emphasised. R. P. Gillies's *German Stories*, a three-volume anthology of short German fictions in English translation, contained such important supernatural tales as 'The First of May; or Wallburga's Night', 'The Warning' and 'The Spectre Bride', the latter a version of the German story that was especially influential upon Washington Irving's 'The Spectre Bridegroom' from *The Sketch Book of Geoffrey Crayon, Gent.* (1819–20). We know, too, that spectres, ghosts and apparitions featured prominently in the conversations that passed between Lewis, Byron and Percy Shelley when Lewis visited Byron, his friend and erstwhile neighbour, at the Villa Diodati in mid-August 1816. 'We talk of ghosts,' Percy recorded in his *Journal at Geneva* on Sunday 18 August; 'Neither Lord B or [sic] M. G. L. seem to believe in them, and they both agree in the very face of reason, that none could believe in Ghosts without believing in God' (Shelley 1997: 156). Lewis proceeded to recite a ghostly ballad that he had composed at the request of his friend the Princess of Wales, a reworking of both Bürger's 'Lenore' and his own 'Alonzo the Brave and Fair Imogine'. In addition to this metrical tale of the unfaithful Mina and the ghost of her dead husband, Lewis also told Byron and Percy four other supernatural tales, 'all grim', the latter noted as he recorded them in his journal, and each of them returning the ghost story to its roots in the older oral tradition of storytelling (Shelley 1997: 157–9).

Although she had not joined the company at Diodati on this particular occasion, Mary Shelley remained fascinated throughout the remainder of her life by Lewis's ghost stories as they had been related to her by Percy. In her stirring call for the re-enchantment of contemporary existence in her essay 'On Ghosts' (1824), for example, she would include the last of them, a tale about the spectral King of Cats, as an appendix, subsequently publishing paraphrases of all four in the second volume of her edition of Percy Shelley's *Essays, Letters from Abroad, Translations and Fragments* in 1840. Beyond the case of *Frankenstein*, the influence of the supernatural tales of Lewis and other Gothic writers in Mary Shelley's oeuvre is perhaps most keenly felt in 'The Invisible Girl', a story of the forbidden love between Rosina and Henry Vernon that was first published in *The Keepsake for MDCCCXXXIII* in late 1832 and which, in its concerns with portraiture, working-class superstitions, mourning, Gothic architectural ruin and apparent acts of haunting, knowingly recalls the conventions of earlier, eighteenth-century Gothic romance. While it is undoubtedly the most spectral of Shelley's tales and short stories, 'The Invisible Girl' ultimately makes recourse to the technique of the explained supernatural in revealing that, contrary to what has long been assumed, the eponymous figure is no revenant haunting the ruined tower on the Welsh coast but the outcast and wretched yet still living figure of Rosina, Henry's lover, herself. Indeed, it was only with Walter Scott's aesthetic critique and practical revision of the explained supernatural during the 1820s that the influence of this earlier Gothic narrative technique would be resisted, challenged and ultimately dismantled. As Scott, commenting on Radcliffe's tendency to rationalise and explain away her spectres, wrote in his Preface to James Ballantyne's Novelists' Library edition of Radcliffe's works in 1824, 'It must be allowed, that this has not been done with uniform success, and that the author has been more successful in exciting interest and apprehensions, than in explaining the means she has made use of' (Scott 1824: xxiv). The concluding chapters in any such a fiction, he went on, those tiresome sections in which the author 'must unravel the skein of adventures which they have been so industrious to perplex, and account for the incidents which they have been at so much pains to render unaccountable', constituted nothing less than the 'torment' of the romance writer and reader alike (Scott 1824: xxiv). In 'Wandering Willie's Tale', consequently, the self-contained ghost story that, in the fashion of 'The Provençal Tale' from *The Mysteries of Udolpho*, Scott included in his novel *Redgauntlet: A Tale of the Eighteenth Century* (1824) that same year, he took care to leave the supernatural for the most part unvanquished. Though the ending of the blind musician's story of his grandfather Steenie Steenson's encounter with the supernatural equivocates somewhat – Steenie may just have easily been tricked by Sir Robert's whistle-blowing pet ape as witness a foul entity squatting on the Laird's coffin – it is ultimately clear that the rational explanation of events peddled by Sir John Redgauntlet has been used to conceal the fact that Steenie has really obtained the receipt for his rent from the ghost of Sir Robert, John Redgauntlet's brother who has been consigned to the fires of hell.

In 'On the Supernatural in Fictitious Composition', the review article of three works by Hoffmann that was published in *The Foreign Quarterly Review* in 1827, Scott elaborated upon, and refined, his views on ghost fiction, celebrating the powers of mystery and obscurity as they might be brought to bear on the representation of the spirit world and claiming that 'The marvellous, more than any other attribute of fictitious composition, loses its effect by being brought much into view' (Scott 1827: 62). The spectre, he here argued, was a figure of radical or absolute otherness, to the extent that 'the exhibition of supernatural appearance in fictitious narrative ought to be rare, brief, indistinct, and such as may become a being to us so incomprehensible, and so different from ourselves' (Scott 1827: 63). These are certainly the qualities with which Scott imbues the apparition in what is probably his best-known piece of short supernatural fiction, 'The Tapestried Chamber; or, The Lady in the Sacque', one of the three short stories that he published in *The Keepsake for MDCCCXXIX* in December 1828. Although Scott's ghost story invokes and alludes to Radcliffe's story of Ludovico in the tapestried chamber throughout, it dispenses with the rational explanation of events that is eventually provided in *The Mysteries of Udolpho*. Indeed, so real a threat is the malevolent spectre of the old woman in the flowing gown that appears before General Browne at Woodville Castle that he summarily departs from his friend's home in terror while Woodville oversees the bricking up of the haunted room in question. Though the story maintains some of the Gothic trappings of earlier supernatural fiction, including its descriptions of the disused wing of the castle, the preoccupation with strange portraits and the intimations of murder and incest, it updates these with the more modern setting of c. 1783, 'About the end of the American war' (Scott 1829: 124). Scott's short ghostly fictions suspend the use of the explained supernatural and take us closer to the terrain of the Victorian ghost story: as Catherine Crowe, one of the Victorian period's most ardent champions of ghost beliefs and fiction, well understood in *The Night Side of Nature* (1848), to dismiss the supernatural as either an electrical hoax, a sleight of hand or a trick of the light was to participate in what she called the 'credulity of the sceptical', an over-eagerness to indulge in scientific explanations and thereby to overlook the real existence of poltergeists and other such supernatural phenomena (Crowe 1848: II, 259).

As Jessica Cox has argued, *The Keepsake*, the literary annual that ran from 1828 to 1857, was crucial to the genesis of the Victorian ghost story insofar as it provided the outlet for such important examples of short Gothic, supernatural or quasi-supernatural fiction as Mary Shelley's 'The Invisible Girl', 'Ferdinando Eboli' (1828) and 'The Mortal Immortal: A Tale' (1833) and Walter Scott's 'The Tapestried Chamber' and 'My Aunt Margaret's Mirror' (1828) (Cox 2016: 54–5). Another important periodical of the 1820s, Cox points out, was *The Terrific*

Register, the cheap, weekly magazine that ran from 1823 to 1825 that the young Charles Dickens enthusiastically read and which included sensationalised accounts of execution, crime, murder, incest, cannibalism, ghosts and apparitions, the influence of which might be traced in Dickens's own ghost stories (Cox 2016: 56). The most culturally significant outlet for short tales of horror and terror in the period, however, was undoubtedly *Blackwood's Edinburgh Magazine*, the publisher William Blackwood's controversial and often provocative answer to the Whiggish *Edinburgh Review* that was founded in October 1817 and which comprised a heady mixture of humour, literary commentary and review, right-wing political opinion and, as Edgar Allan Poe's satirical 'How to Write a Blackwood Article' (1838) makes clear, lurid and sensational short fiction. A mere glance at some of the original literary offerings in *Blackwood's* reveals that very few of these stories contained ghosts or other intimations of the supernatural: the haunting dealt with in Scott's 'Narrative of a Fatal Event' (May 1818) is psychological rather than supernatural in causation; the narrator in Daniel Keyte Sandford's 'A Night in the Catacombs' (October 1818) dreams of spectres but does not encounter them in waking reality; and John Galt's 'The Buried Alive' (October 1821) is a horror story of taphophobia and not unlike the extreme states of claustrophobia explored in William Maginn's 'The Man in the Bell' (November 1821) and William Mudford's 'The Iron Shroud' (August 1830). While Henry Thomson's 'Le Revenant' (April 1827) appears to be narrated by the ghost of a guilty man from beyond the grave, we learn in the end that the narrator has faked his own death and is thus no revenant. Likewise, the spectre that seems to haunt the hangman in William Godwin the Younger's 'The Executioner' (February–March 1832) is no ghost so much as the projection of a guilty conscience; Samuel Warren's 'The Spectre-Smitten' (February 1831) is, like his other contributions to *Blackwood's*, more concerned with the medical, quasi-scientific recording of Mr M—'s extreme physical and psychological reactions to seeing the apparition of Mr T— than indulging its readers in the pleasurable terrors of a well-wrought ghost story.

Amidst so many tales of madness, criminality, anxiety, guilt and corporeal horror, the contributions of James Hogg to *Blackwood's* distinguish themselves through their interests in the spectral and the supernatural, and it is, indeed, with a consideration of Hogg's contributions to the nineteenth-century ghost story, both in *Blackwood's* and elsewhere, that I would like to conclude this chapter. In 'The Mysterious Bride', a story that was published in *Blackwood's* in December 1830, Hogg told the chilling tale of the malevolent ghost of Jane Ogilvie who returns so many years later to wreak her fatal revenge upon the love-smitten son of her murderer, the Laird Allan Sandison. Set in Scotland in the year 1777, this haunting, its narrator emphasises, 'happened in my own remembrance', a claim that definitively breaks with the historical settings of earlier Gothic writing in the same gesture that it draws the story well within the limits of actuality and credibility as M. R. James would later define them (Morrison and Baldick 1995: 115). Ostensibly a continuation of 'The Shepherd's Calendar', the series of tales and essays that Hogg contributed to *Blackwood's* between 1819 and 1828, 'The Mysterious Bride' was one of several stories of ghosts, the supernatural and the prophetic power of dreams that he published in this magazine in a sub-series entitled 'Dreams and Apparitions', standing alongside such supernatural tales as 'George Dobson's Expedition to Hell, and The Souters of Selkirk' (May 1827), 'Tibby Hyslop's Dream, and the Sequel' (June 1827), 'Smithy Cracks, &c.' (July 1827) and 'The Laird of Cassway' (August 1827). Other stories based on Scottish supernatural traditions that Hogg would contribute to *Blackwood's* in the late 1820s include 'Mary Burnet' (February 1828), 'The Witches of Traquair' (April 1828) and 'The Brownie of the Black Haggs' (October 1828), together with the stories in the 'Dreams and Apparitions' series and other pieces that had first been published in *Blackwood's*, these would be anthologised as *The Shepherd's Calendar* in 1829. These stories were all developments of, and elaborations upon, experiments with short supernatural fiction that Hogg had been engaged with at least since 1810, when he published 'Story of the Ghost of Lochmaben, by John Miller' in his weekly periodical *The Spy* (September 1810–August 1811), a story of a vengeful spectre that first appeared on 29 December 1810 and which was extended and published as 'The Wife of Lochmaben' in his *Winter Evening Tales* (1820). Included in this collection's 'Country Dreams and Apparitions' sub-series, 'The Wife of Lochmaben' sat alongside such other tales of apparitions, visions, dreams and uncanny phenomena as 'John Gray o' Middleholm', 'Cousin Mattie', 'Welldean Hall' and 'Tibby Johnston's Wraith'. Throughout his ghost stories, Hogg was keen to document the experiences, supernatural beliefs and superstitious customs of the people of his native Ettrick, often drawing upon oral traditions of supernatural lore, legend and storytelling in order to furnish his readers with accounts of folk belief that were as authentic as they were pleasurable. In so doing, he unwittingly threw off the shackles of earlier Gothic writing even as, in *The Private Memoirs and Confessions of a Justified Sinner* (1824) and elsewhere in his short fiction, he partially situated himself within this very tradition. Setting his ghost stories not in the far-flung reaches of medieval Europe but in the domestic, even quotidian environments of modern-day Scotland, Hogg also turned his back on the explained supernatural, that narrative quirk that so vexed the likes of Walter Scott in the same decade and later Catherine Crowe and M. R. James. In the short supernatural fictions of James Hogg of the 1820s, then, the conditions for the Victorian ghost story had securely set in place. It is to an account of how and why British and American writers of short supernatural fiction across the nineteenth century drew upon, developed and elaborated upon this tradition that the remaining chapters of this volume turn.

Works Cited

Baldick, Chris, ed. *The Oxford Book of Gothic Tales*. Oxford: Oxford University Press, 2009.
Belsey, Catherine. *Tales of the Troubled Dead: Ghost Stories in Cultural History*. Edinburgh: Edinburgh University Press, 2019.
Briggs, Julia. *Night Visitors: The Rise and Fall of the English Ghost Story*. London: Faber, 1977.
Callaghan, Madeleine and Angela Wright. 'Gothic Romanticism and the Summer of 1816', in Dale Townshend and Angela Wright (eds), *The Cambridge History of the Gothic, Vol. II: Gothic in the Nineteenth Century*. Cambridge: Cambridge University Press, 2020, pp. 19–40.
Clery, E. J. *The Rise of Supernatural Fiction, 1762–1800*. Cambridge: Cambridge University Press, 1999.
Cox, Jessica. 'Gothic and Victorian Supernatural Tales', in Dominic Head (ed.), *The Cambridge History of the English Short Story*. Cambridge: Cambridge University Press, 2016, pp. 49–66.
Crowe, Catherine. *The Night Side of Nature; or, Ghost and Ghost Seers*, 2 vols. London: T. C. Newby, 1848.
Handley, Sasha. *Visions of an Unseen World: Ghost Beliefs and Ghost Stories in Eighteenth-Century England*. Abingdon: Routledge, 2016.
Hazlitt, William. *Lectures on the English Comic Writers. Delivered at the Surry* [sic] *Institution*. London: Taylor and Hessey, 1819.
Hoeveler, Diane Long. 'Gothic and Romantic Ghosts in Novels, Dramas, and the Chapbook', in Scott Brewster and Luke Thurston (eds), *The Routledge Handbook to the Ghost Story*. New York: Routledge, 2018, pp. 19–28.
James, M. R. *Collected Ghost Stories*, edited by Darryl Jones. Oxford: Oxford University Press, 2013.
Killick, Tim. *British Short Fiction in the Early Nineteenth Century: The Rise of the Tale*. Abingdon and New York: Routledge, 2016.
Lewis, Matthew Gregory. *The Monk*, edited by D. L. Macdonald and Kathleen Scherf. Peterborough, ON: Broadview Press, 2004.
Macdonald, Jennie, ed. *Schabraco and Other Gothic Tales from The Lady's Monthly Museum, 1798–1828*. Richmond, VA: Valancourt Books, 2020.
Mayo, Robert D. 'Gothic Romance in the Magazines', *PMLA*, vol. 65, no. 5, September 1950, pp. 762–89.

Morrison, Robert and Chris Baldick, eds. *Tales of Terror from Blackwood's Magazine*. Oxford: Oxford University Press, 1995.
Morrison, Robert and Chris Baldick, eds. *The Vampyre and Other Tales of the Macabre*. Oxford: Oxford University Press, 1997.
Potter, Franz J. *Gothic Chapbooks, Bluebooks and Shilling Shockers, 1797–1830*. Cardiff: University of Wales Press, 2021.
Radcliffe, Ann. *The Mysteries of Udolpho*, edited by Bonamy Dobrée, Intro. and Notes by Terry Castle. Oxford: Oxford University Press, 1998.
Scott, Walter. 'Prefatory Memoir to Mrs Ann Radcliffe', in *The Novels of Mrs Ann Radcliffe*. London: Published by Hurst, Robinson, and Co., Printed by James Ballantyne, 1824, pp. i–xxxix.
Scott, Walter. 'On the Supernatural in Fictitious Composition; and Particularly in the Works of Ernest Theodore William Hoffman [sic]' (1827), *The Foreign Quarterly Review*, July 1827, pp. 60–98.
Scott, Walter. 'The Tapestried Chamber; or, The Lady in the Sacque'. *The Keepsake for MDCCCXXIX*, 1829, pp. 123–42.
Shelley, Mary. *Frankenstein; or, The Modern Prometheus*, edited by Maurice Hindle. London: Penguin, 1992.
Shelley, Percy Bysshe. *The Prose Works of Percy Bysshe Shelley*, edited by E. B. Murray. Oxford: Clarendon Press, 1997.
Townshend, Dale. 'Gothic and the Ghost of *Hamlet*', in John Drakakis and Dale Townshend (eds), *Gothic Shakespeares*. Abingdon: Routledge, 2008, pp. 60–97.
Van Woudenberg, Maximiliaan. '*Fantasmagoriana*: The Cosmopolitan Gothic and *Frankenstein*', in Dale Townshend and Angela Wright (eds), *The Cambridge History of the Gothic, Vol. II: Gothic in the Nineteenth Century*. Cambridge: Cambridge University Press, 2020, pp. 41–64.
Walpole, Horace. *The Castle of Otranto*, edited by Nick Groom. Oxford: Oxford University Press, 2014.

Chapter 2

The Ghost Story: 1830–70
Anthony Mandal

In a golden period spanning the mid-1790s to the late 1800s, Gothic novels dominated the shelves of Georgian circulating libraries following the success of Ann Radcliffe and Matthew Gregory Lewis. A brief Gothic renaissance during the late 1810s to the mid-1820s witnessed the appearance of a clutch of titles: Mary Shelley's *Frankenstein* (1818), John Polidori's *The Vampyre* (1819), C. R. Maturin's *Melmoth the Wanderer* (1820) and James Hogg's *Private Memoirs and Confessions of a Justified Sinner* (1824). Despite this passing irruption of the supernatural, the direction of the mainstream novel was by the 1830s clear: towards the quotidian realism that came to distinguish fiction of the 'high Victorian' period. Within this context, as Nick Freeman notes, 'the ghost story developed from an embedded narrative in a novel or miscellany into a distinctive genre of short fiction which encompassed the brief, spooky anecdote and the technically elaborate and psychologically sophisticated tale' (2012: 93). If Victorian fiction in its novel form was eschewing its earlier, fantastical trappings in favour of a newer social realism, its shorter counterpart maintained its links to 'an older popular culture disseminated by broadsheets, ballads, and chapbooks', as 'the means of keeping ghosts, apparitions, and spirits alive within a secular and rationalist society which was almost able to explain them – but not quite' (Bourne Taylor 2012: 242).

Notwithstanding these general changes to the contours of fiction in the first quarter of the nineteenth century, the years 1830 to 1870 demarcate a period of consolidation and diversification in the history of the Victorian ghost story. Alongside the growing market for mainstream novels, the increasingly central role played by periodical culture offered a propitious new home for the supernatural, and a popular new space in which readers could encounter it. Emerging during the waning years of the Romantic Gothic novel, shorter tales focusing on the supernatural and occult experienced sustained popularity over the succeeding century, in no small part a result of the massive growth of both population and print culture from the early nineteenth century onwards (see Mandal 2017).

The emergence of a mass readership triggered a proliferation of publications to meet the demand of new audiences, which themselves drove and were driven by ever more sophisticated print technologies and networks of dissemination (see McKitterick 2009). Outside of the context of print culture and the fiction market, 1830 to 1870 was an era of transition, transformation and turmoil at the social and political levels. The 116-year reign of Georgian monarchs came to an end when George IV was succeeded by his brother William IV in 1830, who was himself followed by the last Hanoverian monarch, Victoria, who would rule from 1837 until 1901. The Roman Catholic Relief Act of 1829 removed the harshest restrictions on Catholicism within Britain, which had huge repercussions for the hegemonic power of the Anglican Church. The Reform Acts of 1832 and 1867 marked a shift in power away from the landed interests towards middle-class capitalists, then urban workers. Following the 1832 Act, disappointed working-class radicals led the charge of the Chartist movement between 1838 and 1857. Geopolitically in the post-Waterloo era, Britain faced the challenges of increasing globalisation, as measured in its responses to the abolition of slavery in the colonies (1833), the Irish famine (1845–52), the Crimean war (1853–6), the Indian Rebellion of 1857 and the 1865 Jamaican uprising, all of which cast looming shadows over British cultural consciousness.

Notwithstanding these challenges, 1830 to 1870 also saw a number of industrial, technological and scientific achievements that further transformed British society and culture. Ongoing mechanisation made Britain a world leader in the manufacture of cotton, sugar, coal and coke, iron and steel. Perhaps capturing the spirit of age most paradigmatically was the Great Exhibition, which ran at the Crystal Palace in London between May and October 1851, and was visited by six million patrons (approximately equivalent to one third of the British population at the time). Within these four decades, the United Kingdom transitioned from a primarily agricultural, rural island into an industrial, imperial superpower, characterised by a scientific, technocratic modernity. Scott Brewster notes that we can place the ghost story at the confluence of these developments and the discourses they generated:

> It prospered amid an array of discourses of the unseen, including the science of optics, the advent of 'invisible' technologies that constituted a form of modern supernatural, and the rise of spiritualism and psychical research. For women writers, the ghost story becomes a tale of increasing visibility and

opportunity: women occupied a prominent role in the growth of the ghost story, exploiting the growing demand for shorter forms of fiction, encouraged by a burgeoning periodical culture. (2020: 224)

From the Folk Tale to the Family Magazine: The 1830s and 1840s

The 1830s marked two key moments in the history of nineteenth-century fiction: the death of Walter Scott (1771–1832) and the emergence into the literary marketplace of Charles Dickens (1812–70) with *Sketches by Boz* (1836). Scott had established himself as a pre-eminent writer of Romantic Scottish literature, beginning with his ballad collections at the turn of the century and shifting to the emergent genre of fiction, including his heavily Gothic *Bride of Lammermoor* (1819), and his short/inset ghost stories 'Wandering Willie's Tale' (1824) and 'The Tapestried Chamber' (1828). As the best-selling novelist of the nineteenth century, it is impossible to underestimate Scott's legacy on the writers who succeeded him from the 1830s and beyond. As far as our history of the ghost story is concerned, Dickens's professional fortunes adumbrate the versatility and adaptability of the genre within the expanding and diversifying marketplace of the mid-nineteenth century.

The presence of Scotland within Gothic writing lingered into the 1830s, in the work of writers like James Hogg (1770–1835) and Catherine Sinclair (1800–64). While his reputation was less esteemed during his lifetime, Scott's compatriot and sometime collaborator Hogg is now recognised as a pioneering exponent of Scottish Romanticism. Most famously, his *Private Memoirs and Confessions of a Justified Sinner* (1824) represents the culmination of his blending of Scottish regional history, theological controversy and Gothic gloom. Alongside this full-length novel, Hogg produced numerous poems, plays and fictions – the latter comprising various short stories, which were often first published in periodicals and later collected in anthologies. Hogg's distinctive combination of Gothic superstition with the periodical tradition reaches its apex with his 1830 tale, 'The Mysterious Bride'. Here, the narrative intertwines love, murder and revenge in an uncannily repetitive framework told through the perspective of its protagonist, the Laird of Birkendelly. The story begins with the journey of the romantic laird on St Lawrence's Eve (9 August) 1777, when he spots 'an elegant and beautiful girl', dressed in white and green. Captivated and surprised, he prophetically speculates that '[s]he must have risen out of the earth, for I never saw her till this breath' (Hogg 1995: 116). Male desire manifests itself through his attempt to catch up with the girl, suggesting both youthful exuberance and sexual threat. Satisfaction is deferred, as he can never catch up with the mysterious young woman despite seeing her on multiple occasions. Even though he is desirous of a meeting, the laird simultaneously experiences something like terror as he closes in on her: 'He now trembled every limb, and, without knowing what he did, rode straight on to the big town, not daring well to return and see what he had seen for three several times' (119). The now-united lovers pledge to meet once a year at St Lawrence's Eve for three years before their final consummation. The laird keeps good to his word, and on the third year is seen setting off to meet his bride. At this point, we learn that the mysterious woman is Jane Ogilvie, who had been engaged to the laird's ancestor, but was then jilted and likely murdered by him. Over the generations, Jane's shade has reappeared to lead each of her quondam suitor's descendants to their demise at the very site of her own death. The curse ends with the death of the current laird, who having no surviving relatives is the end of the family line. Hogg's curious tale presents us with a series of repetitions: the frustrating meetings between the lovers; the doubling of two female love interests and their respective abandonment by their suitors; and finally, Jane's murder multiplied through her own revenge on her killer's descendants on the same day and site of her own killing.

Such cycles of uncanny repetitions of an ineluctable past, from which there is little or no escape, recur in other ghost stories of the 1830s and 1840s. In Abraham Elder's 'The Ghost-Seer' (1839), the eponymous recluse retrospects a youthful encounter he had as a smuggler with a revenue cutter that capsized while in pursuit of his gang. When the smugglers reach the coast, the previously sunken ship reappears with its spectral crew calling their quarry to join them:

> It gave us, to be sure, a very nervous creeping sort of a feel, to think that we were going to be taken prisoners on board a vessel that was not at all a real one, and which was sailed by a crew of men that we had seen drowned with our own eyes, only just the day before. (Elder 1839: 181)

In the anonymous 'The Deaf and Dumb Girl' (1839), a faithless lover, Jules, is haunted by his abandoned mistress while travelling through France when she joins his coach party:

> Her skin was of a deadly white color, and it seemed to cover nothing but bare bones; her lips were thin, so thin indeed, that they scarcely enclosed a perfect set of projecting teeth, and two small eyes sparkled like live coals from the bottom of immense orbits. (Anon. 1839: 38)

After multiple encounters with her, Jules is relieved when she no longer appears and plans marriage to his beautiful and wealthy cousin, at which point he and the narrator part. The tale concludes a month later, with the narrator retracing his journey when he encounters a procession returning from Jules's funeral: here he discovers that the pallid girl was seen in Jules's bedroom precipitating his death, and at the moment of his burial glided into his grave.

A more sympathetic representation of a disability and spectrality appeared a decade later in 'Mabel'. In the frame narrative that opens the story, a visitor to some friends witnesses the chilling spectre of a young woman and her baby:

> its face was that of a young, and would have been that of a handsome woman, but for the livid hue of the lips, and the deadly whiteness of the cheeks; the eyes were lustreless, and the lips appeared to be quivering with extreme cold; the infant's face, hands, and feet were of the same icy hue, and seemed stiffened with cold, as its little body was with swathing bands. (Anon. 1849: 294)

Having shared his encounter with his hosts, the narrator learns her backstory over breakfast: the ghost is that of Mabel, a beloved young girl struck deaf and mute by a childhood disease, who is forced to marry her avaricious cousin Dugdale when her parents die. Having been coerced to yielding the deeds to her property in exchange for their infant child, Mabel flees into the winter night: 'the hapless mother and her infant were discovered about a mile from their home, lying quite dead, and half covered by a drift of snow' (295). Following this, rumours suggest that universal justice has its way, as the scheming Dugdale and his mother are haunted remorselessly by Mabel's ghost to their deaths. The ghosts here act as stark warnings that the moral and legal ties that bind civil society together have been disrupted, their irruption into the everyday world signalling the breach of sympathetic and just feeling.

If Hogg had focused his energies on Scotland's relationship to the supernatural, a generation later Joseph Sheridan Le Fanu would do the same for Ireland. In his fictions, Le Fanu channels his own liminal status as an Anglo-Irish Protestant settler in the largely Roman Catholic nation into accounts of spectralisation and hybridity. Le Fanu is now largely remembered as the leading ghost story writer of his era, especially for his invention of the eponymous femme fatale Carmilla, in his vampire tale of 1871–2; however, he was the author of numerous short stories and over a dozen novels, of which the most famous is *Uncle Silas* (1864). Julia Briggs draws attention to Le Fanu's contribution to the history of the ghost story: 'One obsessive anxiety which Le Fanu dramatizes particularly effectively is the terror of invasion or entrance by some feared or hated object, which may ultimately be connected with sexual fear, or with the neurosis derived from some long-concealed repression' (1977: 48). His first supernatural stories appeared in the *Dublin University Magazine*, beginning with 'The Ghost and the Bonesetter' in January 1835, in which a dead squire steps down from his portrait to alleviate his discomforts in the afterlife. Le Fanu would bring the ghost story to a level of sophistication and finesse that became the hallmark of the mode, and his work would be taken up as the template for the generation of later Victorian writers who followed, most notably M. R. James.

The publication of fiction in periodicals was complemented by the issuing of fiction in parts, which flourished from the 1840s onwards. Parts publication involved the issuing of fiction in regular, typically monthly or weekly, 'fascicles', which were formatted so that they could be bound into volumes once the serial had concluded. Serialisation enabled readers to own a new work of fiction spanning over 600 pages and forty illustrations for 20s paid out over nineteen months, in comparison to the 31s 6d for an equivalent triple-decker format. A number of early Victorian authors availed themselves of fascicle publication, most notably Charles Dickens (*Nicholas Nickleby*, 1838–9; *David Copperfield*, 1849–50) and William Makepeace Thackeray (*Pendennis*, 1848–50; *The Newcomes*, 1853–5). While serialisation in periodicals would eventually eclipse fascicle publishing with the emergence of popular family magazines, it was still being used for long works like George Eliot's *Middlemarch*, which was published in parts between 1871 and 1872. Although serial publication of fiction had been practised since the eighteenth century, the landmark moment was the publication of Dickens's *The Posthumous Papers of the Pickwick Club*, from April 1836 over nineteen months in twenty parts (the last instalment was a double issue). Initially slow sales rocketed following Dickens's introduction of Sam Weller in the fifth number, with circulation climbing to 40,000 copies. In this history of the ghost story, Dickens's inaugural moment was perhaps 'The Story of the Goblins Who Stole a Sexton', originally issued as a story told by mother of the farmer Mr Wardle in Chapter 29 (No. 10, December 1836) of *The Pickwick Papers*. In telling his macabre tale of the violent reformation of the eponymous misanthrope by the goblins and their king, Dickens was adumbrating the successful formula he would perfect with *A Christmas Carol* six years later.

It was the incredible success of Dickens's 'Christmas books' that created a regular seasonal market for supernatural tales. While Christmas gatherings around a good story, and the tradition of the winter's tale, had been well established, Dickens was able to bring together this longer tradition with the expanding print culture of the 1840s in a hitherto unprecedented way. Caley Ehnes has identified the paradigmatic role undertaken by Dickens in stimulating the Christmas ghost story 'tradition':

> Dickens's insistence on publishing literature specifically designed for the Christmas market suggests that he firmly believed that these seasonal traditions were necessary elements of British culture that needed to be preserved and immortalised through literature. The ghost story is the ideal genre for this project. (Ehnes 2012: 20–1)

Published just before Christmas 1843, *A Christmas Carol* sold 6,000 copies in its first day, and a further 2,000 by early January (Shattock 2012: 16). It was followed by four further Christmas books through the decade: *The Chimes* (1844), *The Cricket on the Hearth* (1845), *The Battle of Life* (1846) and *The Haunted Man and the Ghost's Bargain* (1848). Dewi Evans observes:

> Dickens's Christmas ghost stories took the winter's tale in a direction that embraced modern print-cultural innovations, helping to establish the Christmas hearth (rather than simply the winter fireside) as a particularly appropriate spatio-temporal location for the telling of ghost stories. Ultimately, however, their supernatural paraphernalia are employed as vehicles for promoting the values underlying Victorian conceptions of Christmas. (2017: 79)

Building on the appetite for fiction in instalments, publishers also catered to the increasingly literate working classes, most infamously in the form of luridly melodramatic 'penny bloods' (see Mandal 2020: 150–9). At the other end of the spectrum of respectability, the mainstream novel saw the brief re-emergence of Gothic at the end of the 1840s, most notably in what Robert Heilman (2001 [1958]) would call the 'New Gothic' of the Brontë sisters, and which Tamar Heller (2020) has more recently termed 'Domestic Gothic'. In their novels – particularly Charlotte's *Jane Eyre* (1847), Emily's *Wuthering Heights* (1847) and Anne's *The Tenant of Wildfell Hall* (1848) – women are persistently marginalised and forced to haunt the margins of their world, in subjection to social expectations of female submissiveness and to male violence. A number of these spectral figures have become archetypes of Victorian literature: *Jane Eyre*'s 'madwoman in the attic', Bertha Mason; the ghost-child of *Wuthering Heights*, Cathy Earnshaw, who haunts the Yorkshire moors; and the eponymous Tenant, Helen Graham, a respectable woman forced to break the law by taking on a new identity in order to save her child from the influence of her debauched and dissolute husband.

Female spectres can be found in other ghostly stories in the period. In 'The Dark Lady' (1848) by Anna Maria Hall (1800–81), the eponymous ghost appears according to tradition to defend vulnerable and innocent women. Told as a retrospected narrative of her youth by the narrator's Swiss great-grandmother, the story details the domestic tyranny experienced by the beautiful Amelie de Rohean at her uncle's hands. When he prevents Amelie's union to Charles, the son of his sworn enemy, the Dark Lady haunts the count multiple times: first in his bedchamber; then at a collapsing bridge that marks the end of his pursuit of Charles; a possible third time – 'Some said the "Femme Noir" visited him again; I cannot tell; I did not see her; I speak of what I saw, not of what I heard' (Hall 1848: 560); and finally, to take the reformed uncle with her to the afterlife: '"the Femme Noir" appeared again to him – once. She did so with a placid air, on a summer night, with her arm extended towards the heavens.' Similarly, in the anonymous 'The Silver Lady' (1838), the narrator – a soldier garrisoned at the castle of the Baron de Bentheim during the Seven Years' War (1756–63) – meets and falls in love with the baron's daughter, Adelaide. The mystery of the Silver Lady hangs over the house dating back to the Crusades and centring on the persecution and drowning of the daughter of the castle's original owner. The narrator takes up a challenge to spend a night in the castle's haunted chamber, where he meets a seemingly somnambulant Adelaide and plights his troth with a family ring. When it is revealed that the narrator descends from the rightful owners of the castle, the Silver Lady's hidden burial site is unearthed and they discover her perfectly preserved corpse with the narrator's ring on her finger. Initially reeling at the revelation, the narrator realises that his gratitude to the mysterious ghost overcomes his horror:

> when I gazed again upon the remains of this long persecuted and suffering being, lying in her lonely and unholy grave, afar from all the coffins of her race, and thought that to her vigilance and affection I was indebted for the happiness which I now possessed, much of the horror of my retrospection subsided. I felt that she ought rather to appear to me what she really was, the protecting spirit of my love and my fortunes: and the agitation of my mind gradually ceased. (Anon. 1838: 188)

In many ways, 'The Silver Lady' adapts and inverts the infamous story of the Bleeding Nun popularised in Matthew Gregory Lewis's *The Monk* (1796), which linked spectral haunting with carnal desire, brutal violence and generational haunting. Here, however, the much-maligned and brutally mistreated Silver Lady acts as avatar of justice, agent of restitution and enabler of romantic desire for the narrator and her *doppelgänger* Adelaide.

A Golden Age of Ghosts: The 1850s and 1860s

The middle of the nineteenth century witnessed various shifts and transformations in the fiction market. The dominant mode of the 1850s was realism, drawing inspiration from the quotidian experiences of the working and middle classes. The 1860s saw sensation fiction merge realism with a penchant for the criminal, drawing on recent legal controversies and on journalistic reportage, to generate racy, melodramatic narratives that destablised middle-class life. More generally, the era of parts publication was superseded by the rapid expansion of serialisation in magazine format from the mid-1850s onwards. As Shattock notes:

> The founding of house journals by major publishers provided a stimulus to fiction, as serialized stories and full-length novels were added to the mix of articles on politics, literature, art, history, religion, and other topics of general interest in the new magazines. (2012: 11–12)

Graham Law and Robert L. Patten chart the exponential growth of magazines that underpins this thorough permeation through the second half of the century: from 406 in 1860 to 1,033 in 1880 and 2,328 in 1900 (2009: 156–7). New family periodicals like *Household Words* (1850–9) and *All the Year Round* (1859–95), both edited by Dickens, and *Once a Week* (1859–80), joined established titles like the *New Monthly Magazine* (1814–84) and *Blackwood's Edinburgh Magazine* (1817–1980) as the purveyors of new serial fictions and short stories. *Household Words* published a large body of noteworthy ghost stories, among them Elizabeth Gaskell's 'The Old Nurse's Story' (1852) and 'The Poor Clare' (1856); Wilkie Collins's 'A Terribly Strange Bed' (1852), 'The Ostler' (1855) and 'The Dead Hand' (1857); and Dickens's 'The Ghost Chamber' (1857). *All the Year Round* featured ghost stories in even greater abundance than *Household Words*: key titles include Gaskell's 'Lois the Witch' (1859) and 'The Grey Woman' (1861); Amelia B. Edwards's 'The Phantom Coach' (1864); Dickens's 'The Trial for Murder' (1865) and 'The Signal-Man' (1866); and Le Fanu's 'Madam Crowl's Ghost' (1870).

Many of these ghost stories turn to scrutinise intra-familial relations. In 'The Poor Clare' and 'Lois the Witch', Gaskell explores the results of familial breakdown and the cyclical and self-defeating consequences of vengeance, when set against the redemptive arc of forgiveness. Perhaps the most famous of these is her 'The Old Nurse's Story', in which sibling violence forms the source of a generations-long haunting that opens Gaskell's narrative – thus substantively destabilising domestic and family systems, with the home no longer a site of protection or enclosure but of violence and entrapment. A young orphan, Rosamond, and her nurse are admitted into a house governed by Miss (Grace) Furnivall. The house appears to be haunted by supernatural organ-playing in the great hall, while Rosamond repeatedly encounters a spectral child. It is revealed that Miss Furnivall's elder sister Maude had clandestinely married their music teacher and given birth to a daughter, sparking Grace's jealousy, which leads her to reveal the secret to their father. The enraged patriarch casts his daughter and granddaughter into the winter snow, forbidding any servant to assist them, leaving them to their deaths. The narrative reaches its climax with a spectral replay of the scene from a half-century earlier, exposing the reader to the violence of the father and the hatred of the sister towards Maude:

> the lady turned; and I could see that she defied the old man with a fierce and proud defiance; but then she quailed – and then she threw up her arms wildly and piteously to save her child – her little child – from a blow from his uplifted crutch. (1991: 18)

Despite its temporal distancing and supernatural staging, the excessive violence in the scene from the patriarch towards the defenceless and innocent child offers a chilling indictment of the social order. Rebecca Styler suggests that 'Gaskell's tales do not present the primitive returning to haunt the civilised: she rather presents the so-called civilised order as itself built on irrational, primitive principles' (2010: 38). If the Victorian ghost story is the product of a divided society that prioritised particular forms of social community, especially family, Gaskell's tale positions the family itself as a source of danger and dangerous secrets.

In Mary Braddon's 'The Cold Embrace' (1860), a pair of lovers rather than siblings are the locus of the supernatural haunting. A young German artist secretly pledges his troth to his cousin but abandons her, leaving her to drown herself. He arrives back home on the day her body is recovered, and recognises her by his grandmother's ring on her finger. After falling ill for six weeks, he is accosted by his dead cousin's phantom embrace, preventing him from resting:

> Suddenly some one – something from behind him, puts two cold arms round his neck, and clasps its hands on his breast.
> And yet there is no one behind him, for on the flags bathed in the broad moonlight there are only two shadows, his own and his dog's. He turns quickly round – there is no one – nothing to be seen in the broad square but

himself and his dog; and though he feels, he cannot see the cold arms clasped round his neck.

It is not ghostly, this embrace, for it is palpable to the touch – it cannot be real, for it is invisible. (Braddon 1862: 87)

As a distraction, the artist goes to Paris during Carnival, where he indulges himself in the pleasures of a masked ball. Despite thirsting he does not drink and finally finds himself alone, when the phantom embrace occurs again, and he is forced to dance until he drops dead. Here, the young artist's predilection for debauchery ironically becomes the tool for his punishment at the hands of his abandoned posthumous lover.

Young love and family affections come into unintended conflict in 'The Last House on C—— Street' (1856), by Dinah Maria Craik (1826–87). Here, we encounter another retrospected narrative, like 'The Old Nurse's Story', as the narrator tells her grandchildren a story about another house haunted by family tragedy when she was a young woman. Prior to the episodes, she and her fiancé convince their father to stay with them on a holiday in London, while her heavily pregnant mother decides to return home to Bath but promises her husband to meet his wish that if anything is amiss she will let him know 'under all circumstances'. The houseguests experience the same inexplicable phenomenon: a tapping at the window, 'exactly like the sound of fingers against a pane – very soft, gentle fingers, such as, in passing into her flower-garden, my mother used often to tap outside the school-room casement at home' (Craik 1856: 395). In the father's case, it is supplemented with an image of his wife approaching him, and the next evening a message arrives that she died giving birth to a daughter at the precise time of the haunting. Following this, the young lovers break their engagement and grow to become friends instead. In Craik's tale, the focus falls not on vengeance or justice, but rather offers a wistful and plaintive meditation on bereavement, lost love and the impact of time on desire. As Melissa Edmundson Makala notes:

> The return of memory in ghostly form also points to some sort of resolution by the end of the work, though again, happy endings are seldom reached. Because of this spectral presence, characters are forced to learn difficult lessons about their past or present behaviour, and many must come to terms with their pasts through interactions with a ghost. (2013: 89)

By the mid-century, the Romantic Gothic castle had given way to the middle-class family house, which could be found anywhere, from a traveller's byway in a rural retreat to the suburbs of the modern towns and cities. Haunted houses form a staple of the Victorian ghost story, emerging from the pens of Charles Ollier ('The Haunted Manor-House of Paddington', 1841); Dudley Costello ('The Haunted House in Yorkshire', 1845), Le Fanu ('An Account of Some Strange Disturbances in an Old House in Aungier Street', 1853) and Hesba Stretton ('The Ghost in the Clock Room', 1859), as well as anonymous works ('A Night in a Haunted House', 1848; 'Tremewen Grange', 1867; 'The Ghost of Stanton Hall', 1868). The simple title 'A Haunted House' appears multiple times over our period, in tales by Emma Whitehead (1838), Mary Ann Bird (1852), Nancy Thorning Monroe (1854), Louise Kirby Piatt (1855), Emerson Bennet (1859), Margaret Verne (1859) and anonymously (1870). Perhaps one of the most complex of these is Edward Bulwer-Lytton's 'The Haunted and the Haunters; or, The House and the Brain' (1859). In this convoluted tale, the narrator spends a night in an infamous haunted house, during which he witnesses a series of spectral scenes involving a malign shadowy presence. The backstory to the hauntings relates to multiple murders that span a century, and the perpetrator is revealed to have extended his life unnaturally to the present day. After lifting the curse on the house, the narrator has repeated encounters with the murderer, until the latter, named Richards, is able to use the narrator's own psychic abilities to discover his future. At the tale's conclusion, the narrator receives a note from Richards:

> I wished you to utter what was in your mind. You obeyed. I have therefore established power over you. For three months from this day you can communicate to no living man what has passed between us – you cannot even show this note to the friend by your side. During three months, silence complete as to me and mine. Do you doubt my power to lay on you this command? – try to disobey me. At the end of the third month, the spell is raised. For the rest I spare you. I shall visit your grave a year and a day after it has received you. (Bulwer-Lytton 1859: 245)

A similar dynamic between ineffable evil and the inarticulacy in the face of it is found in Rhoda Broughton's epistolary 'The Truth, the Whole Truth, and Nothing but the Truth' (1868), while the story's title ironically suggests a legal deposition. Elizabeth de Wynt secures a beautiful rental property in 32 —— Street, Mayfair, for her friend Cecilia Montresor at a bargain price in the middle of May. Within two weeks of moving, Cecilia and her family begin to experience paranormal disturbances, learning that no one has remained in the property for more than a month. A maid preparing the room for Cecilia's daughter Adela witnesses something that drives her insane. A final letter outlines the conclusion: Adela's sceptical suitor Ralph Gordon, a young officer, offers to sleep in the cursed room. When Adela, her mother and the party arrive at the room, they find him at the point of death:

> There he was, standing in the middle of the floor, rigid, petrified, with that same look – that look that is burnt into my heart in letters of fire – of awful, unspeakable, stony fear on his brave young face. For one instant he stood thus; then stretching out his arms stiffly before him, he groaned in a terrible, husky voice, 'Oh, my God! I have seen it!' and fell down *dead*. Yes, *dead*. Not in a swoon or in a fit, but *dead*. (Broughton 1991: 82)

The haunting seems to cut across a number of social and professional axes, as a modern home in a fashionable district, affecting both female and male victims, the servant and military classes. Articulating a crisis in the modern consciousness, the challenge for Bulwer-Lytton and Broughton seems to be less an ontological one (whether we believe what passes before our eyes) than an epistemological one (how can we express something that pushes the very limits of our understanding?). These narratives also highlight the complex interrelationships between urbanisation and property acquisition during a fluid and uncertain period of capitalism, as noted by Katie Krueger: 'Stories of haunted town homes pivot around tensions regarding the "acquisition of desirable urban property" and the vulnerabilities of fashion-conscious families to haunting, which inevitably reveal the inadequacies of their own socially-mediated roles' (2014: 86).

It was not only the home that formed the locus of supernatural irruptions and existential anxiety in the Victorian period: by the middle of the century, a range of technological innovations clustered together, transforming logistical, communication and transportation networks, both within the British mainland and between Britain and the rest of the world. As E. S. Dallas noted in 1866:

> the railway and the steamship, the telegraph and the penny postage, by daily and hourly bringing us near a vast world beyond our limited circles, and giving us a present interest in the transactions the most distant regions, have enormously increased the number of readers, have of themselves created a literature. (II, 312)

The expansion of the railways not only transformed daily and professional lives, but the British landscape too. Through processes of deferral, railways also reframed the paradigm of travel into a heterotopic encounter that is both decentring and spectralising, such that

> [t]he traveller, engaged in the process of travelling – rather than at the point of arrival – is [...] an individual placed in an uncanny relationship with both

terrain and mode of travel, and his or her vulnerability in transit remain issues hardly touched upon in Gothic criticism. (Hughes 2020: 446)

In a number of her short stories, Amelia B. Edwards (1831–92) locates conveyances as the sites of a kind of premonitory warning. In 'The Phantom Coach' (1864), a recently married man benighted in the winter snow finds respite in a carriage, which he quickly discovers is filled with dead passengers who were caught in a fateful crash some time previously. 'The Four-Fifteen Express' (1864) details the narrator's encounter in a train carriage with an alleged embezzler from the railway company, who it transpires had been murdered some months earlier for the £20,000 he was transporting on behalf of the company. The ghostly encounter enables the narrator to vindicate the dead man and to uncover his killer and the true thief. Edwards's 'No. 5 Branch Line. The Engineer' forms the concluding story of Dickens's collection of five portmanteau stories by different authors, *Mugby Junction*, which was published for the Christmas 1866 issue of *All the Year Round*. In this tragic tale, two lifelong friends fall out over the love of a faithless Italian woman, with fatal consequences for one. An opportunity for revenge presents itself to the survivor some years later, when he is working as an engine driver and plans to destroy the train and their former mistress, who is one of its passengers. At the crucial moment, he is turned away from such actions by the monitory spectral presence of his friend:

> All that I can say – all that I *know* is – that Matthew Price came back from the dead, to save my soul and the lives of those whom I, in my guilty rage, would have hurried to destruction. I believe this as I believe in the mercy of Heaven and the forgiveness of repentant sinners. (Edwards 1866: 48)

The mid-Victorian ghost story is perhaps no better exemplified than in another story in the *Mugby Junction* collection: Dickens's own 'No. 1 Branch Line. The Signal-Man'. Here, the spectrality that emerges from the collision between modernity and subjectivity is given especial poignancy by the eponymous figure, a man trapped by and within his own frames of reference. 'The Signal-Man' is the first story proper in *Mugby Junction*, and it deals with the feelings of alienation and separation from the rest of humanity experienced by the titular railway worker, who seems unable to understand his existential condition when he experiences an uncannily repeated sequence of visions. Initially, the signalman and the narrator, who acts as his interlocutor, are left to surmise whether the spectral hauntings are a product of some kind of physical or mental pathology. The signalman is unsure whether the ghost is warning him about an impending accident and how it can represent the future, given ghosts are usually echoes of an unresolved past. Does the story suggest the pressures of industrialisation and modernity, with its isolated railway setting? The signalman has become almost like an automaton when undertaking his duties:

> He was several times interrupted by the little bell, and had to read off messages, and send replies. Once, he had to stand without the door, and display a flag as a train passed, and make some verbal communication to the driver. (Dickens 1866: 22)

The narrator speaks of '[a] disease' of 'the delicate nerves that minister to the functions of the eye' (23) – suggesting issues of perception. This uncertainty extends to the reader as well, who is unsure about such interpretation, and we join the narrator in experiencing the signalman's anxiety: 'What does the spectre mean?' This becomes, according to Andrew Smith, the pivotal question of the story:

> the ghost serves to raise questions about interpretation i.e. the tale is an alternative manifesto for the ghost story, one which invites the narrator and the reader to dwell on the problems of interpreting the ghost which more formulaic tales do not. What the ghost might actually mean is therefore subservient to the ability to ask the question of what it is supposed to mean. (2010: 45)

As a robot-like product of industrialisation, the signalman is so interpellated into the mechanisms that he operates and is part of that he is unable to step outside the system to interpret it. Adapting and reframing many of the techniques of his predecessors and contemporaries, Dickens uses the structures of the ghost story to enable the reader (unlike the signalman) to step outside and see the system that governed much of modern life by the later 1860s.

Works Cited

Anon. 'The Silver Lady. A Tale', in *The Keepsake for 1839*, edited by F. M. Reynolds. London: Longman and Co., 1838, pp. 159–92.

Anon. 'Mabel'. *London Journal*, vol. 8, no. 203, 13 January 1849, pp. 293–5.

Anon. 'The Deaf and Dumb Girl'. *Atkinson's Casket*, vol. 15, no. 1, July 1839, pp. 37–42.

Bourne Taylor, Jenny. 'Short Fiction and the Novel', in John Kucich and Jenny Bourne Taylor (eds), *The Oxford History of the Novel in English*, vol. 3: *The Nineteenth Century 1820–1880*. Oxford: Oxford University Press, 2012, pp. 239–55.

Braddon, Mary Elizabeth. 'The Cold Embrace' (1860), in *Ralph, the Bailiff and Other Tales*. London: Ward and Lock, 1862, pp. 80–91.
Brewster, Scott. 'The Genesis of the Victorian Ghost Story', in Dale Townshend and Angela Wright (eds), *The Cambridge History of the Gothic*, vol. 2: *Gothic in the Nineteenth Century*. Cambridge: Cambridge University Press, 2020, pp. 224–45.
Briggs, Julia. *Night Visitors: The Rise and Fall of the English Ghost Story*. London: Faber, 1977.
Broughton, Rhoda. 'The Truth, the Whole Truth, and Nothing but the Truth', in Michael Cox and R. A. Gilbert (eds), *The Oxford Book of Victorian Ghost Stories*. Oxford: Oxford University Press, 1991, pp. 74–82.
Bulwer-Lytton, Edward. 'The Haunted and the Haunters; or, The House and the Brain'. *Blackwood's Edinburgh Magazine*, vol. 86, no. 526, August 1859, pp. 224–45.
Craik, Dinah Maria. 'The Last House in C—— Street'. *Fraser's Magazine for Town and Country*, vol. 54, no. 322, 1856, pp. 392–8.
Dallas, E. S. *The Gay Science*, 2 vols. London: Chapman and Hall, 1866.
Dickens, Charles. *The Posthumous Papers of the Pickwick Club*. London: Chapman and Hall, 1837.
———. 'No. 1 Branch Line. The Signal-Man', in 'Mugby Junction', *All the Year Round*, edited by Charles Dickens, Christmas Number, 10 December 1866, pp. 20–5.
Edmundson Makala, Melissa. *Women's Ghost Literature in Nineteenth-Century Britain*. Cardiff: University of Wales Press, 2013.
Edwards, Amelia B. 'No. 5 Branch Line. The Engineer', in 'Mugby Junction', *All the Year Round*, edited by Charles Dickens, Christmas Number, 10 December 1866, pp. 42–8.
Ehnes, Caley. '"Winter Stories—Ghost Stories … Round the Christmas Fire": Victorian Ghost Stories and the Christmas Market'. *Illumine*, vol. 11, no. 1, 2012, pp. 6–25.
Elder, Abraham. 'The Ghost-Seer', in *Tales and Legends of the Isle of Wight*. London: Simpkin, Marshall and Co., 1839, pp. 175–83.
Evans, Dewi. 'The Victorian Ghost Story and the Invention of Christmas', in Scott Brewster and Luke Thurston (eds), *The Routledge Handbook of the Ghost Story*. New York: Routledge, 2017, pp. 78–86.
Freeman, Nick. 'The Victorian Ghost Story', in Andrew Smith and William Hughes (eds), *The Victorian Gothic: An Edinburgh Companion*. Edinburgh: Edinburgh University Press, 2012, pp. 93–107.
Gaskell, Elizabeth. 'The Old Nurse's Story' [1852], in Michael Cox and R. A. Gilbert (eds), *The Oxford Book of Victorian Ghost Stories*. Oxford: Oxford University Press, 1991, pp. 1–19.
Hall, Anna Maria. 'The Dark Lady'. *Littell's Living Age*, vol. 19, 1848, 557–60.
Heilman, Robert. 'Charlotte Brontë's "New" Gothic', in Stephen Regan (ed.), *The Nineteenth-Century Novel: A Critical Reader*. London and New York: Routledge, 2001, pp. 212–15.
Heller, Tamar. 'Victorian Domestic Gothic Fiction', in Dale Townshend and Angela Wright (eds), *The Cambridge History of the Gothic*, vol. 2: *Gothic in the Nineteenth Century*. Cambridge: Cambridge University Press, 2020, pp. 265–84.

Hogg, James. 'The Mysterious Bride', in Robert Morrison and Chris Baldick (eds), *Tales of Terror from Blackwood's Magazine*. Oxford: Oxford University Press, 1995, pp. 115–30.

Hughes, William. 'Gothic and the Coming of the Railways', in Dale Townshend and Angela Wright (eds), *The Cambridge History of the Gothic*, vol. 2: *Gothic in the Nineteenth Century*. Cambridge: Cambridge University Press, 2020, pp. 445–62.

Krueger, Katie. *British Women Writers and the Short Story, 1850–1930: Reclaiming Social Space*. Basingstoke and New York: Palgrave Macmillan, 2014.

Law, Graham and Robert L. Patten. 'The Serial Revolution', in David McKitterick (ed.), *The Cambridge History of the Book in Britain*, vol. 6: *1830–1914*. Cambridge: Cambridge University Press, 2009, pp. 144–71.

McKitterick, David. 'Changes in the Look of the Book', in David McKitterick (ed.), *The Cambridge History of the Book in Britain*, vol. 6: *1830–1914*. Cambridge: Cambridge University Press, 2009, pp. 75–116.

Mandal, Anthony. 'The Ghost Story and the Victorian Literary Marketplace', in Scott Brewster and Luke Thurston (eds), *The Routledge Handbook of the Ghost Story*. New York: Routledge, 2017, pp. 29–39.

———. 'Gothic Fiction, from Shilling Shockers to Penny Bloods', in Dale Townshend and Angela Wright (eds), *The Cambridge History of the Gothic*, vol. 2: *Gothic in the Nineteenth Century*. Cambridge: Cambridge University Press, 2020, pp. 139–61.

Shattock, Joanne. 'The Publishing Industry', in John Kucich and Jenny Bourne Taylor (eds), *The Oxford History of the Novel in English*, vol. 3: *The Nineteenth Century 1820–1880*. Oxford: Oxford University Press, 2012, pp. 3–21.

Smith, Andrew. *The Ghost Story, 1840–1920: A Cultural History*. Manchester: Manchester University Press, 2010.

Styler, Rebecca. 'The Problem of Evil in Elizabeth Gaskell's Gothic Tales'. *Gothic Studies*, vol. 12, no. 1, 2010, pp. 33–50.

Chapter 3

The Ghost Story: 1870–1900
Nick Freeman

When Charles Dickens died in 1870, *The Times* predicted his sudden death would send 'a thrill of sorrow' through the nation and would be, 'for millions [...] a personal bereavement' (Anon. 1870: 1). No other writer had quite the same relationship with his public or made sociopolitical agitation so entertaining. Dickens enthralled his readers, but he sought also to educate them, to school them in the codes of Christian gentility, and to speak out against injustice. Yet there was a darker side to Dickens's work, one which brooded on bullying, violence, imprisonment and mental collapse. He was fascinated by the supernatural, a constant presence in his fiction from 'The Goblins Who Stole a Sexton' in *The Pickwick Papers* (1837), to the homilies of *A Christmas Carol* (1843) and 'The Haunted Man and the Ghost's Bargain' (1848) and finally, 'No. 1 Branch Line: The Signal-Man', the highlight of *Mugby Junction* (1866). A brilliant practitioner of the ghost story, whose conventions he outlined in 'A Christmas Tree' (1850), Dickens used his position as a magazine editor to encourage other writers to produce tales of their own, either individually or as part of collaborative works. *Mugby Junction*, the centrepiece of *All the Year Round*'s Christmas number, included contributions from Charles Collins, Andrew Halliday, Hesba Stretton and Amelia Edwards. Dickens and the ghost story were synonymous, and the novelist is largely responsible for the equation of ghost stories with Christmas that has endured ever since.

Photographs of the author from the 1860s suggest a man burned out by his own energies and older than his years, but Dickens was only fifty-eight when he died, and one wonders where he might have taken the ghost story (and the English novel) if he had lived for another decade or so. The thematic preoccupations and technical accomplishment of 'The Signal-Man' offer several clues. The story dramatises humanity's growing subservience towards machines, with the signalman, his given name subordinated to his function, living in terror of the railway's timetable and the ringing bell in his signal box. Emerging technologies would henceforth be imbued with supernatural potential, with each innovation – the camera, the phonograph, radio, moving pictures, the motor car – quickly commandeered and exploited by Gothic writers.

Dickens's story also depicts a character attempting to cope with profound psychological distress, even trauma, regardless of whether or not a ghost is present. Haunted by a premonition of disaster, the signalman tells the narrator that he is 'troubled' but that his anxiety is 'difficult to impart [...] very, very difficult to speak of' (Dickens 1898: 96). This shift towards the experience of being haunted rather than the immediacy of seeing a ghost characterised much post-Dickensian supernatural fiction and led Vernon Lee to observe in 1880 that 'by *ghost* we do not mean the vulgar apparition which is seen or heard in told or written tales' but 'the ghost which slowly rises up in our mind, the haunter not of corridors and staircases, but of our fancies' (Lee 2006: 309–10, italics in original). Haunted minds and machines combined to offer a terrible sense of dread, making 'The Signal-Man' at once the culmination of Dickens's lifelong interest in the ghost story and the harbinger of many of its later developments.

Despite Dickens's undoubted importance, he was far from the only Victorian Gothic innovator. Most of Gothic's significant practitioners spent the majority of their careers writing novels which were broadly realist or melodramatic, so, inevitably, the practices and experiments of 'mainstream' fiction informed their supernatural storytelling. Few concentrated on the supernatural to the exclusion of other forms. Even Sheridan Le Fanu, whom M. R. James regarded as 'unsurpassed' as a writer of ghost stories (James 2011: 415), wrote works of sensational crime, such as *Uncle Silas* (1864) and, more surprisingly, a verse drama (*Beatrice* [1865]), alongside his ghost and horror tales. In the mid-Victorian period, Dickens had moved between (and combined) realism and fantasy, George Eliot published *Adam Bede* and *The Lifted Veil* in the same year (1859), and Elizabeth Gaskell had written Gothic tales such as 'The Old Nurse's Story' (1852), a work for which Dickens suggested an alternative (though unused) ending, alongside realist novels such as *North and South* (1854).[1]

These practices continued throughout the century. Henry James was a prolific novelist and ghost story writer, reflecting as early as 1865 that good ghost stories 'must be connected at a hundred points with the common objects of life' (James 1921: 110). Mary Braddon, the subject of that James comment, wrote ghost and vampire stories ('The Cold Embrace' [1860]; 'Good Lady Ducayne' [1896]) alongside her more usual sensational crime and mystery novels, while Thomas Hardy's Wessex was the fertile ground for the macabre fantasies 'The Withered Arm' (1888) and 'Barbara of the House of Grebe' (1891). Rhoda Broughton, Le Fanu's niece, moved between sensation fiction, romance and the supernatural terrors of *Twilight Stories* (1873). There were obvious commercial benefits to adaptability but working in different genres allowed writers to cross-fertilise narrative techniques. This meant ghost stories evolved alongside other strands of Victorian fiction, acquiring greater psychological depth in characterisation and, in some hands at least, a self-conscious literariness far removed from the tales in penny dreadfuls.

From 1870 onwards, late Victorian literature was also shaped by major educational reforms. These improved basic literacy rates and created new literary markets but left conservative commentators worrying about the ways in which the influence of new readers might coarsen public taste. As historians such as Peter Keating (1989) and Philip Waller (2006) have shown, the changes led less to a levelling down than to a complex process of stratification, within both the wider literary world and individual genres. One might, for instance, contrast Bram Stoker's 'The Judge's House', first published in *Holly Leaves*, the Christmas number of the *Illustrated Sporting and Dramatic News*, in December 1891, with Rudyard Kipling's 'At the End of the Passage', which was collected in his *Life's Handicap* (1891) after appearing in the *Boston Herald* the previous summer.

The complex hierarchy governing newspaper and periodical markets during the 1890s may imply an immediate distinction between the audiences for these stories, though this is not to suggest mutual exclusivity. Stoker's tale is a highly professional compilation of conventional ghostly ingredients, in which Malcolm Malcolmson, a Cambridge student revising for his Mathematics finals, ignores the wise counsel of local people and rents an old house with a sinister history that belonged to a judge who was 'held in great terror on account of his harsh sentences' (Stoker 1986: 110). His portrait lours from beside the fireplace in a room overrun by preternaturally intelligent black rats. The rodents disrupt Malcolmson's revision, but the plucky Scot refuses to believe he is in danger until, during a terrible storm one night, the judge's spirit emerges from the painting. Malcolmson is found hanged the following morning from the rope of the house's alarm bell as the judge's portrait smiles at him. The story is fast-moving and memorable, possibly because it largely disdains subtlety: few readers would feel at ease alone in a candle-lit, vermin-infested manor house of unsavoury reputation with a Judge Jefferies-like figure glowering at them from the wall and a tempest raging outside. The bleak ending comes as a surprise – Malcolmson puts up quite a fight, throwing his mother's Bible at one of the rats – but the rest of the story is a predictably efficient dramatisation of familiar materials.

Kipling's tale is very different. It is set in India during the hot season, evoking the subcontinent through the telling use of experientially acquired detail rather than pre-packed Gothic props. Instead of Stoker's classic haunted house, its setting is a flimsy bungalow beside a partially built railway. 'The Judge's House' has a simple, linear structure and is told by an omniscient narrator. 'At the End of the Passage' is also told in the third person, but much of its content emerges from conversations between its four characters, young Englishmen who are archetypes of the Indian imperial project: a surveyor, a policeman, a doctor and an engineer. In Stoker's story, the reader sees the rats and the portrait as Malcolmson does, fear being generated by the proven means of exposing them to incidents they are certain to find alarming. By contrast, Kipling locates his horrors in the mind of Hummil, the engineer, who has become crazed by insomnia in the ferocious heat of the Indian summer. Hummil longs to sleep but only if sedated, for his dreams are haunted by something, he says, that 'has made every night hell to me; and yet I'm not conscious of having done anything wrong' (Kipling 1907: 202). Many earlier Victorian tales used the folkloric device of ghosts taking revenge on the living who have wronged them, but Kipling makes cause and effect unclear. Hummil is tormented by 'A blind face that cries and can't wipe its eyes, a blind face that chases him down corridors' (204). Malcolmson ignored the advice of the villagers. Hummil has not tempted Providence so overtly, but he still suffers an awful fate. After another week of torment, he is found dead, his eyes wide open. His colleagues notice mysterious 'grey blurs' (209) in his pupils, and one takes a photograph. Whatever it depicts is too disturbing to reveal; the photographer destroys the photographic negative and the story ends with its central questions unanswered.

'The Judge's House' is designed as a chiller for a winter's night, suspenseful and dramatic when read aloud and requiring little interpretive effort to achieve its impact. 'At the End of the Passage' is less immediately accessible, with the relationship between Hummil and his tormentor mysterious (might the weeping figure be a symbol or embodiment of the India he is engaged in colonising?) and the horrors themselves mentioned almost in passing, as if, like Hummil's face on the final page, they are too terrible to look upon directly. In short, Stoker depicts frightening events while Kipling gives his readers just enough of a glimpse of them to spur their own imaginations. The two texts might both appeal to ghost story connoisseurs, but the wider Victorian public, who perhaps only read such tales as an aspect of Yuletide tradition, would surely regard Stoker's as the 'proper' one. George Gissing remarked that 'nothing is so abhorred by the multitude as lack of finality in stories, a vagueness of conclusion which gives them the trouble of forming surmises' (Gissing 1898: 103) and Kipling's is a case in point – too elliptical, occluded and, in its underlying speculations about the workings of empire, too provocative for easy fireside reading.

What terrifies one generation often has far less dramatic effects upon the next. Gothic writers have always recognised the law of diminishing returns. During the 1880s and 1890s, a number signalled their break with earlier Victorian supernatural fiction by writing parodies of it. In Grant Allen's 'Our Scientific Observations of a Ghost' (1884), a phantom appears to two Oxford medical students and tells them, '"you can't eject a ghost, you know. You may get a writ of *habeas corpus*, but the English law doesn't supply you with a writ of *habeas animam*"' (Allen 1884: 326). Oscar Wilde's 'The Canterville Ghost' (1887) depicted an aristocratic Elizabethan spook haunted, indeed bullied, by the vulgar Americans who buy his ancestral home, with the Irish writer wittily overturning stale convention while simultaneously signalling the imminent eclipse of the Old World by the New. Jerome K. Jerome's *Told After Supper* (1891) was an unforgiving dissection of earlier ghost stories even as it revealed a profound affection for them. Kipling's 'My Own True Ghost Story' (1888) cleverly demonstrated how a credulous observer could be drawn into a supernatural explanation for resolutely ordinary events, as did Kenneth Grahame's 'The Blue Room' (1895), in which a private tutor misinterprets his charges' activities, albeit more light-heartedly than the governess of *The Turn of the Screw* (1898) would do three years later. Elsewhere, the cartoonists of *Punch* used ghostly trappings to satirise politicians haunted by the recurrent problems of government, while the durability of ghost story conceits would be further emphasised by Georgian parodists such as Saki ('The Open Window' [1911]) and Max Beerbohm ('A. V. Laidler' [1916]). All of these texts convey a sense of restlessness and experiment; even as writers showed their impatience with established methods, they could not help recognising how effective those methods could be. H. G. Wells's 'The Red Room', published in Jerome's *The Idler* magazine in 1896, manages to be a parody of the 'haunted room' style of story that could be traced back to Walter Scott's 'The Tapestried Chamber' (1828) that is also a memorable dramatisation of a frightening experience in a candle-lit French castle. The story's denouement reveals that the room is haunted not by a ghost but by fear itself, an idea that would be taken up by later writers, for example H. R. Wakefield in 'Blind Man's Bluff' (1929).

The conventions of the Victorian ghost story, brilliantly enumerated in Dickens's story-cum-essay 'A Christmas Tree', include old rooms draped with tapestries, sinister portraits, sleepless nights, the deceptive flickering of a log fire that throws monstrous shadows, and 'gliding' figures which move silently across otherwise creaking floorboards as the clock strikes midnight. One such figure is a young woman with a 'low, terrible voice' whose antique clothing is soaking wet and whose long fair hair is 'dabbled with moist mud' (Dickens 1997: 11). There are unerasable bloodstains, ominous portents, black carriages pulled by silent, black horses. These ingredients worked in 'The Judge's House' and they have endured up to the present (as shown by the commercial success of Susan Hill's *The Woman in Black* [1983]) because, handled with a modicum of skill, they are guaranteed to provoke unease. Nevertheless, their familiarity bred contempt from some and impatience in other writers who were keen to explore what the ghost story might be capable of if it ceased merely to restage established tropes. By 1895, the children in Grahame's 'The Blue Room' regard an account of a nocturnal storm, a 'white lady', a 'haunted chamber' and a 'murder re-enacted' as 'already worn threadbare in many a Christmas number' (Grahame 1895: 221). Innovation was vital to prevent the ghost story from becoming obsolete.

Experiment took a number of forms, though the dominant style continued to be versions of realism which focused on well observed, often familiar settings and character types which narrowed the gap between the worlds in which the stories take place and those in which they are read. In these works, which connect the supernatural to James's 'the common objects of life', psychologically complex people have frightening and bewildering encounters with mysterious forces which make narrative sense yet defy rational or doctrinal explanation: Victorian ghost story writers asked their largely Christian readership to indulge ideas of the afterlife very different from those instilled by the established churches. A case in point is Le Fanu's 'Green Tea', usually known from its appearance in his influential collection *In a Glass Darkly* (1872), but first published by Dickens in the October 1869 issue of *All the Year Round*. In it, a clergyman, Jennings, is harassed by the spectral figure of a small black monkey surrounded by 'a halo that resembles a glow of red embers' (Le Fanu 1993: 27), apparently the result of his excessive consumption of green tea. The drink's psychoactive properties have unwittingly opened what the Swedenborgians call the 'third eye', making Jennings all too aware of orders of reality which are usually invisible. Worse, it allows evil spirits to perceive him. 'In all situations, at all hours, it is awake and looking at me,' Jennings says. 'That never changes' (26). After three years, eleven weeks and two days of 'torment' – Jennings 'keep[s] very accurate count' (21) – he consults the unconventional physician Dr Martin Hesselius, who offers several theories to account for the monkey's appearance but cannot prevent the ever-more persistent menace from intimidating Jennings even when he prays. Unable to resist its malignant influence any longer, Jennings's sanity collapses and he kills himself before Hesselius is able to help him.

The story's bleak ending is typical of Le Fanu's fiction, going back to early pieces such as 'Strange Event in the Life of Schalken the Painter' (1839), but its focus on psychological disturbance links it with 'The Signal-Man' or the troubled souls who seek the help of Algernon Blackwood's 'psychic doctor' in *John Silence: Physician Extraordinary* (1908) half a century later. Jennings is afraid both of what the monkey does and of what it *is*. It cannot harm him physically, but its demonic appearance and insistent presence are deeply unsettling and appear to bring about a confrontation between the seemingly meek clergyman and parts of his character hidden even from himself. The story suggests Darwin's provocative theories about humans and animals and anticipates Freud in its recognition of the mental undercurrents swirling beneath public selfhood. Le Fanu skilfully fuses the mystery and fear surrounding the monkey's manifestations with a more intimate treatment of the clergyman's anxieties, for even when the monkey is not present, Jennings is traumatised by its past appearances and dreads its return.

Some of the most accomplished late Victorian ghost stories focused on the experience of being haunted rather than the more immediate terror of encountering an apparition. Such tales built on the troubled protagonists of stories such as 'The Signal-Man' or Le Fanu's 'The Watcher' ([1851], revised as 'The Familiar' in 1872) and dwelled on psychological nuance in line with what Virginia Woolf would later identify as a key aspect of 'modern fiction', its concern with 'the dark places of psychology' (Woolf 2008: 11). Margaret Oliphant is particularly notable in this context. Improbably industrious as a novelist, reviewer and publisher's reader, she wrote over a hundred books between 1849 and her death in 1897, cleverly adapting to changes in literary fashion in moving between domestic realist fiction, biography, travel writing and what she called 'stories of the seen and unseen'. Her final such tale, 'The Library Window' (1896), set in a lightly fictionalised St Andrews she calls St Rule's, is among the most sophisticated Victorian ghost stories and has been anthologised regularly.

The young narrator goes to stay with her aunt while convalescing and spends her time reading and sewing as she regains her strength. She becomes drawn to a window in the library of the university college opposite where she sees a young man writing. Her aunt's female friends discuss whether the window – 'a very dead thing without any reflection in it' (Oliphant 1896:3) – has glass or was painted out to avoid the window tax of the later eighteenth century, and this further piques the narrator's curiosity. The narrator is increasingly fascinated by the scholar, not least because Lady Carnbee, an elderly friend of her aunt, hints at a sinister secret concerning his fate. At this point, the narrator is abruptly taken back to London by her mother and does not return to St Rule's, but she never again looks into one window from another, and she lives in terror of the yellow diamond Lady Carnbee bequeaths her. She also believes that the man in the window continues to appear to her; she is sure that when she returned to England, widowed, from India, she saw him in the crowd at the quayside, waiting for her.

'The Library Window' can be read as a ghost story – the narrator sees the man on midsummer's eve, when tradition has it that the veil between the worlds is thin. It could, however, have no supernatural content and depict instead a young woman's psychological deterioration as she slides towards a breakdown from which she never entirely recovers. She is, in her way, as troubled as Dickens's signalman, though whether the cause of the trouble is supernatural or psychological is not revealed, ambiguity adding to the story's haunting effect. 'The Library Window' made assured use of its material – an imaginative, potentially unstable young woman, the socially claustrophobic setting of her aunt's house and the small town outside, a mysterious figure in a college library, a veiled past, and a nod to historical veracity. The result *feels* believable and psychologically convincing; the story's depth and mystery increase with each reading. Like 'The Signal-Man' or *The Turn of the Screw*, its handling of Gothic convention is deft and skilful, demonstrating how writers could transform familiar generic ingredients into sophisticated literary art that raised important political questions. Oliphant's contrast between the narrator's imagination and the scholar's academic activities did not go unnoticed in the age of the New Woman.

If Oliphant's stories had a leisurely style at times reminiscent of Anthony Trollope, Edith Nesbit's ghost stories were more attuned to the brisk tempo of life during the 1890s and Edwardian age. A bohemian socialist with feminist sympathies, a summary which hardly does justice to the complexity of her political and personal outlook, Nesbit wrote poetry and children's books alongside classic ghost stories such as 'John Charrington's Wedding' (1891, collected 1893) in which the title character's determination to marry overcomes death itself. Her female characters often have progressive political attitudes but are confronted by supernatural representatives of patriarchal order, notably the stone statues which seem to be responsible for the death of the young artist in the chilling 'Man-Size in Marble' (1887, collected 1893). Nesbit and Oliphant came from very different literary and political worlds, but their ghost stories share a concern with female experience. This is clearly demonstrated in Nesbit's 'The Shadow' (1905, collected 1910), originally entitled 'The Portent of the Shadow', which starts as a knowing take on Victorian tradition with a group of young women telling each other spooky tales one Christmas night. Alluding to familiar stories by Walter Scott, Rhoda Broughton, Amelia Edwards and Wilkie Collins, the narrator distinguishes between the 'artistically rounded-off ghost story' and accounts of 'real' ghosts, which offer 'no explanation, no logical coherence' (Nesbit 1905: 10). When Miss Eastwich, the housekeeper, is prevailed upon to tell a story, Nesbit takes the reader into much darker territory in recounting a fatal love triangle. Eastwich recalls how, twenty years earlier, she went to live with a male friend and his wife, Mabel, who was struggling through a difficult pregnancy. Slowly, she becomes aware that the couple's new villa is haunted by 'something' that sighs or else 'that would crouch, and sink, and lie like a black pool, and then draw itself into the shadow that was nearest' (22). The husband fears he and Mabel have been cursed and tragedies follow. Nesbit, however, never provides the 'rounding-off' she disparages at the outset of 'The Shadow', leaving it rich in implication. Were Margaret Eastwich and her old friend once lovers? Is the 'curse' a syphilitic infection that is responsible for Mabel's poor health and, in time, the deaths of her husband and child, not to mention Miss Eastwich's barren life? 'The Shadow' might be read as Nesbit's response to Henrik Ibsen's *Ghosts* (1882), one informed by her torturous relationship with her charming but serially unfaithful husband. It may be significant that the story's original publication in *The Index* magazine billed her as 'Mrs Hubert Bland'.

The type of 'real' ghost story which Nesbit contrasts with its more artistic counterpart began to receive serious scientific study with the formation of the Society for Psychical Research (SPR) in 1882. Its researchers, who came from a variety of disciplines, investigated apparitions and haunted houses, along with other peculiar phenomena such as hypnotism, telepathy and mediumship, approaching them in a spirit of objective scientific enquiry rather than blinkered conformism. In 1886, the SPR published the two-volume *Phantasms of the Living*, which documented over 700 encounters with apparitions. It was poorly received by the scientific establishment, but had the probably unintended effect of making writers reflect on the difference between literary ghosts and their 'real' versions. Michael Cox and R. A. Gilbert observe that fictional spectres:

hardly ever lacked motivation [...] they revealed secrets, avenged wrongs, reenacted ancient tragedies, in some cases proffered help and comfort to the living, or bore witness to the workings of divine providence. Most disquieting of all, they could pursue blameless living victims with a relentless and unfathomable malignity. (Cox and Gilbert 1991: xv–xvi)

The phantoms recorded by the SPR were, by contrast, a dull bunch, typically silent and seen so fleetingly that they suggested little if any narrative potential.

Vernon Lee pondered the difference between the two types of ghost in the preface to her collection *Hauntings* (1890), maintaining that in order to invest a story with 'the strange perfume of witch-garden flowers' (Lee 2006: 39), a writer needed a sophisticated handling of atmosphere and nuance. Her earlier essay, 'Faustus and Helen: Notes on the Supernatural in Art' (1880), argued that the supernatural was 'necessarily vague' – she deplored the way writers transformed 'phantoms into mere creatures of flesh and blood'. In her view, the supernatural was 'nothing but ever-renewed impressions, ever shifting fancies', and the most successful ghost stories were 'those in which the ghost is heard but not seen' (Lee 2006: 310). Lee was no idle theorist, and *Hauntings* was a brilliant demonstration of her beliefs.

In 'Amour Dure', Spiridion Trepka, a cocksure young Polish historian, travels to Italy to research the notorious Medea di Carpi, a femme fatale reminiscent of Lucrezia Borgia. For all his intellectual protestations, Trepka is drawn into a strange erotic communion with a portrait of the murderous aristocrat and begins to believe that her spirit is trying to return. Narrating the story through the entries in Trepka's journal, Lee is able to delineate his character, his opinions, and even his research methods while refusing to confirm that Medea is once again abroad. Is Spiridion in the grip of a dangerous infatuation which clouds his scholarly and personal judgement, or might Medea be influencing his behaviour from beyond the grave, trying to find a way to release her spirit from the statue in which it was imprisoned centuries earlier? Perfectly paced, richly imaginative, and imbued with a thoroughly convincing pseudo-historical backstory informed by Lee's detailed knowledge of the Italian renaissance, it sets the tone for the rest of the volume. Another story, 'A Wicked Voice', explores the implications of Lee's belief that ghosts should be auditory rather than visual in depicting a young operatic composer becoming slowly possessed by the spirit of a long-dead castrato. Lee was a deeply learned cosmopolitan aesthete whose work shows little enthusiasm for popular taste. A 2006 scholarly edition of *Hauntings* edited by Catherine Maxwell and Patricia Pulham shows the breadth of her learning and the sophistication of her multilingual allusions; it is safe to say that she would not have been a contributor to *Holly Leaves* or similar Christmas annuals, 'Amour Dure' appearing in the upmarket *Murray's Magazine* instead. Lee's ghosts were as subtle and refined as she was, showing themselves (if they exist at all) only to those of sophisticated intellectual and artistic sensibilities.

Lee had been friends with Henry James until she caricatured him in her novella, *Lady Tal* (1892), and their ghost stories have much in common. James's brother, William, belonged to the SPR, but Henry's stories are more concerned with psychology than with psychic investigation. What he called 'tales' such as 'The Aspern Papers' (1888) and 'The Beast in the Jungle' (1903) have no supernatural elements yet depict profoundly haunted characters whose lives teem with secrets and obsessions. James had written ghost stories since the 1860s, early ones such as 'The Romance of Certain Old Clothes' (1868) showing the influence of Nathaniel Hawthorne, but between 'Sir Edmund Orme' (1891) and his final ghost story, 'The Jolly Corner' (1908), he became increasingly ambitious, using the form as a vehicle for technical experiment, for the revisiting of enduring preoccupations such as the distinction between public and private selves, and for personal reflection. 'The Jolly Corner' imagines its protagonist, Spencer Brydon, an American who has spent his adult life in Europe, haunted by the self he might have been had he remained in the United States. The story made striking use of the motif of the double seen elsewhere in late Victorian Gothic (such as *Strange Case of Doctor Jekyll and Mr Hyde* [1886] or *The Picture of Dorian Gray* ([1890/1891]) but was more ruminative, brooding on unlived and alternative lives in ways which provided a counterpart to James's accounts of his final return to the United States in *The American Scene* (1907). James's fascination with the complexities of thought and perception informed his subtle depiction of the supernatural and influenced in turn writers such as Robert Hichens, who combined Jamesian elements with more overt melodrama in stories such as 'A Sea-Change' and 'How Love Came to Professor Guildea' (both 1900). James's masterpiece was *The Turn of the Screw* in which a young governess becomes convinced that her charges are being directed by the ghosts of her predecessor and her lover. The story has probably generated more critical discussion than any other of its kind, something which has to a degree overshadowed other fascinating works such as 'Owen Wingrave' (1892) and 'The Way It Came' (1896) which James retitled 'The Friends of the Friends' in 1909. The first of these revisits the familiar trope of a character daring to sleep in a haunted chamber to offer an investigation of masculinity, militarism and personal courage, while 'The Friends' takes an experience familiar from the SPR archives of seeming to see the spirit of a loved one at the moment of their death. As one would expect from James, the stories are rich in ambiguity and suggestion while delineating character with a keen and at times unforgiving eye.

Another way to consolidate and develop Victorian traditions of supernatural fiction was to set ghost stories in places that had gone largely unused in earlier works. These might be exotic, as in Kipling's Indian ghost stories, H. G. Wells's 'Pollock and the Porrah-Man' (1895) which opens in what is now Sierra Leone, or the Scandinavia of stories such as M. R. James's 'Count Magnus' and 'Number 13' (1904). In the early twentieth century, Algernon Blackwood, who journeyed widely in North America, Europe and the Middle East, used his experiences to inform stories such as 'A Haunted Island' (1906) set in the Muskoka region of Ontario. John Buchan set weird tales such as 'The Grove of Ashtaroth' (1912) in southern Africa. Stories with British and Irish settings drew inspiration from a rich reservoir of history and folklore, both actual and invented. Le Fanu was a pioneer in this area. A story such as 'The White Cat of Drumgunniol' (1869), another story to appear in *All the Year Round*, tells of an Irish family whose members live in fear of seeing the mysterious feline whose presence inevitably portends their deaths. It could easily have been recorded in the collections of Irish folklorists such as Jane Wilde (the mother of Oscar) or Augusta Gregory. Kathleen Tynan ('The Death Spancel' [1896]), Robert Louis Stevenson, whose 'Thrawn Janet' (1881) is recounted in Scots dialect, and M. R. James, who displayed a remarkable talent for imitating the style of antique documents in stories such as 'The Ash Tree' (1904), a story combining witchcraft and ghostly vengeance which spans the period 1735 to 1890, all broadened the ghost story's compass by engaging with folk narratives. In the preface to his *Collected Ghost Stories* (1931), James observed that he had 'tried to make my ghosts act in ways not inconsistent with the rules of folklore'. He admitted few 'obligations to literature or local legend' (James 2011: 419) but his stories offer masterful pastiches of both.

Ghost stories were not always so exotic in their settings or so concerned with the fabrication of believable folkloric incidents. They could be much more humdrum, exploring how horror (and on occasion, humour) might be created from everyday settings and experiences. Wells's 'The Inexperienced Ghost' (1902), which manages to be at once comic and startling, features the spectre of a teacher killed in a gas explosion who has forgotten how to return to the spirit world. He is described as 'Lean' with:

that sort of young man's neck that has two great flutings down the back, here and here—so! And a little, meanish head with scrubby hair—And rather bad ears. Shoulders bad, narrower than the hips; turn-down collar, ready-made short jacket, trousers baggy and a little frayed at the heels. (Wells 1927: 901)

Richard Marsh's ingenious collection, *The Seen and the Unseen* (1900), features 'The Fifteenth Man' in which a ghost takes part in a rugby match; the watery haunting, 'The Houseboat'; and 'The Photographs', which is set in a London prison and depicts psychic intrusion into the prison's photographic records. Having served a custodial sentence for fraud in 1884, Marsh was able to put personal experience of the penal system to entertaining use. What might be termed 'everyday ghosts' became increasingly familiar literary presences in the twentieth century, notably in the stories of A. M. Burrage and, after the Second World War, Rosemary Timperley and Penelope Lively.

By 1900, the ghost story had long established itself as an art form that could be both popular and sophisticated, traditional and experimental, reassuringly familiar and profoundly strange. It could be esoteric and highly commercial, sometimes simultaneously. Blackwood's *John Silence* was the first book to be advertised on the side panels of London omnibuses; its publisher's initiative made the collection a bestseller despite its recherché content. In essence though, the form continued to be divided between tales in which some form of spirit appeared to the living and others in which the living coped as best they could with the aftermath of traumatic experience, guilt, loss, or the subtle torments of memory. The ghost story kept pace with the 'body horror' of fiction such as Arthur Machen's *The Three Impostors* (1895) in works such as M. R. James's 'Lost Hearts' (1895, collected 1904), but it could also be comic or sentimental at one end of the scale and charged with psychological complexity at the other in works such as 'The Library Window', 'Amour Dure', *The Turn of the Screw* and Kipling's unforgettably moving depiction of parental bereavement, 'They' (1904). As the Victorian age gave way to a new century, the ghost story would continue to evolve even as anthologists such as Lady Cynthia Asquith (*The Ghost Book*, 1927), Dorothy L. Sayers (*Great Short Stories of Detection, Mystery, and Horror*, 1928), Montague Summers (*The Supernatural Omnibus*, 1931), and the anonymous compilers of works such as *The Evening Standard Book of Strange Stories* (1934) and *50 Years of Ghost Stories*, which announced 'staggering value for half-a crown', the following year emphasised its heritage. In some respects, therefore, the Victorian ghost story became a haunting presence in itself, one which continues to exert its influence on contemporary fiction.

Note

1. Laura Kranzler notes in her edition of Elizabeth Gaskell's *Gothic Tales* that 'Dickens wrote a series of increasingly exasperated letters to Gaskell urging her to change the ending so that only the child Rosamond would see the ghostly figures, though everyone sees the phantom child. Gaskell obviously refused' (Gaskell 2000: 344).

Works Cited

Allen, Grant. 'Our Scientific Observations on a Ghost', in *Strange Stories*. London: Chatto & Windus, 1884, pp. 322–41.
Anon. 'Mr Charles Dickens'. *The Times*, 10 June 1870, p. 1.
Anon., ed. *50 Years of Ghost Stories*. London: Hutchinson, 1935.
Cox, Michael and R. A. Gilbert, eds. *Victorian Ghost Stories: An Anthology*. Oxford: Oxford University Press, 1991.
Dickens, Charles. 'A Christmas Tree', in *Selected Journalism 1860–1870*, edited by David Pascoe. London: Penguin, 1997, pp. 3–16.
———. et al. 'Number 1 Branch Line: The Signal-Man', in *Mugby Junction*. London: Chapman and Hall, 1898, pp. 89–110.
Gaskell, Elizabeth. *Gothic Tales*, edited by Laura Kranzler. Harmondsworth: Penguin, 2000.
Gissing, George. *Charles Dickens: A Critical Study*. New York: Dodd, Mead, 1898.
Grahame, Kenneth. 'The Blue Room', in *The Golden Age*. London: John Lane, 1895, pp. 195–212.
James, Henry. 'Miss Braddon', in *Notes and Reviews*. Cambridge: Dunster House, 1921, pp. 108–16.
James, M. R. 'Some Remarks on Ghost Stories', in *Collected Ghost Stories*, edited by Darryl Jones. Oxford: Oxford University Press, 2011, pp. 410–16.
———. 'Preface' to *The Collected Ghost Stories of M. R. James*. In James, *Collected Ghost Stories*, edited by Darryl Jones. Oxford: Oxford University Press, 2011) pp. 418–20.
Keating, Peter. *The Haunted Study: A Social History of the English Novel 1875–1914*. London: Secker & Warburg, 1989.
Kipling, Rudyard. 'At the End of the Passage', in *Life's Handicap: Being Stories of Mine Own People*. London: Macmillan, 1907, pp. 183–212.
Lee, Vernon. 'Faustus and Helen: Notes on the Supernatural in Art', in *Hauntings and other Fantastic Tales*, edited by Catherine Maxwell and Patricia Pulham. Toronto: Broadview Press, 2006, pp. 291–320.
———. 'Amour Dure', in *Hauntings and other Fantastic Tales*, edited by Catherine Maxwell and Patricia Pulham. Toronto: Broadview Press, 2006, pp. 41–76.
Le Fanu, Sheridan. 'Green Tea', in *In a Glass Darkly*, edited by Robert Tracy. Oxford: World's Classics, 1993, pp. 5–40.

Nesbit, E. 'The Portent of the Shadow'. *The Index*, 1905, pp. 10–11, 22–3. Credited to 'Mrs Hubert Bland'.
Oliphant, Margaret. 'The Library Window'. *Blackwood's Magazine*, January 1896, pp. 1–30.
Stoker, Bram. 'The Judge's House', in Michael Cox and R. A. Gilbert (eds), *The Oxford Book of Ghost Stories*. Oxford: Oxford University Press, 1986, pp. 109–24.
Waller, Philip. *Writers, Readers, and Reputations: Literary Life in Britain 1870–1918*. Oxford: Oxford University Press, 2006.
Wells, H. G. 'The Inexperienced Ghost', in *Complete Short Stories*. London: Ernest Benn, 1927, pp. 899–912.
Woolf, Virginia. 'Modern Fiction', in *Selected Essays*, edited by David Bradshaw. Oxford: World's Classics, 2008, pp. 6–12.

Chapter 4

Neo-Victorian Unquiet Spirits: Encounters with Nineteenth-Century Ghosts

Marie-Luise Kohlke

The framing country house setting of Henry James's *The Turn of the Screw* (1898), one of the Victorian age's pre-eminent ghost stories, encapsulates the promise proffered to audiences of this genre: to be deliciously terrified at a comforting temporal remove, safe from the otherworldly terrors consumed with equal relish and trepidation. At the same time, ghost stories underline the speciousness of strict demarcations between past and present, radically eroding any such seeming security. This central paradox is only heightened further when refracted through the dual temporal lens of neo-Victorianism's reimagining of the long nineteenth century (roughly 1789 to 1914) from the vantage point of presentist hindsight. Whether revenants of once-living persons, intangible supernatural entities that were never human to begin with, or other 'existences' manifesting out of their proper time, neo-Victorian ghosts collapse temporal difference into sameness.[1] These unquiet spirits reflect not only prevailing anxieties and iniquities of the past but also the present-day cultural contexts of the stories' production.

This chapter focuses on 'genuine' hauntings or encounters with forms of para-existentiality that cannot be reduced to mere projections of ignorant, deceived or traumatised minds. Paradoxically, however, such spectral encounters confront protagonists and readers with distinctly human rather than necessarily supernatural evils. Through a range of iconic and critically neglected novels and short stories, I explore some significant elements of neo-Victorian ghost stories: a playful use of multi-intertextuality; inversions of the conventional temporal structure of haunting; the introduction of biofiction and/or first-person narration by spectres themselves; a strong focus on gender and gendered abuse; and a wider concern with historical trauma, social justice and (vicarious) witnessing. While further characteristics, such as the lover-returned-from-the-grave trope or the belated punishment of malefactors, are typical features of the ghost story generally, neo-Victorian writers often give these elements unforeseen twists to innovate the form.

Women dominated ghost story writing in the long nineteenth century. Hephzibah Anderson cites a figure of 70 per cent for female authorship of publications in this genre in British and US magazines 'at the height of the form's popularity' (Anderson 2016: n.p.). Unsurprisingly, women writers also preponderate in neo-Victorian reworkings of the form, their most obvious innovation being the shift from the short story to longer prose forms, especially the novel. Following in the footsteps of James's *The Turn of the Screw*, novellas such as Marghanita Laski's *The Victorian Chaise-Longue* (1953), Susan Hill's *The Woman in Black* (1983) and A. S. Byatt's 'The Conjugial Angel', collected in *Insects and Angels* (1992), assume a halfway position in this transition. Further 'genuine' neo-Victorian ghost stories include Toni Morrison's *Beloved* (1987), Michèle Roberts's *In the Red Kitchen* (1990), Joanne Harris's *Sleep, Pale Sister* (1994), Margaret Atwood's *Alias Grace* (1996), Barbara Chase-Riboud's *Hottentot Venus: A Novel* (2003), Audrey Niffenegger's *Her Fearful Symmetry* (2009), Catriona Ward's *Rawblood* (2015) and Lorna Gibb's *A Ghost's Story* (2015), as well as – with qualification – John Harwood's *The Ghost Writer* (2004).[2] In the only two extant collections of neo-Victorian ghost short stories to date that I am aware of – suggesting an emerging trend of renewed interest in the shorter form – women writers likewise outnumber male contributors: in *The Haunting Season: Ghostly Tales for Long Winter Nights* (2022) by seven to one, and in its follow-up, *Winter Spirits: Ghostly Tales for Frosty Nights* (2023), by ten to two. The characteristic woman-centred focus of most of these texts, even if sometimes in whole or part narrated or mediated by a first-person or third-person male perspective, can also be attributed to neo-Victorianism's general feminist leanings and interest in the recovery of marginalised histories. The nineteenth-century 'second sex' provides convenient models of 'Othered' oppressed subalternity, whose experiences have been culturally spectralised. Indeed, ghosts serve as 'particularly powerful and suggestive figure[s] of women's marginal and repressed position in society' (Wallace 2018: 428). Interestingly, though, non-heteronormative identities, an otherwise prominent theme in neo-Victorianism, have made little impact on neo-Victorian narratives of 'genuine' hauntings as yet.

The ghost story's anachronistic rupture of temporal boundaries vitiates any real sense of security, with protagonists modelling readers' own violability to potentially inimical forces beyond their control. Ghost stories thus stage violations of self and subjectivity as well as time, 'Othering' their readers also. Spectral visitants drive home the dismaying realisation that all human life, including one's own body and consciousness, is destined for death, decay and (self)loss. Jeanette Winterson reminds us that as long as 'death is the lived experience of us all', ghost stories function as attempted 'partial answer[s] to the mystery' of our final destination (Winterson 2023: 18), or, as Audrey Niffenegger puts it, as 'little experiments in death' (Niffenegger 2018: ix). The deaths already suffered by ghostly visitants 'create a shiver of pleasure because they are not ours, not yet' (Niffenegger 2018: ix).

At one extreme, then, ghost stories are about attempts to conquer death itself. Hence writers like Jess Kidd in 'Lily Wilt' (2021) use the form to parody postmodernity's obsession with eternal youthfulness and the search for artificial means of somehow eluding ageing and extinction altogether.[3] Focusing on the 'memorial photographer' Walter Pemble, employed by an establishment specialising in postmortem images of 'The Recently Expired' (Kidd 2022: 111), Kidd's story also summons up the ghosts of various nineteenth-century texts.[4] In spite of being warned off from indecent conduct – 'no touching, leering or rubbing yourself against the casket' (Kidd 2022: 111) – Walter promptly falls, in fateful Poesque fashion, for the deceased Lily Wilt whom he has been charged with capturing for eternity. The dead girl's immaculate beauty, lauded in an obituary by the famous author and friend of the family, 'Mr D—', attracts veritable crowds to her parents' home to gaze upon '[h]er mortal shell exquisite and untarnished by natural processes', celebrated as 'The Perpetually Sleeping Beauty' whose charms will never fade (Kidd 2022: 130, 112, 132). Kidd evokes the well-known fairy tale alongside one of Edgar Allan Poe's recurrent themes: the untimely death of exquisite young females. Yet the corpse's depiction also echoes that of the (un)dead Lucy Westenra in Bram Stoker's *Dracula* (1897). Walter compares Lily's face to 'a martyr's' and a saint's but notes 'a certain plump-lipped voluptuousness' to her mouth indicative of far from innocent sensuality (Kidd 2022: 113).[5] Later, the maid Nan Hooley witnesses ghostly tracings of Lily's name on the side of the coffin and admonishes her onetime mistress to 'stay put' and not 'go gallivanting' (Kidd 2022: 115). Walter's developed photographs capture not just the dead Lily's 'supernatural beauty' but also her transparent ghost archly observing the proceedings (Kidd 2022: 117). In a subsequent photographic session, Walter captures the vain seductive spectre in all sorts of provocative poses and succumbs to her promise to be his if he can find a way of reuniting her spirit and body.

Kidd repurposes the well-known trope of old lovers-returned-from-the-grave to draw the living to their death but substitutes a promised new lover. With the help of an esoteric occult tome and criminals paid to steal Lily's corpse, Walter manages to resurrect his love in Frankensteinean fashion, only to be horrified when her immaculate beauty begins to quickly deteriorate. Lily loses her deathly 'alabaster complexion', '[h]er skin sags and her teeth wobble, her eyes sink and her golden hair dulls' (Kidd 2022: 136). In effect, the reanimated Lily becomes a feminine counterpart to the degenerating portrait of Oscar Wilde's Dorian Gray: while her initial postmortem portraits freeze her beauty in time, her resurrected body succumbs to time's ravages. Walter hides Lily away in his attic room in Mrs Peach's lodging house, turning to drink and long walks since he 'dreads […] above all, going home' to his lover (Kidd 2022: 136).

Lily's food cravings soon take a ghastly turn, reducing Walter to catching neighbourhood cats, which his lover consumes alive from 'the wriggling sack' (Kidd 2022: 137) in another allusion to *Dracula* (see Stoker 1997: 43–4). When returning to his lodgings one day to find that his landlady has discovered Lily's presence, Walter summarily dispatches Mrs Peach in order to safeguard the secret of Lily's resurrection. Walter is only saved from his Renfield-like servitude by the Wilts' maid Nan, who confronts him in a tavern and convinces him to have Lily's body secretly returned to her parents' home, after he shows her the most recent likeness taken of his beloved, asking Nan to tell him 'exactly what you see' (Kidd 2022: 138). What Nan sees, however, is left to the reader's imagination. Buried in a closed casket, Lily's ghost confronts the mourning Walter at her graveside, acidly reflecting that 'this is not quite the ending I had planned' and suggesting there is still a way for them to 'be together' (Kidd 2022: 140). Walter obediently hands himself into the law and duly hangs for his crimes, while Nan burns his last photograph of Lily. Kidd thus trenchantly satirises our own culture's overinvestment in an impossible and pernicious feminine beauty ideal that seeks to defy nature.

In more serious vein, many neo-Victorian ghost stories serve the purpose of belated witness-bearing and 'working through' of historical, especially gendered traumas, as in the case of Laski's *The Victorian Chaise-Longue*. Following a difficult birth compounded by tubercular infection, the twentieth-century protagonist Melanie rests on a recently acquired, Victorian chaise-longue and inexplicably wakes in the dying tubercular body of Milly, a nineteenth-century 'fallen woman' and previous occupier of the divan. Deprived of her illegitimate child, Milly is condemned and psychologically tortured by her vindictive sister and a onetime suitor posing as a sympathetic visitor. The titular haunted object of furniture occasions a quasi-timeslip. However, the twentieth-century protagonist is not just temporally transported but also haunted – to the point of total possession – by the unremembered Victorian victim, from whom she struggles to differentiate herself: 'Dare I touch them, these breasts that may be mine and alive, or will they crumple, will they rot if I touch them with my living hands, my hands on long-dead breasts?' (Laski 1968: 124). As in Kidd's story, female corporeality becomes the site of terrifying abjection. As the protagonist relives the terminal sufferings of her period counterpart, her horror (like the reader's) is compounded by the story's open-endedness, refusing the ghost story's typical consolation.[6] While Melanie reflects that 'we are [...] waiting for release, Milly to death and I to life' (Laski 1968: 124), it remains unclear whether the protagonist ever returns to her married life and more sexually liberated own time or perishes in her double's ailing body.[7] Laski innovates the genre by staging an 'inverted haunting', with Melanie functioning as a disorientated ghost of the future within the Victorian past, becoming an unwilling first-hand witness to nineteenth-century women's subjection to punitive sexual discrimination.

Elizabeth Taylor too employs inverted haunting in 'Poor Girl' (1955), adapted for ITV's 'Haunted' series for Christmas in 1974. A story with an early Edwardian setting, 'Poor Girl' nonetheless qualifies as neo-Victorian due to its evident intertextual debt to *The Turn of the Screw*. In a secluded country mansion, Miss Florence Chasty, a young governess in her first position, is charged with educating 'an alarmingly precocious' and 'flirtatious little boy', Hilary Wilson (Taylor 2012: 275), like James's Miles far too worldly-wise for his unspecified years.[8] In 'Poor Girl' too, moral corruption comes in spectral form, though not of the child but of the governess, helplessly seduced by first the son, who treats her with an 'air of dalliance' and makes her 'blush, as if he were a grown man' (Taylor 2012: 275, 276), and then by his father. Lonely and isolated from both the Wilson family and the servants, Florence feels assailed and 'too sealed-up' (Taylor 2012: 276), evoking both fairy-tale and grave-like imagery of being immured in a kind of living death without excitement, genuine romance or self-fulfilment.

Florence continues the line of marginalised, self-effacing female figures in nineteenth-century fiction, like frustrated governesses or disappointed spinsters, who prove particularly prone to hauntings: already 'haunted by lives that might have been', these women mirror the 'ultimate outsider' status of ghosts as 'unable to partake of life in any meaningful way' (Anderson 2016: n.p.). The spectral crisis proper begins when Florence smells an unfamiliar 'heavy scent, dry and musky' in the schoolroom (Taylor 2012: 276); suspecting one of the maids, the governess is mortified by Hilary's assertion that the perfume is diffused by her own clothes. When his mother looks in, she notices 'a crimson smear' on

'Florence's empty teacup' although the governess does not wear lipstick, and when the governess rises to open the window, her skirts rustle sensuously, making Mrs Wilson suspect her of wearing 'silk underwear' and her modest dress of 'concealing frivolity and wantonness' (Taylor 2012: 276). Spectrality becomes the means to critique double moral standards regarding male and female sexual impropriety. Mrs Wilson's reluctant confiding of her suspicions to her wayward husband initiates exactly the behaviour she most fears, as he promptly takes an inappropriate 'warming' interest in the mousy governess (Taylor 2012: 279). A series of further inexplicable phenomena follow, including the residue of cigarette smoke in the schoolroom where no one smokes, a terrifying 'desire, horribly defined, though without direction' that overpowers Florence, and a long string of showy green glass beads, never before seen but strangely 'familiar', appearing at her throat (Taylor 2012: 281, 284). Comparable to Melanie's creeping dissolution of self in Laski's novella, Taylor's governess 'seem[s] to lose the true Florence' (Taylor 2012: 284), overcome by a ghostly Other's presence and personality that manifest through intrusive sensory experiences and material signs, inciting uncharacteristic behaviour and libidinal longings in the haunted protagonist.

When Mrs Wilson discovers her husband in the schoolroom alone with the governess in a state of disarray, Florence finds herself summarily dismissed. Only upon her departure is the nature of the repeated 'curious infraction of the [school]room and of her personality' revealed (Taylor 2012: 284). While leaving, Florence steps aside on the staircase to allow a young woman and girl to pass, watched by a man in the hall whom she recognises as Hilary grown up. The woman's description – wearing an indecently short tunic, a helmet-like hat, silk stockings, green glass beads, and a heady perfume – identifies her as a future occupant of the house, possibly Hilary's flapper wife or else his mistress and the child's governess. Here the spectral future rather than past forcibly confronts Florence with the 'unnatural' circumscriptions of her life.

Catriona Ward's *Rawblood* constitutes perhaps the most complex experiment in neo-Victorian inverted haunting to date, switching between the lead-up to the First World War and multiple nineteenth-century sections focused on the protagonist Iris Villacra's ancestors and people connected to them. Living in virtual isolation at the Dartmoor family seat of Rawblood, with only her father Alonso and an old butler for company, the young Iris is warned to curtail her burgeoning friendship with a local farmer's son, Tom Gilmore, as Alonso tells her of the family curse, 'a disease [...] named *horror autotoxicus*' (Ward 2021: 15, italics in original). The curse ensures that any attachment formed by a Villacra will bring death and destruction to those they love and themselves, haunted to death or driven to murder and self-murder by the Rawblood spectre. An evil in female shape, the ghost 'travels in our blood, passed down' as 'a biological inheritance, as much as a spiritual one', Alonso explains; exuding a sense of overwhelming 'despair' that feels like having 'the living marrow [...] sucked from the world', the ghost has 'taken' all the Villacras who met her terrifying gaze (Ward 2021: 77–8). Yet Ward's story also introduces the possibility that Iris and Tom disturbed an ancient spirit in a secret underground cave with a kind of pagan altar where superstitious villagers leave gifts to obtain supernatural favours. Within this subterraneous space, the teenage Iris (but not Tom) glimpses what 'could [...] be a very thin pale person, curled on the floor', who 'uncurls' to stand upright with 'bony fingers, spread wide; a bare skull peeping through baby-fine hair', a 'white thing' with 'a black mad eye' that comes '[p]adding' towards her (Ward 2021: 28), causing the protagonist to panic and drag Tom from the cavern.

The novel builds up suspense by recounting the haunted lives and violent deaths of Iris's ancestors, as well as characters' repeated visions of a newly dug grave at the foot of a cedar tree dominating the Rawblood grounds. A flashback to 1881, for instance, relates a visit by the doctor Charles Danforth to help his friend Alonso find a cure for the Villacra family's presumed hereditary blood disease. From his bedroom window, occupying just the spot from which he was earlier observed by a mysterious female figure as he walked outside, Charles sees 'unbroken' ground he only just traversed inexplicably 'scarred' by a gaping 'fresh grave':

> Long enough to hold a small woman or an older child. The sight filled me with a peculiar feeling, as if all the sadness in the world had drawn down into that spot. [...] I was on the verge of recalling some monstrous secret of existence. [...] There was something unpleasant about it, as if these feelings belonged to someone else entirely and I was merely a vessel for them. (Ward 2021: 59)

In *Rawblood* too, characters are haunted by a spectre of the future rather than the past, as eventually revealed following Iris's inadvertent killing of Alonso after he tries to strangle her and her subsequent long years of wrongful confinement in the Earlswood Asylum. Her harrowing persecution at the institution is prefigured by Alonso and Charles's cruel experiments on live animals, including the cutting of rabbits' vocal chords to still their cries of pain, and culminates in Iris's extracted consent to her 'Prefrontal Leucotomy' (by making her falsely believe she would be permitted to return to Rawblood thereafter), performed alongside a non-consensual hysterectomy; further experimental procedures follow, until she can no longer speak and the nurses 'don't even use her name anymore' (Ward 2021: 184, 323). The immaterial horrors of the text are eclipsed by the physical suffering induced by unethical male medical science and the violent subjugation of women's bodies.

Eventually, Iris appears to escape and travel home, only to discover the 'monstrous secret' foreshadowed in Charles's haunting. Iris, in fact, died at Earlswood, and the Rawblood Ghost is none other than the dreadfully scarred, mutilated and emaciated Iris herself, unknowingly enacting her despair on all those who brought her into being so as to effect her own undoing: 'I will take them all. Then I will never have been' (Ward 2021: 341). Tom, the friend of her youth, her mother's ghost explains to Iris, left the family ring Iris had gifted him on the altar in the cave – 'That the ones you love may never die' (Ward 2021: 344) – thereby extending her life and suffering indefinitely. Iris haunts herself and others until Tom reunites with Iris's spirit, empathically shares her pain, and lays her corpse to rest beneath the cedar tree, in another unusual twist of the lover-returned-from-the-grave trope.

Neo-Victorian resorts to inverted haunting, then, can also be read as reflections on the continued prevalence of discrimination and violence suffered by women in postmodern Western societies, in which, supposedly, women's rights have been secured, affording them increased protection. Commenting on the inherent subversiveness of female spirits, Robin Roberts thus argues that they 'provide warnings not just to the other living characters in their narratives, but also to their readers' (Roberts 2018: 3). Neo-Victorian spectrality points to a persistent fissure between the progressive ideal of gender equality and women's lived actualities, precipitating new fears of precarity,[9] as also underlined by the recent loss of crucial reproductive and abortion rights in both the United States and parts of Europe, anticipated in Iris's forced sterilisation. As Gina Wisker remarks, 'hauntings in women's ghost stories are not just personal; they exemplify, embody, the social, cultural wrongs which women suffer and have suffered' (Wisker 2022: 262). Hence individual neo-Victorian ghosts represent a wider cultural malaise, so that Iris's spectre becomes a metonym for women's ongoing exposure to systemic forms of gender-based violence.

Unsurprisingly, malevolent female ghosts like Iris constitute a recurrent motif in neo-Victorian ghost stories, seeking retribution on male perpetrators or society more generally for women's unredeemed suffering. In Susan Hill's *The Woman in Black*, another social outcast, Jennet Humfrye, is forced to give up her illegitimate son Nathaniel, passed off as her sister's offspring, only to helplessly witness him die in a tragic accident. Afterwards, literalising the metaphorical living death to which society condemned her, she 'waste[d] away' from distress until 'she looked like a walking skeleton, a living spectre' (Hill 1998: 149). Following her demise, Humfrye's ghost torments the community by causing the deaths of its children by way of coerced expiation, forcing the townsfolk to partake of her unappeased anguish. Hence Humfrye's haunting cannot be reduced to sheer vindictiveness, with critics repeatedly reading it as a post-traumatic re-enactment of her intolerable suffering, an indictment of patriarchal injustice, and a search for vindication for victimised women (see Cook 2014: 152–3; Burkhard 2016; Miquel-Baldellou 2021: 179–81). Ironically, however, the ghost's reclamation of agency and punishment of happy families – including that of the narrator Arthur Kipps, whose wife and son perish due to her manifestation – also inflicts harm on other women.

The same trajectory informs Margaret Atwood's *Alias Grace*, a bio-fiction of the Irish servant and convicted murderer Grace Marks, which raises the possibility of Grace's spirit-possession by her dead friend Mary Whitney at the time of the killings of Grace's employer Thomas Kinnear and his housekeeper-cum-mistress Nancy Montgomery. By implication, Mary, seduced by her employer's son and dying after a botched abortion, seeks to avenge herself – and other powerless servants, like Grace, vulnerable to sexual extortion and assault – on upper-class exploiters (as well as women who willingly submit to their advances). Hence like Hill's novella, *Alias Grace* belongs to those 'tales of women overshadowed in life and avenged in death [that] constitute a category we might call the return of the oppressed' (Belsey 2019: 106). Aptly, the narrative suggests that Grace was sexually abused by her own father, as well as assaulted by various employers and even a doctor in the asylum to which she is temporarily confined.[10] Again, spectral female violence is refigured as traumatic re-enactment. Yet by dispatching Nancy, Mary/Grace also becomes an unwitting patriarchal enforcer of society's double moral standards, implicated in their perpetuation rather than overcoming. Nonetheless, like their spectral Victorian predecessors, neo-Victorian 'ghost women [...] unleash the anger that their living sisters must swallow' (Anderson 2016: n.p.), amplifying expressions of female fury at patriarchal injustice.

It seems no coincidence that the decade preceding *Alias Grace*'s publication witnessed the 'sprawling' sociocultural 'phenomenon' of a child sexual abuse panic in the United States, precipitated by *Michelle Remembers* (1980), 'a book by a Canadian psychologist and his former patient about her memories of child abuse at the hands of satanists' (Yuhas 2021: n.p.). A flurry of prosecutions followed, though many convictions were later overturned on appeal, in some cases only after alleged perpetrators had already served lengthy prison sentences (see Yuhas 2021: n.p.). The panic spread north of the border as well as to Europe, fuelling the subsequent UK satanic ritual abuse panic of the 1990s. As Wisker notes, ghosts 'articulate the unsayable hidden secrets and darknesses of social and cultural moments' (Wisker 2022: 12), including real-world sexual crimes. Neo-Victorian ghosts remind readers that their own societies continue to be haunted by the terrifying spectres of paedophilia and child murder.

The encoding of the 1990s child sexual abuse panic into the neo-Victorian ghost story becomes explicit in Joanne Harris's *Sleep, Pale Sister*, in which the 'hungry' ghost of the murdered ten-year-old Marta Miller seeks vengeance on the perpetrator, the artist Henry Chester (Harris 1994: 374). Harris's novel continues the strand of late Victorian and Edwardian ghost stories by women writers in which 'abused children feature prominently' (Edmundson 2018: 74) but introduces the twist of a sexualised murder not found in predecessor texts. Years earlier, Henry's obsession with female purity precipitated his attempted paedophilic rape of Marta in her mother's brothel, during which he inadvertently suffocated the child while trying to silence her cries for help. Spectrality becomes both a displacement and a kind of oblique 'working through' of the cultural horror of paedophilia that collides with the limits of representability. As in *The Woman in Black*, the horror of *Sleep, Pale Sister* is heightened by the trope of child death, 'a subject that is at once profoundly and universally affecting, not just because of the tragedy of a life unfulfilled, but because the death of children is the death of the future' (Cook 2014: 146). The main story-plot is driven by the dead Marta's desperate desire to return to her mother and reclaim her lost future, by taking over the consciousness and body of Effie, Henry's child-wife, muse and model, who wants to escape her oppressive marriage and enforced infantilisation, which feeds Henry's art. Effie's resulting accidental death and Marta's/Effie's haunting of Henry thereafter – 'at night [...] they came, my darling Erinyes, [...] my darling succubi' (Harris 1994: 357) – lead to the artist suffering a stroke and confessing to his wife's murder. While 'justice' is achieved by his pending execution (though not specifically for Marta's killing), the ghost of the abused child is left unhoused to continue to haunt the extradiegetic future.

Besides the use of intertextuality to heighten its ghostly effects,[11] *Sleep, Pale Sister* 'fuse[s]' its characters with biofictional aspects 'of the relationships between John Ruskin, Effie Gray, and John Everett Millais' (Cox 2019: 62). This points to a further neo-Victorian innovation, previously introduced in Byatt's 'The Conjugial Angel': the use of spectres of real-life persons that conflates the ghost story and biofiction.

Spectrality is doubled in such texts, since readers are aware that not just the ghosts but also the historical figures still living in the diegesis are, in fact, long since dead and hence imaginatively 'reanimated' in the reader's own time. In Byatt's novella, the spiritualist Lilias Papagay arranges séances led by her protégée medium, Sophy Sheekhy, at the house of Alfred Lord Tennyson's sister Emily and her husband Captain Richard Jesse. Emily's life is haunted by her youthful romance with Arthur Henry Hallam, struck down suddenly and immortalised in her brother's elegiac masterpiece, *In Memoriam A. H. H.* (1850), wherein Alfred spectralised Emily's grief, 'in some curious way' turning himself 'into Arthur's widow' (Byatt 1995: 234). When Sophy produces automatic spirit writing that suggests Arthur's ghostly displeasure at Emily's sale of her copy of his posthumously published verse and poems, Emily recalls her younger self's terror of 'the process of his dissolution' upon hearing of Arthur's 'dismembered' body being transported home from Trieste, while his 'heart had been shipped in a separate iron casket': 'The Thing coming so slowly over the sea filled her with horror' (Byatt 1995: 220–1). Thereafter, the dead Arthur's memory became a source of 'moral oppression', with society expecting Emily to steadfastly mourn for her soulmate forever 'entombed in grief', her 'heart [...] sealed up' as if confined to its own funereal chest (Byatt 1995: 222, 229, 241) – and then condemning her when, after nine years of mourning, she chose life and Richard instead.

Byatt presents another version of the lover-returned-from-the-grave[12] to draw the (here subversively uncompliant) living woman to her death or at least to 'death-in-life', reduced to a joyless self-effacing husk, like '[h]er small ghost' that 'appeared from time to time' in her brother's poem (Byatt 1995: 233). Even Emily's eldest son, named after both his mother's dead fiancé and his living father, acts as a haunting reminder of her 'failure of perpetual maidenhood', with Emily reflecting: 'You are accompanied through life [...] not only by the beloved and accusing departed, but by your own ghost too' (Byatt 1995: 236, 242). Byatt's biofiction thus describes an accusatory self-haunting by 'dead' selves as much as a literal conjuring of the dead. The 'approaching annihilation' and 'vanishing' of subjecthood (Byatt 1995: 261), which so appals the aged Alfred Tennyson later in the novella, was forced upon his sister while still young, as it would never have been on her fiancé had Emily died instead. Byatt too, then, employs spectrality in the service of resonant gender critique. When Sophy encounters the mouldering ghost of Arthur in her bedroom (and again in a later séance), the earthbound spirit ironically yearns for the same 'life of sensation rather than thought' that society reproaches Emily for embracing (Byatt 1995: 251).

Arthur's ghost remains confined to the half-life of Tennyson's poetry and the poet's deflected homoerotic 'unappeasable longing' (Byatt 1995: 223), which almost vampirically feeds off his beloved dead friend. In a further inversion of the trope of the lover-returned-from-the-grave, the living man condemns Arthur's spectre to life-in-death, preventing his final dissolution.

In *Hottentot Venus*, Barbara Chase-Riboud employs the ghost itself as the primary, first-person, biofictional narrator,[13] with the novel opening with the eponymous Sarah Baartman of the decimated African Kkoekhoe tribe as she recounts her death in Paris in 1816. Hence the novel presents as a posthumously 'authored' memoir by a triply Othered subaltern: a spectre subjected to racial and sexist abuse in life and death. Collaborative Western imperialism and objectifying science are exposed as murderous ghostings of their dehumanised victims, so that the revenant, in Andrew Smith's terms, 'functions as a conceit for the political projection of spectrality' (Smith 2010: 186). In the dead Sarah's own words, '[w]herever I looked, I was not there' (Chase-Riboud 2003: 258). Through self-narration, the spectre's 'place on the social margins becomes transformed into a position of power' (Smith 2010: 187), as Sarah 're-members' her violated body as a once-living suffering subject. Sarah thus makes herself truly seen beyond the racist Othered projections imposed upon her as one of the 'freaks of nature, [...] things-that-should-never-have-been-born' (Chase-Riboud 2003: 3).

Nonetheless, *Hottentot Venus* lacks the liminal frisson of most ghost stories, since it opts for a realist recounting of the multiple intersectional traumas to which Sarah is subjected: displacement from her homeland, exhibition at freak shows in Britain and France, and financial and sexual exploitation by patriarchal 'masters'. The litany of violation culminates in Baron Georges Léopold Cuvier's Ripperesque dissection of Sarah's corpse to extract her Hottentot apron in a literalised re-enactment of the metaphorical rape of the African continent: 'The baron had arrived at last at the place in Africa he wanted to be, most wanted to possess' (Chase-Riboud 2003: 281). What haunts Chase-Riboud's novel are not incorporeal shadows but the very real, material horrors of colonial violence, as Sarah makes clear: 'I became the body politic of Africa's intercourse with Europe, which consisted of discovery, exploitation, war, extermination and silence' (Chase-Riboud 2003: 312). Only in the final chapters does *Hottentot Venus* pitch over into full-blown Gothic mode in the dissection scene and in the 'Epilogue' that depicts, in condensed form, the merciless revenge the ghost takes on those who abused her in life, 'accelerat[ing] their demises with [...] a maximum of torment' (Chase-Riboud 2003: 308).

Sarah becomes another raging Fury. With real-world justice remaining foreclosed, her spectral vengeance enacts a kind of symbolic justice for irredeemable suffering, a phantasmal 'sop' to readers' outraged sensibilities on her behalf.[14] As audiences are all too aware, the systemic racism and Othering denounced by Sarah's ghost persist in the extradiegetic world long after her remains are laid to rest in her homeland.

The ghost story has become an ineradicable fixture of neo-Victorianism's Gothic imagination. However, its neo-Victorian reiterations resist the wider generic trend towards 'more inward imaginings of terror' (Edmundson 2018: 69), which substitute psychologised projections for external occult entities. Instead, much neo-Victorian fiction opts for 'genuine' supernatural hauntings that paradoxically reflect real-world horrors, inhabiting both the nineteenth-century past and readers' here and now. In particular, the prevalent trope of inverted haunting, involving spectres of the future, emphasises what might be termed the 'transhistoricity' of neo-Victorian spectres and their significance. As Susanne Gruss explains, '[r]ather than uncritically assuming the universal potential of literature to "heal" the wounds of the past', neo-Victorian ghost stories 'point to a prevalence of traumatic memory that cannot (and should not) be over-written by (at best) pseudo-consoling narratives' (Gruss 2014: 135). Hence many neo-Victorian exemplars of the genre deliberately elide reassuring closure, refusing to definitively lay the ghosts or grant them 'transformative potential' (Arias and Pulham 2010: xx), so as to mistakenly suggest transcendence or a final overcoming of historical trauma. Neo-Victorian ghost stories prove most effective when they produce haunted readers, left to question the persistence of inimical gendered and racial violence and injustice into the present day.

Notes

1. My parameters for 'ghost story' are thus broader than those proposed by Michael Cox and Robert Gilbert, who assert that 'each ghost, whether human or animal phantom or reanimated corpse, must unquestionably be dead' (Cox and Gilbert 1992: ix).
2. Although the main text of Harwood's novel does not, strictly, qualify as a 'genuine' ghost story, some of the incorporated tales by Viola Hatherley, the eponymous (fictional) ghost story writer from the 1890s, do.
3. Winterson's *Night Side of the River: Ghost Stories* (2023), though not neo-Victorian, thus includes stories linking the afterlife and otherworldly experiences to digital media, the metaverse and virtual posthumanity, through which '[w]e can become our own haunting' as deathless avatars (Winterson 2023: 304).

4. As Rosario Arias and Patricia Pulham note, neo-Victorianism 'reanimates Victorian genres', including the nineteenth-century ghost story and Gothic texts more generally, so that Victorianism itself 'functions as a form of revenant' haunting present-day textuality (Arias and Pulham 2010: xv; also see Gruss 2014: 123).
5. In *Dracula*, the dying Lucy, 'in a soft, voluptuous voice', immodestly solicits a kiss from her fiancé Lord Arthur Godalming, and, re-encountered as a vampire, her 'voluptuous' and 'wanton smile' seeks to lure him into her deadly embrace (Stoker 1997: 146, 188).
6. Peter Ackroyd deems the ghost story 'oddly consoling', proposing that '[s]ome comfort, some confirmation of an alternative world, may be derived from the presence of ghosts' (Ackroyd 2011: 4).
7. Laski's novella ends ambiguously on 'at last there was nothing but darkness, and in the darkness the ecstasy, and after the ecstasy, death and life' (Laski 1968: 125), which may simply depict the longing for continuity by a dying consciousness.
8. The protagonist's name evokes Florence, Miles's younger sister in *The Turn of the Screw*, and puns on female 'chastity'.
9. The UK's 2022 Femicide Census reports 'that a woman has been killed by a man, on average, once every 3 days, over a 10-year period' (Femicide Census 2022: n.p.).
10. The implication occurs in a dream that the amnesiac Grace recounts to Dr Simon Jordan, charged with helping her recover her memories of the murders to assist in a campaign for her pardon (see Atwood 1996: 280).
11. Jessica Cox, for instance, discusses the influence of Wilkie Collins's *The Woman in White* (1859–60) on Harris's text (see Cox 2019: 58 and *passim*).
12. Byatt already introduced the trope earlier in Lilias's hope for a message from her own mariner husband, Arturo, lost at sea some ten years prior, presumed drowned, as she recites lines from *In Memoriam*: '"Ah, dear, but come thou back to me," said Mrs Papagay to herself, to her dead man' (Byatt 1995: 191). In the novella's closing scene, Arturo quite literally returns from the dead but as a living man.
13. Sarah's self-narration is contextualised with brief interpolated sections from other historical and fictional characters' perspectives. Note that Chase-Riboud's resort to posthumous spectral narration is not entirely new, having already been employed by Joyce Carol Oates in 'Accursed Inhabitants of the House of Bly' (1993), in which the ghosts of Miss Jessel and Peter Quint retell the events of *The Turn of the Screw*. Similarly, parts of Niffenegger's *Her Fearful Symmetry* are narrated by Elspeth, the twin protagonists' dead aunt inhabiting her nieces' flat. Meanwhile, Gibb's *A Ghost's Story* uses a spirit narrator who never was human, acting as the spirit guide 'Katie King' to various nineteenth-century American and British mediums, some biofictional. Katie's self-narration occurs through spirit writing.
14. Baartman's remains were kept on display at the Musée de l'Homme, Paris, until 1985. The novel ends with the 2002 repatriation of Sarah's skeletal remains to South Africa following President Nelson Mandela's request and initial resistance from the French state.

Works Cited

Ackroyd, Peter. *The English Ghost: Spectres through Time*. London: Vintage, 2011.
Anderson, Hephzibah. 'The Secret Meaning of Ghost Stories'. *BBC Culture: Books*, 22 January 2016, n.p. https://www.bbc.com/culture/article/20151204-the-secret-meaning-of-ghost-stories (last accessed 31 December 2024).
Arias, Rosario and Patricia Pulham. 'Introduction', in Rosario Arias and Patricia Pulham (eds), *Haunting and Spectrality in Neo-Victorian Fiction: Possessing the Past*. Basingstoke and New York: Palgrave Macmillan, 2010, pp. xi–xxvi.
Atwood, Margaret. *Alias Grace*. London: QPD: Quality Paperbacks Direct by arrangement with Bloomsbury Publishing, 1996.
Belsey, Catherine. *Tales of the Troubled Dead: Ghost Stories in Cultural History*. Edinburgh: Edinburgh University Press, 2019.
Burkhard, Denise. 'Between Madness, Malice and Marginalization: Reading the Ghost of Jennet Humfrye in Susan Hill's *The Woman in Black* in the Context of Trauma Theory'. *Supernatural Studies*, vol. 3, no. 2, 2016, pp. 9–20.
Byatt, A. S. 'The Conjugal Angel', in *Angels & Insects*. London: Vintage, 1995, pp. 161–290.
Chase-Riboud, Barbara. *Hottentot Venus: A Novel*. New York and London: Doubleday, 2003.
Cook, Michael. *Detective Fiction and the Ghost Story: The Haunted Text*. Basingstoke and New York: Palgrave Macmillan, 2014.
Cox, Jessica. *Neo-Victorianism and Sensation Fiction*. Cham: Palgrave Macmillan, 2019.
Cox, Michael and R. A. Gilbert. 'Introduction', in *The Oxford Book of English Ghost Stories: Chosen by Michael Cox and R. A. Gilbert*. London, New York, Sydney and Toronto: BCA by arrangement with Oxford University Press, 1992, pp. ix–xvii.
Edmundson, Melissa. 'Women Writers and Ghost Stories', in Scott Brewster and Luke Thurston (eds), *The Routledge Handbook to the Ghost Story*. New York and Abingdon: Routledge, 2018, pp. 69–77.
Femicide Census. 'Data Matters – Every Woman Matters', n.d. https://www.femicidecensus.org/data-matters-every-woman-matters/ (last accessed 31 December 2024).
Gruss, Susanne. 'Spectres of the Past: Reading the Phantom of Family Trauma in Neo-Victorian Fiction', in Nadine Boehm-Schnitker and Susanne Gruss (eds), *Neo-Victorian Literature and Culture: Immersions and Revisitations*. New York and Abingdon: Routledge, 2014, pp. 123–36.
Harris, Joanne. *Sleep, Pale Sister*. New York: Harper Perennial, 1994.
Hill, Susan. *The Woman in Black*. London: Vintage, 1998.
Kidd, Jess. 'Lily Wilt', in *The Haunting Season: Ghostly Tales for Long Winter Nights*. London: Sphere, 2022, pp. 109–42.
Laski, Marghanita. *The Victorian Chaise-Longue*. New York: Ballantine, 1968.
Miquel-Baldellou, Marta. '"As Soon As Ever She Died, The Hauntings Began": Revisiting the Victorian Fallen Woman as a Gothic Archetype in Susan

Hill's *The Woman in Black*', *Ex-centric Narratives: Journal of Anglophone Literature, Culture and Media*, vol. 5, 2021, pp. 164–83.

Niffenegger, Audrey. 'Introduction', in *Ghostly: A Collection of Ghost Stories*. London: Vintage, 2018, pp. ix–xii.

Roberts, Robin. *Subversive Spirits: The Female Ghost in British and American Popular Culture*. Jackson, MS: University Press of Mississippi, 2018.

Smith, Andrew. *The Ghost Story, 1840–1920: A Cultural History*. Manchester: Manchester University Press, 2010.

Stoker, Bram. *Dracula*, in Nina Auerbach and David J. Skal (eds), *Dracula: Authoritative Text, Contexts, Reviews and Reactions, Dramatic and Film Variations, Criticism*, Norton critical edition. New York and London: W. W. Norton, 1997, pp. 1–327.

Taylor, Elizabeth. 'Poor Girl', in *Complete Short Stories*, introduced by her daughter Joanna Kingham. London: Virago, 2012, pp. 275–90.

Wallace, Diana. 'The Ghost Story and Feminism', in Scott Brewster and Luke Thurston (eds), *The Routledge Handbook to the Ghost Story*. New York and Abingdon: Routledge, 2018, pp. 427–35.

Ward, Catriona. *Rawblood*. London: Gollancz, 2021.

Winterson, Jeanette. 'Introduction', in *Night Side of the River: Ghost Stories*. London: Jonathan Cape, 2023, pp. 1–18.

Wisker, Gina. *Contemporary Women's Ghost Stories: Spectres, Revenants, Ghostly Returns*. Cham: Palgrave Macmillan, 2022.

Yuhas, Alan. 'It's Time to Revisit the Satanic Panic'. *New York Times*, 31 March 2021, n.p. https://www.nytimes.com/2021/03/31/us/satanic-panic.html (last accessed 31 December 2024).

Part II

Critical Contexts

Chapter 5

Economics
Andrew Smith

Mary Poovey, in *The Financial System in Nineteenth-Century Britain* (2003), identifies visibility as the key issue confronted by Victorian social commentators who sought to reflect on the changing economic practices of the period. The new forms of economic activity initiated by the Stock Exchange, for example, appeared to many to render wealth (and poverty) intangible since money seemed to be made and lost through occulted processes which bore little relationship to the material presence of gold or silver. The prevalence of paper money in the period also raised an issue about visibility, as the promissory note (the bank note) was just that, a promise to pay the bearer a sum in gold or silver rather than being 'real' money. Poovey summarises the situation:

> much of the wealth that fuelled Britain's spectacular growth in the nineteenth century was never available for its possessors to touch or count, for the gold that composed the wealth was characteristically rendered unnecessary by the paper that represented it, while the capital that wealth signified was typically at work elsewhere, awaiting collection at some future date. (Poovey 2003: 2)

Such a system posed particular problems for financial commentators who sought to explain economic processes to 'ordinary Britons' who 'could not visualise how the market worked' (Poovey 2003: 4). This formal problem of visibility reflects its conceptual expression in Marx's account of commodity fetishism. Marx, in 'The Fetishism of Commodities' in *Capital* (1867), argues that manufactured objects are freighted by the life and labour which produced them. How to make this visible requires a particular way of looking at such objects. Marx gives the example of a table and notes that:

> A commodity appears, at first sight, a very trivial thing, and easily understood. Its analysis shows that it is, in reality, a very queer thing, abounding in metaphysical subtleties and theological niceties [...]. Yet, for all that, the

table continues to be that common, everyday thing, wood. But, so soon as it steps forth as a commodity, it is changed into something transcendent. It not only stands with its feet on the ground, but, in relation to all other commodities, it stands on its head, and evolves out of its wooden brain grotesque ideas. (Marx 1977: 435)

The problem that Marx identifies is related to sight. The social critic needs to move beyond that 'first sight' in order to see into the object itself. By shifting the gaze away from the surface another reality can be discerned, one which radically makes visible the subjective endeavours of the worker. As we shall see, this emphasis on forms of seeing plays a significant role in a certain strand of ghost stories which focus on economic matters. This chapter explores a number of such narratives and examines whether their investigation into spectral economies points towards a radical appraisal of the financial system, or works to correct, and ultimately to support, a capitalist economy.

It is important to note that nineteenth-century Britain was subject to periods of acute economic crisis and that this is the key context in which our ghost stories should be understood. The 1840s (the 'hungry forties') and the years 1870–90 (as a consequence of the after-effects of the Franco-Prussian war) were characterised by moments of recession. It was during these periods that money repeatedly became addressed as a topic in the ghost story. Money during a recession seems to become spectral, subject to disappearance and sudden reappearance, and the tales which explore this share something of the cultural ambition noted by Poovey, which is to make the economic system visible. This becomes a notably pressing concern during these economic crises, as the ghost writings of Dickens, Wilkie Collins, Charlotte Riddell and others make clear.[1]

A Christmas Carol (1843) appears to articulate a clear moral message as it explores ways in which Scrooge can find the compassionate grounds on which he can empathise with the plight of others, which will put him back into social circulation and his money into economic circulation. Scrooge is a miser who attempts to hang on to his wealth during a period of economic recession and the narrative requires him to employ his money in such a way that everyone will benefit. For this to happen it requires Scrooge to see money differently, and the spectral intervention of Jacob Marley is the initial facilitator of this.

At one level *A Christmas Carol* seems to indulge a Marxian view of the subject whose subjectivity becomes lost within economic processes which seemingly consume subjects as a requirement for economic exchange. The impersonality of the economic system in effect depersonalises those who play a role within that system. Dickens's tale makes this visible by representing spectres that are held back by the materialism which had ensnared them during their working life. Marley's ghost, for example, appears with a chain that 'was long, and wound about him like a tail; and it was made (for Scrooge observed it closely) of cash-boxes, keys, padlocks, ledgers, and heavy purses wrought in steel' (Dickens 1985: 57). Marley's ghost has imbibed the spirit of their counting-house, as he tells Scrooge: '"My spirit never walked beyond our counting-house – mark me! – in life my spirit never roved beyond the narrow limits of our money-changing hole"' (61). Marley's ghost thus makes visible the physical paraphernalia that support the capitalist economy and which inhabit the 'spirit' both of the workplace and of the subject. Notable in this confrontation is the emphasis which is accorded to sight. Scrooge observes 'closely' Marley's chain, while Marley's '"mark me!"' indicates that Scrooge needs to focus on the consequences of economic activity which destroys the spirit. The objects which Marley has on his chain are made from what '"I forged in life"' (61) and make visible the ideological nature of production which, for Lynn M. Voskuil, requires blindness in order for it to work. For Voskuil, 'this vision of reality – in which products spring spontaneously to life as commodities – is an ideological illusion. But that illusion is the lynchpin of bourgeois production, wilful blindness the key to the system' (Voskuil 2002: 257). How Scrooge can develop a new way of looking at the world becomes central to the story so that he too can move beyond the 'wilful blindness' that has also depersonalised him.

It is noted on Christmas Eve that in the area of Scrooge's counting-house 'The fog came pouring in at every chink and keyhole, and was so dense without, that although the court was of the narrowest, the houses opposite were mere phantoms' (47). After his encounter with the spirits, Scrooge is able to see the world more clearly so that when he awakens on Christmas morning there was 'No fog, no mist; clear, bright, jovial, stirring, cold; cold, piping for the blood to dance to; Golden sunlight; Heavenly sky; sweet fresh air; merry bells' (128). This list of light and noise ('merry bells') is the antidote to the earlier gloom and the potential desolation that might be spread by the ghost of the future which at first sight 'seemed to scatter gloom and mystery' (110). It is Scrooge's transformation which has affected this change. He now sees work and money in a different way and his benign redistribution of money (to Bob Cratchit and others) leads to this transformation. This also, however, begs the question of how radical is this transformation?

At one level the ability to see the economy in a new way is an issue that is central to Marx's notion of commodity fetishism, and Chris

Baldick has noted how Marx's writing uses references to 'ghosts, vampires, ghouls, werewolves, alchemists, and reanimated corpses', because they 'continue to haunt the bourgeois world, for all its sober and sceptical virtues' (Baldick 1987: 121). These are Gothic figures which are used to reflect on Marx's key idea that 'There is a definite social relation between men, that assumes, in their eyes, the fantastic form of a social relation between things' (Marx 1977: 436). Scrooge's new perception appears to break this cycle. He has seen how ghosts are tied to economic factors because the self becomes horrifyingly subsumed within a series of relationships which reflect the impersonal exchanges of the economy itself. Scrooge, however, is a miser who has placed himself in social isolation and put his money beyond use. The coming back to life of Scrooge (before he too becomes a ghost) depends upon his redistributive practice, and this economic circulation supports rather than undermines the capitalist enterprise. Scrooge, in short, needs to become a better capitalist, and putting money back into circulation during a recession is one way in which the tale suggests that poverty can be alleviated. Ghosts do not appear to be quite so radical after all, as the narrative about how to become human emphasises the importance of economic use. These issues about money and spectrality were also explored by Charlotte Riddell in her short story 'The Old House in Vauxhall Walk' (1882), which can be read as critically talking back to *A Christmas Carol*, but which emphasises the role that gender plays in these financial considerations.

'The Old House in Vauxhall Walk' centres on the experiences of the homeless and near destitute Graham Coulton who spends a night in a supposedly haunted house. Coulton comes from a wealthy background but has been left penniless after an argument with his father. A chance meeting with William, a former family servant, who has been living in a house which his wife believes to be haunted, provides Coulton with a bed for the night. Coulton awakens from a dream encounter with the spectral image of the female miser who seemingly haunts the house. He describes seeing

> the outline of a female figure seated beside the fire, engaged in picking something out of her lap and dropping it with a despairing gesture.
> He heard the mellow sound of gold, and knew she was lifting and dropping sovereigns. (Riddell 1977: 91)

This figure is seemingly beyond redemption because, unlike Scrooge, she is unable to use this wealth to alleviate the plight of the poor. Hers is therefore a more tragic plight, which she is aware of: '"Oh! My lost life – for one day, for one hour of it again!"' (92). Coulton notes that the reason for this tragedy is because the money is beyond use and so cannot alleviate the plight of 'the old men and the young children, the worn women with weary hearts, whose misery that gold might have relieved, but whose wretchedness it mocked' (92). It transpires that this is the ghost of the aged Miss Tynan who has been murdered in the house which is owned by her brother (on whom suspicion has fallen). She had once been close to her brother but they had become estranged due to her miserly ways. Her spirit evokes that of Scrooge's pre-redemptive world in which she is seen 'walking slowly across the floor munching a dry crust – she who could have purchased all the luxuries wealth can command' (92–3). Coulton also notes the dilapidated four-poster bed in which she sleeps 'with her claw-like fingers clutching the clothes, as though even in sleep she was guarding her gold!' (94).

The following night, Coulton observes a confrontation between the spirit and a seemingly identical version of her which steps out from behind a mirror and 'at the sight of which the first turned and fled, uttering piercing shrieks as the other followed her' (98). On the following day, Christmas Eve, Coulton returns to the house in the evening and encounters the two robbers who have been responsible for Miss Tynan's murder and who have returned to try and find her money. Coulton is assaulted but the police are called and the robbers apprehended. Later, a loud noise attracts the attention of Mr Tynan who rushes into the room from which it came and finds that the mirror has fallen over and shattered, revealing where his sister had kept her wealth: 'Hundreds, thousands of gold pieces were scattered about, and an aperture behind the glass contained boxes filled with securities and deeds and bonds, the possession of which had cost his sister her life' (100–1). This explains the ghost's horrified response when she see herself reflected in the mirror as her despair acknowledges that it is her very attachment to this money which has depersonalised her and which had made her spectre-like, even in life.

A grateful Tynan shares some of his wealth with Coulton, which enables him to regain the social standing he had lost when he had become estranged from his father. He also becomes reconciled to his father, who is proud of the way in which his son had fought with the robbers. The radical elements of Riddell's tale relate to how it introduces gender into the story of her miser which implicates how men, associated with a public sphere of social status, become rewarded whereas Miss Tynan is excluded from this world. Riddell's tale suggests that the redistribution of money and personal reconciliations can only take place in the male public sphere, which is also a contributory factor in Miss Tynan's despair. The gendered critique of *A Christmas Carol* indicates how these issues about money need to be related to wider social contexts. How far this complicates Dickens's benign reflection on capitalist economics is less clear. Victoria Margree has noted of Riddell's ghost stories that 'It is money that makes ghosts of people in her fictions, and it does so even while they are alive', because the 'miser' loses 'their humanity in their pursuit of wealth, becoming mere spectres of themselves' (Margree 2014: 77). To that degree they appear radical, but ultimately, for Riddell:

> It is not, for her, that the capitalist system itself is immoral; it is rather, that money is haunted by a potential for monstrosity, which it is the responsibility of individual economic actors to resist. In articulating the principles of a feminised financial ethics charged with keeping money's action benign, Riddell defends the capitalist system which she hails as being the best prospect for delivering material and spiritual goods. (Margree 2014: 82–3)

Riddell was a writer not just of ghost stories but also a number of novels about the financial sector including *City and Suburb* (1861), *George Geith of Fen Court* (1865), *The Senior Partner* (1881), *Mitre Court* (1885) and *The Head of the Firm* (1892). Her gendered form of capitalism appears as a critique of a male-controlled system, but even here there is also some ambiguity as her ghost stories often centre on how good, if impoverished, men such as Coulton become rewarded and are able to re-enter the family structure (like Scrooge) whereas her female figures are either irreparably estranged from such family ties, or need a man to enable them to share in their prosperity. Riddell's *The Uninhabited House* (1875) also explores these issues.

The Uninhabited House opens with an account of a court case in which the tenants of River House are attempting to sue its owners for renting them a haunted house. A clerk, Patterson, who works for the law firm defending the case agrees to spend some time in the house in order to discover the origin of these supposedly ghostly activities. It is revealed that the house is haunted by the ghost of a Mr Elmsdale, a disreputable moneylender and a previous owner of the house. In life Elmsdale had tried to financially ruin a Mr Harringford, who had shot Elmsdale. Colonel Morris, the ultimately successfully litigant in the case, recounts his encounter with Elmsdale's ghost. On an evening walk he had heard a noise emanating from within the house, so that:

> I rushed to the nearest window and looked in. The gas was all ablaze, the door of the strong room open, the table strewed with papers, while in an office chair drawn close up to the largest drawer, a man was seated counting over bank-notes. He had a pile of them before him, and I distinctly saw that he wetted his fingers in order to separate them. (Riddell 1971: 107)

This spectral attachment to bank notes represents an attachment to the promissory note, which as discussed earlier, is a spectral, because not quite real, form of money. Those 'wetted' fingers emphasise this attachment and make visible how such an attachment generates forms of depersonalisation. This becomes clear when the discovered and now dying Harringford explains what happened. For him, money becomes a type of curse because although he tells Patterson that '"From the hour I left him lying dead in the library every worldly plan prospered with me"', nevertheless '"I had sold my soul to the devil"' (163), which led to the premature deaths of his wife and children, while he became prematurely aged and lame.

The problem addressed in Riddell's spectral narratives is that of greed. Money which is come by in the wrong way becomes inhabited by a form of malevolence which destroys not only the lives of the principal protagonists, such as Harringford, but also of those closest to them. The destruction of the domestic world, as represented by the deaths of Harringford's family, also indicates that Riddell was conscious of how family life is also implicated in economic considerations. She shares an ambition that we see in Dickens, in which we witness how Scrooge's economically redistributive activities also effect a change that enables him to rejoin his family. Scrooge is able to reflect on his present and the future by seeing a painful image of what he had left behind in his pursuit of money – his fiancée and the family life that marrying her had promised. Elmsdale's ghost also plays a role in this type of family drama.

Patterson is seemingly visited in his dreams by the ghost of Elmsdale who, over a series of nights (which echo Scrooge's visitation by the spirits), leads him to an empty grave while its occupant, the apparently restless spirit of Elmsdale, sits on a nearby tombstone. This figure compels Patterson to look at a figure which seems to have 'no shape or substance' (131) but appears to implicate Harringford. Harringford is subsequently discovered near the house, which haunts him with his crime, and he is revealed to be 'the hiding figure in my dream' (154). When confronted Harringford makes his confession but also, in a desire to make reparation, leaves his money to Elmsdale's daughter who subsequently marries Patterson. Elmsdale's ghost is thus seeking to make sure that Harringford is confronted and money restored to the family. At the end Patterson has some economic security and the promise of a family life. Patterson has also borne witness to how money, when used for immoral purposes, destroys those associated with unscrupulous practices (Elmsdale is a blackmailer) and those who have come by their money by dubious means, such as Harringford. Margree has noted how these financial considerations bear upon the family, because in Riddell's ghost stories,

> men learn to understand the value of money as well as the dangers attached to pecuniary greed; they learn too their responsibilities, both economic and emotional, to others, and in doing so become capable of being husbands and fathers, as well as better brothers and sons. (2014: 71)

This is the lesson learned by both Coulton and Patterson, both of whom have come into money which has been filtered through ghosts of people who have lost their lives due to their miserliness or financial scheming. Using money for positive purposes is ultimately the position which Riddell shares with Dickens. There is thus a moral mission in these texts which seeks to correct the disreputable purposes which colour a particular type of capitalism, without questioning the wider implications of the capitalist system. The labour that Marx sees as spectrally present in the table is not a consideration here, but the issue of paper money is. Elmsdale's ghost is seen counting bank notes and his association with paper money symbolically emphasises the precarious nature of money during periods of economic recession. This is an issue given extended treatment in the anonymously published 'The Ghost in the Bank of England' (1879).

'The Ghost in the Bank of England' is narrated by Andrew Wilson, a recently qualified doctor who has some financial problems. He agrees to take on a wealthy if hypochondriac patient, Julius Mendez, who lives in the West Indies, meaning that Wilson leaves behind his pregnant wife, Annie, in Britain. Mendez believes that he will die before he reaches his fifty-seventh birthday. He also believes that if he survives this birthday by just one day, he will live for another forty years. Wilson, who sees Mendez through his birthday, falls ill with yellow fever and is forced to rest in the West Indies for some months. On his return to Britain he finds that Annie has had the child and is living with her brother Tom. Wilson is still living in some poverty until he discovers a letter sent by Mendez some months before which Annie had not opened, which contains a cheque for £1,000 from the grateful Mendez. Wilson cashes the cheque with a sinister-looking bank teller and uses the money (provided as a bank note) to set up in private practice. All seems to go well until it is discovered that the bank note he used is one that had been listed as destroyed by the bank, which means that Wilson must have used a counterfeit and he finds himself investigated for fraud.

The focus in the tale is not on Wilson but on the story of the mysterious bank teller that he needs to identify in order to clear his name. The solution is provided by Mr Deacon, an octogenarian who lives in the same village as Wilson and who had sixty years earlier worked in the bank. From Wilson's description he is able to identify the teller as Isaac Ayscough, someone whom he had worked with. Some years before, Ayscough had fallen in love with Nancy who was the sister of another cashier, Fred Dawes. Ayscough had tried to make Nancy dependent upon him by secretly implicating Fred in some trouble at the bank, which saw Fred imprisoned. The plan backfires when Fred is found guilty and executed. Nancy is driven insane by her grief and Ayscough is left isolated as he is shunned by the other cashiers and is repeatedly overlooked for promotion. His spectral presence is attributed to the idea that his ghost appears to issue dead bank notes to those who try to cash cheques written by dead people, because they are usually forgeries. It transpires that Mendez's cheque was post-dated and that he in fact died the day after his birthday and so before the date on the cheque.

Wilson is struck by the Gothic nature of this spectral intervention which he also associates with his support of Mendez. He recollects of his time with Mendez that:

> It was almost as if he had decoyed me to his detestable sugar plantation, where all sorts of wild notions and strange practices lingered [...] in order that he might convey to himself the additional years of health and life which had been given to me. (Anon. 1996: 252)

Wilson sees Mendez as a type of emotional vampire, but it is also the work itself which has sucked the life out of him as it was work that was undertaken purely for financial gain. Again, the market depletes those that enter it, and the return of Ayscough is linked to this because it represents the return of a past which is also associated with death and illness due to financial plotting.

Ayscough also represents the inherent spirit of the bank itself which is depersonalised and depersonalising in its transactions. This turns him into a type of automaton whose spectrality makes this depersonalisation visible. Wilson recalls of his encounter with him that 'he was nothing to me save in his capacity of an automaton for paying me a thousand pounds on demand' (264), but he is also menacing as he represents the dead, and yet spectrally alive, nature of the bank itself, so that he appears to possess 'a corpse look which had murdered not only bodies, but brains, hearts and souls' (266). Sara Malton has explored the changing role of banks during the nineteenth century and noted that 'the period's fiction charts an increasing – if tentative – acceptance of the bank's role as both a financial *and* interpersonal mediator; one often responsible for the authentication of individual identity and a guarantor of social legitimacy' (Malton 2012: 138–9, italics in original). The bank contains an archive of personal transactions but it is also part of a wider system of financial regulation which was shaped by legal considerations that established the penalties for economic crimes. Fred Hawes is one victim of this, and Wilson nearly becomes another, meaning that while 'The bank may represent a potential source of social mollification [...] it too must come to terms with its own history, which reveals its embroilment with an inequitable legal system and its resulting responsibility for so many deaths' (Malton 2012: 146). Ayscough is the figure who makes this visible because of his association with crime. For Wilson, 'I know in my inner brain stands the corpse of Isaac Ayscough, in his habit, in his sin, and in his remorse as he lived, honouring with burned bank-notes the cheques of dead men' (286). Ayscough is both punished and punishes. He also makes visible the indelibility of money which has a persistent, if spectral, presence. It is noted that, 'Burn a bank-note as thoroughly as you will, its practices are not destroyed, and may be restored by the process of ghostly cohesion, which, if such a thing be at all, is just as applicable to paper and to engraver's ink as flesh and bone' (286). Money persists and reappears in spectral form as a potentially menacing destructive power.

Wilson is exonerated, largely because the authorities are prepared to entertain more prosaic explanations for the existence of his bank note, such as a possible clerical error or fraud by a cashier. Wilson, however, is haunted by Ayscough's presence:

> I can see him still in fancy as I saw him once in visible fact, receiving what, by the ghostly error of a ghostly clerk, he mistook for a ghostly cheque drawn by a dead man from the hands of one who looked like a ghost, so worn out was I by the shadow of death through which I had so lately gone. (285–6)

The persistence of spectral money also plays an important role in Wilkie Collins's *The Haunted Hotel* (1878), which also reflects upon forms of financial speculation.

The Haunted Hotel was originally published in *Belgravia* magazine in November 1878. When published in book form it was included with another novella, *My Lady's Money*, which also focuses on missing money and financial misappropriation. *The Haunted Hotel* is a complexly plotted detective novel which incorporates a ghost story within it as a way of emphasising that money come by through criminal activity is tainted and haunts the lives of those involved in crime. It therefore shares a view of the dangers of the disreputable acquisition of money which was a feature of Dickens, Riddell and 'The Ghost in the Bank of England'. The plot of the novel centres on the death of Lord Montbarry who is murdered by the alchemist Baron Rivar, who has plotted the murder with his sister, the Countess Narona, who marries Montbarry shortly before he is murdered. Montbarry's death results in an insurance payment of £10,000, which Baron Rivar spends on his alchemical experiments, so that money is used to try and make more money. Montbarry's two brothers and sister, along with Agnes (who had once been engaged to Montbarry), visit the Venetian hotel in which he was murdered. The hotel is also a business venture that requires investors, so that the site of a murder committed for money becomes associated with financial speculation. Those who stay in the room inhabited by Montbarry report having restless nights and the room gains the reputation of being haunted. The economically minded hotel manager 'instantly saw that the credit of the hotel was in danger, unless something was done to retrieve the character of the room' (Collins 1982: 73), a situation that he tries to remedy by changing the room number from 14 to 13A. Montbarry's ghostly presence is initially manifested through unusual smells and in the haunted dreams of those that he was close to and who have come to the hotel. The ghost makes a more direct appearance during an encounter between Agnes and the countess when they suddenly find themselves confronted by the apparition of a severed head:

> The hair on the skull, discoloured like the hair on the face, had been burnt away in places. The bluish lips, parted in a fixed grin, showed the double row of teeth. By slow degrees, the hovering head (perfectly still when she first saw it) began to descend towards Agnes. (97)

This is a spectral vision of a skull which haunts the hotel and Henry, one of Montbarry's brothers, and the hotel manager search the room and find the decomposing head of Montbarry concealed within a chamber in the room where its spectral counterpart appeared. Ever mindful of the financial damage that such a discovery could inflict on the hotel, the manager asks Henry (who has not recognised the head as that of his brother) to keep quiet about it because '"If this frightful discovery becomes known [...] the closing of the hotel and the ruin of the Company will be the inevitable results"' (105). However, some guests see him trying to transport the head to another part of the hotel and it is not possible to keep this secret.

Francis, another of Montbarry's brothers, who has made his money by investing in the theatre, had heard about the supposed ghost before he had visited the hotel and takes an economically pragmatic line on this:

> The circumstances related to him contained invaluable hints for a ghost-drama. The title occurred to him in the railway. 'The Haunted Hotel.'

Post that in red letters six feet high, on a black ground, all over London – and trust the excitable public to crowd into the theatre! (74)

Ghosts clearly sell, and when he is later approached by the countess to see if he might be interested in purchasing a play from her he suggests that she try and write '"a drama with a ghost in it?"' (82). The countess becomes subsequently deranged after the encounter with the spectral head and she forgets that her brother has since died but knows that his experiments had used up all the insurance money. She decides to write the ghost play in order to generate more money for the now deceased brother's experiments. It is an ambition which also points towards the commercial aspects of the theatrical and literary culture of the time, an issue made clear in Francis's reflection on ghost plays. Ironically, she writes a play which recounts the murder plot but dies before she can be brought to justice. The murder of Montbarry and the writing of a play about his ghost indicates how the murder and the financial scheming behind it haunt her and this is reflected in her death when it is seemingly unclear whether she is living or dead. Henry asks the doctor who attends her, '"Is she likely to die?"' because she appears to be breathing heavily, and the doctor replies that '"She is dead [...] Those sounds that you hear are purely mechanical – they may go on for hours"' (119). In the end, she becomes ghost-like as she dies after writing her play about a ghost who not only makes visible the financial ambitions behind the murder but is also a figure within the commercially successful venture of the ghost play.

In *The Haunted Hotel* spectrality is a highly overdetermined concept. The ghost that is produced by a murder makes the murder visible, but poses a potential economic threat to the hotel. The impoverished countess writes a play to make money which includes a ghost within in it in which the ghost becomes real, to the degree that it explains the murder plot. The countess then dies but is still seemingly alive, if ghost-like. These different strands of spectrality are united by their links to the money that has been acquired through illegal or otherwise disreputable ends. The novella is not quite sure how to conclude, as the crime story is solved while the metaphysical presence of the ghost is more difficult to explain. For Francis, that narrative has been based on delusion and the text concludes with 'Is there no explanation of the mystery of The Haunted Hotel? Ask yourself if there is any explanation of the mystery of your own life and death – Farewell' (127). The ghost story is linked to the crime story because both reflect on how the pursuit of money leads to depersonalisation and death. The ghost story thus makes visible what is at work within the crime narrative, as it is also inherently related to forms of financial intrigue.

The texts discussed in this chapter have all addressed concerns about money during periods of economic recession. The ghost provides a way of reflecting on money when money appears to be subject to disappearance and so has become spectral. The radical debate about the spectral presence of labour is not obviously apparent in these narratives as they support benign forms of capitalism, a key feature of the work of Dickens and Riddell. There is, however, a view that the pursuit of wealth depersonalises, and the idea that in a money-based economy human relations become transformed into a relation between things is a feature of Marx's critique. This is the central issue that is addressed by Collins, where it is clear that Montbarry's family have little sympathy with him because they have, like the countess and her brother, effectively depersonalised him. This changes for Henry when he sees the countess's play, because the figure of the spectre enables him to acquire some empathetic understanding of his brother; he tells Francis, '"I felt for him to-night, what I am ashamed to think I never felt for him before"' (123). Repeatedly, the ghost becomes the figure that enables characters to see others in a different light because it changes how they think about money.

This chapter began by outlining Mary Poovey's account of writing on financial matters in the period. She noted that the desire to make the financial system visible was a key ambition of those who reported on economic change. She also argues that such writers often used ideas from fiction to make culturally visible the seemingly mysterious processes of the financial sector. Poovey notes that such writings often employed techniques drawn from 'melodrama, romance, the detective story, and sensationalism' (Poovey 2003: 33) to achieve this. These generic forms became useful when the financial sector appeared to be shaped by supernatural and criminal elements – an impulse which also runs throughout the ghost narratives discussed here. That the starting point for change requires personal reformation is key to understanding how the spectres affect you. Or, as Scrooge acknowledges at the end, '"I will live in the Past, the Present, and the Future. The Spirits of all Three shall strive within me. I will not shut out the lessons that they teach"' (126). Finally, the spirit points towards the possibility of a better life, if not a radical overhaul of the financial system.

Note

1. The coverage and approach in the chapter reflects some of the discussion I make in 'Dickens' Ghosts: Invisible Economies and Christmas' (2005) and *The Ghost Story, 1840–1920: A Cultural History* (2010).

Works Cited

Anon. 'The Ghost in the Bank of England', in *Victorian Ghost Stories*. London: Senate, 1996, pp. 242–87.

Baldick, Chris. *In Frankenstein's Shadow: Myth, Monstrosity and Nineteenth-Century Writing*. Oxford: Clarendon Press, 1987.

Collins, Wilkie. *The Haunted Hotel: A Mystery of Modern Venice*. New York: Dover, 1982.

Dickens, Charles. *A Christmas Carol*, in *The Christmas Books*, vol. 1, edited and introduced by Michael Slater. Harmondsworth: Penguin, 1985, pp. 45–134.

Malton, Sara. 'Recountings: On Dickens's Financial Memory'. *ESC*, vol. 38, no. 2, June 2012, pp. 137–56.

Margree, Victoria. '(Other) Worldly Goods: Gender, Money and Property in the Ghost Stories of Charlotte Riddell'. *Gothic Studies*, vol. 16, no. 2, November 2014, pp. 66–85.

Marx, Karl. *Capital*, in *Karl Marx: Selected Writings*, edited by David McLellan. Oxford: Oxford University Press, 1977, pp. 415–507.

Poovey, Mary. *The Financial System in Nineteenth-Century Britain*. Oxford: Oxford University Press, 2003.

Riddell, Charlotte. 'The Old House in Vauxhall Walk', in *The Collected Ghost Stories of Mrs. J. H. Riddell*, edited and introduced by Richard Dalby. New York: Dover, 1977, pp. 85–101.

———. *The Uninhabited House*, in E. F. Bleiler (ed.), *Five Victorian Ghost Novels*. New York: Dover, 1971, pp. 1–118.

Smith, Andrew. 'Dickens' Ghosts: Invisible Economies and Christmas'. *Victorian Review*, vol. 31, no. 2, 2005, pp. 36–55.

———. *The Ghost Story, 1840–1920: A Cultural History*. Manchester: Manchester University Press, 2010.

Voskuil, Lynn M. 'Feeling Public: Sensation Theater, Commodity Culture, and the Victorian Public Sphere'. *Victorian Studies*, vol. 44, no. 2, Winter 2002, pp. 245–74.

Chapter 6

Ghostly Machines and Mechanical Ghosts: Industrialisation and Victorian Haunting

Bridget M. Marshall

In the chilling opening lines of 'A December Vision' (1850), Charles Dickens depicts a ghostly embodiment of industrialisation spreading across the country, annihilating life in all its forms:

> I saw a mighty Spirit, traversing the world without any rest or pause. It was omnipresent, it was all-powerful, it had no compunction, no pity, no relenting sense that any appeal from any of the race of men could reach. (Dickens 1850: 265)

Dickens's malevolent Spirit of industrialisation destroys not only men, but also the environment:

> It passed through the forest, and the vigorous tree it looked on shrunk away; through the garden, and the leaves perished and the flowers withered; through the air, and the eagles flagged upon the wing and dropped; through the sea, and the monsters of the deep floated, great wrecks, upon the waters. (265)

With these stark descriptions of the devastation of various ecosystems, Dickens presciently depicts the global climate disaster that industrialisation would eventually precipitate. Dickens figures the supposed progress and persistent pressures of industrialisation as an invisible, yet extremely powerful entity, a deadly, inescapable haunting. Like both human workers and machines that worked ceaselessly – sometimes around the clock – in factories, mills and mines, the industrial Spirit 'had its work appointed; it inexorably did what was appointed to it to do; and neither sped nor slackened' (265). This ghost of industrialisation operated just like the factory machines and workers that it represented, relentlessly completing monotonous tasks. As Andrew Smith writes, 'this ideal of the robotic employee suggests alienation from industrialization', demonstrating 'unthinking assimilation to the system' (2010: 45).

Robotic employees – both machines and humans – were mindlessly driving towards their own doom, and this implacable 'Spirit' served as a terrifying image of industrialisation writ large.

This chapter focuses on how nineteenth-century writers deployed ghostly workers and haunted machines in response to the world-altering changes of the Industrial Revolution. Though notably under-studied, the ghostly apparitions of the Victorian era frequently depicted or alluded to industrial developments; haunted tales erupted in response to horrendous labour conditions and fears about the new systems and machines that powered the mills, factories, mines and railways that were transforming the world. The sections that follow will consider, first, the ways that workplaces and workers were equated with ghosts, both in non-fiction and fiction, and then turn to explore how machines – those in industrial spaces and the new transportation technologies – emerged as haunted or ghostly, signalling existing fears and inspiring new ones. Ultimately, the Victorian ghost story introduced new kinds of ghosts that demonstrated the alarming permeability of the border between living beings and machines.

Industrial Workers as the New Ghosts

During the nineteenth century, changes in where and how people lived, worked and moved through the world would transform the ghost story's standard settings and subjects. As rural landscapes gave way to developing industrial towns, entirely new architectural forms and styles sprang up. Huge industrial buildings were frequently described as haunted or ghostly, particularly when they were running at night or when they were eerily empty. For example, during the cotton famine in 1861, when many Manchester mills shut down, Henry Adams described how 'many factories stood still and their gigantic chimneys rose, ghostly and inactive' (qtd in Bradshaw 1987: 61). Early paintings of industrial scenes such as Joseph Wright's *Arkwright's Cotton Mills by Night* (1782) and Philippe Jacques de Loutherbourg's *Coalbrookdale by Night* (1801) also suggest the haunted nature of industrial sites.[1] As the number of people working in industrial settings increased, so too did worries that these places might be haunted by the ghosts of workers who died in accidents. John Ruskin went so far as to suggest that the smoke from factories might be 'made of dead men's souls' (1884: 33). His image suggests that human bodies were consumed like fuel in factories, with human spirits being released through chimneys.

While dead workers were thought to haunt industrial sites, actual living workers were frequently portrayed in both fiction and non-fiction as having ghostly features. Industrial workers were often pale, their skin tone indicating that they were underfed, malnourished, and rarely saw the sunshine due to their indoor work. In his 1845 study *The Condition of the Working Class in England*, Friedrich Engels labelled Manchester's working people 'pale, lank, narrow-chested hollow-eyed ghosts', a description that emphasises the lifeless appearance of their emaciated bodies (1993: 93). Workers' ghostliness was further underscored by the timing of their labour, which often commenced in the early morning hours, even before sunrise, or ran, in some cases, through the entire night. Workers thus were seen haunting their worksites. In Rebecca Harding Davis's short story 'Life in the Iron Mills' (1861), workers at the mill at night are described as 'crowds of half-clad men, looking like revengeful ghosts in the red light' (1861: 433). Her version of the worker-ghost is far more threatening than Engels's seemingly lifeless ghost workers, but in both instances, the ghosts inspire fear not just of the workers, but of the system that has created them.

In his introduction to his collection *Classic Victorian and Edwardian Ghost Stories* (2008), Rex Collings asks, 'when was there a really interesting working-class ghost?' (2008: ii). As he explains, the primary characters in much Victorian fiction were middle- and upper-class people, generally reflecting the authorship of these pieces. While Collings may be correct to say that literature of the time includes very few working-class ghosts, it is quite easy to find them if we look beyond literary sources. Turning to newspaper accounts and local folklore yields an abundance of working-class ghosts haunting mills, factories and especially mines. Coal mining was notoriously dangerous, as horrifying accidents involving machinery, mine collapses and explosions killed workers at alarming rates.[2] Folklorists have documented long-standing ghost beliefs among coal miners, particularly stories of the ghosts of dead miners haunting mines and spectral appearances that warned of impending accidents.[3] Newspaper accounts from across England, particularly in the latter half of the nineteenth century, were filled with stories of ghosts haunting coal mines.[4] Following a series of explosions between 1858 and 1890 that killed over 150 workers, Morfa Colliery in Wales became known as the 'Pit of Ghosts'. As ever larger numbers of workers were endangered and killed by unsafe industrial processes, these ghosts appeared on an industrial scale.

But working-class ghosts were not confined exclusively to haunting real sites of industrial accidents; fiction, too, portrayed the occasional working-class ghost figure. For instance, in Harriet Martineau's

'The Ghost That Appeared to Mrs. Wharton' (1850), a grimy ghostly face appears each night to frighten the title character; later, while visiting a glass factory, the terrified lady discovers that a glass worker there had been using a secret passage and trapdoor that allowed him access to her home. Thus the nightly visits were not from a true ghost, but rather an actual worker. The story suggests, though, that the upper-class lady is in fact haunted by the working class, living in terror of their access to her domestic space.

Working-class ghosts are particularly terrifying in *Life and Adventures of Michael Armstrong, the Factory Boy* (1840), in which Frances Trollope portrays the children who work in mills as ghostly. When Michael first arrives at a particularly brutal mill that operates on a 24-hour system and employs only children, he is horrified, as 'he seemed to feel that the filthy, half-starved wretches before him were so many ghostly representations of what he was himself to be' (1840: 182). These real children are effectively ghosts-of-Christmas-future as the boy considers what the working conditions have done to them and will do to him in short order. Later in the novel, the factory owner, Sir Matthew, is haunted by the ghosts of the children who were maimed or killed in his factory; in his deathbed delirium, he screams, '"take them away from me, I tell you! They are all dirty, beastly factory-children. Their arms and legs are all broken and smashed, and hanging by bits of skin"' (364). This graphic haunting terrifies the aristocratic mill owner, who must face the consequences of the torture that he inflicted upon child workers. In his delirious vision he sees that 'it is not one – it is five hundred' (364) mangled children surrounding him, anticipating the horror of Dickens's narrator ten years later in 'December Vision' who says, 'I saw Thirty Thousand children, hunted, flogged, imprisoned' (1850: 265). In both cases, the horror is further intensified by the fact that it is not merely one single ghost, but many hundreds of ghosts, suggesting the exponential scale of the problem. These ghosts are mass-produced by the factories, mirroring and highlighting the horror of the brutal and large-scale consequences of industrial capitalism.

British industrial ghosts were matched by similar American figures. In Rebecca Harding Davis's *Margret Howth* (1862), a mill owner walking through his mill past the whizzing and clanging machinery 'had a vague sensation of being followed. Some shadow lurked at times behind the engines, or stole after him in the dark entries. Were there ghosts, then, in mills in broad daylight?' (1862: 116). Even while his mill is filled with living people working and machines whirring, he cannot shake the feeling that there is a ghost lurking in the building. Stories of working-class ghosts were also spread through the popular cheap medium of the poetry broadside, as in *The Girl from Yewdall's Mill* (1863), which recounted the local legend of a mill girl who returned in ghostly form to haunt the factory where she once worked. The ghosts of workers were both a local and a global phenomenon, haunting individual sites where bad things happened, but doing so in similar ways as the spread of industrialisation made for similar conditions and scenarios around the world. The idea of a worker turning into a ghost is perhaps best exemplified in James Kirke Paulding's story 'The Man Machine; or, the Pupil of Circumstance' (1826) in which the narrator explains how he began work in a mill at the age of nine and 'by the time I had been there three years, I became sensible that my soul had transmigrated into a spinning jenny, and that I had actually become a piece of machinery' (1826: 24). The remainder of the story is narrated by the man-machine, who is unable to break free of the routines and discipline enforced by his master, the mill overseer. It is a chilling depiction of the utter loss of humanity; even the fact that the machine has a human name (the spinning jenny) suggests the ways that such a machine is haunted.

The notion that humans might be turned into ghosts through industrial labour appears throughout fiction depicting industrial workers. In Elizabeth Gaskell's *Mary Barton* (1848), mill worker John Barton appears as 'a form [that] had glided into sight; a wan, feeble figure' with 'bowed head, sinking and shrunk body', all descriptors that indicate his ghostliness and emphasise the damage that mill labour has inflicted on his body (2000: 428). He is compared unfavourably to a ghost: 'No haunting ghost could have had less of the energy of life in its involuntary motions than he, who, nevertheless, went on with the same measured clockwork tread' (428). Like the implacable ghost of Dickens's 'December Vision', Barton likewise cannot do anything beyond mindless repetition of assigned work. In Dickens, Gaskell and numerous other nineteenth-century depictions of labour, human beings are described as working like 'clockwork'; such descriptions transformed human workers into ghostly, inhuman mechanical devices.

Industrialisation's Machines as Ghosts

Machines have a long history of striking fear into the hearts of humans. In '"This Dreadful Machine": The Spectacle of Death and the Aesthetics of Crowd Control' (2017), Emma Galbally and Conrad Brunstrom explain the importance of one of the most devilish of machines: the guillotine that was a major symbol of the French Revolution. Measured by its productivity, the guillotine was surely a success; it likely killed

17,000 people during the Reign of Terror (June 1793–July 1795). But it also demonstrated how the quest for efficiency and speed (prized goals of the Industrial Revolution) could be applied in supremely ghoulish ways. Several classic ghost stories used the fear of the guillotine as a starting point, such as Washington Irving's 'The Adventure of a German Student' (1824), Alexandre Dumas's 'La femme au collier du velours' ('The Woman with the Velvet Necklace') (1850) and an 1896 story by an unknown British author titled 'From the Guillotine'. Each story centres around a victim of the guillotine who somehow seems to have survived their beheading; only later, when someone looks more closely at a scar or removes a ribbon from their neck, are they revealed to be ghosts, victims of a brutally efficient execution machine. Such stories suggest the deep horror of such mechanical murder devices, and the eerie sense that such means of death were uncanny.

Beyond the guillotine, with its intentionally deadly purpose, other machines of a more mundane variety would also appear as pivotal objects in ghostly tales. In Richard Marsh's stories 'The Adventure of the Phonograph' (1898) and 'The Photographs' (1900), new machines – a phonograph that plays screams from a murder victim and a camera that captures images of a dead woman – essentially create the (possible) ghosts, suggesting the power of these emerging technologies and the eerie possibilities of uncanny interactions between machines and the supernatural. As Nick Freeman writes in his discussion of Marsh's tales, 'Far from undermining the ghost story, technological innovation was to prove a valuable invigorating influence' (2012: 106). Such technologies offered entirely new kinds of ghosts such as those revealed in the practice of spirit photography – in which images of supposed 'ghosts' were produced on daguerreotypes or photographs of live sitters – which was popularised by the work of William Mumler in the United States and then by Frederick Hudson in England.[5] Machines offered new sites for hauntings as well as new potential resolutions for ghost stories. In Phoebe Pember's 'The Ghost of the Nineteenth Century' (1880), a young woman is awakened every night by moaning sounds that she believes emanate from the ghost of a young man who died tragically, only to discover that in fact she is being haunted by 'a modern ghost,' specifically, the local steamboat: 'The sobs that struggled through the air were the steam-throbs of her engine, mellowed by the distance; the agonized and oppressed heartbeats, the beat of her paddle-wheels' (1880: 259). While Pember's 'ghost' turns out to be a machine, the fact that the steamboat is given personal pronouns ('her') and that its sounds are described as heartbeats suggest that there is something ghostly about it; such personification of machines promoted a sense that they were alive.

Nowhere is anxiety about the lifelike aspects of emerging machine technology more forcefully displayed than in the work of Samuel Butler, who raised the possibility that machines might evolve in his essay 'Darwin among the Machines' (1863), and further expounded upon the theory in his dystopian novel *Erewhon; or, Over the Range* (1872). In 'Darwin among the Machines',[6] Butler delineated his concern that with the latest advancements in machinery (such as the railroad), 'we find ourselves almost awestruck at the vast development of the mechanical world, at the gigantic strides with which it has advanced in comparison with the slow progress of the animal and vegetable kingdom' (1913: 43). He anticipates that watches may replace clocks, which would become 'extinct' by applying the theory of evolution to the inanimate world of machines. As even more developed machines appear, Butler suggests that not only will old machines be replaced by new ones, but that humans may well be replaced by machines; as he explains, 'we are ourselves creating our own successors' and 'in the course of ages we shall find ourselves the inferior race' (44). As the letter proceeds, Butler's alarm is apparent as he warns that, 'day by day, however, the machines are gaining ground upon us; day by day we are becoming more subservient to them; more men are daily bound down as slaves to tend them', and he comes to a shocking conclusion: 'Our opinion is that war to the death should be instantly proclaimed against them. Every machine of every sort should be destroyed' (46). Butler put this proposed destruction into action in his novel *Erewhon; or, Over the Range*, in which he depicts a fictional culture (Erewhon) where the inhabitants have destroyed all their machines and have reverted to an earlier, agrarian lifestyle. Three entire chapters are devoted to the 'Book of the Machines', more fully developing the implications of machines taking control, painting a stark picture of Victorians' worst nightmares about ghostly machines.

Machines for Transportation

While Butler certainly took fear of machines to an extreme, ghost stories were an important means through which Victorians grappled with fears of new machines, especially in the realm of transportation, where new methods and speeds transformed how humans and goods moved through the world. As Ralph Harrington explains in 'Transport and Trauma: Uncanny Modernities' (2017), 'Vehicles are as capable of being haunted as houses, cemeteries, or abandoned hospitals' (306); new transportation machines offered new spaces where hauntings could happen. But the advances in transportation were developing at a speed that alarmed

Victorians. Aviva Briefel writes of this in 'Ghost Speed: The Strange Matter of Phantom Vehicles' (2022), where she suggests that 'Victorian narratives express transportation nostalgia through the representation of ghostly conveyances: spectral coaches, ships, trains, and rickshaws', and argues that such ghost stories expose a 'nostalgia for more human(e) modes of transportation' (694–5). Each new technology left behind a ghost of an abandoned technology, and despite supposed advances in speed or access, the newer technologies felt increasingly inhospitable to the humans they were theoretically intended to serve, often creating new and dangerous threats to human safety and well-being.

Butler's plan to destroy all machines may seem extreme, but it reveals the profound impact of ever-evolving and expanding transportation modes, as old machines became 'extinct' along with the people who worked on and with those machines. Anxiety about such extinction is the crux of a ghost story by Wilkie Collins titled 'The Last Stage Coachman' (1843), in which a narrator laments the unpleasantness of train travel and contrasts it with the pleasures of travel in earlier times, by stagecoach. The narrator is then met by an apparent ghost of a coachman, who describes how his life and livelihood were destroyed by the railway. The narrator is shocked as 'a fully equipped Stage Coach appeared in the clouds, with a railway director strapped fast to each wheel, and a stoker between the teeth of each of the four horses' (1843: 211). This ghostly animated stagecoach, helmed by the aggrieved coachman, appears to threaten the railway workers, but the scene dissolves in the face of reality, where the railways actually carry real people on their travels, while the ghostly coachman merely has an imagined vision of revenge. Reading this scene, Briefel writes that the horrid vision depicts how 'a desire for the past quickly transforms into a full-fledged revenge fantasy, garnished with the remains of those associated with technological progress' (2022: 697). Technological progress was thus both admired and feared, and ghost stories demonstrate the striking ways that Victorians coped with rapid change.

As railways spread across the country, so too did ghost stories about those trains. As William Hughes explains in 'Gothic and the Coming of the Railways' (2020), 'supernatural fictions from the mid-nineteenth century through to the later twentieth are undoubtedly freighted with narratives of cursed engines, disappearing rolling stock and phantom expresses' (460). As he details, the mechanical trains themselves sometimes manifest as ghosts, but the ghosts of railway workers and passengers are also quite apt to appear on trains, in stations, and along the many miles of track that connected the countryside. A recent anthology – *The Platform Edge: Uncanny Tales of the Railways* (2019) – features numerous examples of trains as sites for ghost stories; as Mike Ashley notes in his introduction to the collection, some very high-profile accidents and deaths involving trains (especially the death of William Huskisson on the opening of the Liverpool and Manchester Railway in 1830) 'emphasized the inherent danger of steam trains' (7). Railway accidents that killed both rail workers and passengers were shocking events that left behind mangled machines and human bodies, and newspaper accounts spread vivid descriptions of scenes of carnage. Harrington notes that given increasing knowledge of both the opportunities and dangers of train travel, 'Ghosts readily took to the rails and the ghost story thrived in these new environments' (2017: 305). While trains offered luxury and speed to passengers seeking to travel for business or pleasure, they also created new dangers that could not be overlooked; ghost stories provided vivid reminders of the darker side of the new transport's efficiency.

Charles Dickens was a significant supplier of haunted trains; as Harland S. Nelson has explained, throughout his work, Dickens portrays the railway as 'a symbol of the Industrial Revolution' (1974: 51), and frequently that symbol was one not of progress but of fear. In the story collection *Mugby Junction* (1866), Dickens (and the other contributors to the collection he edited) depicts an imagined rail junction crowded with unsettling stories and ghostly apparitions, fully realising the possibilities of the haunted railway. As Jen Cadwallader explains in 'Death by Train: Spectral Technology and Dickens's *Mugby Junction*' (2015), Dickens and his collaborators 'participated in the "spectralization" of the locomotive: a rewriting of technology which marks it as a haunting, alien, uncontrollable force rather than a tool for human betterment' (58). Dickens's own *Mugby* contribution – 'No. I Branch Line: The Signal-Man' – is perhaps the best-known railway ghost story. Considerable scholarship on the tale considers the story's supernatural depiction of what was unfortunately an all-too-mundane occurrence: deadly train accidents. As Jill Matus argues in 'Trauma, Memory, and Railway Disaster: The Dickensian Connection' (2001), the story is deeply connected with Dickens's own experience of being a passenger on a train that had an accident that caused several deaths; she argues that the story is 'a creative way of articulating [Dickens's] personal experience of railway shock' (428). In 'Victorian Railway Accident and the Melodramatic Imagination' (2012), Matthew Wilson Smith also argues that Dickens's terrifying experience in this accident (at Staplehurst in 1865) was a catalyst for the story, but emphasises that there was a broader context to understand: 'the railroad disordered the Victorian world in ways that strain our imagination today and very nearly baffled theirs at the time' (499). Thus it was not merely Dickens's individual experience that gives the story power, but the widespread understanding among his readers that trains were in fact quite dangerous. William Hughes also notes Dickens's likely familiarity with a variety of other well-publicised train accidents that would have informed his writing and inflamed the anxieties of his readers (2020: 457).

In 'No. I Branch Line: The Signal-Man', a railway worker is haunted by a ghost that appears just before deadly accidents, and ultimately he himself is the victim of a third fatal accident. The narrator is haunted by the story and the ghostly apparitions that attempt to warn of, yet cannot prevent, the apparently inevitable deaths of workers and passengers alike. When a signalman fails at his job, people can die, and both the threat of this and the actual occurrence of accidents and deaths haunted workers – in both fiction and real life. The signalman, with his literal life-and-death responsibility for maintaining safety on the railways, was a figure that also inspired an 1880 poem titled 'The Signalman's Dream', by an unknown poet. In it, the titular signalman returns to work after a deadly train accident and finds that he is haunted by the ghosts of the victims of the disaster: 'I see each blood-stained human shred – / The crushed, the slain – these I behold. / They follow me living. When I am dead / I dread the meeting beyond the mould.'[7] Notably, the poem was a response to the Tay Bridge disaster, in which a bridge collapsed under a train, killing everyone on board. The accident had nothing to do with the failure of railway signals or signalmen; however, it is nonetheless the signalman who is haunted by the horror of the events.

The plight of the railway worker was also addressed in the anonymously authored 'A Desperate Run', published in an 1878 Christmas annual called *The Mistletoe Bough* edited by Mary Elizabeth Braddon. In this fast-paced three-page story, an unnamed narrator is awakened by the ghost of a railway worker who delivers a message that he must prevent a train collision. The ghost guides him in what to do and the disaster is successfully averted; the narrator then discovers that the worker died of a heart attack on the job, but his ghost's expert guidance saved the people on the train from a surely deadly collision. The railway worker in this case is portrayed as an exceptionally dedicated employee, managing to complete his appointed duties even after his own death. Of course, this only serves to highlight just how dangerous railways might be, leaving the lives of train riders in the hands of men who might fail, mentally or bodily, to complete tasks that had life or death consequences.

In addition to ghostly rail workers, phantom trains were a popular ghost figure in folklore, newspaper accounts and fiction. Phantom train sightings were often inspired by real-life train disasters, suggesting that they were a trauma response as much as a warning of the real dangers of the new transport technology. Real accidents were an unfortunately regular occurrence and were major news stories. One especially famous incident was the aforementioned Tay Bridge disaster in Scotland, which occurred on 28 December 1879, when the Tay Bridge collapsed beneath a train during a storm. No one survived, and it is believed that seventy-five people died; local legend holds that a 'ghost train' appeared each year on the anniversary of the disaster.[8] As Sage Leslie-McCarthy argues, such anniversary appearances match with a common belief at the time that 'hauntings are a result of strong emotional events having taken place resulting in death, and that the residual emotions cause the event to be repeated, usually on the anniversary of, in this case, the traffic accident' (2008: 280). Thus, while the specific technology was new, the basic sense of how haunting worked was carried over from earlier times.

Phantom trains also appeared in popular non-fiction and fiction writing of the nineteenth century. George Sala, in a *Household Words* essay titled 'Poetry on the Railway' (1855), recalls a recent railway accident in which many passengers and two railway workers were killed, and goes on to wonder, 'suppose the line were haunted!' (1855: 418). The train he proceeds to conjure is particularly gruesome: 'the carriages themselves are mere skeletons – they are all shattered, dislocated, ruined', and the passengers are a 'horrible sight to see!' (418). He finally offers that 'All these sights of horror flit continually past, up and down, backwards and forwards, haunting the line where the accident was' (418). Thus, railway ghosts could appear anywhere and everywhere across the network of rails that covered the countryside. Recollections of railway accidents that they personally witnessed or simply read about surely imbued rail travellers with anxiety for their safety. Such is the case with the phantom train that haunts Lucy G. Moberly's story 'A Strange Night', which appeared in the *South Wales Echo* in 1897. In it, a couple spends the night in an abandoned railway town where they discover a horrifying train accident unfolding as a signalman fails in his job. The narrator describes what he witnesses: 'The sound of the collision was one that I shall never forget, and following upon it came the yet more awful sounds of shrieks, cries, groans–cries of deadly terror, shrieks of agony' (2019: 64). But when the couple rush to provide assistance, there is nothing – no train, no crash, no passengers. They learn the next day that there was a deadly train accident at the site two years prior, and that every night since the event, the people in the town heard the crash over again. They were so disturbed by the event and its nightly re-enactment that they abandoned the town. Despite the fact that 'they were phantom trains, phantom passengers' (67), these terrifying visions forced an entire town to move to a new location.

Other forms of transportation, too, were apt to inspire ghost stories, as demonstrated by Dickens's story 'The Bagman's Uncle' within the *Pickwick Papers* (1836–7), in which the title character discovers the remains of dilapidated and abandoned mail coaches that spring to life; he is treated to an elaborate adventure with the 'ghosts of mail-coaches and horses, guards, coachmen, and passengers' (1986: 766). A similar ghostly coach with passengers appeared in Amelia Edwards's 'The Phantom Coach' (1864). The story's narrator, while waiting to catch a coach in a snowstorm, learns that nine years prior, a mail coach accident caused the death of six people. As he rides the mail coach with silent passengers, he begins to notice that the coach is in a shocking state of decay, discovers that his fellow passengers are ghosts, and realises he is now a passenger in the doomed coach. The narrator survives his ordeal, but it is never clear whether he had a ghostly encounter or an alcohol- or cold-induced hallucination. In either case, he is left shaken, keeping the story to himself for twenty years. Occasional news stories also suggested that such coach-ghosts were not only the subject of fiction, but were part of local legends as well.[9]

In his analysis of Victorian ghosts, Jarlath Killeen claims that 'The ghost, after all, represents a breach in historical progression: in a stark reproach to the Victorian investment in notions of linearity and progress, the ghost is a manifestation of the "past-in-the-present"' (2009: 129). But the thread of stories explored here suggests a contemporary and even forward-looking anxiety in addition to this fear of the past returning. As Victorians viewed the newer, faster pace of daily business, and the utter transformation of landscapes and everyday life, they manifested ghosts in their fiction and folklore to document, confront and possibly exorcise these new fears.

Notes

1. For more on this, see Marshall (2023).
2. See Benson (1989), who claims that 'between 1868 and 1919 a miner was killed every six hours' (43).
3. See numerous examples described in Fraser (1983).
4. The British Library newspapers database contains at least twenty stories describing so-called 'coal pit' ghosts between 1862 and 1895. For one example, see 'Ghost in a Coal Pit', *Newcastle Journal*, 19 November 1862.
5. For more on spirit photography, see Paola Cortés-Rocca's 'Ghost in the Machine: Photographs of Specters in the Nineteenth Century' (2005)

and Jen Cadwallader's 'Spirit Photography and the Victorian Culture of Mourning' (2008).
6. The essay first appeared in Christchurch in the *Press* newspaper, 13 June 1863, p. 1 and was later republished in a variety of collections.
7. I learned of this poem from Erin Farley's 'The Place of Poetry in Victorian Dundee' (2018: 48). See Farley's work for discussion of the wide array of poetry written about the Tay Bridge disaster.
8. See Una McGovern's 'Phantom Trains' (2007). The supposed 'ghost train' on the Tay Bridge appears in numerous modern articles about haunted places.
9. For example, see 'The Phantom Coach,' *The Welshman*, 25 December 1835.

Works Cited

Anon. 'A Desperate Run', in Mike Ashley (ed.), *The Platform Edge: Uncanny Tales of the Railways*. London: British Library, 2019, pp. 47–50.
Anon. 'From the Guillotine' in *The Haunted Manor House and Other Tales*. London: Skeffington & Sons, 1896, pp. 41–50.
Anon. 'Ghost in a Coal Pit'. *Newcastle Journal*, 19 November 1862. British Library Newspapers.
Anon. 'The Phantom Coach'. *The Welshman*, 25 December 1835.
Anon. 'The Signalman's Dream'. *People's Journal*, 10 January 1880, p. 5.
Ashley, Mike. 'Introduction', in Mike Ashley (ed.), *The Platform Edge: Uncanny Tales of the Railways*. London: British Library, 2019, pp. 7–8.
Benson, John. *British Coalminers in the Nineteenth Century: A Social History*. London: Longman, 1989.
Bradshaw, L. D. *Visitors to Manchester: A Selection of British and Foreign Visitors' Descriptions of Manchester from c.538 to 1865*. Manchester: N. Richardson, 1987.
Briefel, Aviva. 'Ghost Speed: The Strange Matter of Phantom Vehicles'. *Victorian Literature and Culture*, vol. 50, no. 4, 2022, pp. 693–720.
Butler, Samuel. 'Darwin Among the Machines', in *The Note Books of Samuel Butler*, edited by Henry Festing Jones. London: A. C. Fifield, 1913, pp. 42–7.
Cadwallader, Jen. 'Death by Train: Spectral Technology and Dickens's *Mugby Junction*', in Adrienne E. Gavin and Andrew F. Humphries (eds), *Transport in British Fiction: Technologies of Movement, 1840–1940*. London: Palgrave Macmillan, 2015, pp. 57–68.
———. 'Spirit Photography and the Victorian Culture of Mourning'. *Modern Language Studies*, vol. 37, no. 2, 2008, pp. 8–31.
Collings, Rex. 'Introduction', in Rex Collings (ed.), *Classic Victorian and Edwardian Ghost Stories*. London: Wordsworth Editions, 2008, pp. i–iii.
Collins, Wilkie. 'The Last Stage Coachman'. *The Illuminated Magazine*, August 1843, pp. 209–11.
Cortés-Rocca, Paola. 'Ghost in the Machine: Photographs of Specters in the Nineteenth Century'. *Mosaic: An Interdisciplinary Critical Journal*, vol. 38, no. 1, 2005, pp. 151–68.
Davis, Rebecca Harding. 'Life in the Iron Mills'. *The Atlantic Monthly*, April 1861, pp. 430–51.

———. *Margret Howth: A Story of to-Day*. Boston, MA: Ticknor and Fields, 1862.
Dickens, Charles. 'Chapter XLIX Containing the Story of the Bagman's Uncle', in *The Pickwick Papers*, edited by James Kinsley. Oxford: Clarendon Press, 1986, pp. 747–66.
———. 'A December Vision'. *Household Words*, vol. 2, no. 38, 1850, pp. 65–7.
———. 'No. I Branch Line: The Signal-Man', in *Mugby Junction*. London: Chapman and Hall, 1898, pp. 89–110.
Dumas, Alexandre. *The Woman with the Velvet Necklace*. Boston, MA: Little, Brown, 1897.
Edwards, Amelia. 'The Phantom Coach', in Rex Collings (ed.), *Classic Victorian and Edwardian Ghost Stories*. London: Wordsworth Editions, 2008, pp. 150–61.
Engels, Friedrich. *The Condition of the Working Class in England*. Oxford: Oxford University Press, 1993.
Farley, Erin. 'The Place of Poetry in Victorian Dundee'. Unpublished PhD thesis, University of Strathclyde Glasgow, 2018.
Fraser, Marianne. 'Warm Winters and White Rabbits: Folklore of the Welsh and English Coal Miners'. *Utah Historical Quarterly*, vol. 51, no. 3, 1983, pp. 246–58.
Freeman, Nick. 'The Victorian Ghost Story', in Andrew Smith and William Hughes (eds), *The Victorian Gothic: An Edinburgh Companion*. Edinburgh: Edinburgh University Press, 2012, pp. 93–107.
Galbally, Emma and Conrad Brunstrom.'"This Dreadful Machine": The Spectacle of Death and the Aesthetics of Crowd Control', in Carol Margaret Davison (ed.), *The Gothic and Death*. Manchester: Manchester University Press, 2017, pp. 63–75.
Gaskell, Elizabeth. *Mary Barton*. Peterborough, ON: Broadview Press, 2000.
Harrington, Ralph. 'Transport and Trauma: Uncanny Modernities', in Scott Brewster and Luke Thurston (eds), *The Routledge Handbook to the Ghost Story*. New York: Routledge, 2017, pp. 301–11.
Hughes, William. 'Gothic and the Coming of the Railways', in Dale Townshend and Angela Wright (eds), *The Cambridge History of the Gothic*. Cambridge: Cambridge University Press, 2020, pp. 445–62.
Irving, Washington. 'The Adventure of the German Student', in *The Works of Washington Irving*, new edition, revised, vol. VII: *Tales of a Traveller*. New York: G. P. Putnam & Company, 1859, pp. 55–62.
Killeen, Jarlath. *Gothic Literature 1825–1914*. Cardiff: University of Wales Press, 2009.
Leslie-McCarthy, Sage. 'Spectral Traffic', in Sue Thomas (ed.), *Victorian Traffic: Identity, Exchange, Performance*. Newcastle upon Tyne: Cambridge Scholars Publishing, 2008, pp. 273–83.
McGovern, Una. 'Phantom Trains', in *Chambers Dictionary of the Unexplained*. Chambers Harrap, 2007. Credo reference: https://search.credoreference.com/articles/Qm9va0FydGljbGU6MzgxMzg2?aid=102631.
Marsh, Richard. 'The Adventure of the Phonograph', in *Curios: Some Strange Adventures of Two Bachelors*. Kansas City: Valancourt Books, 2007, pp. 26–48.
———. 'The Photographs', in *The Seen and the Unseen*. London: Methuen, 1900, pp. 18–60.

Marshall, Bridget M. 'The Haunted Industrialized Nightscape: Factories, Mills, and Ironworks at Night', in Pamela Phillips (ed.), *Enlightened Nightscapes*. New York: Routledge, 2023, pp. 234–51.

Matus, Jill L. 'Trauma, Memory, and Railway Disaster: The Dickensian Connection'. *Victorian Studies*, vol. 43, no. 3, 2001, pp. 413–36.

Moberly, Lucy Gertrude. 'A Strange Night', in Mike Ashley (ed.), *The Platform Edge: Uncanny Tales of the Railways*. London: British Library, 2019, pp. 62–7.

Nelson, Harland S. 'Staggs's Gardens: The Railway through Dickens' World'. *Dickens Studies Annual*, vol. 3, 1974, pp. 41–234.

Paulding, James Kirke. 'The Man Machine; or, the Pupil of Circumstance', in *The Merry Tales of the Three Wise Men of Gotham*. New York: G. & C. Carvill, 1826, pp. 21–42.

Pember, Phoebe Yates. 'The Ghost of the Nineteenth Century'. *Harper's Magazine*, August 1880, pp. 251–60.

Ruskin, John. *The Storm Cloud of the Nineteenth Century: Two Lectures Delivered at the London Institution*. New York: John Wiley, 1884.

[Sala, George.] 'Poetry on the Railway'. *Household Words*, 2 June 1855, pp. 414–17.

Smith, Andrew. *The Ghost Story 1840–1920: A Cultural History*. Manchester: Manchester University Press, 2010.

Smith, Jimmy. *The Girl from Yewdall's Mill*. Philadelphia: T. M. Scroggy, 1863.

Smith, Matthew Wilson. 'Victorian Railway Accident and the Melodramatic Imagination'. *Modern Drama*, vol. 55, no. 4, 2012, pp. 497–522.

Trollope, Frances. *Life and Adventures of Michael Armstrong, the Factory Boy*. London: Henry Colburn, 1840.

Chapter 7

The Ghost Story as Written by Victorian Women Writers
Lucie Armitt

In his Preface to the essay collection *Victorian Hauntings* (2002), Julian Wolfreys reflects on the concept of haunting and spectrality in relation to print culture and the role reading plays in the reanimation of a text: 'We speak of the text as "saying something"', he observes, or 'we substitute the author's proper name in rhetorical formulae such as "Dickens comments" ... as though the text were merely a conduit, a spirit medium if you like, by which the author communicates' (Wolfreys 2002: xii). Wolfreys's playful rhetorical agility becomes serious when applied to Victorian women ghost story writers, whose voices have largely become subsumed by male writers of the period. How to title this essay was surprisingly difficult: 'The Victorian Woman's Ghost Story' would have been a misnomer, for it would have implied a form of possession: the ghost story as *owned* by Victorian women. While some women certainly lived in houses furnished with sumptuous libraries, to what extent did they legally own their contents? Instantly we confront one of the key sociohistorical inequalities of the Victorian period: to what extent were women of that time permitted, by law, to own anything?

Queen Victoria had reigned for thirty-five years before the passing of the 1882 Married Women's Property Act. As Emma Liggins observes, the concept of property and inheritance is intrinsic to many ghost stories and one can no more separate out that historical connection than the fact that the stories published in the later decades of the nineteenth century coincided with 'the formation of the Society for Psychical Research in Britain, which set out to investigate and classify paranormal phenomena and, amongst other things, invited readers of the periodicals to report instances of haunting and hallucinations' (Liggins 2009: iii). This is a time, then, in which readers, not just writers, start to determine what ghosts *meant*. In terms of the connection between social change and the gendered appeal of ghosts, Vanessa D. Dickerson goes further, arguing that their appeal derived from Victorian women's sense of having been cast adrift in an ambitiously intellectual century dominated by the public clamour of masculine voices:

> Factories, railroads, Corn Laws, poorhouses, and doctrines of evolution all evinced the materialism, skepticism, and empiricism that rapidly altered the Victorian world [...] One of the things expected of [the] Victorian woman, a mother, wife, and daughter, was that she control herself and suppress desire and passion [...] It was mete that woman give up, rein in, be silent, be still. (Dickerson 1996: 4)

In effect, Dickerson argues, the Victorian woman *became* a ghost in social terms, not simply through her shadowy public existence, but in coming to inhabit a state of 'in-between-ness', for alongside the necessary self-diminishment, women were called upon to exercise a form of soft, sculpting power as role models of spirituality and morality for their families. Hence, 'At a time when nineteenth-century men pushed on to greater and greater heights in science, technology, and administration, women were expected to ground and center this progress, to be fulcrums for the disequilibrium of change' (Dickerson 1996: 4, 10).

As the complex nature of these competing agendas makes clear, women may have lacked political prominence (despite Queen Victoria, herself, being an enormously powerful global figure), yet they were certainly believed to have power in the private realm. Indeed, Alex Owen's book on spiritualism suggests that these womanly powers extended even beyond the grave, as she examines women's central involvement in spiritualism, a form of faith in which it was believed that one could, via enlisting the services of a spirit medium (the majority of whom were female), contact the souls of the dead. As Owen notes, 'The underlying assumption of the sanctity of home and hearth, of chaste and disciplined family feeling, and of moral scrupulousness between its members contributed to a notion of the domestic circle as the epitome of spiritualist excellence' (Owen 1989: 75). Dickerson goes further, in superimposing the typical Victorian woman's existence onto a ghost's, both being 'figure[s] of indeterminacy, of imperiled identity, of substance and insubstantiality' (Dickerson 1996: 5).

Introducing the history of spiritualism, which arrives in Victorian Britain from the United States of America in 1852, Owen recounts the story of two American girls, Katherine and Margaret Fox, who

> were twelve and thirteen years old, and lived in the family home in rural upstate New York. Their house was reputedly haunted and the eight-year-old daughter of the previous occupant had already experienced frightening occurrences there. But the inexplicable knockings and rappings which broke

out shortly after the Fox family moved in did little to daunt the sisters. On the contrary, they discovered that they could 'talk' to the unseen source of the disturbances by establishing a simple code involving a specific number of raps in response to their verbal questions. It was thereby established that the cause of all the trouble was the spirit of a pedlar who had supposedly been murdered in the house and buried in the cellar. (Owen 1989: 18)

We note that this account takes shape as a family narrative, fully in keeping with the feminine sphere of the domestic interior, enabling the story to be wholly contained by female 'authorship', despite it being a tale of property and disputed possession that would usually belong in the masculine sphere. Furthermore, we note the absoluteness of Katherine and Margaret's storytelling powers. They are entirely self-authenticating: if Katherine and Margaret say they have discovered 'the spirit of a pedlar [...] buried in the cellar', no further recourse to authenticating voices is required. Such a recognition of female authority over the spirit world and its shaping in narrative format makes it all the stranger that, until recently, little sustained challenge has been offered to the tendency to associate the Victorian ghost story with male writers.

That paradoxical invisibility takes us on to other forms of presence, for in order to narrate a compelling ghost story one needs both to implicate oneself in the scenario (there is often a performative nature to the telling even of a written ghost story) and, at the same time, remove oneself from it sufficiently (through hearsay or a lapse of time or voice) to ensure that it becomes the tale of 'another'. What results, perhaps, is a form of cultural ventriloquism, whereby the story that is being told belongs to one character while being told through the voice of another. As Helen Davies observes, in her book on cultural ventriloquism, '"having a voice" has become one of the more compelling motifs of identity politics' (Davies 2012: 2). Davies's usage of the present perfect tense here ('has become') establishes what is a key dyadic methodology of Davies's argument: the complex relationship between looking back and 'talking back' (Davies 2012: 1), alongside the recognition that, in revisiting the past to make points that speak as much about the present as they do the past, such forays risk 'either a "subversive" or "conservative" enterprise'. They 'might challenge the patriarchal, heteronormative, eurocentric discourse of history, but [they] might also repeat it' (Davies 2012: 6).

Victorian spiritualism, similarly, followed this kind of ventriloquising pattern. Owen informs us that,

Until the 1870s the peak of success in the field of spirit communication was the production of the 'direct' spirit voice or writing, a process which culminated in spontaneous speech or messages produced quite independently of the medium although at her behest. (Owen 1989: 41)

Indeed, that such spoken or written messages sometimes required the medium to enter a 'trance [...] thus absenting herself from conscious involvement' (Owen 1989: 41), perhaps positions the medium as dummy rather than ventriloquist. When looking back at Victorian writing itself, however, and more specifically the Victorian ghost story as written by female authors, one recognises precisely such a complex uncertainty about whether what one is reading is indeed 'subversive' or 'conservative' and, undoubtedly, that complexity resides in the use made of the voice in these stories. According to Davies,

> the late nineteenth century was a turning point in ventriloquism; prior to the dummy/ventriloquist stage act, the topic of ventriloquism encompassed the prophecies at the Delphic oracle, accounts of demon possession, the strange mimicries of distant voice ventriloquism and the mysterious utterances of nineteenth-century spiritualism. (Davies 2012: 7)

Importantly, once performed on stage as an 'act', the ventriloquist artists were usually male, a shift that ruptured what had previously been seen as the assumed connection between women and the disembodied spirit voice.

That arrival of the male ventriloquist seems to find an analogy in the again paradoxical relationship between women and narrative voice in Victorian ghost stories. In the stories under examination in this chapter, one cannot help but observe that the narrative voice is persistently male, despite these stories being written by women. In contradistinction to the aforementioned self-authenticating narrative voice of Katherine and Margaret Fox, it is as if the woman writer, perhaps because writing for publication positions her firmly in the public rather than private domain, does not trust that the material she is creating will have authenticity if told through a female voice. Similarly, we also notice how many of these tales follow a kind of hearsay or one-stage-removal dynamic through being either epistolary in form, such as Mary Shelley's *Frankenstein* (1818; 1831), or multi-narrated, such as Emily Brontë's *Wuthering Heights* (1847). Even in the case of these two highly canonical novels, we note that the primary teller/scribe is male. The enforced present-ness of these male narrators undoubtedly complicates the narrative voice's location, such that we forget that these are voices 'thrown' by a female writer. This authorial ventriloquism returns us to the Victorian woman's problematic relationship to property, for even in relation to her own ghost story the Victorian woman writer seems strangely ill at ease. Is this insecure relationship to the voice, however, driven by a lack of faith in self-authentication, or simply a form of self-protection? During an age when, as Elaine Showalter observes, citing Phyllis Chesler, 'insanity is a label applying to gender norms and violations, a penalty for "*being* 'female' as well as desiring or daring *not* to be"' (Chesler 1972: 16; cited in Showalter 1996: 4) and in which the medical profession believed 'that the instability of the female nervous and reproductive systems made women more vulnerable to derangement than men' (Showalter 1996: 73), one can see why women would shy away from using their own voices when narrating tales of ghosts.

In 1850, editing a new, posthumous edition of her sister Emily Brontë's novel, *Wuthering Heights*, Charlotte Brontë (writing as Currer Bell) apologises for the presence therein of, among other things, 'The practice of hinting by single letters those expletives with which profane and violent persons are wont to garnish their discourse', adding that she 'cannot tell what good it does – what feeling it spares – what horror it conceals' (C. Brontë 1978: xxxii). Charlotte continues by affirming the unknowing creativity inherent in what we might describe (though Charlotte does not) as her sister's 'Gothic' vision, similarly utilising Emily's genderless pseudonym:

> Her imagination, which was a spirit more sombre than sunny, more powerful than sportive, found in such traits material whence it wrought creations like Heathcliff, like Earnshaw, like Catherine. Having formed these beings she didn't know what she had done. If the auditor of her work, when read in manuscript, shuddered under the grinding influence of natures so relentless and implacable, or spirits so lost and fallen; if it was complained that the mere hearing of certain vivid and fearful scenes banished sleep by night, and disturbed mental peace by day, Ellis Bell would wonder what was meant ... (C. Brontë 1978: xxxiii)

Alongside the dually pseudonymous approach, we observe how nervously Charlotte refers to the elemental disturbances depicted in Emily's book:

> Having avowed that, over much of *Wuthering Heights* there broods 'a horror of great darkness'; that, in its storm-heated and electrical atmosphere, we seem at times to breathe lightning, let me point to those spots where clouded daylight and the eclipsed sun still attest to their existence. (C. Brontë 1978: xxxiv)

Charlotte's 'Preface' echoes that of Shelley's 'Author's Introduction' to her second edition of *Frankenstein* (1831), in which she begins by asking of herself, 'How I, then a young girl, came to think of and to dilate upon so very hideous an idea?' (Shelley 1985: 55). Shelley's second edition predates Victoria's reign by six years, but in her brave and astute reflection on what will become one of the most influential novels in the history of English literature and, arguably, the bedrock novel of all modern Gothic, she establishes, here, the idea that haunting itself might become seen as the primary metaphor for all creativity:

> Night waned [...] and even the witching hour had gone by before we retired to rest. When I placed my head on my pillow, I did not sleep, nor could I be said to think. My imagination, unbidden, possessed and guided me, gifting the successive images that arose in my mind with a vividness far beyond the usual bounds of reverie ... (Shelley 1985: 58-9)

These images, of course, shape themselves into Victor Frankenstein and his own monstrous creation. Thirteen years after the publication of the first edition, in contradistinction to the Fox sisters, Shelley is keen to conceive this process as an affliction over which she, as author, had no control. She is equally keen to assert her inferiority to the men by whom she was surrounded, paramount among them, of course, Percy Bysshe, whom, as poet, she is at pains to elevate for his 'radiance of brilliant imagery and [...] music of the most melodious verse' in preference to 'the machinery of a story' such as her own (Shelley 1985: 57).

Both Shelley's Introduction and Brontë's Preface stand as testimony to the extraordinary effort it must have taken, simultaneously, to revolutionise the face of English literature whilst desperately trying to downplay their imaginative powers for fear of attracting calumny from their peers. Nevertheless, irrespective of how hard Shelley strives to conceal herself behind her husband (even permitting him to write the 'Preface' to the first edition as if it were by his hand),[1] it is the story Shelley recounts in that Introduction that frames our knowledge of the creation of *Frankenstein*. Recollecting the now well-documented 1816 trip to Switzerland, during which time her 'ghost story' was conceived (Shelley 1985: 57), we are struck by the directness of her voice, in describing how her vision came upon her in her bed in terms that are not very far from being sexual: 'When I placed my head on my pillow, I did not sleep, nor could I be said to think. My imagination, unbidden, possessed and guided me, gifting the successive images that arose in my mind ... The idea so possessed my mind that a thrill of fear ran through me' (Shelley 1985: 58-9). Shelley is, of course, by this time viewed as a woman with a tarnished reputation, having eloped to Europe with Percy Bysshe while he was still married, and thus we see how, in these early decades of the nineteenth century, the woman's published work is viewed as a reflection on its author's moral standing and reputation, alive or dead.

No wonder Charlotte is so keen to reassure us that 'My sister's disposition was not naturally gregarious; circumstances favoured and fostered her tendency to seclusion; except to go to church or take a walk on the hills, she rarely crossed the threshold of home' (C. Brontë 1978: xxxiii).

In fact, through its treatment of ghosts, *Wuthering Heights* reinforces and challenges simultaneously the relationship between the woman, home and domestic seclusion. In the famous scene from Chapter Three, our first-person male frame narrator, Lockwood, is forced to stay overnight because of the tempestuous elements outside. Roused from sleep by a branch rattling at the window, he tries to open the window to dislodge it. Finding the casement locked, he takes what can surely only be seen as an ill-mannered and disproportionate action, 'knocking [his] knuckles through the glass', at which point he finds, in his hand, not a branch but 'a little, ice-cold hand', believed to belong to the ghost of Cathy, Heathcliff's childhood playmate, sweetheart and only love (E. Brontë 1978: 20). Brontë's narrative is, in mid-nineteenth-century terms, similarly shocking to Shelley's Introduction to the 1831 edition of *Frankenstein*, in that here we have a man in his bed, haunted by the ghost of a younger woman (at one point Lockwood describes it as having 'a child's face' (20)), who insists on gaining access to his bedchamber, an action that would most certainly not have been permissible had Cathy been alive. What we also notice is that this ghost is situated outdoors, while he resides within, reversing the stereotypical gender connection between private and public spheres and positioning her as a child of the wild outdoors, an element of Cathy's characterisation that is reiterated again, when Ellen Dean, the housekeeper, recalls an earlier conversation she had with Cathy, by then unhappily married to Edgar Linton. Cathy insists to Ellen:

> 'You should have spoken to Edgar [...] and compelled him to leave me quiet! Oh, I'm burning! I wish I were out of doors! I wish I were a girl again, half savage and hardy, and free; and laughing at injuries, not maddening under them! [...] Open the window again wide: fasten it open! Quick, why don't you move?' (E. Brontë 1978: 107)

This second window encounter reinforces the fact that the model of young womanhood with which *Wuthering Heights* presents us is clearly at odds with the genteel feminine 'norm' we are encouraged to associate with Victorian middle-class life. Though Leonore Davidoff and Catherine Hall acknowledge that, in this period, 'women might work in the garden themselves', and that 'Behind walls and hedges, genteel women could legitimately engage in brisk physical activity and even display some aggression against pests and weeds', in general terms, 'Within garden imagery women were increasingly associated with flowers; their brilliant colouring, fragility, fragrance and existence for decorative purposes only' (Davidoff and Hall 2019: 374). Indeed, it seems to be the transgressive shift into the world of ghosts that, in all these instances, leads to a more progressive, perhaps even a more transgressive, window onto female sensuality. As Jennifer Uglow notes, 'ghost stories seemed to give their writers a licence to experiment, to push the boundaries of fiction a little further' (Uglow 1988: xiv).

Dickerson goes so far as to describe *Wuthering Heights* as a narrative of 'emancipatory supernaturalism' (Dickerson 1996: 104). Nor, perhaps, is *Wuthering Heights* alone in being so. A similar adventurousness surrounds young Rosamond, in Elizabeth Gaskell's 'The Old Nurse's Story' (1852), a tale in which the child is lured by a ghostly playmate out onto the wilds of the Westmoreland Fells, in temperatures so cold that her first-person narrator nurse tells us 'that the air almost took the skin off my face' (Gaskell 2000: 21). That allure is, certainly, feminised in the form of the 'little girl, not so old as [Rosamond] ... but so pretty ... [who] beckoned to [her] to come out; and oh, she was so pretty and so sweet, I could not choose but go' (Gaskell 2000: 22). Though Rosamond's desire is embodied by the girl, in effect she is drawn away from the forbidding masculine enclosure of Furnivall Manor, 'a great and stately house, with many trees close around it, so close that in some places their branches dragged against the walls when the wind blew' (Gaskell 2000: 13). In *Frankenstein*, *Wuthering Heights* and 'The Old Nurse's Story', the Gothic allure of elemental outdoor conditions is as thrilling as it is dangerous and, even in *Frankenstein*, a narrative in which only the male characters are situated in direct confrontation with those elements, it is clear that it is Shelley's own creative response to the Alpine storm that shapes the book's appeal: 'One which would speak to the mysterious fears of our nature and awaken thrilling horror – one to make the reader dread to look round, to curdle the blood, and quicken the beatings of the heart' (Shelley 1985: 57–8).

In the second half of the nineteenth century, married women's financial security takes a significant leap forward in the passing, in 1882, of the Married Woman's Property Act, legislation that allowed, for the first time, a married woman to retain legal ownership over her own property, where previously it had passed automatically into the hands of her husband on marriage. Undoubtedly this act made a major contribution to the financial autonomy of married women, but what is interesting about the ghost story is that it demonstrates that property can bring trouble as much as security. Take, for example, Charlotte Riddell's ghost story 'The Open Door' (1882), published in the same year as the act was passed. The very title is suggestive, implying, rather like the use of windows in *Wuthering Heights*, that a new aperture had opened up for women, facilitating freedom of movement, the crossing of thresholds, facilitated by this socioeconomic shift. Riddell's story, however, is one in which inherited property brings murderous desires; in which the central protagonist is a young male; and in which a threat, not just to property ownership but to life, is posed by a 'devilish' female presence reduced by Riddell, in synecdochic form, to 'an awful figure, with uplifted hand', who flees with her maid 'abroad the very morning' of their discovery (Liggins 2009: iv; Riddell 2009: 57–8).

Property rights are shown to affect our male narrator, too. At the beginning of Riddell's story he is down on his luck, threatened with redundancy, and retains his job only because he makes a bargain with his employer, the owner of the haunted Hall, that he will stay there a fortnight and bring to light its mystery, in return for which he will receive a payment of ten pounds (half his annual salary). That perilous relationship to property extends to an equally perilous relationship to proper ('propre') nouns. Not simply unnamed, Riddell draws especial attention to him being actively 'mis-named' the instant he moves into direct speech:

> 'Sandy!'
> 'What do you want?'
> 'Should you like to earn a sovereign?'
> 'Of course I should.'
> A somewhat curt dialogue, but we were given to curtness in the office of Messrs. Frimpton, Frampton and Fryer, auctioneers and estate agents, St Benet's Hill, City.
> (My name is not Sandy or anything like it, but the other clerks so styled me because of a real or fancied likeness to some character, an ill-looking Scotchman, they had seen at the theatre). (Riddell 2009: 28)

By evoking the wrong name, our anonymous clerk removes himself from the system of patrilineage that attaches itself directly to property ownership. In contrast, he works for a firm carrying a surfeit of names ('Frimpton, Frampton and Fryer') which collectively enacts the affirmation of property rights, being a firm of estate agents. The comparison works to 'un-man' him, in patriarchal terms. Our disadvantaged narrator, then, speaks but is not named and, as is typical in the ghost story, retells his tale retrospectively, from a distance of space and time. He is, in that sense, both there and not there, a ghost in his own tale. Riddell's seemingly disappointing decision, in this year of all years, to tell her story through a male narrator is therefore more complicated than it appears. Liggins argues that writers such as Riddell utilise this genre to bring to light the fact that 'new legislation was only just addressing women's rights to their own earnings and their property' (Liggins 2009: iii) and perhaps it is our narrator's lack of ease in both the house and his own skin that reinforces the inequalities of this fragile situation. He may well enter the haunted room as an estate agent, describing it as 'a good-sized room, twenty by twenty (I knew, because I paced it afterwards), lighted by two long windows', but he still 'ascend[s] the great staircase feeling curiously like an intruder' (Riddell 2009: 44, 42).

Moreover, the ghostly encounter, once it comes, leaves our narrator outwitted. The 'ghost' turns out to be the former owner's young widow. She has murdered her husband in order to secure his estate and, in league with her maid, 'haunts' the house by concealing herself inside, searching for the hidden will that will secure her future. Ironically, securing her own future requires the unfastening of the door, which she reopens whenever anyone shuts it, to give the impression that the house is haunted. Riddell's story maps directly onto the argument put forward by Sandra Gilbert and Susan Gubar, in their landmark discussion of nineteenth-century women's writing *The Madwoman in the Attic* (1979), in which they argue that 'Dramatizations of imprisonment and escape are so all-pervasive' during this period 'that we believe they represent a uniquely female tradition'. Moreover, where women writers of the period begin frequently by emphasising the heavy, entombing architecture of a Gothic house, 'they also use much of the other paraphernalia of "woman's place" to enact their central symbolic drama of enclosure and escape. Ladylike veils and costumes, mirrors, paintings, statues, locked cabinets, drawers, trunks, strongboxes and other domestic furnishings appear and reappear' in these tales (Gilbert and Gubar 1984: 85): certainly they do in 'The Open Door'. The haunted room is enclosed by two doors, the 'haunted' one at the entrance and a locked one at the far end, behind which the murderess and her maid live during daylight hours. It is

> a dreary, gloomy room; the dark panelled walls; the black shining floor; the windows high from the ground; the antique furniture; the dull four-poster bedstead, with dingy velvet curtains; the gaping chimney; the silk counterpane that looked like a pall. (Riddell 2009: 44)

While our hapless narrator suspects, correctly, that the solution to the mystery lies behind the locked door, in secreting himself in a chair concealed by those 'dingy' curtains he fails to realise that he has enwrapped himself within the 'paraphernalia' of 'woman's place' (to recall Gilbert and Gubar). Hence, even his look-out station places him at a gendered disadvantage. While he espies the woman entering the room, and surprises her in the act of searching out the will, the physical struggle that follows leaves him on the wrong side of 'a fight for life' (Riddell 2009: 57) and, though he survives it, he remains haunted by 'a great horror of darkness ... and at such periods I cannot endure to be left alone' (Riddell 2009: 58), while she and her maid escape, unscathed and unpunished. Furthermore, at the owner's behest, the incident is 'hushed up', re-silencing our narrator until the cathartic moment of retelling which constitutes the ghost story (Riddell 2009: 58). Our narrator experiences, too late, what Gilbert and Gubar term 'the explosive violence' typifying the furious heroine of this period, through whom 'the female author enacts her own raging desire to escape' (Gilbert and Gubar 1984: 85).

Physical violence by women against men remains a rarity in writing by women and certainly it is not the most common danger women are perceived to pose to men. Vernon Lee's (Violet Paget's) story 'Dionea' (1890) is that of a foundling, a survivor of a shipwreck, a beauty who becomes accused, by the townspeople, of bearing the evil eye. The story begins in 1873 and spans a fourteen-year period ending in 1887, the recent past at the time of first publication. Writing through a male pseudonym, Lee's tale again intermingles the voices of male and female storytellers. The frame epistolary narrator is an older man, Doctor Alessandro De Rosis, his addressee the much younger Lady Evelyn Smith, Princess of Sabina. Again, the epistolary structure combines distance (of time) and proximity (of voice) with the authority that any patriarchal society would attach to the words of a senior, male figure. Yet, of course, that voice is ventriloquised twice: once through being written by a female author and again through her 'throwing' her voice via adopting a male pseudonym. That layering of names attaches itself to Dionea, too, for although her eponymous status implies an authoritative placement at the heart of the story, Dionea's actual name is seen to be far more difficult to ascertain. On being washed ashore, the name Dionea is stitched into her clothing, but the locals wish, presumably for religious reasons, to rename her Maria. There being 'already twenty-three other Marias, Marietta, Mariuccias, and so forth at the convent', 'Dionea' is reinstated, but the slipperiness of name is reflected in Dionea's problematic relationship with lived identity.

On arrival, her foundling status merits comparison with Brontë's Heathcliff. When Heathcliff first arrives, in Chapter 4 of *Wuthering Heights*, he is described as a 'dirty, ragged, black-haired child' and a 'gipsy brat' who is 'big enough to walk and talk ... yet, when it was set on its feet, it only stared round, and repeated over and over again some gibberish, that nobody could understand' (E. Brontë 1978: 30). In Lee's story, Dionea is described as 'a poor little waif ... doubtless a heathen' and a 'Poor little brown mite!' (Lee 2015: 3–4). Both are introduced, to characters and reader, as 'foreign', in the dual sense of arriving from abroad and being 'strange' or exotic. In 'Dionea', her beauty and unclear origins combine to attract a sense of the uncanny. As a young child, she is 'decidedly pretty, and as brown as a berry'. By eleven she has 'the prettiest face of any little girl in Montemirto'. At thirteen, she is in danger of being expulsed from the convent for 'handling in a suspicious manner the Madonna's gala frock and her best veil of *pizzo di Cantù*' and for being 'seated on the edge of the altar, in the very place of the Most Holy Sacrament' (4, 6, 9). By adolescent maturity, though 'already dubbed La bella Dionea', we are told that if any of the boys or men turn to look at her as she passes, 'it is ... with an expression rather of fear than of love', while 'The women ... make horns with their fingers as she passes' (10). Finally, a contagion also attaches itself to her, for though no man dare pledge his troth to her, 'where-ever she goes the young people must needs fall in love with each other, and usually where it is far from desirable' (10). Such a connection has an etymological root. If we think of the word 'glamour' (originally referring to a witch's magic), or adjectives such as 'enchanting', 'bewitching' or even 'stunning', we see how they all derive from fear of the supernatural power inherent in women's beauty and the 'spell' it casts over (presumed to be) male suitors. Sexual allure can be deadly, and the ghost story plays on that connection to its fullest extent, even, it seems, when written by female authors.

Although these features might, at first, suggest the tale to be a Gothic rather than a ghost story, the ending of 'Dionea' tells us that she, much like Cathy and Heathcliff in *Wuthering Heights*, is said to appear in ghostly form, 'on stormy nights, wandering among the cliffs' (Lee 2015: 26). Moreover, according to the testimony of a local 'sailor boy', even before the shipwreck, he had witnessed her aboard 'a Greek boat ... going full sail ... a robe of purple and gold about her, and a myrtle-wreath on her head ... singing words in an unknown tongue, the white pigeons around her' (26). Dionea is, in these terms, as much a ghost at the start as at the end of the story, spectrality framing her existence throughout. As in *Wuthering Heights*, then, Lee's story forges a clear connection between the tempestuous, elemental outdoors and female supernatural identity. Even the shipwreck is brought on by a 'squall', a 'dreadful storm' borne from what our frame narrator describes as 'a wicked sea, wicked in its loveliness' (3), the primary elemental trait that defines Dionea. The fear of active female sexuality that epitomises 'Dionea' attaches itself, similarly, to Victorian spiritualism.

Owen is at pains to stress that 'Both spiritualists and feminists [of the time] were in tune with a social purity ethic which was waxing during the 1870s and 1880s and which stressed the high moral standards of men and women' (Owen 1989: 34). Nevertheless, the American origins from which British Victorian spiritualism had emerged 'had become identified with "free love" principles' (Owen 1989: 35), a connection that dogged female spiritualists. 'Dionea', published at the end of the so-called 'golden age of English spiritualism' (Owen 1989: 1), seems to have been influenced by the presumed connection between female sexuality, female susceptibility to ghosts and the danger both posed to the male characters involved.

Arguably, even more extreme sexual dangers accrue around Edith Nesbit's story 'The Ebony Frame' (1893), in which witchcraft and passion become the bargaining chips for romance. Again, our point-of-view protagonist is male, but the potency of the story resides wholly in the sensual allure of a painted woman. Our once again unnamed narrator inherits an old house from his deceased aunt. Sitting there on his first evening as proprietor, he takes an interest in a framed picture above the fireplace. It contains 'an exceedingly bad print', but the frame itself 'was not intended for a print, but for an oil-painting. It was of fine ebony, beautifully and curiously carved'. He learns that the frame used to contain another painting, so 'black and ugly it might as well be a chimney-back', and that it had been removed to the attic and the frame reused (Nesbit 2020: 10–11). Inevitably, our narrator's curiosity is piqued, and he searches out the painting and attempts to clean it. Unsuccessful, he realises that he is looking at the reverse of the painting and that its depth is unusually 'thick'; in fact, he is holding two portraits, 'nailed face to face' (12). Uncanniness follows, on the discovery that one side depicts himself, while the other is of 'a woman of the type of beauty beloved of Burne Jones and Rosetti ... her face was turned full forward, and her eyes met those of the spectator bewilderingly' (12–13). That reference to the return of the gaze is the first inclination given of the subject's sensual nature, for as studies of pornography make clear, the gaze and its return determine the nature of the gender politics inherent in scopophilia. As Susanne Kappeler observes, 'in [woman's] look man recognizes himself. In her look, however, he experiences fear and ignorance: he does not like being seen' (Kappeler 1986: 65). In 'The Ebony Frame', not only does the painted image appear to frame the onlooker as much as the painting frames its subject, their unorthodox positioning means that they have been face-to-face in the frame, thus diminishing his spectatorial potency. As the story progresses, her powers extend while his diminish:

I left the bell, I seized the poker, and battered the dull coals to a blaze. Then I stepped back resolutely, and looked up at the picture. The ebony frame was empty! From the shadow of the worked chair came a silken rustle, and out of the shadow the woman of the picture was coming – coming towards me. (Nesbit 2020: 15)

Defining, surely, the revenge of the pornographic object, we also consider that the word 'glamour', originally deriving from witchcraft, has another, more modern meaning. 'Glamour photography' is a euphemism for 'dirty pictures' and 'The Ebony Frame', if nothing else, is certainly a ghost story about a faceless man's fascination with his very own 'dirty picture'. The story might well be subtitled 'Be Careful What You Wish For'.

At the end of her own book, Dickerson bifurcates the chronology of the Victorian woman's ghost story into those written pre- and those post- Charles Darwin's *On the Origin of Species* (1859). One can see why: if one no longer believes in God, why would anyone believe in ghosts, as ghosts cannot exist without belief in an afterlife? And yet, not only did the ghost story continue to flourish after Darwin's theories, it continues to flourish today. For Dickerson, post-Darwin, ghost stories by women were 'written in a climate of change and in education, employment, and suffrage; the passage of the married women's property bills; and the rise of the New Woman' (Dickerson 1996: 133). It is true that, although *Frankenstein, Wuthering Heights* and even 'The Old Nurse's Tale' provide us with characters who are as wild as the elements and, in certain ways, with whom it is perhaps easier for a twenty-first-century reader to empathise than those ventriloquised male-narrated tales set within the suffocating interior of the Victorian mansion, nevertheless, once social reforms begin to gather pace, these same women perhaps need to stifle their male narrators in those confines to bring home to readers just how suffocating they are, whilst simultaneously 'throwing their voice' to protect themselves from accusations of insanity or derangement. As Owen reminds us, writing of Victorian spiritualism, 'Underlying the assumption of the physician's moral superiority was a preoccupation with the "depraved instincts" supposedly manifested in many typical cases of insanity' (Owen 1989: 141–2), and belief in ghosts could easily come under scrutiny in those terms.

Note

1. The 1818 first edition of *Frankenstein* was published anonymously, but carried a 'Preface' authored by Percy Bysshe Shelley.

Works Cited

Brontë, Charlotte. 'Editor's Preface to the New Edition of *Wuthering Heights* [1850]', in Emily Brontë, *Wuthering Heights*. London: J. M. Dent, 1978, pp. xxxi–xxxv.

Brontë, Emily. *Wuthering Heights*. London: J. M. Dent, 1978.

Chesler, Phyliss. *Women and Madness*. Harmondsworth: Penguin, 1972.

Dalby, Richard, ed. *Victorian Ghost Stories by Eminent Women Writers*. New York: Carroll and Graf, 1988.

Davidoff, Leonore and Catherine Hall. *Family Fortunes: Men and Women of the English Middle Class, 1780–1850*, 3rd edn. London: Routledge, 2019.

Davies, Helen. *Gender and Ventriloquism in Victorian and Neo-Victorian Fiction: Passionate Puppets*. Basingstoke: Palgrave Macmillan, 2012.

Dickerson, Vanessa D. *Victorian Ghosts in the Noontide: Women Writers and the Supernatural*. Columbia: University of Missouri Press, 1996.

Gaskell, Elizabeth. 'The Old Nurse's Tale', in Elizabeth Gaskell, *Gothic Tales*, edited by Laura Kranzler. Harmondsworth: Penguin, 2000, pp. 11–32.

Gilbert, Sandra M. and Susan Gubar. *The Madwoman in the Attic: The Woman Writer and the Nineteenth-Century Literary Imagination*. New Haven, CT: Yale University Press, 1984.

Kappeler, Susanne. *The Pornography of Representation*. Cambridge: Cambridge University Press, 1986.

Lee, Vernon. 'Dionea', in Roger Luckhurst (ed.), *Late Victorian Gothic Tales*. Oxford: Oxford University Press, 2015, pp. 3–26.

Liggins, Emma. 'Introduction', in Charlotte Riddell, *Weird Tales*. Brighton: Victorian Secrets, 2009, pp. i–vi.

Nesbit, Edith. 'The Ebony Frame', in *The Collected Short Stories of E. Nesbit*, vol. 1: *Gothic Horror*, edited by S. J. Hills. London: DTC Publishing, 2020, pp. 10–23.

Owen, Alex. *The Darkened Room: Women, Power and Spiritualism in late Victorian England*. London: Virago, 1989.

Riddell, Charlotte. 'The Open Door', in *Weird Tales*, introduced by Emma Liggins. Brighton: Victorian Secrets, 2009, pp. 28–58.

Shelley, Mary. *Frankenstein, or, The Modern Prometheus*. Harmondsworth: Penguin, 1985.

Showalter, Elaine. *The Female Malady: Women, Madness and English Culture, 1830–1980*. London: Virago, 1996.

Uglow, Jennifer. 'Introduction', in Richard Dalby (ed.), *Victorian Ghost Stories by Eminent Women Writers*. New York: Carroll and Graf, 1988, pp. ix–xvii.

Wolfreys, Julian. *Victorian Hauntings: Spectrality, Gothic, the Uncanny and Literature*. Basingstoke: Palgrave, 2002.

Chapter 8

The Victorian Ghost Story and Colonialism
Melissa Edmundson

During Queen Victoria's sixty-three-year reign, the British Empire expanded across the globe in an unprecedented way. By 1876, Victoria had been proclaimed Empress of India and the British controlled vast territories stretching from Canada and the Caribbean to Africa, Asia and Australia. Along with these British incursions into Indigenous lands came numerous colonists who sought to claim both physical territory and natural resources at the expense of Native peoples who had lived on the land for tens of thousands of years. The popular image arose of Victoria's empire as one on which the sun never set, but this system of oppression came at an immeasurable cost of life and livelihood to those whose land was taken from them. Armed conflicts happened throughout Victoria's reign. Soon after ascending to the throne in 1837, Britain fought to establish commercial trading routes in Asia that led to the Opium Wars between China and Britain in 1839–42 and 1856–60. The Indian Uprising, also known as the First War of Indian Independence, began in 1857 and resulted in shocking violence. The Anglo-Zulu War of 1879 was one of many conflicts on an African continent which was being divided by several imperial regimes during what become known as the 'Scramble for Africa'. While these rebellions took place in Africa and Asia, British emigration to other colonies such as Australia and Canada led to the forced removal of Indigenous groups from lands they had inhabited for generations. The stories discussed in the following pages reflect the widespread unrest which occurred because of colonial expansion and focus on narratives from across the empire, from Africa, Australia and India, to Ireland, Canada and the Caribbean. The stories surveyed illustrate how history and literature merge to create unique social commentaries that reveal anxieties about Great Britain's involvement in foreign lands.

These anxieties soon found their way into print. Expanded use of the telegraph meant that news of distant overseas conflicts could reach

Britain much more quickly, often making headline news in major newspapers across the country. The empire was seemingly closer than ever before. The opening of the Suez Canal by the 1870s meant that what had once been remote colonial regions were now more accessible. Places that took several months to reach by ship could now be reached in a matter of a few weeks. This increased contact with imperial territories, coupled with heightened discord between Britain and its foreign subjects, led to further unease about how colonialism would affect British national identity. Worries about blurred geographic boundaries and the blending of cultures began to find their way into the popular literature of the time, such as the adventure romances made famous by Henry Rider Haggard. The Gothic, with its ability to speak the unspoken, likewise became a fitting vehicle to express colonial tensions. Haggard's *King Solomon's Mines* (1885) and *She* (1887) and Joseph Conrad's *Heart of Darkness* (1902) are set in Africa and explore British experience in what became known as the 'Dark Continent'. Several other Gothic novels of the Victorian era, such as Charlotte Brontë's *Jane Eyre* (1847), Emily Brontë's *Wuthering Heights* (1847), Wilkie Collins's *The Moonstone* (1868), Arthur Conan Doyle's *The Sign of Four* (1890), Richard Marsh's *The Beetle* (1897), Florence Marryat's *The Blood of the Vampire* (1897) and Bram Stoker's *Dracula* (1897), explored the dangers of the foreign Other 'coming home' to Britain. Gothic short stories dealing with empire also appeared during the period, a prime example being Rudyard Kipling's 'The Mark of the Beast' (1890).

At the same time that these Gothic works proliferated, the colonial ghost story was also emerging as a subcategory of what Patrick Brantlinger has termed the 'Imperial Gothic'. Brantlinger outlines three defining themes of this Gothic subset: the fear of moral regression and degeneration (what was termed 'going native'); civilisation giving way to barbarism; and declining opportunities for heroism in a modernising world (1988: 230). Building on Brantlinger's work, Tabish Khair sees the Victorian imperial Gothic as one which 'found more space for the colonial Other', a character who was 'often beyond the pale of direct narration' in more mainstream literature of the time (2009: 22). As Britain expanded its empire, the parameters of the traditional English ghost story likewise broadened. Even ghost stories set in Britain during this period reflect the presence of empire. Simon Hay claims that because 'the only-marginally-visible is precisely the central concern of ghost stories in general', these stories are thus 'insistently about Empire' (2011: 10). Colonial ghost stories bring into focus some of the most compelling qualities of the ghost story: fear and anxiety, troubled power dynamics, and the blurred boundaries between self and other. The ghost story became a vehicle to highlight social issues and inequalities within colonial regions and drew attention to the harmful effects of imperialism during Queen Victoria's reign. As the British travelled, they took their ghosts with them, and within colonial regions these ghosts transformed into terrifying forms, ones which show the British haunted by their attempts to conquer new lands and oppress Indigenous peoples.

Colonial ghost stories expand the parameters of the Victorian ghost story. As the European ghost from its beginnings represented unfinished business, unspoken trauma, and a demand to be heard and understood, so, too, did the colonial ghost. However, in colonial regions, the ghost acquires even more meaning as it speaks of historical and cultural violence, instability of power structures, possession and dispossession, fractured identity, and questions of belonging and not belonging within the British imperial project. This undercurrent of unease is a common trait of ghost stories set in the colonies. Ghost stories can be found across the British Empire during the Victorian period. Colonial regions provided the perfect environment for ghost stories to explore cultural fears and more directly interrogate the effects of imperialism. This chapter explores how the colonial ghost story illustrates the impact of imperialism and how the troubled relations between colonised and coloniser are at the forefront of these narratives. In many ways, the colonial ghost mirrors the imperial project itself. These ghosts represent a form of haunted memory and have a lasting impact on those who come into contact with them.

Mapping the Colonial Ghost Story

Colonial ghost stories during the Victorian period are products of individual and cultural unsettlement, displacement and resistance. These ghosts challenge issues of ownership and identity, whether this takes the form of ownership of a piece of land, oppression of Indigenous cultures, or the blurring of white British identity within colonial regions. Encounters between Indigenous peoples and colonisers are fraught with violence and tension and the figure of the ghost rises to remind readers of the lasting trauma that is inherent in such encounters. As such, ghost stories that include aspects of colonialism are fitting examples of Mary Louise Pratt's concept of the 'contact zone', which is defined as a 'social space where disparate cultures meet, clash, and grapple with each other, often in highly asymmetrical relations of domination and subordination – like colonialism, slavery, or their aftermaths' (2003: 4). As the British were the dominant culture, so, too, do ghost stories set in regions of empire focus on the experience of white colonisers. In these stories, experiences and beliefs of Indigenous people are relegated to the margins of the narrative, and established Indigenous belief systems are often reduced to local superstition. Likewise, British characters are the heroes and thus the only ones contemporary readers were supposed to care about. Rarely do we get sympathetic accounts of Native peoples or an insight into their suffering. However, there are frequent hints of unease resulting from the imperial project as both Indigenous and British characters ultimately suffer through their (direct and indirect) contact with empire and what Pratt calls the 'asymmetrical relations of domination and subordination' (4). This contact and the resulting unease surrounding one's place within empire leads to an overwhelming cultural anxiety that pervades these narratives. Violence, or the threat of violence, is ever-present in these stories, especially the unpredictability of violence and fears of losing control in unfamiliar surroundings and amidst unfamiliar people. If the English ghost story prides itself on upsetting the status quo, then this tendency is taken even further in ghost stories set in colonial regions.

Ghostly retribution for misdeeds is a recurring theme in stories with a colonial setting. This revenge is linked to violence done by colonisers to Indigenous peoples. As such, the ghost story becomes more graphic and visceral within colonial spaces and often amplifies the violence found in Eurocentric ghost stories that centre on crime, transgressions, lies and secrets. For instance, Alice Perrin's 'Caulfield's Crime' (1892) is a reincarnation story in which a murdered Indian fakir seeks revenge on an arrogant British Army officer. The story is an exploration of the consequences of brutality, and Perrin neither spares her title character nor provides her readers with a resolution that reinforces official narratives about the glory of empire. The British soldier is clearly the villain and suffers for his crime. There is no room for redemption amidst the killing of the fakir or the torturous death suffered by the title character. This motif of ghostly revenge recurs in other stories from the imperial era including Joseph Conrad's 'Karain: A Memory' (1897) which focuses on the power of local customs and spiritual belief told in the context of a haunting over a past transgression.

Often, the downfall of a settler-invader is linked to the oppression of Indigenous peoples. In Francis Owen's 'The Prophetess' (1907), two workers for the Canadian Pacific Railway encounter a First Nations woman while walking through an isolated mountain forest near Vancouver. The woman is described as an 'apparition', a 'foreboding spectre' and a 'ghostly phantom' (Owen 1989: 56, 57, 58) as she suddenly appears before the men and vents her anger towards them as destructive invaders of her land. Much of the force of the story comes from the woman herself as she voices her experience at the hands of the white invaders:

> 'See these valleys and these mountains [...] they were the home of my people, the hunting ground of my tribe; the land of the red man. They lived and laughed; they basked in the sun; they hunted and they fished; they died in the land of their fathers. But the vile intruder came. He came with his internal devils that scared the fish from the rivers, that shivered the hills to fragments, that filled the mountain streams and hewed down our sacred trees. They drove us before them like sheep and we starved among the rocks.' (57)

This is a rare attempt at a sympathetic rendering of Indigenous experience, particularly considering that the story was published in the early twentieth century. Owen's story encapsulates the trauma of white 'progress' which ultimately leads to destruction and disillusion for all involved, First Nations peoples and settler-invaders alike. The men initially dismiss the woman as 'a poor, crazy Indian' (58), but her warning comes to fruition when Vancouver is destroyed by fire. The fires are ironically started by the settlers themselves, as they burn large piles of timber and debris from the clear-cutting of the land through which the railroad cuts. The woman appears again to the two men, this time in one of the buildings being consumed by flames. She seemingly becomes the ghost that she was described as earlier, and her premonition comes true in one final act of victory and vengeance.

Ghost stories frequently emerge from historical sites of colonial violence, and this spiritual unrest is intimately tied to some sort of dispossession. Numerous Australian stories are set on former Aboriginal massacre sites that become haunted. In these stories, possession of land takes on new meanings. William Sylvester Walker, who was the nephew of the Australian writer 'Rolf Boldrewood' and who wrote under the penname 'Coo-ee', explores the lasting trauma of such a site in 'The Evil of Yelcomorn Creek' (1899). Baines, an outback prospector, and Bobbie, an Aboriginal man, travel to a remote place known for having valuable opals. However, they are unable to capitalise on their findings when the ghosts who inhabit an Aboriginal burial site return to drive them away. Bobbie dies of fright and the ghostly warriors force Baines from the spot, re-enacting a defence of their homeland that brings the past back into the present:

> 'As the battalions of twenty, spear in hand, "heilaman" on left shoulder, foot to foot, shoulder to shoulder, trooped forth, their eyes blazing with the light of battle, they'd stop and bow their heads by Bobbie and cast phantom ashes of the sacred "wambiloa" upon him. And I reckon that made him a ghost like themselves.' ('Coo-ee' 1994: 151)[1]

In an attempt to bury Bobbie, Baines strikes 'a blow' with his pick and sees the rich 'blue deposit, and a lot of different sized opals'. However, this action is met with another '"ghostly awful cry"' that causes Baines to leave immediately, refusing to '"[meddle] with things beyond [his] knowledge"' (151). Likewise, Ernest Favenc's 'The Red Lagoon' (1892) deals with continuing spiritual unrest as the return of those who died violent deaths allows Aboriginal people to reclaim their land by driving settlers away.

As specific sites of unrest, haunted houses were transferred to colonial settings and took the form of Anglo-Indian bungalows, huts in the African jungle and abandoned shacks in the Australian outback. Supernatural activity in these interior settings mirrors much of the unease which arises in exterior locations. Rosa Mulholland's ghost stories express anxieties surrounding property ownership within an Irish context. In 'The Lady Tantivy' (1898), a ghost helps find a lost will and secures the present-day heir's claim to the house. However, the ghostly presence suggests that one's connection (or disconnection) to a home(land) is often tied to feelings of loss and dispossession. Mulholland's 'The Ghost at the Rath' (1866) also features a stolen inheritance and a house whose resident ghost symbolises past unrest that continues to affect the present. The house as a site of past trauma is a recurring trope. Hume Nisbet's 'The Haunted Station' (1894) critiques the Australian penal system and the mistreatment of women and children in isolated bush settings. An English doctor wrongfully accused of his wife's murder is transported to a prison in Western Australia, where he escapes and stumbles upon the abandoned station. After seeing the ghosts of a murdered family who once lived in the house, the narrator chooses to stay at the residence not only for shelter but also to solve the mystery. He remarks, '*I could not leave the house, now that I had taken possession of it*, or rather, if I may say it, now that *the house had taken possession of me*' (Nisbet 1894: 23, italics in original). Indeed, possession and dispossession are central to the story. When he first arrives at the house, he recalls:

> I naturally supposed that I had walked hundreds of miles since leaving the convict settlement, and as I had encountered no one, not even a single tribe of wandering blacks, it seemed impossible to believe that I was not the first white man who had penetrated so far. (14)

According to Ken Gelder, 'these are narratives that symbolically re-enact colonisation: the empty house is a kind of *terra nullius*' that is discovered to be the home of ghosts (1994: xii). Gelder sees this troubled sense of home as an 'insistent theme in Australian ghost stories of not-so-distant crimes that work to give a particular place an unsettling significance, still "felt" by those who traverse or inhabit it' (xviii). Colonial ghost stories betray racist anxieties regarding Indigenous peoples as well, and haunted houses provide convenient sites for these attitudes, such as fears about living near Native peoples in colonial regions. This is particularly the case in Anglo-Indian ghost stories where the British share their households with numerous Indian servants. These narratives follow the formula of a white person being the victim of a crime, usually murder, in which a servant residing in or near the house is then found guilty. Prime examples of this are Rudyard Kipling's 'The Return of Imray' (1891), Alice Perrin's 'In the Next Room' (1893) and B. M. Croker's 'The Chowkedar' (1905).

Retribution also takes the form of reverse colonisation as the ghost returns to right some wrong. These hauntings are typically the result of a British person not taking Native beliefs seriously or believing that they can simply leave their problems behind by returning to the safety of England. The presence of the supernatural within the metropole represents a return of the repressed. Native peoples who were once victims of imperial rule gain power after death and can transgress temporal and geographical boundaries that would not otherwise be available to them. National boundaries and closed borders are of little consequence in the afterlife. In Arthur Conan Doyle's 'The Brown Hand' (1899), the retired British Army surgeon Sir Dominick Holden is haunted by the nightly appearance of the earth-bound spirit of an Indian man whose hand he amputated. The doctor's nephew is able to appease the ghost by offering another 'brown man's hand' (Doyle 1908: 299). Although the story seemingly ends on a positive note, there are underlying racial attitudes that haunt the narrative. Aviva Briefel notes that 'the British characters' superstitious fixation on the severed hand threatens to undermine their Western rationality' (2015: 40). The hand itself also becomes a commodified object that is acquired, traded and used by the British for their own personal gain (2015: 39). Likewise, in 'Lot No. 249' (1892), Conan Doyle bookends the story by musing on 'the strange by-paths into which the human spirit may wander' (1894: 221). Indeed, the narrative transverses multiple borders: colony/metropole, paranormal/science, death/life, ghost/mummy/human. Set two years after the Anglo-Egyptian War of 1882, the story is a not-so-subtle exploration of the consequences of privileged British men using Indigenous resources in an attempt to control something they do not fully understand.

In Kate and Hesketh Prichard's 'The Story of Baelbrow' (1898), the psychic detective Flaxman Low arrives at Baelbrow to investigate the mansion's resident ghost. The ghost is described by the young inheritor of the estate as '"an heirloom"' and '"a family possession"' (Heron 1898: 369), one which differs from the new supernatural threat encountered by visitors to the house. As an object of empire, the reanimated mummy is kept in the house's 'Museum', and thus provides a place for empire to exist within the very heart of the metropole: the British home. The mummy is also more dangerous than the family ghost. As young Swaffam observes, '"[O]ur original ghost was a mere misty presence, rather guessed at from vague sounds and shadows – now we have a something that is tangible, and that can, as we have proof, kill with fright"' (371). Low discovers that a vampire has inhabited the dead Egyptian's body and is using it to prey on the house's occupants. The story melds Gothic creatures into one destructive force: the family ghost becomes a vampire and then a mummy-vampire. However, the 'savage' way that Swaffam kills the creature (by shooting it multiple times and then beating its head in) before setting it on fire and casting it into the sea away from the house – and seemingly away from England – re-enacts the brutal violence historically inflicted on colonial subjects in order to silence and control them. Haunted objects from empire also appear in W. W. Jacobs's 'The Monkey's Paw' (1902). In much the same way as 'The Story of Baelbrow', an object from empire – in this case India – is brought to England with dire consequences. The narrative focuses on a powerful colonial force that asserts its supernatural influence on events through an imperial object. In both stories, these objects – which happen to be bodily remains – are willingly brought into the British domestic space where they wreak havoc.

In H. G. Wells's 'Pollock and the Porroh Man' (1895), the title character becomes a victim of a local medicine man who is a member of the Poro, a secret society in Sierra Leone, West Africa. Pollock is a member of a British expedition whose inexperience and disregard for the local population gets him into trouble. Much like the title character in Alice Perrin's 'Caulfield's Crime', Wells establishes Pollock as a dislikable character who has travelled to Africa to distance himself from scandal at home. While in Sierra Leone he desecrates a local idol by writing his name on it, keeps a local woman as a mistress and shoots the Poro man, all while assuming that none of his actions will lead to any serious repercussions. When the leader of the expedition recognises him as '"one of those infernal fools who think a black man isn't a human being"' (Wells 1927: 485), Pollock is sent back to England to avoid the Poro man's revenge. However, the story makes it clear that leaving the colony can do little to stop the supernatural forces bent on ensuring that Pollock pays for his disregard of local people and their belief systems. In this sense, the Poro man attains even more spiritual power after his death and enacts a revenge that follows Pollock to the supposed safe space of London.

G. M. Robins's 'The Man With No Face' (1902) ties haunting and the phenomenon of second sight directly to colonial violence emerging from harsh conditions on Caribbean sugar plantations. In the story, Violet Shirley recounts her husband's mysterious encounters with a man who repeatedly tries to strangle him. She describes him as 'very horrible' with his face covered by 'a mass of scars' (Robins 2003: 5). As in many ghost stories, the sighting of the apparition is connected to questions of mental instability and the potential loss of British masculine identity, and, consequently, there arises the need to explain away the supernatural visitations by some medical or scientific means. By the story's end, however, the ghost turns out to be very real and therefore even more dangerous. The husband is accidentally killed when the disfigured man enters his hotel room by mistake, the intended victim being the manager of a West Indies sugar plantation. The man's motive is tied to his mistreatment on the plantation:

> He was half-caste, and his face was eaten away by vitriol. His motive in murdering the man Gabbett was clear enough. He owed his disfigurement and much other brutal ill-treatment to him. He had followed him to England to be revenged upon him. (8)

The murder of Shirley is described as 'simply a blunder' (8), but the insinuation of the young Shirley as collateral damage is clear. Those not directly associated with the imperial project can still be harmed by it.

Violence against women drives the plots of several colonial ghost stories. In these works, this violence is closely connected to issues of colonial identity, particularly a male-dominated culture that is bent on maintaining authority and existing power structures through the use of fear, which in turn leads to wider problems of imperial violence against both British and non-British women. Such stories can be found in all regions of empire. Mary Fortune's ('W. W.') 'Mystery and Murder' (1866) and 'The Illumined Grave' (1867) centre around ghostly murdered women and illustrate the close connection between the Gothic and mystery/detective fiction. These bodies return from their graves to claim justice against those who killed them, while the recurring victimisation of women through acts of extreme brutality show British settlement in Australia to be very much unsettled. Through these supernatural returns, Fortune transforms these women into fear-inducing women who demand vengeance. In these stories, domestic violence is connected to the harshness of the outback. Violent deaths and subsequent hauntings are the (super)natural end result for those living in such an untamed and lawless land. Other stories by Australian women use spectrality to critique issues of female autonomy, or lack thereof, such as Jessie Couvreur's ['Tasma'] 'The Rubria Ghost' (1878).

Ernest Favenc's 'Doomed' (1899) faces colonial violence against Indigenous people directly. Five men involved in the senseless killing of an Aboriginal woman and her baby each die violent deaths as they are haunted by the woman's ghost. Before she dies, she swears vengeance on them. The men cannot understand her words, but it is through her anger that her meaning is translated. For Ken Gelder and Rachael Weaver, this is a key component to Australian Gothic:

> The genre turns towards precisely those stories of death and brutality that might not otherwise be told in colonial Australia, playing out one of the Gothic's most fascinating structural logics, the return of the repressed: quite literally, as graves are dug up, sacred burial grounds uncovered, murder victims are returned from the dead, secrets are revealed and past horrors are experienced all over again. (2007: 9)

In other stories, spectral women use their beauty to seduce the living. B. M. Croker's 'If You See Her Face' (1893) describes the recurring presence of a ghostly temple dancer who enacts revenge on an oppressive British colonial official. Croker's portrayal of a female Indian ghost reflects the popular interest in Indian women during the last decades of the nineteenth century. The legend surrounding the palace tells of a rajah who once tortured and disfigured a young woman whose ghost still dances at the palace and who causes the immediate death of any man who looks into her face. The woman finds a morbid pleasure in enacting her dance, changing it from a once objectifying and oppressed act into a gesture of female power over both Indian and British men.

Rabindranath Tagore's 'The Hungry Stones' (1895) features an Indian cotton duty collector who falls under a spell when he visits a 250-year-old palace. He learns that a Bedouin girl had been kidnapped and sold as a slave and that her spirit still haunts the property. The worker is seduced by the voice who cries from the stone floor seeking his help. In the story, reality and delusion become blurred as the man begins to regret his role as an office worker who has assimilated into British professional work and dress. Travelling back to the past and joining the spectral girl would mean that he 'would then be transformed into some unknown personage of a bygone age, playing my part in unwritten history; and my short English coat and tight breeches did not suit me in the least' (Tagore 1917: 15–16). However, there is also danger in following the mysterious voice, as previous men have gone insane after giving in to the fantasy. The worker narrowly escapes a similar fate, but Tagore suggests that his reality is far from satisfying and in either outcome some part of his identity would be lost. The supernatural is not a source for contentment but instead raises personal doubts in this story of innocence lost.

Colonial ghost stories also warn of the dangers to British children. This is a particular concern of Anglo-Indian stories due to the increasing numbers of British families living in India during the Raj period. In Alice Perrin's 'Chunia, Ayah' (1901), a trusted Indian nursemaid is reprimanded by the child's mother and kills the child out of anger. The ayah is then haunted and driven insane by the crying of the ghost child. Florence Marryat's 'Little White Souls' (1883) concerns a British Army colonel's pregnant wife who travels, along with her young daughter, to convalesce in the northern Indian hills (rather than home to England as her husband advises). Her Indian servants warn that their intended residence is haunted by the ghost of a white woman kidnapped by a rajah, but these warnings are dismissed.[2] The narrative upholds racist attitudes towards Indian servants who were seen as difficult, superstitious and manipulative, and Indian men who were perceived as violent, lustful and otherwise dangerous. The white woman was supposedly murdered along with her child and returns to take any children born in the house. However, as the title of Marryat's story suggests, she 'is not satisfied with the souls of black children' (Marryat 1883: 9) and takes the living woman's premature baby. In this case of spectral racism, the ghost upholds contemporary hierarchies that placed whiteness above blackness. These attitudes are upheld on a supernatural level as white children are preferred over black children, even in the afterlife.

Sickness and disease are prevalent in stories set in imperial regions and reflect the British fear of being unsuited for unfamiliar, 'hostile' climates, or, in other words, being somewhere they should not be. In B. M. Croker's 'Her Last Wishes' (1896), the ghost of a young woman who died during a cholera outbreak appears to a visitor who is staying in her former room. Her spirit walks to the site of her grave in a nearby garden, a place which has remained undiscovered since her hasty burial several years ago. In addition to the threat of disease in colonial regions, the story is full of anxieties surrounding British citizens who travel away from their home country and never return. Because the burial site is unknown, the woman is literally 'lost' in India, and it is only through the presence of her ghost that her identity can be restored.

As Britain's empire expanded in the second half of the nineteenth century, so-called 'crisis apparitions' emerged from imperial regions and were frequently connected to sudden deaths that might not otherwise be readily known to loved ones living far apart. R. C. Finucane classifies these ghosts as 'informative' rather than 'purposeless' and surveys instances when apparitions returned to the living with a message about their deaths. In 1848, for instance, a father looked out of his window and saw his son standing outside, only to learn later that his son had died in Australia at the exact time that he was sighted in England (Finucane 1984: 194–5). After its founding in 1882, the Society for Psychical Research published many reports of crisis apparitions who appeared to loved ones from the far reaches of empire. Rudyard Kipling's 'By Word of Mouth' (1887) relates the story of a happily married surgeon whose wife dies of typhoid and returns from the dead to tell an Indian servant that she will see her husband again in a month. Alice Perrin's 'The Summoning of Arnold' (1901) concerns a woman who keeps her promise to return to her husband in India. The husband is found dead from a chloroform overdose at the same time that a telegram arrives relating the message that his wife died while under chloroform on an operating table in England. Ellen Wood's 'A Mysterious Visitor' (1857) directly addresses the events of the Indian Rebellion as Louisa Ordie experiences a ghostly visitation from her husband who died during the Rebellion. These types of otherworldly stories from colonial regions relate to what Roger Luckhurst calls the imperial rumour. He connects the rumour to deeper anxieties about British rule in India and elsewhere as ghosts were seemingly able to move faster than any man-made form of communication, while apparitions which told of deaths from imperial violence became representative of British fears over failed governmental control in these regions (Luckhurst 2004: 199–201, 204–5). During the Victorian period and into the beginning decades of the twentieth century, ghosts transverse fictional and non-fictional narratives as they were used to describe troubled memories and lingering unrest stemming from colonialism.[3]

The (Post)Colonial Ghost Story: Looking Back, Looking Forward

John Lang's 'The Ghost Upon the Rail' (1859) begins, 'It was a winter's night – an Australian winter's night – in the middle of July' (1994: 1), placing the story firmly within a colonial setting while alerting the reader to its conscious shift away from a traditional ghost story set in Europe. This is a place where ghost stories are still told in winter, but the seasons are completely different, and so is the perspective. The ghost represents a return, and the colonial ghost story repeatedly returns to disturb and disrupt expectations. It upsets traditional components of the ghost story. It gives us a way of thinking about the ghost story that transcends traditional settings and scenarios while it likewise transcends geographic, national and cultural borders. If the British imperial agenda was focused on forward movement and growth of British influence in distant lands, then the colonial ghost story represents a pause, a looking backward or sideways to the troubled past and present.

As effective as colonial ghost stories are for revealing the anxieties of the time regarding the imperial project, there are inherent flaws. It is important to note that these stories ultimately do not provide a full picture of the horrors of empire. Although a completely accurate figure will never be known, the British Empire was responsible for the deaths of millions of people, in addition to causing the mass displacement of people from their homelands due to land partition, famine and war.[4] We come closest to recognising the harm done by empire by considering stories written by those who were themselves marginalised within British imperial culture: particularly Indigenous peoples and women, but also colonists and subjects who increasingly distanced themselves – whether voluntarily or involuntarily – from British identity, notably Australians who were transported as part of the penal system, as well as the Irish whose population suffered under years of misrule that led to famine and mass emigration. Regrettably, however, examples of contemporary colonial ghost stories written by Indigenous peoples are difficult to find. In his survey of Australian Gothic fiction, Gerry Turcotte has suggested that while the genre helped colonial writers find a distinctive Australian voice, the Gothic also served to silence Aboriginal people. He writes, 'It is not surprising that Aboriginal writers have tended not to use the Gothic mode since it has generally represented for them a disabling, rather than an enabling discourse' (2009: 285). Historically, Aboriginal people have been portrayed 'as the monstrous figures haunting the Australian landscape, spectres more frightening than any European demon, because they represented a physical threat to settlers and to theories of enlightenment which believed in the civilising presence of Whites' (2009: 285). This depiction of Indigenous people as the monstrous 'Other' likewise holds true for colonial ghost stories set in other major British colonies, particularly India and Africa. What is also evident in colonial fiction from the Victorian period is the blatant racism that is present and the repeated racist depictions of Indigenous cultures. Brantlinger notes:

> Imperialist discourse is inseparable from racism. Both express economic, political, and cultural domination [...] and both grew more virulent and

dogmatic as those forms of domination, threatened by rivals for empire and by nascent independence movements [...] began gradually to crumble in the waning decades of the century. (1988: 39)

So, while colonial stories may at times offer progressive critiques of imperialism through the figure of the ghost, they are still narratives presented from a privileged white point of view.

Stories by British women writers tend to be more sympathetic to Native peoples, and their narratives examine in more detail the harm done to both colonised and colonisers during the imperial era. These stories frequently resist official histories of empire – ones that claim that the imperial project was necessary for solidifying British power and influence – and instead focus on the more problematic effects of colonialism on both Indigenous and British individuals.[5] Yet even these more enlightened views of empire are influenced by racist attitudes towards those who are colonised. Non-white people are typically the sources of fear in these stories, just as they are in stories written by white men. Because of these attitudes, there will always be a blind spot when it comes to Victorian ghost stories that engage with colonialism.

Despite these shortcomings, the colonial ghost story remains a unique product of its time. It allows us to recognise tendencies within the Gothic mode to revisit and reinterpret the historical past through the figure of the ghost. William Hughes and Andrew Smith claim that 'the Gothic is, and has always been, *post*-colonial' and becomes the point where 'disruption accelerates into change, where the colonial encounter – or the encounter which may be read or interpreted through the colonial filter – proves a catalyst to corrupt, to confuse or to redefine the boundaries of power, knowledge and ownership' (2003: 1, italics in original). In the decades following the decline of the British Empire, the colonial ghost story was replaced by the postcolonial ghost story as previously colonised Indigenous peoples added their voices to the history of imperialism and its after-effects. The colonial story thus becomes its own ghost, its presence within the wider literary history of Victorian literature reminding us of how the ghost story has always revealed our troubling pasts as its spectres become symbolic embodiments of social inequalities, cultural anxiety, repressed guilt and historical trauma.

Notes

1. A heilaman is an Aboriginal wooden shield. Wambiloa is a type of wood.
2. In much the same way as ghost stories set in Europe, local people are the source of information about hauntings. However, the class consciousness

that causes many of these stories of local lore to be dismissed is heightened in colonial stories because there is racial bias in addition to other forms of class bias. Colonial servants are frequently dismissed as hysterical or overly sensitive. However, these warnings that are the result of generational knowledge about local sites known to be haunted are usually proved to be true. The British characters, as outsiders, are harmed by their decisions not to believe their servants.
3. The Indian Civil Service officer Malcolm Darling described the lasting influence of the Indian Rebellion in a 1906 letter as 'a kind of phantom standing behind official chairs' (cited in MacMillan 1988: 104). Edward Thompson, in his account of the Rebellion, *The Other Side of the Medal* (1926), likewise describes Indian hostility towards the British as a vengeful ghost: 'Right at the back of the mind of many an Indian the Mutiny flits as he talks with an Englishman – an unavenged and unappeased ghost' (32).
4. For more on these aspects of the British Empire, see Caroline Elkins's *Legacy of Violence: A History of the British Empire* (2022).
5. I discuss women's contributions to the colonial ghost story in *Women's Colonial Gothic Writing, 1850–1930: Haunted Empire* (2018).

Works Cited

Brantlinger, Patrick. *Rule of Darkness: British Literature and Imperialism, 1830–1914*. Ithaca and London: Cornell University Press, 1988.
Briefel, Aviva. *The Racial Hand in the Victorian Imagination*. Cambridge: Cambridge University Press, 2015.
Doyle, Arthur Conan. 'The Brown Hand', in *Round the Fire Stories*. Leipzig: Tauchnitz, 1908, pp. 284–303.
———. 'Lot No. 249', in *Round the Red Lamp*. London: Methuen, 1894, pp. 220–80.
Conrad, Joseph. 'Karain: A Memory', in *Tales of Unrest*. London: T. Fisher Unwin, 1898, pp. 1–79.
'Coo-ee' [William Sylvester Walker]. 'The Evil of Yelcomorn Creek', in Ken Gelder (ed.), *The Oxford Book of Australian Ghost Stories*. Melbourne: Oxford University Press, 1994, pp. 142–51.
Croker, B. M. 'If You See Her Face', in Richard Dalby (ed.), *'Number Ninety' and Other Ghost Stories*. Mountain Ash, Wales: Sarob Press, 2000, pp. 20–5.
———. 'Her Last Wishes', in Richard Dalby (ed.), *'Number Ninety' and Other Ghost Stories*. Mountain Ash, Wales: Sarob Press, 2000, pp. 49–57.
Edmundson, Melissa. *Women's Colonial Gothic Writing, 1850–1930: Haunted Empire*. Basingstoke: Palgrave Macmillan, 2018.
Elkins, Caroline. *Legacy of Violence: A History of the British Empire*. London: Bodley Head, 2022.
Favenc, Ernest. 'Doomed', in James Doig (ed.), *Ghost Stories and Mysteries*. Cabin John, MD: Wildside Press, 2012, pp. 192–5.
———. 'The Red Lagoon', in James Doig (ed.), *Ghost Stories and Mysteries*. Cabin John, MD: Wildside Press, 2012, pp. 140–3.
Finucane, Ronald C. *Appearances of the Dead: A Cultural History of Ghosts*. Buffalo, NY: Prometheus Books, 1984.

Gelder, Ken. 'Introduction', in Ken Gelder (ed.), *The Oxford Book of Australian Ghost Stories*. Melbourne: Oxford University Press, 1994, pp. ix–xviii.

Gelder, Ken and Rachael Weaver. 'The Colonial Australian Gothic', in Ken Gelder and Rachael Weaver (eds), *The Anthology of Colonial Australian Gothic Fiction*. Melbourne: Melbourne University Press, 2007, pp. 1–9.

Hay, Simon. *A History of the Modern British Ghost Story*. Basingstoke: Palgrave Macmillan, 2011.

Heron, E. and H. [Kate and Hesketh Prichard]. 'The Story of Baelbrow'. *Pearson's Magazine*, April 1898, pp. 366–75.

Hughes, William and Andrew Smith. 'Introduction: Defining the Relationship between Gothic and the Postcolonial'. *Gothic Studies*, vol. 5, no. 2, 2003, pp. 1–6.

Jacobs, W. W. 'The Monkey's Paw'. *Harper's Monthly Magazine*, September 1902, pp. 634–9.

Khair, Tabish. *The Gothic, Postcolonialism and Otherness: Ghosts from Elsewhere*. Basingstoke: Palgrave Macmillan, 2009.

Kipling, Rudyard. 'By Word of Mouth', in *Plain Tales from the Hills*. London: Macmillan, 1898, pp. 294–9.

Lang, John. 'The Ghost Upon the Rail', in Ken Gelder (ed.), *The Oxford Book of Australian Ghost Stories*. Melbourne: Oxford University Press, 1994, pp. 1–18.

Luckhurst, Roger. 'Knowledge, Belief and the Supernatural at the Imperial Margin', in Nicola Bown, Carolyn Burdett and Pamela Thurschwell (eds), *The Victorian Supernatural*. Cambridge: Cambridge University Press, 2004, pp. 197–216.

MacMillan, Margaret. *Women of the Raj*. New York: Thames & Hudson, 1988.

Marryat, Florence. 'Little White Souls', in *A Moment of Madness and Other Stories*, 3 vols. London: F. V. White & Co., 1883, pp. 213–43 (vol. 2), 1–19 (vol. 3).

Mulholland, Rosa. 'The Ghost at the Rath', in *The Haunted Organist of Hurly Burly and Other Stories*. London: Hutchinson, 1891, pp. 22–51.

———. 'The Lady Tantivy'. *Temple Bar*, vol. 113, January 1898, pp. 119–27.

Nisbet, Hume. 'The Haunted Station', in *The Haunted Station and Other Stories*. London: F. V. White & Co., 1894, pp. 1–33.

Owen, Francis. 'The Prophetess', in Greg Ioannou and Lynne Missen (eds), *Shivers: An Anthology of Canadian Ghost Stories*. Toronto: Stoddart Publishing, 1989, pp. 53–63.

Perrin, Alice. 'Caulfield's Crime', in Melissa Edmundson (ed.), *East of Suez*. Brighton: Victorian Secrets, 2011, pp. 125–32.

———. 'Chunia, Ayah', in Melissa Edmundson (ed.), *East of Suez*. Brighton: Victorian Secrets, 2011, pp. 159–64.

———. 'The Summoning of Arnold', in Melissa Edmundson (ed.), *East of Suez*. Brighton: Victorian Secrets, 2011, pp. 105–10.

Pratt, Mary Louise. *Imperial Eyes: Travel Writing and Transculturation*. London: Routledge, 2003.

Robins, G. M. 'The Man With No Face', in Richard Dalby (ed.), *The Relations and What They Related & Other Weird Tales*. Mountain Ash, Wales: Sarob Press, 2003, pp. 3–8.

Tagore, Rabindranath. 'The Hungry Stones', in *The Hungry Stones and Other Stories*. New York: The Macmillan Company, 1917, pp. 3–25.

'Tasma' [Jessie Couvreur]. 'The Rubria Ghost', in Ken Gelder (ed.), *The Oxford Book of Australian Ghost Stories*. Melbourne: Oxford University Press, 1994, pp. 85–93.

Thompson, Edward. *The Other Side of the Medal*. New York: Harcourt Brace, 1926.

Turcotte, Gerry. 'Australian Gothic', in Marie Mulvey-Roberts (ed.), *The Handbook of the Gothic*, 2nd edn. Basingstoke: Palgrave Macmillan, 2009, pp. 277–87.

'W. W.' [Mary Fortune]. 'Mystery and Murder', in Ken Gelder and Rachael Weaver (eds), *The Anthology of Colonial Australian Gothic Fiction*. Melbourne: Melbourne University Press, 2007, pp. 31–43.

———.'The Illumined Grave', in Ken Gelder (ed.), *The Oxford Book of Australian Ghost Stories*. Melbourne: Oxford University Press, 1994, pp. 19–35.

Wells, H. G. 'Pollock and the Porroh Man', in *The Short Stories of H. G. Wells*. London: E. Benn, 1927, pp. 483–501.

Wood, Ellen [Mrs. Henry Wood]. 'A Mysterious Visitor', in *Adam Grainger and Other Stories*. London: Macmillan, 1900, pp. 361–93.

Chapter 9

Religion
Alison Milbank

In an essay on supernatural horror, H. P. Lovecraft wrote that:

> occult believers are probably less effective than materialists in delineating the spectral and the fantastic, since to them the phantom world is so commonplace a reality that they tend to refer to it with less awe, remoteness, and impressiveness than do those who see in it an absolute and stupendous violation of the natural order. (Lovecraft 2013: 82)

For Victorian Christians, however, the presence of spectres was not at all commonplace and, indeed, just as problematic as for agnostics. Medieval ghosts in collections which circulated among monastics had an ethical purpose and metaphysical home in Purgatory; they came to warn or ask for prayers. The Reformation removed Purgatory, because it was too much associated with indulgences and salvation by 'works' but they lost with it an origin for the spectral visitant. Protestant theologians cited the warning of the dead Samuel summoned on King Saul's orders by the witch of Endor in 1 Samuel 28, who chastised the king, thus condemning any passage between the living and the dead, while some Reformation writers such as James VI and I in his *Demonologie* claimed it was not Saul at all but a demon who appeared (James R. 1597: 4). Such uncertainty made the ghost of Hamlet's father a problematic visitant at the time of the play's first production.

Although John Wesley, the founder of Methodism, whose family home suffered from poltergeist infestation, viewed ghost stories as reminders of the truth of the supernatural, and used them for pedagogical purposes, such belief had become an embarrassment for Methodists by the nineteenth century (Davies 1997: 257–8). Scandals like the hoax of the Cock Lane ghost of 1762 and the rationalism of much eighteenth-century Anglicanism and Dissent meant that Gothic novels, such as those of Ann Radcliffe, which are full of uncanny events, eventually explained their effects in terms of material causes, apart from her playfully historicist

Gaston de Blondeville (1826), in which the ghost was safely confined to the thirteenth century. Furthermore, Walter Scott, despite including ghost stories within his historical fiction, maintained that belief in ghosts was actually an effect of the loss of a belief in divine revelation, for 'unaided by revelation, it cannot be hoped that mere earthly reason should be able to form any rational or precise conjecture concerning the destination of the soul when parted from the body' (Scott 1830: 4). Radcliffe's authoritative governess in *A Sicilian Romance* (1790) does believe in revelation and advises her charges:

> 'I will not attempt to persuade you that the existence of such spirits is impossible. Who shall say that any thing is impossible to God? We know that he has made us, who are embodied spirits; he, therefore, can make unembodied spirits.' (Radcliffe 1992: 83)

Both Radcliffe's Madame de Menon and Scott, however, warn against ghost-seeing and Scott's spectres, like Radcliffe's, are historicised as part of folklore tradition. Like miracles, which Protestants believed ended with the apostolic age, ghosts had no part in the life of modern Christians. So, the Anglican cleric, Sabine Baring-Gould, for example, who had a strong interest in the ghost tradition, publishing *The Book of Werewolves* in 1865, referred to it as an 'ugly superstition' (Baring-Gould 1865: 116). He frequently presented his own ghost stories in the form of traditional folk tales, as, for example, 'Margery of Quether' (1891), in which a seventeenth-century vampire haunts the church bell-tower, or else he voiced them through an individual, deliberately omitting the kind of confirmatory evidence that would make belief inescapable.

These warnings against passage with the dead were not heeded, however, by the many people who attended séances in the Victorian period or formed the congregations for the developing spiritualist and Swedenborgian churches. These congregations might be fully Christian or quite unorthodox, but the spiritualist movement generally, which spread from the United States in the mid-century, was always religious in character, since it sought to communicate with the dead, and therefore assumed a life beyond the grave (Byrne 2010: 105–6). One of its most interesting features was the material nature of the visitants, who might make noises, manifest themselves visually or touch the participants. As long ago as 1766, the philosopher Emmanuel Kant had decried the visions of Emmanuel Swedenborg precisely because such experiences crossed the divide between phenomenal experience and the spiritual and unknown noumenal (Kant 1992: 357–8). Like British Deists and Unitarians, Kant believed morality more important than fear of hell in determining human action. Hell was noticeably absent from the post-mortem experiences of the spirits conjured by spiritualistic mediums and their physical manifestations have more to do with establishing the reality of an afterlife, which is just that: an after-life continuation of earthly existence rather than a qualitatively different mode of being. No wonder that Henry J. Raymond charged the movement as being 'sheer naturalism under an assumed spiritual form' (cited in Bann 2009: 669).

Yet during the Victorian period, writers of faith contributed with distinction to the ghost story genre and developed it as a mode of theological reflection. As Zoë Lehmann Imfeld has shown, such tales 'suspend ontology and open a space in which theological truth claims are at once immanent and strange' (Imfeld 2016: 167). Although for Protestants one's eternal destiny was fixed at death as either heaven or hell, the supernatural tale provided an opportunity to explore Roman Catholic ideas of a mediatory realm in which a purgatorial purpose might be entertained, where the dead themselves might be suspended, with the possibility of hope and transformation beyond the grave. Moreover, the tendency to speak of the dead as 'sleeping' drew attention to the temporal gap between death and the resurrection, during which the body – and in some iterations of Protestant theology also the soul – slept, awaiting the call of the trumpet of the Last Judgement. Victorian writers were increasingly attracted to belief in some sort of consciousness in this liminal state, including an awareness of events on earth (Wheeler 1994: 68–81). The ghost story therefore had the potential to become a site for exploration of death and judgement, but equally of memory and forgiveness. It allowed the dead to speak but equally expressed their balked attempts at communication.

Open Doors: The Return of Purgatory

This failure to communicate is particularly to the fore in the supernatural tales of Margaret Oliphant, who suffered a number of bereavements, being widowed young and losing children in adulthood, and experienced for herself the distress of loss of connection with the dead. Her Little Pilgrim series of stories from the 1880s begins as a way of narrating the passage from death to the other world, and includes her recently deceased close friend, Eleanor Clifford, as one of the characters. She makes the failure to be able to speak to the living an actual punishment: '"We are here for that; this is the fire that purges us, – to see at last what we have done, and the true aspect of it, and to know the cruel wrong, yet never be able to make amends"' (Oliphant 1885: 45–6). It is likely that Oliphant is responding here to Elizabeth Gaskell's most celebrated tale, 'The Old Nurse's Story' of 1852. In Gaskell's tale, young Miss Furnivall, some years in the past, had betrayed the existence of her sister's clandestine child to her father out of jealousy. They were then thrown out of the house and the child died of cold on the moors, with her spectre now crying for admittance at the window, seeking to lure the little girl now living there in the care of the old nurse. Events repeat when the door is broken open and the spectres of father, daughter and child reappear in the house and re-enact the traumatic scene. This time, Miss Furnivall shows mercy and tries to intercede with her father who is about to strike the ghostly child, but the ghost of her younger self then appears 'with a look of relentless hate and triumphant scorn' (Gaskell 2008: 21). The spectres depart and Miss Furnivall is left paralysed, turning her face to the wall and muttering constantly, 'What is done in youth can never be undone in age' (21). The supernatural mimics the treadmill of bitter memory and regret for events which can never be reversed.

Although Oliphant's 'Old Lady Mary' (1884) suggests that the cycles of regret that torment Gaskell's protagonist can continue into the afterlife, she develops her narrative more hopefully. For Lady Mary is given permission to make the dangerous passage back to earth to observe the life of her god-daughter whose future comfort she had failed to secure, and who has been left destitute. She hopes to communicate the knowledge that a letter conveying her intentions to leave everything to 'little Mary' (Oliphant 1885: 113) lies in a secret drawer in her cabinet. Yet although the child to whom Mary is now governess can see the revenant, Mary herself cannot, leading old Lady Mary to despair. The existence of an unregarded spectre, forced to view her beloved Mary working as a servant in her former home, is evidently part of her purgation, especially since she must haunt the great house as an interloper where she once ruled as mistress. The younger Mary too is distraught by the reports of the haunting and her inability to see her beloved Lady Mary: '"Unseen! Unseen! Whatever we do!"' (208). Yet as she expresses her love and loyalty, the spectre of Lady Mary hears her words and returns to the afterlife, knowing she has been forgiven. This reconciliatory experience enables her purgation, for the story assumes that moral growth and transformation are possible even after death, and she has learnt from her suffering.

The availability of redemption not just in this life but beyond the grave became a concern among some liberal Christians of the period, as they questioned the punitive and eternal nature of divine judgement. F. D. Maurice's tentative questioning of the eternity of hell in his *Theological*

Essays of 1853 lost him his position at King's College, London but was highly influential on the broad church. Writers like Charles Kingsley took Dante's Purgatory of moral transformation and elided it with the punishments of hell to turn the whole of the afterlife to one of development. The poet Dante's journey through the afterlife became a model for Oliphant and is the source for the purgatorial flames in 'Old Lady Mary'. She employed his purgatorial theology of poetic justice and reconciliation to structure her tales of haunting. Lady Mary even essays a delicate Dantesque joke when she first joins the afterlife, about in which of Dante's *cantiche* she has ended up. Oliphant had been raised a Free Presbyterian, but worshipped as an Anglican and she corresponded with F. D. Maurice. She even imports Maurice's hopeful theology into a story with a Scottish setting, 'The Open Door' (1882), which again appears to be in dialogue with Gaskell, for it has a child at its heart who can hear the cries for admittance of a spectre and who is mortally affected by it, just like the little girl in 'The Old Nurse's Story'. The ghost is a boy estranged from his mother who constantly tries to get her to open what is now a mere ruinous archway.

Oliphant's narrator, desperate to lay the ghost and aid his son's recovery, calls in Dr Moncrieff, the local minister, who recognises the voice and cries out: '"She's no here. You'll find her with the Lord. Go there and seek her, not here … He'll let you in, Though it's late"' (Oliphant 1885: 73–4). Then he prays: '"Lord, let that woman there draw him inower [in over]. Let her draw him inower!"' (75). The door between living and dead, heaven and hell, lies open here, like the ruined doorway at which the ghostly Willie throws himself. And there is always hope of salvation, even beyond death, and it is here even mediated through the mother's agency as one of the blessed. When the narrator expresses surprise at finding these Roman Catholic views on the lips of a Presbyterian minister, Moncrieff replies, '"There is just one thing that I am certain of – and that is the loving kindness of God"' (77). Although human freedom means alienation from God and hell are realities, divine compassion renders redemption always possible.

The trope of the open door appears very frequently in stories of this period, and I would argue that it often embodies this idea of theological hope. Charlotte Riddell also wrote a story entitled 'The Open Door' in 1882, which is typical of her style in its prosaic, realist setting and jaunty city clerk protagonist, who stays in a haunted house, abandoned by its owner, to earn some money. A door on the ground floor stands mysteriously open, no matter how often it is closed or locked. It comes to represent the opening of a passage between this world and the next, as in the popular novel by Elizabeth Phelps, *The Gates Ajar* (1868), in which descriptions of the afterlife as a continuation of earthly society, with concerts and family relations, comfort a war widow. Like Phelps, Riddell's moral transformation and growth are focused on the earthly living protagonist, but his development is brought about by the seemingly ghostly incursion. Living criminals are outmanoeuvred by the ghost of the man they murdered, who enacts the justice of Providence.

The apogee of this congress and exchange between living and dead can be found in Oliphant's *A Beleaguered City*, a novella published in 1880. Set in Semur in Burgundy, it describes the incursion of the dead citizens, who expel the living townspeople as a judgement on their selfishness and grasping mercenary character and reoccupy their old city. Presented like a *procès-verbal* in terms of legal testimony, it is narrated in part by the secular mayor, who must organise and house the expelled families. Eventually the dead withdraw, and the mayor returns to his house to find his dead relatives have reorganised the furniture but also left an olive wreath. The art of the story lies in the way that the roles of living and dead are reversed, with the funeral wreath now the tribute of the dead to those still alive. Its power also comes from its realist technique, which makes the reader accept the events as wholly believable, especially given the free-thinking mayoral narrator, the furniture removals witnessed in the various homes, and the novella's pessimistic conclusion. A man left in the hospital pretends to have seen visions, which fool the pious, but life continues as before. So ironically, the dead have grown in wisdom and insight, but the living do not change. The story reworks the Lukan parable of Lazarus and Dives, where the deceased rich man now in torment asks that Lazarus return to warn his descendants, only to be told by Abraham, '"If they hear not Moses and the prophets, neither will they be persuaded, though one rose from the dead"' (Luke 16:30–1).

As in Riddell's story, the dead demonstrate their presence by opening doors:

> 'They were now all open, even the door of my wife's room of which I kept always the key, and where no one entered but myself; the windows also were open. I looked out upon the Grande Rue, and all the other houses were like mine.' (Oliphant 1988: 26)

Despite the negative ending in which the dead do not manage to change the future, they have shown that there is an opening between modes of existence, and the fact of the failure of the dead in enabling justice only aids the reality effect of this passage between worlds.

The Appeal of Catholicism

As well as the broad-church concern with hope beyond the grave of redemption, and congress between living and dead, another reason for renewed attention to Catholic doctrine was the growing prominence of Catholicism in Britain following the Roman Catholic Relief Act of 1829, which removed barriers to worship and allowed Catholics to sit in Parliament. Catholics were more numerous in England, Scotland and Wales as a result of Irish immigration and in 1850 Pope Pius IX restored the diocesan hierarchy in England, with sees and bishops. The French Revolution and Napoleon's persecution of religious orders had also brought monks and nuns to seek refuge in Britain in the early nineteenth century, while the Oxford Movement in the Church of England led to the creation of Anglican religious orders. I have already mentioned that ghost story exchange was a medieval monastic pastime, and due to the fact that the English gentry often lived in former abbeys and priories as a result of Reformation land grabs or royal gifts, monks and nuns were ubiquitous in traditional supernatural tales, haunting the homes of their usurpers or cursing their descendants, as in Charlotte Riddell's novel *The Nun's Curse* (1888). This novel was set in her native Ireland, where Catholics had long been an oppressed majority, and had a strongly religious purpose, in which a range of characters, both Protestant and Catholic, are judged by their degree of mercy and generosity. The nun's curse comes true in the appointment of a rabidly republican parish priest as a result of Protestant misdeeds. Riddell was an Anglican, but she tended to use the supernatural elements in her novels and stories as modes of moral realism, whereby a haunting might execute justice on the reprobate, but on the other hand might help the merciful and generous to providentially directed good outcomes.

The Oxford Movement sought to restore the Catholic inheritance to the Reformed Church of England in terms of ritual and spirituality and imported elements of Catholic practice such as prayers for the dead and private confession as well as religious orders. Its adherents were sometimes tempted to go further, so that some well-known Oxford Movement figures, of whom the most famous was John Henry Newman, became Roman Catholics. One particularly effective ghost story which plays upon the aesthetic and ritualistic appeal of the Catholic Church to Anglicans is 'A Midsummer Night's Marriage', by J. Meade Falkner, published in 1896, at a time when several literary figures associated with the literary *fin de siècle* 'went over to Rome', including Ernest Dowson in 1891, Aubrey Beardsley in 1897 and Wilde himself on his deathbed in 1900 (Mascurel-Murray 2012: 105).

In Falkner's story, after buying an antique ring, a regency undergraduate finds himself waylaid on a journey, taking shelter in an ancient house, ominously called Laffontine Abbey, and thus a former monastery. He stumbles upon a funeral in its chapel and gradually he realises that what is being celebrated is not an Anglican rite but a Catholic requiem mass, his primary cues being that the service is in Latin and prayers are addressed to the saints and angels. The beauty and the power of the ancient rite performed amid clouds of incense is plangently evoked, but because in the nineteenth century Catholic services were still in Latin, the protagonist fails to realise that he is not watching a contemporary requiem but rather one in the Elizabethan period, when Catholicism was proscribed and the celebration of mass celebrated only in secret. Hints of the sixteenth century in the dress and stance of the congregation are interpreted by the protagonist in historicist terms as reminding him of 'kneeling statues of alabaster he had seen on ancient funerary monuments' (Falkner 1896: 856). He even notes with antiquarian interest his ring's crest on the pall over the coffin. That same night he falls in love with the daughter of the house, Cecilia Bejant, and marries her, only to awake next day without his ring and lying on the altar step of an empty ruin.

The recusant past then shadows his life ever after, so when years later he seeks to marry, the service is interrupted by the ghostly Jesuit who performed the ceremony which joined him to Cecilia (who died in 1580); he converts to Catholicism and the long-dead Jesuit appears once more to conduct his funeral. The story offers a hospitable space in which the attraction of Catholicism can be explored and past and present united, but the spectral nature of the rites consigns the old faith to an irrecoverable past, however nostalgically conceived. This is the antiquarian and ecclesiastical ghost story, which will find its apogee in the work of Falkner's fellow scholar, M. R. James, in the next century, in which archaeological discoveries of manuscripts, whistles or equally ancient items, often in church or monastic settings, make the protagonist porous to supernatural incursions of a demonic nature.

The materiality of the object that provokes the haunting in 'A Midsummer Night's Marriage' allies it with the physicality of the other world called up by the spiritualists. Jennifer Bann has argued that the disembodied hand evoked by the medium is 'a literal metonymy' for the movement, and she argues that these ghostly objects only gain in agency throughout the later part of the century (Bann 2009: 670). M. R. James will have a similar hairy demonic hand touch his manuscript in

'Canon Alberic's Scrapbook' (1895). In Falkner's 'Midsummer's Night Marriage' it is the ring which causes the haunting and literally weds its owner to the past. It disappears after its use in the marriage and is presumably taken by Cecilia to her grave. Does Falkner's antiquarianism also wed him to a past without any relation to the present? He explores this more fully in his Gothic novel *The Nebuly Coat* (1903), where Catholicism is honoured but the high church worship of the Anglican choral tradition allows some passage to the future.

An equally engaged approach to Catholicism in the ghost story is taken in another supernatural tale by Elizabeth Gaskell, which allows her to move beyond the moral stasis of 'The Old Nurse's Story'. As someone brought up in the liberal tradition of Unitarianism and married to a minister, she might have been expected to take a negative view of the Roman Catholic Church, but her story 'The Poor Clare', originally published in instalments in the December issues of *Household Words* in 1856, is wholly sympathetic in its treatment of convent life, in stark contrast to the anti-Catholicism of her editor, Charles Dickens, who had been vituperative about papal interference after the restoration of bishoprics (Dickens 1850: 193–6).

Like Falkner, she provides a convincing historic setting, which in this case is the recusant area of Lancashire in the Forest of Bowland, which to this day has some Catholic villages and primary schools. A nurse, Bridget Fitzgerald, brought across from Ireland when her mistress weds a Jacobite squire, curses a visiting aristocrat, Sir Philip Gisborne, because he destroys her dog, Mignon, who had been her only companion after the disappearance of her daughter overseas. Calling down the saints as witness that the poor and helpless have the armies of heaven behind them, she curses Gisborne:

> 'You shall live to see the creature you love best, and who alone loves you, – ay, a human creature, but as innocent and fond as my poor, dead darling – you shall see this creature, for whom death would be too happy, become a terror and a loathing to all, for this blood's sake.' (Gaskell 2008: 46)

The supernatural enters in the specific and prophetic nature of the curse, which does indeed bring about a living punishment in the haunting of Sir Philip's daughter by a demonic doppelgänger; it makes her a terror to herself and someone rejected by her father. Yet the irony of the curse is that it completely rebounds on Bridget, in that the girl is the issue of Sir Philip and her own lost daughter. Gaskell will have had the general Jepthah in mind from the Judges 11, who prays for victory in battle, vowing to sacrifice the first creature that crosses his path on his return;

this proves to be his own daughter, whom he then has killed to fulfil the vow. Similarly horrified by this outcome of her curse falling on her granddaughter, Bridget seeks to atone by joining one of the most austere of religious orders, the Poor Clares, who devote themselves to good works and rely on their neighbours for sustenance. None of this penance avails, however, and the curse is not lifted; for this reason, Rebecca Styler views the tale as one exhibiting a moral rationalism, typical of much Unitarian thought (Styler 2010: 50). Yet Gaskell is no rationalist and is much more attuned here to Catholic sacramental theology. For when Bridget called up the curse it was certainly not the saints and angels who made it happen. Bridget herself confirms this when she replies to the narrator who begs her to lift the curse: '"I defy the demon I have called up. Leave me to wrestle with it"' (Gaskell 2008: 72). It is the powers of evil who have latched on to her wish and created the double; they are both external demonic forces but are also within her. Indeed, Lucy's double existence as both innocent girl and the demon-soul simulacrum is an embodiment of her grandmother's divided will, which cannot truly forgive. 'The evil powers had stricken her dumb ... when she approached confession' (76).

In Catholic theology, unless a confession is sincere, absolution is not possible. And even if it is, there remains the stain of sin and the effects of one's actions, which must be dealt with. Gaskell's Dante study would have apprised her of this sacramental theology, which prevents Guido da Montefeltro from salvation in *Inferno* 27. Only when Bridget, now Sister Magdalen, by a quirk of circumstance finds herself nursing the wounded Sir Philip in a Dutch uprising against their Austrian rulers, does she truly forgive and in so doing expel the demon she has inadvertently conjured. In an act of self-sacrifice, she denies herself food to offer what she has to Gisborne, after which she can confess properly, and the curse is lifted. It seems that Gaskell can imagine the possibility of reconciliation and transformation in a Catholic theological register; outside it, the laws of moral cause and effect are seemingly inexorable, as in the despair of Miss Furnivall at her inability to change the past in 'The Old Nurse's Story'. These theological explorations suggest that Gaskell finds the moralism of Unitarian ethics somewhat unsatisfactory and that she views evil as more complex than individual responsibility, as it creates webs of suffering and injustice.

My third exponent of Catholic theology in the ghost story, J. Sheridan Le Fanu, is usually discussed either as the Protestant Anglo-Irish inheritor of a guilty history or as the heterodox employer of Swedenborg's spiritual cosmology in the ghost stories collected in *In a Glass Darkly* (1872). Swedenborg's Platonism makes this world the plaything of the more real world of spirits, who can possess and direct human agents, as in the haunting of Reverend Mr Jennings by the demonic monkey in 'Green Tea'. Another of the tales in this collection, 'The Familiar', however, has a strong investment in what are broadly Catholic ideas of purgatory, transformation through confession and penitence as well as the intercessory role of the saints shared by Oliphant and Gaskell.

Captain Barton is haunted by the ghost of a sailor he had caused to be flogged so severely he died of his wounds. This man now dogs his footsteps and even sends him a letter in the post, part of the turn to the physicality of supernatural incursion noted in spiritualist practice and ghost stories alike. As with Gaskell, Oliphant and Riddell, Le Fanu's metaphysics makes the haunting undeniably real within the frame of the narrative, so other witnesses see the spectre and the story ends with his presence registered physically as a 'deep indenture, as if caused by a heavy pressure' (Le Fanu 1993: 80) at the foot of the bed of the dead Barton, causing his death by fright. Barton had been an Enlightenment free thinker, but his haunting turns him into an appalled believer:

> 'I *know*,' continued Barton, with increasing excitement, 'that there is a God – a dreadful God – and that retribution follows guilt, in ways the most mysterious and stupendous – by agencies the most inexplicable and terrific, – there is a spiritual system ... malignant and implacable, and omnipotent, under whose persecutions I am, and have been, suffering the torments of the damned!' (Le Fanu 1993: 60)

The deity thus evoked is a dark version of the *Deus absconditus* of Calvinism, in which God's justice cannot be anything but inimical to evil and in which his purposes are inscrutable: 'As we are all vitiated by sin, we cannot but be hateful to God, and that not from tyrannical cruelty, but the strictest justice' (Calvin 1960: Book 3, 23, 3, 950). Barton articulates a typically Calvinist radical determinism, in which God's secret counsel is the cause of all events, and other agents are just that – his instruments.

Although there were Calvinist evangelicals in Britain in the nineteenth century, Irish Anglicanism had a stronger Calvinist element, embodied in its articles, which supported the terrified expression of its doctrines expressed by Barton. And yet his heart is hardened in the sense that despite his best efforts, he cannot pray, as if a demon holds his hands down. And indeed, Satan can be an instrument of God's judgement and testing in Reformation theology. Barton begs the Church of Ireland cleric to whom he confesses all this for 'vicarious supplication – by the intercession of the good' (Le Fanu 1993: 64). This prayer the priest offers to perform, but rather dismisses Barton's experience and the spectre as a self-produced imaginary projection, in typical eighteenth-century rationalist style.

Where a Catholic spirituality enters this unpromisingly Protestant narrative is in the form of a dream, which Barton believes to be a true vision, in which he finds himself in a heavenly landscape, lying with his head in the lap of the daughter of his persecutor, the 'familiar'. We learn later that he had seduced this young woman, who had then been treated harshly by her father and had died broken-hearted. In the dream she provides consolation and intercession as she sings a song 'that told, I know not how – whether by words or by harmonies – of all of my life – all that is past, and all that is still to come' (Le Fanu 1993: 75). He awakes comforted, 'for I knew that I was forgiven much' (76).

So, in complete opposition to the Calvinist nightmare, this dream offers the Catholic intercession of the blessed dead and presents the death Barton must face as a purgatorial ordeal but one that suggests he is not damned but forgiven. His demise takes place when a pet owl flies through the window of the room in which he lies on his sickbed. Owls are figures for desolation in the Old Testament, as in Jeremiah 50.39: 'And the owls shall dwell therein: And it shall be no more inhabited for ever.' In Swedenborg, spirits often take the form of birds or animals (Swedenborg 1873: 209), and here it appears that the owl is the form of the Familiar himself, who brings about Barton's death. Yet Barton's servant hears another calm voice in the room, so that we imagine the presence of the dead girl moving a candle across the room to accompany the body, as was the custom in watching over the dead. Spirits of the father and daughter then enact the roles of the guardian angel and demon who traditionally fight over the dying person, only the outcome has already been decided. The chapter is entitled 'Requiescat', a shortening for the grave epitaph, 'may he rest in peace', which is used primarily by Catholics and Anglicans who accept prayer for the dead. The phrase is used several times in the Latin of the Catholic requiem rite. It suggests a hopeful eternal outcome for the penitent Barton.

To conclude, while the Gothic novel of the eighteenth century negotiated the rationalism of the Enlightenment by staging seemingly real hauntings, which provoked a hesitation about the status of an event that crossed epistemological boundaries, but was either shown to have a natural cause, or else confined to the marvellous, as befitted rational Christianity, the liminal space of Victorian investigation is quite different. This essay has revealed a concern with questioning the absolute divide between heaven and hell among writers from a variety of Protestant denominations, from Oliphant's Presbyterianism to Elizabeth Gaskell's Unitarianism. Paradoxically, a Catholic-inflected theology allows them an open door between living and dead and between salvation and damnation, and the ghost story with its passage between modes of existence is the perfect genre for this exploration. I have argued elsewhere, in contrast to Hillis Miller and other literary historians, that the Victorian supernatural tale becomes more, not less, religious across the century and increasingly hospitable to Catholic practices and sensibility (Milbank 2018: 305). The challenge of materialist accounts of reality forces Protestants to recover a sense of the sacramental in order to allow the material to open to the transcendent and link natural and supernatural worlds. Le Fanu is a strong exponent of this pan-sacramentality, making his Swedenborgian Dr Hesselius affirm that 'the entire natural world is but the ultimate expression of that spiritual world from which, and in which alone, it has its life' (Le Fanu 1993: 8). Such a metaphysics re-enchants the material, so that objects are restored to full presence, for good or ill, and the human subject moves easily, whether aware of it or not, between 'his own hall-door to the light of day, or through the gates of darkness to the caverns of the dead' (Le Fanu 1993: 5).

Works Cited

Bann, Jennifer. 'Ghostly Hands and Ghostly Agency: The Changing Figure of the Nineteenth-Century Spectre'. *Victorian Studies*, vol. 51, no. 4, 2009, pp. 663–85.
Baring-Gould, Sabine. *The Book of Werewolves*. London: Smith and Elder, 1865.
Baring-Gould, Sabine. *Margery of Quether and Other Stories*. London: Methuen, 1891.
Byrne, Georgina. *Modern Spiritualism and the Church of England, 1850–1939*. Woodbridge: Boydell & Brewer, 2010.
Calvin, Jean. *Institutes of the Christian Religion*, 2 vols, edited by John T. McNeill. Louisville: Westminster John Knox Press, 1960.
Davies, Owen. 'Methodism, the Clergy, and the Popular Belief in Witchcraft and Magic'. *History*, vol. 52, no. 266, 1997, pp. 252–65.
Dickens, Charles. 'A Crisis in the Affairs of John Bull'. *Household Words*, vol. 2, 23 November 1850, pp. 193–6.
Falkner, J. Meade. 'A Midsummer Night's Marriage'. *The National Review*, vol. 97, 1896, pp. 851–71.
Gaskell, Elizabeth. 'The Poor Clare', in *Tales of Mystery and the Macabre*, edited by David Stuart Davies. Ware: Wordsworth, 2008, pp. 37–84.
Holy Bible, Authorised Version. Cambridge: Cambridge University Press, n.d.
Imfeld, Zoë Lehmann. *The Victorian Ghost Story and Theology: From Le Fanu to James*. Basingstoke: Palgrave Macmillan, 2016.
James Rex. *Demonologie, in the Form of a Dialogue*. London: James Waldegrave, 1597.
Kant, Emmanuel. *Dreams of a Spirit-Seer Elucidated by the Dreams of Metaphysics*, in *Theoretical Philosophy, 1755–70*, translated and edited by

David Walford and Ralf Meerbote. Cambridge: Cambridge University Press, 1992.
Le Fanu, Sheridan. *In a Glass Darkly*, edited by Robert Tracy. Oxford: Oxford University Press, 1993.
Lovecraft, H. P. *Supernatural Horror in Fiction*, foreword by Alex Rurtagic. Abergele: Wermod and Wermod, 2013.
Mascurel-Murray, Claire. 'Conversions to Catholicism at the fin de siècle: A Spiritual and Literary Genealogy'. *Cahiers victoriens et édouardiens*, vol. 76, 2012, pp. 105–25.
Milbank, Alison. *God and the Gothic: Religion, Romance and Reality in the English Literary Tradition*. Oxford: Oxford University Press, 2018.
Oliphant, Margaret. *Two Stories of the Seen and Unseen: The Open Door, Old Lady Mary*. Edinburgh: William Blackwood, 1885.
Oliphant, Margaret. *A Beleaguered City and Other Stories*, edited by Merryn Williams. Oxford: Oxford University Press, 1988.
Radcliffe, Ann. *A Sicilian Romance*, edited by Alison Milbank. Oxford: Oxford University Press, 1992.
Scott, Sir Walter. *Lectures on Witchcraft and Demonology*. London: John Murray, 1830.
Styler, Rebecca. 'The Problem of "Evil" in Elizabeth Gaskell's Gothic Tales'. *Gothic Studies*, vol. 12, no. 1, 2010, pp. 33–50.
Swedenborg, Emmanuel. *Arcana Caelestia*, 5 vols. New York: Swedenborg Publishing, 1873.
Wheeler, Michael. *Heaven, Hell and the Victorians*. Cambridge: Cambridge University Press, 1994.

Chapter 10

The Victorian American Ghost Story
Jeffrey Andrew Weinstock

Ghost stories inherently reflect anxieties concerning loss and death, and desires for an afterlife and justice. The expression of these general anxieties and desires, however, is inevitably shaped by culturally specific contexts and the personal experiences and tastes of individual authors. This chapter will examine how the ghost story by American authors between roughly 1837 and 1901 was conditioned by and used as a vehicle to address issues including the subordination and abuse of women and children, slavery and its aftermath, spiritualism, and epistemological uncertainty introduced by postbellum scientific advances and the Victorian 'crisis of faith' (see, for example, Meyer 1975).

As Anthony Mandal observes in a British context, the Victorian period 'witnessed the emergence of a mass readership and the proliferation of publications to meet the appetites of its new audiences, underpinned by sophisticated new print technologies and circuits of dissemination' (2018: 29). This was true of the United States as well, the population of which, according to US Census data, increased more than fourfold, from 17 million in 1840 ('Pop Culture: 1840') to 76 million in 1900 ('Pop Culture: 1900'). Keeping pace with the growing population in general and of urban centres in particular, and assisted by improvements in printing and papermaking technologies, modes of transportation, reductions in postal rates and increases in literacy rates, US magazines proliferated at an unprecedented rate during the Victorian period. John Tebbel notes that, at the beginning of the nineteenth century, there were only about a dozen American magazines, while by 1825 there was nearly one hundred (1969: 169). Twenty-five years later, in 1850, there were about 600 and Frank Luther Mott estimates that for every magazine operating in 1850 another seven or so had failed over the preceding two and a half decades – which means that some 4,000 or 5,000 magazines in total were published during the period (1938: 342). Following the American Civil War, which lasted from 1861 to 1865, the United States experienced another boom in magazine publishing. Susan Belasco Smith and Kenneth M. Price explain that, by the 1870s, the number of cheap, weekly magazines in the United States had expanded to over 4,000, with a combined circulation of more than 10 million – a figure equal to a third of the total US population in 1870 (1995: 5–6). During this period, established literary magazines such as *Harper's New Monthly Magazine* and *Atlantic* (later, *Atlantic Monthly*), and women's magazines such as *Godey's Lady's Book*, were joined by other widely circulating magazines such as *Harper's Bazar* (later *Harper's Bazaar*), *Overland Monthly*, *Scribner's Monthly*, *Ladies Home Journal* and *McClure's Magazine*.

In keeping with sensation fiction in general, ghost stories tend to thrive in short form where they can most effectively generate affect, and these US magazines were hospitable homes for ghost stories by American authors. Competing against one another, magazines were hungry for content and ghost stories, perennially popular, were in vogue. In addition, many American authors focused on magazine publication during the period since they remained at a disadvantage in the literary marketplace where longer forms were frequently pirated due to the absence of an international copyright law. This situation created an unfair playing field since American book and magazine publishers could simply pirate British and European titles without paying the authors at all. Market forces, therefore, together with demographic shifts, technological improvement and reading tastes resulted in the proliferation of the American ghost story across the Victorian period.

One other demographic shift pertinent to the development of the Victorian American ghost story worth noting at the outset is the increasing role played by female authors in the genre's development. Authorship in the early American republic was primarily the 'province of gentlemen and clergymen' (Mott 1938: 341) and generally relied upon finding a patron to fund one's writing (Douglas 1977: 96). As the American literary marketplace developed and expanded in the first half of the nineteenth century, women began to play an increasingly central role in commercial publication, coming to the fore in what has been referred to by Fred Lewis Pattee as the 'feminine fifties' (see Pattee 1940) during which authors such as Maria Susanna Cummins, Fanny Fern and E. D. E. N. Southworth dominated the literary marketplace – leading to Nathaniel Hawthorne's famous gripe that 'America is now wholly given over to a damned mob of scribbling women' (see Frederick 1975: 231). Following the Civil War, many more women turned to writing by necessity. The number of men killed during the war is generally estimated at 620,000 – one out of four soldiers that went to war never made it home, and many that did returned physically or mentally impaired ('Civil War

Causalities', 2023). Forced to make a living on their own to support themselves and their families, many women therefore turned to one of the few career options available to them – writing – and the ghost story was an established and popular form. According to Jessica Amanda Salmonson, as much as 70 per cent of supernatural fiction published in American magazines during the Victorian period was by women (1989: x). Ghost stories by women thus proliferated in good measure because they were saleable.

Turning now to the stories themselves, it is important to bear in mind that Victorian American ghost stories were primarily published for profit. While some could be didactic – preaching about the marvels of the world to come or, alternatively, chastening the overly credulous – and some could be extremely artful, as with the late Victorian works of Henry James and Edith Wharton (the latter of which published mostly during the Edwardian period), many were not particularly high-minded as they sought to cash in on a popular genre. Nevertheless, especially when considered together as a body, they offer insight into the 'zeitgeist' of the period and can be grouped into three broad and interconnected categories: tales of abuse and exploitation, contemplations of the meaning of death and the afterlife, and explorations of the limits of human knowledge.

Ghost stories in general often find their basis in situations of abuse, exploitation and victimisation that culminate in death, and the ghost in such tales then manifests either to reveal the crime or to seek revenge directly on the abuser. As such, these tales are forms of wish fulfilment: they express the desire for a universe in which crime is revealed and punished – and for disadvantaged populations in the nineteenth century, spectral revenge was perhaps the best that could be hoped for. This is certainly the case where disempowered women and children were concerned and a large body of Victorian American ghost stories addresses the forms of injustice patriarchal culture excuses and facilitates.

A central figure here is Mary E. Wilkins Freeman.[1] Best known as a regionalist author whose fiction depicted the 'lives, experiences and conditions of lower classes and working people, especially women, in rural new England' ('Mary E. Wilkins Freeman', n.d.), Freeman produced a number of fine Gothic tales that participate with her other works in questioning 'the power structures limiting the roles and choices of her female protagonists' (Diederich 2011: 21). *The Wind in the Rose Bush and Other Stories of the Supernatural*, a volume collecting together her supernatural tales and published by Freeman in 1903, includes several tales of ghostly women and children. Interestingly, Freeman in her ghost stories tends to emphasise not the unchecked brutality of men, which is often the focus of her more realistic writings, but the selfishness or hardheartedness of women. This is the case in the collection's title story, 'The Wind in the Rose Bush', and in 'The Lost Ghost', both first published in Freeman's 1903 collection of supernatural stories.

The protagonist in 'The Wind in the Rose Bush' is an unmarried woman named Rebecca Flint who travels from Michigan to the geographically ambiguous town of Ford Village to take custody of her young niece Agnes three years after the death of Rebecca's brother John. Her biological mother having passed away, Agnes has been living with her stepmother, Emeline. When Rebecca arrives at John's home, Agnes is not present and Emeline is evasive. Strange things then begin to happen: a rose bush shakes violently although the air is still, Rebecca catches a glimpse of a girl she believes to be Agnes but then no one is there, the piano mysteriously plays in the night, Rebecca discovers Agnes's nightgown laid out on her bed, and so on. The upshot of the story is that Agnes has been dead for a year. As tersely communicated to Rebecca by the postmaster, 'Mrs. John Dent said to have neglected stepdaughter. Girl was sick. Medicine not given. Talk of taking action. Not enough evidence. House said to be haunted' (1974: 109).

Freeman's 'The Lost Ghost' is in many respects quite similar. In this tale, an older woman, Mrs Meserve, recounts her youthful experience boarding with two older women, the sisters Mrs Dennison and Mrs Bird – the latter a childless widow described by the narrator as 'a real motherly sort of woman' (1974: 163). As in 'The Wind in the Rose Bush', strange things began to happen – most notably, the narrator sees an apparition outside her bedroom door:

> I saw a little white face with eyes so scared and wishful that they seemed as if they might eat a hole in anybody's heart. It was a dreadful little face, with something about it which made it different from any other ace on earth ... And there were two little hands spotted purple with the cold ... and a strange little far-away voice said: 'I can't find my mother'. (1974: 163–4)

The story eventually comes out that the house had previously been inhabited by a married couple with a daughter. While the father was away on business, the abusive mother ran off with another man leaving the daughter locked in a room, and the child either starved or froze to death. When the father learned what had happened, he tracked the wife down and shot her to death. At the end of the story, Mrs Bird dies and is glimpsed 'walking off over the white snow-path with that child holding fast to her hand, nestling close to her as if she had found her own mother' (175–6).

In both stories, young girls are victimised by cruel mothers or stepmothers who act without constraint. Fathers are either dead or absent and the children are left entirely without protection as neither the law nor the community is able to intervene. In the case of 'The Wind in the Rose Bush', the story comes out, but no justice is served as the abusive and ultimately murderous stepmother disappears. In 'The Lost Ghost', a kind of rough justice is served as the husband murders the iniquitous wife; however, the story appears to end on an optimistic note with the ghost of a childless but motherly woman assuming a maternal role in relation to the ghostly child. The stories together suggest that some women are ill suited for motherhood and, by contrasting positive and negative depictions of motherhood, reinforce conventional understandings of the mother's role within the nuclear family as nurturer and guardian of children.

In contrast to these ghost stories about children abused and neglected by wicked mothers, the violence that men visit upon women in patriarchal culture (as well as upon other men) is a recurring theme in the works of another significant American practitioner of the supernatural tale: Ambrose Bierce. In Bierce's 'The Middle Toe of the Right Foot', for example, first published in the *San Francisco Examiner* in 1890, the reader is introduced to a man named Manton who murdered his two children and his wife, the latter of whom lacked the middle toe of her right foot. Tricked ten years later into revisiting the scene of the crime, he is discovered dead the next morning, apparently of fright. The only clues as to what happened are footsteps in the dust: 'three parallel lines of footprints – light but definite impressions of bare feet, the outer ones those of small children, the inner a woman's. From the point at which they ended they did not return; they pointed all one way' (1964: 182) – the footprint of the woman, of course, lacks the middle toe of the right foot.

Bierce's 'The Moonlit Road', first published in 1907 in *Cosmopolitan* (stretching the Victorian framework slightly), tells the tale of Joel Hetman who tests his wife's fidelity by arriving home from a trip earlier than anticipated. Believing he sees a man running from the house and assuming his wife's infidelity, he strangles her. She later appears to him as an apparition while he is walking home at night, driving him to distraction and, apparently, to the edge of suicide. The twist of the tale is that, through post-mortem narration by the wife, the reader learns that she not only had been faithful to her husband – who or what ran from the house is left uncertain – but that she is unaware that it was her own husband who murdered her. She was not seeking revenge when she manifested before him; rather, she was seeking a means to convey her 'great love and poignant pity' to her husband and son (1964: 148).

In both of these stories by Bierce, women are murdered by violent and possessive men. No explanation for the murders in 'Middle Toe' is provided; the narration only mentions dryly that Manton 'thought it expedient' to do so (1964: 176). In 'The Moonlit Road', Hetman jumps to the conclusion that his wife has been unfaithful and, 'crazed with jealousy and rage, blind and bestial with all the elemental passions of insulted manhood' (1964: 145), chokes the life out of his wife. As in the stories by Freeman, the women in Bierce's tales are afforded no protection from the 'elemental passion of insulted manhood' and their only means of redress is – at least in the case of 'Middle Toe' – revenge from beyond the grave. Unchecked nineteenth-century toxic masculinity can only be countered by supernatural intervention.

It is worth mentioning that the ghost stories by Bierce and others in which women and children are brutalised complicate a commonplace framework for interpreting supernatural tales in which female authors are said to address the 'terrors of the known' – the frustrations and dangers of everyday life as women within patriarchal culture – while men explore the 'terror of the unknown' (see Weinstock 2008: 28). This contrast has an appealing logic to it; it makes sense that authors would draw upon their own experiences as the focus of tales of dread and horror, and men and women experienced and continue to experience the world differently. While this is broadly true, however, it breaks down under closer scrutiny. Many ghost stories by men involve murdered women and children, while some supernatural stories by women – such as Freeman's 'The Hall Bedroom' (1905) and Madeline Yale Wynne's 'The Little Room' (1895), to be discussed below – raise troubling questions about our abilities to make sense of our experiences. Further, Victorian American ghost stories that reference slavery make clear that ghost stories by 'men' refers specifically to generally affluent white men since non-whites, both men and women, were in various ways disenfranchised and subject to exploitation and abuse.

Two American ghost stories that offer an interesting perspective on slavery and its aftermath are Thomas Nelson Page's 'No Haid Pawn' from 1887 and Charles Chesnutt's 'Po' Sandy' from 1888. Page, an apologist for slavery who offered 'idealized memories of a lost Cavalier society' (Martin 1998: 17), is little read today. His haunted house story, 'No Haid Pawn', however, repays close scrutiny as, despite the author's apparent intentions, it highlights the barbarity of slavery. As characterised by Matthew R. Martin, Page helped shape a nostalgic vision of a romantic Old South (1998: 17–18). And yet, as commentators have pointed out, 'No Haid Pawn', included as part of his 1887 collection *In Ole Virginia*, shows 'the dark side of slavery' (Hagood 2013: 139).

The story is about a haunted plantation house called No Haid Pawn – Page's Southern Black dialect version of 'No Head Pond' – built deep in the Virginia swamp. In the lead-up to the story, the white narrator recalls the history of the house. Built by slave labour, 'the negroes employed in the work of diking and reclaiming the great swamp had sickened and died by dozens'. 'The bodies,' continues the narrator, 'it was said, used to float about in the guts of the swamp, and on the haunted pond; and at night they might be seen … rowing about in their coffins as if they were boats' (Page 1887: n.p.). The plantation was then sold to a brutal man from the West Indies who terrorised his slaves, going so far as to decapitate one of them and to display the headless corpse as a form of intimidation.

In conjunction with this history of the plantation house, the narrator also recalls that the region was haunted in another way: by abolitionists. The discovery that the underground railroad (network for those escaping slavery) was active in the region, the narrator explains, created a good deal of excitement: 'It was as if the foundations of the whole social fabric were undermined. It was the sudden darkening of a shadow that always hung in the horizon' (Page 1887: n.p.). Their presence inspired many slaves to run off, including, notes the narrator, 'the most brutal negro I ever knew' (Page 1887: n.p.).

Having provided this background, the narrator turns to his actual story. Frustrated in duck hunting, he decided to try his luck in the remote vicinity of No Haid Pond – the 'name of which inspired dread' for the local population (Page 1887: n.p.). Predictably, he is forced inside the abandoned and dilapidated house by a storm and, as darkness descends, all the legends he has heard seem to be confirmed. A flash of lightening reveals a boat and then a monstrous figure appears in the house with what the narrator perceives to be a 'black and headless trunk' (Page 1887: n.p.). The story's rapid denouement provides no explanation for how the narrator survived; it simply reports that when the house was returned to, it is found to have been burned to the ground and, with overtones of Poe's 'The Fall of the House of Usher' (1839), to have been submerged in the swamp: 'The changed current had washed its way close to the place, and in strange verification of the negroes' traditions, had reclaimed its own, and the spot with all its secrets lay buried under its dark waters' (Page 1887: n.p.).

It seems unlikely that there is any 'actual' ghost in 'No Haid Pawn'. The background the narrator provides sets up an explanation for the purportedly supernatural events: The allegedly haunted house is being used as a stop on the underground railroad and the 'gigantic figure' (Page 1887: n.p.) that confronts him is the escaped slave mentioned earlier, described by the narrator as 'a fine butcher ... and a first-class boatman' (Page 1887: n.p.). It is unclear what the 'headless trunk' is, but one can conjecture a wild pig or something of that nature. Despite this rational explanation, however, the story is nevertheless a haunting one – one that, as Carme Manuel Cuenca observes, functions as 'a terror tale which makes use of one of the most disturbing elements in the slavery system of the Old South: the cruelty with which masters could treat their slaves' (1994: 134). As with the tales of abused women and children in Freeman and Bierce, exploitation and violence against the disempowered serves as the precondition for haunting. This Victorian American ghost story arises directly out of chattel slavery.

Slavery similarly serves as the context out of which haunting arises in Charles Chesnutt's better-known short story, 'Po' Sandy', first published in *The Atlantic* in 1888 and then collected together with Chesnutt's other 'Uncle Julius' stories in *The Conjure Woman* (1889). The stories in *The Conjure Woman* all share the same frame narrative: a white northerner in the South sharing tales of haunting and hoodoo told by ex-slave Uncle Julius McAdoo. In 'Po' Sandy', Uncle Julius attempts to persuade John against using lumber from an abandoned schoolhouse to build a new kitchen by explaining the sad fate of Sandy, a slave owned by Mars Marrabo McSwayne. McSwayne would constantly lend Sandy out to friends and family, selling Sandy's wife during one such occasion. Protesting against McSwayne's treatment of Sandy's new wife, Tenie, Sandy (as rendered by Chesnutt in dialect) wishes that he '"wuz a tree, er a stump, er a rock, er sump'n w'at could stay on de plantation fer a w'ile"' (1888: 607). Tenie, who it turns out is a conjure woman (a type of magician), fulfils Sandy's wish, transforming him into a tree. Unfortunately, trees can be cut down for lumber and such is Sandy's fate. While Tenie is away tending to the plantation's mistress, Sandy is harvested to build a new kitchen for the plantation master and cut into boards with an unusual amount of 'sweekin', enmoanin', engroanin'' (609). The kitchen is built and, as one might expect, becomes the focus of strange activity: the slaves 'could hear sump'n moanin' engroanin' 'bout de kitchen in de night-time, enw'en de win' would blow dey could hear sump'n a-hollerin' ensweekin' lack hit wuz in great pain ensufferin'' (610). After the slaves concluded that the kitchen was haunted, McSwayne disassembled it and used the lumber to build the schoolhouse – itself now rumoured to be haunted – that the story's narrator is now eyeing as raw materials for his own kitchen.

As with all of Chesnutt's 'Uncle Julius' tales, 'Po' Sandy' is told in a light-hearted way, with John and his wife dismissing Julius's tale but nevertheless concluding to use new rather than repurposed lumber in building the kitchen. Like 'No Haid Pawn', however, this ghost story finds its basis in a decidedly dark history. Sandy is worked constantly, let out to his master's family and friends, and given no rest. His first wife is sold while he is away and, whether or not he is actually transformed into a tree, he is treated as something less than human and without depth of feeling. Like lumber – and like the slaves who built No Haid Pawn – he is considered as a dispensable 'raw material' in the creation of white architecture. His ghostly moans therefore are a synecdochic expression of grief for all the slaves whose voices by rights should haunt the American landscape and corridors of power.

The ghosts I have discussed so far all serve very conventional ghostly functions: to highlight the persistence of the past into the present and to hope for a future if not of justice, at least of acknowledgement. They ask us to recognise historical forms of abuse and mistreatment, to mourn the lost, and, to the fullest extent possible, to see that justice is done. Another subset of Victorian American ghost stories, however, is future oriented. Rather than calling attention to legacies of violence, they instead use ghosts to speculate about what is to come in that undiscovered country awaiting us all. Drawing impetus from American Spiritualism, such stories often feature ghostly narrators who speak from the other side, letting readers have a glimpse of what exists beyond the veil of death.

As Ann Braude explains, American Spiritualism in the middle part of the nineteenth century was 'a new religious movement aimed at proving the immortality of the soul by establishing communication with spirits of the dead' (1989: 2). An alternative to traditional Protestantism, Spiritualism provided an optimistic vision not only of the afterlife, but of a new era of progress in which humanity, 'with spirit guidance, would achieve hitherto impossible levels of development' (1989: 6). American Spiritualism went through two waves of popularity; its first blossoming was in the 1850s and then a second wave followed the end of the American Civil War in the 1870s when its promise of an afterlife offered solace to millions of grieving Americans.

American Spiritualist practices of séances and mediums communing with the departed found their counterpart in Victorian ghost stories in which the dead tell their own tales. Prior to the beginning of American Spiritualism, Edgar Allan Poe had experimented with this idea in his 'The Facts in the Case of M. Valdemar' (1845) in which the titular character is mesmerised precisely at the moment of death and his spirit remains entrapped in his body until released from his hypnotic state. An interesting example of post-mortem narration is also provided in Harriet E. Prescott Spofford's fascinating short story 'The Amber Gods' (1863), in which the reader only discovers that the narrator, Yone, is dead with the story's startling last line: 'I must have died at ten minutes past one' (1985: 65). More obvious uses of the conceit, however, are provided by Nathaniel Hawthorne and Elizabeth Stuart Phelps.

A supernatural element is present in a number of Hawthorne's works, although he characteristically calls into question their veracity by suggesting, as he does, for example, in 'Young Goodman Brown' (1835) and *The House of the Seven Gables* (1851), that they may be the result of either ocular deception or romantic reverie. In 'Graves and Goblins', however, included in Hawthorne's 1876 collection *The Dolliver Romance and Other Pieces*, Hawthorne presents a straightforward supernatural piece narrated, as the reader learns in the second line of the tale, by a ghost: 'Now talk we of graves and goblins! Fit themes, – start not! gentle reader, – fit for a ghost like me' (1904: 125). Our spectral narrator explains that ghosts must linger by their graves 'Till purified from each stain of clay; till the passions of the living world are all forgotten; till it have less brotherhood with the wayfarers of earth, than with spirits that never wore mortality' (126). In a way that interestingly looks forward to Act III of Thorton Wilder's *Our Town* (1938), in which the dead slowly lose interest in the world of the living, Hawthorne's narrator discusses the ties that bind the dead to the world and how they slowly fade, as well as how the dead offer inspiration to the living: 'Who has not been conscious of mysteries within his mind, mysteries of truth and reality, which will not wear the chains of language? Mortal, then the dead were with you!' (126).

The dead also have much to say to the living in the works of Elizabeth Stuart Phelps, although the living cannot always hear. The somewhat pessimistic version is in her short story 'Since I Died', first published in *Scribner's Monthly* in 1873. In this surprising tale of same-sex desire, the ghostly narrator lingers around her beloved, attempting futilely to make contact. 'I told you I would come,' she says. 'Did ever promise fail I spoke to you? "Come and show me Death," you said. I have come to show you Death. I could show you the fairest sight and sweetest that ever blessed your eyes' (1989: 232). The narrator then goes on to explain her experience of dying and emerging into a world of meadows and sand and rock suffused by an immense 'Presence' (234–5). Her attempts to communicate her experience and her love, however, fall on deaf ears as she can neither be heard nor seen and, in the end, she is 'beckoned' as the material world fades away (235).

The optimistic version of the afterlife is available in Phelps's much better known *The Gates Ajar* (1868), which was followed by two sequels, *Beyond the Gates* (1883) and *The Gates Between* (1887). As Cindy Weinstein explains, *The Gates Ajar* was written to heal the psychic wounds of massive numbers of women who had lost their husbands, brothers, sons, and fathers in the [Civil] war, and it depicts heaven as a kind of Prozac nation, replete with material goods, nature at its most serene and unthreatening, and classical works of art that leave the viewer refreshed and content. (2012: 58)

The story concerns Mary Cabot, who is notified of the death of her much-loved brother, Royal, during the war. Succumbing to despair, her faith in God and heaven waivers until it is restored by her widowed aunt Winifred Forceythe, who offers an inspiring vision of heaven and the afterlife in which 'the dead do what they enjoy most while awaiting reunion with those they love – play the piano, wear their favorite clothes ... and, if they are Union soldiers, meet President Lincoln' (Showalter 2009: 160). The novel and its sequels were remarkably popular – Elaine Showalter states that the book sold more than 80,000 copies (2009: 161) – and, according to David Blight, *The Gates Ajar* was one of more than eighty books published between 1865 and 1876 on the idea of heaven and an afterlife (Blight 2008).

Hawthorne, it is important to note, was no Spiritualist and, indeed, took a dim view of Spiritualist belief, together with séances, mesmerism and what Taylor Stoehr has called Victorian pseudo-science (see Stoehr 1978). Phelps did affiliate with Spiritualism, albeit as a lens through which to reform Christianity (see Harde 2008). In both cases, though, their stories told from the perspective of the dead demonstrate the influence of Victorian American Spiritualism with its focus on establishing lines of communication between this world and the hereafter. Their ghosts are ultimately hopeful, testifying to the perpetuation of spirit after physical dissolution and, especially in the case of Phelps, offering consolation to the bereaved that their loved ones still exist in another form and are waiting to be reunited with them.

The other side of the same coin consists of Victorian American ghost stories that, rather than seeking to offer solace to the living or to confirm the existence of an afterlife, instead raise questions about the extent to which human beings can trust their senses and arrive at accurate conclusions about the world. As Bret E. Carroll summarises, traditional sources of authority and ways of understanding the world were shaken during the Victorian period. Darwin's theory of evolution and geological studies disputing the biblical account of creation challenged traditional Christian belief. Meanwhile, shifts in American social, economic and political life, including population and immigration growth, the rise of a market economy, the 'proliferation of factories, railroads, and telegraph lines' and the 'emergence of a mass democratic political culture' created the sense that the 'fabric of American life seemed to be unraveling, stretched and torn by forces which promoted selfishness, materialism, fragmentation, and atomization' (Carroll 1997: 3). 'These unsettling developments,' explains Carroll, 'combined to produce spiritual malaise, discomfort, discontent, and above all a search for order among many Americans' (1997: 3).

Many Victorian American ghost stories find their grounding in and reflect this pervasive sense of unease as Americans questioned what could be known with certainty. While not a ghost story per se, Ambrose Bierce's 'The Damned Thing' (1893) raises the possibility that the limitations on the human sensorium prevent us from fully comprehending the world around us. Drawing an analogy with sound, the narration offers one explanation for a deadly attack by what seems to be an invisible monster: that there may be colours the human eye cannot perceive. Bierce's story may have influenced Guy de Maupassant's 'The Horla' (1877) and certainly provided inspiration for H. P. Lovecraft's 'The Colour Out of Space' (1927). A similar scenario is also present in F. Marion Crawford's 'The Upper Berth' (1894) in which the narrator recounts his own harrowing confrontation with an at-times invisible monstrosity.

That space may be unstable is the premise of a handful of haunting tales from the period, including Madeline Yale Wynne's 'The Little Room' (1895), Ambrose Bierce's 'The Spook House' (1889), Elia Wilkinson Peattie's 'The House That Was Not' (1898) and Mary E. Wilkins Freeman's 'The Hall Bedroom' (1905). In Wynne's puzzling story, a house seems to change its configuration, sometimes presenting as a china closet, at other times a little room. Debates over the house then sow the seeds of distrust between husband and wife and among family members. Bierce's story is cut from the same cloth: two travellers seek shelter in a deserted house whose inhabitants had mysteriously disappeared. They stumble into what seems a supernatural room that contains the corpses of the missing family. When the house is later revisited by the sole survivor, the room is no longer there. In Peattie's story, an isolated young mid-western housewife sees a house in the distance, only to discover that it is illusory; a trip to the site reveals only the rubble of the house that once stood there. In Freeman's story, the proprietor of a boarding house shares with the reader the personal journal of one of her boarders who has disappeared. His entries seem to suggest that the room somehow at times permits passage into an alternative realm or world.

These stories by Bierce, Crawford, Wynne, Peattie and Freeman all channel the epistemological uncertainty of the era, raising questions about whether we can trust our eyes and if we are seeing the whole picture, and calling into question assumptions about the consistency of space itself. Not only do they reflect scientific developments confirming the limitations on human vision – X-rays were discovered, for example, in 1895, by German scientist Wilhelm Röntgen – but they also are very much part of the late Victorian questioning of the dualistic belief that the observer can stand apart from and have objective knowledge of the observed.

Nowhere is the epistemological uncertainty of the period more in evidence than in Henry James's class ghost story *The Turn of the Screw* (1898). Told from the perspective of the young and impressionable governess, the question of whether ghosts actually exist or if they are instead projections of the governess as part of a 'neurotic case of sex repression', as Edmund Wilson famously put it in 1934, is ultimately unanswerable. To be fair, the question of 'specter or delusion?' as Margaret L. Carter phrases it in the title of her study (1987), is one often raised by supernatural tales. James's tale, however, as Tzvetan Todorov observes in his study of the fantastic as a genre, sustains that question all the way through, offering no solid evidence that would allow us to resolve the question either way (see Todorov 1975: 43). It thereby seems to reflect the epistemological crisis of the late Victorian period.

The Victorian American ghost story thus shares concerns with other ghost story traditions. It reflects the hopes that justice will be done and for the persistence of spirit after death and it reflects anxieties that we do not fully comprehend our world and may never will. Its specific contours, however, are shaped by American history and social conditions. It reflects not just the victimisation of women and children, but the shameful legacy of slavery and other forms of racial bigotry; it shows the influence of American Spiritualism; and, especially in late Victorian tales, expresses the concern that the ground of tradition is giving way beneath our feet as the forces of modernity sweep us into the twentieth century. American ghost stories are thus part of the broader family of Victorian ghost stories, sharing kinship with other traditions, while at the same time being shaped by specifically American historical forces.

Note

1. While I will focus on Freeman and Ambrose Bierce here, victimisation of women and children is a pervasive theme of Victorian American ghost stories, including in works by Harriet Beecher Stowe, Elia Wilkinson Peattie, Charlotte Perkins Gilman and Edith Wharton. See my *Scare Tactics: Supernatural Fiction by American Women* (Weinstock 2008) study, as well as Dara Downey's *American Women's Ghost Stories in the Gilded Age* (Downey 2014), for a fuller analysis of such tales.

Works Cited

Bierce, Ambrose. 'The Damned Thing', in *Ghost and Horror Stories of Ambrose Bierce*, edited by E. F. Bleiler. New York: Dover, 1964, pp. 32–9.

———. 'The Middle Toe of the Right Foot', in *Ghost and Horror Stories of Ambrose Bierce*, edited by E. F. Bleiler. New York: Dover, 1964, pp. 175–82.

———. 'The Moonlit Road', in *Ghost and Horror Stories of Ambrose Bierce*, edited by E. F. Bleiler. New York: Dover, 1964, pp. 141–9.

———. 'The Spook House', in *Ghost and Horror Stories of Ambrose Bierce*, edited by E. F. Bleiler. New York: Dover, 1964, pp. 76–9.

Blight, David W. 'Lecture 17 – Homefronts and Battlefronts: "Hard War" and the Social Impact of the Civil War'. Yale Open Courses, 2008. https://oyc.yale.edu/history/hist-119/lecture-17 (last accessed 3 January 2025).

Braude, Ann. *Radical Spirits: Spiritualism and Women's Rights in Nineteenth-Century America*. Boston, MA: Beacon Press, 1989.

Carroll, Bret E. *Spiritualism in Antebellum America*. Bloomington and Indianapolis: Indiana University Press, 1997.

Carter, Margaret L. *Specter or Delusion? The Supernatural in Gothic Fiction*. Lewiston, NY: Edwin Mellen, 1987.

Chesnutt, Charles. 'Po' Sandy'. *The Atlantic Monthly*, 1888, pp. 605–11; available at https://chesnuttarchive.org/item/ccda.works00014 (last accessed 3 January 2025).

'Civil War Casualties: The Cost of War: Killed, Wounded, Captured, and Missing'. American Battlefield Trust, 2023. https://www.battlefields.org/learn/articles/civil-war-casualties (last accessed 3 January 2025).

Cuenca, Carme Manuel. 'Thomas Nelson Page's "No Haid Pawn": The Gothic Horror of the Southern Plantation'. *Revista Alicantina de Estudios Ingeleses*, vol. 7, 1994, pp. 133–40.

Diederich, Nicole A. 'The Gothic as Semiotic Disruption: Layers and Levels of Terror and the Abject in Mary E. Wilkins Freeman's "The Wind in the Rose-bush"'. *Journal of the Midwest Modern Language Association*, vol. 44, no. 2, 2011, pp. 21–41.

Douglas, Ann. *The Feminization of American Culture*. New York: Avon Books, 1977.

Downey, Dara. *American Women's Ghost Stories in the Gilded Age*. London and New York: Palgrave Macmillan, 2014.

Frederick, John T. 'Hawthorne's "Scribbling Women"'. *The New England Quarterly*, vol. 48, no. 2, 1975, pp. 231–40.

Freeman, Mary E. Wilkins. 'The Hall Bedroom', in *Collected Ghost Stories*. Sauk City, WI: Arkham House, 1974, pp. 21–38.

———. 'The Lost Ghost', in *Collected Ghost Stories*. Sauk City, WI: Arkham House, 1974, pp. 157–76.

———. 'The Wind in the Rosebush', in *Collected Ghost Stories*. Sauk City, WI: Arkham House, 1974, pp. 90–109.

Hagood, Taylor. 'Ghosts of Southern Imperialism: Caribbean Space, Functions of Fiction, and Thomas Nelson Page's "No Haid Pawn"'. *The Mississippi Quarterly*, vol. 66, no. 1, 2013, pp. 139–60.

Harde, Roxanne. '"God, or Something Like That": Elizabeth Stuart Phelps's Christian Spiritualism'. *Women's Writing: The Elizabethan to Victorian Period*, vol. 15, no. 3, 2008, pp. 348–70.

Hawthorne, Nathaniel. 'Graves and Goblins', in *The Dolliver Romance and Other Pieces*. Boston, MA: Houghton, Mifflin and Company, 1904, pp. 125–35.

James, Henry. *The Turn of the Screw*. New York: W. W. Norton, 2020.

Mandal, Anthony. 'The Ghost Story and the Victorian Marketplace', in Scott Brewster and Luke Thurston (eds), *The Routledge Handbook to the Ghost Story*. New York and London: Routledge, 2018, pp. 29–39.

Martin, Matthew R. 'The Two-Faced New South: The Plantation Tales of Thomas Nelson Page and Charles W. Chesnutt'. *The Southern Literary Journal*, vol. 30, no. 2, 1998, pp. 7–36.

'Mary E. Wilkins Freeman'. Loyola University Chicago Digital Special Collections, n.d. http://www.lib.luc.edu/specialcollections/exhibits/show/autograph-collection/mary-e--wilkins-freeman (last accessed 3 January 2025).

Meyer, D. H. 'American Intellectuals and the Victorian Crisis of Faith'. *American Quarterly*, vol. 27, no. 5, 1975, pp. 585–603.

Mott, Frank Luther. *A History of American Magazines*, vol. 1. Cambridge, MA: Belknap Press, 1938.

Page, Thomas Nelson. 'No Haid Pawn' [1887]. Project Gutenberg Australia, 2006. http://gutenberg.net.au/ebooks06/0606201h.html (last accessed 3 January 2025).

Pattee, Fred Lewis. *The Feminine Fifties*. New York and London: D. Appleton-Century Company, 1940.

Peattie, Elia Wilkinson. 'The House That Was Not', in *The Shape of Fear and Other Ghostly Tales*. Freeport, NY: Books for Libraries Press, 1969, pp. 53–64.

Phelps, Elizabeth Stuart. *The Gates Ajar*. Boston, MA: Fields, Osgood, & Co, 1868.

———. 'Since I Died', in Jessica Amanda Salmonson (ed.), *What Did Miss Darington See? An Anthology of Feminist Supernatural Fiction*. New York: The Feminist Press, 1989, pp. 229–35.

Poe, Edgar Allan. 'The Facts in the Case of M. Valdemar', in *Poe: Poetry, Tales, & Selected Essays*, edited by Patrick F. Quinn and G. R. Thompson. New York: The Library of America, 1984, pp. 833–42.

'Pop Culture: 1840'. United States Census Bureau, n.d. https://www.census.gov/programs-surveys/decennial-census/decade/decennial-facts.1840.html#list-tab-1813000050 (last accessed 2 January 2025).

'Pop Culture: 1900'. United States Census Bureau, n.d. https://www.census.gov/programs-surveys/decennial-census/decade/decennial-facts.1900.html#list-tab-1813000050 (last accessed 2 January 2025).

Salmonson, Jessica Amanda. 'Preface', in Jessica Amanda Salmonson (ed.), *What Did Miss Darrington See? An Anthology of Feminist Supernatural Fiction*. New York: The Feminist Press, 1989, pp. ix–xiv.

Showalter, Elaine. *A Jury of Her Peers: American Women Writers From Anne Bradstreet to Annie Proulx*. New York: Alfred A. Knopf, 2009.

Smith, Susan Belasco and Kenneth M. Price. 'Introduction: Periodical Literature in Social and Historical Context', in Kenneth M. Price and Susan Belasco Smith (eds), *Periodical Literature in Nineteenth-Century America*. Charlottesville and London: University Press of Virginia, 1995, pp. 3–16.

Spofford, Harriet Prescott. 'The Amber Gods', in *The 'Amber Gods' and Other Stories*, edited by Alfred Bendixen. New Brunswick, NJ: Rutgers University Press, 1985, pp. 37–83.

Stoehr, Taylor. *Hawthorne's Mad Scientists: Pseudoscience and Social Science in Nineteenth-Century Life and Letters*. New Haven, CT: Archon Books, 1978.

Tebbel, John. *The American Magazine: A Compact History*. New York: Hawthorn Books, 1969.

Todorov, Tzvetan. *The Fantastic: A Structural Approach to a Literary Genre*, translated by Richard Howard. Ithaca, NY: Cornell University Press, 1975.

Weinstein, Cindy. 'Heaven's Tense: Narration in "The Gates Ajar"'. *NOVEL: A Forum on Fiction*, vol. 45, no. 1, 2012, pp. 56–70.

Weinstock, Jeffrey Andrew. *Scare Tactics: Supernatural Fiction by American Women*. New York: Fordham University Press, 2008.

Wilson, Edmund. 'The Ambiguity of Henry James'. *Hound and Horn*, April–June 1934, pp. 385–406.

Wynne, Madeline Yale. 'The Little Room', in Alfred Bendixen (ed.), *Haunted Women: The Best Supernatural Tales by American Women*. New York: Frederick Ungar Publishing, 1985, pp. 119–32.

Chapter 11

Victorian Christmas Ghosts
Tara Moore

British tradition had linked Christmas and ghosts for centuries. Writing in 1725, ethnographer Henry Bourne noted, 'Nothing is commoner in Country Places, than for a whole Family in a Winter's Evening to sit round the Fire and tell Stories of Apparitions and Ghosts' (Bourne 1725: 76). Writing in the early twentieth century, folklorist Clement A. Miles found that several traditions previously associated with All Souls Day (1 November) and All Saints Day (2 November) had been transferred to the Christmas season over the centuries. Those All Souls holidays relating to the cult of the dead had previously marked the start of the Christmas season in the seventeenth century (Miles 1912: 189).

The origins of oral storytelling circles are challenging to track due to a lack of written evidence. A few existing sketch pieces from the eighteenth and early nineteenth centuries treat it as a set piece of the Christmas celebration (Moore 2009: 82). For example, the slim volume *Round about Our Coal Fire* (1730) lovingly chronicles the country house celebrations of the well-to-do, describing scenes of feasting, games and dancing before coming to the premise of the volume's tales: 'another Entertainment frequently used, which is of the Story-telling Order, vis. of Hobgoblins, Witches, Conjurers, Ghosts, Fairies, and such like common Disturbers' (1796: 14). Such evidence suggests that seventeenth- and eighteenth-century oral ghost traditions drove demand for printed versions of supernatural stories later on (Clery 1995: 2–5).

Early nineteenth-century writers capitalised on the nostalgia for the aristocratic manor house Christmas in their fiction and poetry, and ghosts featured in most of these country house Christmases. Walter Scott imbued ghost stories with vast nostalgic import in his poem known as 'Christmas in the Olden Time', a poem originally published as the introduction to the sixth canto of *Marmion* (1808). The poet harks back to the Yule of the Danes before recreating a fifteenth- or sixteenth-century great hall Christmas gathering. The rich and poor come together to share the squire's boar's head, Christmas pie, mistletoe and entertainment: "'Twas Christmas broached the mightiest ale, / 'Twas Christmas told the merriest tale' (Scott 1887: canto 6, introduction, ll. 6.82–3). The poem's later section focuses on the supernatural, appealing to Scott's friend Richard Heber to set aside more academic studies so that he can consider tales befitting Christmastime, tales containing 'ghost, Goblin and witch!' (Scott 1887: canto 6, introduction, ll. 6.140–1).

Scott's text was frequently excerpted and republished in illustrated volumes for Christmas purchase and consumption throughout the nineteenth century. The longevity of this piece as a stand-alone poem suggests that Scott had tapped into a fruitful wealth of nostalgia for the country house community Christmas.

Washington Irving also identified ghost stories as part of the British country house Christmas in his essay 'Christmas', which appeared in *The Sketch Book of Geoffrey Crayon, Gent.* (1820). The American narrator chronicles the events of the British Christmas celebration like a besotted ethnographer. At one point he comes upon the adults, gathered around the fire in the drawing room, listening to the parson's local tales of folklore and the supernatural. One such tale features a restless crusader entombed in the church who walks around the churchyard during thunderstorms. Telling ghostly tales is just one of the Christmastime gambols the narrator depicts alongside the feasting, the games, the wassail and the mummery of this propertied family.

John Storey has argued that these medieval, big hall scenes represent a frequently hailed version of Merry England 'driven by a utopian nostalgia: an attempt to recreate an imaginary past' (Storey 2008: 29). Storey discredits these literary scenes as true historical accounts of days gone by; instead, they are 'nostalgic fantasies' which idealise 'feudal power relations of the past' for the middle-class audience (Storey 2008: 30). While the boar's head remained out of the reach of most middle-class readers, they could replicate the cheaper aspects contained inside the nostalgic fantasy: the feasting, alcohol consumption and communally told ghost stories.

Due to the tradition and the successful propaganda of these 'big hall' texts, ghosts possessed a corner of Christmas. To the Victorians, Christmastime ghost tales felt de rigueur in the same way that spooky stories are an expected part of the American campfire tradition. The Victorians did not limit themselves to ghosts. Many of the stories of the uncanny produced for Christmas arose from a range of other supernatural possibilities. They might relate stories about dream premonitions and, later, mesmerism.

Early big hall scenes promoted the ghost story concept, but they stopped short of delving into carefully crafted or fully developed stories. Andrew Smith provides a useful distinction between 'stories about ghosts' – inelegant fireside retellings of local legends – and literary ghost stories, which were constructed with some art (Smith 2010: 3). The first type are mere summaries without literary depth, snippets that appear as minimalist, one-dimensional descriptions. In contrast, the literary ghost story steals the light from any existing frame tale. Both types of tales were marketed to Christmas readers.

Charles Dickens and Christmas Ghosts

Christmas went through a momentous transition in the 1840s, and Charles Dickens played a significant role in investing the Victorian Christmas with the old expectations of ghosts. Notably, his ghosts are most often ghosts of ideas or memories rather than ghosts of the deceased. Moreover, his ghosts educate a middle-class readership in how to behave towards the destitute, how to spend and how to celebrate Christmas. Brandon Chitwood argues that Dickens expands Christmas beyond its religious meaning to a cultural meaning, and 'in reifying and reproducing Christmas within the curious genre of the ghost story, [he] expanded the horizons of capitalism itself' (Chitwood 2015: 684). Lines from 'A Christmas Tree' (1850), published in *Household Words*, attest to Dickens's boredom with the worn patterns of ghost stories. Even in the midst of a sentimental essay on Christmases past, Dickens cannot stop himself from pointing out that ghost stories are 'reducible to a very few general types and classes; for, ghosts have little originality, and "walk" in a beaten track' (Dickens 1850: 293), and it is clear from his production of Christmas ghosts that Dickens sought a different track for his spectres. In nearly all his ghost stories, Dickens adapted the pre-Victorian Christmas ghost tradition into a literary ghost story dependent on a 'redemptive ghost', one who learns how to handle middle-class wealth (Moore 2009: 97). According to Colin Dickey, 'Dickens' genius was to wed the gothic with the sentimental, using stories of ghosts and goblins to reaffirm basic bourgeois values' (Dickey 2017).

Early on, Dickens inserted a spectral story into the Dingley Dell Christmas in *The Pickwick Papers* (1836–7). The tale combines a glorified fireside storytelling party with a more developed literary ghost story. The host, Mr Wardle, and his guests relax by the fire after an evening of festivities to their 'invariable custom': 'Every body sits down with us on Christmas eve, as you see them now – servants and all; and here we wait till the clock strikes twelve, to usher Christmas in, and wile away the time with forfeits and old stories' (Dickens 2008: 351–2). Mr Wardle then launches into the story, the same tale his father told at a Christmas fire many years ago. In the story, 'The Story of the Goblins Who Stole a Sexton', goblins use vignettes of humanity to re-educate/ redeem Christmas-hating Gabriel Grub. Here and elsewhere, Dickens's tales imbue Christmas with new expectations of commercialism, charity and goodwill. At the same time, he emphasises the nostalgia of the ghostly tale: Mr Wardle revives his own father's story from Christmas past.

Like *The Pickwick Papers*' goblins, the spirits in *A Christmas Carol* are largely conductors-cum-counsellors rather than dead people walking again. The ghostly tutors reinforce a lesson: Christmas capitalism is a requirement of proper Victorian behaviour (Chitwood 2015: 683). Robert Tracy identifies the spirits as 'theatrical illusionists, literary artists, presenting a series of dramatic vignettes [...] which will work upon Scrooge' (Tracy 1998: 124). The same might be said for the spectral figures in subsequent Christmas books: the cricket in *The Cricket on the Hearth* (1845) and the spirits of the bells in *The Chimes* (1844). They reveal or stage scenes of life to make a rhetorical argument in favour of hope, generosity or charity. The protagonist views the tableaux as a voyeur, and the same lesson that the spirits teach the protagonist is similarly consumed by the reader, the secondary observer.

Scrooge's visitations have received the lion's share of critical examination, but this essay will look instead at another of Dickens's Christmas hauntings, the one that takes place in *The Haunted Man and the Ghost's Bargain* (1848). The ghost in the last of Dickens's Christmas books is an 'evil spirit' of the protagonist Redlaw, a lonely chemistry professor (Dickens 1848: 41). Helen Growth describes Redlaw's ghost as 'a terrifying embodiment of the fragmentation of his psyche – a figure that ultimately forces him to recognise the distortive moral effects of his narcissistic dwelling on past wrongs' (Growth 2007: 51). In one engraving by John Leech, the spirit hangs over Redlaw's chair like a menacing doppelgänger. The spirit confers 'a contagious "gift" of memory oblivion', removing memories of sorrow and pain (Ingleby 2013: 99). As part of the arrangement, Redlaw will infect others with this condition, cancelling memories of sorrow and trouble in those he physically encounters.

Redlaw quickly comes to see the bargain as a curse as he learns to value the lost memories. He recognises how the loss of memories embitters those around him, especially the poor. Redlaw begins a journey from scene to scene, and he and the reader observe the effects his curse has on his neighbours. After Redlaw enters their rooms, one loving couple turns resentful and selfish; a doting father spurns his sick adult son; the repentant son hardens his heart. Viewing these tableaux teaches Redlaw the value of past trouble: pain nurtures compassion and softer feelings.

After making his own visitations as voyeur, Redlaw regrets his decision. Fortunately, the ghost offers him a remedy. The working-class woman and angel in the house Milly Swidger can wipe away the effects of Redlaw's curse. She retraces his steps room by room: 'She came among them like the spirit of all goodness, affection, gentle consideration, love, and domesticity' (Dickens 1848: 160). As a symbol of Victorian female purity, the uneducated Milly serves like the bronze serpent from the Old Testament. All who see her regain their memories of sorrow and the resulting appreciative contentment. As a result of his new knowledge, Redlaw enlarges his social circle by becoming a fatherly figure to a poor student and a benefactor of the working-class people around him. Redlaw also vows to 'reclaim' a heartless waif who has been portrayed as little more than an animal (185).

Dickens uses his ghost's lesson to expertly blend poignant scenes with his own brand of Christmastime values. In *The Haunted Man*, the narrator tells the audience, 'Christmas is a time in which, of all times, in the year, the memory of every remediable sorrow, wrong, and trouble in the world around us, should be active with us [...] for all good' (184–5). Dickens's ghosts force the protagonist and the reader to interpret the tableaux, and thereby participate in self-reflection and meditation.

The narrative concludes with a 'big hall' Christmas scene reminiscent of Scott's and Irving's narratives, one that Victorian readers had already been trained to associate with the idealised, traditional Christmas. Redlaw reinstitutes the huge holiday gathering in the college's disused great hall. The redeemed Scrooge only celebrates with people from his own class; in contrast, Redlaw takes the more emotionally vulnerable step of opening his doors to everyone (Ingleby 2013: 99). Redlaw invites the full cast of characters, people from lower-middle and working-class backgrounds.

The visual representation of Redlaw's final 'big hall' scene re-enacts the Christmas storytelling circle, the readership scenario most associated with spectral Yuletide narratives. In Clarkson Stanfield's original engraving, the reader views the story from the perspective of the hearth itself (see Figure 1). Storytelling circles are inherently associated with the hearth, but the hearth scene usually appears to stage right or stage left; Stanfield situates the hearth in an entirely novel position, as a frame through which the reader views the characters' heart-warming,

Figure 1 Clarkson Stanfield's final plate in Charles Dickens's *The Haunted Man and the Ghost's Bargain*. Scan provided by Tara Moore.

communal gathering. The reader inhabits the fire itself, and from there views the reconstituted big hall gathering: Redlaw; his servants the Swidgers and their kin; the Tetterbys; and Redlaw's two new dependents, his impoverished student and the waif.

Stanfield's plate is the sixth hearth scene depicted in *The Haunted Man*, and it serves as a visual bookend to the story. Its composition hearkens back to imagery depicted on the first story plate, the image that opens Chapter 1 (see Figure 2). That earlier shadow hearth scene by John Tenniel depicts a child holding a book up to the firelight while reading, possibly sharing the story with the nurse and siblings assembled in the fire's glow. That image, which Dickens details in the text a few pages later, shows how the firelight and the imaginative moment can transform the shadow of the fire tongs so that the shadow on the wall

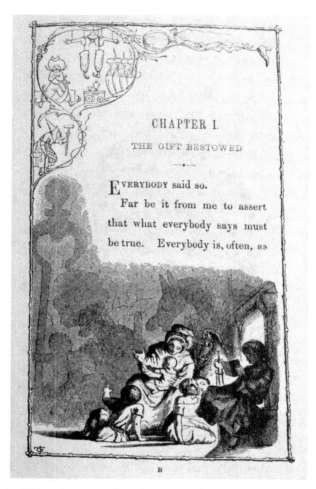

Figure 2 John Tenniel's image for Chapter 1 of Charles Dickens's *The Haunted Man and the Ghost's Bargain*. Scan provided by Tara Moore.

becomes that of a man-eating giant (Dickens 1848: 9). Tenniel's fire tongs appear in the foreground of Stanfield's final engraving of the big hall celebration. Dickens and his collaborators use the fireside's visual icons to frame this story at its beginning and to echo back to that storytelling circle at the story's end.

Both scenes idealise a fireside kinship and suggest a community knitted together by stories and spectres. Dickens took great pains with his illustrators in *The Haunted Man and the Ghost's Bargain*, and the collaboration between the artists and the writer emphasise an additional lesson beyond the values of Christmas. While most Christmas frame tales narrate or otherwise depict a scene of oral storytelling, Tenniel's illustration demonstrates the new technology of the book as a replacement for oral tradition at the fireside. Thus, the images within this ghost tale educate the reader on how to consume Christmas stories.

The Fixation with Frame Tales

When depicted in a story, the narrative rendering of the storytelling circle expresses nostalgia for the oral tradition even as it acts as a frame tale for the main act, the ghost story. In Victorian stories, the frame tale is usually briefly described: aristocratic or upper middle-class characters gathered in an opulent setting, possibly even a Christmastime setting. Once the setting is established, one speaker delves into a ghostly narrative, usually one with which they have a close family connection or first-hand experience. This ghost tale takes over from there and provides the scare, but the frame tale also plays a key role in this equation. Authors might rely on frame tales to structure collections of stories, or they might use them to open a stand-alone ghost story (Moore 2009: 86).

Dickens adapted the storytelling circle for the second generation of his Christmas offerings, the Christmas numbers that took the place of his earlier annual Christmas books. The Christmas numbers allowed Dickens to commission pieces from various authors and relieved him of the exhausting role of writing another Christmas book. As editor, Dickens usually included ghost stories in the late December numbers as well as the extra Christmas numbers of his weekly periodicals *Household Words* (1850–9) and *All the Year Round* (1859–70). By his third Christmas number, Dickens was implementing a frame tale structure to stitch together the pieces he had commissioned to fill the special number. This storytelling circle format would characterise many of his subsequent special numbers.

Elizabeth Gaskell published her Gothic story 'The Old Nurse's Tale' (1852) in a Christmas number that immediately establishes its frame tale storytelling approach in the title: *Round of Stories by the Christmas Fire*. The frame tale introduces a family who sit 'in a goodly circle by the Christmas fire', and the participants take turns telling tales (Dickens 1883: 650). Gaskell's story begins as the old nurse takes her turn. During her tale she addresses the younger family members gathered around the fire – 'my dears' – as she launches into the story of their mother, presumably the mistress of the house, and how she survived a haunting as a small child living in a remote Yorkshire manor house with a guilt-ridden, elderly relative (Gaskell 2000: 11).

Elizabeth Gaskell creates a Gothic ghostly tale in 'The Old Nurse's Tale', complete with one ghost playing an organ when storms blow in and a relentless ghost-child who tempts the living child of the house out into the frozen landscape, luring her towards an icy death. The Gothic setting of Gaskell's tale – organ music, a lonely moor and a decayed east wing – contrast with the cosiness of the frame tale that the nurse hints at in her opening remarks. The nurse breaks from her story to speak directly to her listeners: 'There never was such a baby before or since, though you've all of you been fine enough in your turns' (Gaskell 2000: 11). By referencing the story circle early on, Gaskell hints at the happy resolution of the story. We know from the outset that the little child of the story will end up a beloved mother to grown-up children, all safely gathered together in economic comfort and emotional security. Whatever Gothic horrors she experiences with her nurse will be distant memories. A happy ending is assured.

Authors and publishers like Dickens and Gaskell marketed an idealised Christmas reading circle experience for middle-class readers who did not have access to that country house setting or a community of listeners and orators. Of course, many readers bought books or periodicals to share with their reading circle in the midwinter evenings, but even lone readers could now access a community of storytellers by purchasing a volume for Christmas or a Christmas number.

Many pieces use the frame tale to suggest that the embedded story is a 'found story' based on a manuscript or the testimony of an associate, a narrative deception with a long history. Horace Walpole initiated the 'found story' conceit when he published the first edition of *The Castle of Otranto* (1764). Walpole's duplicitous introduction tricked at least one reviewer who failed to notice the telling clue of the first edition's Christmas Eve publication date and initially praised the 'ingenious translator' (Review of *The Castle of Otranto* 1765: 50). Following in Walpole's footsteps, Rhoda Broughton's narrators attest to the truth of each story of ghosts, mesmerism, dream premonitions and eerie burglaries in her collection *Tales for Christmas Eve* (1873). The narrators indicate where they encountered the ghost-witness, also known as a percipient, but narrators otherwise protect their sources. While hinting at the existence of a real witness lends the story legitimacy, the narrator prevents the story from being traceable to its origins. Narrators therefore blot out full names of towns or people with dashes or vague references to locations. M. R. James was still using this worn pretence in the early twentieth century when he claimed that 'The Story of a Disappearance and an Appearance' (1919) came directly from a series of old letters in his possession: 'There is no doubt about their authenticity. [...] The only point which they do not make clear is the identity of the writer' (James 1919: 109). The conceit allowed readers to pretend that the narratives stemmed from real life.

Catherine Crowe capitalises on the legitimising power of the frame tale when she depicts a country house Christmas in the first lines of *Ghosts and Family Legends: A Volume for Christmas* (1859). Crowe's cachet as a Victorian author has greatly declined, and she is 'virtually unknown in the twenty-first century' (Kim 2021: 294). Nonetheless, Crowe was an excellent judge of what her audience wanted since she was 'an incredibly successful nineteenth-century author whose popularity at one point rivalled Dickens's' (Kim 2021: 277). In Crowe's Christmastime volume, the narrator lifts the curtain on stories told 'last winter in a large country mansion in the north of England' (Crowe 1859: 3). By chronicling these stories, Crowe hopes her book 'may prove a not uninteresting companion for a Christmas fireside' (4). The book opens with brief details about the gathering, but it is enough to indicate a country house ghost story circle: the leisured guests meet each night during a late December house party and tell story after story of apparitions and prophetic dreams. This is the updated version of the 'big hall' Christmas circle without the boar's head.

What follows in Crowe's volume is a bounty of 'stories about ghosts' – inelegant summaries that lack artistry and depth. The speakers gush about ghostly appearances, curses and prophetic dreams at a frenetic rate. The narrative design captures a sense of tales recounted in a conversational setting. The 'stories about ghosts' read as clunky rather than artful. Ruth Heholt attributes the volume's disjointed style to the fact that Crowe truly believed in ghosts and wished to present her tales as evidence to the scientific community; as a result, the volume's style emulates the bare, jumpy pattern of stories collected from an oral tradition (Heholt 2014: 47–9).

The early chapters in this *Volume for Christmas* recount stories told for eight consecutive nights. Then Crowe moves beyond the country house circle and relates individual ghost stories that require deeper narrative contexts to unpack. These longer, slightly more artful stories also rely on the frame tale formula of wealthy tellers encountered in upmarket settings. The frame tales remain important since they add elevated class status to the story.

One such tale is Crowe's 'The Swiss Lady's Story', the tale of a ghost who startles servants and children on the stair, then disappears through the wall at a certain landing. The Swiss lady's story begins as a tale of two orphans adopted by their unpleasant, rich uncle. Alfred attempts to ingratiate himself with the uncle, but the uncle bequeaths his estate to

Louis who has left to become a soldier. Louis is eventually presumed to be dead, so Alfred inherits the estate by default. Over time, Alfred sells his first house in Geneva, and it becomes a rental. Sadly for the new owner, the house gains the reputation of being haunted, and uncanny experiences drive away renters. When an English family rents the house, the women, young boys and female servants see a ghostly figure in uniform, but the father of the family never sees it. A daughter of the house translates the ghost's silent movements to suggest that he wants a wall torn down. Heholt has noted that the story's male ghost is 'Entirely removed from any position of power' and he needs women 'to act for him' (Heholt 2014: 54).

The English father becomes convinced that the ghost exists even though he cannot see it, and the entire family hopes to propitiate it. One of the children suggests that they might find money beyond the ghost's wall. No one dismisses the possibility, presumably because of the familiarity of this plot point in Victorian ghost narratives (Crowe 1859: 283). When the English renters demolish the wall, they find skeletal remains. In a show of superstitious policing, the authorities gather testimony from people who saw the spirit. As a result, the authorities decide that the miserly Alfred had murdered his brother Louis and hidden his body rather than hand over the inheritance when Louis returned unexpectedly after being presumed dead (294–6). This story has more depth than the stories about ghosts that precede it in the volume. Crowe creates a tale of wills, leases and rental agreements, all tied up with a ghost that seems one with the house itself, disappearing into the wall as he does. Women and children are presented as being more receptive to ghostly appearances while men bear the financial burden of hauntings without being able to experience the spectre for themselves.

In the frame tale, the Swiss lady narrator recounts the story to Crowe when the two meet on a steamboat in Switzerland. The Swiss lady attests to the veracity of the tale by claiming to be related to several of its participants, since her mother was the English girl who finally communicated with the ghost. British readers would have enjoyed reading about the plucky English family who solved a Swiss murder mystery that had stumped the locals. Moreover, the Swiss lady's story shows that in the laying of the ghost, her English family made powerful allies and became enmeshed in Swiss society, a society into which she herself has married. Such a tale gives lonely readers sitting by their fire a ghostly thriller embedded within an elevated class setting.

The country house Christmas frame continued as a staple for decades. Henry James's most famous ghost story, *The Turn of the Screw* (1898), opens with a carefully wrought Christmas circle connection. The Gothic horror of the governess's and the children's narrative may blot out memories of the story's opening page; however, *The Turn of the Screw* begins on Christmas Eve amidst a country house Christmas party. One guest hesitantly mentions a manuscript in his possession, a testimony from a governess he knew. He sends to town for the old pages and then reads the chilling tale to his eager audience over the course of several late December evenings (James 1981: 4–11). As in Crowe's tale, the storytelling circle is an extended, multi-night experience.

Jerome and the Late-Century Parodies

Victorian authors and audiences were so familiar with the frame tale format that late-century samples spoofed it. Parodies of ghost stories were common in and out of Christmas reading at the end of the century (Freeman 2012: 100). Comic writer and author of *Three Men and a Boat* (1889) Jerome K. Jerome put his hand to a parody with a duodecimo volume *Told after Supper* (1891). Jerome knew he was repeating a well-worn theme, and his preface plays around with the concept: 'Whenever five or six English-speaking people meet round a fire on Christmas Eve, they start telling each other ghost stories. [...] It is a genial, festive season, and we love to muse upon graves, and dead bodies, and murders, and blood' (Jerome 1891: 15–16).

Jerome's tales are comical rather than eerie. Their author presumes the novelty of ghosts has been exhausted, so he takes the line of being completely bored by the need to produce more tired ghost stories. The volume's tone echoes Dickens's similar observation made forty years earlier in 'A Christmas Tree'. Jerome makes no effort to frighten; instead, the narrator quips about the ubiquitous nature of Christmas Eve ghosts, a belaboured and threadbare tradition, according to him. Jerome's snide comments position him as superior to the custom, but entirely immersed in it as well. He opens with a section highlighting the frame tale, entitled 'How the Stories Came to Be Told'. The narrator joins friends at his uncle's row home in Tooting – a London suburb – for Christmas Eve dinner and serious drinking. The guests share ghost stories during their bouts of sobriety, and the volume offers these stories as embedded texts.

The volume ends by shifting back into the frame tale. The Christmas Eve party dissolves, and the narrator, supposedly Jerome himself, eagerly heads upstairs to spend the remainder of the night in a room supposedly haunted every Christmas Eve. There the character Jerome meets the Ghost of the Blue Chamber, the star of one of the earlier embedded texts known to have murdered several annoying street musicians. After a relaxed chat, the ghostly encounter ends with a ridiculous scene: the ghost tricks Jerome into walking into the street dressed in only his nightclothes, to the shame of his family. Jerome prefaces his report of the ghost with a long, meta-explanation about how 'we literary men of the new school have one praiseworthy yearning [...] never to appear in the slightest degree egotistical' (Jerome 1891: 123). The embarrassing, trouserless conclusion simultaneously flaunts Jerome's self-mockery and casts faith in ghosts in a comical light. Overall, Jerome gives a tongue-in-cheek performance.

M. R. James: Continuing the Christmas Reading Scenario

Christmastime ghosts saw some developments at the end of the century and up until the First World War. The well-worn reading fad elicited parody in some quarters, as demonstrated by Jerome. In others, it reached a new creative level. Christmas ghosts inhabit M. R. James's early twentieth-century collections, including *A Thin Ghost and Others* (1919). The author pens a preface that emphasises the escapism of Christmas ghosts: 'the tales make no pretence [sic] but to amuse [...] perhaps also some one's Christmas may be the cheerfuller for a storybook which, I think, only once mentions the war' (James 1919: i). Contemporary reviewers echoed James's hopes. One wrote, 'many a fireside will enjoy Christmas all the more for the thrills received' from the volume (Webb 1920: 143). Another wrote, 'A flavour of olde times, of long-past Christmases, and of Yule logs and snapdragons – though these are never mentioned – comes with this delightfully blood-curdling book' (Harper 1920: 60). Post-war readers seeking nostalgic Christmas escapism now knew where to turn.

The Christmas reading scenario remains at the forefront of the stories' production. This volume is filled with more authentic thrills than most ghost stories offer, probably because the tales avoid stereotypes and forge their own path. 'The Story of a Disappearance and an Appearance'– the only tale in the collection to depict a Christmas setting – is told through a collection of eighty-year-old letters. The correspondent/narrator, W. R., writes to his brother in the days before Christmas 1837 to regretfully excuse himself from their manor house Christmas plans. He must forgo that pleasure to investigate a missing persons case – that of their uncle, a rural vicar with the personality of a martinet.

The letters themselves turn into Christmastime reading for the brother who receives them at the heart of his family's holiday celebration.

He may even read them around the fire to his family. The imagined 'big hall' Christmas reading scenario set in 1837 adds a thrill to James's real readers seeking to access Christmas traditions of storytelling in 1919. By perusing the beguiling letters, James's reader poses as the country house squire/brother. The reader gets a part in the play.

The letters start innocuously enough. W. R. hopes that he might wrap up the business and join the rest of the family by Christmas Day. Then the letters suddenly veer away from that cosy scene to detail the police search and W. R.'s own inquiries. After two days of fruitless searching, W. R. describes his eerie dream of a particularly vicious Punch and Judy show, one that causes him to compare Punch to Satan and a vampire. In the dream a hooded figure pursues Punch in a weird and troubling attack. W. R. details his dream in a letter to his brother. A subsequent letter wraps up the mystery with a Gothic, supernatural finale. W. R.'s final letter describes the haunted Christmas Day church service and a second, uncanny Punch and Judy experience.

Ironically, W. R. first tries to read the final instalment of *Pickwick Papers* after church, but he falls asleep over it. The medium he consumes instead on this Christmas afternoon is the cursed Punch and Judy show performed just outside his window after he awakens. The reference to Dickens's novel serves as a world-building detail for 1837. It also contrasts W. R.'s desired Christmas Day reading (jolly Pickwick) with the ghost story's shocking conclusion.

James's depiction of a rural Punch and Judy show channels Gothic horror. W. R. watches as the public performance deteriorates into inexplicable, terrifying chaos during the puppet show's traditional hanging scene. It seems a figure with a bag on his head had appeared in the show box. One performer dies in the show box, and the other takes off running. The fleeing puppeteer falls into a pit and dies. Some bystanders claim to have seen a third spectral figure fleeing the show box too. Later, the missing uncle's body is found buried in the same pit with his head covered in a bag and his throat mangled. W. R. ends the story without resolving the mystery, but clues suggest that the murdered vicar returned to take his revenge on the Punch and Judy performers.

This Christmastime ghost enacts a type of corporeal, hands-on agency that is lacking in earlier ghosts. Jennifer Bann notes that Dickens's Jacob Marley is merely a catalyst to another character's change (Bann 2009: 663). Crowe's ghost silently approaches the women of the house, requesting that they demolish the wall that hides his body. Many of the ghosts prepared for Christmas reading indicate their problem and wait for living observers to take action on their behalf – find their body, find their gold, live better lives – but later ghosts appear to gain agency

(Bann 2009: 664). In James's spectral tale, the vicar's spirit hopes that law enforcement or his nephew will take the correct action and find his killers. When the living appear to give up the effort, the ghost acts to kill his murderers and reveal the hiding place of his own corpse. He literally lifts the one murderer like a puppet behind the Punch and Judy curtain in a terrible variation of the entertainment. Both brothers, W. R. and his correspondent reading in the heart of a 'big hall' Christmas, must adjust to the fact that their relative has taken corporeal form and meted out wrathful revenge.

Conclusion

Throughout the nineteenth century the tradition of the Christmas ghost story was intrinsically tied to the Christmas storytelling gathering. In many cases, the set-up for telling the story was as important as the ghostly content of the tale itself. Plenty of ghost stories were printed without the beloved frame; nonetheless, these narratives existed within the known context: the expectation of how one ought to read such a story. The cosiness of the Christmas storytelling circle cannot be overstated. Readers treasured the ironic reading experience, a snug setting in which to hear unsettling content. Authors and readers wished to recreate that ironic experience for more than a century. The hero of *The Pickwick Papers* is just one such character who performs the Christmastime dream on behalf of his audience. Mr Pickwick enjoys the Christmas Eve gambols and feasting at Dingley Dell, then joins a fireside storytelling circle arranged beside 'a huge fire of blazing logs'. '"This," said Mr. Pickwick, looking round him, "this is, indeed, comfort"' (Dickens 2008: 351). Dickens's eager readers and many more like them throughout the long nineteenth century sought out Christmas ghost stories as a way to access that same idealised holiday delight.

Works Cited

Bann, Jennifer. 'Ghostly Hands and the Ghostly Agency: The Changing Figure of the Nineteenth-Century Spectre'. *Victorian Studies*, vol. 51, no. 4, 2009, pp. 663–85.

Bourne, Henry. *Antiquitates vulgares; or, the Antiquities of the common people, giving an account of several of their opinions and ceremonies, etc.* Newcastle: John White, 1725.

Broughton, Rhoda. *Tales for Christmas Eve.* London: Richard Bentley and Son, 1873.

Chitwood, Brandon. 'Eternal Returns: *A Christmas Carol*'s Ghosts of Repetition'. *Victorian Literature and Culture*, vol. 43, 2015, pp. 675–87.
Clery, E. J. *The Rise of Supernatural Fiction, 1762–1899*. New York: Cambridge University Press, 1995.
Crowe, Catherine. *Ghosts and Family Legends: A Volume for Christmas*. Leopold Classic Library, 1859.
Dickens, Charles. *A Christmas Carol*. London: Chapman and Hall, 1843.
———. 'A Christmas Tree'. *Household Words: A Christmas Number*, 1850, pp. 289–95. https://archive.org/details/householdwords02dicklond/page/294/mode/2up (last accessed 3 January 2025).
———. *The Haunted Man and the Ghost's Bargain*. London: Bradbury & Evans, 1848.
———. *The Pickwick Papers*. Oxford: Oxford University Press, 2008.
———. 'The Poor Relation's Story', in *The Christmas Books and Reprinted Pieces*. New York: John B. Alden, 1883, pp. 650–9.
Dickey, Colin. 'A Plea to Resurrect the Christmas Tradition of Telling Ghost Stories'. *Smithsonian Magazine*, 15 December 2017. https://www.smithsonianmag.com/history/plea-resurrect-christmas-tradition-telling-ghost-stories-180967553/ (last accessed 3 January 2025).
Freeman, Nick. 'The Victorian Ghost Story', in Andrew Smith and William Hughes (eds), *The Victorian Gothic: An Edinburgh Companion*. Edinburgh: Edinburgh University Press, 2012, pp. 93–107.
Gaskell, Elizabeth. 'The Old Nurse's Tale', in Laura Kranzler (ed.), *Gothic Tales*. London: Penguin, 2000, pp. 11–32.
Growth, Helen. 'Reading Victorian Illusions: Dickens's *Haunted Man* and Dr. Pepper's "Ghost"'. *Victorian Studies*, vol. 50, no. 1, 2007, pp. 43–65.
Harper, Edith K. Review of *A Thin Ghost and Others* by M. R. James. *The Occult Review*, vol. 31, 1920, p. 60.
Heholt, Ruth. 'Science, Ghosts and Vision: Catherine Crowe's Bodies of Evidence and the Critique of Masculinity'. *Victoriographies: A Journal of Nineteenth-Century Writing, 1790–1914*, vol. 4, no. 1, 2014, pp. 46–61.
Ingleby, Matthew. 'Chemistry versus Biology: Dickens, Malthus, and the Familiarized Doppelganger'. *Victorian Review*, vol. 39, no. 2, 2013, pp. 97–113.
Irving, Washington. *The Sketchbook of Geoffrey Crayon, Gent*. New York: G. P. Putnam, Hurt and Houghton, 1867.
James, Henry. *The Turn of the Screw*. New York: Bantam Dell, 1981.
James, M. R. *A Thin Ghost and Others*. New York: Longmans, 1919.
Jerome, Jerome K. *Told after Supper*. London: The Leadenhall Press, 1891.
Kim, Katherine J. 'Catherine Crowe, Charles Dickens, and Perceptions of Female Insanity'. *Dickens Quarterly*, vol. 28, no. 3, 2021, pp. 277–9.
Miles, Clement A. *Christmas in Ritual and Tradition Christian and Pagan*. London: T. Fisher Unwin, 1912.
Moore, Tara. *Victorian Christmas in Print*. New York: Routledge, 2009.
Review of *The Castle of Otranto, a Story* by Horace Walpole. *The Critical Review, or Annals of Literature*, vol. 19, 1765, pp. 50–1.
Round about Our Coal Fire: Or Christmas Entertainments [1730]. H. Fenwick, 1796.
Scott, Walter. *Marmion: A Tale of Flodden Field in Six Cantos*. London: Macmillan, 1887.

Smith, Andrew. *The Ghost Story, 1840–1920: A Cultural History*. Manchester: Manchester University Press, 2010.

Storey, John. 'The Invention of the English Christmas', in Sheila Whiteley (ed.), *Christmas, Ideology and Popular Culture*. Edinburgh: Edinburgh University Press, 2008, pp. 17–31.

Tracy, Robert. '"A Whimsical Kind of Masque": The Christmas Books and Victorian Spectacle'. *Dickens Studies Annual*, vol. 27, 1998, pp. 113–30.

Webb, B. Review of *A Thin Ghost and Others*. By M. R. James. *The Bookman*, 1920, p. 143.

Part III

Authors

Chapter 12

Charles Dickens
Scott Brewster

Dickens's final supernatural tale, 'No. 1 Branch Line: The Signal-Man' (1866) asks the central question that underlies all of his ghost stories: '"What does the spectre mean?"' (Dickens 2010: 100). Andrew Smith observes that 'Dickens's ghosts are always about something other than just being ghosts' (Smith 2010: 33), but what is that 'something other'? In Dickens's fiction and journalism, ghosts fulfil a variety of functions: sources of diverting fireside entertainment, designed to induce 'an agreeable creeping up our back', as Dickens observed in 'A Christmas Tree' [1850] (Dickens 1997: 12); agents of justice, vengeance, moral guidance or social critique; or symptoms of physical or psychological illness. Ghosts are 'something' to reckon with, even if they are a thing of nothing, but what do they have to tell us? As the signalman anxiously admits, this question 'troubles me so dreadfully' (Dickens 2010: 100). Although they generate fascination, attract profound belief and prompt serious scientific scrutiny, spirits remain an unresolved question in Victorian culture. As Dickens reflects in 1848, ghosts are '[d]oubtful and scant of proof at first, doubtful and scant of proof still' (Dickens 1996: 83), but throughout his career he continued to pursue, or come to terms with, the enigmatic spectre.

A Christmas Carol (1843), Dickens's best-known ghost story, may provide a partial, albeit perplexing, answer in the phantasmal shape of Jacob Marley, replete in his clanking chains but unmistakeably modern in sensibility. To some degree, Marley stands in 'a long tradition of the limited dead' (Bann 2009: 663), a spirit come from beyond the grave to tell of endings rather than beginnings. Of course, in this tale ghosts have comedic and homiletic qualities, reinforcing a benign but ultimately conservative vision: Scrooge must revert to tried-and-tested forms of community, generosity and fellowship, reconnecting with a cherished past and doing good in the present. Yet, just as it does for the signalman and his curious visitor, the apparition makes Scrooge stare uncertainly into the darkness. While Marley is 'dead as a door-nail', this not to affirm absolute closure. This definitive judgement deals in metaphor and its deferral of precise, unequivocal meaning, as the narrator admits: 'I don't mean to say that I know, of my own knowledge what there is particularly dead about a door-nail.' Marley's name survives on the door of the warehouse, constantly bringing Scrooge's late lamented partner back to life: 'Sometimes people new to the business called Scrooge Scrooge, and sometimes Marley, but he answered to both names. It was all the same to him' (Dickens 2006: 9). Nevertheless, although apparently interchangeable with his living partner, Marley (being dead) is also irreducibly separate. This commerce, or permeability, between the living and the dead is charted by the Victorian ghost story. Spectres, the intimate dead, represent an ending and a starting point, at once reminding us of former days and vigorously inhabiting the present. They are, above all, something to reckon, and think, with. From the early interpolated tales in *The Pickwick Papers*, to the Christmas books and the epistemological uncertainties of his final stories, the nature of ghost-seeing and the allegorical meaning of spirits is never settled for Dickens. In a period often preoccupied by the invisible and unseen, the ghost represents for Dickens a figure of doubtful *and* privileged perception.

Early in the nineteenth century, the self-contained ghost story typically appears as an interlude lending variety and changes of pace and intensity to larger narratives, epitomised by 'Wandering Willie's Tale', an episode in Walter Scott's *Redgauntlet* (1824). Dickens's first ghost stories are inset tales centred on the intimate storytelling circle, which became a staple feature of the form, and they establish the formal and thematic characteristics of his later supernatural tales. In *The Pickwick Papers* (1837), ghost stories are festive entertainments at Dingley Dell, anticipating Dickens's Christmas books in the next decade. The playfulness distinguishing many of these early ghost stories offers a marked contrast to the solemn, meditative turn of his later supernatural fiction. In 'The Bagman's Story', Tom Smart stops at a roadside inn, 'a strange old place' presided over by a 'buxom widow' (Dickens 2003: 187). Liberally fortified with hot punch, Tom discovers a 'queer' chair in his room gradually assuming the form 'of a very ugly old man, of the previous century, with his arms a-kimbo' (189–90). The widow's 'guardian', this haunted chair enlists the traveller's help in warding off an unwelcome suitor and, for his assistance, the enterprising Tom is rewarded by marrying the woman himself. While many attribute these events to intoxication or expedient invention, the story suggests that receptiveness to the dead may prove beneficial, and 'the past might haunt us for our own good' (Wood 2017: 94). 'The Story of the Bagman's Uncle', recounting a fantastic adventure that involves travelling back to bygone days and unlikely feats of derring-do in Edinburgh, offers less tangible instruction or reward. As Jack Martin awakens in a dilapidated coach, his wondrous journey may be explained more prosaically as a drunken dream. Although not 'of a marvellous or romantic turn' (Dickens 2003: 647), he holds nonetheless to the veracity of his haunting experience, feeling privileged to be the only living person to enjoy a night-time excursion with the 'ghosts of mail-coaches and horses, guards, coachmen, and passengers' (659).

In 'The Story of the Goblins Who Stole a Sexton', the supernatural or ghostly takes on a homiletic function, even if the narrative remains predominantly in the comic key. Set in an 'old abbey town', the story carries a wry disclaimer: coming from so long ago, the tale 'must be a true one, because our great grandfathers implicitly believed it' (380). Gabriel Grub the sexton is an 'ill-conditioned, cross-grained, surly fellow' in the manner of Ebenezer Scrooge. Merrily going to dig a grave on a twilit Christmas Eve, Grub treats festive cheer in the community as 'gall and wormwood' (381). Disturbed by goblins in the churchyard, who vault irreverently over the gravestones, the sexton is identified as 'the man with the sulky face and grim scowl' who struck a young boy 'in the envious malice of his heart' (385) and is then taken underground to learn his lesson. As with Scrooge's spectral visitations, Grub is shown visions of honest toil, patient suffering and constant 'affection and devotedness' (389). Resonantly for *A Christmas Carol*, the first scene depicts frugal domestic harmony that quickly becomes clouded as family members begin to die; the demise of the angelic youngest child is a clear forerunner of Tiny Tim. This supernatural encounter induces a change in the haunted protagonist. Back in the upper human world, the repentant Grub leaves town, but his return a decade later, a 'ragged contented, rheumatic old man' (390), happy to relate this instructive tale for the public good, recalls Washington Irving's 'Rip Van Winkle' (1819).

Contrastingly, 'A Madman's Manuscript' foregrounds the uncertain relation between psychological instability and spirit-seeing which would become a recurrent concern in Dickens's writing on the supernatural. Confined in an asylum, the narrator is constantly visited by the spectre of his dead wife, whom he attempted to murder before being declared insane: 'I see, standing still and motionless in one corner of this cell, a slight and wasted figure with long black hair, which streaming down her back, stirs with no earthly wind, and eyes that fix their gaze on me, and never wink or close.' While specifying that the phantom appears 'when I start up from my sleep', his perception is shaped by the 'madness ... mixed up with my very blood, and the marrow of my bones' (151). Afflicted by the 'pestilence' of inherited mental illness, the 'old spirits' passed down the family line impelled him to attack his unhappily married bride, in order to prevent psychological disorder being passed onto future generations. For all the method in this 'madness', however, the reader is invited to view the ghost either as an agent of justice, or merely as a symptom of the narrator's guilt or delusion.

Nicholas Nickleby (1839) again situates the ghost story within a storytelling competition. 'The Baron of Grozwig' performs a didactic function, albeit its 'laudable example' (Dickens 2003: 86) is somewhat equivocal. When contemplating desperate measures to escape financial ruin after a life of uninhibited pleasure and moral turpitude, the eponymous nobleman is confronted by a 'wrinkled hideous figure', the spectral 'Genius of Despair and Suicide' (82–3). Instead of hastening the act of self-destruction, however, the spectre's appearance prompts a moment of contemplation: its gloomy counsel encourages the baron to count his blessings and reflect that '"nothing is too bad to be retrieved"' (84). Spirits restored (as it were) through his insouciant response to haunting, the baron laughs the admonitory ghost to scorn and resolves to '"put good face on the matter"', bringing his wife and in-laws 'to reason' and leaving behind 'a numerous family' (85).

Master Humphrey's Clock (1840–1) features a supernatural tale revolving around the interweaving of ghosts, obsession and unassuageable guilt seen in 'A Madman's Manuscript'. Like a number of Dickens's protagonists, who are prisoners of the past and unable to escape crimes of thought and deed, the narrator of the 'found' tale, 'The Clock Face: A Confession Found in a Prison in the Time of Charles the Second', is haunted by the living and the dead. Having taken charge of his nephew when the boy's parents die, the narrator develops a strange fascination with the child that is not purely motivated by financial gain. The boy's intent gaze reminds him of his sister-in-law, whose (presumably disapproving) gaze 'haunted me'; even in the condemned cell, her 'fixed and steady look comes back upon me now like the memory of a dark dream and makes my blood run cold' (Dickens 1978: 88). About to murder his nephew to banish this memory, he looks at the boy's face and sees that '[h]is mother's ghost was looking from his eyes' (89). The consequences of his actions blur the boundary between reality and delusion, tormenting him with dreams of capture and the discovery of the child's body. Visited by a former military comrade, he becomes utterly distracted and confesses to the crime: this ending portrays haunting as a symptom of psychological, as well as moral, disorder.

Dickens has often been regarded as 'inventing' the Christmas ghost story, a development giving major impetus to the form through the Victorian period, and continuing in robust health up to the present day. Yet he inherited rather than inaugurated the Yuletide tale of phantoms, an abiding part of popular tradition across the British and Irish Isles stretching back to the fifteenth century. Thomas K. Hervey's *The Book of Christmas* (1836) makes the 'blazing fire' in winter a perfect place to 'awaken those impressions of the wild and shadowy and insubstantial, to which tales of marvel, or of terror, are such welcome food' (Hervey 1888: 237–8). For Hervey, the winter tale is not solely about pleasurable frights: it is connected to Christmas 'observances which had a direct tendency to propagate a feeling of brotherhood and a spirit of benevolence' (1888: 26). Dickens's strongest literary precedent was Washington Irving's *The Sketchbook of Geoffrey Crayon, Gent* (1820). A pioneer of the ghost story, Irving immerses his eponymous New World visitor in the winter customs of the old country, helping to revivify Christmas traditions for an English readership. Although acknowledging that he may have succumbed to nostalgic 'fallacy', Irving's traveller celebrates England's 'holyday customs and rural games of former times', when the world seemed 'more homebred, social, and joyous, than at present' (Irving 2014: 169). Christmas epitomises this vision of communality, serving a familial and wider social function: it is 'the season for kindling not merely the fire of hospitality in the hall, but the genial flame of charity in the heart' (173). Such warmth will eventually thaw Scrooge's icy heart, even if this fireside is also the stage for winter tales of terror. Invited to join the seasonal festivities at Bracebridge Hall in rural Yorkshire, Crayon participates in a feast of music, decorative colour, lavish fare and cherished tradition that wears its feudal origins lightly. The Squire, who anticipates Fezziwig in *A Christmas Carol*, is 'a bigoted devotee of the old school, and prides himself upon keeping up something of old English hospitality' (181). From bringing in the boar's head to wassailing, the merriment echoes back 'the joviality of long departed years' (217). Against the charge of 'garrulity' and writing for mere amusement, Crayon pleads that his account of Christmas 'gambols' has been in the service of moral improvement, prompting 'a benevolent view of human nature' and making the reader 'more in good humour with his fellow beings and himself' (218). While Dickens's Christmas tales can be said to serve similar enlightening and celebratory purposes, they move gradually from comedy and social critique to brooding introspection.

'A Christmas Tree', from the Christmas number of *Household Words* in 1850, recalls the toys, decorations and pleasures of childhood. In an 'old house', Dickens conjures the classic scenario for the ghost story:

> There is probably a smell of roasted chestnuts and other good comfortable things all the time, for we are telling Winter Stories – Ghost Stories, or more shame for us – round the Christmas fire; and we have never stirred, except to draw a little nearer to it. (Dickens 1997: 11)

Similarly, 'Nurse's Stories', published in *All the Year Round* in 1860, returns to early days and recalls Dickens's youthful imagination being nourished by a diet of sensational and supernatural tales. Indeed, Harry Stone has called the Christmas ghost stories 'fairy-tales' whose 'machinery' (the manipulation of time, personification and animism) cloaks horror and suffering in 'joyful affirmation' and enables protagonists to learn the error of their ways and impart a moral lesson (Stone 1999: 11–12).

Dickens's Christmas spectres have clear intentions to instruct, entertain and act as the catalyst for seasonal goodwill and transitory harmony. The Preface to *A Christmas Carol* gently acknowledges its homiletic spirit, but presents haunting in hospitable terms:

> I have endeavoured in this Ghostly book to raise the Ghost of an Idea which shall not put my readers out of humour with themselves, with each other, with the season, or with me. May it haunt their houses pleasantly, and no one wish to lay it. (Dickens 2006: 6)

Far from homely, the abode of Scrooge, 'a squeezing, wrenching, grasping, clutching, covetous old sinner [...] warning all human sympathy to keep its distance', is haunted unpleasantly. Definitely out of humour with the season, and with others, Scrooge condemns anyone celebrating Christmas to be 'boiled with his own pudding, and buried with a stake of holly through his heart' (10–11). Unsurprisingly, perhaps, he returns home on Christmas Eve to find his door knocker resembling Jacob Marley's face, 'with ghostly spectacles turned up on its ghostly forehead' (17), anticipating his former partner's role as a ghostly portal that night. Marley's shade confounds Scrooge's best efforts to dismiss the apparition as humbug, the product of digestive disorder or a derangement of reason: as Marley stresses, the living man should not doubt the evidence of his senses (21).

Wound in a chain made of 'cash-boxes, keys, padlocks, ledgers, deeds, and heavy purses wrought in steel' (19), Marley laments that this encumbrance was 'forged in life', since his spirit 'never roved beyond the narrow limits of our money-changing hole' (22–3). Andrew Smith suggests that many Dickens ghost stories function 'as allegories about how individuals negotiate their way around the financial system even whilst that system appears to psychologically "possess" them' (Smith 2010: 34), and Marley seems to typify such possession. Shackled to the financial system, money made him lifeless before death, and he is doomed to carry this burden in the world beyond. Yet this returning spectre seems to transport us momentarily, even impossibly (Marley is 'only' a ghost, after all) beyond the dead weight of capitalism, which veils itself behind the magical aura of objects. A thing of nothing that will melt into air, the restless Marley materialises to estrange Scrooge's vision and open him to a form of social critique. Although the spirits who follow Marley fulfil a predictable homiletic role, they do not walk the formulaic 'beaten track' described by Dickens in 'A Christmas Tree' (Dickens 1997: 12). Reversing and accelerating time, these phantoms are mobile, leading Scrooge beyond his customary habits and ingrained prejudices. They wander far and wide, taking Scrooge on enlightening journeys that expose not only his losses and regrets, but also the stark social and economic inequalities around him, epitomised by the figures of Ignorance and Want, who are 'wretched, abject, frightful, hideous, miserable' children (Dickens 2006: 61).

As he awakens to 'an altered life' on Christmas morning, vowing to live '"in the Past, the Present, and the Future"' (2006: 77), Scrooge's charity and fellow-feeling returns us to Irving's sentimental account of traditional festive entertainments. This localised resolution nonetheless leaves the economic underpinning of that society intact. Scrooge's belated largesse, designed to promote non-transactional ties and affection, cannot remedy wider social problems. As Dewi Evans notes, while Dickens was in part provoked to write *A Christmas Carol* as a response to the *Second Report of the Children's Employment Commission* (1842), the story 'constituted the invention of a new commodity for middle-class consumers to purchase at Christmas'. Priced at five shillings, out of reach of most potential readers, the book can be seen as 'designed to assuage the anxieties of a middle-class readership', selling a fairy tale of 'stability and cohesion' (Evans 2017: 81) during a time of significant social unrest in England. A veiled awareness of these limitations to ghost-seeing may account for the increasingly dark tone of his Christmas stories.

In *The Chimes* (1844), ghosts visit a figure who lacks Scrooge's wealth and relative privilege. The street-porter Toby Veck, however, does cross the path of the upper orders, including the heartless political economist Filer, the condescending Alderman nostalgic about 'good old times' (Dickens 2006: 108) but arrogantly dismissive about want and starvation in the present day, or the patrician Sir Joseph Bowley MP, claiming to be the poor man's friend but utterly indifferent to the reality faced by working people. This conceit enables a satirical examination of hypocrisy and inequality reminiscent of *A Christmas Carol*, but here the central protagonist feels the consequences of poverty directly.

Despite his straitened circumstances, Toby is optimistic rather than haunted at the year's end, with his daughter Meg to be married on New Year's Day to her strong-minded lover Richard, a young man with 'certain' employment 'for some time to come' (98). He also displays seasonal spirit and selfless generosity to the 'turbulent and rebellious spirit' Will Fern, who faces imprisonment, and Fern's orphaned niece. Initially indignant about the rumour that his beloved bells are haunted, or 'connected with any Evil thing' (92), Toby's night-time 'swoon' (122) in the bell-tower affords him ghostly visions of unhappy futures for his family and friends, as the hope and charity of his immediate present descends into despair. In the belfry, 'the dread and terror of the lonely place, and of the wild and fearful night that reigned there, touched him like a spectral hand' (127). First goblins sport, 'leaping, flying, dropping, pouring from the Bells without a pause', and when this 'swarm' fades away, the Spirits of the Bells present visions of possible events to come. Fern's desire to rectify social injustice turns him to insurrectionary activity, and Toby helplessly watches as his 'blighted' child Meg is left without work and eventually abandons her child before drowning herself. As Toby hears the chimes 'ring the joy-peals of the New Year: so lustily, so merrily, so happily, so gaily', the spell is broken and prompts him to declare that '"I know we must trust and hope, and neither doubt ourselves, nor doubt the good in one another"' (157). Amid the marriage celebrations of Meg and Richard, the reader is urged to 'endeavour to correct, improve, and soften' the 'stern realities from which these shadows come' (161).

Progressively, however, Dickens's Christmas stories become less certain about the ghost's didactic or homeopathic capacity. In the final Christmas book, *The Haunted Man and the Ghost's Bargain* (1848), the shadows of *The Chimes* return but acquire a more introspective and sombre cast. When the lonely chemist Redlaw, whose solitary lifestyle already makes him seem haunted, encounters his spectral mirror image, this 'dread companion' (2006: 338) offers him the chance to forget the pain of the past, the memory of 'sorrow and trouble', and to relinquish its 'intertwisted chain of feelings and associations' (343). As a result of this wish being granted, Redlaw destroys painful memories in others, but also banishes their compassion, sympathy and kindness. The phantom's bargain has made Redlaw 'infectious', and this 'poison' (343) means that rancour, '"[s]elfishness and ingratitude spring up in my blighted footsteps"' (370), very different from Scrooge's walking with ghosts. The narrative ensures a modest restoration of seasonal spirit, with Redlaw revealing his affliction on Christmas morning; his experience is ascribed a 'natural' explanation, with the ghost being merely 'the representation of his gloomy thoughts' (408). Familial connections and cherished memories are renewed, demonstrating that Christmas is a moment when 'the memory of every remediable sorrow, wrong, and trouble in the world around us, should be active within us' (407). This suggests, uncomfortably, that we *should* be haunted, since pain and loss keep us alive to the present and the future. Such understanding has been enabled by the spectre, a relic of bygone times that challenges us and will not leave us alone.

After his Christmas tales, Dickens's approach to ghosts subtly changes. Spectres become associated with a broader range of uncanny and occult phenomena, and his supernatural stories display increasing self-reflexivity. In addition to his fiction and editorial responsibilities, Dickens's journalism played an important role in public debates on the supernatural. His attitude to ghosts was equivocal; as Louise Henson comments, while he put 'well-attested ghost stories' into circulation, he advocated rigorous enquiry into ghosts, and responded suspiciously to 'bald credulity and superstitious belief' (Henson 2004: 44). Dickens's review of Catherine Crowe's *The Night Side of Nature* (1848) exemplifies this scepticism towards reported sightings of spirits: 'in vast numbers of cases they are known to be delusions superintended by a well-understood, and by no means uncommon disease' (Dickens 1996: 83). In his rejection of Crowe's credulity, Dickens demonstrates his adherence to earlier medical accounts of ghost-seeing. Both Walter Scott's *Letters on Demonology and Witchcraft* (1830) and David Brewster's *Letters on Natural Magic* (1832) sought to explain ghosts as optical illusions produced by 'the deceived or diseased eye of the beholder' (Smajić 2010: 4). Spectres were tricks of the eye that could be explained in physiological or psychological terms and, as Srdjan Smajić observes, 'optical theory' would become a 'staple' of the ghost story form in the nineteenth century (Smajić 2010: 45). Dickens's mesmeric 'treatment' of Augusta de la Rue in 1845 also shaped his conception of ghosts, which he regarded as the consequence of a disturbed nervous system (Henson 2004: 46–7). Yet Dickens's dismissal of Crowe masks uncomfortable affinities in their approach to ghosts. While treating accounts of apparitions seriously, she claims that the phenomena under investigation would one day be 'reduced strictly within the bounds of science' (Crowe 2000: 22). Equally, Crowe deploys methods similar to those used by Dickens in gathering material on the supernatural, collecting 'real' ghost stories and perusing philosophical and medical texts. As Dickens's later stories demonstrate, any psychological 'explanation' for ghosts is scarcely an answer: the spectre merely raises new questions that test scientific theory and spiritual belief.

'To be Read at Dusk' (1852) engages with the contemporary debates outlined above about the relationship between mental health and the supernatural. Set in the Swiss Alps, it features two framed tales shared by German and Swiss couriers who deny they are talking of ghosts, but cannot find an alternative term for their inexplicable experiences. The frame narrator is a silent English auditor who, unlike these European travellers, may position himself as less susceptible to superstitious lore. More an account of uncanny premonition, or sinister mesmeric influence, than a ghost story, the first tale concerns a young bride on honeymoon on the Riviera 'haunted' by a dream of a man's face staring from the darkness. To her barely concealed terror, this creature of imagination materialises as the mysterious Signore Dellombra ('of the shadow' in Italian), who befriends the woman's husband before carrying her away. Premonition, or foresight, also lies at the heart of the second tale. In this instance, it can be read as an example of phantasms of the living, which would be researched by the Society for Psychical Research in the 1880s. This phenomenon involved an encounter with the apparitions of living people who 'may be on the very brink and border of physical dissolution' (Gurney, Myers and Podmore 1886: xxxv). The German courier who relays the story hails, according to his former English employer, from 'a sensible country, where mysterious things are inquired into and are not settled to have been weighed and measured – or to have been unweighable and unmeasurable – or in either case to have been completely disposed of, for all time – ever so many years ago' (Dickens 1978: 108). Hesitations in this declaration may be explained by the fact that the Englishman has just seen the phantom of his brother, whom he subsequently discovers has fallen mortally ill. Both men are aware of this premonition, a form of thought transference, or perhaps ghost-walking, before life has ebbed away. As these strange narratives end, the frame narrator sits alone in the silence, the group having departed 'as if the ghostly mountain might have absorbed them into its eternal snows' (109). Ghostliness lingers as an eerie after-effect, and the narrator retreats inside to hear a more down-to-earth anecdote from the American traveller he has previously avoided.

Dickens returns to the inset story in 'The Ghost in the Bride's Chamber', which appears in *The Lazy Tour of Two Idle Apprentices* (1857). The book, published in sections in *Household Words*, records a walking tour of north-west England undertaken by Dickens and Wilkie Collins, who use the pseudonyms Francis Goodchild and Thomas Idle. While mainly a light-hearted diversion, Dickens's ghost story represents an intriguing reflection on the nature of ghost-seeing and ghost-writing, the very basis of the supernatural tale. Staying in an old house, the travellers encounter a group of 'noiseless old men' (Dickens 1978: 110) who silently accompany the landlord and waiter, and one of this strange number relates the story of the haunted room. After a tale of cheated prospects, marital cruelty, murder and the pursuit of 'dark trade' (123), the lugubrious man reveals himself to be the ghost of the murderer hanged at Lancaster Castle. Forced, as in his later years, to remain in the house, 'evermore to live with a rope around this neck' (122), the wraith haunts the chamber along with his victims. In an echo of 'A Madman's Manuscript', the phantom of his young bride, 'a white wreck again' (126), urges him to 'live' through each night. Such punishment will end only if 'two living men, with their eyes open, could be in the Bride's chamber at One in the morning' (127). Since Idle has already been charmed to sleep, this hope is dashed, as on the previous occasion when two men dared to spend the night in the bedroom, and only one stayed awake: '[t]o him alone, I was an awful phantom making quite a useless confession' (129). Resigned once more to sharing his story with a single witness, the phantom reflects that his situation may be eternal.

Seized with 'indescribable dread', Goodchild breaks the spell cast by 'fiery lines extending from the old man's eyes to his own' (125) and flees with his groggy companion, leaving the ghost to his lonely vigil. There is nothing final to say in this frightening episode, unlike the life-changing transformations that mark most of Dickens's Christmas stories, but the spectre's account remains painfully open. Futilely, he shares his tale with one of the living who cannot lay the ghost to rest or authenticate its reality, and whose evidence can be discounted as subjective or delusional. As the ghost acknowledges, to make an impression is the perennial problem for returning spirits: '"When I appear, the senses of one of the two will be locked in sleep; he will neither see nor hear me; my communication will ever be made to a solitary listener, and will ever be unserviceable. Woe! Woe! Woe!"' (129). He faces the despair of never finding absolution, and the flesh-and-blood witness cannot present irrefutable proof of ghosts. In this moment of narrative aporia, the ghost story has journeyed a long way from the cosy fireside celebrated by Dickens's early tales.

'To be Taken with a Grain of Salt', originally published in the Christmas number of *All the Year Round* in 1865 and later known as 'The Trial for Murder', offers a strange twist to the interrogative or investigative approach to ghosts. The story's variant titles imply two differing valuations: a tale to be viewed sceptically, even dismissively, or one that is involved with the serious business of the daytime world. In this 'case', a ghostly murder victim silently guides the prosecution in court, intruding on a legal system supposedly devoted to the objective, dispassionate pursuit of truth. Open to strange 'psychological experiences', the narrator knows Brewster's work and has minutely followed a case of 'Spectral Illusion occurring within my private circle of friends' (Dickens 1991: 55). In this procedural vein, his account of the trial initially eschews the typical trappings of the supernatural tale. On 'a bright autumn morning' he first receives a mental picture, 'impossibly painted on a running river', of the murder scene in 'chambers in Piccadilly' (56). Following this 'curious sensation', he sees from the window a ghostly tableau: two men, one of 'lowering appearance' and the other with 'the colour of impure wax' (57), walk in oddly abstracted fashion amidst the living world of the street around them. Although he has been mildly out of sorts – 'I was not ill, but I was not well' (57) – there is nothing to account for these events, since he possesses no prior knowledge of the actors in this drama. When the waxen man materialises again in his bedroom, the image is communicated to his valet seemingly through 'some occult manner' of thought transference (58).

Summoned for jury service at the Old Bailey, the courtroom shrouded in a 'black vapour hanging like a murky curtain outside the great windows', the narrator immediately recognises the prisoner as the man he had seen in Piccadilly. Although the prisoner objects strongly to his presence, the narrator becomes Foreman of the jury and thinks he can count thirteen members rather than twelve. After a miniature presented as evidence shows the murder victim to be the apparition encountered in the narrator's chambers, the spirit intervenes regularly in the proceedings, invading the jury's dreams, highlighting corroborating evidence, shaping judgements and inducing inexplicable 'trepidation or disturbance' (62) in the court room. In his final words from the dock, the prisoner declares that before his capture, the Foreman had '"*somehow got to my bedside in the night, woke me, and put a rope round my neck*"' (64, italics in original). This dramatic turn ascribes prodigious psychical or occult powers to the narrator, making him the haunter of the guilty man. As in 'To Be Read at Dusk', the narrator is rendered ghostly.

'No. 1 Branch Line: The Signal-Man' draws on various contemporary conceptions of the supernatural, including 'theories of spectral illusion, clairvoyance and psychic sympathy, and notions of suggestion and expectation' (Henson 2004: 57). Although these perspectives may account for the haunting it relates, the tale has a troubling excess that no conventional orders of knowledge can explain. The story is also shaped in part by Dickens's experience as a surviving passenger in the Stapleford rail disaster in 1865, alluded to by the 'violent pulsation' of a passing train (Dickens 2010: 91) felt by the narrator. As Catherine Aird has shown, the development of the rail network brought new fears, such as 'commotion shock' to rural areas (Aird 2012: 25). Epitomising the speed and power of modernity, the railway is also a site of the uncanny, a return to the superstitious past. On first sight the cutting seems tomb-like to the narrator, making him feel that 'I had left the natural world' (Dickens 2010: 92). In this lonesome spot, the signalman resembles 'a spirit, not a man', and the narrator speculatively attributes his distracted manner to 'infection in his mind' (93). Yet such an observation may be down to the eye of the beholder: the signalman has originally wondered if his unexpected visitor is the phantom who haunts him with its warning of impending danger. Strange counterparts, they appear to inhabit an otherworld.

The narrator deploys optical theory in attributing the signalman's disturbed vision to a 'disease of the delicate nerves that minister to the functions of the eye' (97), and the patient seems to accept this judgement, calling his experience a 'cruel haunting of *me*' (100). The 'imaginary cry' can be interpreted as an effect of 'the wind in this unnatural valley while we speak so low, and to the wild harp it makes of the telegraph wires' (97). In truth, this is hardly a comforting diagnosis, given that the haunted sensorium generated by modern technology represented both excitement and uneasiness for Victorian culture. As Steven Connor remarks, the supernatural would become 'entangled with the "real world" of science and progress [...] in its mirroring of the communicational technologies of the second half of the nineteenth century' (Connor 1999: 211). Like messages transmitted by the telegraph and the telephone, ghosts could emerge from silence and invisibility, returning to the living world from unaccountable distances. The ghostly bell in the signal box is audible *and* visible only to the signalman, who finds himself enmeshed in a network circulating indecipherable messages that also elude the narrator, even with the benefit of hindsight. In *Household Words* in 1850, Frederick Knight Hunt reflected on the mixture of anticipation and dread associated with telegraphy and the ringing of the electric bell: '[t]he greater part of the dispatches sent by this wonderful invention in England relate, we believe, to occasions of disaster and surprise' (Hunt 1850: 245). Dickens's tale, however, is not reducible solely to the shock or surprise of modernity: the two men are already marked by its assault on the senses. When they peer into the tunnel, they look into the darkness of the future, anticipating what might arrive; but each instance of haunting, including the narrator's account of the signalman's death, represents an aftermath, the trace of what remains. Perhaps this is what the spectre finally 'means': it obliges us, perhaps like Scrooge, to think of the past, live with our memories in the present, and anticipate the incalculable future, where ghosts still wander.

Works Cited

Aird, Catherine. 'Dickens and Railway Spine Neurosis'. *The Dickensian*, vol. 108, no. 486, 2012, pp. 25–8.

Bann, Jennifer. 'Ghostly Hands and Ghostly Agency: The Changing Figure of the Nineteenth-Century Specter'. *Victorian Studies*, vol. 51, no. 4, 2009, pp. 663–85.

Connor, Steven. 'The Machine in the Ghost: Spiritualism, Technology and the "Direct Voice"', in Peter Buse and Andrew Stott (eds), *Ghosts: Deconstruction, Psychoanalysis, History*. London: Macmillan, 1999, pp. 203–25.

Crowe, Catherine. *The Night Side of Nature: Or Ghosts and Ghost Seers*. Ware: Wordsworth, 2000.

Dickens, Charles. *The Supernatural Stories of Charles Dickens*, edited by Michael Hayes. London: John Calder, 1978.

———. 'To be Taken with a Grain of Salt', in Michael Cox and R. A. Gilbert (eds), *The Oxford Book of Victorian Ghost Stories*. Oxford: Oxford University Press, 1991, pp. 55–64.

———. Review: *The Night Side of Nature; or, Ghosts and Ghost Seers* by Catherine Crowe. *The Examiner*, 26 February 1848, in *Dickens' Journalism: The Amusements of the People and Other Papers: Reports, Essays and Reviews 1834–51*, vol. II, edited by Michael Slater. London: J. M. Dent, 1996, pp. 80–91.

———. 'A Christmas Tree' [1850], in *Selected Journalism 1850–1870*, edited by David Pascoe. Harmondsworth: Penguin, 1997, pp. 3–16.

———. *The Pickwick Papers*, edited by Mark Wormwald. London: Penguin, 2003.

———. *Nicholas Nickleby*, edited by Mark Ford. London: Penguin, 2003.

———. *A Christmas Carol and Other Christmas Books*, edited by Robert Douglas-Fairhurst. Oxford: Oxford University Press, 2006.

———. 'No. 1 Branch Line: The Signal-Man', in Michael Newton (ed.), *The Penguin Book of Ghost Stories*. London: Penguin, 2010, pp. 91–104.

Evans, Dewi. 'The Victorian Ghost Story and the Invention of Christmas', in Scott Brewster and Luke Thurston (eds), *The Routledge Handbook to the Ghost Story*. London and New York: Routledge, 2017, pp. 78–86.

Gurney, Edmund, Frederic W. H. Myers and Frank Podmore. *Phantasms of the Living*, vol. 1. London: Trübner & Co. 1886.

Henson, Louise. 'Investigations and Fictions: Charles Dickens and Ghosts', in Nicola Bown, Carolyn Burdett and Pamela Thurschwell (eds), *The Victorian Supernatural*. Cambridge: Cambridge University Press, 2004, pp. 44–63.

Hervey, Thomas K. *The Book of Christmas*. Boston, MA: Roberts Brothers, 1888.

Hunt, Frederick Knight. 'Wings of Fire'. *Household Words*, vol. 2, 1850, pp. 241–5.

Irving, Washington. *'The Legend of Sleepy Hollow' and Other Stories*. London: Penguin, 2014.

Smajić, Srdjan. *Ghost-Seers, Detectives, and Spiritualists: Theories of Vision in Victorian Literature and Science*. Cambridge: Cambridge University Press, 2010.

Smith, Andrew. *The Ghost Story 1840–1920: A Cultural History*. Manchester: Manchester University Press, 2010.
Stone, Harry. '*A Christmas Carol*: Giving Nursery Tales a Higher Form', in Elton E. Smith and Robert Haas (eds), *The Haunted Mind: The Supernatural in Victorian Literature*. Lanham, MD: Scarecrow Press, 1999, pp. 11–18.
Wood, Claire. 'Charles Dickens and the Ghost Story', in Scott Brewster and Luke Thurston (eds), *The Routledge Handbook to the Ghost Story*. London and New York: Routledge, 2017, pp. 89–97.

Chapter 13

Rudyard Kipling
Minna Vuohelainen

Kipling's 'enchanted land'

In his autobiography *Something of Myself* (1937), Rudyard Kipling (1865–1936) describes how his authorial 'Personal Daemon' first came to him 'early' in his career when he was struggling, 'bewildered among other notions, and said; "Take this and no other"' (Kipling 1937: 208–9). The result of following the Daemon's advice was Kipling's earliest ghost story, 'The Phantom 'Rickshaw' (1885), of which he writes: 'Some of it was weak, much was bad and out of key; but it was my first serious attempt to think in another man's skin' (1937: 209). 'When your Daemon is in charge, do not try to think consciously', Kipling concludes: 'Drift, wait, and obey' (210). This account of the genesis of Kipling's earliest ghost story is notable for two reasons: its description of his authorial drive and craft as a 'Daemon' confirms his attraction to the Gothic mode; and it gives a special place in his authorial journey to the ghost story, arguably the most prominent subgenre of the Gothic mode during the Victorian period (Briggs 2000: 122).

As B. J. Moore-Gilbert notes, Kipling's work demonstrates a sustained inclination towards the Gothic, a 'well-established genre in Anglo-Indian fiction' that offered 'a medium to express the sense of estrangement […] characteristic of the exiled community' and made use of the 'often extraordinary nature of Indian surroundings' (Moore-Gilbert 1986: 188). From the beginning of his authorial career, Kipling wrote both Gothically inflected stories that contained no discernible ghostly encounters, such as 'The Strange Ride of Morrowbie Jukes' (1885), and stories making knowing use of traditional ghost story conventions such as 'The Phantom 'Rickshaw' (see Vuohelainen 2021). It is this latter body of work that this essay explores. Kipling's fascination with spectral encounters persisted throughout his writing career despite his professed 'ambivalence about the supernatural' (Pamboukian 2004: 429).

In *Something of Myself*, he notes that his was not 'a type of mind that dives after [...] "psychical experiences"' – a sentiment perhaps most famously articulated in his poem 'The Road to Endor' (1919), which warns about the dangers of the spiritualist craze sweeping Europe in the aftermath of the First World War (Kipling 1937: 215).

As a professional author and a time-pressed journalist, Kipling was, despite his scepticism, attracted to the ghost story for several reasons. The genre was best suited to the short form, in which Kipling excelled. It operated through a set of recognisable conventions, which appealed to an author writing under pressure and to tight deadlines, and its brevity suited the needs of Kipling's journalistic calling, which often demanded short contributions suitable for periodical publication. Its frequent testing of generic and narrative conventions encouraged literary experimentation and anticipated the emergence of the modernist short story in the early twentieth century. Its engagement with spectrality and its suggestive narrative gaps were well placed to address topics central to Kipling's authorial vision, including colonial unease, the uncomfortable and often violent nature of intercultural encounters, the centrality of loss and grief to modern life, and the experiences of belonging, marginality, transit and exile. Finally, its tendency to locate hauntings in characteristic settings that played a central role in the story appealed to Kipling's 'fundamentally spatial' literary imagination (McBratney 2011: 24).

This essay explores a range of Kipling's ghost stories from a period of twenty years following the publication of 'The Phantom 'Rickshaw', with a focus on Kipling's attempts 'to think in another man's skin' and particularly in his *place*. That place, in Kipling's Victorian-era ghost stories, is almost exclusively India. In *Something of Myself*, he describes an Indian landscape haunted by the past:

> The dead of all times were about us – in the vast forgotten Muslim cemeteries round the Station, where one's horse's hoof of a morning might break through to the corpse below; skulls and bones tumbled out of our mud garden walls, and were turned up among the flowers by the Rains; and at every point were tombs of the dead. Our chief picnic rendezvous and some of our public offices had been memorials to desired dead women; and Fort Lahore, where Runjit Singh's wives lay, was a mausoleum of ghosts. (Kipling 1937: 42)

As a fundamentally 'place minded' (Tally 2019: 1) author who 'straddl[ed] two cultures' (Strack 2005: 50), Kipling draws on his cultural hybridity and spatial awareness in ghost stories that respond imaginatively to Henry James's well-known contention that fiction in this genre 'must be connected at a hundred points with the common objects of life'

(James 2005: 119). In Kipling's Victorian-era ghost stories, the colonisers' feelings of anxiety, insecurity, alienation and exile manifest through characteristic Anglo-Indian settings, including the cheerless colonial home, the 'Dark World' of the coloniser's mind, the liminal, unpredictable frontier zone, the closed world of the military barracks, and the place of entertainment where colonial officials seek, usually unsuccessfully, an escape from the futility of their lives (Kipling 1999: 27). While the ghost story form made these familiar settings strange to Kipling's original Anglo-Indian readers, non-colonial readers may have felt that these (to them exotic) settings instead troubled the otherwise familiar genre of the ghost story. This essay explores a range of Kipling's ghost stories with a focus on their characteristic spatialities to argue that what Andrew Lang called Kipling's 'enchanted land, full of marvels and magic that are real', is essential to an appreciation of Kipling's contribution to this genre that commanded sustained popularity and commercial appeal during the Victorian period and beyond (Lang 1971: 71).

Uncanny Returns and Unhomely Homes

Despite Kipling's relatively dismissive assessment of 'The Phantom 'Rickshaw' as 'weak, [...] bad and out of key', this early story, produced when the author was still in his teens, establishes many of the central themes that would continue to characterise his ghost stories over the coming decades (Kipling 1937: 209). Human relationships, domestic lives and a sense of anxiety and exile are central to a number of Kipling's Anglo-Indian ghost stories, including 'The Phantom 'Rickshaw' (1885), 'By Word of Mouth' (1887), 'At the End of the Passage' (1890) and 'The Return of Imray' (1891). As Moore-Gilbert observes, Kipling draws on Gothic tropes 'to explore the deeper anxieties' of an exiled Anglo-Indian community experiencing nostalgia for the 'metropolitan homeland' and a 'sense of deprivation' in its colonial existence (Moore-Gilbert 1986: 190, 44).

Published in December 1885 in the *Quartette*, a publication jointly authored by the Kipling family and printed by the *Civil and Military Gazette* (*CMG*), Kipling's then-employer, 'The Phantom 'Rickshaw' is a Christmas tale that knowingly deploys many of the recognised conventions of the ghost story while simultaneously reinventing them through its Anglo-Indian setting. Initially told entirely in protagonist Jack Pansay's voice, the story subsequently acquired a framing structure introducing Kipling's distinctive narrative voice and questioning Pansay's sanity. The storyline is a common one: Pansay's callous flirtation with and subsequent rejection of married Mrs Keith-Wessington leads her to die of a broken heart, only to return to haunt him until he comes to realise his error; in the process, Pansay loses everything that he cares for, including his reputation, his sanity, his new fiancée and his life. What lifts the story from others in a similar vein is its setting in colonial Simla, a holiday site familiar to Kipling's Anglo-Indian audience but exotic to British readers, and the profound strangeness of the haunting that follows Pansay in the form of the eponymous 'yellow-panelled 'rickshaw' pulled by four ghostly '*jhampanis*' (rickshaw bearers) wearing 'black and white liveries' (Kipling 1999: 27, 31). 'So there *were* ghosts of 'rickshaws after all,' Pansay reflects on the absurdity of his experience, 'and ghostly employments in the other world!' (36).

The story demonstrates Kipling's precocious understanding of the relationship between place and memory, and of cultural hybridity. As Pansay embarks on a new, more serious relationship following Mrs Keith-Wessington's death, he acknowledges, as he visits their old haunts with his new fiancée, that 'every inch of the Jakko road bore witness to our old-time walks and talks' (35). The ghostly rickshaw with its unwelcome passenger begins to intercept Pansay at various well-known, mundane Simla locations and landmarks, bringing '[e]veryday, ordinary Simla' into conflict with the 'dark labyrinths of doubt, misery, and utter despair' which Pansay is experiencing because of his lingering guilt (45, 43). This early story allows Kipling to establish many of the key principles of his subsequent ghost story craft: Anglo-India as a trademark setting; the possibility that colonial life might expose the Anglo-Indian community to local superstitions and mental strain; the ability of familiar places to trigger haunting memories; the realisation that it may not be possible to escape India even in death; an interest in modes of transport as conduits into another world; and the juxtaposition of the horror of colonial existence with its mundane details, which questions the imperial mission by turning the 'workaday Anglo-Indian world' into a 'world of shadows' (44).

'The dead travel fast, and by short cuts unknown to ordinary coolies', Pansay remarks of his haunting (37). 'By Word of Mouth', published in the *CMG* on 10 June 1887, is another relatively formulaic ghost story centred on lost love and an unexpected encounter with the spectral. This 1,600-word story is a good example of the extreme brevity Kipling was able to achieve in his journalistic 'turnovers', which required him to 'write short' (Kipling 1937: 66). Unlike 'The Phantom 'Rickshaw' with its doomed extramarital affair, 'By Word of Mouth' takes as its premise the untimely end of a happy marriage, brought about by poor hygiene and a medical oversight. Dr Dumoise and his wife have led a quietly happy life – so much so that their wilful 'retire[ment] from the world after their marriage' has led to the couple being dubbed the 'Dormice' – until a typhoid epidemic claims Mrs Dumoise's life (Kipling 2001: 229). Her death cuts Dumoise loose from his bearings, and he goes on a walking tour 'in the heart of the hills, [where] the scenery is good if you are in trouble', staying at a 'bitterly cold' *dâk*-bungalow on his way home (230, 231). These modest, staffed guesthouses offered free but often uncomfortable accommodation to government officials, and feature in other examples of the genre such as Kipling's 'My Own True Ghost Story' (1891), discussed below, and B. M. Croker's 'The Dâk Bungalow at Dakor' (1893) as places of discomfort, anxiety and exile.

In 'By Word of Mouth', this transitory accommodation serves as a reminder of Dumoise's recent loss of a happy home and provides an opportunity to leave his newly rootless life behind, as his bearer returns with news from the dead Memsahib of a promised meeting 'next month at Nuddea' in faraway Bengal (231). The message presages Dumoise's as yet unknown transfer to a typhoid station in Nuddea, which he accepts in full knowledge of his own impending death. Despite its extreme simplicity, the story anticipates Kipling's later stories about reunion in death, such as 'Mrs Bathurst' (1904), discussed below, and 'A Madonna of the Trenches' (1924). Unlike these later stories, however, it foregrounds the utmost importance of a stable home life to Anglo-Indian officials such as Dumoise, who has relied on this safety net for his sanity.

'At the End of the Passage' (1890) and 'The Return of Imray' (1891) explore the fates of colonial professionals who have no prospect of experiencing such domestic felicity. These stories from the early 1890s occasion a shift away from conventional ghost story tropes towards a complex combination of haunting, the Gothic and the macabre. They depict the colonial home as a site of disintegration, precarity and horror, anticipating Joseph Conrad's *Heart of Darkness* (1899).

'At the End of the Passage', published in the *Boston Herald* on 20 July 1890 and then in August 1890 in *Lippincott's Magazine*, exposes the fundamental solitude of Anglo-Indian life. Worn down by 'overwork and the strain of the hot weather', the central character Hummil, a colonial engineer, inhabits a cheerless bachelor bungalow, his comfortless and suffocating life only occasionally enlivened by the visits of other, similarly beleaguered colonial professionals (Kipling 2003: 341). Even the furniture accentuates Hummil's lonesome existence: a 'worn and battered little camp-piano – wreckage of a married household that had once held the bungalow' acts as a ghostly trace of a happier but now vanished domesticity, while a tune played on the piano – 'something that might once have been the ghost of a popular music-hall song' – recalls life back in England (333). Kipling makes effective use of the pathetic fallacy, suggesting Hummil's deteriorating mental health through descriptions of a 'dense dust-storm' and a 'brown purple haze of heat', which seem to presage 'the earth [...] dying of apoplexy' (334, 328). With his face 'white and pinched', 'his eyes [...] unnaturally large', and bearing 'himself rigidly as a corpse', Hummil already looks like a ghost or a corpse when he confesses to terrifying nightmares in which a 'blind face' 'chases him down corridors' in 'a place down there' (335, 337, 340, 339). Eventually, however, the 'echoing desolation of his bungalow' produces visions of a sinister double 'born of overwork', which initially 'slides away [...] like a ghost' but eventually comes to sit at Hummil's table and share his daily life (341). Apart from 'cast[ing] no shadow' (341), this 'harbinger of death' (Luckhurst 2019: 287) is not a traditional ghost but a vision recalled by Hummil's peculiar living conditions at the far reaches of the empire.

The conclusion of 'At the End of the Passage' leaves Hummil's cause of death open, his descent 'into the Dark Places' suggesting both a supernatural experience and death from the colonial 'horror' later experienced by Joseph Conrad's Kurtz (342). 'The Return of Imray', published in *Life's Handicap: Being Stories of Mine Own People* in 1891 and initially titled 'The Recrudescence of Imray', also plays on the question of the unhomeliness of the colonial home while articulating the dangers of intercultural encounter. The narrator recounts how Imray has 'disappear[ed] from [...] the little Indian station where he lived', allowing Strickland of the Indian Police, a recurring character in Kipling's work, to take possession of his now-vacant 'desirable bungalow' (Kipling 1891: 225, 227). The defining features of Imray's former residence are its superb, 'heavily thatched' roof and 'neat', newly 'repainted' ceiling-cloth (227). This seemingly attractive feature is quite literally a whitewash, however, for it not only 'harbour[s] all manner of rats, bats, ants, and foul things' but conceals Imray's decaying corpse (228).

Like 'At the End of the Passage', 'The Return of Imray' contains a degree of uncertainty about its central haunting, which blends elements of the supernatural ghost story and the non-supernatural Gothic. The narrator feels that the bungalow, which he is visiting as Strickland's guest, is 'occupied' by 'a fluttering, whispering, bolt-fumbling, lurking, loitering Someone', while Strickland's faithful dog Tietjens refuses the interior of the dwelling (231, 230). However, the story leaves the reader uncertain whether the bungalow is haunted by Imray's 'insubstantial and speechless' ghost returning to seek justice or the vermin swarming on his grotesquely decaying body (Macfarlane 2016: 90). In either case, the story challenges any notion of the security and sanctity of the colonial home, spotlighting the precarity of Anglo-Indian life even in places of supposed safety.

Imperial Frontiers and Colonial Nightmares

Such anxieties about overwork and betrayal are also characteristic of stories set in places of Anglo-Indian professional or military life and the places of entertainment designed to provide relief from duty and toil. 'My Own True Ghost Story' (1888) and 'The Lost Legion' (1892) both explore sensations of vulnerability in the colonial hinterland, 'simultaneously promot[ing] and def[ying] imperial discourse' (Generani 2016: 20). 'Haunted Subalterns' (1887), 'The Rout of the White Hussars' (1888), 'The Broken-Link Handicap' (1887) and '"Sleipner", Late "Thurinda"' (1888) are all slight, early stories set within the characteristic colonial settings of the army barracks and the racecourse. These relatively under-explored stories combine Kipling's peculiar strand of humour, an uneasy colonial laughter (see Smith 2010), and the supernatural (or *faux*-supernatural) into the characteristically Victorian genre of the comic ghost story.

The anxiety of colonial vulnerability and betrayal haunts 'My Own True Ghost Story', published in the *Week's News* on 25 February 1888. Despite its jocular tone and reassuringly rational conclusion, this story anticipates Kipling's later depiction of India's haunted landscape in *Something of Myself* by detailing the multiplicity of (mostly malevolent) ghosts associated with specific locales:

> There are, in this land, ghosts who take the form of fat, cold, pobby [swollen] corpses, and hide in trees near the roadside till a traveller passes. Then they drop upon his neck and remain. There are also terrible ghosts of women who have died in child-bed. These wander along the pathways at dusk, or hide in the crops near a village, and call seductively. [...] There are ghosts of little children who have been thrown into wells. These haunt well curbs and the fringes of jungles, and wail under the stars, or catch women by the wrist and beg to be taken up and carried. These and the corpse ghosts, however, are only vernacular articles and do not attack *Sahibs*. No native ghost has yet been authentically reported to have frightened an Englishman; but many English ghosts have scared the life out of both white and black.
>
> Nearly every other Station owns a ghost. There are said to be two at Simla, not counting the woman who blows the bellows at Syree *dâk*-bungalow on the Old Road; Mussoorie has a house haunted of a very lively Thing; a White Lady is supposed to do night-watchman round a house in Lahore; Dalhousie says that one of her houses 'repeats' on autumn evenings all the incidents of a horrible horse-and-precipice accident; Murree has a merry ghost, and, now that she has been swept by cholera, will have room for a sorrowful one;

there are Officers' Quarters in Mian Mir whose doors open without reason, and whose furniture is guaranteed to creak, not with the heat of June but with the weight of Invisibles who come to lounge in the chairs; Peshawar possesses houses that none will willingly rent; and there is something – not fever – wrong with a big bungalow in Allahabad. The older Provinces simply bristle with haunted houses, and march phantom armies along their main thoroughfares. [...]

In [...] dâk-bungalows, ghosts are most likely to be found, and when found, they should be made a note of. (Kipling 1888: 32–3)

Amidst such perceived hauntedness, it is perhaps not surprising that the narrator thinks to have stumbled upon the titular 'true ghost story' while staying at a *dâk*-bungalow in the course of his travels. These 'objectionable' temporary dwellings, he notes, are 'generally very old, always dirty', host 'a fair proportion of the tragedy of our lives out here', and have 'handy little cemeteries in their compound' to remind guests of the high mortality rates and violence characteristic of colonial existence (33, 34).

During the night, conscious of his vulnerability in this isolated location, the narrator hears what sounds like a group of doolie-bearers, and then a game of billiards, outside his room. The following morning, he is briefly led to believe that he may have witnessed a ghostly re-enactment of a 'lost imperial past' (Smith 2010: 162), when a death had taken place in what was once a 'billiard room for the *Sahibs* who built the Railway. [...] But the *Sahibs* are all dead now' (38). 'I had my ghost – a first-hand, authenticated article', the narrator reflects gleefully: 'I would write to the Society for Psychical Research – I would paralyse the Empire with the news!' – only to realise that the sound had been produced by 'a restless little rat [...] running to and fro inside the dingy ceiling-cloth' (39). Light in tone and rational in its conclusion, the story nonetheless foregrounds the precarity and troubled history of Anglo-Indian life through the uneasy night the narrator spends at the *dâk*-bungalow. It also suggests that the British presence has increased the number of India's ghosts through death and violence.

'The Lost Legion', first published in the *Strand Magazine* in May 1892, shares this sense of colonial insecurity but also articulates tension between 'national and colonial identities' and a feeling that the Indian landscape oozes history and blood (Smith 2010: 2). In this story, the ongoing trauma of the Indian Rebellion of 1857 continues to haunt the British imagination (Welby 2015: 6). The story follows a British squadron of cavalry on a secret mission into the 'death-trap' of the 'hills of Afghanistan', where they are to apprehend a rebel leader (Kipling 2009: 94, 91). The Britons' success depends on 'silence and speed', but after passing a 'very graveyard of little cairns', they find themselves 'stalked by a full regiment in the rear' (94, 97, 98). It is only when they find the Afghan tribesmen too terrified to defend their own that they come to realise that their companions are in fact a 'Dead Regiment' of 'Native Irregular Horse' who had joined with the rebels of 1857, only to be betrayed and slaughtered by the Afghan tribe that is still causing trouble thirty years later (101, 91). The story's conservative logic assuages colonial anxieties by firstly punishing the rebel regiment of 1857 with death and then allowing them 'much credit' for their repentance in death of their desertion and the vengeance they take by supporting the present-day cavalrymen in their mission (102). While 'the memory of the deed is now dying', the story also suggests that the very landscape continues to hold memories of past violence, and, obliquely, that the empire's gains in the troubled frontier region have been slow (92).

If 'The Lost Legion' conceals its anxiety with reassurance about the righteousness of Britain's imperial mission, several of Kipling's lesser-known ghost stories use humour to address such anxieties. 'Haunted Subalterns', first published in the *CMG* on 27 May 1887, recounts an anecdote in which the eponymous subalterns, Horrocks and Tesser, find themselves subjected to entertaining but inconvenient hauntings. Horrocks is disturbed by 'two white Things hopping about his rooms and jumping up to the ceiling', while Tesser finds his bed stripped and his banjo played by an unseen intruder (Kipling 2001: 247). The story treats the otherwise harmless hauntings lightly, associating them as a matter of course with India: 'It stands to reason,' Horrocks remarks, revealing his prejudices, 'that such a beastly country should be full of fiends and all sorts' (250). At the same time, however, unease is bubbling under the surface, for 'Man can't feel comfy with a regiment that entertains ghosts on its establishment', and there is speculation that the subalterns may be guilty of a crime that has made them subject to this ongoing disturbance: 'haven't you done something – committed some murder that has slipped your memory – or forged something ... ?' (247, 249). While the narrator dismisses these concerns with a wink at the end of the story, the spectres they raise are those of colonial guilt and military insubordination in the closed world of the army barracks rife with anxiety and superstition.

'The Rout of the White Hussars', published in *Plain Tales from the Hills* in 1888, similarly exposes disarray within army ranks but also undermines military authority. This story explores the White Hussars' response to a new colonel, 'a mean man and a bully' who 'ought never to have taken the Command', deciding to replace a much-loved drum-horse, a symbol of the regiment's identity, with a younger animal (Kipling 2001: 171, 169). The drum-horse is seemingly put down, its fate making apparent the soldiers' equally low value in the colonel's eyes as disposable cannon fodder. The story details the humiliating panic occasioned by the 'resurrection' of the drum-horse, whose 'ghost' returns to base with a skeleton on its back (178, 174). The knowing narrator has helped to prepare the hoax: the drum-horse is in fact alive and well and its seemingly spectral return overturns the colonel's unpopular decision. Echoing Kipling's *Barrack-Room Ballads* and his notoriety as the voice of the hooligan, the story foregrounds the anarchic resourcefulness of the lower ranks of the Anglo-Indian army.

Horses, so fundamental to Anglo-Indian life as modes of civil and military transport, are also a central presence in 'The Broken-Link Handicap', first published in the *CMG* on 6 April 1887, and '"Sleipner", Late "Thurinda"', which appeared in the *Week's News* on 12 May 1888. Both stories make use of racecourse settings as places of entertainment that provide Anglo-Indians with momentary respite from the everyday. Like 'The Rout of the White Hussars', 'The Broken-Link Handicap' is a *faux*-ghost story. The story commences with a cynical warning: 'Understand clearly that all racing is rotten [...]. In India, in addition to its inherent rottenness, it has the merit of being two-thirds sham' (Kipling 2001: 122). The story concerns a jockey, Brunt, who rides a reliable winner but whose 'nerve had been shaken' by the 'awful butchery' he has survived at a previous race (124). The owner of a rival horse is able to exploit Brunt's trauma by making use of the 'astounding peculiarity' of how sound travels on the racecourse to send what seems a ghostly whisper into Brunt's ear at a crucial point in the race, regardless of any potential injury (123).

A similar callousness can be found in '"Sleipner", Late "Thurinda"', a story about a horse given away after a fatal accident, whose subsequent owners find her to be haunted by the horse and rider who had died in the accident. Those who now ride Thurinda see and hear the ghost of the dead horse pressing at her heels, leading her to be renamed 'Sleipner' after the eight-legged horse of the Norse god Odin. Unlike the mythical Sleipner, however, Thurinda is not a reliable mount: those riding her are liable to experience accidents, and the 'infernal mare' (Kipling 1909: 155) is eventually put down. While playfully conflating the idea of a gift-horse and a nightmare, the story, like 'The Rout of the White Hussars' and 'The Broken-Link Handicap', asks serious questions about the 'rottenness' of Anglo-Indian life. The racecourse, while supposedly offering opportunities for temporary respite and relaxation, is instead shown to be a microcosm of Anglo-Indian life in its cynicism, cruelty, greed and indifference to the well-being of men and animals, perhaps in reflection of a recklessness resulting from a sense of life's precarity.

Modernist Travels

Kipling left India for England in 1889. Fifteen years later, he described his 'discovery of England' in terms reminiscent of his perception of India's hauntedness:

> To me it is a land full of stupefying marvels and mysteries; and a day in the car in an English county is a day in some fairy museum where all the exhibits are alive and real and yet none the less delightfully mixed up with books. For instance, in six hours, I can go from the land of the *Ingoldsby Legends* by way of the Norman Conquest and the Barons' War into Richard Jefferies' country, and so through the Regency, one of Arthur Young's less known tours, and *Celia's Arbour*, into Gilbert White's territory. Horses, after all, are only horses; but the car is a time-machine on which one can slide from one century to another [...]. You who were born and bred in the land naturally take such trifles for granted, but to me it is still miraculous [...] in England the dead, twelve coffin deep, clutch hold of my wheels at every turn, till I sometimes wonder that the very road does not bleed. *That* is the real joy of motoring – the exploration of this amazing England. (Kipling 2004: 150–1)

Kipling's immediate post-Victorian ghost stories share this delight in 'technologies of mobility' (Rix 2016: 60) that act 'as conduits for supernatural phenomena' (Pamboukian 2004: 430) and for unexpected communication with the unseen world. While shifting firmly towards a modernist aesthetic, '"Wireless"' (1902), '"They"' (1904) and 'Mrs Bathurst' (1904) nonetheless build on the relationship between place, memory and haunting so central to Kipling's Anglo-Indian ghost stories.

'"Wireless"', published in the American *Scribner's Magazine* in August 1902, develops the themes of 'The Finest Story in the World' (1891), an earlier story that explores the possibility of reincarnation and memory of one's past lives. In '"Wireless"', however, Kipling develops these ideas with a firm connection to place and the ghost story tradition by describing the titular wireless experiment with its peculiar outcome as resembling 'a spiritualistic séance' (Kipling 2002: 237). The story turns on the notion that 'like causes *must* beget like effects', with the circumstances of the story's setting seemingly inviting a spectral echo of the past (232). The narrator is visiting a 'glittering' chemist's store lit by 'kaleidoscopic lights' and filled with 'the flavours of cardamoms and chloric-ether', of 'pastilles and a score of drugs and perfume and soap scents', to witness a wireless experiment (227). This enchanted setting, the '[b]itter cold' winter's night, and the painful 'cough' of the consumptive druggist Mr Shaynor recall, it is suggested, a trace of the dead Romantic poet Keats, whose poetry, previously unknown to him, Shaynor begins to recite in a 'machine-like' trance (222, 231). The narrator implies that Shaynor has been 'snatched' by 'the Powers – whatever the Powers may be – at work – through space – a long distance away' to be used as a human wireless receiver, somehow in tune with the dead poet, whose circumstances in life had so closely mirrored Shaynor's (235, 225). The combination of place and technology calls forth the haunting.

'Mrs Bathurst', published in September 1904 in the middlebrow British *Windsor Magazine* and in the American *Metropolitan Magazine*, similarly uses modern technology, in this case the cinema and the railway, to bring about what may be understood as a spectral encounter. Like the earlier 'By Word of Mouth', 'Mrs Bathurst' can be read as a ghost story about a 'destined reunion' in death (Stinton 1988: 55). Unlike the earlier, very simple story, however, 'Mrs Bathurst' is puzzling in the extreme. Its disjointed, elliptical narrative brings together four men at a loose end, whose aimless chatter relies on shared memories and understandings that the reader is not privy to. The conversation drifts to the unexplained desertion of naval warrant officer Vickery after he has seen early film footage showing a certain Mrs Bathurst alighting from a train at Paddington Station in London, 'lookin' for somebody' (Kipling 2002: 270). Vickery is convinced that she is looking for him, and insists on watching the haunting footage again and again, the cinema enabling the repeated return of the ghostly Mrs Bathurst. As it happens, one of the men has reason to believe that the dead body found next to a railway line is Vickery's. As Stinton notes, the suggestion is that Vickery has gone looking for Mrs Bathurst 'at the end of the line', knowing her to be dead, but whether he is responsible for her death remains unclear (Stinton 1988: 66).

The ghostly experience in '"They"', published in *Scribner's Magazine* in August 1904, is also enabled by modern technology, in this case the motor car. The narrator spends much of the story in transit motoring through the English countryside, seemingly leaving the modern world for a landscape of 'hidden villages', 'Norman churches', 'stone bridges built for heavier traffic than would ever vex them again' and 'a mile of Roman road' (Kipling 2002: 239). The motor car, seemingly in possession of a mind of its own, takes the narrator 'clean out of [his] known marks', through the 'confusing veils of the woods' and 'into a gloomy tunnel where last year's dead leaves whispered and scuffled about [his] tyres' (239). This seemingly accidental journey takes the narrator on three separate occasions to 'an ancient house of lichened and weather-worn stone [...] flanked by semi-circular walls' and guarded by 'horsemen ten feet high with levelled lances [...] all of clipped yew' – defences that suggest that this 'House Beautiful', 'so out of the world', may be a forbidden space (240, 248, 241). It is only at the end of his third visit that the narrator comes to realise that the 'shy' children fleetingly glimpsed during his visits are in fact ghosts lingering in some strange limbo in 'this place [...] made for children', and that his own dead child is amongst them (242, 243).

An intensely personal story, '"They"' draws for its setting on Bateman's, the Kiplings' family home in Sussex, and for its plotline on the death of Kipling's daughter Josephine in 1899. The realisation of the narrator's loss and grief places his sense of being 'utterly lost' and the repeated reminder that he comes 'from the other side of the country' within the generic context of the ghost story dealing with experiences of loss and mourning (243, 245). The story's suggestion that it is comforting for those who 'have borne [and] lost' to 'walk in the wood' recalls Dr Dumoise's walking tour in 'By Word of Mouth', while the narrator's conclusion that he 'must never' return confirms Kipling's own scepticism about spiritualism (256, 248, 257): 'I have seen too much evil and sorrow and wreck of good minds on the road to Endor to take one step along that perilous track', Kipling asserts in *Something of Myself* (Kipling 1937: 215).

As Fred Botting notes in his analysis of heterotopic ghost stories, the genre has the capacity to 'transport readers into remote and unreal places' while being 'read in a specific place in the present, thereby disturbing a sense of reality' (Botting 2000: 9). Kipling's Victorian-era ghost stories accomplish this by making their Anglo-Indian readers aware of the strangeness of familiar settings via ghostly encounters, while simultaneously making the familiar genre of the ghost story newly strange to British audiences through their Anglo-Indian settings. The Victorian ghost story, characterised by Kipling's distinctive narrative voice, cultural hybridity and scepticism about spiritualism, afforded the author opportunities for literary experimentation that informed his emergence as a genuine 'innovator and a virtuoso in the art of the short story' (Rutherford 2001: viii). By the early twentieth century, Kipling's creative 'Daemon' (Kipling 1937: 208) was driving him towards a complex modernist aesthetic that nonetheless maintained its setting in that 'enchanted land' where place, memory and haunting meet (Lang 1971: 71).

Works Cited

Botting, Fred. 'In Gothic Darkly: Heterotopia, History, Culture', in David Punter (ed.), *A Companion to the Gothic*. Oxford: Blackwell, 2000, pp. 3–14.

Briggs, Julia. 'The Ghost Story', in David Punter (ed.), *A Companion to the Gothic*. Oxford: Blackwell, 2000, pp. 122–31.

Generani, Gustavo. 'Kipling's Early Gothic Tales: The Dialogical Consciousness of an Imperialist in India'. *Irish Journal of Gothic and Horror Studies*, vol. 15, 2016, pp. 20–43.

James, Henry. 'from an unsigned review, "Miss Braddon", *Nation*, 9 November 1865, i, 593–5', in Norman Page (ed.), *Wilkie Collins: The Critical Heritage*. New York and London: Routledge, 2005, pp. 119–20.

Kipling, Rudyard. 'The Phantom 'Rickshaw', in *The Man Who Would be King and Other Stories*, edited by Louis Cornell. Oxford: Oxford University Press, 1999, pp. 26–48.

———. 'By Word of Mouth', in *Plain Tales from the Hills*, edited by Andrew Rutherford. Oxford: Oxford University Press, 2001, pp. 229–33.

———. 'The Broken-Link Handicap', in *Plain Tales from the Hills*, edited by Andrew Rutherford. Oxford: Oxford University Press, 2001, pp. 122–6.

———. '"Sleipner", Late "Thurinda"', in *Abaft the Funnel*. New York: B. W. Dodge, 1909, pp. 141–60.

———. 'The Haunted Subalterns', in *Plain Tales from the Hills*, edited by Andrew Rutherford. Oxford: Oxford University Press, 2001, pp. 247–51.

———. 'The Rout of the White Hussars', in *Plain Tales from the Hills*, edited by Andrew Rutherford. Oxford: Oxford University Press, 2001, pp. 169–78.

———. 'My Own True Ghost Story', in *The Phantom 'Rickshaw & Other Eerie Tales*. Indian Railway Library No. 5. Allahabad: A. H. Wheeler; London: Sampson Low, Marston, Searle, & Rivington, 1888, pp. 32–40.

———. 'At the End of the Passage', in Michael Cox and R. A. Gilbert (eds), *The Oxford Book of Victorian Ghost Stories*. Oxford: Oxford University Press, 2003, pp. 328–45.

———. 'The Return of Imray', in *Life's Handicap: Being Stories of Mine Own People*. London and New York: Macmillan, 1891, pp. 225–39.

———. 'The Lost Legion', in *War Stories and Poems*, edited by Andrew Rutherford. Oxford: Oxford University Press, 2009, pp. 91–102.

———. '"Wireless"', in *The Wish House and Other Stories*, edited by Craig Raine. New York: Modern Library, 2002, pp. 222–37.

———. 'Mrs Bathurst', in *The Wish House and Other Stories*, edited by Craig Raine. New York: Modern Library, 2002, pp. 259–74.

———. '"They"', in *The Wish House and Other Stories*, edited by Craig Raine. New York: Modern Library, 2002, pp. 239–57.

———. 'To Filson Young, April 1904. Text: Filson Young, *The Complete Motorist*, 1904, pp. 285–8', in *The Letters of Rudyard Kipling*, vol. 3: 1900–10, edited by Thomas Pinney. Basingstoke: Palgrave, 2004, pp. 149–52.

———. *Something of Myself: For My Friends Known and Unknown*. London: Macmillan, 1937.

Lang, Andrew. 'Mr Kipling's Stories', in Roger Lancelyn Green (ed.), *Kipling: The Critical Heritage*. London: Routledge and Kegan Paul, 1971, pp. 70–6.

Luckhurst, Roger. *Corridors: Passages of Modernity*. London: Reaktion, 2019.
McBratney, John. 'India and Empire', in Howard J. Booth (ed.), *The Cambridge Companion to Rudyard Kipling*. Cambridge: Cambridge University Press, 2011, pp. 23–36.
Macfarlane, Karen E. 'Here Be Monsters: Imperialism, Knowledge and the Limits of Empire'. *Text Matters*, vol. 6, no. 6, 2016, pp. 74–95.
Moore-Gilbert, B. J. *Kipling and 'Orientalism'*. Beckenham: Croom Helm, 1986.
Pamboukian, Sylvia. 'Science, Magic and Fraud in the Short Stories of Rudyard Kipling'. *English Literature in Transition, 1880–1920*, vol. 47, no. 4, 2004, pp. 429–45.
Rix, Alicia. '"Disturbing Traffic": Kipling's Stories'. *Critical Quarterly*, vol. 58, no. 4, 2016, pp. 50–67.
Rutherford, Andrew. 'General Preface', in *Plain Tales from the Hills*, edited by Andrew Rutherford. Oxford: Oxford University Press, 2001, pp. vii–xi.
Smith, Andrew. *The Ghost Story, 1840–1920: A Cultural History*. Manchester: Manchester University Press, 2010.
Stinton, T. C. W. 'What Really Happened in "Mrs. Bathurst"?' *Essays in Criticism*, vol. 38, no. 1, 1988, pp. 55–74.
Strack, Daniel C. 'Who Are the Bridge-Builders? Metaphor, Metonymy, and the Architecture of Empire'. *Style*, vol. 39, no. 1, 2005, pp. 37–53.
Tally, Robert T., Jr. *Topophrenia: Place, Narrative, and the Spatial Imagination*. Bloomington: Indiana University Press, 2019.
Vuohelainen, Minna. 'Traveller's Tales: Rudyard Kipling's Gothic Short Fiction'. *Gothic Studies*, vol. 23, no. 2, 2021, pp. 181–200.
Welby, Lizzy. *Rudyard Kipling's Fiction: Mapping Psychic Spaces*. Edinburgh: Edinburgh University Press, 2015.

Chapter 14

J. Sheridan Le Fanu
William Hughes

When Montague Rhodes James published the first twentieth-century anthology of J. Sheridan Le Fanu's supernatural fiction, *Madam Crowl's Ghost and Other Tales of Mystery*, in 1923 it was no doubt with a consciousness that the Irish author's specifically Victorian reputation had for some time been in decline (James 1923: vii). In attempting to revive that reputation, however, the well-meaning James arguably initiated a process which has unduly limited access to the breadth of the author's short fiction – and this despite the inclusion of a helpful, if incomplete, bibliography as an Epilogue to the volume (James 1923: 265–77). To supplement the stories of *Madam Crowl's Ghost*, James recommended his readers to approach Le Fanu first through *In a Glass Darkly* (1871) and then 'go on to *Uncle Silas* and *The House by the Churchyard*' (James 1923: 277). Thus was a rudimentary canon established, and from the breadth of a writing career that spanned some twenty-seven years, a premium was further placed upon Le Fanu's later works as being both the most sophisticated and the most accessible to twentieth-century readers. This situation has been perpetuated into the current century, as the range of texts considered, for example, in Crawford et al.'s significantly titled collection *Reflections in a Glass Darkly* (2011), amply illustrates. A revision of the Le Fanu canon as a critical institution is thus overdue, and in this reconsideration attention must necessarily be paid to those works which predate the 'earlier stories' whose impact was, in James's words, somewhat lessened by 'the mannerisms of the forties and fifties' (James 1923: viii). There is another Prologue to be written, in other words, a necessary critical preface which fully acknowledges the relevance of Le Fanu's earliest works.

Amongst the extensive writings of J. S. Le Fanu (1814–73), the Purcell Papers are, paradoxically, perhaps the least well known to twenty-first-century readers. This situation is somewhat surprising, given the status of these twelve stories, which were published in the *Dublin University*

Magazine between 1838 and 1840, as the earliest examples of the author's dexterity as a writer of both short fiction and ghost stories.[1] Indeed, this critical neglect is all the more perplexing, given that the individual after whom the narrative cycle is named – the Roman Catholic priest Father Francis Purcell – can rightly be considered a direct rhetorical ancestor of Dr Martin Hesselius, the German physician around whom the stories of the better-known collection *In a Glass Darkly* (1871) circulate. A possible motivation for the comparative neglect of the Purcell Papers might be their different geographical settings. The Purcell Papers are, with one exception, set in provincial Ireland – and even this exceptional component is framed by a narrative told to Purcell in Ireland. *In a Glass Darkly* casts its geographical net more widely, its four stories being enacted variously in the metropolitan capitals of England, Ireland and France, as well as in provincial France and rural Styria. A more likely explanation, though, is the consistent supernatural content of *In a Glass Darkly*, the stories of which involve ambiguous visual and aural phenomena, a repetitive haunting, a predatory vampire and a murder plot based upon vivisepulture. The Purcell Papers, by comparison, is a considerably more eclectic body of work, embracing as it does the conventional ghost story, ambivalent tales of the demonic, macabre comedy, family intrigue and historical adventure, all punctuated by a consciousness of the controversies and cultural tensions which underwrote Irish politics in the early Victorian period.

It is this latter intimacy between the political and the literary that provides an element of distinction to the Purcell Papers that Le Fanu's later writings arguably lack. In the highly politicised discourses of academic Irish studies, much has been made of the implication of Le Fanu's place in a London-based publishing culture founded upon English tastes and withal favouring narratives set in English milieux (McCormack 1991: 845). This publishing culture, without doubt, exerted a profound effect upon Le Fanu's later fiction, and shaped particularly those novels which the author was pressured by his London publisher to set in near contemporary times and locate within identifiably English settings (Tilley 2014: 130).

In the case of the early Le Fanu, however, this implication seems hardly fair: the *Dublin University Magazine*, with its often-sectarian eye to civil polity and reportage of rural outrage and urban intrigue, was no mere echo of a London paradigm. Though Elizabeth Tilley (admittedly echoing earlier commentators) insists that 'the Irish "colour" of the *DUM* ... was not particularly strong' (Tilley 2014: 130), the *Dublin University Magazine* was undeniably freighted with items of Irish interest. These included, for example, in the first issue (dated January 1833) alone, 'Writers on Irish Character', 'The Irish Bar As It Was, and As It Is', 'Perils of the Irish Poor' and 'The Irish Bench – Mr Justice Burton' as well as a report entitled 'University Intelligence' which prioritises the internal affairs of the University of Dublin. Indeed, speaking on behalf of 'our Irish periodical' and specifically addressing 'our Irish readers' (Anon. 1833: 87), an editorial column in the first issue suggested that:

> We are persuaded that within the bosom of our country there is talent sufficient, and more than sufficient, to support a periodical fully equal to any of those in any other country. This talent we trust to bring into efficient operation in our Magazine, and thus, by opening at home a channel for those communications which have hitherto occupied the pages of foreign reviews and periodicals, to prevent the literary resources of our country being drained away to increase the already too abundant treasures of the sister island. (Anon. 1833: 88)[2]

It is hardly surprising, therefore, that Le Fanu, who was born and educated in Dublin, and who participated willingly in the editorial as well as creative culture of the Irish capital, should regard himself as being capable of deploying, with the sharpness of local knowledge, 'the experience of past ages to guide our own ignorance and weakness, and [to] employ the observations of other times in enabling us to form a correct estimate as to the results of our own' (Anon. 1833: 89).

This editorial emphasis upon the relevance of the past to the present may well have exercised as profound an influence upon the early Le Fanu as the contractual obligations imposed by Richard Bentley were to impose upon the later author. In the case of the Purcell Papers, the memoirs of the fictional priest, selected and published at some point following his death, evoke what seems to be, at first sight at least, an eighteenth-century past for the early Victorian reader. That past, though, is heavily freighted with the profound civil, religious and cultural changes which were to divide and reshape Ireland from time of the Glorious Revolution of 1688–90 to the Éirí Amach or Rebellion of the United Irishmen in 1798. The Purcell Papers are, withal, a reflection upon this historical situation, conditioned by the uncertainties of a culture undergoing significant changes in the early years of the reign of a new monarch, and with the events of 1798 still very much a part of living memory in Ireland. The tales that make up the Purcell Papers thus balance contemporary and historical politics, interrogate the breadth of sectarian identities, interface urban intellectualism with traditional folk-knowledge, and are written with an undoubted consciousness of the presence of history and mythology on both sides of a conflicted contemporary culture.

The Purcell Papers thus express the somewhat complex relationship between the anglicised culture of educated Protestant Ireland and its Roman Catholic – and often rural – Other. For the most part, these are Irish narratives ostensibly collected in the manner of Sir Walter Scott's assembly of demotic Scots legendry – Scott is indeed mentioned explicitly at the close of 'Scraps of Hibernian Ballads', the eighth of the Purcell Papers – though they are almost certainly the product of the author's own imagination rather than a diligent record of oral folk culture, even where the fictional Purcell himself might protest otherwise when reporting a demotic ballad which was allegedly sung 'at weddings, wakes, and the like' (Le Fanu 1839: 754, 755). Le Fanu's ostensible commitment to the recording of folkish mythology is not unproblematic, however. Purcell is constructed, as Aoife Dempsey asserts, as something of a 'proto-folklorist', though his records often exhibit a perceptible element of intellectual condescension – an indulgent tolerance, as it were, of the superstitions and folk-beliefs of his co-religionists. His accounts, in one respect, impose a degree of control over the waywardness of indigenous mythology. Though nominally a Roman Catholic priest, Purcell – as the imaginative expression of an Irish Protestant author writing for an Irish Protestant journal – is heavily implicated in what Dempsey terms the 'Protestant stewardship of Irish culture and Irish life' (Dempsey 2022: 27).

The supposedly demotic narratives recounted by Purcell are, in turn, further conditioned through the intervention of the late priest's *'residuary legatee'* (Le Fanu 1838: 50, italics in original), a legal executor who both selects and contextualises these already mediated superstitions and folk beliefs before they are finally presented to the reader by way of a Dublin journal committed to the Protestant cause. It can be argued, therefore, that the ghosts, spirits, devils and family legends which populate these twice-mediated tales might potentially be of less interest to the literary and cultural scholar of Victorian Ireland than the subtle implications embedded in their narration. Certainly, there can be no doubt that Purcell's stories are influenced by, and expressive of, the sectarian politics of a period in which the Protestant population of Ireland perceived a threat to existing polity from the Roman Catholic population at home and the liberal establishment in London (Dempsey 2022: 24–6). It is equally evident, however, that in subtly mobilising contemporary concerns, these narratives engage simultaneously in a complex negotiation between the past and the present, between the 'old' Ireland and its fearfully anticipated successor – and, indeed, in some detail, interrogate further the place occupied by Roman Catholic institutions and identities, past and present. The Purcell Papers are far more than mere ghost stories, and Purcell himself much more than a convenient device by which purportedly historical, demotic and rural narratives might be conveyed to a contemporary, educated and urban readership.

The glib association of the Purcell Papers with Le Fanu's later reputation as an author of supernatural fiction has somewhat obscured the nature of works framed within the memoirs of this rural cleric. Not all of the Purcell Papers embody a supernatural content. Of the twelve 'extracts', as they are consistently subtitled in the *Dublin University Magazine*, two – 'Scraps of Hibernian Ballads' (June 1839) and 'An Adventure of Hardress Fitzgerald, A Royalist Captain' (February 1840) – embody no element of the marvellous and are essentially tales of adventure underwritten by the rhetorical fervour of a historical Irish, rather than contemporary British, cultural identity. The notion of a discrete Irish identity, bound up not merely with Roman Catholicism but also with a mythologised ambience of chivalry and *noblesse oblige* in historical times permeates the other narratives within the cycle, defining their heroes, condemning their villains, and underlining their separation from any English milieu. These are in essence Irish stories, not imitations of their Scottish or English counterparts, and they represent the work of an author not yet enmeshed in the culture of London publishing.

The remaining ten extracts are dominated by tales of intrigue or adventure – these preoccupations, needless to say, being shared to a greater or lesser extent by Purcell's explicitly supernatural narratives. There is, without doubt, a distinctive Gothic heritage in the family intrigue that underwrites the fifth extract, 'Passage in the Secret History of an Irish Countess' (November 1838), a condensed anticipation of Le Fanu's 1864 novel, *Uncle Silas*. 'The Last Heir of Castle Connor' (June 1838), the third extract, opens with an optimistic prospect of regeneration within 'an ancient Irish family' (Le Fanu 1838: 713), a Roman Catholic dynasty whose ancestral lands had been forfeited in 'the storm of confiscation' following the victory of William III (Le Fanu 1838: 713). This hopeful scenario is fatally disrupted through the arrival of a mysterious tempter who ends the familial line by provoking the eponymous last heir into a duel, an event which the young Purcell – a friend of the family – was to witness. 'The Bridal of Carrigvarah' (April 1839), the sixth narrative, likewise embodies no supernatural content, though its depiction of a dark and vulpine servant's revenge upon his master is replete with Gothic tension. There is a clandestine marriage, a fatal challenge prompted by a lady's honour, a poignant encounter between the priest and the bereaved wife in which the honour of another scion of Roman Catholic descent is affirmed, and the disreputable servant, having squandered his ill-gotten wealth in 'profligate extravagance' sinks finally to 'the character of an informer' against his own countrymen during the 1798 Rebellion (Le Fanu 1839: 411, 413–14, 416–17, 418).

Relatively few of the Purcell Papers can thus be classified unequivocally as ghost stories: indeed, 'Strange Event in the Life of Schalken the Painter' (May 1839), the seventh extract, is probably the only narrative in the cycle in which a supernatural entity is observed by more than one person. Of the other narratives which may be deemed to fall comfortably within the purlieu of the ghost story, 'The Fortunes of Sir Robert Ardagh' (March 1838) embodies an implied but still debatable supernatural script, albeit it with a freighting of stylistic horror, where 'The Ghost and the Bone-Setter' (January 1838) and 'The Drunkard's Dream' (August 1838) are premised upon the faulty perception of an inebriated witness. Like 'The Ghost and the Bone-Setter', 'Jack Sullivan's Adventures in the Great Snow' (July 1839) and 'The Quare Gander' (October 1840) are comedic pieces which, nonetheless, draw upon an ostensible belief in supernatural phenomena amongst rural Roman Catholics. These latter are, perhaps, those likely to be of least interest to Gothic scholars. The former narrates the assumed death of the titular figure during a blizzard, the hasty remarriage of his wife to a younger man, and the fear of the newlyweds when the supposed ghost of Sullivan attempts to enter his former home a week later, once the snow has melted. 'The Quare Gander' is a comedic revision of the possibility of reincarnation, the supposed recipient body of the departed soul being that of a goose destined for the market. In this extract, as well as in 'Jack Sullivan's Adventures in the Great Snow', Roman Catholic priests are represented not as scheming Jesuits but rather as figures almost as gullible as their parishioners. These are demotic tales, represented in a stylised version of rural speech, and the well-spoken Purcell plays no direct role in the working through of their ironically comedic plots.

Purcell, like the later Hesselius, is implicated in the first of the tales which bear his name, albeit only by dint of being the recipient of a narrative told by the ghost-seer's son. In 'The Ghost and the Bone-Setter', Purcell's literary executor – whose religious affiliations are notably *not* disclosed – introduces the conceit of the series with loving, though never sycophantic, care.[3] Of the first extract he intimates:

> It is one of many such; for he was a curious and industrious collector of old local traditions – a commodity in which the quarter where he resided mightily abounded. The collection and arrangement of such legends was, as long as I can remember him, his *hobby*; but I had never learned that his love of the marvellous and whimsical had carried him so far as to prompt him to commit the results of his enquiries to writing, until, in the character of

residuary legatee, his will put me in possession of all his manuscript papers. (Le Fanu 1838: 50)

The customary Protestant prejudice which associates priestcraft with superstition is here undermined somewhat by the executor, given that the narratives which are to follow the emphatically titled 'The Ghost and the Bone-Setter' are immediately dismissed as marvels and whimseys rather than actual horrors. The temperate rationality of Purcell is further emphasised by the sentence which follows immediately after this opening gambit. The residuary legatee continues, anticipating perhaps an objection from a reader located on either side of the sectarian divide:

> To such as may think the composing of such productions as these inconsistent with the character and habits of a country priest, it is necessary to observe, that there did exist a race of priests – those of the old school, a race now nearly extinct – whose habits were from many causes more refined, and whose tastes more literary than are those of the alumni of Maynooth. (Le Fanu 1838: 50)

This single sentence locates Purcell's literary executor within an identifiable point in Irish history, this being the transition between the eighteenth and nineteenth centuries. St Patrick's College at Maynooth, north of Dublin, was founded in 1795 as the first seminary on Irish soil within which Roman Catholic priests might be trained. Constructed on land belonging to the sympathetic Duke of Leinster – a Protestant – its establishment was in part underwritten by the British government so as to reduce the Roman Catholic Church's reliance upon clergy trained on a European continent the culture and politics of which were then dominated by revolutionary France.[4] The government's apparent patronage of the Roman Catholic cause was, needless to say, a controversial move in a country in which some voters were already anticipating the possible advantages and disadvantages of the political and parliamentary Union that was to finally come in 1800. In context, the needs of a specifically *British* nation at war had been, in Irish Protestant eyes, prioritised over Irish – and sectarian – imperatives. Hence, a discernible level of suspicion might well be aroused at the prospect of an institution which might recruit its students from an assertive Catholic bourgeoisie that was also perceived as aspiring to the eclipse of the established and primarily Protestant landed order. Speaking in the House of Lords, for example, the Earl of Clare decried the funding advanced to the Maynooth seminary, specifically noting that 'The school was merely calculated for the education of youth of a middle class, the consequence of which was, the parents of those of higher distinction would not send their children there' (Anon. 17 Apr. 1799). Those Roman Catholics 'of higher distinction' appear to have been perceived as potential allies for the preservation of a social order on the verge of transferring qualification from a sectarian to a financial prerogative. If these upstart priests, the scions of bourgeois or tradesmen families, might be regarded as being the cultural and intellectual inferiors of their Protestant neighbours, they might necessarily be regarded also as being potentially as dangerous to the Roman Catholic elite as their counterparts trained in post-Bourbon France. The account of Clare's speech, published in a Dublin periodical, *Saunders's News-Letter*, continues, intimating how:

> The noble Earl entered into an examination of the conduct of the Roman Catholic Clergy of this Seminary, in the course of which his Lordship depicted in very severe terms the sedition of Dr Hussey, who, instead of acting as a Minister of the Gospel, and a preacher of peace, had been the author of a diabolical pamphlet, which went to commit Catholic against Protestant, and to create rebellion in the country. (Anon. 1799)

Maynooth in its early years, it seems, was – to the fearful Protestants of *fin de siècle* County Dublin, at least – a byword for disorder and unrest, with rumours of foreign infiltration within the town (Anon. 3 Feb. 1797), agrarian terrorism (Anon. 28 Jan. 1797) and even open rebellion (Anon. 27 Jul. 1798), with one early student of the seminary, Francis Hearn, being judicially executed for unspecified 'treasonable practices' (Anon. 1799). There would thus seem to be something of an ironic touch of nostalgia invested in the now-deceased persona of the late Father Purcell, a representative, seemingly, of the more peaceful times before 1798, and a gentleman whose erudition and temperance would seem to distance him from the brash contemporary world of bourgeois aspiration.

This apparent nostalgia for less complicated times is a central theme of the Purcell Papers. Purcell's memoirs frequently recall hard times – times of poverty and precarious inheritance, of violence in word and in deed, and of cynicism with regard to familial or marital connections. These are times, though, in which the conflicts of the present day feel comparatively muted – and even where political betrayal is evoked, a historic and patriotic devotion to a culturally discrete Ireland is prioritised over the sectarian divisions associated with the reader's nineteenth-century milieu.[5]

This imagined past is called up from Purcell's own youthful experience, from narratives told to him by his contemporaries, be they peasant co-religionists or educated Protestants. In those stories which lack supernatural content, the only ghost to be found is the metaphorical ghost of departed times and departed manners – manners appendant to a form of Roman Catholicism somewhat more palatable to Ascendancy tastes, characterised by polite restraint and conspicuous bravery, moderated through the temperate leadership of the hereditarily wealthy and the lineally noble. The peasants portrayed in these fictions may alternate between the crude and the comical, but they signally fail to display the naked ambition and entrepreneurship apparently associated with the rising Roman Catholic bourgeoisie in the opening years of Victoria's reign. The loyalty of these simple folk is to a country conveniently emblematised by patrician leadership underwritten by *noblesse oblige* and chivalrous devotion. This is the devotion that would bring 'ten thousand Irish boys' to stand with Lord Edward Fitzgerald (1763–98), a Protestant nationalist and, for the bard of 'Scraps of Hibernian Ballads', 'the bravest gentleman, an' the best that ever stood' (Le Fanu 1839: 754). Similar enthusiasm is exhibited upon the return of the eponymous 'Last Heir of Castle Connor' (Le Fanu 1838: 714). Gallantry is a constant theme across the Purcell Papers, with masculine and military honour established as a prerogative to be defended even unto death (Le Fanu 1840: 145, 157, 159), whilst betrayal for personal gain attracts deepest contempt (Le Fanu 1839: 411, 413–14, 416–17, 418).

This is the Ireland of an imaginative past, therefore, populated by landlords closer to the soil than to commerce, and by peasants loyal to patrician families who have held tenure for generation (Le Fanu 1838: 714). It is an idyll where the priesthood engages not in sedition but upholds instead a locally paternalistic relationship based upon dependence rather than competition. Any uneasy relationship with the distant government of London rests not upon active coercion but a sense of that power seeking to usurp local custom. Hence, Purcell's ostensible memories overlook the tense sectarian culture which followed the Glorious Revolution, and project instead an idyll that never really existed, a fantasy regarding a different type of Roman Catholicism – something resembling feudal times, almost, and with a nostalgic ambience more frequently expressed in late eighteenth-century Gothic fiction than in the early Victorian short story.[6]

What may thus be considered an eighteenth-century generic inheritance punctuates the Purcell Papers. The opening of the second extract, 'The Fortunes of Sir Robert Ardagh' (March 1838), evokes a residual Ireland, an arboreal space 'in which some fragments of aboriginal wood have found a refuge' (Le Fanu 1838: 313). This eighteenth-century environment has, admittedly, lost 'its oldest and grandest trees' to the woodsman's axe, though Purcell is lyrical in his description of its 'wild and pleasing peculiarities of nature – its complete irregularity – its vistas'. The 'tyrant pruning hook', indeed, is all that represses this obscure corner of Ireland, though the reader is soon brought to the realisation that, even in the eighteenth century, things are not as they once were. The memoir continues, with a sudden turn that cuts hard into the substance of the contemporary idyll implied by Purcell's opening sentence:

> But now, alas, whither have we drifted? – whither has the tide of civilization borne us? – it has passed over a land unprepared for it – it has left nakedness behind it – we have lost our forests, but our marauders remain – we have destroyed all that is picturesque, while we have retained everything that is revolting in barbarism. (Le Fanu 1838: 313)

A similar framing likewise structures the opening of 'The Last Heir of Castle Connor' (June 1838):

> There is something in the decay of ancient grandeur to interest even the most unconcerned spectator – the evidences of greatness, of power, and of pride that survive the wreck of time, proving, in mournful contrast with present desolation and decay, what *was* in other days, appeal with a restless power, to the sympathies of our nature. (Le Fanu 1838: 713)

The emphatic 'our' is significant here. Purcell later talks, with unalloyed regret, of those families ruined 'in the cause of a lost country and a despised religion' (Le Fanu 1838: 713), and though the conceit is that the addressee of this aside *ought* to be a co-religionist, the incorporation of the narrative in a Protestant journal implicates quite another readership. Where 'The Ghost and the Bone-Setter' is, beyond its appointed opening, a comedic tale of superstition related by an inebriated peasant, 'The Fortunes of Sir Robert Ardagh' – like 'The Last Heir of Castle Connor' – narrates the decline of an ancient and noble Irish family, and though Ardagh's religious affiliation is never specified, his having 'served in foreign armies' might suggest recusant status (Le Fanu 1838: 314). There is something of Ann Radcliffe here, a memory of glories departed which might, nonetheless, be partially restored – and which, with that restoration, might promise a more congenial present thereafter. If Purcell himself can be considered, in his literary executor's words, a priest of 'the old school, a race now nearly extinct' (Le Fanu 1838: 50), such sentiments may equally be attached to the declining grandees of Ireland. These latter seemingly pose no substantial threat to the Protestant ascendancy and, indeed, might well have been – or might well be, if revived and integrated into national life – an agency of social control over their less-fortunate co-religionists.

Purcell himself is something of an ecumenicalist, remarking in 'Strange Event in the Life of Schalken the Painter' of one 'Captain Vandael, whose father had served King William in the Low Countries, and also in my own unhappy land during the Irish campaigns' (Le Fanu 1839: 579), that 'I know not how it happened that I liked this man's society spite [sic] of his politics and religion: but so it was' (Le Fanu 1839: 579). An explanation for this comfortable acceptance might be sought, perhaps, in the manner in which the amiable cleric has similarly gained affectionate admission to the circle of readers who subscribe to the *Dublin University Magazine* by way of his good manners and – for the most part (Le Fanu 1840: 390) – understated beliefs.

Purcell's amiability, though, is but one factor in his seemingly easy admission into the confidence of an overwhelmingly Protestant readership. If his mode of description occasionally touches upon a Radcliffean paradigm, the priest's rational behaviour in those few stories which feature, or else suggest, the actual presence of a ghost or demon, locates him firmly within the conventions of the so-called explained supernatural. In the case of Terry Neil, who narrates his father's experiences to Purcell in 'The Ghost and the Bone-Setter', it is the ghost-seer's own free admission of his progressive inebriation – 'a small taste iv the pottieen' (Le Fanu 1838: 51) leads to him having 'dhrunk about a pint of sperits' (Le Fanu 1838: 52) – that undermines the reliability of his ancestor's ghost story.[7] By contrast, 'The Drunkard's Dream' (August 1838) – a narrative whose fleeting visions of hell are floated upon the excessive consumption of commercially produced whiskey rather than home-distilled poteen – is narrated directly to the priest, who admits to a certain prejudice regarding the reputation of the individual concerned and the reliability of his testimony. Purcell is aroused from his sleep in order 'to visit the death-bed of a presumptuous sinner, to endeavour, almost against my own conviction, to infuse a hope into the heart of a dying reprobate – a drunkard but too probably perishing under the consequences of some mad fit of intoxication ...' (Le Fanu 1838: 152). Purcell, however, arrives apparently too late at the drunkard's bedside, finding 'the blue and swollen features of the drunkard', Pat Connell, now 'fixed and livid' in death, his countenance displaying 'a ghastly and rigid expression of despairing terror such as I never saw equalled' (153). The priest's prayerful attempts to comfort the dead man's family, however, are disrupted when the corpse suddenly revives, becoming an emblem of spiritual as well as physical depravity, a grotesque un-dead body which, now that 'the human tenant had deserted it' had become 'the horrible sport of demoniac possession' (154). The shocked priest, however, is mistaken. This is no demoniac possession but an awakening from alcohol-induced catalepsy, as the priest himself realises when 'the spell was broken – superstition gave way to reason: the man whom all believed to have been actually dead, was living!' (154).

From this point, Purcell's narrative adopts the redemptive and hopeful tone of Christian moralism. Ceding control of the revived body to the attending medical practitioner for the moment, the priest subsequently returns in order to hear the man's confession and, he hopes, to return him to sober, industrious and pious habits. The nature of the drunkard's confession, though, recalls again the supernatural ambience that characterises Purcell's initial response to his revival. The confession, which is elicited without the customary ritual of the sacrament, intimates that the drunkard, having returned home intoxicated, left his bed and, on walking down to the first landing of his ramshackle dwelling, fell through the floor and into a judgemental tribunal intent on committing him to eternal punishment in hell. The drunkard is permitted to 'depart for a season' (Le Fanu 1838: 155) on the promise of his return, delivered by a magisterial figure whom he assumes to be no other than the Prince of Darkness.

Though the attentive priest appreciates 'the impressiveness which always belongs to the narration of an *eye-witness*' (Le Fanu 1838: 155, italics in original), it is made clear that he does *not* believe that his parishioner has been granted an insight into the destiny reserved for the unrepentant sinner. Purcell considers Connell's vision of hell representative of 'vulgarly received notions of the great place of punishment, and of its presiding spirit', even though it strikes him with 'awe, almost with fear' (155). Significantly, in his retrospect Purcell remarks that he received the drunkard's confession 'long before Vatheck [sic] and the "Hall of Ebles" [sic] had delighted the world (155).[8] On reflection, Purcell's awe appears that of a literary man swayed by an evocation of the sublime – notwithstanding his misspelling of the name of Beckford's Caliph and the place of his eternal punishment – rather than that of a simple believer in visions and portents. His response to Connell's desperate question regarding his eternal destiny – 'is there any hope; is there any chance at all? or, is my soul pledged and promised away for ever' (155–6) – is as pragmatic as it is casuistic:

> In answering him I had no easy task to perform; for however clear might be my internal conviction of the groundlessness of his fears, and however strong my scepticism respecting the reality of what he had described, I nevertheless felt that his impression to the contrary, and his humility and terror resulting from it, might be made available as no mean engines in the work of his conversion from profligacy, and of his restoration to decent habits, and to religious feeling. (156)

Purcell's closing words are significant, and underline once more his location within the politics of Le Fanu's early Victorian Ireland rather than the fictional priest's eighteenth-century equivalent. Purcell becomes a sort of honorary Protestant here, not just in terms of his judiciously sceptical attitude to the marvellous and the portentous, but also in his commitment to a work ethic based upon temperance and personal betterment. It would seem that the cleric is prioritising the physical well-being of his parishioner – 'decent habits' notably precede 'religious feeling'– and is utilising this crisis not to ensnare him in the church's profitable cycle of spiritual prophylactics but rather to improve his situation through the discipline of redemptive labour. Purcell thus distinguishes himself from another Roman Catholic cleric mentioned in his memoirs, an individual keen to offer ostensibly spiritual solutions to human problems – at a price (Le Fanu 1839: 106). Purcell succeeds in part. Connell's 'good resolutions' did not fail but were to 'gather strength by time' and Purcell observes:

> ... when I saw that man shake off the idle and debauched companions, whose society had for years formed alike his amusement and his ruin, and revive his long discarded habits of industry and sobriety, I said within myself, there is something more in all this than the operation of an idle dream. (Le Fanu 1838: 156)

The priest's summation of the former drunkard's change of habits is notably ambiguous as to whether Connell's evident improvement may be attributed to divine patronage or personal endeavour. There is notably no statement from Purcell regarding Connell's subsequent attendance upon the requisite ceremonies of his faith: the priest encounters the former drunkard outside his workplace or else the family dwelling, but apparently not in God's house itself.

Connell, though, ultimately fails to eschew both superstition and bad company, even though he became, for a time, 'a good workman, and with his better habits he recovered his former extensive and profitable employment' (Le Fanu 1838: 156). In essence he fails to achieve that final stage of independence that would free him not merely from alcohol – he yields to the temptation of alcohol upon the return of a companion of his youth – but also from superstition, for he is caught by Purcell on the landing from which he supposedly fell into hell during his vision 'strengthening the floor with a view to securing himself against such a catastrophe' (156). Purcell's indulgent smile and simple blessing – 'God bless his work' (156) – ironically accentuate the incompleteness of Connell's ostensible 'conversion'. Connell dies by falling down the same stairs whilst intoxicated, his wife having conveniently witnessed her husband's departure from the room by the flickering light of the fire accompanied by another figure. The priest attempts to suggest this was Connell's shadow but leaves the house 'in a state of horror which I could not describe' (157). He seems hardly convinced that the tragedy that has just come to an end is the 'coincidence' which his rationality insists it should be, concluding 'it was then a mystery. Was the dream verified? – whither had the disembodied spirit sped? – who can say? We know not.' (157).[9]

Purcell must thus be considered a far more complex figure than his literary descendent, Hesselius. His presence within the narratives issued in his name is more protracted than that of the German physician, and his direct intervention into, and interpretation of, the lives and deaths of his counterparts more profound. Beyond this, though, his signal importance lies in his mobilisation of the cultural unease of the first years of the reign of Queen Victoria, a period when the Protestant confidence of the Glorious Revolution was fading, the relatively recent memory of the 1798 Rebellion underwriting a pervasive sense of unease at the dawning of a new age. Under government exercised from a city geographically and culturally distant from Protestant Dublin, the accession of a young and inexperienced ruler in 1837 might prove as opportune as the sporadic distraction provided by the mental indisposition of George III – himself an opposer of extending political rights to Roman Catholics. The Purcell Papers are thus as relevant to the scholar of Victorian Irish culture as well as to Gothicists: as is the case with almost all ghost stories, their narratives of the supernatural, of contested belief and of human reactions to the uncanny embody an historical context, the sober and introspective reflection of which contrasts markedly with the excitement and grotesquerie of the events portrayed. Other scholars will, no doubt, find further fuel for argument and analysis in this unjustly neglected body of early work from a writer who was rightly identified by M. R. James as one who stood 'in the first rank as a writer of ghost stories' (James 1923, vii).

Notes

1. The twelve tales originally published in the *Dublin University Magazine* were subsequently issued in a posthumous three-volume collection in 1880, with the assistance of Le Fanu's brother and the permission of the author's eldest son (Graves 1880: xxxi). 'Billy Malowney's Taste of Love and Glory', the final narrative in the 1880 collection, embodies no explicit connection to the linking figure of Purcell, though it is admittedly a narrative couched in demotic speech and reported by an educated interlocutor.

2. See, also, Aoife Dempsey's persuasive analysis of the place of the *Dublin University Magazine* as an expression of 'Irish Protestant exceptionalism within a wider conception of "Britishness"' (Dempsey 2022: 19–21).
3. The editor, commentator or witness who links a series of short fictions appears to be a device favoured by Le Fanu (Dempsey 2022: 45, 47–8, 130–1). Le Fanu also deployed named milieux, such as Chapelizod near Dublin (Le Fanu 1851: *passim*) or the eponymous but fictional English village in *Chronicles of Golden Friars* (1871), to connect what might otherwise be disparate short narratives.
4. The College was legally established under *An Act for the Better Education of Persons Professing the Popish or Roman Catholic Religion* (35 Geo. III. c. 21) and admitted its first students in the autumn of 1795.
5. Elsewhere, however, in the *Dublin University Magazine*, the hardships as well as the victories of the Glorious Revolution are celebrated in more explicitly sectarian terms: see, for example, 'The ◊ will be Trumps Again' (Anon. 1838: *passim*).
6. This type of mythmaking is not uncommon in the *Dublin University Magazine*: see, for example, 'The Orphans of Dunasker' (Anon. 1838: 235–6).
7. Drawing on the derogatory tradition of the 'Irish bull' or malapropism, Neil later describes his father as 'an industhrious, sober man, an' an example of inebriety to the whole parish' (Le Fanu 1838: 53).
8. This suggests that Connell's experience occurs prior to 1786 and the first English edition of *Vathek*, published anonymously as *An Arabian Tale*.
9. The abuse of alcohol by the rural working classes is a recurrent theme in the Purcell Papers, and is raised also in 'The Quare Gander' (Le Fanu 1840: 392) and briefly in 'Jim Sullivan's adventures in the Great Snow' (Le Fanu 1839: 105).

Works Cited

Anon. [i.e. William Beckford]. *An Arabian Tale, From an Unpublished Manuscript with Notes Critical and Explanatory*. London: Published for J. Johnson, 1786.

Anon. 'Dublin'. *Saunders's News-Letter, and Daily Advertiser*, 28 January 1797, p. 2, col. 2.

Anon. 'Dublin'. *Saunders's News-Letter, and Daily Advertiser*, 3 February 1797, p. 2, col. 2.

Anon. 'Dublin, June 20th'. *Kentish Gazette*, 27 July 1798, p. 1, cols 3–4.

Anon. 'Francis Hearn, Late a Student of the College of Maynooth', *The Kentish Chronicle*, 8 November 1799, p. 3, col. 2.

Anon. 'House of Peers. Monday, April 15th'. *Saunders's News-Letter, and Daily Advertiser*, 17 April 1799, p. 2, cols 1–2.

Anon. 'New Year's Day, or Our First Number'. *Dublin University Magazine*, 1 January 1833, pp. 87–90.

Anon. 'The Orphans of Dunasker', chapter 13, 'The Twelfth of July'. *Dublin University Magazine*, 11, 1838, pp. 284–90.

Anon. 'The ◊ will be Trumps Again'. *Dublin University Magazine*, 11, 1838, p. 49.

Crawford, Gary William, Jim Rockhill, and Brian J. Showers, eds. *Reflections in a Glass Darkly: Essays on J. Sheridan Le Fanu*. New York: Hippocampus Press, 2011.

Dempsey, Aoife Mary. *Joseph Sheridan Le Fanu*. Cardiff: University of Wales Press, 2022.

Graves, Alfred Percival. 'Memoir of Joseph Sheridan Le Fanu'. In Joseph Sheridan Le Fanu, *The Purcell Papers*, 3 vols. London: Richard Bentley and Son, 1880, vol. 1, pp. v–xxxi.

James, Montague Rhodes. 'Prologue. By the Editor', in J. S. Le Fanu, *Madam Crowl's Ghost and Other Tales of Mystery*, edited by M. R. James. London: G. Bell and Sons, 1923, pp. vii–viii.

Le Fanu, Joseph Sheridan. 'An Adventure of Hardress Fitzgerald, A Royalist Captain'. *Dublin University Magazine*, 15, 1840, pp. 145–58.

———. *In a Glass Darkly*, 3 vols. London: R. Bentley and Son, 1872.

———. 'The Bridal of Carrigvarah'. *Dublin University Magazine*, 13, 1839, pp. 405–18.

———. 'The Drunkard's Dream'. *Dublin University Magazine*, 11, 1838, pp. 151–7.

———. 'The Fortunes of Sir Robert Ardagh'. *Dublin University Magazine*, 11, 1838, pp. 313–24.

———. 'The Ghost and the Bone-Setter'. *Dublin University Magazine*, 11, 1838, pp. 50–4.

———. 'Ghost Stories of Chapelizod'. *Dublin University Magazine*, 37, 1851, pp. 85–98.

———. 'Jim Sullivan's Adventures in the Great Snow' *Dublin University Magazine*, 14, 1839, pp. 103–7.

———. 'The Last Heir of Castle Connor'. *Dublin University Magazine*, 11, 1838, pp. 713–30.

———. *The Purcell Papers*, 3 vols. London: Richard Bentley and Son, 1880.

———. 'The Quare Gander'. *Dublin University Magazine*, 16, 1840, pp. 390–4.

———. 'Scraps of Hibernian Ballads'. *Dublin University Magazine*, 13, 1839, pp. 752–6.

———. 'Strange Event in the Life of Schalken the Painter'. *Dublin University Magazine*, 13, 1839, pp. 579–91.

McCormack. W. J. 'Irish Gothic and After', in Seamus Deane (ed.), *The Field Day Anthology of Irish Writing*, 3 vols. Londonderry: Field Day Publications, 1991), vol. 2, pp. 842–6.

Tilley, Elizabeth. 'J. S. Le Fanu, Gothic, and the Irish Periodical', in Christina Morin and Niall Gillespie (eds), *Irish Gothics: Genres, Modes, and Traditions, 1760–1890*. Basingstoke: Palgrave Macmillan, 2014, pp. 130–46.

Chapter 15

Margaret Oliphant
Valerie Sanders

Margaret Oliphant's supernatural story of 1880, 'Earthbound', opens with a recently bereaved family gathered together at Christmas discussing ghosts and spiritualism. Although this is a familiar scenario for a Victorian ghost story, the narrator says the 'commonplace ghost-stories, which are among the ordinary foolishness of Christmas did not suit with the more serious tone in which their thoughts flowed'. Instead, the older people talk about 'those sensations and presentiments that seem sometimes to convey a kind of prophecy, only understood after the event, of sorrow on the way', while the younger discuss spiritualism and other 'new-fangled fancies' (Oliphant 2000: 140). This generational divide allows Oliphant (1828–97) to capture that mixture of belief and scepticism that was characteristic not just of herself, but also of many nineteenth-century authors who, for various reasons, tried their hand at the supernatural story.

Oliphant's reasons for being intrigued by spectral presences were both personal and poignant. In some ways she may seem an unlikely author of ghost stories, associated as she is with the realist social comedy of the Carlingford novels, such as *Salem Chapel* (1863) and *Phoebe, Junior* (1876), featuring middling to lower-class families who live humdrum lives as nonconformist ministers and shopkeepers with socially aspirational daughters. It was not, indeed, until the final decade of her life that she applied herself to the writing of supernatural tales, and this perhaps for the most painful of biographical reasons. From the loss of her ten-year-old daughter Maggie in Rome in 1863 to that of her youngest son Francis Romano ('Cecco') in 1894, Oliphant was confronted with an unthinkable succession of close family bereavements. Not one of her six children survived her, and as she assembled her fragments of autobiography, prompted by the need for reflection on the deaths of Maggie, Cyril and Cecco, she could not help speculating as to where they were.[1] 'The more I think of it,' she says in her *Autobiography* (1899), 'the less

I am able to feel that those who have left us can start up at once into a heartless beatitude without caring for our sorrow' (Oliphant 2002: 39). Some of the last stories she wrote verge on dystopian fantasy as she strains to visualise entering this 'heartless beatitude': hence the recurrent image of the 'open door' in so many of her stories, signifying a two-way entry point for the dead. The door is either a portal for their entry into the afterlife or for their return to earth on unfinished business: business often frustrated by a failure of communication between the dead and the living. More than anything, Oliphant's stories explore the frustrations of trying to convey messages or interpret them as the two parties strain to make contact.

As Melissa Edmundson argues, many nineteenth-century women's ghost stories are written from the sidelines, and 'tend to show a more developed sympathy for the complexities of human relationships', eschewing 'outward manifestations of brutality and horror' (Edmundson 2018: 69). This is certainly true of Oliphant, whose ghostly presences divide broadly into two types. The majority want to help the living (often their relatives) by warning them of trouble or danger, and in this sense are benign ghosts, while the minority are more concerned with their own needs. Few, if any, are malign, or intent on traumatising their seers. Many of her stories also feature discussions between clergy, doctors, scientists and servants as to the nature of what they have seen. As Srdjan Smajić suggests, 'Ghost stories are narratives about people who cannot *see* otherwise than with their bodily eyes, and who invoke science more often than religion when they see something unexpected, something possibly not of this world' (Smajić 2010:47).

As it develops, Oliphant's interest in the supernatural, though driven by personal grief, extends beyond the circumstances of her own bereavements. Both her adult sons, Cyril (1856–90) and Cecco (1859–94), led curiously inert lives, despite the privileged Eton education she had worked to subsidise. While Cyril was a drinker, Cecco inherited his father's tubercular constitution; both were indolent by nature, and (unlike their mother) disinclined to dedicate themselves to a career. Oliphant was left with little to console her, while at the same time yearning to find some means of making sense of her loss. There were, however, other examples to hand, especially Eleanor ('Nelly') Clifford, a Windsor neighbour about whom Oliphant wrote five stories featuring a 'Little Pilgrim' travelling into the afterlife. Unlike the Oliphant sons, Nelly had lived to some purpose in her own community, and was therefore rewarded with a quick passage to Heaven (a word, incidentally, rarely used by Oliphant). In the first story, 'A Little Pilgrim in the Unseen', first published in *Macmillan's Magazine* in 1882, the Pilgrim paradoxically awakes into death as if she had 'risen up with a delicious sense of daring, and of being all alone in the mystery of the sunrise, in the unawakened world which lay at her feet to be explored, as if she were Eve just entering upon Eden' (Oliphant 1883: 5). In this intuitively female version of the afterlife, the Pilgrim mostly feels kinship with other women and children, and even meets Oliphant's daughter Maggie, now transformed into an angelic figure fully resigned to God's purposes. It seems significant that Oliphant's husband, Frank, who had died in Rome in 1859, leaving her pregnant with Cecco, never figures as someone she yearns for, or tries to find in the afterlife. In the first two 'Little Pilgrim' stories, the word 'husband' occurs only twice (and in a generic context), while 'child' is mentioned fifty-three times.

Of all the stories Oliphant wrote about the afterlife, 'A Little Pilgrim' is perhaps the one that most transparently reveals her need, not just to be reassured about the peacefulness and even happiness of the life to come, but also to connect with those she mourned, albeit through a mediator. But while this offers insight into what Oliphant explores in her ghost stories, and what she demands of them, the story by no means permanently resolved her perplexity about the meaning of death, or her own frustrations at being unable to speak to her children and understand what happened to them. Altogether she wrote nine 'classic' ghost stories, but her full oeuvre in this field includes one three-volume novel with supernatural elements (*The Wizard's Son*, 1884) and a number of long short stories or novellas, some published in book form, of which *A Beleaguered City* (1880) is the most substantial. This and many of her other supernatural stories were first serialised in journals, and most narrate attempts by a ghostly figure to contact the living, usually via one selected individual. Interactions between the two parties vary from the almost sociable to the frustratingly baffling. Rarely spine-chilling, her supernatural tales essentially explore emotional longing and inertia in bereaved or dysfunctional families. 'The Open Door' is typical in terms of the father's absence from home while his son's condition worsens; another example is 'The Portrait' (1885), narrated by a man whose mother died at his birth. Where events happened long ago, as in this mother's death, Oliphant remains interested in the lasting repercussions of bereavement within families where the survivors find it difficult to talk to one another.

In most of Oliphant's ghost stories, the spectre is matched with a living person who has reached a point of stagnation in their life, while the spatial arrangement of the home where these frustrated ghostly connections take place seems in itself to become part of the theatre of illusion so intriguing to Oliphant. As Leila Walker observes, Oliphant 'used her ghost stories to create a safe rhetorical space in which to explore a shifting relationship between gender, power, property, and space' (Walker 2009: 178). Most of these stories are set in a specific domestic location where an unhealed rift remains, like the lingering aftertaste of a misunderstanding or a betrayal, and the majority of Oliphant's seers are initially doubters. What apparently interests her most is the process by which they become convinced that they have seen *something*, although common sense tells them this is unlikely. Alongside this runs the challenge of sharing this experience with other people in their household who may be anywhere on the spectrum between fervent belief and scoffing scepticism.

'The Open Door' (1882)

Perhaps her most urgent examination of the existence of ghosts occurs in 'The Open Door', whose narrator, Colonel Mortimer, is desperate to discover an explanation for his son Roland's agitation about a supposed ghost-child crying for help. A rationalist, he sets out to investigate, telling himself, 'This is the thing that human nature trembles at – a creature invisible, yet with sensations, feelings, a power somehow of expressing itself' (Oliphant 2000: 189). When he tries to enlist other men, including a clergyman and a butler, to accompany him into the murky grounds of his rented country house in Scotland, they all represent a position on the spectrum of un/belief, the most scientific, Dr Simson, admitting '"I can't tell what to think of it"' (Oliphant 2000: 198). Nor does the story itself deliver a clear explanation. They speculate that the crying voice of a 'prodigal' son is the result of ventriloquism or reverberation, while the presence of bread crusts on the floor may indicate that someone has been 'lodging' there. Either way, there is known to be a housekeeper's son who arrived after his mother's death and begged to be admitted. The 'open door' of the title is part of the ruined former house, and leads nowhere, neatly symbolising the frustrations of access into the afterlife. '"Father will know,"' Roland insists (181), but the father himself is at a loss. This is either a gateway to nothing, or a meaningful portal between two worlds. While Mortimer decides it is 'wisest to accept' his son's explanation 'as if it were all true' (179), Oliphant remains uncertain.

Doors and windows, as entry and exit points, not just to the home, but also to the past of ghosts and the future of seers, repeatedly tease those involved in these tense transactions. This is a recurrent feature of Oliphant's supernatural tales, stressing her preoccupation with boundaries between the dead and the living. Both in her autobiographical observations and in individual stories, she senses that these mysterious portals can be alternately flimsy and impenetrable. They torture her characters with their proximity and frustrating glimpses of passages to and from the worlds of the living and the dead, which nevertheless exclude the emotionally needy. This frustration applies equally to the supernatural presences who have urgent messages to convey, and to their intended recipients, who sense that someone is trying to reach them. Overall, perhaps, Oliphant's most persistent theme in her ghost stories is the barrier to communication. Their outcomes rarely achieve a solution that is anything more than a compromise. They end in anticlimax, frustrating multiple attempts at connection and explanation.

Like many other ghost stories, Oliphant's focus is on problematic relationships among the living which trigger or underlie their supernatural encounters. These are often relationships between the young and old, potential lovers, or (in an exaggerated version of these) thwarted connections between ancestors and living members of the same family. The ghost is more likely to be a relative or someone who has lived in the house before, rather than a complete stranger, and they often have a resonance for the seer, appearing at a moment of crisis in their lives, as we see in 'The Open Door'. Seers, in Oliphant's tales, are fairly evenly divided between men and women, children and adults, sceptics and believers. Inevitably, a further dimension of her stories is the seer's increasing isolation and desperation as their connection with the supernatural exacerbates or exposes an emotional need within themselves, especially if they sense a reciprocal need in the spectral presence. Sometimes, in her stories, a character's first meaningful experience of sexual attraction comes with a ghostly meeting, as with Oliphant's male seers in 'The Lady's Walk' and 'Earthbound', or the unnamed young girl in 'The Library Window', who becomes obsessed with her vision of a male scholar writing in a spectral library across the road from her aunt's house in the fictional St Rule's (based on St Andrews). The secrecy of these relationships is reinforced by the seers' solitary outdoor walks (if they are men) and their indoor vantage points (if they are young women or girls).

'The Library Window' (1896)

'The Library Window' is a late composition in which a young female narrator describes her hidden observation post overlooking the street as lying within 'the deep recess of the drawing-room window'. It has a curtain that half falls over it, which clearly shields her, both from drawing-room visitors, and from being seen from the library window opposite; but her space is soon crowded by her aunt's friends, a group of 'three or four old ladies', whom she describes as 'pressing into my recess, pressing upon me, a row of old faces, peering into something they could not understand' (Oliphant 2000: 366). Already they seem like ghosts, intruding on the narrator's romantic yearning for a relationship with the mysterious scholar who gradually flickers into life in the window across the street. Like Roland in 'The Open Door,' she is frail and fanciful, with 'a sort of second-sight', and like him, frustrated by the generation gap which obstructs trust and meaningful communication, both between the ghost and the seer, and the seer and their relatives (364–5). This is another of Oliphant's attempts to rationalise how and why some people are more susceptible than others to tenuous communications with supernatural presences, and one that she explores from both ends of the age spectrum. If the girlish narrator of 'The Library Window' finds her space has been invaded by old ladies, Old Lady Mary (in her eponymous story), feeling guilty about a young, neglected legatee, is placeless and invisible to all but a baby and a housemaid who appear to have sensed her presence. Through the displacement and invisibility of her female and child seers and ghosts, Oliphant seems to be reflecting their cultural insignificance according to the social assumptions of the age.

Oliphant's seer-ghost relationships, however, span all categories of class, gender and age. Some of what they see is depersonalised into an object of some kind: thus the narrator of 'The Library Window', feeling suffocated by her aunt's 'old half-blind ladies' (Oliphant 2000: 370), is rewarded at first by the expanding vision of an empty room containing a writing desk like her father's (372). 'I used to see more and more of the room as the days went on,' she narrates (373), her broadening view the opposite of the old ladies' diminishing sight. It may be no coincidence that when she is in her private viewing space she is often reading or holding a book, and she eventually perceives books on the floor in the ghostly room, and a large picture with a gilded frame. Oliphant's ghost stories, though written at different times, are connected via patterns of shared images: not just the doors and windows already mentioned, but portraits and pictures, which superimpose other times and identities over the ghost-seers. 'The Portrait' (1885) refers to a picture of the male protagonist's dead mother, which contrasts with the real-life presence of his father, sitting at a writing-table, just as the narrator of 'The Library Window' seems to see her father's writing desk. The writing father in possession of a room of his own sends its own Woolf-like message about the space and freedom of male self-expression and the right to study, which contrasts pointedly with the girl's furtive reading in the curtained window-seat at the edge of her aunt's drawing-room.

When the library window finally reveals a man in the room, busily writing, his back is towards her, outlined against the 'dim gilding' of the picture frame (Oliphant 2000: 378) and unresponsive to her stare. As if to stress her invisibility, on a subsequent sighting, the narrator's curtain hangs 'a little more over' her than usual (382), and her heart gives 'a great jump,' like the 'sudden leap' made by Philip Canning, the ghost-seer of 'The Portrait' when he hears a door opening and shutting in the house (Oliphant 2000: 295). The girl-narrator's invisibility makes her a ghost in the writing man's room, as well as he in hers, even as she prides herself on having the superior vision of youth, unlike the half-blind old ladies who insist the library window has been blocked in. Interestingly, this blocked window, a form of cancelled access into the afterlife, repeats an image from 'The Open Door', where Dr Simson, at the end of the story, 'with his stick penetrated an old window which had been entirely blocked up with fallen soil' (Oliphant 2000: 209–10). While not a window opening on to a room, it leads Simson and Mortimer into 'a little hole' (210) where someone has been sleeping rough. The sexual imagery of this scene adds an uncomfortable further dimension to Oliphant's gendered exploration of the supernatural in everyday life, as does the polarisation of intuitive sensory perception and rational scientific endeavour. What makes Oliphant's writing more inclusive, however, is that her men too can be sensitive ghost-hunters, as we see, both in 'The Portrait' and 'The Lady's Walk' (1882–3). The latter seems prefigured by 'Earthbound' (1880), where the seer, Edmund Coventry, also sees a ghostly woman walking in the grounds of the estate.

'The Lady's Walk' (1882–3, 1897)

The two versions of 'The Lady's Walk' (first serialised first in *Longman's Magazine* (1882–3) and later published as a novel in 1897) implicitly pair the ghostly lady associated with the Ellermore estate in Scotland where the narrator, Mr Temple, is a house guest, with the family's eldest daughter, Charlotte. Known as 'Chatty', Charlotte Campbell is a 'sister-mother' to her otherwise motherless siblings, and believes that the lady whose footsteps are often heard on a particular pathway is the family's 'guardian angel'. So long as the footsteps are heard, the family is safe; but as Temple hears, 'It is always death that is coming when she goes away' (Oliphant 1897: 25). He feels the same about Chatty herself, perceiving with 'a little shudder how entirely the whole thing would collapse if by any chance Chatty should be decoyed away' (Oliphant 1882: 6). Like herself, the ghost was an eldest daughter of the family, and Temple notices that both women have a habit of wringing their hands in a particular way. In the short story version, Chatty becomes 'white, white', and 'worn and pale' (Oliphant 1883: 348). At this point, shattered by the suicide of her eldest scapegrace brother, Colin, and the sale of the family estate, she acknowledges that she and the ghostly woman are the same: '"It has come to me all in a moment to see that She is just like me after all"' (Oliphant 1883: 352). Reinforcing the point, Temple notes that after seeing her stricken father to bed, 'she comes downstairs 'like a ghost through the dim-coming shadows' (357). The message this story seems to reinforce is that neither the benign ghost nor the sister-mother Chatty/Charlotte is able to protect the family from the sadness that befalls them in the death of Colin, the decline of the father and the threatened loss of their estate. It was a delusion that the family ever thought they could fend off the vagaries of Providence by clinging to a naive superstition, and she has sacrificed her own identity and independence by believing in it. If they were trusting in lifelong divine protection through the warnings of a personal ghost, religion, in this instance, lets them down. Nevertheless, the ghost directly speaks to Temple at the end, urging him to do something to help Charlotte, but though he would gladly marry her, she declines his offer. When she says it is 'out of her power' (Oliphant 1883: 364), she leaves the reader with a suspicion that she may be so aligned with her ghostly double that she is unable to contemplate an earthly relationship. At the end of 'Earthbound', a more visible ghostly woman in white with a black fichu similarly declines the hero's offer, though he does manage to persuade the flesh-and-blood daughter of the house, Maud, to marry him.

Ultimately, the message that so insistently communicates itself to the reader of these stories is concerned less with the existence of ghosts than with a family's unrealistic expectations of its mother-figures. Charlotte has become so 'anxious,' like the lady herself – a term reiterated several times in the closing pages – because she is desperate to protect the family. Oliphant suggests in this story that this is very much the mother's role, and Charlotte sees herself as deputising for her dead mother. As for the lady, as Charlotte finally admits, '"Perhaps to die does not make a woman wise any more than life does"' (Oliphant 1883: 352), an axiom that certainly applies to another of Oliphant's female ghosts, 'Old Lady Mary'. The difference here is that Lady Mary could have done something useful and practical for her godchild, whereas Charlotte and the lady could not save the family, any more than Oliphant could, from the heartbreak caused by a feckless son.

'Old Lady Mary' (1884)

Over time, Oliphant divides her attention between petitioning revenants haunting their old homes, and the recently dead entering the afterlife with all the uncertainty of a new arrival at an unfamiliar institution whose rules and codes of behaviour need to be explained. Her afterlife is a curiously sociable place with friendly guides offering advice on useful matters, such as making return visits to the living in order to set something right. We see this especially in 'Old Lady Mary', where the eponymous protagonist wants to show her family where she has hidden her will. The reason Lady Mary has failed to provide for her companion and godchild (known as 'little Mary') is that, not expecting to die (although she is over eighty), she has delayed making a will. Without it, her property will go to a wealthy grandson. One day she does, in fact, make a simple will, leaving everything to Mary. She even has it witnessed by her two servants (without telling them what it is), and then hides the will, for a 'joke' in the secret drawer of an old Italian cabinet (Oliphant 2000: 220). Although it is some time before she finally dies, the 'joke' remains undiscovered until the anticlimactic ending when one of the vicar's sons accidentally discovers the secret drawer with the will inside it. Even then, little Mary's future is left undisclosed, as the story ends with old Mary's return to the world of the afterlife which she left in order to right things in her former home.

Although on the surface this feels like a very different story from 'The Lady's Walk', in that part of it, at least, is narrated from the ghost's perspective, this too focuses on the notion of a woman's responsibility for the welfare of her family, and a widowed woman at that, who ignores her lawyer's advice. Lady Mary, like the Lady of the walk, returns from the dead to do what she can to put things right, and like Oliphant herself in her *Autobiography*, she reviews her life to ascertain whether she has made the best of it. Full of remorse, Lady Mary, whose declining years had been so full of gentle, harmless routines, now finds herself an ignored witness to household consultations about the future.

Unlike the stories previously discussed, this is one where there is no mystery about the origins or identity of the ghost. The reader knows throughout who the ghost is and why she has returned. Oliphant therefore sacrifices the eeriness of 'The Open Door' and 'The Lady's Walk' for emphasis on the ghost's sense of guilt and shame for her irresponsibility, and the mentoring process she undergoes at the hands of a male spirit (her former husband?) who awakens her conscience. Like so many of Oliphant's other ghost stories, it features the image of the open (or closed) door as emblematic of the portal between the living and the dead: in this case frustratingly epitomised in the notion of the secret drawer, described as 'the little door that opened into the secret place' (Oliphant 2000: 244), which she cannot open to reveal the will. There is also a door between Lady Mary's bedroom and little Mary's, and the godchild 'dreamed a dozen times over that she heard Lady Mary's soft call through the open door' (253). Not that the door is kept open, as it has now been 'shut closely and locked' (253) by the new family, as if to close off all notion of connection between the previous inhabitants and the present. For little Mary it is as if she has also been locked out of both past and future, her sense of belonging somewhere and being part of a family. The second half of this story thus shifts from focusing on her godmother's attempts to release the will, to what will become of the homeless god-daughter. What most frustrates her and gives the story an unexpected twist is that a complete stranger becomes the ghost-seer.

All seems positive when Lady Mary is given some kind of divine authorised pass to return to earth: 'The door opened,' the narrator announces, 'and she felt herself free to come out' (228). But this is only the first of several portals she must pass through, while also suffering the realisation that when she enters a room in her old house, no one sees her, except a baby, a dog and eventually Connie, the sensitive youngest daughter of Mrs Turner, the wealthy woman whose family are renting the house. 'It is hard to be left out in the cold when others go into their cheerful houses,' the narrator observes, 'but to be thus left outside of life, to speak and not be heard, to stand, unseen, astounded, unable to secure any attention!' (240). Both Marys are thus marginalised, neither of them finding a place in the onward life of the house.

Being merely rich, the Turners are assumed to be vulgar, and indeed once Connie begins to see Lady Mary's ghost, the ghost-seeing becomes coarsened by gossip. Oliphant draws attention to this by referring to 'various vulgar effects', adding, 'A housemaid became hysterical, and announced too that she had seen the lady' (265). Given that Oliphant's ghosts are mostly seen by sensitive young people who live in isolated country houses, or who are at least middle class, the socially downward slide of Lady Mary's household marks her further degradation. Employing another disturbing suggestion, which seems to anticipate the advent of the vampire, little Mary wastes away while Connie stabilises and recovers. As the doctor puts it, '"That little Connie Turner is as well as possible; she has handed over her nerves to Mary Vivian"' (267). It is as if the vulgarly rich family who have taken over the house have somehow sucked out the vitality of their more refined predecessors, and even assumed communication with Lady Mary, who remains stubbornly invisible to her god-daughter, although she somehow senses the ghost's presence. Oliphant calls it 'this visionary double life' (269): in other words, Mary senses her godmother is close to hand although she never sees her as the servants and Connie claim to have done. Mary's frustration with Connie's ignorant speculation as to what her godmother must have left causes her suddenly to seize the child 'with a pressure that hurt Connie', imploring her not to say anything (269–70). At this high pitch of emotion, Mary starts to sound like the governess in Henry James's as yet unpublished *The Turn of the Screw* (1898), and Connie like one of the children, as she shouts '"There, there! Don't you see her?"' (270). Mary's cry to God in this scene, imploring him to let her godmother know that she has never blamed her (271), breaks a spell, in that Lady Mary realises she has been forgiven, and the vicar's sons find the will. As an ending, this is abrupt and almost farcical. It makes a nonsense of all the anguish suffered by both Marys, and shows that, in the end, disengaged bystanders have casually uncovered the mystery. When Old Lady Mary returns home to her new friends in the afterlife and asks the momentous question 'What is death?' it seems typical of Oliphant's habit of retreating from metaphysical clarification, that 'no one made any reply' (273).

A Beleaguered City (1879–80)

Oliphant's earliest contribution to the genre, *A Beleaguered City*, is also her longest, and in some ways her least typical.[2] I have chosen to discuss it last as its engagement with the 'unseen' is on an operatic scale, affecting the inhabitants of an entire town, and because this is a shared experience, the existence of ghosts seems to be authenticated. Potentially any member of the crowd can become a seer, though certain individuals emerge as being more susceptible than others to connections with the unseen. Families are separated for much of the story, which largely focuses on the men, tracing their mass expulsion from their homes by an invisible crowd of the dead, a force-field of hostile energy shrouded in darkness, whose presence is heralded by signs and wonders, bells and trumpets, and the opening and closing of gates and portals, like the coming of Judgement Day. At the most terrifying moment of communication, the illuminated word 'Sommation' (summons) appears on the great door of the cathedral, apparently a message from the dead ordering the people to leave the town, for 'us who know the true signification of life' (Oliphant 2000: 21).

The story is set in the French town of Semur (which Oliphant visited in 1871) and narrated by the self-important mayor, Martin Dupin, assisted by an expanding group of eyewitnesses who include his wife and mother. Modern photographs of the town show that the Cathedral of Nôtre Dame does indeed loom over the landscape, a presence reflected in the tale's preoccupation with the secularisation of modern sceptics like Dupin, contrasted with a spectrum of believers, from the parish priest to the visionary Paul Lecamus, who dies in a state of religious ecstasy after a momentary spiritual connection with his dead wife. The brief scene that follows (narrated by Dupin's wife, a believer) is like a mass rising of the male townsmen as if called to account by the resurrection: 'With a start and universal movement the sleeping men got up from where they lay – not one but every one, coming out of the little hollows and from under the trees as if from graves' (Oliphant 2000:79). As a communal experience, believed to be triggered by a decision to reduce the number of masses said at the Hospital of St Jean tended by Catholic sisters, it plunges the whole town into turmoil, but Oliphant's focus on the men's collective terror and consternation, prompting them to re-evaluate their instinctive scepticism, reads like an indictment of their spiritual emptiness and cavalier cynicism.

Underlying the whole experience is the frustration of not knowing who is trying to communicate with the living and what they want. The group exchange operates at cross-purposes: beyond the sound and fury of the darkness and clanging gates, neither side can reach out to the other, except via momentary visions (like Lecamus's) or symbolic gestures, such as the olive branch laid on the portrait of the Dupins' dead daughter, Marie. Yet the demands are insistent and overwhelming. A whole city is being held to account for what appears to be the snubbing of a religious sisterhood. Then when the darkness lifts after three days and everyone returns home, the townspeople rapidly recover from their ordeal. Indeed the fuss about the neglected masses seems to the mayor himself (as it may to the reader) remarkably trivial as a reason for triggering a bespoke Judgement Day for the inhabitants of Semur: 'And now they would insult the Great God Himself by believing that all He cared for was a little mass in a convent chapel' (Oliphant 2000:102). The whole episode is further downgraded by the alleged revelations of Mère Julie, a market woman who claims to have seen angels, and a hospital patient, Pierre Plastron, who insists 'St Jean himself had interfered on behalf of the Sisters' (103). Cynicism returns, at least in Martin Dupin, notwithstanding his collection of eyewitness accounts and dutiful attendance at the cathedral's Te Deum.

Ultimately it remains a conundrum for the reader too. As the lengthiest of Oliphant's ghost stories (except *The Wizard's Son*) and the one containing the most eyewitnesses to a collective supernatural event for which there seems to be no other plausible explanation, *A Beleaguered City* is also her most frustrating. Its principal narrator is a self-satisfied sceptic, and its women mostly saintly believers. Gullibility and cynicism seem to cancel each other out in what reads less as the exposure of an irreligious community than as the instigation of a debate about the credibility of the supernatural. With this we return to the fundamental question, probed not just in Oliphant's ghost stories, but also in those of her contemporaries. Does the supernatural actually exist, and if so, how can it be explained?

Conclusion

At its most plangent, Oliphant's quest in her supernatural stories is perhaps best summarised by the words of Paul Lecamus, the visionary of *A Beleaguered City*, when he asks: '"How can one go away who loves you, and never return nor speak, nor send any message – that is the miracle"' (Oliphant 2000: 52). For him this silent absence is more of a 'miracle' than the heavens opening and the gates of Paradise rolling back. The fact that everyone in Semur is punished and feels the presence of an invisible force seems to reinforce the message that what they experienced was real: the dead can return to communicate with the living. For Oliphant indeed her ghost stories are essentially about the yearning of both sides to remain in touch. In most of her stories, only one person communicates directly with the unseen, although the ghostly presence is generally in or around an inhabited house, implying that something is wrong with the family relationships of the living or their history. Most of Oliphant's ghosts are trying to right a wrong, or draw attention to an injustice or moral failing. They are rarely evil or vindictive, but equally their messages are generally unclear. They speak little, if at all, and they rarely achieve anything momentous. Even the great drama of *A Beleaguered City* quickly subsides as the inhabitants return to their old ways. There is a futility of effort on both sides (the seers and the ghosts), perhaps confirming what Oliphant explores in her 'Carlingford' novels of small-town life: that people become agitated for a while about a matter of urgency which then subsides. In this respect, both men and women, whether ghosts or seers, like the people of Semur, return to their mundane lives, briefly disturbed, occasionally improved, but ultimately unsure of what they have just experienced.

Notes

1. The three children of Oliphant's who survived childhood were Margaret (Maggie) (1853–64), Cyril (1856–90) and Francis Romano, known as Cecco (1859–94). Her husband was Francis Wilson Oliphant (1818–59).
2. 'A Beleaguered City' was first published in *The New Quarterly Review* IX (January 1879), pp. 73–149. It was republished in book form by Macmillan in 1880.

Works Cited

Edmundson, Melissa. 'Women Writers and Ghost Stories', in Scott Brewster and Luke Thurston (eds), *The Routledge Handbook to the Ghost Story*. New York and London: Routledge, 2018, pp. 69–77.

Oliphant, Margaret. 'A Beleaguered City', in *A Beleaguered City and Other tales of the Unseen*, edited by Jenni Calder. Edinburgh: Canongate Classics, 2000, pp. 1–105.

———. 'A Little Pilgrim in the Unseen'. *Macmillan's Magazine*, May 1882, pp. 1–9 (reprinted by London: Macmillan and Co., 1883).

———. *The Autobiography of Margaret Oliphant* (1899), edited by Elisabeth Jay. Peterborough, ON and Ormskirk: Broadview Press, 2002.

———. 'Earthbound'. *Fraser's Magazine*, January 1880, in *A Beleaguered City*, edited by Jenni Calder. Edinburgh: Canongate Classics, 2000, pp. 137–70.

———. 'Old Lady Mary'. *Blackwood's Edinburgh Magazine*, January 1884, in *A Beleaguered City*, edited by Jenni Calder. Edinburgh: Canongate Classics, 2000, pp. 211–73.

———. 'The Lady's Walk'. *Longman's Magazine*, December–January 1882–3, pp. 229–52; 341–64.

———. *The Lady's Walk* by Mrs. Oliphant. London: Methuen & Co., 1897.

———. 'The Library Window'. *Blackwood's Edinburgh Magazine*, January 1896, in *A Beleaguered City*, edited by Jenni Calder. Edinburgh: Canongate Classics, 2000, pp. 363–402.

———. 'The Open Door' (1882), in *A Beleaguered City* (2000), edited by Jenni Calder. Edinburgh: Canongate Classics, 2000, pp. 171–210.

———. 'The Portrait'. *Blackwood's Edinburgh Magazine*, January 1884, in *A Beleaguered City*, edited by Jenni Calder. Edinburgh: Canongate Classics, 2000, pp. 275–312.

Smajić, Srdjan. *Ghost-Seers, Detectives and Spiritualists: Theories of Vision in Victorian Literature and Science*. Cambridge: Cambridge University Press, 2010.

Walker, Leila. 'Ghosts in the Home: Margaret Oliphant's Uncanny Response to Feminist Success', in Tamara S. Wagner (ed.), *Rereading Nineteenth-Century Women Writers*. Amherst and New York: Cambria Press, 2009, pp. 177–95.

Chapter 16

Charlotte Riddell
Helena Ifill

When Charlotte Riddell died in 1906, obituaries at the time recognised her as a 'writer of considerable reputation' ('Obituary' 1906: 446) whose 'best-known novels' concerned 'city and commercial life', and whose 'short stories were far less successful than her novels' ('Obituary. Mrs J. H. Riddell' 1906: 5). Yet, while some recent critical attention has been paid to Riddell's City novels (Colella 2016; Henry 2018), it is her shorter works, and especially her supernatural fiction, which has brought her back to the awareness of academic and general readers, and seen her recognised as the 'Irish [...] queen' of 'the nineteenth-century ghost story' (Barrett 2017: 25).[1] Riddell's novels are characterised by depictions of urban life, financial speculation and insecurity, and the fortunes of businessmen and office workers; her most popular novel during her lifetime, *George Geith of Fen Court* (1864), has an accountant as its hero. Similar interests are apparent in Riddell's ghost stories, which makes her writing distinctive, even as she utilises settings, plots and tropes that are common features of the genre. Two of her most famous stories, for example, *The Uninhabited House* (1875) and 'The Open Door' (1882), are narrated by clerks and begin with extended descriptions of office life. The first part of this chapter discusses the recurrent and distinguishing features of Riddell's supernatural fiction, and particularly her facility with the haunted house narrative.

Like many Victorian women writers, Riddell uses the haunted house narrative to explore anxieties about domesticity and marriage, but she often does so from a male perspective; all but one of her first-person ghost story narrators are male, the exception being Peg Vernam in *The Haunted River* (1877). Critics have convincingly shown how even though Riddell's stories 'ostensibly revolv[e] around male characters', they 'express concern with women's particular vulnerability in an economic climate dominated by and thus geared toward men' (Bissell 2014: 76). Others have suggested that Riddell's male protagonists, who are often financially struggling, are placed 'in conventional positions of femininity' (Smith 2010: 93, n. 8), or that their situation in a haunted house means that 'the men are transformed by, quite as much as they are transforming of, this feminised space' (Margree 2014: 70). Riddell's stories certainly show concern for the position of women and their reliance on men in Victorian society, and demonstrate men experiencing vulnerability and assuming 'conventionally feminine characteristics, such as imagination, empathy, and a desire to nurture' (Margree 2014: 74). Riddell's stories are also, however, reflections upon masculinity and the expectations placed upon men in Victorian society. Considering how and why such a prolific female writer as Riddell repeatedly explores the house and home from a male perspective can, as the final part of the chapter shows, broaden our notions of how women engage with and use the haunted house narrative.

There are certainly recurrent themes and features in Riddell's ghost stories, including an interest in money and middle-class life and a focus on the experiences of young men. Nevertheless, an overview of Riddell's supernatural oeuvre reveals plenty of variety in terms of content, narrative and setting. Central characters include a cab driver, a female professional artist, a Scottish minister and a general practitioner; ghosts include a neglected child, an abused wife, a money lender and several entities that are not strictly ghosts, including a banshee and the devil. In general, the manifestation of a spirit, if not actively benign, leads to the protagonist's moral and financial enhancement, but not always. In 'A Terrible Vengeance' (1889), for example, a man is trampled to death by the wet footprints of the woman he murdered, and in 'Sandy the Tinker' (1880) a Scottish minister encounters 'the Evil One' and is manipulated into causing the death of a member of his congregation. In 'Old Mrs Jones' (1882), the eponymous ghost scares a woman into premature labour, and burns down the house it haunts, while in 'The Last Squire of Ennismore' (1888), the dissolute squire walks willingly into sea with someone who leaves 'the print of a cloven foot' behind (Riddell 2008: 73). Riddell also makes use of psychic phenomena in stories such as 'Forewarned, Forearmed' (1874), in which a recurrent dream proves to be precognitive and helps the protagonist to prevent a murder, and 'Why Dr Cray Left Southam' (1889), in which the doctor's suspicions about a poisoner are confirmed by a disembodied voice urging him to '*Look at his eyes!*' (Riddell 2008: 220). Riddell sets supernatural events in the typical suburban townhouse and country ancestral home, but also, to offer just a few examples, in a boarding house, a mill house, on a farm, at a wedding, and on a stretch of road which is unremarkable except for 'a figure dressed in black [which] would dart out on any passer-by, and keep beside him for a mile or more, no matter how fast he ran' (Riddell 1878: 62). Although, or perhaps because, she is the 'novelist of the City', Riddell's stories also include several instances of unnerving or sublime natural environments such as the 'bogs' in 'Diarmid Chittock's Story' (1899) which could 'engulf a whole army' (2008: 256), and the disused canal in *The Disappearance of Mr Jeremiah Redworth* (1878), which has become overgrown to the extent that a body could be hidden 'in some sedge-covered bay, half weed, half slime, beside [a] weird sheet of water bordered by a vegetation which is almost tropical in its rank luxuriance' (Riddell 1878: 56). These images of water and vegetation consuming the human may seem particularly disturbing to a city-dweller.[2]

Many of Riddell's stories are set in southern England (often London, but also real and fictional commuting towns and counties such as 'Meadowshire' in 'The Open Door'). However, the Carrickfergus-born Riddell unsurprisingly has several stories which are set in Ireland (including 'Diarmid Chittock's Story' and 'The Last Squire of Ennismore', mentioned above), feature Irish protagonists or draw on Celtic folklore.[3] In 'Hertford O'Donnell's Warning' (1867), for example, the eponymous protagonist, is a 'young Irishman' (Riddell 2008: 129) working as a surgeon in London, who hears 'a low, sobbing, wailing cry' (136). Although disconcerted, O'Donnell recognises this as his family's banshee, to which he responds with grim humour: 'It's a mighty queer thing to think of, being favoured with a visit from a banshee in Gerrard Street; and as the lady has travelled so far, I only wish I knew whether there is any sort of refreshment she would like to take after her long journey.' (137). This may be Riddell's affection for her heritage, but it also reveals her assumption that descriptions of Ireland and its people will fascinate her majority-English readership. O'Donnell, for example, is 'Irish' in a way that 'is objectionable to the orthodox and respectable and representative English mind' (131), but has 'a pleasant brogue', and rode 'like a Centaur over the loose stone walls in Connemara' before moving to London (133).

These different characters, settings and scenarios mean that Riddell's stories have an impressive variety and range. However, she most often wrote in the subgenre of the haunted house narrative, and her skill as a ghost story writer lies partly in her ability to move within relatively restrictive generic conventions without becoming monotonously repetitive. Her haunted house stories include 'A Strange Christmas Game' (1867), 'The Open Door', 'The Old House on Vauxhall Walk', 'Walnut-Tree House' (all 1882), as well as the novellas *The Uninhabited House* and *Fairy Water* (1873). 'Nut Bush Farm' (1882) and *The Haunted*

River could be better termed 'haunted grounds' narratives, as the ghost mostly appears on land around the house, but it still prevents the protagonist from settling in the building they intended to make home. In these stories a first-person narrator tells the story of a scary experience that they can now relate from the relative comfort of temporal distance, or a third-person omniscient narrator describes the experience of the protagonist. The ghost usually reveals the circumstances or location of its death to someone who has unwittingly moved into its former residence or knowingly gone there to uncover the truth about mysterious reports. While this structure is quite straightforward, Riddell frequently plays with narrative reliability and perspectives. In 'A Terrible Vengeance', for example, the third-person omniscient narrator describes two gentlemen observing an unhappy lower-class couple passing a country inn. It is only later revealed that one of the men, Mr Murray, has been 'keeping company' (Riddell 2008: 319) with the woman in the couple, Lucy, and, it is heavily implied, drowned her shortly after this scene. Much of the narrative is focalised through Murray's manservant, and Murray dies before he can confess to the magistrate whom he asks to see, meaning that the reader never fully knows the circumstances of Lucy's death. Despite the many uncertainties in the story, one thing the reader can be comparatively sure of is that it is Lucy's spirit enacting the 'terrible vengeance' of the title, as Murray is followed everywhere by small wet footprints from the day after he sees Lucy to the day of his death.[4]

This (relative) certainty about the existence of the ghost is a common feature in Riddell's stories, which is important when considering how she is situated within the developing literary tradition of the ghost story. In her exploration of Victorian and Modernist haunted house narratives by women writers, Emma Liggins explains that:

> As the ghost story began to reflect new understandings of psychology, trauma and repression, women writers of the ghost story increasingly made use of the unexplained supernatural to address their fears about modernity. [...] Unlike the multidimensional Gothic narratives of Radcliffe and her imitators, the short story [...] lends itself to the unexplained supernatural, which increasingly underpins representations of the haunted house and women's perceptions of its unhomeliness. (2020: 8–10)

Riddell's ghost stories are examples of the unexplained supernatural, in that apparently supernatural events do not turn out to have natural causes, unlike the kind of Gothic fiction popularised by Ann Radcliffe. They do not, however, have the sense of open-endedness and uncertainty that often accompanies stories of the unexplained supernatural, exemplified in texts such as Mary Elizabeth Braddon's 'The Shadow in the Corner' (1879) in which it remains unclear whether a young woman's death is due to supernatural influence or suicide. In Riddell's ghost stories the reasons behind supernatural events *are* explained, in the sense that there really is a ghost with a motive for its appearance. This may mean that Riddell's fiction lacks one type of psychological complexity that Liggins identifies in Victorian women's ghost stories, but her ghosts are tangible and influential in ways that have palpable (often financial) repercussions. The ghosts and their motivations, as well as the protagonists' connections to the haunted houses, represent responses to modernity which are quite distinct from the kind of domestically focused women's ghost stories that Liggins discusses, making them interesting in their own right, as shown below, rather than as a step on the way to modernist sophistication.

As well the fact that the ghost's existence is rarely questionable in a Riddell narrative, plenty of room is given to uncovering the ghost's motivation and what happened to it that led it to haunt a certain place. This aligns Riddell's supernatural fiction with the popular Victorian genre of sensation fiction and the emerging genre of detective fiction.[5] Like sensation and detective novels, several of Riddell's stories (such as *Fairy Water* and 'The Open Door') feature a missing will or are preoccupied with inheritance. They also include murder (both old Lord Ludlow in 'The Open Door' and Miss Tynan in 'The Old House in Vauxhall Walk' are stabbed), suspicious death (Mr Elmsdale in *The Uninhabited House* is a presumed suicide until the appearance of his ghost suggests otherwise) and sudden disappearances, such as the eponymous character in *The Disappearance of Mr Jeremiah Redworth*, Jeremy Lester in 'A Strange Christmas Game' who goes missing one Christmas morning, or Mr Hascot in 'Nut Bush Farm' who is presumed to have abandoned his family for a young woman. In three of Riddell's stories, 'The Open Door', *The Uninhabited House* and 'The Old House in Vauxhall Walk', a young man investigates the mystery of a haunted house, actively turning detective; in others ('Nut Bush Farm', 'A Strange Christmas Game') residents are driven to detection as their homes are rendered uninhabitable by hauntings. Often the protagonist must speak to local residents, family members, friends and enemies of the deceased, servants and tradespeople, in order to piece together the ghost's story. As with much detective fiction, there is a drive to uncover truth and restore order, and Riddell's ghosts play an important role in this as they indicate, by their very presence, that there is a mystery that needs solving, and often contribute to its resolution; this may be by replaying scenes from their lives, appearing near the scene of their death or unburied corpse, or indicating the hiding place of important documents.

Riddell produced four supernatural novellas as Routledge Christmas Annuals between 1873 and 1878: *Fairy Water*; *The Uninhabited House*; *The Haunted River*; *The Disappearance of Mr Jeremiah Redworth*. As Liggins notes, 'the 1840s to the 1940s encompasses the rise and subsequent popularity of' the short ghost story (2020: 10), as opposed to the Gothic novel, and, while several mid-Victorian writers did produce longer ghost stories (for example, Wilkie Collins's *The Haunted Hotel*, 1878, and Charles Dickens's *A Christmas Carol*, 1843), Riddell is unusual in publishing so many.[6] These novellas are all variations on the haunted house narrative, so not drastically different to her shorter fiction, but it is worth considering what Riddell did with the extra space she needed to fill as sole author of a Christmas special.[7]

Riddell spends more time creating a general atmosphere of unease (the extract about the disused canal in *The Disappearance of Mr Jeremiah Redworth*, above, is just a small part of an extended unsettling description of the land and waterways between the home of Mr Redworth and the place he was murdered), but she does not string out the scary and supernatural elements in her novellas. In fact, with the exception of *The Uninhabited House*, Riddell postpones the appearance of the ghost until quite late in the narratives. In *The Disappearance of Mr Jeremiah Redworth*, for example, the majority of the story focuses on the repercussions within Mr Redworth's family and local community after he leaves his house one morning, supposedly planning to walk to a neighbouring town, and does not return. The supernatural is introduced slowly, over a third of the way into the story, when one character comments that the nearby Taunton Hall has a reputation for being 'haunted' ever since a previous squire 'elected to be buried in his own garden' without consecration (Riddell 1878: 35). A haunting directly linked to Redworth's disappearance does not occur until sometime later, when his 'figure' is seen, looking 'as erect as ever, umbrella in hand' (73), in the grounds of Taunton Hall before vanishing. Not long after, a 'man' the driver recognises as Jeremiah Redworth is seen '*walking* and keeping up easily' with a galloping horse and cart as he passes the Hall (80, italics in original), where it turns out that Redworth was murdered. Similarly in *The Haunted River*, the ghost is not mentioned until chapter five, and not seen by the narrator until chapter ten (out of twenty); in *Fairy Water*, the haunting of Crow Hall is not mentioned until chapter four (of ten).

Rather than including more ghostly elements, Riddell introduces more sustained humour and social observation in her supernatural novellas. Melissa Edmundson has noted 'the success with which [Riddell] blended economic concerns with the haunted-house motif, making what otherwise would be dry, didactic economic commentary entertaining for mass audiences, who could learn and have a good read at the same time' (2010: 53). Riddell's supernatural stories (which tend to have happy endings) are in fact noticeably more humorous and light-hearted than her novels, which were often accused of having an atmosphere of 'extreme and untempered gloom' ('George Geith' 1865: 291), suggesting her recognition that ghost stories are intended to amuse and entertain as much as to teach moral lessons or scare readers. This is particularly true of the novellas. *Fairy Water*, for example, is narrated by 'H. Stafford Trevor, barrister-at-law' who, rather than practising his 'profession', 'dines out' by vocation (Riddell 2018: 20). This allows for dry remarks about the different social groups Stafford moves among, such as Bohemians who serve their meals 'on stone-china, with wit for *sauce piquante*' (29). The narrator of *The Uninhabited House* spends several pages poking fun at Miss Blake – an Irishwoman with poor dress sense, 'the most fearful' changeable accent, and no 'thought of paying the debts she owed to anyone, unless she was obliged to do so' (Riddell 2018: 179–80). While instances such as these could be seen as padding, Riddell uses them to convey a message to her readers, and they support the momentum of the plot. In *Fairy Water*, for example, the description of bohemian lifestyle carries with it a warning that, amidst the jollity at table, there is 'for an unbidden guest the skeleton – Debt' (Riddell 2018: 29). Moreover, the narrator's cross-class connections become important for the final stages of the plot which involves an item of the middle-class heroine's furniture being sent to a lady's house. In *The Uninhabited House*, we learn that Miss Blake is in her desperate position (which adds to her comically exacting and grasping behaviour) because when they were younger, she and her sister scorned the chance to marry 'a curate, a doctor, a constabulary officer, and the captain of a government schooner', and instead travelled to England to aim for 'rich husbands' above their station. Failing in that aim, and conned by their 'trustee', the sisters find themselves 'on the verge of beggary' with no skills by which to earn a living (Riddell 2022: 53–4); this warns against the pride, naivety and unpreparedness of the sisters, and leads to the younger sister's marriage to Mr Elmsdale, who will become the story's ghost.

Moral messages and warnings relating to money and financial conduct are central to almost all of Riddell's supernatural stories, particularly her haunted house narratives. Several critics have observed how money becomes associated with, and indeed helps to generate, a fearful atmosphere at least as much as the ghosts themselves. Margree, for example, argues that '[i]n Riddell's ghost stories, it is rarely the supernatural that is productive of Gothic effect, but instead in economic relationships a potential for monstrosity is seen to reside' (2014: 82). This is particularly true of 'The Old House in Vauxhall Walk' which features the ghost of a woman who becomes a miser, 'contaminated with the most despicable and insidious vice poor humanity knows' (Riddell 2008: 92). Bissell notes that Riddell's ghost stories 'feature a plethora of financial shocks, ruined subjects, and economically driven spirits' and argues that the 'terrifying menace of Victorian economics' is far scarier than the ghosts themselves (2014: 74). Ghosts are often murdered for money, or have morally questionable relationships to money during their lives. In 'The Old House in Vauxhall Walk', for example, the miser is murdered by thieves, and in *The Uninhabited House*, Mr Elmsdale the money lender is murdered by a business associate.

However, while Riddell's stories do show 'the diabolical tendency of money to turn friends into betrayers and lovers into destroyers' (Margree 2014: 82), money is also often used as an expression of emotional bonds, both positive and negative. In numerous stories fortunes and estates are shared or withheld through the writing of a will (which usually goes missing), indicating affection, respect and duty (or lack thereof) towards the living who are left behind. In 'The Open Door', for example, the ghost of old Lord Ladlow indicates – through the open door – the scene of his murder and the hidden will that restores his inheritance to his nephew, who 'loved the old man tenderly' (Riddell 2016: 49). Ladlow had previously disinherited the nephew in favour of his 'young wife' who, it becomes clear, has not been 'the source of happiness [Lord Ladlow] expected', has compromised 'his honour' in a way that is never revealed (49–50), and then murdered him. This indicates the changing affections of the old Lord, and hints at a story of marital discord which has 'destroyed his peace' (50). In *Fairy Water*, Captain Geoffrey Trevor is so concerned that 'someone might yet win' his wife Mary's 'affection when he [is] dead and forgotten' (Riddell 2018: 39) that he makes a will which completely disinherits her, and revokes her parental rights, if she marries again (49); part of the story revolves around the search for the replacement will he made revoking this expression of jealous possessiveness. While Riddell's ghost stories do warn of the damage that an attachment to money can cause, they also show how money becomes a means of exerting control and expressing the depth and tone of emotional attachments, often revealing a desperate need to control and retain possession of a loved one.

Bissell argues that 'if dead hands can exert their influence on the living through the instrument of legal wills, then Riddell's fiction suggests that post-death existence remains mired in this troubling equation of identity with material goods' (2014: 79). Troubling as this may be, it also shows Riddell's consciousness, and frank acknowledgement, of the emotional and psychological impact of the possession or loss of money; financial security is desirable and, precisely because it is so precarious, one of the most important gifts that a person can give. This is something that Riddell was acutely aware of. As a young woman she and her mother were left with 'but a small jointure' at her father's death, as their home 'passed into other hands' (Black 2011: 16), and they moved to England where Riddell pursued a writing career to support them.[8] Riddell's husband, Joseph Hadley Riddell, a civil engineer, was repeatedly unsuccessful in business and eventually died heavily in debt in 1880, meaning that Riddell continued to have to write to ensure financial security.[9] As Margree puts it, 'Riddell experienced both prosperity and pennilessness; she knew what it was to be vulnerable to a fiscally imprudent male relative, and she knew both the good that money could bring and the disaster that might ensue from its reckless pursuit' (2014: 69).

Money and morality are not just intertwined in negative ways in Riddell's ghost stories. While her numerous rich but corrupt characters confirm that 'ownership of wealth is not in itself a virtue' (Smith 2010: 72), Riddell offers material enhancement as a reward for the hard work, bravery and compassion shown by her heroes who discover the truth about the ghosts in their respective stories. In 'The Old House in Vauxhall Walk', Graham Coulton, who sees the miser's ghost, subsequently catches the thieves who murdered her, finds her hidden gold and is able to reconcile with the father who had turned him out at the start of the story. In *The Uninhabited House*, Henry Patterson the clerk ghost hunter discovers the murderer, earns the love of the dead man's wealthy daughter, is rewarded with 'a partnership in [an] established firm' (Riddell 2022: 175) and named his uncle's heir. Whelan sees this pattern in Riddell's stories as typical of the 'Victorian suburban ghost narrative', which 'provides a middle-class male hero the opportunity to order the space of a haunted house that has been disrupted by a specter, and, through a fantasy of excluding this specter, to reassert (the readers') middle-class values' (2002: 134). The rewarding of her heroes is a further demonstration of Riddell's keen awareness of the security and resultant contentment that a healthy financial position can provide, and, more specifically, of the pressures placed on young men, who cannot take their place in society as breadwinners and homemakers until they are able to offer these qualities to women in their care.

Several of Riddell's stories begin with young or financially unstable men in positions where they are unable to exert the authority and control that Victorian society associated with masculinity, or the independence required to achieve these qualities. For example, Phil Edlyd in 'The Open Door' is fired by his frustrated employer when he asks for payment to uncover the mystery of the door, and Graham in 'The Old House on Vauxhall Walk' is '[h]ouseless – homeless – hopeless' after arguing with his father (Riddell 2009: 99). The ghost, and the mystery surrounding it, offers a chance for the young man to develop bravery and show his worth in an alternative manner from the means that have so far proved unproductive to him. For example, Graham refers to ghost hunting and searching for the 'missing treasure' as 'work' (111) that is a preferable alternative to joining the army, declaring 'one may as well be picked off by a ghost as a bullet' (110). However, Riddell's young male protagonists often end up facing a real, flesh-and-blood villain as well as experiencing a ghostly encounter; while the miser's ghost is harmless (and in fact gives him the clue of where to find the treasure), Graham is shot in the shoulder by home invaders. The encounter with the ghost and her murderers leaves Graham richer and wiser. He shows his development by returning to make peace with his father, announcing that he has made his 'fortune' and that he 'mean[s] to strive and make a better thing of my life than I should ever have done had I not gone to the Old House in Vauxhall Walk' (115). Similarly, Phil, with the help of the ghost, confronts a living foe and finds the treasure, also getting shot in the shoulder.[10] Consequently, Phil can show his sweetheart Patty's father that he is 'good for something' (Riddell 2009: 50) and move away from the city to 'manage' a farm 'and make both ends meet comfortably' (58).

Other stories offer variations on this plotline, with men who begin somehow lacking in their lives, and end with the means to achieve greater wisdom, financial security or a suitable marriage, often all of these. In 'Walnut-Tree House', for example, the protagonist Mr Stainton is rich after working 'goldfields' (Riddell 2009: 7) abroad and inheriting the titular property, but is 'utterly alone' in the world until his encounter with a child ghost leads him to meet and fall in love with its now grown sister (9). Along the way he employs an old servant that the previous owner left to the workhouse and vows, much like Graham Coulton, 'I will not so misuse the wealth which has been given me' (17).

These examples show that Riddell's stories are concerned with domesticity and marriage, but in quite a different way from the stories of many other women ghost story writers. For the majority of Riddell's protagonists, the haunted house is not a home in which their domestic happiness is disrupted, but a house which they do not own, or of which their ownership is questionable in some way (not simply because there is a ghost in residence). In 'The Open Door', 'The Old House in

Vauxhall Walk' and *The Uninhabited House*, the protagonist stays in a house with permission of the owner to uncover the truth about the hauntings. Similarly Mr Stainton in 'Walnut Tree House' has returned from overseas and moves into the house he has inherited at short notice, camping out in the former library for the first night (8). In 'Nut Bush Farm', Jack, the married narrator, has received compensation after an 'accident in [his] employers' service', which has resulted in medical advice that he must 'give up office work and leave London altogether' (Riddell 2009: 60). He rents a farm in the countryside, which he believes will also improve the health of his 'nervous, impressionable' wife and 'delicate weakling of a child' (60) but is unable to bring his family to the farm he has rented due to its haunting by the ghost of the previous tenant. The fact that he is renting (the likely condition of the majority of Riddell's readers) means that the farm and land are not really his, and any sense of propriety is undermined by both the visitations of the former tenant (as Margree has discussed, 2014: 75–6), and the fact that his landowner, Miss Gostock, frequently tells him how to farm the land, walks on the property and refuses to share knowledge relevant to his tenancy.

As part of her argument that by encountering ghosts Riddell's male protagonists 'cultivate conventionally feminine qualities', Margree demonstrates that the narrator becomes more '*imaginative*' and '*impressionable*' during the course of the story (2014: 76, italics in original). However, the opening of 'Nut Bush Farm' shows that Jack already possesses what could be seen as feminine qualities, and that it is not only his wife that has sensitive nerves. When visiting the countryside, the narrator describes how, after his 'long illness', the 'sweet, pure air seemed to have braced up my nerves and given me fresh energy' (Riddell 2009: 61–2), and when he first sees the farm, he perceives it 'like a fairy scene' (64), suggesting he is already quite imaginative. There are also indications early on that he feels pressure to conform to standards of masculinity: his desire that his 'boy' should 'get more like other lads' is telling (64), as is his claim that '[i]t is unnecessary to say I did not believe in ghosts or anything of that kind' (60), which evasively relies on assumptions about rational masculinity, rather than directly saying that he did not believe. We also learn that Jack regrets his youthful decision to 'come up to London to see the lions and seek my fortune', and cherishes 'the meadows and the cornfields, and the cattle, and the orchards, and the woods and the streams, amongst which my happy boyhood had been spent' (61). This is a man who has not flourished under the pressures of the City, and seeks somewhere he can establish a link with his 'happy boyhood', while providing the home, stability and income required by his family. As much as cultivating feminine traits, Jack can be seen to gain an opportunity to achieve positive masculine traits. While he does fall 'into a womanly faint' when he finally sees the ghost of Mr Hascot (Margree 2014: 76), this is followed by his firm decision that 'no man should have implored my help with such passionate earnestness without avail, and if indeed one had appeared to me from the dead I would right him if I could' (Riddell 2009: 85).[11] He goes on to save Hascot's wife from the workhouse and uncover the murderer; his encounter with the ghost prompts him to take control in a way that he has felt unable to before. Riddell's ghost stories are frequently concerned, therefore, with what makes a good man, and with the development of men who will eventually take their place as heads of families, protectors of women and contributors to the social good.

Despite her predominant concern with male characters, Riddell's stories contain some notable female characters whose social position means they take on masculine roles. One is Miss Gostock, mentioned above, who owns Nut Bush Farm, wears 'a man's broad-brimmed straw hat, a man's coat, and a woman's skirt' (Riddell 2009: 65), wears 'her hair short like a man' (66), and takes shots of brandy in the morning. We are given the impression that 'there was a time' when she did not behave in such a way, but that unspecified 'trouble' (69) has led to her independent state and disregard of gender expectations. For all of her brash unconventionality the narrator, though sometimes amused by her, also views her with respect and some affection, and he hates himself 'for the suspicion' (90) that she might be the murderer (which she is not). Trouble also leads Peg Vernam, the *The Haunted River*'s narrator, to act in the role of head of the household when she and her younger sister are orphaned. Concerned to see her sister happily married, Peg does not consider conventional domestic happiness for herself (having been unlucky in love in her youth), takes over their business and financial cares and pursues a financially profitable career as an artist, which she achieves. Another unconventional woman is Helena Elmsdale in *The Uninhabited House*, who proposes to the narrator rather than waiting for him to overcome his scruples about her superior position as an heiress. While Riddell's depictions of men striving to become good brothers,[12] husbands and fathers to the women who are reliant on them is undoubtedly influenced by Victorian gender conventions, her unconventional female characters show that, when men fail in this role, women are capable of supporting themselves, even if it means diverging from the norm.[13]

Riddell's ghost stories work firmly within the literary conventions of the genre, and are resolutely Victorian in their valorisation of heteronormative, patriarchal relationships. Yet Riddell's engagement with contemporary gender expectations and relations, and insistence on exploring the challenges that young men face in pursuing the ideal of securing a house that they can make a home, not to mention her occasional assertion that sometimes women need to take on this role, makes her stories distinct. Victorian women's ghost stories are often seen, in contrast to men's, to reflect more upon the vulnerable position of women within the home, 'transform[ing] domestic space into a place of terror that threatens marital relations and women's lives and sanity' (Liggins 2020: 2). In Riddell's haunted houses, it is most often single men's lives, sanity and marital prospects (rather than current relations) that are threatened. Her sustained experimentation with masculine personas and male narrative perspectives partly reflects Riddell's sense that she 'under[stood] men well' and had 'much in sympathy with them' ('The Ladies' Corner' 1890: 3). However, it also offers a way of exploring male insecurities and concerns – particularly those of young men who are contemplating existing or near-future positions as homemakers and breadwinners – and reveals a concern with how positive masculine traits could be cultivated, so that the women and children under their care could also enjoy domestic stability and happiness.

Notes

1. Recent publications edited and introduced by leading academics in the field include the Victorian Secrets edition of Riddell's 1882 collection *Weird Stories* (Liggins 2009), the British Library's *Haunted Houses*, which includes *The Uninhabited House* and *Fairy Water* (Andrew Smith 2018), and a Broadview edition of *The Uninhabited House* (Melissa Edmundson 2022). The most extensive collection available at the time of writing is Wordsworth Editions' *Night Shivers: The Ghost Stories of J. H. Riddell* (2008). Mrs J. H. Riddell is the name she most often published under during her career.
2. They also make Riddell's fiction an excellent, untapped source of eco-Gothic writing, something which there is unfortunately not space to discuss here. Emily Alder (2023) has begun this work, discussing 'Walnut-Tree House' with a focus on the suburban setting and issues such as fuel economy.
3. 'Conn Kilrea' (1899), features a young soldier, serving in England, from Moyle (part of County Antrim, where Riddell was born).
4. Sarah Bissell asserts that Riddell's 'mild' and 'mundane' ghosts are not particularly scary (2014: 73), but Riddell is capable of creating some chilling moments. Here, and in *The Disappearance of Mr Jeremiah Redworth*, Riddell uses the idea of a supernatural presence effortlessly following a living person to great effect (something revisited in cinema in *It Follows*, 2015).

5. Sensation fiction was the most popular genre of the 1860s. Its leading authors Mary Elizabeth Braddon and Wilkie Collins both wrote novels featuring amateur and professional detectives, and Collins's *The Moonstone* (1868) is often seen as the first detective novel. They also wrote numerous ghost stories. Andrew Smith has discussed the resonances between Riddell's and Collins's fiction (see Smith 2010: 71). Riddell's ghost stories also draw on other modes and genres. A realist attention to detail and the day-to-day lives of lower-middle-class subjects is apparent in works such as *The Uninhabited House*, and *The Haunted River* could even be read as a supernatural *künstlerroman* because Peg's encounter with a ghost and the atmospheric grounds it haunts form an important step on the way to her successful career as an artist. This pre-dates Riddell's semi-autobiographical *künstlerroman A Struggle for Fame* (1883).
6. Riddell's supernatural novellas have not, with the exception of *The Uninhabited House*, been recovered to the extent of her shorter ghost stories, perhaps because shorter works are easier to anthologise, or because the novellas do not fall so purely into the genre of the ghost story as the presence of the supernatural is less concentrated. Nevertheless, these four stories are worthy of more critical attention, and not just as expanded short stories.
7. *Fairy Water* is slightly more complicated than Riddell's shorter works, as it has two main plotlines (one with a missing will, one with a haunting) that ultimately interlink. *The Disappearance of Mr Jeremiah Redworth* is less stringently a haunted house narrative as the murdered man does not die in his own home or its grounds, unlike Riddell's other stories in the genre.
8. Her mother died in 1856 just as Riddell saw some literary success, a sad irony that Riddell drew on in her 1883 novel, *A Struggle for Fame*.
9. For more on Riddell's financial situation, see Henry (2018: 179–215).
10. While it is often assumed that the woman in the house is the lord's wife, Phil's description of her as 'not a lady' (Riddell 2016: 82), and the specification that 'dowager and her maid went abroad' (84), lead me to read it as the maid who infiltrates the house.
11. Graham Coulton similarly faints from fear before developing his resolve to confront the thieves (Riddell 2016: 156).
12. There is not space to discuss sibling relationships here, but men such as John Lester in 'A Strange Christmas Game' and Jack in 'Nut Bush Farm' are joined by their sisters in the ghostly adventure, and rely on their practicality and emotional support.
13. This is a recurrent theme in Riddell's novels. In *Mortomley's Estate* (1874), for example, the heroine saves her husband's business after his nervous breakdown following financial ruin.

Works Cited

Alder, Emily. 'Domestic EcoGothic: The Haunted Houses of Riddell, Nesbit, and Mulholland'. Paper presented at Gothic Women Conference, University of Dundee, 29–31 August 2023.

Anon. 'George Geith'. *Saturday Review*, vol. 19, no. 489, 1865, pp. 290–1.

———. 'The Ladies' Corner'. *Pall Mall Gazette*, 18 February 1890, p. 3.
———. 'Obituary'. *The Gentleman's Magazine*, vol. 301, no. 2110, 1906, pp. 441–7.
———. 'Obituary. Mrs J. H. Riddell'. *Aberdeen Journal*, 27 September 1906, p. 5.
Barrett, Mike. 'Charlotte Riddell's *Weird Stories*'. *The Green Book: Writings on Irish Gothic, Supernatural and Fantastic Literature*, vol. 9, 2017, pp. 24–32.
Bissell, Sarah. 'Spectral Economics and the Horror of Risk in Charlotte Riddell's Ghost Stories'. *Victorian Review*, vol. 40, no. 2, 2014, pp. 73–89.
Black, Helen C. *Notable Women Authors of the Day: Biographical Sketches*. Brighton: Victorian Secrets, 2011.
Colella, Silvana. *Charlotte Riddell's City Novels and Victorian Business: Narrating Capitalism*. New York: Taylor & Francis, 2016.
Edmundson, Melissa. 'The "Uncomfortable Houses" of Charlotte Riddell and Margaret Oliphant'. *Gothic Studies*, vol. 12, no. 1, 2010, pp. 51–67.
Henry, Nancy. *Women, Literature and Finance in Victorian Britain: Cultures of Investment*. Basingstoke: Palgrave Macmillan, 2018.
Liggins, Emma. *The Haunted House in Women's Ghost Stories: Gender, Space and Modernity 1850–1945*. Basingstoke: Palgrave Macmillan, 2020.
Margree, Victoria. '(Other)Worldly Goods: Gender, Money and Property in the Ghost Stories of Charlotte Riddell'. *Gothic Studies*, vol. 16, no. 2, 2014, pp. 66–85.
Riddell, Charlotte [Mrs J. H.]. *The Uninhabited House and The Haunted River*. London: George Routledge and Sons, n.d.
———. *The Disappearance of Mr. Jeremiah Redworth*. London: George Routledge and Sons, 1878.
———. *Night Shivers: The Ghost Stories of J. H. Riddell*, edited by David Stuart Davies. Ware: Wordsworth Editions, 2008.
———. *Weird Stories*, edited by Emma Liggins. Brighton: Victorian Secrets, 2009.
———. *Haunted Houses: Two Novels by Charlotte Riddell*, edited by Andrew Smith. London: British Library, 2018.
———. *The Uninhabited House*, edited by Melissa Edmundson. Peterborough, ON: Broadview Press, 2022.
Smith, Andrew. *The Ghost Story 1840–1920: A Cultural History*. Manchester: Manchester University Press, 2010.
Whelan, Lara Baker. 'Between Worlds: Class Identity and Suburban Ghost Stories, 1850 to 1880'. *Mosaic*, vol. 35, no. 1, 2002, pp. 133–48.

Chapter 17

Vernon Lee
Ardel Haefele-Thomas

What was haunting Vernon Lee at the end of the Victorian age? This is a question I have been considering, researching and writing about for well over a decade. And, each time I return to Lee, I catch glimpses of queer, trans and deliciously decadent possibilities that I had not yet considered.[1] In *Queer Others in Victorian Gothic: Transgressing Monstrosity* (2012), I argued that Lee's decadent queer Gothic was a coded defence of their own literary and artistic community of friends as well as a defence, on a much larger scale, of sexual and gender outlaws who came under intensifying legal and medical scrutiny in the latter half of the nineteenth century in England.[2] From the very public arrest of Fanny and Stella (Ernest Boulton and Frederick Park) in 1870 on the charges of cross-dressing in order to commit sodomy, through the passing of Section 11 to the Criminal Law Amendment Act in 1885 which made any public or private sexual acts between men illegal, the 1889 Cleveland Street scandal in which a male brothel catering to gentlemen was raided and numerous arrests were carried out, to the sodomy trials of 1895 sentencing Oscar Wilde to hard labour at Reading Gaol, Lee's friends and loved ones and the extended decadent aesthete art and literary communities were under attack in England. This is in part why Lee chose to live in Italy.

When considering Vernon Lee within the contexts of the Victorian ghost story, it is essential to read their ghost stories within the parameters of this specific *fin de siècle* cultural climate; however, it is equally important that we recognise that Lee's prolific writing career bridged the Victorian and the modern eras. Vernon Lee lived and wrote in both of these centuries, and Lee's ghost stories, while situated within the Victorian period, also hark back to prior centuries, thus adding another complex layer to time and place. 'Oke of Okehurst; Or, The Phantom Lover' (1886) takes place in the Kentish countryside in the 1880s, but time collapses into the same location in the seventeenth century. 'Amour

Dure' (1887) is set in Italy in 1885; however, the story focuses on the spectre of a sixteenth-century femme fatale. Lee's *fin de siècle* present was always imbued with the past. Jack Halberstam posits that:

> Queer uses of time and space develop ... in opposition to the institutions of family, heterosexuality, and reproduction. They also develop according to other logics of location, movement, and identification. If we try to think about queerness as an outcome of strange temporalities, imaginative life schedules, and eccentric economic practices, we detach queerness from sexual identity ... (Halberstam 2005: 1)

In their preface to the 1890 edition of *Hauntings: Fantastic Stories*, Lee signals what, a century later, Halberstam calls this 'outcome of strange temporalities' and 'imaginative life schedules' when they write:

> Indeed we live ourselves ... on the borderland of the Past, in houses looking down on troubadours' orchards and Greek folks' pillared courtyards; and a legion of ghosts, very vague and changeful, are perpetually to and fro, fetching and carrying for us between it and the Present. (Lee 2006: 39)

Lee's ghost stories also function against these very set normative Victorian institutions: family, heterosexuality and reproduction. What makes Vernon Lee's ghost stories so queerly decadent is their nostalgia for the past via the haunting of the present as they embrace the 'strange temporalities' and 'imaginative life schedules' in their rejection of Victorian heteronorms and cisnorms. Here, in the twenty-first century, what can Vernon Lee's Victorian ghost stories, imbricated with all of these time slippages, tell us about then as well as now?

In Jim Sharman's film adaptation of *The Rocky Horror Picture Show*, Dr Scott anxiously states, '"We've got to get out of this trap. Before this – decadence – saps our wills"' (Sharman 1975). In this twentieth-century queer Gothic cult classic, Dr Scott mocks the nineteenth-century German sexologist Richard von Krafft-Ebing whose medical models for normalcy in *Psychopathia Sexualis* (1877) were based on strict ideas of cisgender masculinity and heterosexual behaviour. Marriage and sex were for reproductive purposes and not for pleasure. Dr Scott panics in the face of the fabulously trans and pansexual mad scientist Frank-N-Furter, the newly created Adonis-like Rocky, and all of the 'freak' occupants of the isolated country house; the coterie exemplifies queer decadence. Yet, the doctor's alarm signifies precisely late Victorian fears of and disdain for decadence in art, literature and culture (and in all honesty, he underscores the socially conservatives' 1970s alarm stemming from the very public LGBTQI2+ liberation movements of that decade). For some conservative nineteenth-century thinkers, the fear was that decadence would bring about the downfall of proper society. It is crucial that we remember this when we consider Lee's decadent ghost stories, and the 'traps' that their writing (as well as the productions of other decadent writers and artists) was perceived to create. Decadent writers like Lee, Walter Pater and Wilde were seen as a menace to normative society, and they were under attack from thinkers around Europe whose works were readily imported into England. The tensions were running high amongst numerous intellectuals at the *fin de siècle*.

In 1857, the French scientist Bénédict Augustin Morel published his studies of degeneration, devolution and hereditary taint; and in 1876 the Italian criminal anthropologist Cesare Lombroso mapped Morel's ideas onto his theories of criminals and degeneration (Hurley 1990: 193–5). Krafft-Ebing admired Lombroso and utilised his criminal classification models on degeneracy to construct his own study of 'the pathological manifestations of the sexual life' in *Psychopathia Sexualis: With Especial Reference to Antipathic Sexual Instinct* published in German in 1877 (Krafft-Ebing 1877: 384). Quickly, degeneration and hereditary taint, criminality and any and all types of sexual and gender 'transgressions' became melded together. Vernon Lee and many of their friends and acquaintances, though, presented a growing late-Victorian resistance against the tyranny of heteronormative and cisnormative legal, medical and sexological classifications constructed to monitor and restrict cultural production.

John Addington Symonds, the English poet and literary critic who was also homosexual, had read Krafft-Ebing's tome on various 'psychopathic' sexualities, and wrote a heartfelt letter of rebuttal. Symonds posited that, perhaps, men who had sex with men (urnings) were not neurotic because of their homosexuality, but because society shunned them as sick, criminal or both, which, in turn, made them anxious (Haefele-Thomas 2019: 100). In response, Krafft-Ebing removed Symonds's name from the epistle and then included it in one of his later editions of *Psychopathia Sexualis*.

In 1892 Max Nordau, the conservative Hungarian doctor and social critic, wrote *Degeneration* which he dedicated to Lombroso:

> Now I have undertaken the work of investigating (as much as possible after your method), the tendencies of the fashions in art and literature; of proving that they have their source in the degeneracy of their authors, and that the enthusiasm of their admirers is for manifestations of more or less pronounced moral insanity, imbecility, and dementia. (Nordau 1895: viii)

Nordau specifically calls out authors like Oscar Wilde (this English translation was first available two months before Wilde's sodomy trials) and Algernon Charles Swinburne as not only decadent, but queer artists, and in so doing, equates decadence with queerness; this queer decadence leads to degeneration.³ And, with Nordau's caustic take on decadent artists and writers, Vernon Lee entered into the *fin de siècle* culture wars by directing 'Deterioration of Soul' as their rebuttal to Nordau:

> We need only search our own souls for the queer comradeship of outlawed thought; and are we not made more lenient towards the vapourings of neo-mystics, the egotism and depravity of decadents, the uncleanliness of realists, by knowing that Professor Nordau would like, if he could, to set up a Holy Office and an Index Expergatorious, and to commit to the flames the books, to the *maison de santé* the bodies, of all of the writers whom, in the name of an immutable and officially consecrated psyche-logical science, he has condemned as degenerate? (Lee 1896: 938)

'Deterioration of Soul' is not one of Lee's ghost stories; however, it sheds light on their writing about spectral encounters at the *fin de siècle*. Lee's tone in the essay fluctuates between outraged and satirical; and the decadent descriptions, language and situations found in the two ghost stories I will examine also flirt with satire *and* outrage over the unattainable. The 'queer comradeship of outlawed thought' comes to life in Lee's Gothic tales. The impossible and nostalgic longing for those long dead in 'Amour Dure' and 'Oke of Okehurst' is fraught with the danger of loving outside of the norms. In their Introduction to *Hauntings: Fantastic Stories*, Vernon Lee writes that these stories:

> are of no genuine ghosts in the scientific sense [...] My ghosts are what you call spurious ghosts (according to me the only genuine ones), of whom I can affirm only one thing, that they haunted certain brains, and have haunted, among others, my own and my friends. (Lee 2006: 39–40)

Lee writes the introduction specifically to friends Arthur Lemon and Flora Priestly; however, Lee's words can be taken to signal a larger sexual and gender outlaw community at the *fin de siècle*. Lee's ghost stories exemplify modes of a love that 'dare not speak its name', amplified since, in many ways, in the Victorian era, loving a ghost would have been safer than loving queerly in the flesh. Lee's queer and trans decadent ghost stories are haunted by the current events at the time of the writing, regardless of their being set in the past; they exemplify a *fin de siècle* queer anguish. And the emotional anguish felt by those haunted in these two stories is, I argue, indicative of queer anguish in Victorian Britain.

Magnificent Obsessions: 'Amour Dure' (1887)

What could be more luscious, deadly and decadent than falling in love with the ghost of a gorgeous 300-year-old scheming Italian murderess, Madonna Medea de Carpi of Urbania? This is precisely what brings about the demise of Vernon Lee's young Polish historian, Spiridion Trepka, in 'Amour Dure: Passages from the Diary of Spiridion Trepka'. His diary opens with a yearning: 'I had longed, these years and years, to be in Italy, to come face to face with the Past' (Lee 2006: 86). In 'Amour Dure' – much like 'A Wicked Voice' written three years later which is a decadent queer and trans spectral tale also set in Italy – Lee embodies an affected male narrator who has been dispatched to Italy from northern Europe to create something brilliant. Spiridion Trepka finds himself on a scholarship there in order to generate a second innovative tome on art criticism. Trepka is self-deprecating concerning his own art, much as Lee was. In Spiridion's first diary entry, it is notable that Lee signals the Polish historian as a stand-in, if you will, for themselves:

> Is this folly? Is it falsehood? Am I not myself a product of modern, northern civilization; is not my coming to Italy due to this very modern scientific vandalism, which has given me a travelling scholarship because I have written a book like all those other atrocious books of erudition and art-criticism? (86)

This could be about Lee who, in 1880 had impressed the London literary world with an immense study of art criticism of eighteenth-century Italy; there is a sense that Lee plays with the reader, inviting us to conflate Spiridion Trepka and Vernon Lee. And as the story of obsession and haunting unfolds, we need to consider not only Trepka's literal murderous ghost, Medea de Carpi, but also the various 'spurious ghosts' that haunt Lee as they write.

Briefly, the story follows Spiridion as he begins to explore Italian history because he wants to be transported to the decadent past. In his research and ramblings, he stumbles on the history of one Madonna Medea de Carpi of Urbania who seduced and enchanted every man she came into contact with, and, once married to each one, murdered them. While Trepka studies the story of this enchantress who lived three hundred years prior to his visit, he becomes obsessed with Medea and her story to the point he begins to hallucinate, forgets to eat, and lives each day to look upon the few images of her he has found. Ultimately, whether in obsessed fevered dreams or in some haunted reality, she rises from the grave to lure him, on Christmas Day, to his death; he is found stabbed and frozen next to a statue of one of Medea's husbands.

In 'Amour Dure', time and space are well bent. While on the surface Spiridion and Medea's imagined affair is heterosexual, there is certainly nothing normative about it – for normative would also include a reality and timeline of the reproductive and the familial in accordance with Halberstam's juxtaposition of queer time to normative time. *Fin de siècle* decadent aesthetics are certainly not interested in normative production – or reproduction, for that matter. A love story between a 300-year-old woman corpse/ghost and a living breathing man becomes queer indeed. Throughout the diary entries, Spiridion becomes more and more restless and impatient and belligerent with the living people surrounding him – most of them other men of letters – who work to dissuade him from his obsession. Their heteronormative peer pressure, though, does not force him back onto the proverbial straight and narrow, but rather pushes him further down a queer haunted path in search of Medea's ghostly embrace.

The aesthetics of 'Amour Dure' are incredibly queer whether Spiridion writes of one of his acquaintances or of the small statue and one portrait he has found of the late Medea. Spiridion notes the following in his diary dated 20 October:

> I have been seeing a good deal of late of the Vice-Prefect's son: an amiable young man with a love-sick face and languid interest in Urbanian history ... This young man ... wears extremely long and tight trousers, which almost preclude his bending his knees, a stick-up collar and an eyeglass, and a pair of fresh kid gloves stuck in the breast of his coat ... This person frequently entertains me with his amori, past, present, and future; he evidently *thinks me very odd* [emphasis mine] for having none to entertain him with in return; he points out to me the pretty (or ugly) servant girls and dressmakers as we walk in the street, sighs deeply or sings in falsetto behind every tolerably young-looking woman, and has finally taken me to the house of the lady of his heart, a great black-moustachioed countess, with a voice like a fish-crier ... (53–4)

Any allusion to Wilkie Collins's iconic gender outlaw Marian Halcombe in *The Woman in White* (1859–60) aside, Spiridion's description is laced with queer and trans innuendo and possibility. His description of the Vice-Prefect's son, with his tight pants, sticking-up collar, eyeglass and kid gloves, portrays a decadent aesthete. He sings falsetto and his true love combines a masculine moustache and a shrill (often read as feminine) voice; she defies norms concerning femininity and beauty. In Spiridion's October entry, we also find out that he has no women lovers from his past or his present, nor does he mention any future ambition about joining the heterosexual economy. This is, of course, prior to Spiridion meeting Medea in the dusty histories of Urbania, falling in love, and then succumbing to her ghost. More to the point, Spiridion

Trepka falls for whom he should not – someone society in the present deems must not be loved.

In his 22 December entry, Spiridion underscores this idea when he writes, 'you were right when you felt that you were not made for any earthly *amori*' (70). That same night, he steals away from his boarding house to visit the church where he has seen Medea's apparition. Spiridion sneaks into the church where he awaits a signal from the cloaked Medea and then follows her behind the altar and out into the night where she disappears.

His secretive encounter with Medea connotes numerous queer male encounters, specifically, in public spaces in urban Britain-like alleyways, underground meetings, pubs, parks and public toilets. For men seeking sexual encounters with men, there was always a danger of following the enticing shrouded figure: could it be another man also looking for romantic and/or sexual connection? Could it be a blackmailer waiting to entrap? Could it be a murderer? For Spiridion, it is the latter.

Two days before he perishes, Spiridion writes:

> Ambition, love of art, love of Italy, these things which have occupied my spirit, and have yet left me continually unsatisfied, these were none of them my real destiny. I have sought for life, thirsting for it as a man in the desert thirsts for a well; but the life of the senses of other youths, the life of the intellect of other men, have never slaked that thirst. Shall life for me mean the love of a dead woman? (71)

Thirty-five years following Lee's narration as Spiridion Trepka, Lee wrote this about Venice, the Floating City, in 'Out of Venice at Last' (1925): 'I was never quite free from regrets and from longings, or the delusive happiness which is streaked with them ... the things which Venice offers to the eye and the fancy conspire to melt and mar our soul ...' (Lee 2006: 340). Lee's longing and regrets mirror Spiridion's summation of Italy as a whole. They are both left 'thirsting as a man in the desert thirsts for a well'.

'I'm in love with your ghost'[4]: 'Oke of Okehurst; Or, The Phantom Lover'

Unlike Spiridion, the narrator of 'Oke of Okehurst; Or, The Phantom Lover' is not the person seduced by a ghost of someone long dead. Rather, he serves as an observer who relates the complete breakdown of a marriage through a strangely queer and trans Gothic spectral haunting. 'Oke' begins with Vernon Lee's note to Count Peter Boutourline, a poet and friend who resided in Russia. Lee penned the dedication in July 1886 from Kensington on a trip to England, and, thus, it is the one ghost story not written in nor set in Italy. The letter begins with Lee's reminding him of the story of Mrs Alice Oke of Okehurst, named after her relative, Alice Oke, who lived there two centuries prior to this story. After the enclosed memo, Lee begins the tale as though speaking directly to the reader; they directly become our young unnamed male narrator who is a portrait painter. The story commences with, 'That sketch up there with the boy's cap? Yes; that's the same woman [...] The most marvelous creature [...] an artificial and perverse sort of grace [...] There was something exquisite and uncanny' (Lee 2006: 105–6). This opening not only signals a gender disruption, but flags Alice Oke as 'different'. Our narrator, who had been living in London, has fallen out of favour with a wealthy woman he painted and has thus fallen on hard times. When he is in this vulnerable financial state, a Tory squire from Kent, Mr Oke of Okehurst, hires him to come to the country estate for a few months to paint himself and his mysterious wife. Although the family home is isolated and in a desolate country locale, the narrator is impressed with the beauty of the home: 'It was, without exception, the most perfect example of an old English manor-house that I had ever seen ...' (111). From here, the story follows the narrator's recollections of the months spent at Okehurst engaged in portraiture and being brought into the confidences of the squire and his 'peculiar' wife. As the tale unfolds, we learn that the current Alice Oke is obsessed with the 1626 story of the 'other' Okes of Okehurst, including a love triangle between them and the 'bad boy' poet Christopher Lovelock. The story of 1626 culminates in the murder of Lovelock, and the story of the late 1880s ends with the current Mr Oke attempting to murder Lovelock's ghost; but, instead, he shoots and kills the current Alice Oke and then turns the gun on himself, thus ending the Oke family line. In witnessing these events, the reader is left to rely on the narrator – Vernon Lee – to interpret this bizarre murder ghost story.

In describing his first impressions of Mrs Oke, the narrator, like Spiridion, recalls images like Collins's Marian Halcombe – a beautiful and graceful woman who is unexpectedly masculine and yet more intriguing because of it:

> She was very tall; and I suppose people would have called her thin. I don't know, for I never thought about her as a body – bones, flesh, that sort of thing; but merely as a wonderful series of line, and a wonderful strangeness of personality. Tall and slender, certainly, and with not one item of what makes up our notion of a well-built woman. She was as straight – I mean she had as little of what people call figure – as a bamboo; her shoulders were a trifle

high, and she had a decided stoop ... But this bamboo figure of hers had a suppleness and a stateliness ... there was in it something of the peacock and something also of the stag; but above all, it was her own. (114)

Our narrator employs masculine descriptors – stags and peacocks – to describe the gender-fluid and unconventional main character. The utilisation of 'stag' with 'peacock' is jarring – one strong and stately and the other beautiful and shrill, signalling further complexities within masculinities. It is important to note, also, that while the narrator discusses the 'unusual' qualities of Alice Oke, he also tells the reader that he is 'a rather unusual kind of man' (113). These portrayals of himself and Alice Oke in juxtaposition with Mr Oke who exudes a very staid, heteronormative and conservative (not just politically but emotionally) air are strikingly queer, and become more so as the ghost story unfolds.

As Alice Oke becomes more comfortable with our narrator, she allows him into the one room where nobody else dare to venture alone – her yellow drawing room. Like all good country house ghost stories, this room is 'that room' – the one imbued with hauntings and ghosts of the past. Unlike the rest of the very English country mansion described in tones of dark, sombre beauty, the drawing room is bright, painted in warm shades of yellow, and opens out to the lawn. There is something of the heat of Mediterranean climates about Alice Oke's drawing room, which is another signal that Alice Oke may not truly fit into an English mould, but, rather, a more stereotypically passionate Italian one. The narrator notes that 'it reminded me more of an Italian room than an English one' (126). This room is where Mrs Oke spends hours of her time, seemingly languishing there, and it is where the narrator opts to begin sketching her for his painting. It is in this room while he sketches that Alice Oke decides to share the long-dead Lovelock's poetry while she wears the original Alice Oke's dress (she has gone into drag as the seventeenth-century mistress of the house). This image both delights and terrifies our narrator when he writes that she gave him

> a delightful picturesque shudder [...] I pictured to myself Mrs. Oke sitting in that yellow room – that room which no Oke of Okehurst save herself ventured to remain in alone, in the dress of her ancestress, confronting, as it were, that vague, haunting something that Seemed to fill the place – that vague presence, it seemed to me, of the murdered cavalier poet. (Lee 2006: 130)

Throughout the story, Mrs Oke cross-dresses on various levels – whether she is in women's garb circa 1600 or in men's attire from that same time period. There is something about her that is not of the current time of the tale. The narrator writes, 'There was a waywardness, a strangeness, which I felt but could not explain – a something as difficult to define as the peculiarity of her outward appearance …' (116–17). The narrator often refers to her as 'strange' or 'peculiar' – and what is curious is that she is married to such an ordinary man. They are first cousins by relation, which, of course, is not unusual at all as far as marriage arrangements at that time. And, although it is clear that Oke is horribly in love with his wife, she dismisses him and only truly comes alive when she is dressed up and dreaming about the past, her ancestors and a dead disreputable poet. There is a great mystery surrounding the original Alice Oke, and as Lee's tale unfolds, Mrs Oke takes the artist even further into her confidence to tell him the horrible story of family scandal and murder.

Mr Oke attempts to silence Alice Oke as she tells the painter the story of their ancestors from two and a half centuries prior. Mr Oke, in frustration, says, 'I can't understand how people can talk about murders in their families, and ghosts, and so forth' (120). Alice Oke insists on keeping the portraits of the ancestors up because, for her, they represent the two people who were *not* boring in their family. Mr Oke represents conservatism, the traditional and the heteronormative – he wishes for heirs, but also comes to the realisation that they will never have any – the line dies with these two. Alice goads him about his morality and about his embarrassment concerning the two ancestors long dead. Slowly, the story comes out to our narrator. The Oke of Okehurst family had been historically honourable when a young poet, Christopher Lovelock, was disgraced because of a love affair at Henry VIII's court, finds himself in his uncle's small abode in Kent next to the Okehursts. He becomes friends with the married couple, but it soon becomes clear that Lovelock is attempting to seduce Alice. Taking matters into their own hands, husband and wife murder him on Cotes Common, a desolate place on their property: 'one evening as he was riding home, Lovelock had been attacked and murdered, ostensibly by highwaymen, but was afterwards rumoured, by Nicholas Oke, accompanied by his wife dressed as a groom' (121). As he dies, Lovelock recognises the groom as his woman love and cries out against her.

As the story progresses, Alice grows listless and, as the narrator notes, occupied with a 'strange self-engrossment and stranger mania about people long dead' (131). On one occasion, Mrs Oke becomes animated enough to take our narrator for a carriage ride which transforms her from the languishing lady in the yellow drawing room to a skilled driver of horse and cart as she whisks them away to Cotes Common, the site of the past murder. Once they arrive at the spot, we are told that the 'distant look' that had been in her eyes prior to the outing were now 'strangely eager and fixed ... this woman positively frightened me' (135). On their return home, William Oke nearly has a nervous breakdown when he learns of their trip, and our narrator observes that, outside, the 'mists were beginning to rise, veiling the park-land ... It was damp and cold, and I shivered' (135). The spectre of the murdered Lovelock coupled with Alice Oke's newly 'eager and fixed' countenance bring a sense of Gothic foreboding to the grounds of Okehurst.

William Oke would clearly do anything to get his wife out of the constant reverie she has fallen into, which includes her ramblings about Lovelock and the original Mrs Oke, so he throws a grand masquerade ball to enliven her spirits. As the guests arrive, the narrator notes that Mrs Oke has strangely vanished, and he assumes she has been overcome with fatigue and taken herself back to her drawing room. However, just as they are all filing into dinner, the following happens:

> the door opened and a strange figure entered, stranger than any of these others who were profaning the clothes of the dead: a boy, slight and tall, in a brown riding-coat, leathern belt, and big buff boots, a little grey cloak over one shoulder, a large grey hat slouched over the eyes, a dagger and pistol at the waist. It was Mrs. Oke, her eyes preternaturally bright, and her whole face lit up with a bold, perverse smile. (138)

Everyone is stunned into silence until they begin to applaud, and the narrator comments that 'there is something questionable in the sudden appearance of a young married woman, the mistress of the house, in a riding-coat and jack-boots' (138). As she takes her seat, she explains the story of Lovelock's murder by her and William's ancestors, and yet she sends up a toast to the dead poet: '"To the health of the poet, Mr. Christopher Lovelock, if his ghost be honouring this house with its presence!"' (138). Later, it becomes clear that Alice Oke also embodies the dead Lovelock – that within her own body, she is the ancestor Alice Oke as well as Lovelock. She is fluidly gendered as she embodies three people: herself in the late Victorian era and Alice and the poet in 1626. This makes not only a ghostly (two thirds) triangle, but one that truly lives within queer time and place. This is not the heteronormative Victorian model; rather, these ghosts of past delectable sexual transgressions and murder haunt the present Victorian moment – and more to the point, they haunt the normative home of William Oke the Tory from Kent. This decadence is not only to be pushed aside back into the murky past but must be eradicated entirely. Lee could very well be playing with outlawed ideas about masquerade – not only people seeming to be someone or something they are not within the framework of a party that allows this behaviour, but also very much about masquerade being another marker of queerness in nineteenth-century England. Especially for people assigned male at birth, as in the case of Fanny and Stella who were arrested dressed as women on the assumption that they were ready to commit sodomy, 'masquerading' was dangerous indeed.[5] This is the stew that Lee leaves us with, embodied within Victorian Alice Oke who clearly rejects her contemporary time frame. Rather, she embraces the ghosts haunting her Victorian present so that she can flee back to a past over two hundred years gone.

The narrator writes the following:

> I sometimes felt ... an intense and impotent desire to enlighten this man about his wife's character. I seemed to understand it so well, and to understand it well seemed to imply such a comfortable acquiescence; and it seemed so unfair that just he should be condemned to puzzle for ever over this enigma, and wear out his soul trying to comprehend what now seemed so plain to me. But how would it ever be possible to get this serious, conscientious, slow-brained representative of English simplicity and honesty and thoroughness to understand ... (140)

While the narrator does call out Alice Oke's 'vanity' and 'love of morbid excitement', there are two other layers to this quote. The first is that William Oke's staid position as the upstanding English gentleman – an example of absolute normativity in this case – is completely undermined as unintelligent and simple. The second is more interesting in that the narrator refers to his paradoxically 'intense' and 'impotent' desire to explain Alice Oke since he understands her 'so well'. Why does the narrator understand Alice Oke? Does he, too, live within this queer world? Does he understand her because he is like her? What is this 'morbid excitement'? It is as though there is coded language and a coded agreement between the narrator and Alice Oke – this type of code very openly appears again, as noted earlier, in Lee's dedication, three years later, to Mary Wakefield. The narrator knows because he is in the know. The literal ghost haunting this tale may be Lovelock, but the ghosts haunting 'Oke of Okehurst' are those of the present Victorian moment when queerness, queer desire and gender transgressions *must be ghosted in order to survive.*

As the story races to the conclusion, Alice Oke retreats more and more to the yellow room, forgetting sustenance, foregoing sleep and mumbling about Lovelock visiting her. All of this causes her husband more anguish and anxiety. As the narrator sketches her one day in this progressing condition, she says to him, '"Such love as that ... is very rare, but it can exist ... it can survive the death, not merely of the beloved, but of the lover"' (150). In a jealous frenzy, William Oke locks his wife in her room to prove her affair with Lovelock. He imprisons her and then beckons our narrator to play voyeur with him as they stand outside the window to spy on her actions. How many times in the past – and even in our present – have queer and trans people been arrested, violated and murdered because someone was gazing on voyeuristically without our consent? As they look in at Alice, they see her on the sofa, her head thrown back, and a red rose in her hand as though a lover were kissing her neck. Oke pushes the narrator aside as he bursts into the room to shoot Lovelock's spectre, which is, in fact, just his own wife; he turns the gun on himself, failing to commit suicide cleanly, and dies several days later of an infection. And, as our narrator tells us, he only has sketches of Alice Oke of Okehurst, and not a completed painting. We are, however, left with this queer decadent ghost story as our portrait.

'Don't Dream It, Be It'[6]

At an LGBTQI2+ authors lecture at the San Francisco Public Library in 2016, the famous US lesbian pulp writer Ann Bannon commented that authoring lesbian pulp fiction in the 1950s placed her in a paradoxical position. On one hand, she was able to create a robust queer life and spend her days with her characters. On the other, the formula for these stories demanded punishment on the page. LGBTQI2+ authors in the 1950s could construct lavish, sexy and romantic queer fictional lives, and readers had a safe, deliciously trashy space to devour these cheap novels. Various social and cultural issues surrounding queer people, coming out, romance and sex could be explored fully and in detail in a time when being queer and/or trans was still illegal. How could this be? As Bannon explained, as long as, in the last two pages, the author killed the queer characters, imprisoned them or destroyed them in some way, the novels could be published. And they were published by the hundreds! There could not be a positive outcome, but as Bannon noted in her lecture in 2016, there could certainly be loads of delicious queer goings-on along the way (Ann Bannon, SF Public Library, 9 June 2016). I have dragged the present (and the twentieth-century example) into this as a lens through which to reconsider or continue questioning Vernon Lee's work and Vernon Lee's motives in these Victorian ghost stories.

Was Lee a prototype for this sort of undercover writing that was very obviously decadent and queer in plot and description? Does the form of the Victorian ghost story allow Vernon Lee to explore these queer and trans possibilities in both coded and overt ways as long as there is a tragic ending? Spiridion dies – his body found torn apart and frozen on Christmas morning. Alice Oke is murdered by her husband for her forbidden desires. In many ways, Lee's writing is not literally about the ways that queer and trans people were seen as monstrous, but Lee's writing via queer decadent Gothic modes heightens that sense that we must take note of how, on an emotional level, it may have felt to be queer in Victorian England: studied like a diseased specimen; looked upon as a criminal; seen as a decadent deviant – and hence a useless – member of society – superfluous. What decadent ghosts are these? Perhaps Lee is telling us that what we are left with are the ghosts of possibility. They tell us it is possible to dream it. Lee's contemporary, E. M. Forster, wrote the following in his male romance *Maurice*, which was written in 1913 but only published posthumously in 1971: 'Dedicated to a Happier Year' (Forster 1971: 5). Both of these queer authors knew we were yet to come and that we could use their guidance. So, perhaps they dreamed it. And it is down to us to *Be It*.

Notes

1. 'Queer' is still the most utilised umbrella term to encompass lesbian, gay, bisexual, transgender, queer, intersex, asexual and Two Spirit (in the Americas) (LGBTQI2+) people. However, there is also, at least in the United States and Canada, a lot of discussion around 'queer' as an umbrella term for diverse sexualities and 'trans' as an umbrella term for diverse gender expressions and identification.
2. There are various arguments about Vernon Lee as a lesbian or Vernon Lee as a trans masculine figure. I think the 'or' is a false binary – especially considering the time Lee lived in when sexual orientation and gender expression and identity were, in many ways, much more fluid – or were exchanged much more freely. For this essay, I am settling on the neutral pronoun in order to hold a queer and trans space for Vernon Lee.
3. In the British Library's note to this online archival piece, there is a discussion about the theories of Nordau and Lombroso being used against queer aesthetes like Wilde, Swinburne and Pater. The website notes specifically that their theories were eventually discredited. This note is no longer available to view, but see the second edition of *Degeneration* on The Internet Archive: https://archive.org/details/degenerationtrfr00norduoft/degeneratio ntrfr00norduoft/ (last accessed 22 January 2025).
4. Song lyrics, The Indigo Girls (Ray and Saliers 1992).
5. I am not arguing that Fanny and Stella embraced women's clothes as strictly a form of drag. There is growing research around considering them in more of a trans feminine light. See Simon Joyce's 'Two Women Walk into a Theatre Bathroom: The Fanny and Stella Trials as Trans Narrative' (Joyce 2018).
6. From *The Rocky Horror Picture Show* (Sharman 1975).

Works Cited

Bannon, Ann. LGBTQ+ Authors Series at the San Francisco Public Library, 9 June 2016.

Forster, E. M. *Maurice*. New York: W. W. Norton, 1971.

Haefele-Thomas, Ardel. *Queer Others in Victorian Gothic: Transgressing Monstrosity*. Cardiff: University of Wales Press, 2012.

———. *Introduction to Transgender Studies*. New York: Columbia University Press, 2019.

Halberstam, Jack. *In a Queer Time and Place: Transgender Bodies, Subcultural Lives*. New York: New York University Press, 2005.

Hurley, Kelly. *The Gothic Body: Sexuality, Materialism, and Degeneration at the Fin-de-Siècle*. Cambridge: Cambridge University Press, 1990.

Joyce, Simon. 'Two Women Walk into a Theatre Bathroom: The Fanny and Stella Trials as Trans Narrative'. Special issue on Trans Victorians (edited by Ardel Haefele-Thomas), *Victorian Review*, vol. 44, no. 1, Spring 2018, pp. 83–98.

Krafft-Ebing, Richard von. (1877) *Psychopathia Sexualis: With Especial Reference to Antipathic Sexual Instinct: A Medico-Forensic Study*, 10th edn. London: Forgotten Books, 2012.

Lee, Vernon. 'Deterioration of Soul'. *The Fortnightly Review*, CCCLIV, New Series, 1 June 1896, pp. 928–43.

———. 'Oke of Okehurst; Or, The Phantom Lover', in *Hauntings and Other Fantastic Tales*, edited by Catherine Maxwell and Patricia Pulham. Peterborough, ON: Broadview Press, 2006, pp. 105–53.

———. 'Amour Dure', in *Hauntings and Other Fantastic Tales*, edited by Catherine Maxwell and Patricia Pulham. Peterborough, ON: Broadview Press, 2006, pp. 41–76.

———. 'Hauntings: Fantastic Stories', in *Hauntings and Other Fantastic Tales*, edited by Catherine Maxwell and Patricia Pulham. Peterborough, ON: Broadview Press, 2006, pp. 37–40.

———. 'Out of Venice at Last', in *Hauntings and Other Fantastic Tales*, edited by Catherine Maxwell and Patricia Pulham. Peterborough, ON: Broadview Press, 2006, pp. 339–41.

Nordau, Max. *Degeneration*. London: William Heinemann, 1895.

Ray, Amy and Emily Saliers (The Indigo Girls). 'Galileo'. *Rites of Passage*. Epic Records, 1992.

Sharman, Jim, dir. *The Rocky Horror Picture Show* [film]. Michael White Productions/20th Century Fox, 1975.

Chapter 18

Henry James
Luke Thurston

'[T]he trap set by the artist,' wrote Henry James in 1899, 'occupies no different ground ... from the offer of her charms by the lady. [...] When we do respond to the appeal, when we *are* caught in the trap, we are held and played upon ...' (James 1987: 339). Over the whole long course of James's writing, there is a steadily growing preoccupation with the question of 'infatuation' – in the sense of sex, of psychopathology, of the writer's obsessive relation to his craft or his audience – and thus a growing awareness of the seductive powers of art. It was for this reason that James was never content with the legacy of the Victorian novel if that meant no more than an all-encompassing bland documentary realism, which was why he always preferred the exuberant grotesquerie of Dickensian style to what he disdainfully labels the 'empirical' novels of Trollope (James 1987: 59). Now, the Victorian ghost story (Dickens is a case in point) showed dramatically – and of course often with lurid vulgarity, hugely complicating James's fastidious and yet fascinated relation to it – precisely how much more literature could do than merely offer reports on common-sense reality.

To write ghost stories was thus for James never a mere bagatelle, something to be sneered at by serious, grown-up writers of Great Literature, though at times some of his comments – especially after the embarrassing public sensation of *The Turn of the Screw* (1898) – might lead one to suppose he thought precisely that. Although in his later years, after the key crisis of 1895 which I will argue is central to understanding his most important ghost stories, there is little doubt that James concentrates his main literary ambitions on the novel, the ghost story still served him as a precious way to express the more ludic and experimental possibilities of what he called the 'prose picture' (James 1987: 339).

Jamesian ghost stories also offer useful windows onto the different stages of his writing life with its extended metamorphosis from the mid-Victorian to the Edwardian period. Although of course there are consistent preoccupations and themes across all Jamesian fiction, I will argue that because his ghost stories often coincide with, or even function as responses to, a personal crisis in the author's life, they offer especially intense visions of his primary concerns, what fundamentally drove him to live the strange life he led as an exiled bachelor dedicated to the craft of writing but also caught up in a complex, shifting network of passionate emotional bonds. The ghost story, for James, shone a surprising and estranging sidelight on emotional connectivity – his own and, it turned out, everyone else's.

It makes obvious sense, then, to read the ghost stories in chronological order as a counternarrative to the various phases and developments of James's work. And if that notion of ghostly counternarrative brings with it an implicit contrast between quotidian ego and nocturnal alter ego, between 'morning sunshine [and] dubious twilight' (James 1962: 59), that apparently Gothic dualism will prove highly relevant: there is a real sense, as we will see, in which the Jamesian ghost story centres on the figure of split selfhood made eternally famous by James's close friend Robert Louis Stevenson.

We will explore three clusters of stories: firstly, from the very beginning of James's career, then from the 1890s, that decade of 'modern' neo-Gothic extravagance, and lastly from the period after the major crisis for James caused by the disastrous opening night of his play *Guy Domville* in January 1895.

The first of our scenes is set in 1867, with the youthful James still living at the family home in Cambridge, Massachusetts, recovering from illness, while outside the whole country was attempting to recover from the Civil War, a conflict in which two of James's brothers had fought and been badly traumatised. A decade later, James would write that 'the Civil War marks an era in the American mind. It introduced into the national consciousness a certain sense ... of the world being a more complicated place than it had hitherto seemed, the future more treacherous' (quoted in Lee 1987: 85). A story James wrote in this traumatic and transitional period is given a title playfully harking back to the novels of Hawthorne (who had only recently died, in 1864), 'The Romance of Certain Old Clothes'. And the opening line of the story seems a deliberately comic evocation of a lost world before the shock of modernity: 'Toward the middle of the eighteenth century there lived in the Province of Massachusetts a widowed gentlewoman, the mother of three children' (James 1962: 297). We are 'in the direct line of Hawthorne', thinks Leon Edel (Edel 1985: 17), and the antebellum setting, suggesting peaceful social inertia, is soon unsettled by Gothic shadows. From the moment when the rival daughters are introduced, some of the key features of the

Jamesian ghost story can be seen emerging. The dead father had been an American besotted with English culture, and so had named his daughters after Shakespearean characters: 'Upon the elder he had bestowed the romantic name of Viola; and upon the younger, the more serious one of Perdita, in memory of a little girl born between them, who had lived but a few weeks' (James 1962: 297). If we follow the names back to *Twelfth Night* and *The Winter's Tale*, we discover in those plays endless signs of something at the heart of the Jamesian ghost story: the idea of the groundless and antagonistic nature of the self. The near anagrammatic equivalence of Viola and Olivia in *Twelfth Night* is a clue to how the play shows identity, especially feminine identity, as caught up in masquerade and mimetic rivalry, in the knowing assumption and usurpation of desire and selfhood: when asked if she is mistress of the house, Olivia replies, 'If I do not usurp myself, I am' (Shakespeare 1985: 64). And in the later play too, Perdita appears in disguise, 'in borrowed flaunts' (Shakespeare 1966: 90), her identity masked, substituted, self-usurped. But Perdita's name, signifying 'the lost female', is in turn borrowed by James and given a ghostly twist as the name 'of a little girl born between them', a ghostly double that both divides and spectrally links the two sisters. Later, when Perdita's imminent death leads her to carefully plan how to prevent her sister from taking her place by marrying her husband, the figure of an uncanny shadow again intervenes between feminine identities. It occurs to Perdita that it is really her clothes and jewellery, not her husband, that Viola is after, but then, 'At this moment, the thought of her sister's rapacity seemed to cast a dark shadow between her and the helpless figure of her little girl' (James 1962: 311). The shadow is now cast by female desire and its annihilatory envious mirroring, but we should note the key role of the child here: just as the spectral 'lost girl' first divides and haunts the sisters, so Viola will usurp her sister's identity as wife and mother through the medium of the female child. The latter, whom the story gives no name because her role is merely functional, is caught in the net of adult desire when Viola expertly simulates the maternal role, thus of course in turn duping the witless husband and gaining access to the object of her desire: her sister's stuff.

As well as its playful allusions to Shakespeare, this early story by James is permeated, almost to a parodic extent, by the themes and motifs of Gothic fiction. When Viola is caught in front of the mirror in borrowed flaunts, 'in Perdita's cast-off wedding veil and wreath' and pearls (307–8), the ghosts of Bertha Mason and Miss Havisham are in the room too, and the mirror scene of feminine rivalry will repeat itself on through Gothic fictions from *Rebecca* (1938) to *The Haunting of Hill House* (1959) and beyond.

This first ghost story by James is in many ways not a ghost story at all, and of course the later Prefaces will make explicit James's dissatisfaction with the generic label. The characters lack the minimal depth to generate the realist frame required by the uncanny, with their Shakespearean names and formulaic narrative roles effectively distancing the sisters from readerly engagement: thus when Viola is vengefully slain by Perdita's old frocks there is little trace of shock or horror. Although the American setting and Hawthornean stylistics of the tale add to the sense that it is in essence a parody of 'American Gothic' – and we could therefore see it as part of James's writerly detachment from his own origin and culture – it nevertheless announces some of the central motifs and preoccupations of the later 'genuine' ghost stories: feminine subjectivity, rivalry and control, the mediation of adult sexual bonds through the dangerous supplement of the child.

By the time James published 'The Ghostly Rental' in 1876, much had changed and his self-transformative move from America to Europe had at last occurred. The narrative is again set in antebellum Massachusetts, and again it can be seen as a playful and parodic simulation of Hawthornean Gothic. The sense of the kinship of horror and laughter runs through the story – 'I laughed ... but I confess I shuddered too' (James 1962: 67) – signalling a Jamesian uncertainty about the dubious, perhaps illicit, pleasures of the ghostly, an uncertainty that will persist in his later writing. Some of the major motifs of the later stories are visible here: the pairing of a homely and an uncanny dwelling, the significance of staircases and thresholds as transitional spaces. When the narrator finds himself lurking in a graveyard, 'feeling very much like a restless ghost myself' (68), it becomes clear that the central conceit of the story, in which an individual lodges fraudulently in a family house by duping her father into the fantasy of paying off an imaginary debt, can be interpreted as almost a piece of playful autobiography. The sense of a restless desire to escape from the familiar confines of a known world is constantly suggested by James's writing, and although we are many years before Freud's article on the uncanny, there is already a clear inscription of *Unheimlichkeit*:

> There was something very singular in this gesture; it seemed to denote resentment and dismissal, and yet it had a sort of trivial, familiar motion. Familiarity on the part of the haunting Presence had not entered into my calculations and did not strike me pleasantly. (76)

Of course, the story's bathetic denouement, revealing the 'Presence' to be in fact 'a large fair person, of about five-and thirty' (83), serves to undercut and ironise the earlier 'singular' unsettling of realism, and the notional glimpse of the father's ghost on the staircase is not enough to restore the magic.

These early stories, then, although they anticipate some of the features of the definitive Jamesian ghost story, are little more than ironic disengagements from American literary traditions. By the 1890s, when the great stories are written, James is a famous author living in England and vividly conscious of the cultural and social upheaval taking place in that delirious decade. If we turn to 'Sir Edmund Orme' (1891) with the fake ghost from 'The Ghostly Rental' in mind, we can gauge how much has changed: what the later story does so brilliantly is find a new way to make the ghost 'authentic' by linking it to an emerging sense of subjectivity as irreducible to the alienating surfaces of social identity. The scene is Victorian Brighton, a glittering parade of social and sexual intersubjectivity where everything, from fashion to gossip to 'looks, movements and tones' (James 1963: 121), is caught in the seductive play of signifiers. And the ghost corresponds to precisely what *eludes* this Wildean masquerade of social reality, to a hidden dimension which James links again to the mother–daughter relation but also, crucially, to the new 1890s subculture of the occult and mediumship. The social parade of display and seduction is thus traumatically breached by the libidinal signals of the female body:

> ... Mrs Marden, looking away from me. 'Ah!' she suddenly panted, in the next breath, rising to her feet and staring at her daughter ... She stood a few seconds, with the queerest expression in her face; then she sank back upon the seat again and I saw that she had blushed crimson. Charlotte ... came straight up to her and, taking her hand with quick tenderness, seated herself on the other side of her. The girl had turned pale – she gave her mother a fixed, frightened look. (122–3)

The flow of blood to and from the female face, the panting and the significant gaze all correspond to an orgasmic connection to something repressed from superficial social reality. The narrator is pulled into this asocial libidinal dimension in a directly eroticised manner: 'She drew me down beside her and for a moment I felt her hand pressing my arm in a way that might have been an involuntary betrayal of distress and might have been a private signal' (123). The dimension of supernatural communication is private, trouncing the merely conventional signifying power of language, and it is no surprise to learn that Mrs Marden has 'intuitions' and 'uncanny promptings' (124), that she is in touch with a psychical reality more authentic and truthful than the cliché-ridden 'reality' of social discourse. It is thus that the narrative dramatises the breakthrough of an ordinary person to a new dimension of inner-worldly truth, with a soupçon of deranged, socially taboo enjoyment: 'if Mrs Marden was mystifying I can scarcely say she was alarming. I couldn't imagine what she meant, but I wondered more than I shuddered... . She struck me as hopelessly right' (126). Since the ghost appears whenever desire for the daughter manifests itself, the narrator can both relish and disavow its presence as a queer taste of forbidden pleasure: 'though I knew nothing about him but that he was Sir Edmund Orme I felt his presence as a strong appeal, almost as an oppression' (133–4). With Jamesian subtlety, the name of the ghost merges desire for aristocratic authenticity with the sense of an alternative selfhood – 'or me' – embodying a pure enjoyment unhindered by the gaze of social morality.

The sense of the supernatural as a framework for an imaginary escape from social visibility and censorship becomes an important feature of the Jamesian ghost story. In 'Sir Edmund Orme' the narrator is vividly aware of the peculiar enjoyment available away from the laws of social legibility. Reflecting on his relation to the motherly Mrs Marden, he is sure that 'our privacy was all-sufficient. We communicated so closely and completely now, and with such silent reciprocities ...' (142). This psychical proximity and full communication is clearly against the rules of a social censorship that makes ordinary relationships a matter of half-truths and strategies; and it burgeons, for the narrator, into the confession of properly transgressive desire: '[Sir Edmund Orme] looked strange, incontestably, but somehow he always looked *right*. I very soon came to attach an idea of beauty to his unmentionable presence, the beauty of an old story of love and pain' (145).

Because the ghost is not subject to external social scrutiny, the narrator can identify him (never 'it') with a Gothic orgasmic intensity absent from modern reality, corresponding indeed to an inner-worldly truth wholly unrecognised by that reality. It is thus that the ghostly *ménage à trois* of the narrator, Sir Edmund and Mrs Marden opens onto what James will memorably call the 'cure of souls' at the heart of literary creation. The occult teamwork of their ghostly project, in other words, has been hugely therapeutic for the haunted mother: 'For herself she felt it to be a good time, a sort of St Martin's summer of the soul. She was better than she had been for years, and she had me to thank for it' (147).

This idea of the supernatural as a threshold to a deeper, more authentic level of the psyche becomes another key theme of the later stories. What gives the ghostly in James its power is the possibility that this other psychical scene is not compatible with the ordinary, subject-centred syntax of representation. At the lurid climax of 'Sir Edmund Orme', any sense of curative soul-baring is eclipsed by an indecipherable outbreak of jouissance:

> Was the sound I heard when Chartie shrieked – the other and still more tragic sound I mean – the despairing cry of the poor lady's death-shock or the articulate sob (it was like a waft from a great tempest), of the exorcised and pacified spirit? (151)

The jagged syntax and strained hyperbole speak of a challenge to legibility and communicative rationality far removed from the standard Jamesian repertoire of stylistic mastery. And this challenge to authorial dominion is profoundly, irreconcilably, ambiguous: as three voices blend in this final orgasmic scream, how can we distinguish between haunting and exorcism, between the penetrative shock of the ghost and its therapeutic pacification?

As James attempted during the 1890s to shift from writing mainly as a novelist to writing for the theatre, he entered a difficult period when for almost the first time he began encountering hostility and rejection. Even before the bad opening night of his play *Guy Domville* in 1895, which for James was nothing less than a life-changing catastrophe, the short story served him as a good medium in which to think through and work over the kind of problems of social and sexual identity he saw as suitable material for the public art-form of the theatre. It is for this reason that we need to take seriously James's caution about the generic label 'ghost story' – indeed, some of the texts assembled under that heading in modern editions, including some that clearly do not involve anything we would normally consider a ghost, might be better described in different terms, perhaps as 'psychical cases'. The Prefaces James wrote in 1909 shed light on this generic uncertainty as the author reflects on the uncanny process of writing these stories. He is discussing the genesis of 'The Private Life':

> This piece of ingenuity rests for me on such a handful of acute impressions as I may not here tell over at once; so that, to be brief, I select two of the sharpest. Neither of these was, in old London days, I make out, to be resisted even under its single pressure; so that the hour struck with a vengeance for 'dramatize it, dramatize it!' ... from the first glimpse of a good way to work together the two cases that happened to have been given me.
>
> [...] So at least one could but take the case – though one's need for relief depended, no doubt, on what one (so to speak) suffered. (James 1909: xii–xiii)

The combination of confession and non-disclosure is pure Gothic, and directly continuous with the metafictional tropology James frequently uses in his narratives, notably in the frame narratives, where the document left in a locked drawer or the secret doings in a forbidden chamber are essential mechanisms to generate the Gothic split between normative verisimilitude and its uncanny psychical other. If the 1890s stories are not, as the earlier American tales had been, simply parodies of the ghost story, they are not simply content to be 'straight' ghost stories either. When James speaks of 'taking the case' we need to hear a double ventriloquism: part Sherlock Holmes, part Sigmund Freud. There is a mystery to be solved, and the 'question of evidence' (James, 'The Way It Came' 1964: 391), whether in terms of detective or therapeutic epistemology, looms large, especially in the story 'The Friends of the Friends', with its deaths and enigmas. Kneeling by the dead body of her friend and love-rival, the protagonist underscores the Gothic epistemology of desire and non-disclosure: 'Death ... had made her, had kept her silent. It had turned the key on something I was concerned to know' (387).

If the case is to be taken, then, by the Freudian-Jamesian detective who tells the tale, it is as a result of a strange psychical pressure, almost amounting to an auditory hallucination. On one side is the repeated command to 'dramatise it!', voicing the permanent Jamesian obsession with public celebrity and lucrative success; on the other, an unmistakable metaphorics of sexual desire, tension and compulsion ('sharpest', 'pressure', 'relief', 'suffered'). These stories explore above all the puzzles of the sexual psyche, and the sense of aesthetic and libidinal urgency conveyed by James makes it clear that 'taking the case' involves a writerly passion of sharpness and intensity, a passion itself mysterious, not to be 'told over'. 'The Private Life' (1892) is primarily an expression of this epistemophilic passion rather than a ghost story, since it focuses on the thinly veiled 'cases' of Robert Browning and Frederick Leighton, stars of the Victorian art world who perplex the Jamesian narrator by seeming to be psychically split between the banal conventional ego of quotidian reality and a mysterious alter ego locked in the secret chamber of artistic creation. A striking feature of this psychical investigation is its playful departure from the conventional surfaces of Victorian gender identity. At the opening of the story the narrator presents the following celebrity gathering:

> we had by a happy chance the *fleur des pois*: Lord and Lady Mellifont, Clare Vawdrey, the greatest (in the opinion of many) of our literary glories, and Blanche Adney, the greatest (in the opinion of all) of our theatrical. (James 1963: 189)

In this pick of the bunch of artistic personalities, it is unclear who is male and who female, as the chiming pairs – Lord and Lady Mellifont, Clare Vawdrey (who is male) and Blanche Adney (who is female) – deliberately blur the conventional lexicon of gender. In another story, 'Owen Wingrave' (published in 1892), although gender is not playfully muddled in this way, the narrative surface is constantly and playfully troubled by ripples of queer desire. The house at the centre of what amounts to a family nervous breakdown is named 'Paramore', signalling an erotic subtext at odds with normality (para + amore: 'alternative love'). Spencer Coyle, the tutor of young Owen, is pleasantly surprised when his pupil 'passed his hand entreatingly into his companion's arm, permitting himself thus a familiarity unusual between master and pupil' (James, 'The Way It Came' 1964: 31). We need to attend carefully here to the way James re-edits the original magazine text when it is republished in the New York edition. In the 1892 text, 'Owen Wingrave smiled down at his small but erect instructor'; in 1909, 'erect' has disappeared. In 1892, Spencer Coyle reflects that Owen's attitude 'was really a stiff obsession'; but in 1909, 'it was a monomania' (32–3).[1] It does not require Freudian ingenuity to see in this censoring of 'erect' and 'stiff' a concerted effort by James to suppress the erotic dimension of the adult–child relation which in the Wildean 1890s had taken a distinctively queer turn.

If 'The Private Life' and 'Owen Wingrave' are less ghost stories than they are psychical investigations, then, the latter in particular nonetheless has some stylistic motifs that anticipate James's mostly authentically ghostly ghost story, *The Turn of the Screw*. Paramore is presented somewhat playfully as a haunted house, 'with its old grey front which came forward in wings so as to form three sides of a square', which is duly dubbed 'uncanny' by the perceptive Mrs Coyle (James 1964: 30). Owen himself complains that the source of his anxiety is the family home: 'Oh, the house – the very air and feeling of it. There are strange voices in it that seem to mutter at me – to say dreadful things as I pass' (34). And Mrs Coyle uses a significant expression to describe the strange, quasi-incestuous relationship between Owen and the assertive, socially toxic Kate Julian: 'They're a quaint pair!' (48) Quaint, rooted in old French *cointe*, has unmentionable implications, and will be recognisable in the name of one of the infamous spectres at Bly: 'quaint pair', we might say, anagrammatically prefigures Peter Quint.

The stories written by James in the early 1890s thus focus above all on the mysteries of other minds and the unfathomability of selfhood and sexuality. As he entered his fifties, James suffered a number of painful bereavements, above all the deaths of his sister Alice in 1892 and of his dear friend Constance Woolson in 1894. These personal disasters were matched by what he saw as the artistic catastrophe that occurred to him in January 1895, when at its premiere his play *Guy Domville* met with guffaws and catcalls from the London audience. For Leon Edel, James's sense of his cherished play's failure constituted a 'black abyss' that led to a complete transformation of his life and work: he left London and gave up his ambitions to be a successful playwright, dedicating himself to the less hazardous business of writing novels and tales, thus addressing a smaller, more discerning audience (Edel 1985: 425–68). As I have argued elsewhere, this crisis was also a turning point for the Jamesian ghost story that resulted in it reaching a wholly new level of literary importance and psychical significance (Thurston 2012: 73–95).

One of James's first tasks after the *Guy Domville* disaster was to complete a story he had begun earlier for magazine publication. Entitled 'The Way It Came' (which James later changed to 'The Friends of the Friends'), it can be seen as a bridge between the earlier stories, with their focus on the social ramifications of gender identity and sexual relations, and the later more radical explorations of those themes. What is crucial in this story, and what makes its investigation of the psyche less disturbing than the later texts, can be easily formulated: *there are no children*. At the centre of this story is the question of what constitutes a bond or rapport between two individuals, a man and a woman, who are caught up in a network of social relations outside the family. The Jamesian conceit of a pair who never meet offers a striking picture of heterosexual non-relation:

> It was at any rate the very liveliest of all the reasons why they ought to know each other – all the lively reasons reduced to naught by the strange law that had made them bang so many doors in each other's face, made them the buckets in the well, the two ends of the see-saw ... so that when one was up the other was down. [...] They were in a word alternate and incompatible ... (James 1964: 377)

The playful tone of the narrative does not diminish the importance of the question of the relation between ordinary social contact and properly meaningful bonds. Because the former can be documented and historicised, it inhabits the realist horizon of everyday life and its literary reflection in the novel, whereas the latter remains somehow unaccountable, impossible to represent (both members of the non-couple refuse to be photographed and made part of documentary history). And into this gap between realist social existence and fantasmatic connectedness steps the ghost, posing 'the question of evidence' (391) as it is an impossible convergence of the two. The supposed relation between the woman and the man cannot sustain the illusion that they inhabit a single, shared reality: 'you describe the scene – so far as you describe it at all – in terms that are incomprehensible' (393).

The question of the comprehensibility and consensuality of reality is crucial to James's late work. The strange, often overlooked short novel *The Other House* (1896), which James wrote in a state of great disarray and depression, is an important step towards *The Turn of the Screw* because it resituates the problem of identity and relationships in the novelistic domain of the family, specifically at the level of the relation between adults and children. James's initially playful idea for what he had first planned as an Ibsenite play was to confront a good and a bad heroine, with the dutiful Jean Martle opposing the wayward Rose Armiger. The political implications of this opposition are made clear by an early discussion of babies:

> 'I suppose it's very lovely,' Jean remarked with growing confidence.
> 'Lovely! Do you think babies are ever lovely?'
> Taken aback by this challenge, Jean reflected a little; she found, however, nothing better to say than, rather timidly: 'I like dear little children, don't you?'
> Miss Armiger in turn considered. 'Not a bit!' she then replied … (James 1948: 9–10)

Rose's challenge is both to her counterpart and to the gender script that defines and constrains their identities, and makes their social significance coterminous with their potential to produce and care for children. This departure from the script echoes Owen Wingrave's refusal to conform to the family tradition of military masculinity, but whereas the free-thinking young man was merely punished by a conventional spectre of patriarchal authority, the feminist Rose's fate is more complex, and far more disturbing. With macabre insistence, the narrative focuses on Rose's weird relation to the baby Effie (whose father Tony has promised to its dead mother never to remarry while Effie is alive). Brandishing the child like a strange fetish object, Rose is possessed by the uncanny force of the oral drive:

> 'You look at her like an ogre!' Rose laughed, moving away from [Tony] with her burden and pressing to her lips as she went a little plump pink arm. She pretended to munch it; she covered it with kisses; she gave way to the joy of her renounced abstention. (154)

The key to the weirdness of this story is visible here (James decided not to include it in the New York edition and it is rarely even mentioned by James critics). All of this flirtatious joshing with the baby would be quite unremarkable, that is, were it not for that fact that at the end of the novel Rose murders the child by drowning her in the river. James prevaricated over this blood-chilling climax, at one stage having Rose merely poison the baby who could then be given a life-saving antidote, but then restored the full horror of Rose as psychotic fantasist.

The Other House is therefore an intriguing precursor of *The Turn of the Screw*, in terms of the thematics of sexual identity and the gender script, and because of the radically different narrative choices made by James in constructing his two texts. The first obvious difference is that the later text is a framed narrative, with the embedded tale, as a homodiegetic fiction, opening up a complex play of the real and the imaginary, the intuited and the wished-for (in *The Other House*, by contrast, we are confronted by the simple diegetic reality of the woman we had pictured as a feisty heroine being in fact a cold-blooded killer).

What the two texts have in common is a challenge to the gender script, above all to the idea of children as a mediating site of feminine identity and desire. The governess in *The Turn of the Screw* is a version of the 'extra' or supplementary female seen elsewhere in James as a disruptive challenge (either difficult, like Kate Julian, or psychotic, like Rose Armiger). She is neither lady nor servant, neither caught in the fantasy masquerade of middle-class marriage-brokering nor consigned to the drab realism of servants. What her homodiegetic narrative captures so brilliantly is the impossibility of her position as on one side the protector of heteronormative reality from the disruptive attacks of unconstrained libido, and on the other a desiring subject whose fantasy life is itself enigmatically traversed by that libido. What is revealed to her is both the fictionality of 'natural' gender roles – one afternoon she sees Bly 'like a theatre after the performance, all strewn with crumpled playbills' (James 1964: 86) – and, more horrifically, her own unaccountable enjoyment in confronting this opening beyond 'nature' onto something *more real than reality*: 'I greatly preferred, as a safeguard, the fulness of my own exposure' (87). This means that the governess is profoundly *unheimlich*, both a protective homely mother figure and a strange, guilty thrill-seeker. Generations of James critics have tried to firmly position her as either good Jean or evil Rose, either sane saviour of unblemished reality or ghostly fantasist obsessed with the bodies and desires of the children.

What makes *The Turn of the Screw* one of the most powerful Victorian ghost stories is the way James turns the governess's narrative into an exploration of the unfathomable depths of human subjectivity beneath the conventional gendered surface of reality. Because she is not simply a monster like Rose Armiger, the governess is unable to manipulate that surface in the interests of her fantasmatic desire, but is above all desperate to redeem the possibility of a consistent reality, both for herself and for others. After her sight of Quint on the tower, a vision both ultra-real and quasi-fantasmatic, she cannot bear to share it with the mundane Mrs Grose: 'my real beginning of fear was one, as I may say, with the instinct of sparing my companion' (39). Her initially straightforward task of protecting the children against a criminal sexuality figured as Quint and Jessel is complicated not only by her obsessive sense of the children as active participants in that fantasmatic criminality but, more radically, by the opening up of a new sense of sexuality itself – as no longer definable, locatable within 'nature' but as coming from some invisible but ubiquitous elsewhere. If she cannot 'fence about' (50) that other domain and contain it, her failure both energises her narrative and jeopardises its representational power: 'I scarcely know how to put my story into words that shall be a credible picture of my state of mind' (53). It is this fundamental challenge to Victorian realism, an early chapter in the reinvention of realism that will continue with modernism, that makes *The Turn of the Screw* uniquely important.

The main task of the final phase of James's career was producing his three greatest novels, and that task left little room for much else. The stories with a ghostly theme he did find time to write seem mostly minor diversions, self-mocking though occasionally piquant. 'The Real Right Thing' (1899) has biographer George Withermore, working at the very desk recently used by his now deceased subject Ashton Doyne, enjoying the idea that the great man's spirit is with him in the room while he writes. When one day he senses with distress that Doyne's ghost has disappeared, he has intense exchanges with Doyne's widow on how to get through to the ghost and understand the 'dim signs out of his horror' (James, 'The Real Right Thing' 1964: 484). Concluding that being given to the world by a biographer is against the wishes of the ghost, Withermore abandons the book. The story touches lightly on aspects of the radical unravelling of representation and selfhood in *The Turn of the Screw*, but the overall tone is bittersweet comedy.

An even more light-hearted sketch of old age and the proximity of death comes in 'The Third Person' (1900), in essence a piece of satirical mock-Gothic comedy. Two elderly spinster cousins discover a box of Gothic documents that gives them access to a rich history of villainy and bravado sealed away from the pretty village they have moved to. This discovery duly produces a cavalier rogue of a ghost which the old ladies endow with an imaginary sexual rapacity, a kind of libidinal bonus they see as a special treat: 'They had got, in short, more than was vulgarly, more than was even shrewdly supposed – such an indescribable unearned increment as might scarce more be divulged as a dread than as a delight' (James 1964: 151). But, of course, there is no free lunch even in Gothic parody, and the rest of the story reveals how the fantasmatic lover, visiting and abandoning each of the frustrated women in turn, ends by dividing them and making them fall back on dim memories of little slices of enjoyment, such as the moment when Amy got away with smuggling through the customs her racy Tauchnitz novel.

The very last of James's ghost stories, by contrast, returns to the full seriousness and significance seen in the 1890s texts. This is 'The Jolly Corner' (1908), written as a direct response to James's trip back to America, after almost three decades, in 1904–5. The return to his roots reopens fundamental questions for James, and this story explores them: questions of gender identity, sexual desire, the relation between adult and child subjectivity, the source of creativity. Thus Spencer Brydon's identity is split between a theatrical performance of masculinity at his modern property, where he can simulate manly know-how in front of the builders and his old girlfriend Alice, and a very different kind of ego that opens for him in his old house 'on the jolly corner', a place that harbours an undying spectral enjoyment incompatible with repressive adult selfhood. James's text has lyrical passages that strive to conjure up a taste of that lost but unforgotten ecstasy. Entering the old hallway, he hears:

> ... the dim reverberating tinkle as of some far-off bell hung who should say where? – in the depths of the house, of the past, of the mystical other world that might have flourished for him had he not, for weal or woe, abandoned it. (James 1964: 209)

This Jamesian self, opening to the vibrations of experience and imagination beyond the limitations of legible reality, is at the heart of the engagement with the supernatural that preoccupied him throughout his life. What is crucial to see is how this sense of selfhood is profoundly linked to the process of *creativity* in James. Charles Feidelson notes the importance of what James called 'ciphering out' in that process: 'To "cipher out" was to discover all the ramifications of what was presented to him, "to let one's self go to it"' (Feidelson 1953: 48). The letting go of the self, the opening to the other, is the indescribable core of James's ghost stories.

Note

1. For the original 1892 text, I refer to *Ghost Stories of Henry James*, edited by Martin Schofield (Ware: Wordsworth, 2001).

Works Cited

Edel, Leon. *Henry James: A Life*. New York: Harper & Row, 1985.
Feidelson, Charles. *Symbolism and American Literature*. Chicago: University of Chicago Press, 1953.

James Henry. *The Novels and Tales of Henry James: The New York Edition*, vol. 17. New York: Scribner, 1909.

———. *The Critical Muse: Selected Literary Criticism*, edited by Roger Gard. London: Penguin, 1987.

———. 'The Romance of Certain Old Clothes', in *The Complete Tales of Henry James*, vol. 1: *1864–1868*, edited by Leon Edel. London: Hart-Davis, 1962, pp. 297–319.

———. 'The Ghostly Rental', in *The Complete Tales of Henry James*, vol. 4: *1876–1882*, edited by Leon Edel. London: Hart-Davis, 1962, pp. 49–86.

———. 'Sir Edmund Orme'; 'The Private Life', in *The Complete Tales of Henry James*, vol. 8: *1891–1892*, edited by Leon Edel. London: Hart-Davis, 1963, pp. 119–51; pp. 189–227.

———. 'The Way It Came' ('The Friends of the Friends'), in *The Complete Tales of Henry James*, vol. 9: *1892–1898*, edited by Leon Edel. London: Hart-Davis, 1964, pp. 371–401.

———. 'The Turn of the Screw'; 'The Real Right Thing', in *The Complete Tales of Henry James*, vol. 10: *1898–1899*, edited by Leon Edel. London: Hart-Davis, 1964, pp. 15–138; pp. 471–86.

———. 'The Third Person', in *The Complete Tales of Henry James*, vol. 11: *1900–1903*, edited by Leon Edel. London: Hart-Davis, 1964, pp. 133–69.

———. 'The Jolly Corner', in *The Complete Tales of Henry James*, vol. 12: *1903–1910*, edited by Leon Edel. London: Hart-Davis, 1964.

———. *The Other House*, ed. Leon Edel, London: Hart-Davis, 1948.

Lee, Brian. *American Fiction 1865–1940*. Harlow: Longman, 1987.

Shakespeare, William. *The Winter's Tale*, edited by J. H. P. Pafford. London: Methuen, 1966.

Shakespeare, William. *Twelfth Night*, edited by Elizabeth Story Donno. Cambridge: Cambridge University Press, 1985.

Thurston, Luke. *Literary Ghosts from the Victorians to Modernism: The Haunting Interval*. New York: Routledge, 2012.

Chapter 19

M. R. James
Roger Luckhurst

Montague Rhodes James (1862–1936) was a quintessential figure of the late Victorian and Edwardian establishment elite. After preparatory school in Surrey, he was a King's Scholar at Eton College (1873–82), the ancient institution which was and remains one of the small clutch of public schools that has generated England's ruling class. He then moved to King's College at the University of Cambridge for his BA degree (this was the college to which Eton schoolboys traditionally transferred). A few jolly years as a precocious young scholar were followed by election to the Fellowship of the College, and the role of Dean, while also taking on the directorship of the Fitzwilliam Museum, the university's central collection, at a very young age.

His obsessive drive to catalogue the manuscript collections of all the Cambridge college libraries was legendary, as was his extensive collection and collation of biblical apocrypha, a fascination which had begun in childhood (his father was a priest; Eton library had materials reaching back to its founding in the fifteenth century). He became the affable and sociable Provost of King's in 1905, then Vice Chancellor of Cambridge University in 1913. It would seem that the traumas of the Great War, the awful losses of a generation of young Cambridge men at the front, and the onerous public duties tied to the role prompted James to return to Eton College in 1918 as Provost.

He continued to collect the honours and awards of the English elite. He was elected a member of the elite Club of Nobody's Friends in 1917, an exclusive society founded in 1800 to connect Protestant high church clerisy with establishment networks at the heart of government. A group created to preserve the continuity of the English settlement between monarch, Church of England and the state, the club had been formed at the height of establishment panic about the effect of the French Revolution on the exercise of political power in Britain, and espoused 'sacral royalism' (Rowell 2000: 24). James was elected by the

King to the Order of Merit in 1930, its members restricted to twenty-four for their meritorious service to the nation in the arts and sciences. He remained Provost of Eton until his death in 1936, and was buried in Eton's churchyard. He had lived exclusively in all-male communities throughout his life, remaining unmarried, and had been housed in august Gothic structures that radiated deep history, security and the continuity of tradition.

His writing of ghost stories was always a distinctly marginal practice in James's professional career. The existence of these tales might initially seem odd and dissonant with the rest of his intellectual life – his university and Anglican religious circles had little patience with lowly Spiritualism and its claim to communicate with ghosts, although it was slightly more indulgent of the Society of Psychical Research, formed by the eminent Cambridge don Henry Sidgwick in 1882. If the SPR was intent on scientising the supernatural and seeking empirical proof of the survival of the human personality after death, James's tales were in contrast self-consciously produced as 'entertainments' in the Victorian spirit of Charles Dickens's Christmas special issues produced every December for *Household Words*. James's stories were initially delivered to Cambridge's Chit-Chat Club, which met late on Saturday nights in college rooms and where papers were read to a small circle over coffee and 'whales' – that is, anchovies on toast (Parry 2021). Later, and more famously, James developed a Christmas Eve tradition to read out a new story to invited guests in his rooms at King's or Eton, where they were received by the light of a single candle amidst other, more rambunctious activities, such as games of 'grab' – wrestling on the carpet – which James particularly enjoyed ('The iron grip of his fingers will be remembered by anyone who played the game of Grab when he was one of the grabbers', S. G. Lubbock recalled (1939: 12)). One or two of his earliest tales appeared in print in the 1890s, but haphazardly, and without any apparent sense of James wishing to build a literary career in this sphere. His descriptive catalogues and scholarly editions of biblical apocrypha, in contrast, were published at a prodigious rate. His first book of stories had to be actively sought out by the publisher Edward Arnold, who then asked James to pad out his initial meagre offering with any others he might have on his desk. His four collections of tales were *Ghost Stories of an Antiquary* (1904), *More Ghost Stories of an Antiquary* (1911), *A Thin Ghost and Other Stories* (1919) and *A Warning to the Curious* (1925), all then put together with four additional pieces as his *Collected Ghost Stories* (1931). Although all his collections were published after the death of Victoria, they seem quintessential products of the 'long' nineteenth century, James investing in the consolations of institutional and religious tradition against assaults of modernity, a stance only reinforced by the traumas of the Great War. James's output of ghost stories is a small body of work, often strange, donnish and obtuse, yet which have been hugely influential.

The stories were formed by the tradition of the 'club tale', which John Clute describes as 'a tale told by one man to other men in a sanctum to those of similar class and outlook, who agree to believe the story for their mutual comfort, and who themselves may (or may not) tell a tale in turn' (Clute 2023). Immediate models for James might have been Robert Louis Stevenson's *The Suicide Club* (1878) or *New Arabian Nights* (1882) or even the gentle mockery of the whole tradition long embedded in popular culture by Dickens and Wilkie Collins in Jerome K. Jerome's *After Supper Ghost Stories* (1891), produced for the *Idler* magazine in a tone of cynical despair at the formulaic ghosts of the genre (see Fiss 2023). Contemporaneous 'ghost' stories framed as tales told to a close circle include H. G. Wells's *The Time Machine* (1895) and Henry James's maddening *The Turn of the Screw* (1898). The sense that these club tales might generate more stories within the community is demonstrated in the minor trend among James's fellow dons of publishing slim story collections. His lifelong Eton and King's friend A. C. Benson was perhaps the most famous of these fellow ghost-story writers (alongside his brothers E. F. Benson, who attended King's College, and R. H. Benson, also at Eton but then Trinity College, Cambridge). The chaplain of King's College, E. G. Swain, published *The Stoneground Ghost Tales* (1912), and the Master of Jesus College, Cambridge, the Shakespearian scholar Sir Arthur Gray, published his collection, *Tedious Brief Tales of Granta and Gramarye* under the pseudonym Ingulphus in 1919.

Yet despite James's comic embrace in his stories of the figure of the fustian, recondite don or amateur antiquarian, each protagonist often hoist by his own myopic dabblings in ancient manuscripts, artefacts or in churches at dusk, his ghost stories have come to be regarded as central to the latter stages of the golden age of the English ghost story, dated by some as between 1840 and 1920, with James a pivotal figure in the transition from Victorian to Modernist ghost story forms (Smith 2010; Thurston 2012). In his important study *Supernatural Horror in Literature* (1927), H. P. Lovecraft named James as one of the four masters of the English 'Weird Tradition' (after Arthur Machen, Algernon Blackwood and Lord Dunsany). The Weird tends to eschew the conventions of the Gothic or the ghost story for something more focused on (as Lovecraft put it) 'a certain atmosphere of breathless and unexplainable dread' (1973: 15). James's stories are rarely conventional hauntings as such. But James did not return Lovecraft's favour: James despised the vulgar explicitness of the horror emerging from America, all sex and violence, which he called in his 1929 essay 'Some Remarks on Ghost Stories' 'merely nauseating' (James 2013: 414). He advocated instead for a philosophy of tales that opted for indirection, reticence and evasion.

The Englishness of James's tales has been reinforced by the belated insertion of his stories into the category of 'folk horror', a retrospective construction of uneasy works set in rural landscapes where the hubris of modernity begins to unravel after stumbling across alarming continuities of pre-modern, surreptitious old ways – paganism, witchcraft or pre-Reformation beliefs. James's most well-known tales, '"Oh, Whistle, and I'll Come to You, My Lad"' (1904) and 'A Warning to the Curious' (1925), fit this model well. The category of folk horror, typically starting out from Robin Hardy's film *The Wicker Man* (1973), has incorporated the BBC TV adaptations of M. R. James tales into its corpus, with Jonathan Miller's atmospheric version of 'Oh, Whistle', broadcast in 1968, and a subsequent chain of Christmas versions of James's tales released between 1971 and 1978 (see Scovell 2017 and Moon 2018). This television tradition was revived again by writer and actor Mark Gatiss's own Christmas adaptations, intermittently released from 2005 onwards. In 2015, Robert Macfarlane, one of the leading figures of new landscape writing in Britain, turned first to James's story 'A View from a Hill' for outlining that unnerving experience of being snared by the eeriness of the English countryside.

Although distinct in their donnish tones, it proves really quite hard to say what James's stories are ever actually *about*. James himself resolutely offers no direct avenues to outflank his cheery, chatty, clubbable persona. His autobiography, *Eton and King's* (1925), subtitled *Recollections, Mostly Trivial*, declares openly that he will avoid any sober explorations of the inner life or any po-faced passages of self-reflection, even if we get one or two inadvertent (or are they calculated?) glimpses into a disturbed dream-life and symptoms of obsessional neurosis from his boyhood years. The mask of solemn private duty and silly public sociability rarely slips. The bulk of his surviving letters, recently published, reveal startlingly little (James 2022). The tales themselves seem to conform to a gentle self-mockery of the figure of the pernickety antiquarian, that anachronistic amateur, now sidelined by professional historians yet still rootling around in obscure byways of the past. 'A considerable part of the appeal of antiquarianism,' Rosemary Sweet suggests in her study of its rise in the eighteenth century, 'was the refuge it offered from the uncertainties of contemporary life and its promise of stability and even resistance to further change' (Sweet 2004: 36). This refuge in forms and conventions of both knowledge and storytelling prompted the discerning Gothic critic David Punter to once call James's stories 'shockingly bland' (Punter 1996: 68). Others, however, find their apparent superficialities provoke a compulsion to try to tease out some hidden mechanism.

The tales often read like five-finger exercises in the artistic and moral conventions of Gothic fiction: they *are* bland in this way, in their repetition of tropes and plot devices. Typically, they involve smugly complacent protagonists who over-reach the proper bounds of knowledge and disturb from long slumber a nasty historical secret – often figured as a persecutory spectre or demonic figure woken by the hapless antiquarian prying into musty books or spaces. In 'Count Magnus' (1904), we are told of Mr Wraxall that 'his besetting fault was pretty clearly that of over-inquisitiveness' (James 2013: 64), and his longing for one last, illicit look in the mausoleum of the demonic Swedish count will be the death of him. The same happens to Parkin in '"Oh, Whistle and I'll Come to You, My Lad"', the 'young, neat and precise' (James 2013: 76) Cambridge don indulging in a spot of amateur archaeology on the Suffolk coast, who finds a pipe in the ruins and foolishly blows into it, summoning something ancient and predatory. Parkin is called 'something of an old woman' in his pedantic refusal to countenance the supernatural at the start of the story; a sure sign of a sharp metaphysical or spiritual lesson to come (James 2013: 76). Sometimes it is naked acquisitiveness that is punished, as in 'The Treasure of Abbot Thomas' (1904), or as indicated in the very title of 'A Warning to the Curious'. This later story concerns a quest to decode the whereabouts of an Anglo-Saxon crown, with fatal results for the obsessive antiquarian, Henry Long, who tracks it down to an early Christian church in Suffolk only to encounter a spectral sentinel set to guard the treasure.

When set in ancient churches on the European mainland, as in his first story and template for much that followed, 'Canon Alberic's Scrapbook' (1895), the additional Gothic framework of stolid English Protestants encountering histrionic Roman Catholic superstition is also in operation. James also has a fondness for returning to instances of lingering pre-modern belief. 'The Ash-Tree' (1904) concerns a generational curse on the family and country seat of Sir Matthew Fell, who condemned a local woman to death at the height of the witch trials. The story combines the evocation of a fearful era of English religious extremism and superstition – anathema to modern Protestantism in the wake the Civil War – with the conventions of folklore about multi-generational curses cast on aristocratic families by the populations they had driven off common land to create the private estates in the eighteenth century.

The so-called lucks and curses in folklore about aristocratic families was a strong theme in English antiquarianism (Lockhart 1938). So far, so familiar.

One of James's central themes is also quintessentially Gothic: persecution. Key Gothic texts involve relentless, sometimes supernatural pursuit by an implacable Other, from William Godwin's *Caleb Williams* (1794) to his daughter Mary Shelley's *Frankenstein* (1818). Often, the Other is a double that seeks to blacken or destroy the protagonist, as in James Hogg's *The Private Memoirs and Confessions of a Justified Sinner* (1824), Edgar Allan Poe's 'William Wilson' (1839) or Henry James's 'The Jolly Corner' (1908). In M. R. James's stories, antiquarian inquiry frequently unleashes various forms of supernatural persecution. As soon as Dennistoun is in possession of Canon Alberic's scrapbook, he seems to inherit from the jumpy and paranoid sacristan the squat, monstrous creature with 'taloned' hands and eyes of 'beast-like hate' (James 2013: 9) that somehow accompanies the manuscript. There is a similar structure in 'The Tractate Middoth' (1911) or in the lurking thing inside the hedge-maze in 'Mr. Humphreys and His Inheritance' (1911). 'Count Magnus' ends with the pursuit of Wraxall out of Sweden and across the seas to England, where the enigmatic man in the hat who has followed him the whole way runs him down to his death. 'Oh, Whistle' has James's most emblematic pursuit over the long stretch of beach, the landscape broken up by groynes that only feebly hold up the progress of the figure in pursuit along that crumbling Suffolk coast. 'The pursuer' is first envisioned as 'a figure in pale, fluttering draperies, ill-defined' (James 2013: 85), before finally rearing up out of the second bed in Parkin's hotel room.

Pursuit is everywhere in James's tales, from the runic curse issued in the Reading Room of the British Museum in 'Casting the Runes' (1911) to the drama played out in the weirdly animated image of child abduction witnessed in snapshots in 'The Mezzotint' (1904). On a lesser scale, it spills into James's 1932 essay 'The Malice of Inanimate Objects', where he speaks in a jocular but uneasy tone about those 'dreadful days, on which we have to acknowledge with gloomy resignation that our world has turned against us', and quotidian objects – 'the collar stud, the inkstand, the fire, razor, and ... the extra step on the staircase' – declare war on man's complacent ease (James 2013: 397). Mr Wraxall in 'Count Magnus' asks plaintively, 'What is this that I have done?' (James 2013: 73), and this might be the abiding question readers also ask of texts that seem to carry a repeated signature of exorbitant punishment.

One answer to this question has, of late, been to tie this structure of persecution or paranoia to repressed homosexuality. Sigmund Freud understood paranoia as a psychical mechanism of repression of the desire for the father in the male infant. To defend against this taboo, the psyche defensively reverses the valence of love for the father and turns it into the relentless hate of a persecutory figure, and pushes it from the inner psychic world to the outer material world: 'What was abolished internally returns from without' (Freud 1991: 210). This becomes a psychic structure in men who desire other men in cultures that suppress this form of sexual desire.

It was Eve Kosofsky Sedgwick, the pioneering queer theorist, who translated this mechanism of the paranoid return of the repressed into the structure of the early Gothic, arguing that the narrative of persecution, of what she termed 'homosexual panic', had its principal literary expression in British culture in the Gothic (Sedgwick 1985 – see the chapter 'Toward the Gothic: Terrorism and Homosexual Panic'). Sedgwick argues that the policing of socially fostered bonds of homosocial brotherhood became particularly fraught in the late nineteenth century, finally bubbling to the surface in the trial and imprisonment of Oscar Wilde in 1895 (see Sedgwick 1990). M. R. James's fictions, all produced in milieux of homosocial confraternities, might have felt this pressure in the exclusively male environments of Eton and King's. Descriptions of the games of Grab, young men wrestling on the hearthrug with James, take on a decidedly camp tone in this frame. And the tales might also carry all the symptoms of panic, repression and persecution precisely *because* James objected to any explicit thematic of sex in Gothic tales or ghost stories.

M. R. James and his circle were disgusted with their Cambridge contemporary, Robert Ross, the man who had already seduced Oscar Wilde by the late 1880s. James's friend E. F. Benson dunked Ross in a college fountain and Ross left Cambridge without taking his degree soon after. Later, James fought with the bisexual and markedly unrepressed John Maynard Keynes over the running of King's College. Yet James was also lifelong close friends with figures like A. C. Benson, now regarded as a closeted gay writer. Benson's early memoir of Cambridge, *From a College Window* (1906), featured a portrait of James as 'Perry', 'a *savant* with a great reputation; but he makes no parade of his works' (Benson 1909: 58). Significantly, Benson was roused to defend Perry against the accusation made by a woman friend 'that he hated women' because he closeted himself from the round of normal, polite (and implicitly heterosexual) conventions of social visiting (Benson 1909: 59). For Benson, Perry 'has a perfect right to choose his own circle', and avows that the man's college room 'doors are open day and night' to that circle of male friends (James 2013: 61). James's intense homosocial bond with the young illustrator James McBryde has been explored by all of James's biographers (including, most overtly in terms of sexuality, in Mark Gatiss's 2013 TV documentary on James). Arguably, *Ghost Stories of an Antiquary* only came into print to memorialise the young man's early death as a place to showcase his incomplete illustrations for the volume. James openly avowed his love for McBryde in the preface to the volume: 'Those who knew the artist will understand how much I wished to give a permanent form even to a fragment of his work' (James 2013: 407). But this was expressed in a form that might just as well be a passionate restatement of the homosocial and fraternal bond fostered by the ethos of Arnoldian public school education. No hanky-panky need be inferred from this tribute.

When it comes to reading this blurred space between homosocial love and homosexual panic in the fictions, that spectral creature conjured from Parkin's spare bed in 'Oh, Whistle' is a key scene. Setting out for the coast of Suffolk from his Cambridge college, Parkin objects to the idea of sharing his room with a fellow don in a prissy yet initially rather evasive way. So, is the persecutory figure that writhes out of the twisted bedclothes at the end of the story a paranoid return of the repressed from without? Might all these other monastic antiquarian obsessives be suffering this kind of displacement of desire and its persecutory return? Is this what the close homosocial bonds of these performed club tales simultaneously reveal and conceal?

Queer theory has levered open one answer to the question posed by James's male characters, 'What is this that I have done?' But even Sedgwick was clear that not all secrets are always sexual secrets. This is a perversity, as Michel Foucault might say, that we might have *implanted* in the stories with a highly specific hermeneutic of sexual suspicion. And, although this fault line between the homosocial/homosexual is undoubtedly productive for reading James's stories, I think the answer to 'What is this that I have done?' carries a much wider set of resonances that are inevitably multiple and overdetermined. His vengeful spectres are tangled knots of meaning. The masochism of James's repetitive narrative structure of complacent protagonists exorbitantly punished might bring us back round to reading these tales as expressing the guilt and anxiety that roiled under the apparently effortless expression of superiority and power of the Eton- and Cambridge-educated ruling class in the late Victorian and Edwardian period.

Critical paradigms in history and the humanities have become increasingly committed to decolonial thought and to pulling apart the inextricable material and conceptual coupling of modernity with coloniality (see Mignolo and Walsh 2018). In this context, more could be made of the violent colonial history with which M. R. James's family were entwined. As Hugh Paget outlined in 1945, the James family were among the oldest settlers of the English colony of Jamaica in the West Indies. After defeating and displacing the Spanish settlers, Richard James was the first English child born into this new settlement of English colonists, and he was later granted 400 acres of sugar plantation in 1692, which successive generations built up to over 1,000 acres, worked for vast profits by around 3,000 slaves. Paget, in his sketch of the family history, admits that he has skated over 'the important part which the James family played in the Maroon War of 1795–6' – that is, the war fought by the settlers against a slave revolt supported by escaped slaves who hid in the interior and harried the planter settlements with guerrilla tactics (Paget 1945: 272–3). The aristocrat Horace Walpole, often regarded as the founder of the English Gothic, knew the wealthy and foppish heir of this James fortune in the 1780s (the family fortune briefly very badly affected by a destructive hurricane that destroyed crops in 1781). This was because a tradition had grown up in the James family of sending back sons to be educated in Eton and either Cambridge or Oxford University before returning to the colony. The records of the large payments in reparations at the abolition of slavery in the 1830s show many beneficiaries in the intertwined Haughton and James families of Jamaica, as documented in the online database of the Centre for the Study of the Legacies of British Slavery. Yet M. R. James's father Herbert (another old Etonian) was not the direct heir of this wealth and struggled financially to send his sons to Eton and Cambridge (Cox 1983). Even so, Montague Rhodes James carried much of this family history in his very name, and his life followed in its long-established pattern of elite education.

James's stories do not involve anything as overt as plundered colonial artefacts, as in Wilkie Collins's *The Moonstone* (1868), or any number of tales of curses attached to Ancient Egyptian objects that flowered after the British occupation of Egypt in 1882 (see Luckhurst 2011). For monstrous eruptions of the Caribbean Gothic, we would need to go to the pulp horrors of Henry St Clair Whitehead (2012), written while he was an Episcopalian archdeacon of the Virgin Isles in the 1920s. But what *does* come back from the past in James's tales is everything an embedded member of the Protestant English elite might cause to shiver: pre-Reformation beliefs; Roman Catholic superstition, priestcraft and demonology; witchcraft as an emanation of Puritan panic; heterodox pursuits and satanic textual traces; pagan survivals. What is inherited carries with it curses marked by class *ressentiment*, as in the revenging witch of 'The Ash-Tree' or the poacher on enclosed land in

'The Mezzotint' who steals away the sole male heir of the family seat. The spectres glimpsed in James are thin, hungry and seemingly always implacably angry. Another answer to 'What is this that I have done?' is that these protagonists have inherited unthinkingly a narrow isthmus of privilege that is actually menaced on all sides in an era when the British Empire was at its most expansive, yet also starting to have fever dreams about decline and fall. The historian Christopher Clark (2012) has used the metaphor of Europe sleepwalking towards the catastrophe of war in 1914, and James's club tales might be regarded as cosy and conventional entertainments entirely cocooned from the vast geopolitical shifts of the era in which they were composed. The anxious tone of the stories, however, hints at uneasy dreams being constantly tugged towards nightmares of dispossession.

This is a distant reading, rather than one that focuses in on the fine grain of textual detail. But this I think is necessitated by the strange bracketing of wider experience figured in the antiquarian protagonists of James's tales and repeated in the stage of their first telling among a closed group of like-minded men. Although that frame does not often obtrude into the tales themselves – except in the form of the empty 'I' that often passes these narratives on – Darryl Jones is right to emphasise 'the profoundly *institutional* context in which James himself, and his stories, were grounded' (Jones 2018: 135). One last distant reading of the insistent masochistic imagination of these punitive ghost stories, which also reflects their evocation of the culture of the Combination-Room, might be to tie this back directly to the ethos of Eton College itself.

For much of the nineteenth century, the French referred derogatively to *le vice anglais*, meaning the distinct English predilection amongst its ruling class for flogging and being flogged. They were not entirely wrong to do so. While French schools banned corporal punishment early, flogging became intrinsic to the English public school ethos so influentially espoused by Thomas Arnold at Rugby School, and memorialised in Thomas Hughes's *Tom Brown's Schooldays* (1857). In Hughes's book, beating is a central rite of passage from errant boyhood to muscular-Christian manhood. Reports of vicious cruelty in the public school system periodically appeared in the press, but Thomas Arnold defended the use of the birch and the cane in boys up to the age of fifteen, seeing it as instilling 'a manly sense of duty' (Arnold 1845: 370). Defences commonly invoked biblical justification, as in the homiletic 'spare the rod and spoil the child'.

In his history *The English Vice* (1978), Ian Gibson calls Eton College 'the *sanctus sanctorum* of the English worshippers of the rod'

(Gibson 1978: 71). Here, floggings took place in the lower school in front of the assembled boys, the victim bent over a special whipping block, shirt-tails lifted, buttocks displayed. And although legends became attached to particularly effective schoolmasters adept at these 'executions' as they were called, there was also a system of delegating punishment beatings to senior boys, thus incorporating a sadomasochistic dynamic into the heart of the college's complex systems of hierarchy and differentiation. Winston Churchill recalled of his prep school in Ascot that 'Flogging with the birch in accordance with the Eton fashion was a great feature in its curriculum. But I am sure no Eton boy ... ever received such a cruel flogging as this headmaster was accustomed to inflict' (cited Gibson 1978: 66). Ian Gibson observed that even into the 1970s, one hundred years later, Britain was still being 'run by people who were beaten in public schools' (Gibson 1978: 94).

Eton also produced the most notorious instance of the slippage of flagellation from the instilling of moral purpose in boys into sexual fixation and fetish in young men and adults. The poet and masochistic flagellant Algernon Swinburne arrived at Eton in 1849, and was beaten relentlessly by his tutor, the Reverend James Leigh Joynes (a master also recalled by James's Eton contemporary, A. C. Benson). Swinburne went on to produce his mock-epic poem, *The Flogging-Block*, celebrating at length the sexual delights of the cane and the birch, and later contributed to the private circulation of flagellomaniac pornography, *The Whippingham Papers* (1887) (as Steven Marcus has recorded [1966], there were staggering amounts of this kind of pornography produced in Victorian Britain). By the late nineteenth century, the new science of sexology began to construct this kind of masochism as a sexual perversion, a problematic deviation or arrest in heteronormative development. There were extensive case histories in the pioneering work of both Krafft-Ebing and Havelock Ellis. Freud later explored the idea of 'moral masochism', less directly an expression of sexuality, and more a kind of relation to the world: 'The suffering itself is what matters; whether it is decreed by someone who is loved or by someone who is indifferent is of no importance. It may even be caused by impersonal powers or by circumstances' (Freud 1995: 279). In this economy, 'even the subject's destruction of himself cannot take place without libidinal pleasure' (Freud 1995: 283).

James's stories of vengeful spectres and the perversely gleeful pursuit of clueless men unto death keeps asking of the punishment that rains down on their bewildered protagonists, 'What is this that I have done?' The repetitive structures of his stories cloak the sources of their compulsion and the affable authorial persona only redoubles this occlusion.

But if we look harder at the invisible frames of these tales, their ghosts and spectres can acquire the colour and texture of the troubled histories they seem to work so hard to conceal of an old world on the brink of a precipitate fall from grace.

Works Cited

Arnold, Thomas. 'On the Discipline of Public Schools', in *The Miscellaneous Works of Thomas Arnold*. London: Fellowes, 1845, pp. 361–79.

Benson, A. C. *From a College Window*. London: Smith and Elder, 1909.

Clark, Christopher. *The Sleepwalkers: How Europe Went to War in 1914*. Harmondsworth: Penguin, 2012.

Clute, John. 'Club Story'. *The Encyclopedia of Science Fiction*. https://sf-encyclopedia.com/entry/club_story (last accessed 7 January 2025).

Cox, Michael. *M. R. James: An Informal Portrait*. Oxford: Oxford University Press, 1983.

Fiss, Laura Kasson. *The Idler's Club: Humour and Mass Readership from Jerome K. Jerome to P. G. Wodehouse*. Edinburgh: Edinburgh University Press, 2023.

Freud, Sigmund. 'Psychoanalytic Notes upon an Autobiographical Account of a Case of Paranoia' (1911), in *Penguin Freud Library*, vol. 9: *Case Histories 2*. Harmondsworth: Penguin, 1991, pp. 129–223.

———. 'The Economic Problem of Masochism', in Margaret Ann Fitzpatrick Hanly (ed.), *Essential Papers on Masochism*. New York: New York University Press, 1995, pp. 274–85.

Gibson, Ian. *The English Vice: Beating, Sex and Shame in Victorian England and After*. London: Duckworth, 1978.

James, M. R. *Eton and King's: Recollections, Mostly Trivial, 1875–1925*. London: Williams and Norgate, 1926.

———. *Collected Ghost Stories*, edited by Darryl Jones. Oxford: Oxford World's Classics, 2013.

———. 'A Warning to the Curious' (1925), in *Collected Ghost Stories*, edited by Darryl Jones. Oxford: Oxford World's Classics, 2013, pp. 343–57.

———. 'Canon Alberic's Scrapbook' (1895), in *Collected Ghost Stories*, edited by Darryl Jones. Oxford: Oxford World's Classics, 2013, pp. 3–13.

———. 'Casting the Runes' (1911), in *Collected Ghost Stories*, edited by Darryl Jones. Oxford: Oxford World's Classics, 2013, pp. 145–64.

———. 'Count Magnus' (1904), in *Collected Ghost Stories*, edited by Darryl Jones. Oxford: Oxford World's Classics, 2013, pp. 63–75.

———. 'Mr. Humphreys and His Inheritance' (1911), in *Collected Ghost Stories* edited by Darryl Jones. Oxford: Oxford World's Classics, 2013, pp. 197–220.

———. '"Oh, Whistle, and I'll Come to You, My Lad"' (1904), in *Collected Ghost Stories*, edited by Darryl Jones. Oxford: Oxford World's Classics, 2013, pp. 76–93.

———. 'The Ash-Tree' (1904), in *Collected Ghost Stories*, edited by Darryl Jones. Oxford: Oxford World's Classics, 2013, pp. 35–47.

———. 'The Mezzotint' (1904), in *Collected Ghost Stories*, edited by Darryl Jones. Oxford: Oxford World's Classics, 2013, pp. 24–34.

———. 'The Tractate Middoth' (1911), in *Collected Ghost Stories*, edited by Darryl Jones. Oxford: Oxford World's Classics, 2013, pp. 129–44.

———. 'The Treasure of Abbot Thomas' (1904), in *Collected Ghost Stories*, edited by Darryl Jones. Oxford: Oxford World's Classics, 2013, pp. 94–110.

———. *Casting the Runes: The Letters of M. R. James*, edited by Jane Mainley-Piddock. London: Unbound, 2022.

Jones, Darryl. 'M. R. James', in Scott Brewster and Luke Thurston (eds), *The Routledge Handbook of the Ghost Story*. Abingdon: Routledge, 2018, pp. 134–41.

Lockhart, J. G. *Curses, Lucks and Talismans*. London: Geoffrey Bles, 1938.

Lovecraft, H. P. *Supernatural Horror in Literature*. New York: Dover, 1973.

Lubbock, S. G. *A Memoir of Montague Rhodes James*. Cambridge: Cambridge University Press, 1939.

Luckhurst, Roger. *The Mummy's Curse: The True Story of a Dark Fantasy*. Oxford: Oxford University Press, 2011.

Macfarlane, Robert. 'The Eeriness of the English Countryside'. *The Guardian*, 10 April 2015. https://www.theguardian.com/books/2015/apr/10/eeriness-english-countryside-robert-macfarlane (last accessed 7 January 2025).

Marcus, Steven. 1966. *The Other Victorians: A Study of Sexuality and Pornography in Mid-Nineteenth Century England*. London: Weidenfeld & Nicholson, 1966.

Mignolo, Walter D. and Catherine E. Walsh. *On Decoloniality: Concepts Analytics Praxis*. Durham, NC: Duke University Press, 2018.

Moon, Jim. 'M. R. James: The Presence of More Formidable Visitants'. *Folk Horror Revival: Field Studies*, 2nd edn. Durham: Wyrd Harvest Press, 2018, pp. 305–27.

Paget, Hugh. 'The Early History of the Family of James of Jamaica'. *Jamaican Historical Review*, vol. 1, 1945, pp. 260–73.

Parry, Robert Lloyd. 'An Invitation to the Chit-Chat', in *Ghosts of the Chit-Chat*. Dublin: Swan River, 2021, pp. xi–xxv.

Pfaff, Richard. W. 'James, Montague Rhodes'. *Oxford Dictionary of National Biography* (2004), online. www.oxforddnb.com (last accessed 28 June 2023).

Punter, David. *The Literature of Terror: The Modern Gothic*. London: Longman, 1996.

Rowell, Geoffrey. *The Club of 'Nobody's Friends' 1800–2000: A Memoir on its 200th Anniversary*. Edinburgh: Pentland, 2000.

Scovell, Adam. *Folk Horror: Hours Dreadful and Things Strange*. Leighton Buzzard: Auteur, 2017.

Sedgwick, Eve Kosofsky. *Between Men: English Literature and Male Homosocial Desire*. New York: Columbia University Press, 1985.

———. *Epistemology of the Closet*. Berkeley: University of California Press, 1990.

Smith, Andrew. *The Ghost Story 1840–1920: A Cultural History*. Manchester: Manchester University Press, 2010.

Sweet, Rosemary. *Antiquaries: The Discovery of the Past in Eighteenth-Century Britain*. London: Hambledon, 2004.

Thurston, Luke. *Literary Ghosts from the Victorians to Modernism*. Abingdon: Routledge, 2012.
Whitehead, Henry S. *Voodoo Tales: The Ghost Stories of Henry S. Whitehead*. London: Wordsworth, 2012.

Part IV
Places

Chapter 20

Haunted Landscapes
Emma McEvoy

Haunting in Victorian ghost stories tends to take place inside rather than outside. Ghosts are particularly drawn to the domestic space, the realm where the stories are most likely to be read, and they gravitate (or levitate) towards bedrooms especially. However, notwithstanding the general orientation towards domestic interiors, there are some significant instances of stories which set their hauntings outdoors. These are often tales in which witnesses (usually the tellers of the story or the inset story) have strayed into strange locales on which they look with a dispassionate eye. Frequently the stories are concerned with those who are déclassé, scapegoated or dispossessed, cast out in a place that is understood to be marginal or even beyond the social realm. Such stories are often concerned with wider social structures and economies. In the countryside more than in domestic houses, people from different classes and occupations, with radically different outlooks, can be brought together. The urbanite meets the rural dweller, gentry encounter labourers, those from industrial and agricultural economies eye each other askance, and the imperialist and the colonised come into contact. In the Victorian ghost story, landscape often functions, to use an anthropological term, as a contact zone where differences are explored.

The haunted landscapes of the Victorian ghost story are intimately linked with the sociopolitics of their day. However vacant they may seem to be, they are political and social spaces, owned, shaped, adapted and fought over; those set in England testify to the widespread and very recent changes taking place within and around them. These are landscapes based on fault lines. They may, as Charlotte Riddell's 'Nut Bush Farm' (1882) does, speak of lost rural economies, or, like Amelia B. Edwards's 'Was it an Illusion?' (1881), consider the depredation of industry and the transformation of rural communities, or, like Dickens's 'No. 1 Branch Line: The Signal-Man' (1866), focus on the incursion of the railway, or they may, as is the case with Bithia Mary Croker's tales

'If You See Her Face' and 'To Let', from the 1893 collection *"To Let"*, have much to say about British imperialism. Problematic, questioning and sometimes radically emptied out, the landscapes featured in this chapter also respond, indirectly, to new ideas about the natural world and our relation to it, in the light of insights into the 'deep time' of the earth's processes, revealed by geology, the discoveries of extinct species in the realm of palaeontology, and the 'laws' of life emerging from the biological sciences.

A landscape, by definition, is a site viewed through the perspective of art. Deriving from theatre originally, the term made its way to the field of visual art and then into the literary lexicon. In literature, landscapes may be seen through a number of lenses, many of which come with much cultural baggage. They might be envisaged through a mode with an exceptionally long literary history (such as the pastoral) or one more recent (the Gothic), one deriving originally from philosophical enquiry (like the Sublime) or art theory (such as the picturesque). Typically, the haunted landscapes of Victorian ghost stories are contested sites which draw on a number of traditions of representation, appropriating and challenging them. Frequently, these modes are forced into fruitfully problematic disjunction, either through their narrators' perplexed telling or the interpolation of other voices, or a mixture of both. The stories considered here question constructions such as the merry pastoral of old England, the Radcliffean Sublime and Providential (specifically Christianised) Nature, and are involved in prolonged and painstaking debate with the writing of the Romantic poets, in particular William Wordsworth.

The majority of the haunted landscapes of Victorian ghost stories are to be found in the British Isles, with many locales distinctly over-represented across the genre. As Jarlath Killeen points out, 'areas deemed part of the Celtic world' prove to be 'particularly potent sources of horror for the English imagination' (Killeen 2009: 91). Killeen notes that Ireland, Scotland and Wales 'operated as spaces harbouring the atavistic [...] spaces on the edge of the known world, straddling this world and the next, and it was easily imagined that weird and terrible things could happen there' (Killeen 2009: 92). Cornwall also occupied a distinct place within the British imagination. Joan Passey points to nineteenth-century perceptions of the Cornish 'as a "mysterious race", distinct from the surrounding English race [...] separate geographically, culturally and historically [their] difference [...] exaggerated by their ancientness' (Passey 2023: 1–2), and notes that for many Victorian writers (as well as those writing later), 'Cornwall is the end of the land, the end of time and the end of civility' (Passey 2023: 3). However, the haunted landscapes of

Victorian ghost stories are not only to be found in areas associated with the 'Celtic' world. They are also situated throughout England, particularly in places considered marginal, unproductive or those associated with pre-industrial economies. Regions where there is an acknowledged survival of folklore are most likely to harbour haunted landscapes.

In this chapter, I look at tales written between the 1850s and the first decade of the twentieth century. Most of the stories are set in England but three of them look beyond its borders, with one set in the Arctic and two in India. I am interested in the way these stories re-examine ideas about Nature, the immanence of the divine in the material world, the human relation to the natural world and human materiality. I am also interested in the more political aspects of haunted landscapes: the ways that they relate to issues of class, frame debates about ownership and dispossession, or problematise imperial logic. I conclude by looking backwards from M. R. James's *Ghost Stories of an Antiquary* (1904) to consider the indebtedness of twentieth- and twenty-first-century folk horror to the Victorian ghost story.

'The Old Nurse's Story'

Gaskell's 'The Old Nurse's Story' (1852) exemplifies the classic geography of the ghost tale, recounting a journey taken (a generation earlier) by the narrator with her charge, away from the known world and a cosy, lower-middle-class life towards the unfamiliar, the hostile and the threatening. The nurse and the child, Rosamond, are taken beyond 'all signs of a town, or even a village', and find themselves 'inside the gates of a large wild park', where the 'old oaks' are 'all white and peeled with age', the 'trees dragged against the walls' of the great house, and the carriageway is untended and 'moss-covered' (Gaskell 2003: 3). The story ventures further still, moving beyond the house into the wilds of the Cumberland Fells that lie behind and above it. The landscape of the Fells is intimately linked to the tale's themes of dispossession and anomalous class positioning. It is a space beyond the social world of the great house, where the unacknowledged daughter of the beautiful, haughty Maude is fostered in a farmer's cottage. Here, eventually, both mother and daughter die. Ejected from the great house by the old lord, the child freezes to death and Maude goes mad.

The haunted landscape of the Fells is related through a number of traditions of representation. Implicitly, it is compared to the landscapes which feature in the Gothic romances of an earlier generation. However, where the mountains for novelists such as Ann Radcliffe are a source of the sublime, a lifting up towards God, Gaskell's Fells are a forbidding and dangerous place. Neither does the landscape sit comfortably within the particular version of the picturesque customised for Victorian fiction. Although the nurse avails herself of some of its terms, pointing out that the air is health-giving, 'fresh' and 'sharp' (7), and the snow 'white' and 'dazzling' (8), she also notes, with uncharacteristic understatement, that the Fells are 'bleak, and bare enough' (7). This is not merely a 'view', but a harsh environment in which life is difficult and the economy unproductive. As one of the characters points out, what killed the child ghost was not her violent grandfather but 'the frost and the cold' (15).

In Gaskell's story, issues about Christian behaviour and duty are interrogated through the depiction of the relation between the landscape and the ghosts. The Fells are presented as a Christian landscape, more specifically as a Christmas landscape. The tale takes place in the weeks around Christmas and the child under a bush in the snow evokes depictions of the Christ child. The references to the shepherd bringing Miss Rosamond back home and to the ghost asking for shelter reinforce the Christian reading. However, the landscape both exceeds and problematises this perspective, most notably in the image, presented twice, of the mother and child beneath a holly tree. The image is redolent of the Madonna and child, particularly as the holly is associated in numerous traditional carols with the blood of Christ and the Christian covenant. The holly, however, also has pagan resonances. Gaskell's tale plays with these contrasting traditions, presenting a twisted Christian image that is suggestive of both the nativity and the pietà, in which the mother under the holly is 'all crazy and smiling' and 'nursing a dead child – with a 'terrible mark on its right shoulder' (15). The two very different modes of reading this landscape leave the readers, as well as the characters in the tale, with a keen interpretative dilemma. Are the mother and child vulnerable figures who need Christian charity or threatening white ladies of folklore? Are they to be welcomed in or kept out in the landscape to which they seem to belong?

'No. 1 Branch Line: The Signal-Man'

Charles Dickens's 'No. 1 Branch Line: The Signal-Man' also features a haunted landscape in which previous certainties are dislodged and different rules operate. It is both a disturbing and disturbed place, formed by the inroads of the industrial economy into the rural world. The story is set in an 'extremely deep, and unusually precipitate' railway cutting ('made through a clammy stone') with a tunnel and a signalman's hut, where the conscientious railway worker of the title is tormented by what he insists are prophetic visions of victims of crashes.

Like Gaskell's, Dickens's landscape signifies simultaneously at a number of levels. It is realistic, a credible depiction of the cutting with its 'dripping-wet wall of jagged stone, excluding all view but a strip of sky' (Dickens 1894: 313). However, the 'solitary and dismal' place is also relayed in Gothicised terms: it is a 'great dungeon', its 'massive architecture' described as 'barbarous' and 'depressing', the 'gloomy red light' redolent of descriptions of hell (313). The story then makes use of a further register, as the landscape is presented in suggestively pre-Christian terms: 'So little sunlight ever found its way to this spot, that it had an earthy deadly smell; and so much cold wind rushed through it, that it struck chill to me, as if I had left the natural world' (313). The term 'natural' here functions not only in opposition to the industrial but simultaneously to the *super*natural. The cutting is described in terms reminiscent of the landscape of myth, particularly that associated with prophecy. One of the most obvious parallels is with Aeneas' descent to the underworld and his encounter with the Cumaean Sibyl in the sixth book of Virgil's *Aeneid*. The cutting is an updated version of the Sybil's cave, a thin place, in which contact may be had between the spirit world and that of mortals. The overlay of the mythic onto the realistic and Gothic-inflected description lends credence to the signalman's story, providing a counterpoint to the narrator's (troubled) rationalism.

'Was it an Illusion?'

Amelia B. Edwards's 'Was it an Illusion?' also has a despoiled industrialised landscape at its centre. Here too, the haunting takes place before a middle-class observer who is a stranger to the area and its mores. The haunted landscape is encountered at the very beginning of the tale and presented as without value, either aesthetic (in the eyes of the onlooker) or economic. An 'open meadow' lost in 'a fleecy bank of fog' (Edwards 2003: 241), it exists on the threshold of other areas but forms no part of any of them. It is entered via a 'barren slope' where there are the remains of a 'deserted mine' (240), skirted by the parkland of the squire and terminated by the 'smoke-grimed hamlet' of Pit End, with its 'gaunt buildings clustered at the mouths of the coalpits' (243). Although geographically at the centre of the area that is the locale of the tale, this is a marginal place, outside the different lives lived in the area. It is the path not taken by any except the imperfectly sketched murder victim at the centre of the story, the one seeking to punish him for taking it, and those who (like the narrator) are lost.

Behind the tale, the subverted narratives of Romantic childhood loom large. Symbolically and metonymically, the haunted landscape relates to the economic and social exclusion of the murder victim, the illegitimate son of the schoolmaster, described by one of the characters as 'stupid, wilful, and ill brought-up [...] as backward as a child of five years old' (253). A boy 'with a passion for fishing' and 'a habit of slipping away at school-hours' (254), his ghost is glimpsed as a shadow outside the schoolyard, as well as on the path on which he takes his final walk, fishing rod in hand, pursued by the father who is to murder him (and who, interestingly and somewhat paradoxically, is still alive when his spectre appears). This is a story in which Wordsworth's 'The Idiot Boy' is not allowed to roam free and has no parent anxious about him. Wordsworth's 'There was a Boy' is perhaps the poem with which the story is most intertextually linked. The tale reads almost as a dark parody of its more sublime aspects. Unlike the child in that poem, the schoolmaster's son is not buried in the churchyard. Instead of the image of an 'uncertain Heaven received / Into the bosom of the steady lake' entering 'unawares' into the mind of a boy, the story presents the reader with the image of a boy's corpse, pegged down by a pitchfork into the mud of the drained tarn (Wordsworth 1984: 134, ll. 24–5 and l. 22).

Edwards's story is not merely interested in the landscape as representative of the boy and his relation to the society he is unwilling and/or unable to inhabit, it is also interested in the landscape itself and the relationship of humans to it. The landscape is a forsaken world, lost by the economically active, or those who only value the grounds they own, or who, like the narrator, find it unprepossessing because of their own cultural prejudices. It is a landscape of industrial despoilation, as is made terribly apparent at the climax of the tale when, as the result of a fissure linked to mining activity, the tarn drains away. At the climax of the tale, the tarn is transformed into 'an oblong, irregular basin of blackest slime, with here and there a sullen pool' (251) into which the miners venture, 'black with clotted slime' (252). As well as an example of 'discovery' that 'murderers always believe [...] impossible' (254), a stunning image of the bringing to light of that which was hidden, the image of the muddied tarn with the corpse of the boy brings together the complementarily destructive forces – cultural, social, political – that run through the story. The image links parental neglect and abuse, a boy with no voice, a punitive unimaginative education system, absentee landlordism, the industrial economy and environmental destruction.

'Nut Bush Farm'

Much of the power of 'Was it an Illusion?' derives from its juxtaposition of the haunted landscape associated with the boy's former freedom with the site of absence, destruction and abjection where his corpse lies. In Charlotte Riddell's 'Nut Bush Farm', the spot where the corpse of Mr Hascot lies has very different associations. It is a 'deep excavation' 'that from 'top to bottom [...] was clothed with nut trees [which] grew on every side, and in thick, almost impenetrable masses' (Riddell 2009: 80–1). Hascot's ghost is fond of walking along a beech tree walk, the straight line indicative of his practicality and unswerving moral rectitude. The landscape in which his body is found is, by contrast, exuberant, riotous, fertile.

If Edwards's 'Was it an Illusion?' keeps the Wordsworthian vision dear, 'Nut Bush Farm' is decidedly ambivalent on the subject of Nature. Although the landscape of Riddell's tale is one in which old economies and old-fashioned pastoral are enshrined, it is also fey, possessing some of the threatening overtones of Shakespeare's *A Midsummer Night's Dream*. In a remarkable passage, the narrator wakes in the middle of the night and looks 'out over a landscape' preternaturally bright, 'bathed in the clear light of a most lovely moon' (79). This is a world transformed, for which the narrator resorts to the language of magic, telling of 'the full charm and beauty of night [...] a mystic spell on tree and field and stream' (79), the 'fairy light and [...] fairy scene' (79) and the 'witching glamour' (80). It is a world out of linear time, through which the narrator passes in a state of suspended and obscure emotion ('still the same secret feeling' [80]), where he is granted insights into cyclical time. Reaching the nut bushes, he starts thinking of

> the boys who must have gone nutting there, of all the nests birds had built in the branches so closely interlaced, of the summers' suns which had shone full and strong upon that mass of foliage, of the winters' snows which had lain heavy on twig and stem and happed [*sic*] the strong roots in a warm covering of purest white. (81)

Despite provoking a 'keen and subtle pleasure' (79), the landscape is ultimately a disturbing one, so much so that the narrator declares that afterward he 'cannot endure the silvery gleam of the queen of night' (82). In Riddell's tale, the nocturnal jaunt enables the narrator to lose his diurnal self, access his intuitions and liberate his stifled imagination. These gains, however, are all associated with death. The seeming idyll granted to the narrator before the nut bushes is interrupted by his sudden realisation of how the murder could have been committed and where the corpse is. Rather than a curtailment of the magic of the landscape, the moment of envisaging death and killing is intimately linked with it. The reader is not presented with a vision of 'Nature', providing and providential, but a landscape emptied out, with no divine overseeing. It might be fecund, but it is ultimately uncaring. Moreover, it is opposed to human cultivation. The nut bushes grow 'luxuriantly' (81) but they 'threatened ere long to push their way between the trunks of the great trees, which were the beauty and the pride of my lovely farm' (81). This is not a place where humans are succoured; here they moulder. The nut bushes thrive and hide corpses. The merry greenwood is a place where unwary travellers may meet their death.

'decomposed beyond recognition'

Many ghost stories of the period point up the opposition of the natural world to the human world, associating the landscape not only with death, but more broadly with fragmentation of the human. The image of the transformed tarn with the corpse, 'decomposed beyond recognition', in 'Was it an Illusion?' suggests revenge by the earth as water eats away at the body of the boy. In R. H. Benson's 'Father Macclesfield's Tale' (1907) too, the depiction of the human in the landscape is far from reassuring. The tale draws on a tradition that sees the outside world functioning as a liminal place between life and death which provides the means for a spirit to depart (as in Dinah Mulock's 'The Last House in C_ Street', 1856). In Benson's tale, the lingering in the mortal world of a 'convinced infidel' (Benson 2003: 459) is signalled in a series of incidents that take place on the laurel walk outside his house. First, his likeness becomes manifest, only to disappear shortly afterwards, leaving the disturbance of some leaves as testimony to his presence. Then a strange hare is seen. Finally, 'a little column of leaves, twisting and turning and dropping and picking up again in the wind' is linked to the departed man's presence (464). Where is the dead man? Is he part of the landscape? Has his materialism condemned him to a material but non-sentient afterlife?

In many stories, the association of the landscape with the post-human is not merely developed at the level of plot but also insinuated at the level of description. In Gaskell's 'The Old Nurse's Story', for example, the landscape is no mere pathetic fallacy, illustrative of the more terrifying aspects of the ghostly figures. Rather than the landscape taking on their characteristics, the story's characters assume aspects of the landscape. The terms in which the landscape is described prove slippery, contagious and too mobile, effecting disturbing category shifts. Its language of whiteness and cold is extended to the human figures within it, alarmingly not only to the child ghost but also to the endangered young Rosamond. In the landscape which she describes as 'pretty and white' (Gaskell 2003: 10), she becomes 'white' and 'stiff' and 'cold' (10). A similar language of shifting deathly whiteness can be found in Arthur Conan Doyle's 'The Captain of the "Pole-star"' (1883), a tale of Arctic exploration, where British sailors and the story's narrator become aware of a strange, amorphous presence, a 'wreath of mist' (Conan Doyle 2003: 299) outside the ship. As Gaskell's child ghost both inhabits and is an embodiment of the landscape of the Fells, this spectre too is uncannily allied to the 'expanse of spotless white' (288), the 'great motionless ice fields [...] with their weird hummocks and fantastic pinnacles' (291). Likewise, in R. S. Hawker's 'The Botathen Ghost' (1867), the ghost who haunts the Cornish landscape seems to emanate from it. Its signifiers become hers; she has a 'pale and stony face' and 'strange and misty hair' (Hawker 2003: 69).

Margaret Oliphant's 'The Open Door'

Whereas in some tales the alterity of the landscape undermines or at least unsettles the concept of a God-governed world, in others the otherness of the natural world is made the means of gesturing to the truth which lies beyond it. In Margaret Oliphant's 'The Open Door' (1882), the portrayal of the natural world as unmeaning creates the opposing possibility: another world full of meaning. Like many of the stories discussed in this essay, Oliphant's 'The Open Door' carefully distinguishes between the landscape of haunting and other landscapes. In this case, a distinction is made between the landscape travelled by the narrator and his companions, and the space which the ghost inhabits. The ghost hunters move through a 'darkness [...] so complete that all marks, as of trees or paths, disappeared' (Oliphant 2021: 97). Their feet sink 'noiselessly into the slippery grass' (97), they hear 'some rustle in the dead leaves, or creeping creature', and the hoot of an owl on 'the still brooding of the air' (98). As in Gaskell's and Dickens's tales, the language of an outmoded Gothic is summoned up only to be superseded by a new, more compelling mode of horror. The narrator points out that such traditionally blood-freezing phenomena are relatively comforting in that they act as 'signs of the livingness of nature' (97). The truly scary landscape in 'The Open Door' is one of profound emptiness. The tale provides a (literally) brilliant deconstruction of the haunted house, compared with which the former Gothic mode is homely. The spectre stands howling on the other side of a 'vacant blank doorway, blazing full of light' (106). This is a frame without an interior, a 'way of entrance, unnecessary, leading to nothing' (110). Here the spirit's question is not answered, and his appeal is not met until the clergyman converts the open door into a portal from which the spirit of the tortured and torturing spirit can depart.

'ghosts outside Europe'

The character Colvin in Perceval Landon's 'Thurnley Abbey' (1908) asserts that there are 'few ghosts outside Europe – few, that is, that a white man can see' (Landon 2003: 470). However, some Victorian ghost stories – particularly those written later in the century – do feature ghosts beyond Europe, and such spirits become more prevalent as the age of exploration and colonialism goes on. The ghost of 'The Captain of the "Pole-star"' is certainly one that a number of white men see, not least because she is a Cornish ghost. In Conan Doyle's story, there are no humans – living or dead – other than the British, and no stories other than theirs. The Arctic is a blank slate on which the benighted love story between the two outsize players can be written, a playground for an extra-territorial enactment of the Cornish sublime.

By contrast, the stories in Bithia Mary Croker's 1893 collection *"To Let"* are concerned with the colonial encounter and feature Indian as well as British ghosts. Croker's India-set stories have some memorable landscapes, seen here through the eyes of expatriates. In 'The Khitmatgar' (1893), the drunkard and cheat Jackson meets his end shortly after comparing the 'great, barren, scorched compound' with his memories of the (English) 'cool green park at home' (110). Reminiscent of some of the troubling landscapes of J. Sheridan Le Fanu's work is the encroaching, dark and 'feverish' (128) landscape which reaches right to the door of 'The Dâk Bungalow at Dakor' (1893) in the story of that name and contributes to its 'forlorn, desolate, dismal' atmosphere (125). Neither of the stories mentioned above, however, features *haunted* landscapes; these are to be found in the title story, 'To Let', and 'If You See Her Face'.

The haunted landscapes of Croker's tales are intensely politicised spaces, where British and Indian figures interact. The space in 'If You See Her Face' is a garden notable for its beauty and its fecundity, with 'long shady walks paved with white marble, immense bushes of heliotrope and myrtle, delicate palms, fine mango trees, peach trees, and orange trees' (Croker 1893: 190). The garden's elegance is associated and juxtaposed with both 'the bare, desolate, barren country that lay outside its walls' (190) and the 'hidden atrocities, and crimes that had been done here' (191), in particular the Tiger Rajah's torture and disfiguring of a dancing girl. The clearly delimited landscape enables the story to make a parallel between different systems and times. It both testifies to a past economy of luxury, tyranny and arbitrary control over life associated with the Tiger Rajah and highlights present iniquities performed by the administrators of the British Raj, in particular Daniel Gregson. The garden is central to what Preeshita Biswas calls 'the intellectual and spatial displacements of the imperial agents' (Biswas 2021), the fixedness of place being the means for the victim of the past to visit the oppressor of the present. The ghost of the nautch girl dances here; seeing her, Gregson, seated in the open hall of the palace, meets his death.

In Croker's 'To Let', the haunting starts on a verandah 'fully twelve feet wide, roofed with zinc [which] overhung a precipice of a thousand feet' (12). Here, the horrified narrator and her sister-in-law witness a tragedy of the previous generation. A young man rides onto the verandah to visit his fiancée on the eve of their marriage, but the night is stormy; the horse slips and he plunges to his death. The verandah is presented as a liminal zone in the story, situated between the house (an overdetermined European space) and the garden (associated with the native servants), as well as the British-owned property and the wider landscape. The precipitation of the young man into the landscape below breaches both these boundaries. What follows reinforces the sense of the ineffectiveness of colonial boundaries in relation to the reality of the physical environment.

If the story of the death of a would-be bridegroom and the suicide of the fiancée is a familiar European folk narrative, Croker adds to it a coda that has much to say about issues of belonging within a specifically Indian setting. The haunting continues within the broader landscape, as a line of ghostly native servants brings the young man's corpse up the hill and, ultimately, into the house. Earlier in the story this landscape is introduced as a 'glorious view, across a valley, far away, to the snowy range' (12), which is disconcertingly valued in monetary terms ('we said to one another that "the verandah alone was worth half the rent"' [13]). However, at the tale's climax, the landscape is not conveyed as a European landscape and, indeed, is barely the object of the narrator's gaze. Not only is she not able to see the landscape, but she only witnesses the scene played out upon it through the actions of the Indian servants. She sees 'lights moving rapidly to and fro, evidently in search of something', and hears 'a low buzzing murmur' as the corpse is found, followed by 'the "hum-hum" of coolies carrying a burden', noting that '[n]earer and nearer the lights and sounds came [...] Many steps and many torches – faint blue torches held by invisible hands' (32). Themes of belonging and foreignness are to the fore in this scene. The details of their humming and the invisibility of their hands naturalise the labourers' relation to the land. Their certainty in the darkness is contrasted with the fearfulness of the British women standing above, their sure-footedness implicitly contrasted with the fatal ineptness of the fallen fiancé. As Biswas points out, by the end of the tale the narrator and her sister-in-law 'are made to realize that they are irredeemably "other" to and othered by the Indian landscape'.

Folk Horror

The landscape of Croker's 'To Let' and the political claims made of it are underwritten by ideas about Nature and naturalness. Those of M. R. James's collection *Ghost Stories of an Antiquary* (1904) are, by contrast, profoundly human-made places, which have been shaped by human activity – not merely of the recent past but of that more distant. They are powerful locales which are capable of carrying the past into the present. The underlying landscape in '"Oh, Whistle, and I'll Come to You, My Lad"' is a medieval site whose patterns and orientation are etched on everything around it, from the present-day Burnstow to Professor Parkins's bedroom at the Globe inn. James's landscapes seem to have an agency of their own, usually malignant. They are places in which the past is not merely embedded but embodied. The fusion of history and the landscape within James's landscapes is such that in 'The Ash-Tree', the witch has become one with the tree. Investigation of such landscapes frequently provides the trigger for calamitous events. When Parkins excavates the landscape round the ruins of the Templar church, it very nearly destroys him. As Gabriel Moshenska points out, this is a 'distinctively archaeological version of the Freudian *unheimlich* or uncanny' in which 'excavation and transgression, revelation and the uncanny' are connected (Moshenska 2012: 1198, 1199).

It is certainly possible to claim, as many have, that M. R. James is the progenitor of modern folk horror. Stories such as '"Oh, Whistle, and I'll Come to You, My Lad"' and 'The Ash-Tree' are notable for that 'deep mapping of place, connecting layers of history, ecology, folklore and memory' that, as Andrew Hurley (2019) writes, are characteristic of both nature writing and folk horror. As Robert Macfarlane points out, like later creators of folk horror, 'James looked forwards, and saw the English countryside not only as a place of beauty, calm and succour, but also as a green and deeply unpleasant land' (Macfarlane 2015). James, however, was not the first to present this vision.

The fusion of folklore and landscape, so characteristic of folk horror, can be found in the stories discussed in this essay too. As Catherine Spooner points out, in relation to Gaskell's 'northern Gothic', place is 'constructed not just through landscape, but also through the accumulation of legends and folklore that inform local identity' (Spooner 2018: 29). It is not only M. R. James's Count Magnus who appears at a traditional folkloric site of haunting (in this case, a crossroads); the ghost of Riddell's 'Nut Bush Farm' lurks by a bridge, the Botathen ghost frequents standing stones, and that of 'Was it an Illusion?' has a fondness for boundaries – all traditional sites of folkloric haunting. Similarly, the witch of 'The Ash-Tree' is not the first malignant figure to emerge from a landscape which she has become part of. In the stories of Gaskell, Hawker and Conan Doyle too, we see murderous white ladies unsettlingly at one with their environments.

The tales discussed in this chapter interweave folklore, history and violence to stunning effect and, notably, they insist on the agency of the landscape. In Edwards and Hawker's tales in particular, this sense of agency is linked to the ancientness of the landscape. The corpse in the tarn in 'Was it an Illusion?' testifies not merely to the industrial present but also to prehistory and is reminiscent of the bog bodies found over the centuries in Lancashire and Cheshire. Edward Cust, writing about such a body found at Leasowe, Cheshire in 1864, claimed for it (wrongly in this case) 'an antiquity beyond any existing parchments', writing that it provided evidence for 'pre-historical, aboriginal Britain' (Giles 2020: 38). Arguably, the treatment of the boy's corpse in Edwards's story hints at supposed ancient custom and ritual, suggesting atavistic and disturbing tendencies in people of the modern world. In Hawker's 'The Botathen Ghost' the landscape is a particularly potent force that seems to bestow ancientness on a ghost of a young girl who has only recently died. She becomes a pagan presence, to be dispatched not merely with prayer but with a staff made of rowan, a tree that traditionally provides protection against evil spirits. In these stories, the embodying of folkloric elements within the landscape not only creates a sense of uncanniness but also provides a glimpse of alterity, suggesting that in such places, a radically different, but somehow consonant, logic operates.

Many of the concerns that characterise twentieth- and twenty-first-century folk horror are to be found in the stories discussed in this essay. The tales examine the, sometimes terrifying, self-sufficiency of the Earth.

They focus on the materiality of humankind, insisting on the frailty of human physicality. They point to the precariousness of the boundary between the sensate and insensate, the thinking and non-thinking. They gesture to atavism in far-flung places left behind from modernity, where folk belief is embedded within the land, ready to erupt violently and transport the past back into the present. Here, we encounter a sense of otherness. Modern rational belief proves to be contingent; Christian belief is usurped by pagan practice. Folk horror is no twentieth-century invention. It begins with the work of writers such as Gaskell, Dickens, Hawker, Riddell, Edwards, Oliphant, Conan Doyle and Croker.

Works Cited

Benson, R. H. 'Father Macclesfield's Tale', in Michael Cox and R. A. Gilbert (eds), *The Oxford Book of Victorian Ghost Stories*. Oxford: Oxford University Press, 2003, pp. 459–65.

Biswas, Preeshita. 'Visions: "If You See Her Face You Die": Orientalist Gothic and Colonialism in Bithia Croker's Indian Ghost Stories'. *ABO: Interactive Journal for Women in the Arts, 1640–1830*, vol. 11, no. 2, 2021, Article 3.

Croker, Bithia Mary. 'To Let', in *"To Let"*. London: Chatto & Windus, 1893, pp. 1–38.

———. 'If You See Her Face', in *"To Let"*. London: Chatto & Windus, 1893, pp. 181–94.

———. 'The Dâk Bungalow at Dakor', in *"To Let"*. London: Chatto & Windus, pp. 114–44.

———. 'The Khitmatgar', in *"To Let"*. London: Chatto & Windus, pp. 90–113.

Dickens, Charles. 'The Signal-Man', in *Christmas Books*. London: Chapman and Hall, 1894.

Doyle, Arthur Conan. 'The Captain of the "Pole-star"', in Michael Cox and R. A. Gilbert (eds), *The Oxford Book of Victorian Ghost Stories*. Oxford: Oxford University Press, 2003, pp. 283–302.

Edwards, Amelia B. 'Was it an Illusion?', in Michael Cox and R. A. Gilbert (eds), *The Oxford Book of Victorian Ghost Stories*. Oxford: Oxford University Press, 2003, pp. 239–55.

Gaskell, Elizabeth. 'The Old Nurse's Story', in Michael Cox and R. A. Gilbert (eds), *The Oxford Book of Victorian Ghost Stories*. Oxford: Oxford University Press, 2003, pp. 1–18.

Giles, Melanie. *Bog Bodies: Face to Face with the Past*. Manchester: Manchester University Press, 2020.

Hawker, R. S. 'The Botathen Ghost', in Michael Cox and R. A. Gilbert (eds), *The Oxford Book of Victorian Ghost Stories*. Oxford: Oxford University Press, 2003, pp. 65–73.

Hurley, Andrew Michael. 'Devils and Debauchery: Why We Love to Be Scared by Folk Horror'. *The Guardian*, 28 October 2019. https://www.theguardian.com/books/2019/oct/28/devils-and-debauchery-why-we-love-to-be-scared-by-folk-horror (last accessed 8 January 2025).

James, M. R. 'The Ash-Tree', in *Ghost Stories of an Antiquary*. Harmondsworth: Penguin, 1960, pp. 52–68.

———. '"Oh, Whistle, and I'll Come to You, My Lad"', in *Ghost Stories of an Antiquary*. Harmondsworth: Penguin, 1960, pp. 106–30.

Killeen, Jarlath. *Gothic Literature 1825–1914*. Cardiff: University of Wales Press, 2009.

Landon, Perceval. 'Thurnley Abbey', in Michael Cox and R. A. Gilbert (eds), *The Oxford Book of Victorian Ghost Stories*. Oxford. Oxford University Press, 2003, pp. 466–79.

Macfarlane, Robert. 'The Eeriness of the English Countryside'. *The Guardian*, 10 April 2015. https://www.theguardian.com/books/2015/apr/10/eeriness-english-countryside-robert-macfarlane (last accessed 8 January 2025).

Moshenska, Gabriel. 'M. R. James and the Archaeological Uncanny'. *Antiquity*, vol. 86, no. 334, 2012, 1192–201.

Oliphant, Margaret. 'The Open Door', in *The Open Door and Other Stories of the Seen and Unseen*, edited by Mike Ashley. London: British Library Publications, 2021, pp. 75–120.

Passey, Joan. *Cornish Gothic, 1830–1913*. Cardiff: University of Wales Press, 2023.

Riddell, Charlotte. 'Nut Bush Farm', in *Weird Stories*, edited by Emma Liggins. Brighton: Victorian Secrets, 2009, pp. 59–97.

Spooner, Catherine. '"Dark, and cold, and rugged is the North": Regionalism, Folklore and Elizabeth Gaskell's "Northern" Gothic', in William Hughes and Ruth Heholt (eds), *Gothic Britain: Dark Places in the Provinces and Margins of the British Isles*. Cardiff: University of Wales Press, 2018, pp. 27–43.

Wordsworth, William. 'The Idiot Boy', in William Wordsworth and Samuel Taylor Coleridge, *Lyrical Ballads*, edited by R. L. Brett and A. R. Jones. London and New York: Methuen, 1984, pp. 86–101.

———. 'There was a Boy', in William Wordsworth and Samuel Taylor Coleridge, *Lyrical Ballads*, edited by R. L. Brett and A. R. Jones. London and New York: Methuen, 1984, pp. 134–5.

Chapter 21

Maritime Ghost Stories
Joan Passey

The sea has always been haunted. Maritime ghost stories have a long tradition, with Samuel Taylor Coleridge's *Rime of the Ancient Mariner* (1798) being the most immediately recognisable and emblematic, where a man is cursed to wander the world, eternally telling his story of meeting with the manifestation of death at sea. Tamás Bényei describes Coleridge's *Rime* as 'the ultimate ghost text', as ghost stories are 'transferential narratives, in which the point is the iteration and the interaction, the transmission of the story' whereby 'the story seems to replay itself, using its tellers as mediums' (Bényei 2016: 22). If we take that to be true then maritime ghost stories are the ultimate ghost stories, as they make visible and explicit those mechanisms of transmission, through the oral legends of grizzled sea dogs to the maritime circulation of ideas and products around the world.

This chapter will provide an outline of the cultural factors influencing the spectral seascape in the Victorian imaginary, to contextualise an illustrative survey of maritime ghost stories at the end of the century, including Arthur Conan Doyle's 'The Captain of the "Polestar"' (1890), Francis Marion Crawford's 'The Upper Berth' (1894) and 'The Screaming Skull' (1908), and Margery Williams's 'The Last Mitchell' (1905). While the fluidity of the sea and the spectrality of ghosts work to resist a contained, coherent tradition, an illuminating series of inheritances emerge which can provide insight into how the Victorians conceived of human (and non-human) engagements with watery spaces.

The Gothic is submerged in the seascape, as Emily Alder explains:

> intersections between the Gothic and the sea are so visible that the main question is why they are so rarely examined. Ships can be isolating, claustrophobic structures; ocean depths conceal monsters, secrets, bodies; the sea and its weather provide storms, sunsets, and remote locales for sublime and terrifying experiences; deep water is a useful metaphor for the interiority of the

self; the ocean's precarious surface interfaces between life and death, chaos and order, self and other. And the list could go on. (Alder 2017: 1)

Throughout the nineteenth century, tales of maritime disaster were hugely popular and collected in 'anthologies' of horrors.[1] These anthologies continued well into the twentieth century, attracting readers with sensational tales of terror at sea, failed expeditions, shipwrecks, starvation and cannibalism. These narratives appealed to the same thirsts as contemporaneous penny dreadfuls, with the added benefit of being ostensibly real. The rise of sensation fiction, literacy and affordable, accessible print media is inextricable from the development of maritime transportation technologies, whereby large-scale disaster became both increasingly commonplace and more visible. Thus, stories of seascapes, smuggling, wrecking and shipboard travel are ubiquitous across the nineteenth-century literary tradition and throughout the cultural imagination. At the end of the century, amidst the long dusk of empire, maritime disaster is imagined as the ultimate threat to British imperial, military and trading might.

A popular account of the horrors of the sea, Fletcher S. Bassett's *Sea Phantoms; Legends and Superstitions of the Sea and of Sailors* (1892) capitalised on the public thirst for both saltwater horror tales and ghost stories. Bassett notes that the maritime spectre is flexible and multivalent, from 'the ancient Greek navigators, accustomed to materialize all physical phenomena, [who] often beheld apparitions on land and at sea' (Bassett 1892: 31). Tracking apparitions at sea, from Apollo comforting the Argonauts to Walter Scott via *The Tempest*'s Ariel, Bassett documents the long history of 'sea phantoms' in mythology, folklore, fiction and real-life accounts. Saints appear as apparitions on ships in the Middle Ages (Bassett 1892: 32). Reginald Scot and Erasmus reference ghosts and ghostly lights in the sixteenth century, Joseph Addison describes sea ghosts in the eighteenth century, and Percy Bysshe Shelley references sea spirits in 'Prometheus Unbound' (1820) and 'Revolt of Islam' (1818). Bassett's ambitions are both temporally and geographically expansive, charting the pervasiveness of sea spectres across the British Isles, Spain, Italy and China. Alongside this long chronology, Bassett lists myriad spectral tropes, embracing apparitions as diverse as ghost ships, sea spirits, manifestations of god(s), the Virgin Mary, the Holy Ghost, St Elmo's fire/will-o'-the-wisps/corpse lights or other lights acting as portents of doom, the appearance of strange shapes in the fog, spectral cities, impossible fantasy islands, ghost women searching for their drowned children, spectral sea creatures/giants, and sea witches playing dice. These apparitions of humans, non-humans, objects and places serve many functions, allying with mariners or threatening them, causing general mischief, or warning of the death of loved ones elsewhere.

Bassett's miscellany exemplifies the pervasiveness of the maritime ghost and particular interest in the topic in the nineteenth century, with Bassett claiming that '[n]ineteenth century science has not thoroughly dispelled the mariner's belief in the supernatural character of these weird lights' (Bassett 1892: 38). If anything, these scientific discourses and technological advancements nurture rather than undermine maritime ghosts, and nineteenth-century ghost stories draw richly from anxieties about the speed of progress, the specialisation of the sciences, psychical investigations, and conflicts between scientific and religious thought. Maritime ghosts also gain prevalence in the nineteenth century due to their ability to respond to fears surrounding maritime and imperialist expansionism and an increasingly globalised world. Maritime ghosts are bound up in nationalist ideas of the protection of borders and boundaries through the sea as leaky container, frequently undermining or upholding militaristic authority, and responding to a 'universal' fear of the Ocean as something that links as well as separates nations. In a review of Bassett's survey, James Maitland draws specific attention to the global significance of maritime tales, as, '[l]ike fairy stories and children's rhymes, sea yarns are common to every nation' (Maitland 1892: 804). Further:

> Sailors of every nationality share the belief in the sea-serpent, in the ill-luck which attends a voyage begun upon a Friday, the fatality which follows the slaughter of a petrel or an albatross, or drowning of a black cat. The mermaids of to-day are but the sirens of ancient Greece modernized; every people has a tradition of an ark, an Argo and a phantom-ship like the 'Flying Dutchman'. (Maitland 1892: 804)

Maritime stories are transhistorical and global in their reach, resisting and puncturing historical and temporal containers. Nineteenth-century mermaids are, effectively, revenants of the sirens of Ancient Greece, reanimated, made new, transformed. The endurance of maritime legend is a ghost story in its own right, preserving and influencing and shaping attitudes towards the seascape.

The popular association between the maritime and the ghostly is at its most apparent in proliferations of sightings and retellings of the legendary *Flying Dutchman* – a ship doomed to sail the seas for eternity. Print references date back to the end of the eighteenth century, and Walter Scott was the first to refer to the ship as specifically a pirate ship in 1812. The legend was adapted into an English melodrama entitled *The Flying*

Dutchman; or the Phantom Ship by Edward Fitzball in 1826, and later the Gothic novel *The Phantom Ship* (1839) by Frederick Marryat. Richard Wagner adapted the tale into the opera *The Flying Dutchman* in 1843, Washington Irving took inspiration from the legend for *The Flying Dutchman on Tappan Sea* in 1855 and John Boyle O'Reilly borrowed from the legend for *The Flying Dutchman* in 1867. The future King George V claimed to have spotted the phantom ship in 1881. The enduring popularity of the narrative, and its many iterations throughout the nineteenth century, suggest that it appealed to a populace anxious about maritime activity and mortality at sea.

Marryat's novel features Philip Vanderdecken's efforts to rescue his father who is cursed to be the Captain of the Bewitched Phantom Ship after killing a crewman. This is a classic narrative of efforts to lay a ghost to rest, and Vanderdecken sails around the world in his search, encountering myriad supernatural horrors, a breadth of narratives enabled by maritime travel and maritime folklore. The novel was critically panned, but remains formative in the popularisation of nautical horror fiction. Fact blurs into fiction in the novel and in its reception and subsequent tales of Marryat's own life at sea. Marryat's daughter, Gothic author Florence Marryat, retells a maritime ghost story in her biography of her father, reporting that Frederick Marryat saw the apparition of his brother at sea, only to later find out it was at the exact moment he died. A review in *Cornhill Magazine* recognises this trope, as 'Marryat's daughter tells a ghost story which, though of a type sufficiently familiar, is so circumstantially authenticated as to deserve a special record' (Anon. 1873: 183). Nick Freeman recognises this type as 'friend of a friend folklore', after Henry James's 'The Friends of the Friends' (1892), where apparitions let loved ones know about their death elsewhere (Freeman 2012: 103). This form continues in the maritime ghost tradition with Margery Williams's 'The Last Mitchell' (1905), where Williams's protagonist sees the apparition of a stranger before he drowns at sea, and only ceases seeing him *after* he is dead. Freeman tracks the development of the ghost story across the nineteenth century, pointing out that '[g]hostly fiction, like other literary modes, typically follows a cycle of innovation, imitation, decline, burlesque and revival' (Freeman 2012: 98). Maritime ghost stories are no different, beginning with earnest non-fiction reportage and the documenting and dissemination of folk tales at the beginning of the century, and becoming homages, pastiches or critiques of those early tropes later in the century. The 'friend of a friend folklore' is emblematic of this, moving from folklore to the wider ghost story tradition to Williams's inverting of the trope. Florence Marryat's retelling of her father's life at sea as the sort of maritime ghost stories he wrote further complicates the relationship between fiction and non-fiction emblematic in the maritime ghost story and its frequent appeals to the 'authenticated'. The popularity of the *Flying Dutchman* mythos likely contributed to the speculation surrounding the *Mary Celeste*, an American merchant brigantine discovered deserted in the Atlantic Ocean in 1872. The case has never been solved, inspiring a wealth of speculation and legend that emerged nigh instantaneously. Arthur Conan Doyle himself penned an influential retelling of the story in 1884, entitled 'J. Habakuk Jephson's Statement', taking the form of a doctor's diary.

Maritime ghost stories frequently take the form of a found ship's log, diary, journal or newspaper report. Mina pastes newspaper clippings of shipwrecks into her diary in *Dracula* (1897). *Frankenstein* (1818) opens and closes with a ship captain's report. Crawford's 'The Screaming Skull', a mariner's ghost story, ends with a newspaper clipping reporting his death. Arthur Conan Doyle's 'The Captain of the "Pole-star"' (1890) takes the form of the ship doctor's logbook. The Gothic has, since its origins, enjoyed a relationship with the notion of 'truth' at times generative and playful, at times challenging, and the 'found document' of the maritime ghost story tradition is a direct inheritor of the 'found manuscript' of Horace Walpole's *The Castle of Otranto* (1764), calling into question the ways we perceive and validate the 'real'. Maritime ghost stories surge in popularity amidst scientific investigation of both maritime space and the supernatural. Watery and supernatural worlds provide challenge to, and imaginative space for, empirical inquiry and what may lie 'beyond' our realm of understanding, our perceived reality and our inhabitable worlds. In the maritime ghost stories which I survey below, those encountering maritime ghosts take on the role of psychical investigators, performing experiments, and documenting and verifying their findings.

'The Captain of the "Pole-star"' is one of the most anthologised nineteenth-century maritime ghost stories. Doyle's story takes the form of a shipboard doctor's logbook, describing the events on board a Scottish whaling vessel travelling further and further north as the year closes in, increasingly enclosed by the ice sheet. The crew are haunted by a terrible noise and a gruesome phantom flitting across the ice, and become possessed by superstitious fear as the captain loses his wits, apparently consumed by grief for a lost love he seems to see on the ice flats. Doyle's story is part of a polar tradition and an expedition tradition, fuelled by voracious public interest in real-life reports from expeditions – particularly those gone awry. Katherine Bowers describes the significance of the perception of polar regions as horrifying places in the nineteenth century, forged by expedition narratives, gory speculation and reports of John Franklin's final expedition in 1845. Bowers argues that polar space 'pushes beyond the bounds of the civilized mind, and, in doing so, becomes gothic space', and is reimagined, reinscribed and homogenised across the nineteenth century (Bowers 2017: 71).

The sea – and the Arctic sea in particular – is an alien, inhospitable unreality, a sublime and liminal space challenging rational perception and stretching the limits of the imagination. We are introduced to an ice field that 'cannot be smaller than an English county', and 'fish' over ten feet in length (Doyle 1893: 1–3). They are 'a good nine hundred miles' from another settlement and '[n]o whaler has ever remained in these latitudes till so advanced a period of the year' (Doyle 1893: 2). As opposed to the claustrophobia and entrapment of the land-based Gothic, in the maritime and oceanic Gothic too much space becomes oppressive. They are carving out new ground, conquering new frontiers of both land and knowledge, and straining against what is possible and known. Ghosts become more plausible at sea.

Life at sea has the capacity to be horrific enough without supernatural interference. Beyond the spectre, the crew are at 'real' threat from a mad captain and dwindling supplies of food. Being at sea is precarious, detached from home, safety and resources, and this makes the crew vulnerable to other unknowable forces. Like 'The Upper Berth', this narrative specifically involves reliance on the ship's doctor and captain. The narrator doctor of the 'Pole-star' states that 'I have always found that [the Captain] will tolerate from me what he would resent from any other member of the crew' (Doyle 1893: 2). These authoritative and patriarchal figures are at the top of the ship's hierarchy, and thus other men depend on their capacity for rationality and problem solving. Yet, Captain Craigie is an increasingly irrational man, described as a supernatural creature in his own right, somewhat 'fey' (6, 19), 'a seer and expounder of omens' (6), and the doctor marvels at the 'superstition' of his Celtic crew, describing it as an 'epidemic' – something contagious and potentially fatal (6). The doctor begins tranquilising the crew with 'sedatives and nerve-tonics', pathologising their superstition in a positivist approach to supernatural phenomena (6). It is a ship of hysterics, as the ice field is both solid and liquid, a space between life and death, sanity and insanity, the natural and the supernatural, defying categorisation. The long spectre on the ice fields becomes a manifestation of the horrors of shipboard life, of the isolation of a seafaring existence, as the Captain is haunted by the loved one he left behind, furious at the doctor's reports of his own beloved. The Captain 'jumps ship', abandoning life at sea for a seemingly preferable death.

Like the sea itself the captain seems to be suspended in a liminal state between life and death, a conceptual rather than literal skeleton crew. He states that he has 'more to bind me to the other world than to this one' (3). He tells the doctor that 'the thought of death was a pleasant one to him' (5). The Captain 'has devoted himself to whaling simply for the reason that it is the most dangerous occupation which he could select, and that he courts death in every possible manner' (10). He is attracted to a life at sea because he is drawn to and seeks out death, with the maritime, polar environment offering both attraction and repulsion.

'Pole-star' makes reference to the proliferation of popular print media surrounding maritime disaster, as the doctor claims that his lover, Flora, 'no doubt [...] scans the shipping list in the Scotsman every morning to see if we are reported from Shetland' (17). Footnote explanations reinforce the validity of the logbook as scientific document, and it is signed off by the doctor's father, a man of some repute, who evidences its veracity through his own initial cynicism, before offering further sources to substantiate the narrative. Crucially, 'Pole-star' demonstrates that a haunted ship is not just a haunted house at sea, but that the maritime ghost story is a distinct form shaped by the specifics of nautical histories and literary traditions.

'The Upper Berth' (1894) by Francis Marion Crawford provides a variation on what Nick Freeman acknowledges is a common form by the end of the nineteenth century, transplanting the spending 'a night in a room' no one can manage to stay in narrative onto a ship (Freeman 2012: 94). This form, adopted by H. G. Wells in 'The Red Room' (1896) and Rhoda Broughton in 'The Truth, the Whole Truth, and Nothing but the Truth' (1868), to name but two, tends to feature a sceptic voluntarily staying in a haunted room that has caused others to flee with horror. These narratives can either champion rationality (Wells) or punish the arrogant rejection of superstition and/or supernatural forces (Broughton).

Crawford was a prolific writer of novels and short stories, deemed 'rubbish' by George Gissing (Coustillas 1978: 423) and envied by Henry James, who denigrated his literary qualities but admired his output. Crawford published across a huge range of subjects, primarily historical fiction, but it was his maritime horrors that were most critically acclaimed. M. R. James stated that 'horrid story of "The Upper Berth", which (with "The Screaming Skull" some distance behind) is the best in his collection of *Uncanny Tales*, and stands high among ghost stories in general' (James 2013: 415). James's praise is significant for the maritime ghost story tradition, as it becomes apparent that 'The Upper Berth' has some uncanny similarities to James's 'Oh, Whistle, and I'll Come to You, My Lad' (1904).

Four years before Henry James's *The Turn of the Screw* (1898), 'The Upper Berth' opens with a gathering of friends sharing tales (Kitahara 2006: 183). The guests become weary, and the night threatens boredom, when the imposing and charismatic Brisbane offers a tale from his life at sea. The unknown narrator rejoices at Brisbane's offering, and we hear the rest from Brisbane's perspective, losing all contact with the framing narrative. Brisbane is immediately cast as a sort of swaggering hero from a boy's own adventure novel, impressive and jaded. He claims a 'tone peculiar to men who think no more of crossing the Atlantic than taking a whisky cocktail at downtown Delmonico's' (Crawford 1894: 12), differentiating Brisbane's rugged, seafaring masculinity from the more metropolitan audience gathered around him. The steward immediately cowers when Brisbane announces he is to stay in berth 105, and Brisbane injects retrospective asides into his narrative to build tension – 'Ugh! how I hate that state-room!!' (14); 'I was wrong, however, and did the man injustice' (15) – putting him in the position of authority over the reader as well as the cosmopolitan listeners and snivelling crewmen. This reinforces the status of the gruff old salty sea dog archetype, occupying the position of rationality and scepticism otherwise played out by the doctor, scientist or lawyer in Gothic fiction.

Brisbane approaches the transatlantic crossing – which would have been a novelty to most readers – as humdrum, where '[o]ne passage across the Atlantic is very much like another' and 'one whale is very much like another whale' (17–18). Crawford satirises the public interest in tall maritime tales with a narrator who rejects the novelty of such escapades. When he meets his strange roommate he thinks him 'a little odd. There are three or four of his kind on every ocean steamer' (19). Crucially, Brisbane is a man for whom the strange is mundane and the curious banal and he is therefore perfectly suited to confront any supernatural happenings.

An odd bunkmate charges from the room in the dead of night and is never seen again, presumed dead having gone overboard. The ship's surgeon warns Brisbane to move out of the room, and Brisbane refuses, assured of his own immunity to such epidemics of hysteria. That night he encounters 'something that had the shape of a man's arm, but was smooth, and wet, and icy cold', 'endowed with a sort of supernatural strength', that 'smelled horribly of stagnant sea-water' (43–4). Undeterred, he asks that the surgeon spend the next night in the berth, and is promptly rejected:

'Have you any reasonable explanation of these things to offer?' he asked. 'No; you have not. Well, you say you will find an explanation. I say that you won't, sir, simply because there is not any.'

'But, my dear sir,' I retorted, 'do you, a man of science, mean to tell me that such things cannot be explained?'

'I do,' he answered, stoutly. 'And, if they could, I would not be concerned in the explanation.' (51)

Crawford is engaging with what Jennifer Bann identifies as a turn in the ghost story tradition in the nineteenth century (Bann 2009: 663–4). Bann argues that the cultural preoccupation with spiritualism and psychical investigation in the latter half of the century changed the shape of spectres and attitudes towards them, as writers became less interested in passive spooks and more intrigued by scientific engagement with active forces. Freeman argues that this critical engagement with proving and disproving supernatural entities arises from a contemporaneous anxiety with the afterlife amidst the secularisation of Britain. Ghost stories present a means of discussing the afterlife without wading into religious discourse, or rather, with the later influence of spiritualism, a means of engaging with a religious discourse outside of, contrary to, and in some ways overlapping with Christianity:

> the nineteenth century was a time of high mortality rates, very public displays of death and mourning and, at the same time, an increasing scepticism regarding Christian teachings. Even as Darwin and others challenged the notion of the Bible's literal truth, the ghost story allowed writers to explore the mystery of life after death without having to engage in religious controversy. (Freeman 2012: 106)

It is no coincidence that the maritime tale in particular offers the ideal form for playing out these ideological anxieties around the science and theology of life and death. When the four men disappear from the ship they are never seen again, with the oceanic space mirroring the unknowable afterlife. The scale and frequency of maritime disaster meant that the maritime world and maritime tales were intimately associated with and evocative of mortality. Further, there are parallels between emerging and specialising scientific quests to study the supernatural world, and the seascape. Both involve plunging into dark abysses, unknowable spaces, where human life cannot be sustained. Both pose unique challenges to equipment, both are places where our tertiary laws seem not to apply. Thus, Brisbane launches a very scientific and carefully monitored inquiry into his slimy spectre, seeking out an assistant for his 'investigation' in the form of the ship's captain. This is an echo of the *Pole-star*'s doctor fervently documenting the happenings aboard in the midst of supernatural chaos.

Brisbane and the Captain proceed to methodically deconstruct the room with the help of a carpenter. Both continually reiterate that this is a serious inquiry for serious people and meticulously set up the room for the night. They distrust what they see, wondering if the tiny bolts on the porthole are unravelling themselves: '"It moves!" he exclaimed, in a tone of conviction. "No, it does not," he added, after a minute' (Crawford 1894: 62). Eventually, the cabin lurches, and they are attacked by 'something ghostly, horrible beyond words', 'like the body of a man long drowned', 'the slippery, oozy, horrible thing' with 'dead white eyes' in its 'dead face', a 'dead thing' (66–7). This reiteration of 'death' lays the foundations for the story's final lines: '[t]hat is how I saw a ghost – if it was a ghost. It was dead, anyhow' (69–70). This conclusion reinforces the reading of 'The Upper Berth' as a narrative that uses the maritime to consider the impossibility of investigating the afterlife. Death is something we grapple with in tangible, abject ways, but even with Brisbane's rigorous investigation it remains unknowable, and his final position is ambivalent.

'The Upper Berth' is a likely influence on M. R. James's 'Oh, Whistle, and I'll Come to You, My Lad' where a lone traveller (academic instead of sailor) is displaced by a journey (the east coast of England rather than a transatlantic crossing) and unexpectedly shares his twin room with something terrible, only to be saved (somewhat) by a military man crashing into his room. Both even significantly feature swaying, mobile bedsheets, and both are haunted by the latent eroticism of a man sharing his bedchamber with something transgressive. The berth is also a version of the haunted bedroom, a recurrent trope that Freeman aligns with 'bedtime reading' becoming 'a growing pastime in an increasingly literate nineteenth-century Britain, the content of stories often echoed the circumstances of their consumption, and transformed the bedroom from traditional place of safety and repose to a site of unrest and horror' (Freeman 2012: 94–5). The shipboard berth, however, is not a traditional place of safety, and the uncanny effects are doubled.

Nick Freeman notes that the ghostly tale shifted in the nineteenth century from spectral incidents in longer novel forms to the short story form in particular, meaning that 'freeing the ghostly encounter from the demands of intricate novelistic plotting allowed for bravura effects which did not need to be dulled by explanation or formal neatness' (Freeman 2012: 94). The maritime ghost story in particular is both a fitting form for these narrative developments, and actively contributes to these developments through the popularity and proliferation of nautical fiction. Nautical fiction offers the irrationality of life at sea as antidote to the earlier focus on rational explanations and resolutions. Narratives at sea are often temporary scenes, liminal journeys or ephemeral moments. In sea narratives our characters are frequently dislocated from the 'real' as bound to solid ground. They are flung into a space so very 'other', alien, hostile to human life. The sea is uninhabitable and allows for narrative experimentation and challenges to realism.

'The Screaming Skull' (1908) has striking similarities to Crawford's earlier tale. It is the narrative of a grizzled seaman, told to an eager audience. However, we are flung into the tale without a framing narrative, and it becomes apparent that this ghost story constructs a sort of virtual reality, taking the form of a first-person present-tense account directed to us, the reader, who is the listener, sat in the Captain's cottage by the sea, and offered tobacco and beverages and taken on a journey around the house. The surreal, immersive effect is amplified by Crawford's appeal to naturalistic speech. The Captain's report is fragmented, occasionally distracted, punctuated by the apparent sound of the sea, a storm, and the screams of the skull. The Captain knows the reader/listener, referring to shared memories and experiences. 'We' are entrapped and entrusted – 'I suppose you are like me in that, and we are just like other people who have been to sea' (Crawford 1911: 61). 'We' are also a grizzled seafarer! While 'The Upper Berth' relies on Brisbane's jaded *otherness* to the listeners (us included), emphasising the horror of his own visceral response to confronting something terrible at sea, 'we' share the peculiarities of the Captain in 'The Screaming Skull'. We are cast as the expert, and Crawford makes access to tall tales of the high sea more democratic. This befits the ghost story and the Gothic more broadly – a genre that repeatedly rejects enclosure, categorisation and elitism or efforts to govern its topics and readers.

The Captain tells us about his cousin's difficult marriage with his wife. The wife then dies, and the cousin dies not long after, on the beach, with teeth marks on his throat, and a human skull nearby. Later, the Captain becomes haunted by the skull – it screams at night, and he cannot seem to dispose of it. It keeps coming back, the return of the repressed, howling inarticulately. He tries to give it a Christian burial, and adamantly refuses to be frightened of it, or to consider it a supernatural event or haunting. He states that:

> There may be ghosts, or there may not be. If there are, I'm not inclined to believe that they can hurt living people except by frightening them, and, for my part, I would rather face any shape of ghost than a fog in the Channel when it's crowded. No. What bothered me was just a foolish idea, that's all, and I cannot tell how it began, nor what made it grow till it turned into a certainty. (54–5)

And later:

> I ought not to be nervous. I've sailed in a haunted ship. There was a Man in the Top, and two-thirds of the crew died of the West Coast fever inside of ten days after we anchored; but I was all right, then and afterward. I have seen some ugly sights, too, just as you have, and all the rest of us. But nothing ever stuck in my head in the way this does. (57)

Crawford presents us with a ghost story within a ghost story. While maritime stories often rely on the horror of what is possible at sea, 'The Screaming Skull' is specifically about a land-based horror as experienced by someone desensitised *by* maritime horrors. It is a horror story told by a narrator who refuses to experience the events as horrific, and expects the reader/listener to be similarly desensitised, satirising the reading public's exposure to terrible tales. However, it is this scepticism that seals the Captain's fate – having survived a haunted ship he is killed by his own hubris in his own bedroom, as the story ends with a newspaper reporting his death at the same hands (teeth?) as the thing that killed his cousin. The rational, sceptical Captain is made an irrational fool by his refusal to accept the empirical evidence before him – evidence verified by a reliable second witness: the reader.

While 'The Captain of the "Pole-star"', 'The Upper Berth' and 'The Screaming Skull' are narrated by men with experience at sea, Margery Williams's maritime ghost story, 'The Last Mitchell', is narrated by a housewife, and takes place almost entirely within her home. Williams is perhaps most famous for her later children's story *The Velveteen Rabbit* (1922), but her earlier work was significantly more horrific, with her werewolf novel *The Thing in the Woods* (1914) becoming a noted influence on H. P. Lovecraft. 'The Last Mitchell' tells the story of a young family, the Allans, moving to the Cornish coast. They become aware that the house they are staying in was owned continuously by the historic Mitchell family, until Old Jethro Mitchell expelled Young Jethro Mitchell for scandalous behaviour, breaking the line of inheritance and opening up the property to be rented by interlopers. Mrs Allan becomes convinced the house pines for its lost heir. She sees an apparition wandering through the house, and confirms its identity as Young Jethro by a photograph found behind a cabinet, but feels no fear in his presence. One day their housemaid declares that 'corpse lights' have appeared along the beach, forewarning the death of three local men. Jethro appears once more to Mrs Allan, but this time she is repulsed and horrified by his presence, and concludes that Jethro must be dead. Later that night a ship wrecks against the shore, the locals help, and Mr Allan returns, carrying the body of a drowned man, who Mrs Allan recognises as Jethro, the last Mitchell, returned home. Jethro's return is thwarted by the wreck, then ensured by the intervention of helpful bystanders. Jethro is the return of the repressed, washed up on the shores. The sea is recurrently framed as giving up its ghosts and secrets, later motivating the return of the yacht in Cornwall in Daphne du Maurier's *Rebecca* (1938). The living hauntings represent Jethro as existing in a liminal space between life and death embodied by the liminal coast, the liminality of the shipwreck sinking beneath the surface, and the suspension of Jethro's identity caused by his expulsion by his family. Mr Allan jokes about the house being possibly haunted:

> 'The kind of ghosts that crawl up pipes and through crevices, and stalk along the passages, particularly in damp weather. Greenish, scummy ghosts, with phosphorescent eyes, that come through locked doors and grip you by the throat when you're asleep – Ghosts —.' (Williams 1905: 91)

These are distinctly watery ghosts, dependent upon the idea of water being both essential to life and fatal and threatening. The phosphorescent eyes allude to the 'corpse-lights' that forewarn of death on the coast. Corpse lights, sometimes referred to as will-o'-the-wisps, jack-o'-lanterns or corpse candles, have a long folkloric history, appearing above or near water as portents of a watery death. The corpse lights are a spectral manifestation of a death to come, thwarting the linear trajectory of time, reinforcing the inevitability of mortality. They are an articulation of a rich history of efforts to *interpret* the strangeness of phenomena at sea to survive it, to navigate it. Much maritime folklore is an effort to understand the natural world and the tempestuousness of the waves, as storytelling as epistemological mode is a form of scientific investigation of empirical effects. Mrs Allan, crucially, uses a form of modern technology, the photograph (a light-based technology, to boot) to complete her investigation into the supernatural phenomena and identify (and put to rest) the ghost. Mrs Allan, a wife and a mother, assumes the same role as the captains and doctors aboard Conan Doyle and Crawford's ships, demonstrative of the capacity of the maritime ghost story to adapt to appeal to new cultural concerns – in this case, the development of women's ghost stories in the nineteenth century to render women active rather than passive agents.

The seas have, historically, been imaginatively riddled with all shapes and sizes of ghouls and monsters, sluicing through maps and cartographies, terrorising Odysseus, daubed onto Greek and Roman pottery. The Victorians did not reinvent the sea as a frightening place – it has been feared throughout human history – but contact with the sea became more immediate, reports of it were more present, the dangers of it more tangible to more people, our needs more dependent on its whims. Our relationship with the sea is transhistorical and culturally relative, and much of how we understand the seascape now has been shaped by the peculiarities of the Victorian cultural imaginary, the rise of the maritime technologies and imperial expansionism. The Victorians did not invent being scared of the sea, but they did reimagine it very specifically as bound up in anxieties about the rational and the irrational, scientific progress and positivism. These ideas come to shape and define the Victorian maritime ghost story.

Note

1. Archibald Duncan's six-volume anthology *The Mariner's Chronicle: Containing Narratives of the Most Remarkable Disasters at Sea* (1804–34), William Henry Giles Kingston's *Shipwrecks and Disasters at Sea* (1873) and Fletcher S. Bassett's *Sea Phantoms; Legends and Superstitions of the Sea and of Sailors* (1892) are some such examples. Keith Huntress's anthology *Narratives of Shipwrecks and Disasters, 1536–1860* (1974) gathers together many more of these narratives and demonstrates their enduring popularity.

Works Cited

Alder, Emily. 'Through Oceans Darkly: Sea Literature and the Nautical Gothic'. *Gothic Studies*, vol. 19, no. 2, 2017, pp. 1–15.
Anon. 'Sea Novels. – Captain Marryat'. *The Cornhill Magazine*, February 1873, pp. 170–90.
Bann, Jennifer. 'Ghostly Hands and Ghostly Agency: The Changing Figure of the Nineteenth-Century Specter'. *Victorian Studies*, vol. 51, no. 4, 2009, 663–85.
Bassett, F. S. *Sea Phantoms; Legends and Superstitions of the Sea and of Sailors*. Chicago: Morrill, Higgins & Co, 1892.
Bényei, Tamás. 'Ghosts in the Age of Spectrality: The Irrelevance of Ghosts and Late Victorian Ghost Stories', in Irena Grubica and Zdeněk Beran (eds), *The Fantastic of the Fin de Fin de Siècle*. Newcastle upon Tyne: Cambridge Scholars Publishing, 2016, pp. 17–38.
Bowers, Katherine. 'Haunted Ice, Fearful Sounds, and the Arctic Sublime: Exploring Nineteenth-Century Polar Gothic Space'. *Gothic Studies*, vol. 19, no. 2, 2017, pp. 71–84.
Coustillas, Pierre. *London and the Life of Literature in Late Victorian England: the Diary of George Gissing, Novelist*. Brighton: Harvester Press, 1978.
Crawford, F. Marion. 'The Upper Berth', in *The Upper Berth*. New York: G. P. Putnam and London: The Knickerbocker Press, 1894, pp. 3–70.

———. 'The Screaming Skull', in *Wandering Ghosts*. New York: The Macmillan Company, 1911, pp. 41–96.

Doyle, Arthur Conan. *The Captain of the Polestar: And Other Tales*. London: Longmans, 1893.

Duncan, Archibald. *The Mariner's Chronicle: Containing Narratives of the Most Remarkable Disasters at Sea*. New Haven, CT: G. W. Gorton, 1834.

Freeman, Nick. 'The Victorian Ghost Story', in Andrew Smith and William Hughes (eds), *The Victorian Gothic: An Edinburgh Companion*. Edinburgh: Edinburgh University Press, 2012, pp. 93–107.

Huntress, Keith Gibson. *Narratives of Shipwrecks and Disasters, 1536–1860*. Ames: Iowa State University Press, 1974.

James, M. R. 'Some Remarks on Ghost Stories', in *M. R. James: Collected Ghost Stories*, edited by Darryl Jones. Oxford: Oxford University Press, 2013, pp. 410–16.

Kingston, William Henry Giles. *Shipwrecks and Disasters at Sea*. London: Routledge, 1873.

Kitahara, Taeko. 'Framing the Supernatural: Henry James and F. Marion Crawford'. *The Japanese Journal of American Studies*, vol. 17, 2006, pp. 183–200.

Maitland, James. 'BOOK REVIEWS: Sea Phantoms; Legends and Superstitions of the Sea and of Sailors'. *Belford's Monthly*, vol. 9, no. 53, October 1892, p. 804.

Williams, Margery. 'The Last Mitchell'. *Temple Bar: A Monthly Magazine for Town and Country Readers*, July 1905, pp. 90–111.

Chapter 22

The Victorian Haunted House
Emma Liggins

In the hugely influential *The Night Side of Nature, or Ghosts and Ghost Seers* (1848), a compendium of banshees, poltergeists, white ladies and wraiths, and the places they frequented, the popular Victorian writer Catherine Crowe included a chapter on 'haunted houses'. Whilst these are often typecast as uninhabited, dismal, 'antique, mysterious-looking buildings', the collected stories suggest that newer 'prosaic' houses could just as easily acquire an 'evil reputation' (Crowe 2001: 218). Crowe's text has often been a starting point for analysis of the ghostly. Ruth Heholt notes the 'mundan[ity]' and 'unemotional' tone of the stories Crowe tells, perhaps more folkloric than fearful: 'there is little atmosphere, no characterisation [...] no one seems scared of the ghosts mentioned, and they lack mystery or menace' (2021: 171). This slightly misleading appraisal does not take account of Crowe's sense of place, nor what her compendium offers in terms of the troubling of the domestic. The haunted house is a 'troubled house', a place of secrets, disruption and violence, associated with 'deed[s] of darkness' in Crowe's influential formulation (Crowe 2001: 237, 244). It can harbour skeletons hidden under the floorboards, issue forewarnings of deaths and funerals, and resonate with uncanny noise, such as phantom footsteps and the rustling of silks in passageways (238, 271, 330). Crowe's advice for sceptics, 'if these shadowy forms be actually visitors from the dead, I think we cannot too soon lend an attentive ear to the tale their reappearance tells us' (Crowe 2001: 351), reiterates the importance not only of spectral narratives but of 'reappearance', of the manifestation of the dead in specific haunted sites.

The home is one of the most significant haunted places in the Victorian ghost story. Conceptualisations of domesticity cast a shadow across the nineteenth century, as what it meant to be 'at home' or safe in the private sphere continued to be contested. The instability of the domestic and the contradictions of the domestic ideal have been considered by Susan Fraiman, who notes that 'the desire for domestic continuity and security ... [often] arises ... within histories of danger and dislocation' (2017: 10). As I have argued elsewhere, haunted house narratives explored feelings of insecurity and dread in an era when gender divisions and relations with servants were being questioned (Liggins 2020: 4–5). Separate-spheres ideology, inheritance rights and household hierarchies are often shown to be fractured, or unravelling, in the haunted house narrative, and the myth of the happy Victorian family exposed as fraudulent. The ghost story allowed writers to reimagine the dangers, brutality and rivalries of domestic space and to explore the reverberations of the patriarchal past. As Kate Krueger argues, 'the pervasiveness of Victorian ghost stories revolving around the haunted house point to the vulnerability of that location' (2014: 58), where the vulnerability of the domestic ideal is endlessly reinvented and updated to reflect current concerns.

Spatial theory continues to offer a significant and fruitful perspective on the supernatural. Readings of Victorian Gothic have drawn on the ground-breaking work of Gaston Bachelard and Henri Lefebvre, and their philosophical reflections on the rules and regulations of private space. Bachelard's vision of the house as an oneiric realm of lost memories (1964: 20, 36) has helped to transform understandings of domestic interiors and the symbolic significance of specific rooms and passageways. Lefebvre's commentary on the division of space into 'accessible space for normal use' and 'forbidden territories' (1991: 193) raises questions about why certain areas or passageways might be out of bounds. Ghost stories often dwell on 'secret rooms, rooms that have disappeared' (Bachelard 1964: 20), their existence lost from memory. Historians have noted the spatial divisions of the Victorian house, which separated family and servants, or male and female, in an attempt to preserve hierarchical harmony and privacy (Hamlett 2010: 209–10). This harmony is disrupted by ghosts who emerge from secret recesses, manifest in corridors, peer through windows and breach family/servant boundaries. Crowe suggests that ghosts favour liminality, frequently seen or heard in dark bedrooms, on staircases, in passageways or on thresholds, with 'windows and doors ... opened in spite of locks and keys' (2001: 223). Discussing 'the self as haunted and the haunting role of place', Julian Wolfreys reiterates the undeniable connections between dwelling and the uncanny (the border between familiar/unfamiliar) where 'being in place' can be understood in terms of the duality of the present and memories of the past (2018: 21). Wolfreys's reading of haunting in relation to the 'subject-place problematic' (2018: 2) highlights the defamiliarising nature of dwelling, where forbidden, inaccessible spaces contain hidden secrets.

Borrowing from Crowe's taxonomy of place, this chapter considers spectrality and the troubling of the domestic in relation to the haunted house as both a site of secrets and an architectural construct symbolising lost histories. At a time when buying, renting and inheriting property were key concerns, haunted house narratives depict buildings in a state of decay or in terms of an unsettling newness, where new tenants or heirs intent on renovation and fashionable furniture instead have to confront the horror of the past. I analyse British and Irish stories produced between the late 1860s and 1900, by familiar names such as Joseph Sheridan Le Fanu and Henry James and forgotten names such as Lettice Galbraith and Lucas Malet. The stories chosen all linger on architectural descriptions of rooms, passages and features of the estate, such as churchyards, family vaults and 'fatal' ponds, showing how the uncanniness of dwelling suffuses the setting. 'All ghost stories require a death', argues Victoria Margree (2019: 69), with the haunted house animated by the dead bodies and the lost stories of both former and future inhabitants. As these readings suggest, unlocking spectral spaces provides access to the stories of disgraced or forgotten women, family antagonisms and fears about inheritance and property ownership.

The Irish Ghost Story and Architectural Decline

Typical of the mid-Victorian Gothic, the ghost stories of Irish writer Joseph Sheridan Le Fanu often begin with evocative descriptions of decaying, melancholy castles and foreboding estates miles from anywhere. The family history is only gradually revealed, as the silences and strangeness of the house prompt servants to draw out the lost narratives of deceased family members. Jarlath Killeen has written of the Irish Protestant fascination with antiquarianism, folklore and superstition (Killeen 2006). Mirroring the conflicting religious and political forces in nineteenth-century Ireland, ghost stories by Irish Protestant writers emphasise the social changes and crumbling of the 'Big House' or ancestral mansion of the landed class (Killeen 2006). Le Fanu's 'Squire Toby's Will' (1868) opens with the inviting description of the 'dilapidated and weather-stained' black and white house (2020: 173) on the York–London road. Transposed from Ireland to England to appeal to the English market (Cadwallader 2016: 22), the mysterious Gylingden Hall with its glimmering windows is a declining Big House, resonating 'so many signs of desertion and decay' (Le Fanu 2020: 173). Viewed from the bottom of a 'sombre and lifeless avenue', it is 'overgrown like a churchyard', framed by ancient elms. The excess of adjectives signalling architectural and ancestral decline coupled with the repetition of the word 'ancient' is typical of the haunted house narrative. The 'melancholy' trees around the 'forlorn' Hall which 'shroud the old place from view' associate the decaying house with death and secrecy, even before the reader gets to the 'ruinous' chapel which serves as 'burying-place' (174) for the family where 'so many of the old Marston race returned to dust and were forgotten' (177). The death of the old squire of the title, Toby Marston, leaves a state of 'insolvency' in his estates which can only be resolved by the 'deadly feud' (175) between his embittered sons, Scroope and Charlie, who both desire 'possession of the house' (178). The house is 'mildewed' with 'rotting floors', with the anthropomorphised wind 'howl[ing] and sobbing', banshee-like, 'through its empty galleries' (174). Like a disgraced woman, the house is later described as 'fallen Gylingden' (199). This 'rotting' and 'sobbing' of the Irish family prefigures a dispute about succession, inheritance and dispossession.

The haunted house is both akin to and of itself the burying place, the mausoleum, for the declining Victorian family. Linking the ghostly to death and funerary practices, Crowe argued that, 'in those cases where the unseen visitant appears to be the spirit of a person deceased, we see evidences of grief, remorse, and dissatisfaction, together with, in many instances, a disposition to repeat the acts of life' (Crowe 2001: 292). In Le Fanu's story the haunting takes the material form of a seemingly possessed bulldog, perhaps embodying the spirit of the dead Squire. The dog is kept locked up in the house and haunts Charlie's dreams at night, stretching himself with 'odious caresses' (Le Fanu 2020: 186) on his bed. Grief and dissatisfaction are also manifest in unobserved mourning rituals which transform the Hall into a 'troubled' and 'disorderly' (200) house, disrupted by steps in the passages, whispers in the galleries and threatening voices which make the servants panic. Cooper, the butler, and the younger son Charlie visit the Marston 'burying-place' (181) where the dead Squire lies without an epitaph or a stone kist, observing the dog stretch himself upon the grave. The secret room of the Hall is a tapestried bedroom now declined into a lumber room with 'mildewed' paper where Charlie ostensibly wishes to keep the dog but is also directed there by his nightmares to find legal papers. In the wall is a small papered-over press, containing a parchment deed, leaving Gylingden to the elder son. Spectrality is invited by the family's refusal to attend the Squire's funeral or to offer refreshments to the mourners, showing 'no sign of decent respect from Gylingden Hall' (197). A phantom mourning coach then drops two spectral men in black cloaks who enter the Hall and take the 'great liberty' of going upstairs without 'asking leave of anyone' (197), flouting the traditions of the house.

In Crowe's collection, ghostly visitors also appear in broad daylight; one housemaid lets in a lady in fawn-coloured silk and shows her upstairs before realising she has vanished (251). To Cooper the voices and the visitors are accusatory, '"You weren't at the funeral; I might take your life, I'll take your ear"' (201). They also herald the approaching death of the younger son, who will be punished for disrespecting tradition.

In Le Fanu's 'Madam Crowl's Ghost' (1870), the young female servant narrator arrives at night-time at Applewale House in rural Ireland, described like Gylingden in terms of its tree-lined avenue, old-fashioned shutters, glimmering windows and 'locked up' rooms (Le Fanu 2020: 226). The ageing, 'wizened' Madam Crowl, with her claw-like pointed nails and fetish for satin and velvet, is ghoul-like whilst dying and terrifies the servants. In this house of secret closets, there is a symbolic straitjacket previously used to restrain the 'troublesome' Madam Crowl for her madness. Her bedroom is a shrine to her former youth, with its big looking-glass and twenty-two candles; she anticipates the eponymous ghoul of Mary Elizabeth Braddon's 'Good Lady Ducayne' (1896) who refuses to die, clinging to the past with vampiric persistence. Drawing the curtains of her bed to see her new employer, the narrator likens her to an effigy, 'stretched out like the painted lady on the tomb-stean [sic] in Lexhoe Church' (233), unnatural, puppet-like, 'like a thing on wires' (234). Her feverish tales about killing a boy link to the story of the dead heir, her stepson, replaced by her own son to secure inheritance of the Applewale estates. Once dead she remains 'shrouded and coffined' (236) in the house before her delayed and poorly attended funeral, as her grandson ominously neglects funerary rituals. Her mirror moves into the servant's chamber. The hidden room is a locked closet in a recess, used to keep valuables and store what is forgotten. The narrator sees the spectre of Madam Crowl approach this spot in the night; further investigation reveals 'the tracing of a door in the wainscot, and a keyhole stopped with wood' (239), behind an old empty press. These traces of a violent past, locked away from view, conceal ancestral secrets. Behind the door within the door, is a vault 'dark as pick [sic]' (239) in which the candlelight shows up the bones of the lost child, which crumble to dust once poked by the squire. It is one of many Victorian ghost stories where the discovery of a decaying body hidden within the walls leads to the telling of a lost story in order to exorcise the evil reputation of the house.

The crumbling Irish mansion, visibly decaying on the outside and enclosing decay within, testifies to the dishonouring of lost traditions and the dangers of not observing the burial rites of ancestors. Feuds over the possession of property may be resolved through death and the finding of lost wills and bones, but this architectural/bodily decay casts long shadows. The endings of Irish Gothic fiction, Killeen argues, suggest that 'the expulsion [of the primitive past] is never really complete', reinforcing a 'cultural hesitancy between the future and the past, the real and the supernatural' (Killeen 2006). In 'Squire Toby's Will' the 'faded splendour' (179) and lost traditions of 'the old place' and the son's sense that his lost father is 'bullying' him (180) from beyond the grave add to this trouble. The story ends with the 'horribly ominous' (208) vision of three men walking in the dark to the burial ground and the discovery of the master's hanged body behind the door in the lumber room, with the spectral family reunited in their observation of death rituals. On Madam Crowl's death, her grandson will 'discharge' the servants. Madam Crowl's ghost points the way to the boy 'shut up to die thar in the dark' (240), exposing the guilt about a twisted inheritance and fears about the family. This unlocking of the past, suggests editor Xavier Aldana Reyes, 'serves to rationalise the feelings of disgust and fear towards an elderly woman' (Le Fanu 2020: xi); the recognition of her sensationalised madness and 'troublesome' desire for possession as a marginalised woman also paves the way for a new order. The traces of the ancient families, spectralised into the old squire as phantom dog and the stepmother as fiendish revenant, are removed from the haunted house to the family vault. Both stories end with the superstitious servant prospering in the future, contemplating the architectural decline of the Irish family and its doomed bloodline.

The Dangers of the New Home

Women writers sometimes explored the dangers of the new home in stories which linger on the perils of inhabiting modern space. The acquisition of rented property by the nouveau riche, showing their class status through their 'desirable' residences, is punished by violence, anxiety and insanity. A recurring feature in Crowe's *The Night Side of Nature* is the house with 'a rent so low' as to attract a series of owners, none of whom can endure the 'strange circumstances' (Crowe 2001: 219) of haunting. Krueger notes the subgenre of 'stories of haunted townhomes [*sic*]', in which fashion-conscious families are vulnerable to spectral disturbance (2014: 86). Rhoda Broughton's often anthologised tale 'The Truth, the Whole Truth and Nothing but the Truth', from her collection *Twilight Stories* (1873), is unusually structured around the exchange of letters between two fashionable married women. The mysteriously cheap rented property in Mayfair is chosen by Bessy De Wynt for her exiled friend Cecilia Montresor for its pretty drawing rooms, rose-coloured curtains and other 'important little trivialities' (Broughton 2009: 3) like ormolu garden gates. This femininised space, celebrated as 'a palace at the cost of a hovel' (3), becomes a 'terrible, hateful, fatal house' (10), haunted by a phantom targeting tenants duped by the cheapness of the property. Bessy's 'utter disbelief in ghosts' (9) is challenged by the death of the suitor of Cecilia's visitor, Adela, leaving the young woman unmarried and the house empty. The ghost's appearance induces 'unutterable stony horror' (7) in the terrified housemaid and Adela's suitor, yet the inhabitants remain 'utterly in the dark' (8) as to what has been seen. Ghostly noises, 'loudly audible all through the thin walls and floors of a London house' (8), reach the women in the drawing room from Adela's haunted bedroom, as if they are unprotected by the fragility of the house itself. Adela's private space is laid open for male investigation, the absence of Cecilia's husband also adding to the vulnerability of the family. Reading the story in terms of flawed gender norms and frivolity, Krueger notes the unsettling ending: 'the ghost is never exorcised so the haunting does not end' (Krueger 2014: 97). It is also significant that the terrified housemaid is sent to an asylum, where she maintains 'an absolute, hopeless silence' (10), disrupting by her absence the smooth running of the household hierarchy. The low rent invites an unnameable supernatural presence, which ensures a continuing stream of terrified tenants. The story can be read in terms of 'domesticity's doubleness' (Fraiman 2017: 15), exposing the difficulties of running a modern household and the dangers of renting a 'fatal house' with an undisclosed past.

In E. Nesbit's 'The Mystery of the Semi-Detached' from *Grim Tales* (1893), the desirability of the semi-detached house in a suburban street invites another horrifying vision of future violence. New housing developments and 'a wave of suburban expansion' after 1890 made cheaper, smaller houses newly available to the rising middle classes (Hapgood 2005: 5, 8). In this story the opening description of the streets near the haunted house reflects this convenience of modernity. The unnamed 'ineligible' 'City young man' who waits 'in a dusty suburban lane' for his lover is positioned between 'a row of big elms' and 'some eligible building sites' in view of 'the twinkling yellow lights of the Crystal Palace' (Nesbit 2006: 139), between the urbanisation of the pavement and lamp posts and the 'really quite rural' ground near the cemetery. His lover's house, described in the language of property sales as 'desirable, commodious, semi-detached' (139), is also strangely dark, 'no sign of life, no lights even in the windows', with a 'wide open' front door leading into the dark hall, although this is later attributed to careless servants who '*will* run out if they're left' (140). Nesbit's Gothic tales often make use of an open door beckoning in a passer-by to be confronted with death from another time period, as in the later tale 'The House of Silence' (1906). In these dark houses, a step away from the lights of London, silence becomes eerie; this house has 'a gloomy and deserted air' with 'no light anywhere' (140), the tiny rooms empty of people. Checking the rooms with a lit match for signs of burglary, he is unprepared for the spectral revelation in the back bedroom: his sweetheart, her 'throat ... cut from ear to ear' (140). And yet this defeminised object is not his sweetheart, but a stockbroker's daughter, whose death will be reported on 21 October, the date visible on the almanac when the suitor entered the bedroom on a May evening. The stockbroker is the next inhabitant of 'that fatal house' (141), a house of death as well as a 'really remarkably cheap and desirable semi-detached residence' (141), whose repeated commodiousness is no protection from an urban threat. What is uncanny is the suitor's description of the haunted room; he lists the female paraphernalia visible around the body, the scarf, gloves, hairpins and handkerchief, all of which match up with the 'odds and ends lying about' (141) left by his sweetheart, yet it is the spirit of another woman's dead body from a different family lying on the bed 'in a white loose gown' (140). The goriness of the spectral scene harks back to scenes from the sensationalised press; the suitor reads about the death from 'a quiet distant suburb' after the 'removal' of his new wife (141). Dead women in Nesbit's ghost stories, argues Margree, are deployed 'to negotiate fear of death' traumatising male ghost-seers (2019: 100). If a vision of the future betrays a repressed desire, this could be read as the suitor's fears of his own behaviour if allowed into a woman's bedroom. Moreover, it also reiterates the vulnerability of houses which do not stay locked against intruders, contradictory 'place[s] of safety' and 'the utmost danger' (Wisker 2022: 157) aligned with suburban unknowability.

Black Magic and Lost Women in 1890s Ghost Stories

By the 1890s, conversations about the haunted house had shifted to incorporate scientific and psychological explanations for uncanny phenomena. The Society for Psychical Research, formed in 1882, set out to investigate the haunted house and communications with the dead. A growing interest in spirit photography, spiritualism and scientific practices offered new ways of visualising and accounting for spectrality in an age of greater secularisation (Cadwallader 2016: 6, 12). Andrew Lang, a folklorist and member of the SPR, collected haunted house narratives in his popular *The Book of Dreams and Ghosts* (1897). Framed by the workings of 'modern science' and 'scientific experiment', his stories differ from Crowe's in their acceptance of 'the possibilities of occasional hallucinations' (1897: vii, 198). His awareness of the changing dynamics of the ghost story are expressed in his belief: 'The usual process is, given an old house, first a noise, then a hallucination, actual or pretended, then a myth to account for the hallucination' (1897: 201–2). Myths which can be attached to the old house might include enduring Victorian concerns – disputes about money, lost children, fears about servants, buried secrets of past violence – but to suggest that these might manifest in a potentially 'pretended' vision gestures towards an explanation for the ghostly based on repressed desire. Lang contends that 'apparitions in haunted houses are very seldom recognised as those of dead persons, and, when recognised, the recognition is usually dubious' (1897: 201). In his examples, connections between hauntings and family members often remain uncertain. The lady in black sighted by new inhabitants of an 1880s desirable residence is never traced back to a figure from the past, and seemed 'quite unable to speak' to clear up the mystery (1897: 199). The associations between ghosts and the 'old' house persevere, even as the old house was mythologised and remediated in a different form for a more sceptical age.

Lettice Galbraith's 'A Ghost's Revenge', from her little-known collection *New Ghost Stories* (1893), updates the haunted house narrative to include sinister aspects of the occult and fears about the devil in the form of a disgraced female ancestor. The spectral scenes occur in heavy snow on two fatal New Year's Eves, five years apart, when late-running trains struggle to deliver male visitors to the desolate spot of perpetual winter. Galbraith evokes the Gothic trope of the trepidatious approach, an 'almost impassable' road with poor visibility rendered 'desperately bad' by heavy snow, a 'lonely road which lay between the railway and the haunted house' (Galbraith 2023: 108), connecting civilised modernity to the unknowable dangers of the past. Gerald Harrison initially arrives on a 'beast of a night' at a 'desolate hole' (94) in a northern rural location to visit his friend Philip Granville. Granville, the anxious new owner of Ravenshill Hall, 'wrapped in shadow and silence' (109), is haunted by a presence in his property which threatens male owners on the last night of the old year. The queerness of the 'accursed' Hall, its 'bad name' (96), is of a piece with its resistance to renovation; despite spending a lot of money on furniture and repairs on a house which has 'stood empty for years' (96), Granville is still in danger, like Broughton's female tenants, of being 'driven out' or 'evict[ed]' by a phantom. Into the sanctified library organised around masculine leisure, with its tobacco, books and spirit decanter, comes a female demon; the servants report hearing 'shriek upon shriek of demoniacal laughter' (98) coupled with their master's agonised cries. His dead body is recovered from the pond in the grounds, with his eyes 'fixed in a wide stare of indescribable horror' (98). Despite attempts to dismiss the past, 'Horror was in the air. Old superstition reasserted its sway with renewed strength' (99). The 'old oak' of the Hall, symbolising tradition and the lure of the ancient, is of a piece with the 'ominous bell' ringing in the new year from the 'old grey tower' of the church, which 'loom[s] up behind' the rectory (109). These Gothic bells ring out the doom of the male owners who cannot atone for the denial of rights to the lost female ancestor.

In his potent argument about ghost stories as 'fictions of historical collapse', Nick Freeman contrasts the continuity of the house, both 'historical artefact and a contemporary residence', with its spectral inhabitants who lack the 'ability to develop and adapt', trapped by their 'historical fixedness' (Freeman 2018: 328). This clash between historical and contemporary is particularly relevant here, where the renovated house remains cursed by a disgraced spectral woman from the past, trapped by her fixed desire for revenge. The churchwarden explains, rather elliptically, that years earlier, Katharine Deverel cursed the man who robbed her of her husband's name, and their son of his lawful inheritance:

> 'Though I lose my immortal soul ... I'll hev revenge. You may tak' my child's birthright, you my slur ma fair name, but no man ... shall live to see a new year dawn wi'in these walls. I'll die on Deverel land.' (100–1)

She was found drowned in the pond in the grounds, 'with the dead baby still clasped in her arms' (101), a symbol of lost inheritance. Ignoring its function as a site of death, the next owner, Jack Chamberlayne, wants to fill up the pond to make way for a new tennis court, seeing the 'family ghost' as a bonus to the house 'going for a mere song' (102), the house's ominous cheapness again figuring unfinished spectral business (Krueger 2014: 87). The 'fatal pond' (111), rather like Le Fanu's graveyard, buries the secrets as well as the decaying bodies of ancestors who exert a terrifying magnetic pull on the new inhabitants. History repeats itself as the New Year curse lures Jack towards a watery grave. The 'wild awful cry' in the library evokes human sacrifice or terrible fear, before the moon reveals the uncanny figure of Jack, with his 'fixed' (111) eyes of horror slowly 'following the ghostly vision' across the lawn, as if in a hypnotic trance. This also evokes the spectral vision of the exiled mother and her (potentially illegitimate) child who lure out the living in Elizabeth Gaskell's 'The Old Nurse's Story' (1852). What is waiting outside the Victorian home, a purgatorial realm of disgraced women, threatens domestic stability and succession in the haunted house narrative.

Galbraith's fiction also reflects the *fin de siècle* fascination with black magic and its rituals; 'occult transmission' is a key context for the 1890s (Thurschwell 2001: 5). Her later story, 'The Blue Room' (1897), explores the effects of an incubus summoned by spells to the bedroom of an old house by inhabitants who are 'meddling with sorcery' (Liggins 2022: 190). In 'A Ghost's Revenge', the 'doomed' and 'devilish' house is the site of 'black work' (Galbraith 2023: 108), where 'there is no baulking the Deverel curse. It will have its victim' (108); both house and curse operate in terms of demonic malevolence. Approaching the house to rescue his friend Jack, Gerald hears the 'fiendish laughter' of the past female Deverels and their exultant chant, 'we shall have him tonight!' (110). The fire in the library, with its 'fierce, lurid glow', strikes at the heart of masculine privilege and power; it is interpreted by the servants as the feat of 'the devil's spawn' (114). The old oak and 'the great carved bedsteads', sites perhaps of sexual violence, burn quickly until the Hall is 'a heap of smouldering ashes enclosed in four, grim, smoke-blackened walls', a 'bare tottering shell' (114), not a modern place for tennis and theatricals. Significantly, in the Gothicised portrait gallery, 'Deverel after Deverel … shrivelled and cracked away from their frames, to go down calm and unflinching … into that burning fiery furnace' (113), in a hellish and triumphant strike against the family. In 'The Blue Room', the disgraced female ancestor Lady Barbara Mertoun, pictured in her 'bloom' in the portrait gallery, has not been buried in the family vault but 'by herself in the churchyard … all alone' (Galbraith 2023: 118), both spaces having the capacity to signal female exile from the family. Although the end of 'A Ghost's Revenge' sees Gerald lionised as the hero who 'had braved the Deverel ghosts and baulked them of their prey' (114), Jack struggles to 'efface' his experiences through marriage (115), his state of nervous exhaustion and traumatic refusal to speak suggesting that the haunting has left him broken. In both stories the workings of black magic serve to resurrect lost female histories and restore women's names in the family genealogy.

Henry James's *The Turn of the Screw* (1898), one of the most well known late Victorian examples of the haunted house narrative, can also be read in relation to a lost female history. Distinctive for its unsettling descriptions of the Udolpho-like Bly with its crenellated towers signalling 'grandeur' and a knowingly fake 'gingerbread antiquity' (James 1992: 136), the story centres on the potentially hallucinatory vision of its unnamed governess narrator who seeks to protect the children from encounters with the corrupt ghosts of the dead valet Peter Quint and his governess lover Miss Jessel. Andrew Smith has usefully discussed the text's spectral sightings in relation to the traces of history, in which 'the historical essence of the place becomes evoked through the prevailing mood' (2010: 129). This 'notion of place' (Smith 2010: 129), of a house 'spectrally freighted with possibilities', is important; the ghost-seer's emotional reactions are conditioned both by what they see and what they want to see. The governess, like the narrator of 'Madam Crowl', approaches the house and its secrets with awe, at first admiring its flowers and bright prospect but later experiencing the house at night, with its ominous noises and spectres framed in windows. The original illustrations to the 1898 edition in *Colliers' Weekly* dwell on Bly as a Gothic castle, including an iconic image of the governess peering down a dark staircase, candle in hand, which clearly influenced screen adaptations such as *The Innocents* (1960) (MacLeod 2016: 20). Her tour of the house by her young charge Flora takes her past 'empty chambers and dull corridors, on crooked staircases that made me pause and even on the summit of an old machicolated tower which made me dizzy', experiencing this 'castle of romance' 'room by room and secret by secret' (127); the equation of space and secrecy produces the dizziness of enraptured architectural delight. The deaths of the servants Quint and Miss Jessel may suggest 'strange passages and perils, secret disorders' (152), as James plays with the conventions of Gothic secrecy. This 'big ugly antique but convenient house, embodying a few features of a building still older, half-displaced and half-utilised' (127), is a winning combination of old and new, which only half-displaces the past, as the secrets of the dead leak out.

The grounds of Bly are often the site of spectral encounters, as ghosts are glimpsed through windows, on the tower, across the lake. The Sea of Azof, by which the black-clad spectre of the former governess appears, becomes another 'fatal pond'. This could symbolise the suicidal impulses of a servant 'found drowned', a stereotypically Victorian fate for seduced women. Across the lake Miss Jessel is 'an alien object … a figure whose right of presence I instantly and passionately questioned' (154). Distanced from, yet mirroring her governess replacement, the spectre is 'a figure of quite as unmistakable horror and evil: a woman in black, pale and dreadful – with such an air also, and such a face! – on the other side of the lake' (156). This encounter evokes feelings of loss and fears about 'shield[ing]' the young charges (160), with the new governess's despairing sobs linked to her desire for salvation. Associated with the watery depths, hallucinatory reflections and the fears of what might rise to the surface for Flora, the spectral Miss Jessel 'fixed the child … with a kind of fury of intention' (158). Shari Goldberg has discussed James's interest in 'mourning without grief' in his short fiction, where 'a dead girl can be kept alive through …

[memorialising] gestures' (2018: 515). In mourning for herself, or for her ill-fated relationship, the visible blackness of the phantom governess directly impacts on the vulnerable female onlookers at Bly. This 'fallen woman in black' is, according to Catherine Belsey, 'exactly the kind of phantom a susceptible governess who has read ghost stories might expect to see' (2019: 232). Spectral encounters with Miss Jessel precede an appreciation of her lost life, '"Poor woman – she paid for it"', laments Mrs Grose (159). The ways in which the spectres seek to 'fix' their gaze on the new governess is uncanny, the strange freedom of spectrality demanding a consideration of their unspoken histories, which remain tantalisingly obscure.

The little-known novella *The Gateless Barrier* (1900) by Lucas Malet, pseudonym of Mary St Leger Kingsley Harrison, offers an alternative example of the lost ancestor concealed within the architecture, here a masculinised aesthetic domain. In the modernist mode of Henry James and Vernon Lee, Malet's fiction is distinctive, argues Talia Schaffer, for its 'beautiful descriptions of hideous subjects', her interiors displaying 'a shimmering drapery of symbols' which resonate death and a fascination for Catholic rituals (Schaffer 2000: 200; Delyfer 2015). Stoke Rivers, an old English house soon to be inherited by Laurence Rivers after his uncle's death, is a place of dark oak panelling, antiques, 'rich sombre hangings of dark blue, crimson, or violet' (Malet 2015: 8) and erotic art. Growing increasingly hot and enervating, it is suffused by 'the musky odour of orchids' (15). The old-new characteristics of the architecture, apparent in the electric light and heating which clash with the 'old-fashioned character' (8), beckon the modern heir towards revelation:

> In this strange and unearthly radiance, Stoke Rivers seemed to call upon Laurence, to challenge his admiration, to assert its existence and its claim upon his heart, with a singular power ... It laid hands on his past and his future alike. It refused to be taken lightly ... It would force him not to disregard its secrets. (49)

Luring him in from the 'bright, vacant, silent corridor' (15), the secret room is hidden behind a tapestry curtain, depicting 'a naked and reluctant woman' (9). Crossing this sacred threshold is like entering a Bachelardian dream-space, an idealised yellow drawing room full of instruments, old china ornaments and a view of the Italian garden. The spectral Agnes Rivers, widow of Laurence's ancestor and namesake (killed in a naval battle in 1803), occupies this secret room, symbolising the attractions of the past in the face of the 'vacancy' of the modern. Out of 'the unyielding glare of the electric light' (37) served by automaton-like servants, this nostalgic attraction is more potent. In her 'house of dream-memory ... lost in the shadow of a beyond of the real past' (Bachelard 1964: 37), the ghost 'searches vainly for lost things' (35), guiding the living towards a locked escritoire of faded love-letters and her forgotten story. The 'enforced secrecy' (34) of the hidden room offers 'a dangerous degree of personal liberty', as Laurence's dalliances with the phantom 'fairy-lady' (referred to by the parson as a 'Scarlet Woman' because of her rose-pink dress visible through the windows) are more desired than exchanges with his fashionable and trivial American wife. Yet this drawing room is also one of Malet's macabre 'spaces of illness and death' (Benson James 2019: 43). Agnes's missing coffin and mouldering skeleton hidden within the wall, her letters about the bonds of propriety and prohibited marriage before her lover is killed, show the decay and despair behind the beautiful exterior and the 'lost things' to be recovered. The spectre is the only female presence in a house without women; the exchange between the hidden room and the nearby graveyard is another familiar Gothic trope, with missing coffins suggesting hidden threats to the patriarchal bloodline.

Lefebvre's notions of the 'ambiguous continuity' between separate spaces, of the permeability of boundaries and barriers (1991: 87), offer a useful perspective on a story which lingers on the crossing of thresholds between the vacant corridors and 'the room of strange and delectable meetings' (Malet 2015: 76). The notion of 'the gateless barrier' is evoked in the request to the phantom, to 'try to cross the gulf which seems to lie between us' (34). This transgressive act is, in the ghost's words, 'to force some barrier which I have neither the strength nor the right to force', a forbidden barrier imagined as 'ancient and venerable' (103) which, once crossed, allows for illicit conversation. Kirstin A. Mills has discussed Malet's exploration of 'crossing a physical and cognitive boundary' in relation to contemporary Theosophist notions of the supernatural fourth dimension, 'a realm existing outside of, and yet able to intersect with, the three-dimensional space that humans naturally perceive' (2021: 614, 620). This ritualistic crossing and Laurence's serving of the 'mysterious sacramental feast' (Malet 2015: 104) of bread and wine in the ornate dining room, to a ghost who cannot eat, borders on black magic, 'a very dangerous experiment' (103), linked to passages which also recall the giving up of the soul. The fire which partly destroys the wing blackens the tapestry, 'purged the offence' (119) of the explicit paintings, and the room 'stained by smoke' with its pretty furniture destroyed signals the end of the old. Malet's drawing of spectres into the material realm may attest to the rationalisation of the supernatural in the 1890s (Mills 2021: 615) but it also shows the perils of inhabiting patriarchal space.

After the fire the spirit 'could never again be subjected to the indignity of dwelling' (Malet 2015: 115), leaving the new heir to control his environment differently. The story ends next to Agnes's new-made grave in the 'age-old' (121) churchyard, her place in the family acknowledged, and the yellow drawing room 'rebuilt' for Laurence's use, 'a valediction to the old dynasty and a recognition of the new' (60).

Conclusion

The secret rooms, gloomy corridors, fatal ponds and incomplete family vaults of the Victorian haunted house symbolise the darkness of domesticity and the difficulties of inheritance. The architecture itself harbours secrets, curses and decaying skeletons, relics of a patriarchal past which must be recognised and sometimes atoned for. The haunted house, as Crowe intimates, is both prosaic and mysterious, crumbling into decline or newly renovated, situated away from modernity in deep rural seclusion or no less terrifying for occupying space on the borders of the city. According to Wolfreys, the ghost story can redirect us to the 'difference' of dwelling, what 'haunts and returns' in interiors, rooms, hallways (2018: 34). Spaces which refuse to be owned by their new owners or offer up the secrets of the past to family and staff encourage a return to the forbidden and the forgotten. To cross the threshold into the unknown, to go beyond the gateless barrier, is an act of necessary transgression, in order to access lost histories and gain a new understanding of the family and of domestic space.

Works Cited

Bachelard, Gaston. *The Poetics of Space*, translated by Maria Jolas. New York: Penguin, 1964.

Belsey, Catherine. *Tales of the Troubled Dead: Ghost Stories in Cultural History*. Edinburgh: Edinburgh University Press, 2019.

Benson James, Louise. 'Hysterical Bodies and Gothic Spaces: Lucas Malet's "moral dissecting-room"', in Jane Ford and Alexandra Gray (eds), *Lucas Malet: Dissident Pilgrim*. London: Routledge, 2019, pp. 33–51.

Brewster, Scott and Luke Thurston, eds. *The Routledge Handbook to the Ghost Story*. London: Routledge, 2018.

Broughton, Rhoda. 'The Truth, the Whole Truth and Nothing but the Truth', in *Twilight Stories*, edited by Emma Liggins. Brighton: Victorian Secrets, 2009, pp. 1–12.

Cadwallader, Jen. *Spirits and Spirituality in Victorian Fiction*. Basingstoke: Palgrave, 2016.

Crowe, Catherine. *The Night Side of Nature, or Ghosts and Ghost Seers*. Ware: Wordsworth, 2001.

Delyfer, Catherine. 'Visible/invisible/visuel: spectralité et hantologie dans *The Gateless Barrier* de Lucas Malet'. *Polysèmes*, vol. 13, 2015 (online). https://journals.openedition.org/polysemes/315 (last accessed 18 October 2024).

Fraiman, Susan. *Extreme Domesticity: A View from the Margins*. Columbia: Columbia University Press, 2017.

Freeman, Nick. 'Haunted Houses', in Scott Brewster and Luke Thurston (eds), *The Routledge Handbook to the Ghost Story*. London: Routledge, 2018, pp. 328–37.

Galbraith, Lettice. 'A Ghost's Revenge', in *The Blue Room and other Tales*, edited by Alistair Gunn. London: Wimbourne, 2023, pp. 93–115.

———. 'The Blue Room', in *The Blue Room and other Tales*, edited by Alistair Gunn. London: Wimbourne, 2023, pp. 116–38.

Goldberg, Shari. 'Henry James's Black Dresses: Mourning without Grief'. *Nineteenth-Century Literature*, vol. 72, no. 4, 2018, pp. 515–38.

Hamlett, Jane. *Material Relations: Domestic Interiors and Middle-Class Families in England, 1850–1910*. Manchester: Manchester University Press, 2010.

Hapgood, Lynne. *Margins of Desire: The Suburbs in Fiction and Culture, 1880–1925*. Manchester: Manchester University Press, 2005.

Heholt, Ruth. *Catherine Crowe: Gender, Genre and Radical Politics*. London: Routledge, 2021.

James, Henry. *The Turn of the Screw*, in *The Turn of the Screw and Other Stories*, edited by T. J. Lustig. Oxford: Oxford University Press, 1992, pp. 113–26.

Killeen, Jarlath. 'Irish Gothic: A Theoretical Introduction'. *Irish Journal of Gothic and Horror Studies*, vol. 1, 2006 (online). https://irishgothicjournal.net/wp-content/uploads/2018/03/jarlath-killeen1.pdf (last accessed 9 January 2025).

Krueger, Kate. *British Women Writers and the Short Story: Reclaiming Social Space*. Basingstoke: Palgrave Macmillan, 2014.

Lang, Andrew. *The Book of Dreams and Ghosts*. London: Longmans, Green, 1897.

Le Fanu, Joseph Sheridan. 'Madam Crowl's Ghost', in *The Gothic Tales of Sheridan Le Fanu*, edited by Xavier Aldana Reyes. London: British Library, 2020, pp. 225–41.

Le Fanu, Joseph Sheridan. 'Squire Toby's Will', in *The Gothic Tales of Sheridan Le Fanu*, edited by Xavier Aldana Reyes. London: British Library, 2020, pp. 173–210.

Lefebvre, Henri. *The Production of Space*, translated by Donald Nicholson Smith. Oxford: Blackwell, 1991.

Liggins, Emma. *The Haunted House in Women's Ghost Stories: Gender, Space and Modernity, 1850–1945*. Basingstoke: Palgrave Macmillan, 2020.

———. '"Meddling with Sorcery": Hypnotism, the Occult and the Return of Forsaken Women in the 1890s Ghost Stories of Lettice Galbraith'. *Women's Writing*, vol. 29, no. 2, 2022, pp. 177–95.

MacLeod, Kirsten. 'Material Turns of the Screw: The *Collier's Weekly* Serialization of *The Turn of the Screw* (1898)'. *Cahiers victoriens et édouardiens*, vol. 84,

2016. https://journals.openedition.org/cve/2986 (last accessed 9 January 2025).
Malet, Lucas. *The Gateless Barrier*. New York: Yurita Press, 2015.
Margree, Victoria. *British Women's Short Supernatural Fiction, 1860–1930: Our Own Ghostliness*. Basingstoke: Palgrave Macmillan, 2019.
Mills, Kirstin A. 'The Supernatural Fourth Dimension in Lucas Malet's *The Carissima* and *The Gateless Barrier*', in Clive Bloom (ed.), *The Palgrave Handbook of Steam Age Gothic*. Basingstoke: Palgrave Macmillan, 2021, pp. 613–29.
Nesbit, E. 'The Mystery of the Semi-Detached', in *The Power of Darkness: Tales of Terror*. Ware: Wordsworth, 2006, pp. 131–3.
Schaffer, Talia. *The Forgotten Female Aesthetes: Literary Culture in Late-Victorian England*. Charlottesville and London: University Press of Virginia, 2000.
Smith, Andrew. *The Ghost Story, 1840–1920: A Cultural History*. Manchester: Manchester University Press, 2010.
Thurschwell, Pamela. *Literature, Technology and Magical Thinking, 1880–1920*. Cambridge: Cambridge University Press, 2001.
Wisker, Gina. *Contemporary Women's Ghost Stories: Spectres, Revenants, Ghostly Returns*. Basingstoke: Palgrave Macmillan, 2022.
Wolfreys, Julian. *Haunted Selves, Haunting Places in English Literature and Culture, 1880– Present*. Basingstoke: Palgrave Macmillan, 2018.

Chapter 23

Haunted Libraries and Museums
Darryl Jones

'The Burden of Dead Books', a 1919 ghost story by Arthur Gray, opens with these words:

> By its air of reverend quiet, its redolence of dusty death, in the marshalled lines of its sleeping occupants, and in the labels that briefly name the dead author and his work, an ancient repository of books, such as a college library, suggests the, perhaps, hackneyed similitude of a great cemetery. (Gray 2009: 67)

Gray spent a lot of his time in libraries. He was the Master of Jesus College, Cambridge, and a distinguished Shakespeare scholar, who published his sole volume of ghost stories, the unappealingly titled *Tedious Brief Tales of Granta and Gramarye*, under the pseudonym 'Ingulphus' (Ingulf, or Ingulphus, was the eleventh-century Benedictine Abbot of Crowland in Lincolnshire, whose historical writings are notoriously unreliable). Gray was one of a number of influential Cambridge University figures who wrote ghost stories in the late nineteenth and early twentieth centuries. M. R. James, most famously, was Provost of King's and, for a time, University Vice Chancellor; but there was also A. C. Benson (Master of Magdalene), E. G. Swain (Chaplain of King's), Percy Lubbock (Pepys Librarian at Magdalene) and, a little later, A. N. L. Munby (Librarian of King's). E. F. Benson, R. H. Malden and H. W. Tatham all graduated from King's with Firsts in the Classical Tripos; F. M. Mayor, a graduate of Newnham, came from a distinguished Cambridge family (her uncle, J. E. B. Mayor, had taught M. R. James). Other figures, such as Vernon Lee or Henry James, had looser affiliations with the Cambridge world.

Collectively, these writers, and others like them (see Pardoe 1991), defined the parameters of what is often referred to as the antiquarian ghost story, characteristically set in a gentlemanly world of scholarship, amongst libraries, archives and museums, in the colleges of ancient universities, or cathedral closes, or remote country houses or churches. Sometimes, as the title 'The Burden of Dead Books' implies, these stories reveal the dangers, fantasies, frustrations or discontents of the scholarly life. In Gray's story, Matthew Makepeace, a Fellow of Jesus, gets a mysterious visitor to his rooms, who tells him some disturbing truths:

> Getting old is a sad affair, sadder even than dying. I think that you are sixty, and I don't think that just now you are quite in your best health. Has the world gone well with you? In five, ten years, will it go better? You have written a silly book that nobody will read, and you are ashamed of it. You have wasted your years of manhood in twisting ropes of sand. And the solitude, Matthew! My heart bleeds to think what your solitude will be. What friend have you to smooth the downhill course? Who cares for the friend of dead books? (Gray 2009: 86–7)

'The Burden of Dead Books' is the story of a tired life and an exhausted discourse. As the phrase 'perhaps, hackneyed' suggests, by 1919 Gray recognised that the library/cemetery simile was a widely deployed one, in danger of becoming a cliché, and more generally that the library had become a commonplace setting for ghost stories (see Kirk 2016). Gray, therefore, comes at the very end of my story, a kind of terminus. In this chapter I want to look at the development of the library and (to a lesser extent) the museum as loci of fear across the Victorian ghost story, examining a number of uses to which these settings are put, and some of the concerns, anxieties and phenomena which these stories reveal or conceal.

Libraries

In 1907, the Edinburgh University Librarian William K. Dickson wrote appreciatively to M. R. James about his ghost stories. He was a particular admirer of 'Canon Alberic's Scrap-book' (1895), in which Dennistoun, a curator at a thinly fictionalised version of the Fitzwilliam Museum in Cambridge (of which James was the Director from 1893 to 1908), discovers a priceless manuscript collection in the library of a remote Pyrenean cathedral, and in doing so inadvertently releases a demon. 'Perhaps,' Dickson wrote, 'it makes a more intimate appeal to a librarian!' (Dickson 1907). There are good reasons to set ghost stories in libraries.

Writers, as Alice Crawford and Robert Crawford argue in *Libraries in Literature*:

> imagine and metamorphose collections of books, giving libraries of all sorts a heightened metaphorical presence. [...] Not unreasonably, people think

of libraries as full of books, rather than of books as full of libraries. Yet for imaginative writers the lure of the library as a resource, a destination for their work, a place of reverie or haunting or even mockery, has long been strong in fiction. (Crawford and Crawford 2022: 1–2)

The fictional library, we shall see, is regularly 'a place of reverie or haunting'. Libraries, the critic Deidre Lynch writes, are often figured as Gothic spaces, in which the past and present interpenetrate, and where 'readers [...] learn to associate the textual and the spectral' (Lynch 2001: 30):

> In a Gothic novel, to enter the chambers a household sets aside for its reading and writing is to be recruited into a genealogical plot. The secret cabinets of Gothic libraries house memorials and legacies. To visit them is to stumble on wills made by dead fathers; long lost certificates of marriage, musty manuscripts. (Lynch 2001: 29)

The conditions Lynch describes here are exactly those which animate one of the most interesting ghost stories of the earlier nineteenth century, James Hogg's 'Welldean Hall' (1820). In Hogg's story, the estate of the miserly Laird of Welldean is sold off after his death. When a book dealer arrives to evaluate Welldean's 'valuable library', he has a spectral encounter:

> as he approached an oaken book-case in the middle of a large division, he perceived an old man standing before it, of a most forbidding and threatening aspect. [...] He looked at the old man again, and thought he discerned the spokes of the book-case through his body. (Hogg 1820: 250, 251)

Are we seeing the ghost of the Laird here, or the ghost of his bookcase? Or, in keeping with Lynch's conflation of 'the textual and the spectral', is there no difference between the two? The Laird's heir calls in Dr Leadbetter, 'the great metaphysical minister of the parish', to investigate the library: 'But, doctor, it is only on this condition, that whatever you may discover in that library, you are to make known only to me. My late uncle's hoards of wealth and legal bonds have not been discovered, neither has his will' (Hogg 1820: 252, 254). When Dr Leadbetter investigates the oaken bookcase, he is physically assaulted by an invisible force. Eventually, a key written in pencil on the inside boards of a book is deciphered, and the Laird's will, bonds and thousand-pound notes are found interspersed amongst the leaves of the books; a concealed drawer in a bookcase is full of gold.

In Charlotte Riddell's *The Uninhabited House* (1875), an avaricious ghost also haunts his library. River Hall, a seemingly desirable, well-appointed house on the banks of the Thames on the outskirts of London, is impossible to let to tenants as it has a reputation for being haunted. The house was formerly the property of Robert Elmsdale, a tight-fisted businessman and moneylender, who is believed to have committed suicide in his library, and returns in spirit form to '"that dreadful room"' because, one of his creditors says, '"He thought a great deal of money, and has come back for it. He can't rest, and won't let me rest till I have paid him principal and interest – compound interest"' (Riddell 2018: 236, 317). In an influential argument, Andrew Smith has suggested that:

> The nineteenth century was subject to moments of acute economic crisis, and it is noteworthy that images of spectrality take on a particularly economic dimension during such periods. [...] Paper money was perceived as spectral money (not 'real' money), which like the ghost had a liminal presence. (Smith 2010: 5)

Thus, one of the great representative literary works of the 'hungry forties', a decade of depression and starvation, is the most celebrated of all English ghost stories. Charles Dickens's *A Christmas Carol* (1843) is a tale of spectral misers and avaricious businessmen who cannot let go of the wealth they have hoarded, even after death. 'Bookkeeping' is the function of both a librarian and an accountant, and a number of nineteenth-century ghost stories conflate the spectrality of paper money (and other financial documents: wills, bonds, promissory notes, IOUs) with the spectrality of books and libraries. Financial papers can be hidden amongst the leaves of books, or written on their pages, as in Hogg or, later, M. R. James. In *The Uninhabited House*, Elmsdale's ghost haunts his library, '"counting over bank notes. He had a pile of them before him, and I distinctly saw that he wetted his fingers in order to separate them"' (Riddell 2018: 216).

As Penny Fielding has noted in an important study of M. R. James, the very word 'library' was up for contention across the nineteenth and into the twentieth century, an unstable signifier: 'The library's metonymic position as a signifier of "culture", at a time when that very word was a contested issue, allowed it to become a repository of books but also of competing social fears and desires' (Fielding 2000: 752–3). The library, Fielding writes, 'is both a space and a system' (Fielding 2000: 756). It is a place for the housing of books and manuscripts, but also a form of knowledge in itself.

'If truth is not to be found on the shelves of the British Museum,' Virginia Woolf famously asks in *A Room of One's Own* (1929), on visiting the celebrated Reading Room of what was perhaps the world's greatest library, 'where, I asked myself, picking up a notebook and a pencil, is truth?' (Woolf 2015: 20). M. R. James, an old family acquaintance, would have agreed. He set a pivotal scene of possibly his most famous story, 'Casting the Runes' (1911), in 'the Select Manuscript Room of the British Museum' (James 1911: 107). 'Casting the Runes' enacts a clash of two forms of knowledge, the institutional and the occult; in the British Museum, the disreputable occultist Karswell passes a demon-summoning runic parchment to his respectable academic nemesis, Dunning. As Christopher Frayling writes:

> There are many urban legends about the old Reading Room: the one about the occultist Aleister Crowley trying to prove that he had achieved invisibility by walking through the room stark naked – and then thinking he *had* proved it because no-one took any notice; [...] and the one about certain books in the restricted section that are *so* contagiously evil that the Archbishop of Canterbury, or his representative, has to stand over you when you are consulting them. But the most powerful legend of all is the one about the casting of the runes [...]. (Frayling 2005: xx)

As 'both a space and a system', the library was further contested around the turn of the nineteenth and twentieth centuries. Was it a private collection, belonging to wealthy individuals like the Laird of Welldean (or, in another context, to *Pride and Prejudice*'s Mr Bennet, who retreats into his library as it is a symbol and guarantor of his gentlemanly status, which the novel renders increasingly precarious) or to closed institutions like Cambridge Colleges? Or was it an open, public space, like an exhibition or a museum? This tension is played out at the beginning of *A Room of One's Own*. Before she heads, with her pencil and notebook, to the British Museum Reading Room, Virginia Woolf is refused access to the library of Trinity College, Cambridge:

> here I was actually at the door which leads into the library itself. I must have opened it, for instantly there issued, like a guardian angel barring the way with a flutter of black gown instead of white wings a deprecating, silvery, kindly gentleman, who regretted in a low voice as he waved me back that ladies are only admitted to the library if accompanied by a Fellow of the College or furnished with a letter of introduction.
> That a famous library has been cursed by a woman is a matter of complete indifference to a famous library. Venerable and calm, with all its treasures safe locked within its breast, it sleeps complacently and will, so far as I am concerned, so sleep forever. Never will I wake these echoes, never will I ask for that hospitality again, I vowed as I descended the steps in anger. (Woolf 2015: 6)

Virginia Woolf and Margaret Oliphant are linked across generations. Woolf's very question of women's access to libraries informs one of the most important of all Victorian ghost stories, Oliphant's 'The Library

Window' (1896). Like Woolf many years later, Oliphant took out a reader's ticket for the British Museum Reading Room, in her case on moving to London in 1852. In a *Blackwood's* article of 1855, she wrote about the woman librarygoer, in what is surely a self-portrait:

> There she is – behold her! – in the library of the British Museum, with her poke bonnet, her india-rubber overshoes; perhaps – most likely – some sandwiches in that pocket. [...] There she sits all the dull November day, the London fog peering in at her through the big windows, nobody blowing a trumpet to clear the way as she goes home through the dingy streets of Bloomsbury [...] putting up with an omnibus, and perhaps carting her notes in her little bag or basket. (Jay 2022: 106)

In *Three Guineas* (1938), Woolf in her turn writes angrily about Oliphant's lot as a Victorian woman writer:

> Has it not on the contrary smeared your mind and dejected your imagination and led you to deplore the fact that Mrs. Oliphant sold her brain, her very admirable brain, prostituted her culture and enslaved her intellectual liberty in order that she might earn her living and educate her children? (Woolf 2015: 170–1)

'The Library Window' registers, in its indirect manner, the discontents and frustrations of the Victorian woman intellectual.

The story is set in St Andrews (here renamed St Rule's, after one of the university town's medieval towers), a place Oliphant knew well. Its narrator, a young girl, is staying with her aunt in a house opposite the university library. She becomes fascinated by one of the library's windows, through which she begins to see a room slowly taking shape, with a writing desk, bookshelves and a man who sits writing every night, whom she takes to be a librarian. What seems to fascinate the narrator, Elizabeth McCarthy has written, 'above all else is the scholar's absorption in his work' (McCarthy 2010: 108): 'Is he still there? is he writing, writing always? I wonder what he is writing!' (Oliphant 2019: 32). But the window and the room do not exist. Like many Victorian ghost stories by women, 'The Library Window' is a tale of domestic entrapment, which comments obliquely on the life and social position of women (see Dickerson 1996) – in this case, denied access to knowledge and education.

As Elisabeth Jay has observed, by the standards of the ancient British and Irish universities around the *fin de siècle*, St Andrews was actually rather progressive (Jay 2022: 107). It first admitted women as full students in 1892, four years before the story was published, and in 1896 it opened the first university-owned women's hall of residence in these islands. All the Scottish universities, in fact, started to award degrees to women in the 1890s, followed shortly afterwards in 1905 by Trinity College Dublin. Oxford opened its doors to women as full members in 1920; Cambridge (due in no small part to the influence of M. R. James, one of the university's most powerful figures, who did everything he could to block change) not until as late as 1948.

'The Library Window', though, is set many years earlier, in the first half of the century: the narrator, a young girl at the time of the story, is now an elderly widow. Jay points out that the King James Library at St Andrews was in reality not quite as draconian in barring women as some other libraries – the Wren Library at Trinity College, Cambridge, for example; the library that Virginia Woolf curses. The first record of a woman borrowing a book under her own name from the King James is as early as 1835 (Jay 2022: 107). Nevertheless, 'The Library Window' makes it clear that university libraries are exclusively masculine spaces: '"there are no women-servants in the Old Library"', the narrator is told (Oliphant 2019: 17). During a discussion of whether the library window is real, or a *trompe l'oeil* painted in to avoid the window tax, Mr Pitmilly suggests a solution, only to check himself when he realises the impossibility of what he is proposing: '"You could so easily satisfy yourself, Mrs. Belcarres, if you were to –"' (20). The unfinished (silent, spectral) conclusion of that sentence is 'go into the library'. Generations of women, the story implies, have been thwarted, or haunted, by their inability to enter a library.

M. R. James, conversely, spent his life in libraries. He was the most eminent anglophone codicologist of his day, a man of simply phenomenal learning, who dedicated his scholarly life to cataloguing the medieval manuscript collections of many great libraries: he catalogued the collections of sixteen Cambridge colleges, and those of a variety of other libraries, including Eton College, Lambeth Palace, the J. P. Morgan Library, the John Rylands Library, Aberdeen University Library, plus many other smaller libraries and collections. At the time of his death in 1936, he left unfinished a vast project – a catalogue of the medieval manuscripts of Cambridge University Library (see Jones 2022: 114). His biographer Richard William Pfaff suggests that James was attempting in his cataloguing to reconstruct 'a *bibliothèque imaginaire* of the whole of medieval England' (Pfaff 1980: 58), which he carried in his mind.

James's ghost stories have been described as 'a kind of imaginative surplus or by-product of his formal scholarship, to which they are intimately connected' (Jones 2022: 115). Many of his best stories – and particularly those in his first two collections, *Ghost Stories of an Antiquary* (1904) and *More Ghost Stories of an Antiquary* (1911), written while he was still at King's College, Cambridge – are set in and around libraries and archives of various kinds. We have already looked at 'Canon Alberic's Scrap-Book' and 'Casting the Runes'. 'Lost Hearts' (1895) is the tale of a Regency occultist, Mr Abney, whose 'library contained all the then available books bearing on the Mysteries, the Orphic poems, the worship of Mithras, and the Neo-Platonists' (James 1904: 33). At the end of the story, he is discovered dead in his library, killed by the ghosts of the children he has ritually sacrificed. Like 'The Library Window', 'The Tractate Middoth' (1911) is in part a story about women's access to libraries. Here, Cambridge University Library itself is transformed into a labyrinth, whose mysteries involve deciphering the meaning of a hidden code, '11334' (James 1911: 67). This turns out to be a library classmark, for a book which, as in 'Welldean Hall', conceals a will. John Eldred, a Cambridge graduate, has access to the library; his cousin, Mary Simpson, does not, and so needs to employ the help of a man on the inside, an assistant librarian. The book at 11.3.34 (to give its proper classmark) is protected by a terrifying spider-spirit. In 'Mr. Humphreys and His Inheritance' (1911), the protagonist inherits a country house which contains both an impressive library and a mysterious maze, each of which is an emblem for the other. 'The drawing up of a *catalogue raisonné* would be a delicious occupation for winter' (James 1911: 243), he thinks, and sets about simultaneously cataloguing his library and mapping his maze, and in doing so frees a spirit from Hell, which manifests itself in the library, crawling out of a hole in the map. For James, the library and the labyrinth were emblems not only for one another, but for the universe, an unseen order full of malignant spirits whom we should not disturb.

The researcher who stumbles upon a ghost in the archives is a classic figure in the ghost story. In Vernon Lee's 'Amour Dure' (1887), for example, Spiridion Trepka, a Polish scholar, travels to the Italian town of Urbania to research a book. In the archives, he discovers the correspondence of Medea da Carpi, a fifteenth-century noblewoman who may have murdered both of her husbands, and who seems to have been irresistible to all men. As he uncovers her story, he, too falls in love with her, and summons her ghost back from the dead: he receives 'a letter addressed to me in curious handwriting which seemed strangely familiar to me, and which, after a moment, I recognised as that of the letters of Medea da Carpi at the Archives' (Lee 2006: 65). Trepka comes to understand that, as a historian, the past is as real to him as the present; that he lives among the dead: 'Those pedants say that the dead are dead, the past is past. For them, yes; but why for me? [...] Why should there not be ghosts to such as can see them?' (69).

'Am I mad? Or are there really ghosts?' Trepka asks himself (65). As Oliver Tearle has pointed out, there are a number of parallels between Lee and Henry James (Tearle 2018: 151), most notably a fascination with European high culture (Lee spent much of her adult life living in and writing about Italy), and a categorical ambiguity as to the reality of the supernatural. Often, as in 'Amour Dure', or James's 'The Real Right Thing' (1899), the very solitariness and inwardness of archival research breaks down any binary distinctions between objective reality and solipsistic fantasy. As Stephen Matterson argues in his extremely sophisticated reading of 'The Real Right Thing', the later James often deploys an 'intense use of the supernatural form in order to convey an interior truth of the displaced self. [...] At his most corrosively introspective, James turns to Gothic, to the language of the supernatural tale, as the medium of the story'(Matterson 2010: 213).

In James's story, George Withermore, a young writer, is commissioned to write a biography of Ashton Doyne, a recently deceased man of letters. Working in Doyne's library, reading 'diaries, letters, memoranda, notes, documents of many sorts', Withermore comes to believe that Doyne's spirit is there with him, a benign, helpful presence 'among the books and papers, a hushed, discreet librarian' (James 1996: 121, 127). He is '"personally in the room"', Doyne's widow attests: '"He *is* with us"' (126). 'There were moments, for instance,' Withermore comes to feel, 'when, as he bent over his papers, the light breath of his dead host was as distinctly in his hair as his own elbows were on the page before him' (127). But as Withermore's research progresses, Doyne's spirit suddenly turns resentful, antagonistic and frightening: 'He strains forward out of his darkness; he reaches toward us out of his mystery; he makes us dim signs out of his horror' (132). Doyne's ghost appears to Withermore at the library door: 'On the threshold – guarding it... . Immense. But Dim. Dark. Dreadful' (133).

'The Real Right Thing' is a great ghost story, but it is also a major comment on the literary life, the private and public self, the intrusive nature of biography, and the ethics of research. These were subjects which clearly exercised James, and to which he returns several times in his fiction, in stories such as 'The Author of "Beltraffio"' (1884), 'The Private Life' (1892), 'Sir Dominic Ferrand' (1892),'The Great Good Place' (1900), and perhaps most famously in 'The Aspern Papers' (1888). In 1914, two years before his death, James wrote to his nephew Harry:

> My sole wish is to frustrate as utterly as possible the post-mortem exploiter – which, I know, is but imperfectly possible. Still one can do something, and I have long thought of launching, by a provision in my will, a curse not less

explicit than Shakespeare's own on any such as try to move my bones. [...] One can discredit and dishonour such enterprises even if one can't prevent them, and as you are my sole and exclusive literary heir and executor you will doubtless be able to serve in some degree as a check and a frustrator. (Cited in Edel 1972: 145)

Henry James was drawn closer to the world of the supernatural in part through the example of his brother William, who was fascinated by the subject. William James was an early member of the Society for Psychical Research, and its president in 1894–5. At the beginning of the chapter on 'The Reality of the Unseen' in his landmark work *Varieties of Religious Experience* (1902), William wrote:

Were one asked to characterize the life of religion in the broadest and most general terms possible, one might say that it consists of the belief that there is an unseen order, and that our supreme good lies in harmoniously adjusting ourselves thereunto. (James 1987: 55)

There is an unseen order – and we need to stay on the right side of it. As 'The Real Right Thing' suggests, the relationship of biographer to subject is an intimate one, 'an intercourse closer than that of life', like 'a pair of lovers' (James 1996: 124, 126). But, as the story shows, there are some things the dead do not want us to know. The library ghost story can often be, in the title of one of M. R. James's best late ghost stories, 'A Warning to the Curious'.

Museums

In his 1899 novel *Pharos the Egyptian*, the Anglo-Australian novelist Guy Boothby imagines a dialogue between his protagonist, Cyril Forrester, and a mummy Forrester encounters in the British Museum:

It might have been saying, 'Ah, my nineteenth-century friend, your father stole me from the land of my birth, and from the resting-place the gods decreed for me; but beware, for retribution is pursuing you, and is even now close upon your heels. (Boothby 1899: 49)

Pharos the Egyptian is unambiguously a narrative of colonial retribution, as the novel's Gothic Immortal, a revived Ancient Egyptian high priest, destroys European civilisation via a devastating pandemic, of which Forrester himself is the major vector. '"The plague which is now destroying Europe was decreed by the gods of Egypt against such nations as have committed the sin of sacrilege"', Pharos tells him (Boothby 1899: 356).

The museum is a representative nineteenth-century institution, powerfully implicated in the century's world of imperial conquest. Colonialism, Elizabeth Edwards, Chris Gosden and Ruth Phillips write, 'was profoundly material and [...] colonized and imperial centers were critically linked by a traffic in objects' (Edwards, Gosden and Phillips 2006: 3) The British Museum was founded in 1753, but gained particular impetus from 1822 after the deciphering of the Rosetta Stone (a British Museum artefact since 1802) by Jean-François Champollion began the nineteenth century's 'Egyptomania' craze (see Tyldesley 2005: 53–68; Moser 2006). Sir Robert Smirke's neoclassical British Museum building on Gower Street, Bloomsbury was constructed between 1823 and 1846. The Victoria and Albert Museum in South Kensington was established in 1852. Next door to it, the Science Museum opened in 1857. South Kensington's third great Victorian museum, the Natural History Museum, London's cathedral to Darwinism, opened in 1881. Museums, then, were the most spectacular outward and visible embodiments of what Thomas Richards has termed the 'imperial archive', an accumulation and nexus of information, classification and control (see Richards 1993). Museums, therefore, also became an imaginative locus for empire's anxieties, discontents and paranoid fears, for the return of the colonised, often in Gothic or supernatural form (see Arata 1996; Bulfin 2018).

Of all the major Victorian writers of the supernatural, Arthur Conan Doyle was the most avowedly imperialist in outlook and politics. 'I am an Imperialist,' he wrote to the *Irish Times* in 1912, 'because I believe the whole to be greater than the part, and I would always willingly sacrifice any part if I thought it to the advantage of the whole' (Doyle 1986: 164). A number of Conan Doyle's most important supernatural tales, therefore, have museum settings or elements. In 'The Ring of Thoth' (1890), the Egyptologist John Vansittart Smith of Gower Street is researching Egyptian artefacts in the Louvre Museum (established 1793), where he encounters an Ancient Egyptian Gothic Immortal bent on reviving a mummy. In 'Lot No. 249' (1892), an Oxford student and occultist has gathered together his own private museum of colonial plunder: 'It was such a chamber as he had never seen before – a museum rather than a study. Walls and ceiling were thickly covered with a thousand strange relics from Egypt and the East' (Doyle 2016: 215). In one of his last works, *The Land of Mist* (1926), the rogue scientist Professor George Edward Challenger, 'British Museum Assistant, 1892. Assistant-Keeper of Comparative Anthropology Department, 1893.

Resigned after acrimonious Correspondence same year', investigates a haunted house in Dorset, and has a terrifying encounter with the ghost of Dr Rupert Tremayne, a 'mad doctor' who 'had been in India all his life' (Doyle 1952: 11, 409).

'The Brown Hand' (1899) is one of Conan Doyle's most straightforward ghost stories, and is once again an unambiguous tale of colonial retribution. It is the story of Sir Dominick Holden,

> the most distinguished Indian surgeon of his day. In the Army originally, he afterwards settled down into civil practice in Bombay, and visited, as a consultant, every part of India. His name is best remembered in connection with the Oriental Hospital which he founded. (Doyle 2016: 370)

Sir Dominick returns to England and buys 'an ancient manor house upon the edge of Salisbury Plain', where he keeps his own very particular private museum of imperial plunder: 'bloated organs, gaping cysts, distorted bones, odious parasites – a singular exhibition of all the products of India' (370, 375). Sir Dominick's nephew, a member of the Society for Psychical Research who investigates haunted houses, visits his uncle, and has a ghostly encounter:

> The moon shone upon the side of his face, and I saw that it was chocolate-brown in colour, with a ball of black hair like a woman's at the back of his head. He walked slowly and his eyes were cast upwards towards the line of bottles which contained those gruesome remnants of humanity. He seemed to examine each jar with attention, and then to pass it on to the next. When he had come to the end of the line, immediately opposite my bed, he stopped, faced me, threw up his hands with a gesture of despair, and vanished from my sight. (376)

This is the ghost of an Indian beggar whose hand Sir Dominick has amputated. The Indian wants to keep his hand, because 'according to his religion it was an all-important matter that the body should be reunited after death, and so make a perfect dwelling for the spirit', but Sir Dominick, in true colonial fashion, insists on ownership, claiming it for the imperial archive (a part sacrificed to the whole, as Conan Doyle would have said). '"But remember, Sahib"', the Indian tells him, '"I shall want it back when I am dead"' (378).

'Museums,' Vernon Lee wrote in 1881, are 'evil necessities where art is arranged and ticketed and made dingy even as are plants in a botanic collection' (Hoberman 2003: 467). They are part of a Victorian system of classification and taxonomy, she implies, and not primarily spaces of art or culture. The ghost story can serve to frustrate this taxonomic urge, to render it incomplete. Lee's story 'A Wedding

Chest' (1904) opens with an entry from the 'Catalogue of the Smith Museum, Leeds':

> No. 428. A panel (five feet by two feet three inches) formerly the front of a *cassone* or coffer, intended to contain the garments and jewels of a bride. [...] Bequeathed in 1878 by the widow of the Rev. Lawson Stone, late Fellow of Trinity College, Cambridge. (Lee 2006: 229)

And so we end where we began, in the shadowy world of Cambridge dons and their ghostly lives. In 'A Wedding Chest' there is a major, puzzling gap in signification: the missing story of how the Reverend Stone came into the possession of the titular artefact, which is drenched in the blood of the Italian Renaissance. But this, as I have suggested, is a major component of the spectrality of the ghost story, a genre which is often characterised by its use of silences, absences, elisions and lacunae – *things which are not there.*

Works Cited

Arata, Stephen. *Fictions of Loss in the Victorian Fin de Siècle: Identity and Empire.* Cambridge: Cambridge University Press, 1996.

Boothby, Guy. *Pharos the Egyptian.* London: Ward, Lock & Co., 1899.

Bulfin, Ailise. *Gothic Invasions: Imperialism, War, and Fin-de-Siècle Popular Fiction.* Cardiff: University of Wales Press, 2018.

Crawford, Alice and Robert Crawford, eds. *Libraries in Literature.* Oxford: Oxford University Press, 2022.

Dickerson, Vanessa D. *Victorian Ghosts in the Noontide: Women Writers and the Supernatural.* Columbia: University of Missouri Press, 1996.

Dickson, William K. Letter to M. R. James, 19 May 1907. Cambridge University Library MS Add. 7481/D38.

Doyle, Arthur Conan. *The Professor Challenger Stories.* London: John Murray, 1952.

———. *The Unknown Conan Doyle: Letters to the Press.* London: Secker & Warburg, 1986.

———. *Gothic Tales*, edited by Darryl Jones. Oxford: Oxford University Press, 2016.

Edel, Leon. *Henry James: The Master 1901–1916.* London: Hart-Davis, 1972.

Edwards, Elizabeth, Chris Gosden and Ruth B. Phillips, eds. *Sensible Objects: Colonialism, Museums and Material Culture.* Oxford and New York: Berg, 2006.

Fielding, Penny. 'Reading Rooms: M. R. James and the Library of Modernity'. *MFS: Modern Fiction Studies*, vol. 46, no. 3, Fall 2000, pp. 749–71.

Frayling, Christopher. 'Introduction' to Tony Earnshaw, *Beating the Devil: The Making of Night of the Demon.* Bradford: National Museum of Photography, Film and Television, 2005, pp. xx–xxiv.

Gray, Arthur ['Ingulphus']. *Tedious Brief Tales of Granta and Gramarye*. Cambridge: Oleander Press, 2009.
Hoberman, Ruth. 'In Quest of a Museal Aura: Turn of the Century Narratives about Museum-Displayed Objects'. *Victorian Literature and Culture*, vol. 31, no. 2, 2003, pp. 467–82.
Hogg, James. 'Welldean Hall', in *Winter Evening Tales: Collected Among the Cottagers in the South of Scotland*, vol. 2. Edinburgh: Oliver and Boyd; London: G. and W. B. Whittaker, 1820, pp. 245–321.
James, Henry. 'The Real Right Thing', in *Complete Stories 1898–1910*, edited by Denis Donoghue. New York: Library of America, 1996, pp. 121–34.
James, Montague Rhodes. *Ghost Stories of an Antiquary*. London: Edward Arnold, 1904.
———. *More Ghost Stories of an Antiquary*. London: Edward Arnold, 1911.
James, William. *Varieties of Religious Experience*, in *Writings 1902–1910*, edited by Bruce Kuklick. New York: Library of America, 1987.
Jay, Elisabeth. 'Margaret Oliphant's "The Library Window"', in Alice Crawford and Robert Crawford (eds), *Libraries in Literature*. Oxford: Oxford University Press, 2022, pp. 102–13.
Jones, Darryl. 'M. R. James's Libraries', in Alice Crawford and Robert Crawford (eds), *Libraries in Literature*. Oxford: Oxford University Press, 2022, pp. 114–27.
Kirk, Tanya, ed. *The Haunted Library: Classic Ghost Stories*. London: British Library, 2016.
Lee, Vernon. 'Amour Dure' in *Hauntings and Other Fantastic Tales*, edited by Catherine Maxwell and Patricia Pulham. Peterborough, ON: Broadview Press, 2006, pp. 41–76.
Lynch, Deidre. 'Gothic Libraries and National Subjects'. *Studies in Romanticism*, vol. 40, no. 1, Spring 2001, pp. 29–48.
McCarthy, Elizabeth. '"The voice out of the unseen": Love, Death and Mourning in the Writing of Margaret Oliphant', in Helen Conrad O'Briain and Julie Anne Stevens (eds), *The Ghost Story from the Middle Ages to the Twentieth Century*. Dublin: Four Courts, 2010, pp. 97–111.
Matterson, Stephen. '"The Consecration of his enterprise": Henry James' "The Real Right Thing"', in Helen Conrad O'Briain and Julie Anne Stevens (eds), *The Ghost Story from the Middle Ages to the Twentieth Century*. Dublin: Four Courts, 2010, pp. 203–16.
Moser, Stephanie. *Wondrous Curiosities: Ancient Egypt at the British Museum*. Chicago: University of Chicago Press, 2006.
Oliphant, Margaret. *The Library Window*, edited by Annmarie S. Drury. Peterborough, ON: Broadview Press, 2019.
Pardoe, Rosemary. *The James Gang: A Bibliography of Writers in the M. R. James Tradition*. Chester: Rosemary Pardoe, 1991.
Pfaff, Richard William. *Montague Rhodes James*. London: Scolar Press, 1980.
Richards, Thomas. *The Imperial Archive: Knowledge and the Fantasy of Empire*. London: Verso, 1993.
Riddell, Charlotte. *Haunted Houses*, edited by Andrew Smith. London: British Library, 2018.

Smith, Andrew. *The Ghost Story 1840–1920: A Cultural History*. Manchester: Manchester University Press, 2010.

Tearle, Oliver. 'Vernon Lee', in Scott Brewster and Luke Thurston (eds), *The Routledge Handbook to the Ghost Story*. London: Routledge, 2018, pp. 150–8.

Tyldesley, Joyce. *Egypt: How a Lost Civilization Was Rediscovered*. London: BBC Books, 2005.

Woolf, Virginia. *A Room of One's Own and Three Guineas*, edited by Anna Snaith. Oxford: Oxford University Press, 2015.

Chapter 24

Pyramids
Andrew Smith

Ludwig Horace Holly's account of his first encounter with Ayesha in Rider Haggard's *She* (1887) is politically and psychologically complex. He notes that

> the curtain was drawn, and a tall figure stood before us. I say a figure, for not only the body, but also the face was wrapped up in soft white, gauzy material in such a way as at first sight to remind me most forcibly of a corpse in its grave-clothes. And yet I do not know why it should have given me that idea, seeing that the wrappings were so thin that one could distinctly see the gleam of the pink flesh beneath them. I suppose it was owing to the way in which they were arranged, either accidentally, or more probably by design. Anyhow, I felt more frightened than ever at this ghost-like apparition, and my hair began to rise upon my head as the feeling crept over me that I was in the presence of something that was not canny. (Haggard 1995: 106)

The account raises a number of issues about British attitudes towards Egypt during the period. Ayesha may not be an explicitly Egyptian queen (the novel is vague on its precise geography; somewhere in East Africa) but iconographically she represents the popular image of the female mummy at the time. The image is one of an alluring (that 'gleam of pink flesh') but possibly dead, or 'not canny' body that is, in its gauzy white clothes, more 'ghost-like' than the 'corpse' that it initially seems to resemble. Holly's male gaze is also an erotically curious one despite his metaphysical uncertainty over whether she is alive or not. As the moment develops it becomes clear that Ayesha is also unclear whether she is fully alive because as she tells Holly, "'I dwell among the caves and the dead [...] I have lived, O stranger, with my memories, and my memories are in a grave that mine hands hallowed'" (107). Ayesha's reference is to her 2,000-year wait for the return of her lover, Kallikrates, a return which will take her out of her death-in-life existence. Holly's view of Ayesha, however, and her perception of her plight are not as reciprocal as this moment suggests because Holly's view of her is not just erotically charged but also politically loaded. To understand how Ayesha can be read as a political projection (one which, as we shall see, has implications for how Egyptian ghosts are more generally represented), requires an examination of the colonial context which shapes these projected imaginings.

Ailise Bulfin has noted that the initial popularity of mummy stories coincided with the completion of the Suez Canal in 1869 and that 'From 1869 when the canal opened, gaining further momentum after the 1882 occupation, numerous tales positing the irruption of vengeful, supernatural, ancient forces' were published (Bulfin 2011: 412). The canal was commercially crucial to Britain as it enabled goods to be moved between Europe and South Asia, without ships having to make the extensive detour around the African coast. In 1875 Benjamin Disraeli, then Prime Minister, consolidated British interest in the canal by buying significant quantities of shares in the Canal Company. In order to protect this asset Britain took military control over the canal in 1882, but the British presence in Egypt looked to many like an illegitimate occupation. An additional concern related to the extensive archaeological excavations, which had begun earlier in the nineteenth century, in the Valley of the Kings, and while this had generated a British cultural craze for Egyptian-style designs (notably in jewellery, crockery and buildings), it had also generated some unease at what looked suspiciously like grave-robbing. The Egyptian Question, as it was known from the 1880s, was one which raised questions about the legitimacy of British colonialism in the area and it is this very ambivalence about the occupation and the ongoing archaeological excavations that underpins many of the ghost stories discussed here.

The ambivalence about the legitimacy of Britain's occupation of Egypt permeates the culturally conflicted representation of dead undead mummies who, while ostensibly Gothically othered, often seem to have right on their side as they seek restitution for having been unearthed from their graves. These figures complicate the idea of the ghost in the ghost story because the repeated emphasis given to reincarnation (as in *She*) suggests that the dead do not really die but are serially re-embodied. When we do find more conventional spectres, they too tend to be spirits who have the right to live again on special occasions. These issues are gendered, as female mummies are often contrasted with their male counterparts.

Ayesha is seemingly a dead undead figure who at the end of *She* is apparently subject to a reincarnated return. Holly's gaze which sees Ayesha as erotically exposed constitutes what Bradley Deane has referred to as an act of 'Imperial Striptease' (Deane 2008: 381), which imagines Egypt as a woman who needs to be dominated. For Nolwenn

Corriou the process of unwrapping the mummy (a popular public spectacle during the period), which is suggested in Holly's gaze, reflects the archaeological excavations which also removed 'a number of layers of time' to expose the past (Corriou 2015: 4); while Eleanor Dobson notes that 'the mummified female body functions as a site of both sexual and imperialistic desire' (Dobson 2017: 19–20). These bodies, like Ayesha's, elude British attempts to conquer them, which demonstrates how 'fictional British protagonists are ultimately denied the possession of Egypt, symbolized by these dangerous, titillating and, ultimately, unattainable female forms' (Corriou 2015: 23). Male mummies are rather different and represent dangerous, vengeful, figures which pose a more direct challenge to British rule. An analysis of tales such as Grant Allen's 'My New Year's Eve Among the Mummies' (1879), Rider Haggard's 'Smith and the Pharaohs' (1913), Arthur Conan Doyle's 'Lot No. 249' (1892), 'The Story of Baelbrow' (1898) by Kate and Hesketh Prichard and Bram Stoker's *The Jewel of Seven Stars* (1903, revised 1912) demonstrates how the Egyptian dead undead provide a specific way of thinking about colonial ghostly returns during the period.

Grant Allen's 'My New Year's Eve Among the Mummies' is written in a jocular tone even as it makes serious points about the scientific advances made in ancient Egypt. The narrator is 'a wanderer and a vagabond' (Allen 2016: 61), who is visiting Egypt with his fiancée, Edith, and his prospective in-laws. His attachment to Edith is purely pecuniary and he is easily distracted by the sight of more alluring Egyptian women. One night, unable to sleep, he goes for a walk and enters a pyramid where he encounters a woman, the princess Hatasou, who resembles a dancer that the narrator had earlier been enraptured by. The pyramid is populated by the spirits of eminent Egyptians who are enjoying a banquet that they are permitted to hold on New Year's Eve every 1,000 years. Hatasou asks her father, King Thothmes XXVII, to welcome the interloper although Thothmes is sceptical about whether the narrator could enjoy their banquet because '"Savages have no feelings"' and "are [...] incapable of appreciating"' the complexity of the '"Egyptian sensibility"' (69). This prompts the narrator to state:

> 'I am an English tourist, a visitor from a modern land whose civilization far surpasses the rude culture of early Egypt: and I am accustomed to respectful treatment from all other nationalities, as becomes a citizen of the First Naval Power in the World.' (69)

However, this is not a position recognised by Thothmes as the tale generates a version of Ancient Egyptians which associates them with discoveries such as chloroform, watches and gaslight. Hatasou explains to the narrator that the point of embalming their bodies is to enable them to be reinhabited on occasions such as their banquets, meaning that '"We are made into mummies in order to preserve our immortality"' (71). The mummy thus becomes a very specific formation of the spectral in which they are simultaneously alive and dead, as in Holly's first glimpse of Ayesha. The narrator and Hatasou seemingly fall in love and the narrator decides to allow himself to be killed and mummified so that he might see her again. When he awakens he finds himself with a nurse in attendance and it transpires that he had been in a malaria-induced coma and that his vision of the Egyptians may, or may not, have been caused by hallucination. Allen's tale is often flippant in the way that it addresses a culture clash between the modern western world and Ancient Egypt, but its employment of a romance plot as a way of bridging these worlds constitutes a popular device in tales about romantic liaisons with dead undead mummies. The Ancient Egyptians represent formations of spectrality which are specific to these types of narrative. Like the ghost they are a dead undead presence, but also it is not clear if they are 'real' or not. They are not, in romance stories, troubling vengeful entities, although the different attitudes towards the narrator that we witness in Hatasou and Thothmes are attributable to gendered formations of a seductive princess and a dangerous patriarch. It is clear that Hatasou can be read as generated out of a projected need which demonstrates how Egypt is bound up with orientalist colonial projections. The ambivalent nature of this projection (the desire to be dead, or differently alive, to escape an engagement) again echoes the very ambivalence that was articulated by the Egyptian Question. Hatasou is unattainable as Ancient Egypt itself slips from the grasp of the narrator. For Deane, 'The Egyptian Question is raised again and again through the sexual/political allegory of' a possible 'marriage, but it is never answered' because 'the mummies and their suitors remain suspended' (Deane 2008: 385). As we shall see, this issue of suspense has implications for how these tales represent time as fundamentally cyclical. The dead keep coming back because they are endlessly reincarnated, but they do not always come back as the same, as their grievances are often of a contemporary nature, an issue addressed in Haggard's 'Smith and the Pharaohs'.

Haggard's tale was published in 1913, so some time after the time scale covered in this volume, but it addresses issues about the Egyptian Question which are rooted within earlier Victorian anxieties about British colonial interests and can be read as a reflection on those ongoing Victorian concerns. It is also a tale which, like *She* and Grant's tale, centres on a female mummy. The tale focuses on the obsession that one James Ebenezer Smith, a senior clerk in a London bank, develops with a cast of a sculptured head of a woman that he encounters in the British Museum. At the sight of this sculpture 'that face [...] awoke within him all kinds of wonderful imaginings, some of them so strange and tender that almost they partook of the nature of memories' (Haggard 1921: 5). Smith's success in a financial speculation enables him to fund various vacation-time excavations in Egypt, partly prompted by this encounter in the British Museum. He discovers a new tomb within a hill and standing on it one night he speculates about whether the ghosts of the entombed 'still come forth at night and wander through the land where once they ruled?' (14). He contemplates the possibility that 'the *Ka*, or Double, eternally haunted the place where its earthly counterpart had been laid to rest' (15). The tale notes that Smith's 'mind, or rather his imagination – of which he had plenty – went off at a tangent' (15), before he seemingly sees a procession of Ancient Egyptians moving up the road. The reference to the imagination is revealing because it implicates the idea of projection within these visions.

Some research reveals that the tomb was occupied by Ma-Mee, a member of the royal household, and artefacts relating to her include the original of the sculpture that had been the basis of the cast which Smith had seen in the British Museum. A priest had attempted to rob the tomb shortly after it had been constructed and although he had been killed by the guards, the priest had left, undiscovered, the mummy's severed hand with two rings on the fingers, which is also found by Smith. The mantle of thief is later taken on by Smith who, finding himself in an unoccupied part of the Cairo Museum (whose director had helpfully identified some of Smith's artefacts), 'stopped and looked about him like a thief' (34), before taking a ring from the severed hand and putting it on his own. Absorbed by his research Smith finds himself locked into the museum for the night and in need of a place to sleep. After finding such a place, the room comes alive with spectral entities, the *Ka*s, of the Ancient Egyptians, many of whose bodies are held in the museum in mummified form. Smith recognises the *Ka*s of Osiris, Ramses II and other major Pharaohs. Among the congregation he discovers Ma-Mee, 'only ten times more beautiful than he had ever pictured her [...] She appeared to be somewhat moody, or rather thoughtful, for she leaned by herself against a balustrade, watching the throng without much interest' (47). As in Grant's tale, these are spirits who are permitted to convene on an occasional basis (once a year, for one hour), during which they discuss issues considered important to their position as Ancient Egyptians. The issue of tomb-robbing becomes the topic of their debate.

The spirit of one King Metesuphis begins the discussion:

> 'The matter that I wish to lay before you is that of the violation of our sepulchers by those men who now live upon the earth. The mortal bodies of many who are gathered here to-night lie in this place to be stared at and mocked by the curious.' (52)

He likewise notes that their sacred objects and writings have also been stolen. The debate leads them to discuss how they might avenge these acts. A son of Rameses, Khaemuas, advocates taking revenge on such violators, before discovering Smith hiding in the room, who is described as '"one of the worst of these vile thieves"' (54). Smith is acutely aware of the danger he faces because 'He was about to be convicted in a court of which all the kings and queens of Egypt were the jury' (55). Smith acknowledges that while these figures are 'very majestic ghosts' nevertheless as 'a gentleman of the modern world' he 'would not show the white feather before a crowd of ancient Egyptian ghosts' (56). The spectre of Ma-Mee's husband is struck by the resemblance between Smith and the court artist, Horu, who produced the likeness of Ma-Mee that Smith had discovered in her tomb. The husband was aware of a possible romantic attachment developing between Ma-Mee and Horu which resulted in Horu being sent to carve 'statues in the deserts of Kush' (57) until he either died of a fever, or was poisoned. The other ghosts also note the likeness and contemplate whether Smith is a possible reincarnation of Horu (which also links with Smith's initial feelings on the sight of the cast, that 'they partook of the nature of memories' [5]). Khaemuas is unmoved by this possible defence because even if this is a reincarnated Horu in his living form he is '"a violator of the hallowed dead"' (60). The presiding judge, Menes, decides that while the spirit (the *Ka*) of the priest who originally violated Ma-Mee's tomb should be hunted and destroyed, Smith had acted out of ignorance and love for Ma-Mee and should be allowed to go free.

Ma-Mee tells Smith, whom she sees as the reincarnated Horu, that she had not been married to the Pharaoh and was his mistress and therefore Horu's love for her had not transgressed Egyptian laws. She wishes him well and they kiss before she disappears and Smith wakes up in the museum. Smith departs the museum as soon as it opens and is mistaken for a ghost by the attendant opening the museum, who 'uttered a yell of fear' (68) and looks the other way as Smith makes good his escape.

Deane has noted similarities between Allen's tale and Haggard's because with both Hatasou and Ma-Mee 'the Egyptian woman is presented as the ideal partner in an eternal union' (Deane 2008: 391). The resurrection of the pharaohs represents an attempt to stop time because

Egyptian time is endlessly repeated, or reincarnated. These narratives, which reach out for an 'eternal union', are personal because they are romance stories but also political because 'time is encoded into the narrative structure of these stories' in which 'repetition and doubling offer no advance' so that 'our expectations of closure are coyly forestalled' in what becomes a 'fantastic corollary to the British occupation of Egypt' (Deane 2008: 384–5). Ancient Egypt thus uncannily returns because it has not been mastered by an illegitimate British presence which in Haggard's tale is put on trial and is only exonerated due to accidental grave-robbing. Making Smith a reincarnation of Horu turns him into a type of victim (possibly murdered by Ma-Mee's partner) rather than the perpetrator of British colonial rule (to the extent that this is also manifested through archaeology). Britain is judged and reassuringly found not guilty but after his encounter with Ma-Mee, Smith 'never returned to Egypt' (Haggard 1921: 33) in part because he is now satisfied that the mystery of his feelings for Ma-Mee has been clarified, even if he is also forced to acknowledge that she is, in any literal way, unattainable.

Haggard's tale is more explicit than Allen's concerning the level of colonial guilt which is reflected in these projected representations of female mummies. Smith is quite a different protagonist than Allen's man-of-the-world narrator. Smith is a rather solitary figure whose pursuit of romance is specifically located within his precise archaeological interests, whereas Allen's narrator is interested in the exotic and unattainable Hatasou because she favourably compares to the quotidian and all too attainable Edith. In both, however, the reality of the encounters is in some doubt as they can be attributed to a malarial coma (Allen) or dreams produced by a restless night in a museum populated by mummies and their artefacts (Haggard). Read as visions these are projected ghosts and the emphasis given to projection identifies the very mechanism which implicates the idea that these ghosts represent cultural anxieties which are closer to home than Ancient Egypt. Corriou argues that these female mummies which 'represent the colonial in the shape of a woman [...] makes sense in the context of the emergence of the New Woman since this figure also appeared as a threat to patriarchal Victorian society' (Corriou 2015: 12). Ayesha is clearly more of a femme fatale than either Hatasou or Ma-Mee, but her ambivalent representation (Holly is both appalled and beguiled by her) can in part be attributed to the demonisation of powerful women, which reflects reactionary concerns about the emerging authority associated with the New Woman at the time. This identifies how political these gendered projections are. For Maria Fleischhack they also reflect ideas about the self which were being developed in psychology, which is illustrated by how these ideas are 'projected onto archaeological contexts in which modern individuals are confronted by the very artefacts that they seek to unearth' (Fleischhack 2017: 258). Smith finds the woman behind the cast. Allen's narrator finds the antidote to a deadening life with Edith. These are not neutral discoveries but acts of projected desire. Ghosts in these instances fulfil a need which can be read psychologically. Fleischhack concludes that 'the ancient Egyptian exposes the layers of the psyche of the modern Self (often alarmingly similar to the psyche of the ancient Other) just as they themselves have been physically excavated from their resting places' (268). In Freudian terms this suggests the restless unmet desires that we more broadly witness in the Gothic culture of the time in texts such as the *Strange Case of Dr Jekyll and Mr Hyde* (1886) and *Dracula* (1897). The texts discussed so far also incorporate an erotic element which also suggests this version of the self, but with the added context of colonial guilt which ultimately makes these women unattainable because they cannot be contained within conventional romantic, or domestic, plots. The representation of the female mummy thus creates points of contact with desire and guilt, which we do not see in representations of male mummies. Doyle's writings provide an example of this difference.

Doyle's contribution to mummy fiction consists of the romance tale 'The Ring of Thoth' (1890), and 'Lot No. 249' (1892). The later tale focuses on a male Egyptian mummy owned by an Oxford student named Edward Bellingham. He specialises in Eastern languages and possesses a mummy known only as 'Lot No. 249', its designation at the auction from which Bellingham had purchased it. Bellingham seems like a recluse who is only interested in his studies, although he is engaged to the beautiful Eveline, the sister of a fellow undergraduate named Monkhouse Lee. Before we meet Bellingham he is introduced via a discussion between two medical students, Jephro Hastie and Abercrombie Smith, who are heavily involved in the athletic life of the college, which stands as a counterpoint to Bellingham's intellectual interests. It is noted of Hastie and Smith that 'they were open-air men – men whose minds and tastes turned naturally to all that was manly and robust' (Doyle 2016: 131). Smith has just moved into his college rooms and Hastie tells him about his near neighbours, Lee and Bellingham, and notes of the latter, '"There's something damnable about him – something reptilian. My gorge always rises at him"' (132). Later, Lee asks for medical assistance from Smith because Bellingham has fainted in his room. The issue of healthy 'manly' bodies and the bodies encountered by Smith develops tensions about masculinity and health which run throughout the tale. Before helping Bellingham, Smith is distracted by the mummy in Bellingham's room which appears to have half climbed out of its sarcophagus which had been placed on a table in the middle of the room. It is noted that the mummy was 'a horrid black, withered thing, like a charred head on a gnarled bush', which 'was lying half out of its case, with its clawlike hand and bony forearm resting upon the table' (136). Smith takes the unconscious Bellingham's pulse and records its very high rate which suggests that he has collapsed from fear. His face is 'most repellent' and 'absolutely bloodless white', with fear (137). It is also noted that 'He was very fat, but gave the impression of having at some time been considerably fatter, for his skin hung loosely in creases and folds' (137). Thus the tale moves from healthy, athletic bodies to emaciated or once-large bodies which are associated with illness.

When Bellingham revives he attributes his fainting to being in the presence of what is otherwise, for him, a harmless mummy that he bought at auction. In reality he has found a way of bringing the mummy back to life and this is what has disturbed him. The mummy would have been six foot seven in life and Bellingham's ability to control it initially enables him to employ it to seek revenge on anyone who appears to challenge him, which includes Lee who, appalled by some of Bellingham's attitudes, calls off Bellingham's engagement to his sister. Smith and Hastie help rescue Lee from a river into which the mummy had pushed him. Smith warns Bellingham about his future conduct, only for Smith to narrowly escape the mummy the following evening as it pursues him down a country lane. Smith confronts Bellingham and threatens to shoot him unless he disposes of the body by dismembering and burning it, and forces him to destroy the incantation which had brought it back to life. The final lines note that Bellingham left Oxford after this event and was rumoured to be in what was then called the Soudan.

The striking elements of Doyle's tale relate to the competing formations of masculinity and the use of a mummy to conduct personal vendettas. Bellingham is not physically capable of carrying out his revenge on Lee and Smith and uses the mummy as a type of hyper-masculine tool through which he can attack them. There is little sense of the colonial guilt which informed the tales of Allen and Haggard. The mummy is a nameless thing, closer to a zombie in its inhuman physical aggression. The triumph of Smith at the end is because of the defeat of the othered masculinities associated with Bellingham and the mummy. This is a victory secured at gunpoint, which symbolically endorses a violent intervention. The point is to eradicate the mummy and its history (its accompanying documents). To come to this conclusion is to read the narrative from Smith's position, which at an ostensible level the tale champions. It is, however, possible to read the story in a way which is more sympathetic to some of the issues associated with the Egyptian

Question, which requires seeing the tale as focusing on the acquisition of an Ancient Egyptian artefact which is exploited for personal gain. While the tale suggests that it is not possible to sympathise with the mummy, who represents an unappeasable violence, it is possible to condemn Bellingham for his exploitation of it. The dehumanisation of the mummy thus functions on two levels; it is the Gothic 'monster' of the text, but it is also dehumanised and made servile by Bellingham, which reflects the danger of colonial aggression – a topic also addressed in 'Smith and the Pharaohs'.

While the romance plots positions female ghosts as projections which symbolise the unattainability of Egypt, a tale such as 'Lot No. 249' can be read as a revenge narrative in which the mummy, while carrying out Bellingham's orders, is also attacking a privileged world of Oxford students as a tacit assault on the British establishment. Read politically, the spectre of Egyptian revenge can be seen as occupying a number of plot positions (such as Bellingham's revenge narrative), which also hints at the type of political and personal ambivalence about Egypt that we witnessed in Allen and Haggard. This is a view of the mummy which is also explored in 'The Story of Baelbrow' by Kate and Hesketh Prichard.

'The Story of Baelbrow' was published in a series of stories centring on Flaxman Low, a psychic investigator who in this tale has been brought in to examine some seemingly paranormal activity taking place in a 300-year-old mansion called Baelbrow, near Bael Ness, a fictional promontory on the coast of East Anglia. The house is owned by the Swaffam family but has been lent out over the summer to one Professor Jungvort and his family. The Professor is able to consult material held in the family library and his daughter, Lena, who is engaged to Harold Swaffam, is able to meet regularly with her fiancé. The house had always had a benign ghost but this changed when there was an escalation in unusual activity which culminated in the death of a housemaid, which prompted the Professor to invite Flaxman Low to investigate. The Professor tells Low that he had seen '"a figure, not unlike the human figure, but narrow and straight"' (Prichard 2016: 199) as it headed towards a room known as the museum which contains artefacts from the senior Mr Swaffam's extensive travels abroad. The Professor had also noted that this figure had about it '"a flutter of something detached, which may have been a handkerchief"' (199), which, it transpires, is the clothing of a mummy. Before that link is made it is revealed that the maid may have died of fright as a result of anaemia and a weak heart. Her body was largely unmarked except for a small wound below her ear which will later prove revealing.

Doyle's tale had focused on masculinity and had included a story about Lee's sister being in danger from Bellingham. In 'The Story of Baelbrow' there is a similar narrative about the possible dangers confronted by Lena and the housemaids. The challenge posed to masculinity in Doyle is readdressed in this later tale when we are introduced to Harold Swaffam who is initially described as 'a dark-browed young man with a bull neck, and strongly marked features' (201–2). His attitudes reflect his coarse physicality when he asserts that '"It is my opinion that the women in this house are suffering from an epidemic of hysteria"' (202), a view that Low refutes by pointing out that the maid had not died of hysteria. Harold is later attacked by this strange ghost who wears bandages and who is described as having 'a high-nosed, dull-eyed, malignant face, the eye-sockets hollow', and as possessing 'darkened teeth' (208). This face of a male mummy evokes Bellingham's mummy in 'Lot No. 249', and its corpse-like facial features stand in obvious contrast to the beautiful female mummies which we have encountered in Allen and Haggard.

These tales about male mummies foreground issues about male violence. Harold recovers from his attack but has been bitten below the ear. Low is now able to deduce that their monstrous opponent is an overdetermined Gothic figure who is a ghost, a vampire and a mummy. Low's explanation is that a vampire ghost had taken up residency in the form of a mummy that the senior Mr Swaffam had acquired. Low and Harold enter the museum where they find the mummy in an attitude which resembles that of the first sight of Bellingham's mummy: 'Half in and half out of an oblong wooden box in a corner of the great room, lay a lean shape in its rotten yellow bandages' (211). Harold pushes the mummy back into the box where it takes on 'a life-like posture' and seems to mockingly smile at them. The dispatching of the mummy is notable for the level of violence involved:

> For a moment Swaffam stood over the thing; then with a curse he raised the revolver and shot into the grinning face again and again with deliberate vindictiveness. Finally he rammed the thing down into the box, and, clubbing the weapon, smashed the head into fragments with a vicious energy that coloured the whole horrible scene with a suggestion of murder done. (212)

The level of aggression implicates a form of colonial violence which is associated with Harold's hyper-masculinity. The mummy is an innocent victim here because it has been inhabited by the spirit of a restless vampiric spirit which has come from the British burial ground on which the house is built. As with Bellingham's mummy, it is animated by a force which it cannot control in a battle which is staged between various competing forms of masculinity. The mummy, however, can also be seen as symbolically enacting a form of revenge against its objectification as an artefact, which evokes the reflections on tomb-robbing in 'Smith and the Pharaohs'. The final lines of 'The Story of Baelbrow' also reflect on this context when the remains of the mummy are burned in a canoe pushed out to sea. It is noted that 'the history of that dead thing ended 3000 years after the priests of Armen laid it to rest in its appointed pyramid' (212). The remains of that mummy are now, as in Doyle's tale, a long way from its appointed grave. These tales about male mummies have a level of violence in them which provides a different way of thinking about the Egyptian Question. These mummies must be destroyed, but they are also hapless victims, and while their violence can be attributed to outside agents (Bellingham, a spectral vampire), read in symbolic terms they can be read as revenge narratives which incriminate tomb-robbing as a cause of unrest. Stoker's *The Jewel of Seven Stars* brings together issues of tomb-robbing with romance and the novel's two endings illustrate the fundamental ambivalence with which the Egyptian Question was addressed.

Stoker's novel centres on the resurrection of an Egyptian queen named Tera. The mummy had been acquired by an Egyptologist named Abel Trelawny. His investigation of her tomb coincides with, back in England, the death of his wife during childbirth. The daughter, Margaret, survives but seems to have a strange affinity with Tera as the mummy seems to possess the now youthful Margaret in a series of incidents which culminate in Tera's resurrection. The narrative is told from the point of view of Malcolm Ross who is in love with Margaret and whom Margaret had summoned when distressed at finding her father unconscious one night. The plot revolves around Trelawny's attempts to gather the material that he requires to generate Tera's resurrection. His assault has been occasioned by the emanation of Tera's spirit as if it had become aware of some, presumably hostile, activity taking place. One of the main issues relates to the assessment of the type of queen that Tera may have been. The hieroglyphics in her tomb indicate that she may have been a type of dangerous sorcerer and it is noted that she has been spectrally responsible for a number of deaths of people who had violated her tomb. She therefore appears as a revengeful spirit but her seeming periodic inhabitation of Margaret evokes the pattern of the romance plots found in Allen and Haggard. The novel suggests that the lovelorn Ross is simply unable to read Tera as a threat because his love of Margaret makes him incapable of discerning the threat posed by Tera/Margaret. At one level the novel maintains the view that Tera, like Ancient Egypt, is unattainable, a position which characterises these tales that centre on romance. Tera, however, is like Count Dracula as she functions as an invasive presence who enters into the human world, but only with the object of exploiting it for her advantage. Ross eventually is struck by the presence of two Margarets, 'the old Margaret whom I loved at first glance' and the 'new Margaret, whom I barely understood, and whose intellectual aloofness made an implacable barrier between us' (Stoker 1996: 87). Haggard's Ayesha comes back into focus here. In *She* Ayesha is, for Holly, both erotically alluring and intellectually chilling (because her Darwinian ideals are at odds with Holly's search for spiritual truth). Ayesha also challenges Holly's voyeuristic view of her because her beauty becomes a source of terror to him. These tensions between voyeurism and a rebellion against this objectification, in which a mummy is merely an object, are also addressed in Stoker's novel.

Tera's body is unwrapped in preparation for the resurrection. At the sight of her naked body Ross sees 'the image of Margaret as my eyes had first lit on her' (204). He goes on to note that viewing the body in this way 'was indecent; it was almost sacrilegious! And yet the white wonder of that beautiful form was something to dream of' (203). Ross's erotic reverie is not shared by Margaret/Tera, who sees the process as '"cruel, cruel"' (199), although her father attempts to mollify her because they are men of science whereas '"They didn't have women's rights or lady doctors in ancient Egypt, my dear!"' (199). The problem is that Ross's view participates in the politically problematic projections which we have witnessed in the earlier romance narratives. His version of Margaret/Tera is equally unattainable, which evokes the very ambivalence about the Egyptian Question which has shaped these representations. Stoker's novel however, has two endings which resolve this ambivalence depending on how they separate Margaret and Tera.

In the 1903 ending Tera is resurrected and everyone else, except Ross, is killed. This is in keeping with the revenge narratives which typically characterise these tales and is made possible because this is also Tera's revenge against the violation of her disrobing; although clearly, given her earlier pattern of revenge against those who have robbed her tomb, they have fundamentally misread her. The resurrection fails in the 1912 ending and Margaret and Ross marry. Margaret thus becomes obtainable because she is no longer possessed by Tera. The difference in these two endings reflects the very ambivalence of the Egyptian Question. One is a revenge narrative, whereas the 1912 ending simply sidesteps the issue by having Margaret restored to her English identity and so free to marry Ross, unencumbered by the spectral presence of Ancient Egypt.

Ghosts in tales about Ancient Egyptians are a different type of revenant than those found in the typical Victorian ghost story. They represent the spectral return of dead undead mummies who often, notably in romance tales, function as projections associated with desire and an ambivalent response to British colonialism. The tales about male mummies are more violent, but are also linked to the complicated, and often conflicting, view of Egypt at this time – that it is there to be conquered, but that the resistance to British authority has a moral and political legitimacy. The Ancient Egyptian revenant, dressed up as a reanimated mummy, is ultimately a product of a political ambivalence which pricked the Victorian conscience.

Works Cited

Allen, Grant. 'My New Year's Eve Among the Mummies', in Andrew Smith (ed.), *Lost in a Pyramid & Other Classic Mummy Stories*. London: British Library, 2016, pp. 59–78.

Bulfin, Ailise. 'The Fiction of Gothic Egypt and British Imperial Paranoia: The Curse of the Suez Canal'. *English Literature in Transition, 1880–1920*, vol. 54, no. 4, 2011, pp. 411–43.

Corriou, Nolwenn. '"A Woman is a Woman, if She had been Dead Five Thousand Centuries!": Mummy Fiction, Imperialism and the Politics of Gender'. *Miranda: Multidisciplinary peer-reviewed journal on the English-speaking world*, no. 11, 2015, pp. 1–16.

Deane, Bradley. 'Mummy Fiction and the Occupation of Egypt: Imperial Fiction'. *English Literature in Transition, 1880–1920*, vol. 51. no. 4, 2008, pp. 381–410.

Dobson, Eleanor. 'Sleeping Beauties: Mummies and the Fairy-Tale Genre as the Fin de Siècle'. *Journal of International Women's Studies*, vol. 17, no. 3, 2017, pp. 19–34.

Doyle, Arthur Conan. 'Lot No. 249', in Andrew Smith (ed.), *Lost in a Pyramid & Other Classic Mummy Stories*. London: British Library, 2016, pp. 127–70.

Fleischhack, Maria. 'Possession, Trance and Reincarnation: Confrontations with Ancient Egypt in Edwardian Fiction'. *Victoriographies*, vol. 7, no. 3, 2017, pp. 257–70.

Haggard, Henry Rider. *She*. Ware: Wordsworth, 1995.

———. 'Smith and the Pharaohs', in *Smith and the Pharaohs and Other Tales*. New York: Longmans, Green & Co., 1921, pp. 1–68.

Prichard, Kate and Hesketh Prichard. 'The Story of Baelbrow', in Andrew Smith (ed.), *Lost in a Pyramid & Other Classic Mummy Stories*. London: British Library, 2016, pp. 195–212.

Stoker, Bram. *The Jewel of Seven Stars*. Oxford. Oxford University Press, 1996.

Notes on Contributors

Lucie Armitt has recently retired as Professor of Contemporary English Literature at the University of Lincoln. Her principal single-authored publications are *Fantasy* (2020), *The Twentieth Century Gothic* (2011), *Fantasy Fiction: An Introduction* (2005), *Contemporary Women's Fiction and the Fantastic* (2000), *Readers' Guide to Essential Criticism: George Eliot* (2000), *Theorising the Fantastic* (1996) and *Where No Man Has Gone Before: Women and Science Fiction* (1991). She is also co-author (with Scott Brewster) of *Climates of Fear: Gothic Travel Through Haunted Landscapes* (2022).

Scott Brewster is Associate Professor in English at University of Lincoln. He is co-author, with Jeffrey Andrew Weinstock, of *The Routledge Introduction to the American Ghost Story* (2024), and co-author, with Lucie Armitt, of *Gothic Travel through Haunted Landscapes: Climates of Fear* (2022). He also co-edited, with Luke Thurston, *The Routledge Handbook to the Ghost Story* (2017), and has published widely on Gothic and the ghost story, including recent essays on M. R. James, James Hogg, Margaret Oliphant, Bram Stoker, and Gothic criticism in the twentieth century. He is an Editorial Board member of *Gothic Nature*.

Melissa Edmundson is Senior Lecturer of English at Clemson University and specialises in women's supernatural fiction. She is the author of *Women's Ghost Literature in Nineteenth-Century Britain* (2013) and *Women's Colonial Gothic Writing, 1850–1930: Haunted Empire* (2018). She has edited several editions for Handheld Press, including *Women's Weird: Strange Stories by Women, 1890–1940* (2019) and *Women's Weird 2: More Strange Stories by Women, 1891–1937* (2020). Her single-author critical editions include the supernatural and imaginative short fiction of D. K. Broster, Clotilde Graves, Elinor Mordaunt, E. Nesbit, Alice Perrin, Charlotte Riddell and Helen de Guerry Simpson.

Nick Freeman is Reader in English at Loughborough University. He has published widely on the literature and culture of the *fin de siècle* and its aftermath, along with contributing to many reference works on Gothic and supernatural themes. These include *The Routledge Handbook to the Ghost Story* (2018), *The Blackwell Encyclopaedia of the Gothic* (2012) and *The Victorian Gothic: An Edinburgh Companion* (Edinburgh University Press, 2012). More recent work has included selections of A. M. Burrage's ghost stories, *The Little Blue Flames*, for the British Library (2022), and Elizabeth Walter's Welsh horror stories, *Let a Sleeping Witch Lie* (2024).

Ardel Haefele-Thomas serves as the Chair of LGBTQ+ Studies at City College of San Francisco. They are the author of *Queer Others in Victorian Gothic: Transgressing Monstrosity* (2012), *Introduction to Transgender Studies* (2019) and *Transgender: Contemporary World Issues Handbook* (2019). Haefele-Thomas is the editor of *Queer Gothic: An Edinburgh Companion* (Edinburgh University Press, 2023). Their forthcoming works are a four-volume edited set entitled *Queer and Trans Britain: Historic Documents 1790–1918* and a monograph, *AIDS Gothic: The Intersection of Gothic Modes and Disease*. They have published numerous essays on Gothic – specifically queer and trans Gothic with a focus on intersectionality.

William Hughes, formerly Professor of Literature in English at the University of Macau, is now an Honorary Fellow of the University of East Anglia, Norwich. He is the author, editor or co-editor of twenty-three books, including *Beyond Dracula: Bram Stoker's Fiction and Its Cultural Context* (2000), *That Devil's Trick: Hypnotism and the Victorian Popular Imagination* (2015), *Key Concepts in the Gothic* (Edinburgh University Press, 2018), *The Dome of Thought: Phrenology and the Nineteenth-Century Popular Imagination* (2022), *Key Concepts in Victorian Studies* (Edinburgh University Press, 2023) and, with Nick Groom, *The Vampire: An Edinburgh Companion* (Edinburgh University Press, 2025). He is currently writing a monograph on Victorian spiritualism for Manchester University Press.

Helena Ifill is a Senior Lecturer in English Studies at the University of Aberdeen. She has published widely on Victorian popular fiction, especially sensation fiction, the Gothic and the interactions between literature and the medical sciences. Her monograph *Creating Character: Theories of Nature and Nurture in Victorian Sensation Fiction* was published in 2018. She is an editor of *Victorian Popular Fictions* and a series editor for Key Popular Women Writers (Edward Everett Root). Her current research explores the interactions between doctors and patients in popular fiction, and she is currently preparing a monograph on Charlotte Riddell.

Darryl Jones is Professor of Modern British Literature and Culture at Trinity College Dublin. He has written widely on nineteenth- and early twentieth-century popular fiction, with a particular interest in horror and supernatural fiction. His most recent book is *Horror: A Very Short Introduction* (2021), and he is general editor of *The Oxford Sherlock Holmes* (9 vols), for which series he edited *The Hound of the Baskervilles*. His biography of M. R. James, *For the Dead Remember*, will be published in 2025. His next book is *M. R. James and the Ghost Story Men: A Cambridge Tale*.

Marie-Luise Kohlke is Senior Lecturer in English Literature at Swansea University, Wales, UK, and Founding Editor of the open-access *Neo-Victorian Studies* e-journal. She is series co-editor (with Christian Gutleben) of Brill-Rodopi's Neo-Victorian Series, including *Neo-Victorian Biofiction: Reimagining Nineteenth-Century Historical Subjects* (2020), and has co-edited a 2022 special issue of *Humanities* (with Elizabeth Ho and Akira Suwa), titled *Neo-Victorian Heterotopias*, as well as publishing articles and chapters on neo-Victorianism, trauma literature and theory, and gender and sexuality. She is currently working on a Brill *Handbook on Neo-Victorianism* (also with Gutleben) and on neo-Victorian timeslip children's and young adult fiction.

Emma Liggins is Reader in English Literature in the Department of English at Manchester Metropolitan University. Her publications include *The Haunted House in Women's Ghost Stories, 1850–1945: Gender, Space and Modernity* (2020). She has also published an article on Vernon Lee and the supernatural in *Gothic Studies* (2013), a chapter on modernist women's ghost stories in *British Women Short Story Writers: The New Woman to Now*, edited by Emma Young and James Bailey (Edinburgh University Press, 2015) and a chapter on 'The Edwardian Supernatural' in *Twentieth-Century Gothic: An Edinburgh Companion* (Edinburgh University Press, 2022). She is now working on a new study of Victorian and Edwardian death spaces.

Roger Luckhurst is Geoffrey Tillotson Chair of Nineteenth-Century Studies, Birkbeck, University of London. Publications include *Gothic: An Illustrated History* (2021), a scholarly edition of Arthur Conan

Doyle's *Round the Red Lamp* (Edinburgh University Press, 2023) and *Graveyards: A History of Living with the Dead* (2024).

Emma McEvoy is a Senior Lecturer at the University of Westminster. She is the author of *Gothic Tourism* (2016) and *The Music of the Gothic 1789–1820* (2025) and the editor, with Catherine Spooner, of *The Routledge Companion to Gothic* (2007).

Anthony Mandal is Professor of Print and Digital Cultures at Cardiff University. His publications include *Jane Austen and the Popular Novel: The Determined Author* (2007), (as co-editor) *The Reception of Jane Austen in Europe* (2007/2014) and (as editor) Mary Brunton, *Self-Control: A Novel* (2014). Current projects include the *Palgrave History of the Gothic: The Business of Gothic Fiction, 1764–1835* and *The Feminist Literary History of Women's Writing in the British Isles: The Orlando Volumes*, vol. 2: *1790–1900*.

Bridget M. Marshall is Professor of English at the University of Massachusetts, Lowell. She is the author of *Industrial Gothic: Workers, Exploitation and Urbanization in Transatlantic Nineteenth-Century Literature* (2021) and *The Transatlantic Gothic Novel and the Law, 1790–1860* (2011). She is currently editing Mary Elizabeth Braddon's novel *The Factory Girl* (1863) for publication in the Gothic Originals series.

Alison Milbank is Professor of Theology and Literature at the University of Nottingham. She is the author of two monographs on the Gothic: *God and the Gothic: Religion, Romance and Reality in the English Literary Tradition* (2018) and *Daughters of the House: Modes of the Gothic in Victorian Fiction* (1992) and many articles on horror and fantasy. Other books include *Dante and the Victorians* (1998) and *Chesterton and Tolkien as Theologians* (2007). She is currently writing a genealogy of Anglican writing on natural agency and divine immanence.

Tara Moore is an Associate Professor of English and the director of First Year Writing at Elizabethtown College in central Pennsylvania, where she teaches workplace writing and young adult literature. She has published two volumes on Christmas books and culture: *Victorian Christmas in Print* (2009) and *Christmas: The Sacred to Santa* (2014). She also edited the *Valancourt Book of Victorian Christmas Ghost Stories* (2016). Moore is a regional director for the Jane Austen Society of North America. She has penned essays about Jane Austen, Charles Dickens and young adult literature.

Joan Passey is a Senior Lecturer in English at the University of Bristol where she specialises in the representations of seas and coasts in literature, and the Gothic from the eighteenth century to the present. Her monograph *Cornish Gothic, 1830–1913* was published in 2023, and she co-edited *Dark Tales: Reconsidering Shirley Jackson's Short Fiction* (2024) with Robert Lloyd. She is currently working on queer ecologies of the Gothic and queer ecologies in the nineteenth century. She has edited anthologies for the British Library and regularly appears on BBC Radio.

Valerie Sanders is Professor Emerita at the University of Hull, with research interests in Victorian life writing and women's writing. Recent publications include *Margaret Oliphant* (2020) in Edward Everett Root's Key Popular Women Writers series and the volume on Life Writing in Routledge's *Literary and Cultural Criticism from the Nineteenth Century* (2022). She has an essay on Harriet Martineau in a Cambridge University Press essay collection, *Nineteenth-Century Literature in Transition: The 1830s* (2024) edited by John Gardner and David Stewart, and is currently preparing a chapter on Charlotte Brontë and dress for a *Routledge New Companion to the Brontës*.

Andrew Smith is Professor of Nineteenth-Century English Literature at the University of Sheffield where he co-directs the Centre for the History of the Gothic. He is the author or editor of twenty-six published books including *Dickens and the Gothic* (2024), *Gothic Fiction and the Writing of Trauma, 1914–1934: The Ghosts of World War One* (Edinburgh University Press, 2022), *Gothic Death 1740–1914: A Literary History* (2016), *The Ghost Story 1840–1920: A Cultural History* (2010), *Gothic Literature* (Edinburgh University Press, 2007, revised 2013), *Victorian Demons* (2004) and *Gothic Radicalism* (2000). He is a past president of the International Gothic Association.

Luke Thurston is Director of the David Jones Centre at Aberystwyth University and a former Fellow of Robinson College, Cambridge. He is the author of *James Joyce and the Problem of Psychoanalysis* (2004), *Literary Ghosts from the Victorians to Modernism* (2012) and *Understanding Sublimation in Freudian Theory and Modernist Writing* (2024). He is the translator of Jean Laplanche's *The Unfinished*

Copernican Revolution (2020) and the co-editor of *The Routledge Handbook to the Ghost Story* (2018).

Dale Townshend is Professor of Gothic Literature in the Manchester Centre for Gothic Studies, Manchester Metropolitan University. HIs most recent publications include the three-volume *The Cambridge History of the Gothic* (co-edited with Angela Wright and Catherine Spooner, 2020–1) and *Matthew Gregory Lewis: The Gothic and Romantic Literary Culture* (2024).

Minna Vuohelainen is Reader in English at City St George's, University of London. Her publications include the monograph *Richard Marsh* (2015) and the essay collections *Interpreting Primo Levi: Interdisciplinary Perspectives* (2015, with Arthur Chapman) and *Richard Marsh, Popular Fiction and Literary Culture, 1890–1915: Rereading the Fin de Siècle* (2018, with Victoria Margree and Daniel Orrells). She has edited special issues of *Victorian Periodicals Review* on the *Strand Magazine* (with Emma Liggins, 2019) and *Victorian Popular Fictions Journal* on 'Mapping Victorian Popular Fictions' (2019), and produced four critical editions of Marsh's fiction for Valancourt.

Jeffrey Andrew Weinstock is Professor of English at Central Michigan University, the *Los Angeles Review of Books* editor in charge of horror, the founder and president of the Society for the Study of the American Gothic, and the general editor of *American Gothic Studies*. He has published thirty-two books and more than a hundred essays and book chapters on the Gothic, horror, monsters, cult films, and other related topics. Among his book publications are *Gothic Things: Dark Enchantment and Anthropocene Anxiety* (2023), *Giving the Devil His Due: Satan and Cinema* (2021), *The Monster Theory Reader* (2020) and *The Cambridge Companion to the American Gothic* (2018). He has also published two textbooks with Broadview Press: *The Mad Scientist's Guide to Composition* (2020) and *Pop Culture for Beginners* (2022). Visit him at JeffreyAndrewWeinstock.com.

Index

Ackroyd, Peter, 79n6
Adams, Henry, 100
Alder, Emily, 332–3
Allen, Grant
   'My New Year's Eve Among the Mummies', 381–2
   'Our Scientific Observations of a Ghost', 55
America, 160–74, 288
Anderson, Hephzibah, 67, 70, 74
Arias, Catherine, 206–7
Aris, Rosario, 78, 79n4
Armitt, Lucie, 7, 114–28
Arnold, Thomas, 309
Ashley, Mike, 107
Atwood, Margaret, *Alias Grace*, 74

Bachelard, Gaston, 348, 360
Baldick, Chris, 88
Bann, Jennifer, 153, 189, 340
Bannon, Ann, 282
Barrett, Mike, 255
Bassett, Fletcher S., 333–4
Belsey, Catherine, 74, 359
Benson, A. C., 306
Benson, R. H., 'Father Macclesfield's Tale', 324
Benson James, Louise, 360
Bényei, Tamás, 332
Bierce, Ambrose, 171
   'The Middle Toe of the Right Foot', 164, 165
   'The Moonlight Road', 164, 165
Bissell, Sarah, 255, 262–3
Biswas, Preeshita, 327
Black, Helen C., 263
Blackwood, Algernon, 63
Blight, David, 170
Boothby, Guy, *Pharos the Egyptian*, 373–4
Botting, Fred, 222
Bourne, Henry, 176
Bourne-Taylor, Jenny, 34
Bowers, Katherine, 336–7
Braddon, Mary Elizabeth, 52–3
   'Good Lady Ducayne', 351
   'The Cold Embrace', 43–4
Brantlinger, Patrick, 130, 141–2
Braude, Ann, 168
Brewster, Scott, 8, 35–6
Briefel, Aviva, 106, 135
Briggs, Julia, 4, 17, 38–9
Brontë, Charlotte, 118, 120
Brontë, Emily, *Wuthering Heights*, 117, 118, 120, 121, 124–5, 127
Broughton, Rhoda, 53, 184
   'The Truth, the Whole Truth, and Nothing but the Truth', 45–6, 352–3
Bulfin, Ailise, 380

Bulwer-Lytton, Edward, 'The Haunted and the Haunters', 45
Butler, Samuel, 105
Byatt, A. S., 'The Conjugial Angel', 75–7, 79n12
Byron, Lord, 27

Cadwallader, Jen, 107
Carroll, Bret E., 170–1
Carter, Margaret L., 172
chapbooks, 23, 26
Chase-Riboud, Barbara, *Hottentot Venus*, 77–8
Chesnutt, Charles, 'Po Sandy', 165, 167–8
Christmas, 39–40, 56, 87–9, 176–92, 199–203, 241, 320
Chitwood, Brandon, 178
Clark, Christopher, 309
Clery, E. J., 17
Clute, John, 301
Coleridge, S. T., 332
Collings, Rex, 101
Collins, Wilkie, *The Haunted Hotel*, 94–6, 97
colonialism, 3, 7, 12, 54, 77, 129–45, 210–20, 374, 379–92
Connor, Steven, 207
Conrad, Joseph, 'Karain: A Memory', 132
Cook, Michael, 75
Corriou, Nolwenn, 380–1
Cox, Jessica, 29–30, 75
Cox, Michael, 59–60, 78n1
Craik, Dinah Maria, 'The Last House on C—— Street', 44
Crawford, Alice, 365–6
Crawford, Francis Marion
  'The Screaming Skull', 342–3
  'The Upper Berth', 338–41
Crawford, Robert, 365–6
Croker, B. M.
  'Her Last Wishes', 139
  'If you See Her Face', 138
  'To Let', 327–8
Crowe, Catherine, 29, 185, 203, 347, 348, 350, 352
  'The Swiss Lady's Story', 185–6
Cuenca, Carme Manuel, 167
Cust, Edward, 329

Dallas, E. S., 46
Davidoff, Leonore, 120–1
Davies, Helen, 116, 117
Davis, Rebecca Harding
  'Life in the Iron Mills', 101
  Margaret Howth, 102
Deane, Bradley, 380, 382, 384–5
degeneration, 272–3
Dempsey, Aoife, 228
Dickens, Charles, 1, 8–9, 30, 36, 39–40, 47, 51, 56, 107, 110, 178–83, 195–209
  A Christmas Carol, 1–2, 7, 86–8, 91, 97, 179, 195, 200–1, 367
  'A December Vision', 99, 102
  Master Humphrey's Clock, 198
  Nicholas Nickleby, 198
  The Chimes, 201–2
  The Haunted Man and the Ghost's Bargain, 179–83, 202–3
  The Pickwick Papers, 178–9, 190, 196–8
  'The Signal-man', 47–8, 51–2, 107–8, 195, 206–7, 320–1
  'To Be Read At Dusk', 204–5
  'To Be Taken With A Grain of Salt', 205–6
Dickey, Colin, 178
Dickerson, Vanessa D., 4–5, 114–15, 121, 127
Dickson, William K., 365
Dobson, Eleanor, 381
Doyle, Arthur Conan, 135, 374–5
  'Lot No. 249', 386–8

'The Brown Hand', 135, 375, 336–8
'The Captain of the "Pole-star"', 325, 326

economics, 85–98
Edel, Leon, 286, 293–4
education, 53
Edmundson, Melissa, 7, 44, 75, 78, 129–45, 242, 260–1
Edwards, Amelia B., 47, 110
  'No. 5 Branch Line. The Engineer', 47
  'Was it an Illusion?', 321–2
Edwards, Elizabeth, 374
Ehnes, Caley, 40
Elder, Abraham, 'The Ghost-Seer', 37
Engels, Friedrich, 101
Evans, Dewi, 40, 201

Falkner, J. Meade, 'A Midsummer Night Marriage', 152–4
Favenc, Ernest, 138
Feidelson, Charles, 298
Fielding, Penny, 367
Finucane, R. C., 140
Fleischhack, Maria, 385–6
folk horror, 328–30
Forster, E. M., 283
Fraiman, Susan, 348, 353
Frayling, Christopher, 368
Freeman, Mary E, Wilkins, 162
  'The Lost Ghost', 163–4
  'The Wind in the Rose Bush', 163, 164
Freeman, Nick, 5, 6, 34, 51–65, 104, 335, 338, 340, 341, 356
Freud, Sigmund, 306, 310
  'The Uncanny', 2, 288, 328

Galbraith, Lettice
  'A Ghost's Revenge', 355–7

'The Blue Room', 357
Gaskell, Elizabeth, 154
Mary Barton, 103
'The Old Nurse's Story', 42–3, 121, 127, 149, 184, 319–20, 324–5, 356
'The Poor Clare', 154–5
Gelder, Ken, 134–5, 138
Gibson, Ian, 309–10
Gilbert, R. A., 59–60, 78n1
Gilbert, Sandra, 123, 125
Gissing, George, 55
Gosden, Chris, 374
Grahame, Kenneth, 'The Blue Room', 56
Gray, Arthur, 364
  'The Burden of Dead Books', 364, 365
Growth, Helen, 179
Gruss, Susanne, 78
Gubar, Susan, 123, 124
guillotine, 103–4

Haefele-Thomas, Ardel, 10, 270–84
Haggard, Henry Rider
  She, 379–80, 391
  'Smith and the Pharaohs', 382–6
Halberstam, Jack, 271
Hall, Anna Maria, 'The Dark Lady', 41
Hall, Catherine, 120–1
Handley, Sasha, 17–18
Hapgood, Lynne, 353
Hapgood, Taylor, 165
Harrington, Ralph, 105, 107
Harris, Joanne, *Sleep, Pale Sister*, 75
haunted houses, 347–63
Hawker, R. S., 'The Botathen Ghost', 329
Hawthorne, Nathaniel, 161, 169, 170, 286
Hay, Simon, 5, 130

Hazlitt, William, 21
Heholt, Ruth, 185, 186, 347
Heller, Tamar, 40
Henson, Louise, 203
Hervey, Thomas K., 199
Hill, Susan, *The Woman in Black*, 73–4
Hoeveler, Diane Long, 23
Hogg, James, 36
   'The Mysterious Bride', 30–2, 36–7
   'Welldean Hall', 366
Hughes, William, 5, 9, 46–7, 106, 108, 142, 225–40
Hunt, Frederick Knight, 207
Hunt, Leigh, 21
Hurley, Andrew, 328

Ifill, Helena, 9–10, 255–69
Imfield, Zoë Lehmann, 148
industrialisation, 99–113
Industrial Revolution, 35, 107
Ingleby, Matthew, 179
Irving, Washington, 177, 199

Jacobs, W. W., 136
James, Henry, 10, 52, 61–2, 211–12, 285–99, 372–3
   Guy Domville, 291, 293, 294
   'Owen Wingrave', 292–3
   'Sir Edmund Orme', 289–91
   'The Ghostly Rental', 288–9
   'The Jolly Corner', 298
   The Other House, 295–6
   'The Private Life', 291–2
   'The Real Right Thing', 297, 371–2, 373
   'The Romance of Certain Old Clothes', 286–8
   'The Third Person', 297–8
   The Turn of the Screw, 66, 70, 172, 186–7, 296–7, 357–9
   'The Way It Came', 294
James, M. R., 10, 23–6, 62, 184–5, 188–90, 225, 238, 300–13, 338, 364, 365, 368, 370–1, 373
   'Canon Alberic's Scrapbook', 305
   'Count Magnus', 304, 305
   '"Oh, Whistle and I'll Come to You, My Lad"', 304, 307, 328, 341
   'The Malice of Inanimate Objects', 305
   'The Story of a Disappearance and Appearance', 188–90
   'The Tractate Middoth', 371
James, William, 373
Jay, Elisabeth, 369, 370
Jerome, Jerome K., 187–8
Jones, Darryl, 11–12, 309, 364–78

Kant, Emmanuel, 147
Kappeler, Susanne, 126
Keating, Peter, 53
Keepsake, The, 29
Khair, Tabish, 130
Kidd, Jess, 'Lily Wilt', 68–9
Killeen, Jarlath, 110, 318, 349, 352
Kim, Katherine J., 185
Kipling, Rudyard, 9, 55, 140, 210–24
   'At the End of the Passage', 54–5, 214–15
   'By Word of Mouth', 213–14
   'Haunted Subalterns', 218
   'Mrs Bathurst', 221
   'My Own True Ghost Story', 216
   '"Sleipner," Late "Thurinda"', 219
   Something of Myself, 210, 211, 222
   'The Broken-Link Handicap', 219
   'The Lost Legion', 217–18

'The Phantom 'Ricksaw', 210, 212–13
'The Return of Imray, 215–16'
'The Rout of the White Hussars', 218–19
'They', 221–22
'Wireless', 220–21
Kohlke, Marie-Luise, 6, 66–81
Krafft-Ebing, Richard von, 271–2
Kranzler, Laura, 64n1
Krueger, Katie, 46, 348, 353

landscape, 317–31
Lang, Andrew, 212, 222, 354–5
Lang, John, 'The Ghost Upon the Rail', 140–1
Laski, Marghanita, *The Victorian Chaise-Longue*, 69–70
Law, Graham, 42
Lee, Vernon, 10, 60–1, 270–84, 375–6
   'Amour Dure', 60, 274–6, 371–2
   'Deterioration of Soul', 273
   'Dionea', 124–6
   'Oke of Okehurst; Or, The Phantom Lover', 276–82, 283
Le Fanu, J. S., 38–9, 155, 158, 225–40, 349
   'Green Tea', 56–7
   In a Glass Darkly, 225, 226
   'Madam Crowl's Ghost', 351, 351
   'Squire Toby's Will', 349–51
   'Strange Event in the Life of Shalken the Painter', 235
   'The Drunkard's Dream', 235–8
   'The Familiar', 156–7
   'The Fortunes of Sir Robert Ardagh', 233–4
   'The Ghost and the Bone-Setter', 230–1, 235
   'The Last Heir of Castle Connor', 234

Lefebvre, Henri, 348, 360
Leslie-McCarthy, Sage, 109
Lewis, Matthew, 27
   The Monk, 21–3, 41
libraries, 365–73
Liggins, Emma, 11, 114, 122, 123, 258, 267, 347–63
Lovecraft, H. P., 146
Lubbock, S. G., 301
Luckhurst, Roger, 10, 140
Lynch, Deidre, 366

McBratney, John, 211
McCarthy, Elizabeth, 369
McEvoy, Emma, 11, 317–31
Macfarlane, Karen E., 215
Macfarlane, Robert, 328–9
magazines, 25, 30, 31, 36–42, 53, 61, 67, 160–1, 225–6, 227
Maitland, James, 334
Malet, Lucas, *The Gateless Barrier*, 359–61
Malton, Sara, 93, 94
Mandal, Anthony, 6, 34–50, 160
Margree, Victoria, 90, 91–2, 256, 261–2, 263, 265, 266, 349, 354
Marryat, Florence, 335
   'Little White Souls', 139
Marryat, Frederick, *The Phantom Ship*, 335
Marsh, Richard, 63, 104
Marshall, Bridget M., 7, 99–113
Martin, Matthew R., 165
Martineau, Harriet, 101–2
Marx, Karl, 85–6, 87–8
Matterson, Stephen, 372
Matus, Jill, 107
Maxwell, Catherine, 60
Mayo, Robert D., 25
Milbank, Alison, 8, 146–59
Miles, Clement A., 176
Mills, Kirstin A., 360

Moberly, Lucy G., 'A Strange Night', 109–10
Moore, Tara, 8, 176–92
Moore-Gilbert, B. J., 210, 212
Moshenska, Gabriel, 328
Mott, Frank Luther, 160, 161
Mulholland, Rosa, 134
museums, 373–6

Nelson, Harland S., 107
neo-Victorian, 66–81
Nesbit, Edith, 58
    'The Ebony Frame', 126–7
    'The Mystery of the Semi-Detached', 353–4
    'The Shadow', 59
Niffenegger, Audrey, 68
Nisbet, Hume, 'The Haunted Station', 134

Oliphant, Margaret, 9, 148–51, 241–54, 368–9
    'A Little Pilgrim in the Unseen', 242–3
    Autobiography, 241–2
    'Earthbound', 241
    'Old Lady Mary', 149, 249–51
    A Beleaguered City, 151, 251–3
    'The Lady's Walk', 247–8
    'The Library Window', 57–8, 245–7, 369–70
    'The Open Door', 150, 244–5, 247, 325–6
    'The Portrait', 247
Owen, Alex, 115–16, 116–17, 126, 127
Owen, Francis, 'The Prophetess', 132–3

Page, Thomas Nelson, 'No Hand Pawn', 165–7
Paget, Hugh, 308
Pamboukian, Sylvia, 210, 220

Passey, Joan, 11, 318, 332–46
Pattee, Fred Lewis, 161
Patten, Robert L., 42
Pember, Phoebe
    'The Ghost of the Nineteenth Century', 104
    'The Man Machine; or, the Pupil of Circumstance', 103
Perrin, Alice, 139, 140
    'Caulfield's Crime', 132
Pfaff, Richard William, 370
Phelps, Elizabeth Stuart
    'Since I Died', 169
    The Gates Ajar, 169–70
Phillips, Ruth, 374
Poe, Edgar Allan, 166, 168
Poovey, Mary, 85, 97
Potter, Franz J., 22–3
Pratt, Mary Louise, 130
Price, Kenneth M., 161
Prichard, Kate and Hesketh, 'The Story of Baelbrow', 135–6, 388–9
Pulham, Patricia, 60, 78, 79n4
Punter, David, 304
pyramids, 379–92

Radcliffe, Ann, 23, 28, 146–7, 234
    A Sicilian Romance, 147
    The Mysteries of Udolpho, 19–21
Raymond, Henry J., 148
religion, 146–59, 230–3, 234, 235–8, 340
Reyes, Xavier Aldana, 352
Riddell, Charlotte, 9–10, 152, 255–69
    Fairy Water, 262
    'Nut Bush Farm', 265–6, 323–4
    The Disappearance of Mr Jeremiah Redworth, 260
    'The Old House in Vauxhall Walk', 88–90, 262, 264

'The Open Door', 121–4, 150–1, 262
The Uninhabited House, 90–2, 261, 263, 366–7
Rix, Alicia, 220
Roberts, Robin, 73
Robins, G. M., 'The Man With No Face', 137
Rowell, Geoffrey, 300
Ruskin, John, 100
Rutherford, Andrew, 222

Sala, George, 109
Salmonson, Jessica Amanda, 162
Sanders, Valerie, 9, 241–54
Schaffer, Talia, 359
Scott, Walter, 21, 28–9, 36, 147, 228
  'Christmas in the Olden Time', 176–7
seascapes, 332–46
Sedgwick, Eve Kosofsky, 306
Shakespeare, William, 287
Sharman, Jim, *The Rocky Horror Picture Show*, 271, 282
Shattock, Joanne, 42
Shelley, Mary, *Frankenstein*, 26, 117, 118–19, 121, 127
Shelley, P. B., 27
Showalter, Elaine, 118, 170
Society for Psychical Research, 59–60, 61, 62, 140, 204, 301, 354–5, 373
Smith, Andrew, 5, 7, 12, 48, 77, 85–98, 99, 142, 178, 195, 200, 216, 217, 256, 263, 357–8, 367, 379–92
Smith, Matthew Wilson, 107
Smith, Susan Belasco, 161
spiritualism, 115–16, 125–6, 168–70, 172, 211, 222, 241, 340

Spofford, E. Prescott, 'The Amber Gods', 168–9
Spooner, Catherine, 329
Srdjan, Smajić, 203, 242
Stinton, T. C. W., 224
Stoker, Bram
  Dracula, 69
  The Jewel of Seven Stars, 390–1
  'The Judge's House', 53–4
Stone, Harry, 200
Storey, John, 177
Strack, Daniel, 211
Styler, Rebecca, 43
Sweet, Rosemary, 303–4
Swinburne, Algernon, 310

Tagore, Rabindranath, 'The Hungry Stories', 138–9
Taylor, Elizabeth, 'Poor Girl', 70–1
Tearle, Oliver, 372
Tebel, John, 160
technology, 105–6
'The Ghost in the Bank of England', 92–4
Thurston, Luke, 4, 10, 285–99
Townshend, Dale, 5–6, 17–33
Tracy, Robert, 179
transportation, 106–9
Trollope, Frances, *Life and Adventures of Michael Armstrong, the Factory Boy*, 102
Turcotte, Gerry, 141

Uglow, Jennifer, 121

Voskuil, Lynn M., 87
Vuohelainen, Minna, 210–24

Walker, Leila, 243–4
Walker, William Sylvester, 'The Evil of Yellowmoron Creek', 133–4

Wallace, Diana, 67
Waller, Philip, 53
Walpole, Horace, 308
　The Castle of Otranto, 18–19, 184, 335
Ward, Catriona, *Rawblood*, 71–3
Weaver, Rachel, 138
Weinstein, Cindy, 169–70
Weinstock, Jeffrey Andrew, 8, 160–75
Wells, H. G.
　'Pollock and the Porroh Man', 136–7
　'The Inexperienced Ghost', 62–3
　'The Red Room', 55
Whelan, Lara Baker, 263
Wilde, Oscar, 55
Williams, Margery, 'The Last Mitchell', 343–4
Wilson, Edmund, 172
Winterson, Jeanette, 68, 78n3
Wisker, Gina, 73, 75, 354
Wolfreys, Julian, 114, 348, 361
women's writing, 40–1, 67, 114–28, 137–8, 142, 161–2, 165, 186, 255–6, 352–3
Wood, Clare, 196–7
Wood, Ellen, 140
Woolf, Virginia, 57, 367–8
Wordsworth, William, 'The Idiot Boy', 322
Wynne, Madeline Yale, 171

Youhas, Alan, 74–5

www.ingramcontent.com/pod-product-compliance
Lightning Source LLC
LaVergne TN
LVHW052015230825
819359LV00004B/118